Programming Microsoft Dynamics® CRM 4.0

Jim Steger, Mike Snyder, Brad Bosak, Corey O'Brien, Philip Richardson (Sonoma Partners)

PUBLISHED BY
Microsoft Press
A Division of Microsoft Corporation
One Microsoft Way
Redmond, Washington 98052-6399

Library of Congress Control Number: 2008935422

Printed and bound in the United States of America.

1 2 3 4 5 6 7 8 9 QWT 3 2 1 0 9 8

Distributed in Canada by H.B. Fenn and Company Ltd.

A CIP catalogue record for this book is available from the British Library.

Microsoft Press books are available through booksellers and distributors worldwide. For further information about international editions, contact your local Microsoft Corporation office or contact Microsoft Press International directly at fax (425) 936-7329. Visit our Web site at www.microsoft.com/mspress. Send comments to mspinput@microsoft.com.

Acquisitions Editor: Ben Ryan
Developmental Editor: Devon Musgrave
Project Editor: Lynn Finnel
Editorial Production: ICC Macmillan, Inc.
Technical Reviewer: Elliot Lewis; Technical Review services provided by Content Master, a member of CM Group, Ltd.
Cover: Tom Draper Design

Body Part No. X14-95064

Contents at a Glance

Table of Contents

Foreword

Welcome to the world of developing business solutions with Microsoft Dynamics CRM!

For a long time, professional developers building business applications have been forced to choose between two equally unappealing alternatives when designing their solution—either buy an off-the-shelf package and have their hands tied with closed, proprietary designs; or build their own solution from scratch using commonly available technology and spend the majority of the project implementing the "basics" (again!) such as storage, security, and a user interface framework.

Microsoft Dynamics CRM is committed to providing a third way—a flexible architectural model that combines the power of the Microsoft platform with the appeal of a familiar Microsoft Office–style user experience and configurable business process. More important, although the power and value of Microsoft Dynamics CRM are most easily applied to sales, service, and marketing scenarios, the product's capabilities easily provide a platform for enabling a wide range of business processes and applications.

Put simply, Microsoft Dynamics CRM makes delivering the basics easy and lets you apply your energy and creativity where it matters the most—solving unique problems and helping the business succeed with intelligent solutions.

In the end, the most important element of any business application development project is *you*—the developer. With this book, the authors make it easy for you to benefit from their years of practical experience working with customers and other Microsoft partners to deliver high-value CRM solutions. They explain what you need (and want) to know before you start in on your Microsoft Dynamics CRM development project and how to get the most out of the time that you spend. Their ability to provide clear, concise guidance across the entire range of developer capabilities in CRM is a tremendous asset for anyone building custom solutions with the product.

If you're just getting started as a developer working with CRM, this book will give you the strong foundation in the core architecture, processes, and development capabilities to be a great Dynamics CRM developer.

If you've already had some experience with the product, this book is a handy reference that provides ideas and samples to stimulate your own creativity and help tackle common challenges.

I hope you find this guide both as informative and useful to read as I have during my collaboration with the authors. In the end, this book is just a first step. Whether you enjoy building business applications for the technical challenge or for the opportunity to help the world run a little smoother, I'm confident that Microsoft Dynamics CRM can help you reach your project goals faster and more effectively.

Welcome to the next generation of business application development—happy coding!

Andrew Bybee
Principal Program Manager
Microsoft Dynamics CRM
Microsoft Corporation

Acknowledgments

We want to thank all of the people who assisted us in writing this book. If we accidentally missed anyone, we apologize in advance. We would like to extend a special thanks to the following people:

- **Elliot Lewis** Elliot served as our technical reviewer for the book. Elliot's keen eye helped refine the book's approach and ensured the accuracy of its contents. We are all very appreciative of the effort and feedback Elliot provided.
- **Andy Bybee** Andy provided overall guidance and support for the book within Microsoft. He also was gracious enough to provide the book's foreword.

In addition, we want to thank these members of the Microsoft Dynamics CRM product team who helped us at one point or another during the book project:

Kam Baker
Andrew Becraft
Rohit Bhatia
Matt Cooper
Jim Daly
Rich Dickinson
Ajith Gande
Barry Givens
Humberto Lezama Guadarrama
Nishant Gupta
Allen Hafezipour
Peter Hecke
Akezyt Janedittakarn
Steven Kaplan
Jeff Kelleran
Amit Kumar
Donald La
Amy Langlois
Chris Laver
Patrick Le Quere
Dinesh Murthy
Kevin Nazemi
Michael Ott
Ramanathan Pallassana
Irene Pasternack
Dave Porter
Dominic Pouzin
Manisha Powar
Michael Scott
Nirav Shah
John Song
Derik Stenerson
Craig Unger
Praveen Upadhyay
Mahesh Vijayaraghavan
Sumit Virmani
Brad Wilson
Charlie Wood
Tobin Zerba

Thank you to the following Sonoma Partners colleagues who assisted with reviewing the content and providing feedback:

Brian Baseggio
Matt "MattDawg" Dearing
Jeff Klosinski
Bob Lauer
Andy Meyers
Blake Scarlavai
Matt Spezzano
Matt Weiler

Of course, we also want to thank the folks at Microsoft Press who helped support us throughout the writing and publishing process:

- **Ben Ryan** Ben again championed the project and was an invaluable resource for the logistics and planning.

- **Devon Musgrave** Devon provided initial review for the book and provided insight and direction with the book's schedule.
- **Lynn Finnel** Lynn, our project editor, provided the day-to-day guidance and coordination of the editing process.

We also wanted to extend our thanks to the rest of the production team who provided editorial feedback.

Jim Steger's Acknowledgments

I wish to thank my wife, Heidi, for her patience and for continuing to support me during this arduous process again. I want to thank both of my children, who continue to grow, impress, and motivate me. I also received input from numerous members of the Microsoft Dynamics CRM product team, and I want to extend my thanks to them as well. Finally, I wish to express my gratitude to my associates at Sonoma Partners who really stepped up their efforts and understanding while I was forced to prioritize my writing over some of my day-to-day duties.

Mike Snyder's Acknowledgments

I want to thank my wife, Gretchen, who supported me during this project. Writing this book required a significant time commitment above and beyond my normal work responsibilities, but Gretchen remained supportive from start to finish. I want also to thank my children for not deleting my completed work as they learned to play games on daddy's computer! I want to recognize my parents and my wife's parents who assisted my family with various babysitting stints. Finally, thanks to all of my coworkers at Sonoma Partners who allowed me the time and understanding to work on this book.

Brad Bosak's Acknowledgments

I would like to thank my family and friends for being supportive and understanding during the writing process. I'd also like to thank my coworkers at Sonoma Partners for their patience during the busy work days and also for their input and ideas. Finally, I'd like to thank Mike and Jim for the opportunity to help write this book.

Corey O'Brien's Acknowledgments

I would like to thank my wife, Pilar, for supporting me during the writing of this book. She tirelessly took care of our newborn son, Dylan, throughout the late nights and weekends while I was writing. I'd also like to thank my parents and my wife's parents for happily helping with babysitting duties whenever we asked. I'd also like to thank all of my coworkers at

Sonoma Partners for understanding that the growling was due to lack of sleep and not anything they'd done wrong.

Philip Richardson's Acknowledgments

I'd like to personally thank the CRM customers and partners who are a constant source of inspiration for the Dynamics CRM team at Microsoft. During my tenure on the CRM team they helped fuel my passion for the product with constant e-mails, instant messages, and meetings at various conferences. On a personal note, I'd like to thank my wife, Ellie, who is ever supportive of my profession regardless of the unusual working hours which it demands. Finally, I'm ever appreciative of Sonoma Partners for asking me to contribute to this book.

Introduction

If your organization has customers, you need a software system to help you manage your customer information. Unfortunately, many companies today are stuck using antiquated customer systems that don't integrate with Microsoft Office Outlook, aren't available from the Web, and can't be accessed via mobile devices. Even worse, some companies rely on Outlook contacts and Microsoft Office Excel files for precious customer data, making team collaboration on these records very difficult.

You probably already know that Microsoft offers a Customer Relationship Management (CRM) software solution as part of its Dynamics family. Microsoft Dynamics CRM is an easy-to-use application that businesses of all sizes and types can utilize. One of Microsoft Dynamics CRM's most important benefits is its native integration with other Microsoft productivity tools: Outlook, Excel, and Microsoft Office Word. Microsoft Dynamics CRM allows organizations to manage their sales, marketing, and customer service information more efficiently, leading to higher sales revenue and improved customer satisfaction.

But just as important as Microsoft Dynamics CRM's integration with other Microsoft tools, Microsoft Dynamics CRM offers developers a powerful customization and programming platform that you can use to satisfy almost any business requirement. This book provides a detailed explanation of the key areas in the Software Development Kit (SDK) and the Web-service–based Application Programming Interfaces (APIs). This book includes plenty of code samples and examples on topics such as form scripting, plug-ins, workflow assemblies, customizing the user interface, and more.

Programming Microsoft Dynamics CRM 4.0 was written by the consulting firm Sonoma Partners. Our firm has written several other successful titles for Microsoft Press, such as *Microsoft Dynamics CRM 4.0 Step by Step* (2008) and *Working with Microsoft Dynamics CRM 4.0, Second Edition* (2008). We tried to bring our real-world customer experiences to the writing process and share the most relevant information we think you'll need to program with the latest version of Microsoft Dynamics CRM 4.0.

Who This Book Is For

We wrote this book for professional developers who want to use the Microsoft Dynamics CRM SDK and its APIs to extensively customize the software application. We assume that you're comfortable working with .NET solutions and Web services. In addition, we also assume that you have a basic understanding of how to navigate the Microsoft Dynamics CRM interface and you understand its configuration capabilities. If you're looking for a detailed explanation of the Web-based configuration tools that Microsoft Dynamics CRM offers, please refer to *Working with Microsoft Dynamics CRM 4.0, Second Edition*, which explains these topics in great detail. If you're brand new to Microsoft Dynamics CRM, and you want to learn how to navigate through the user interface (from an end-user perspective), you can refer to *Microsoft Dynamics CRM 4.0 Step by Step*, which explains various day-to-day tasks such as creating accounts, logging a phone call, tracking an e-mail, and so on.

What This Book Is About

We divided this book into 15 chapters:

Chapter 1, "Microsoft Dynamics CRM 4.0 SDK Overview," introduces the Microsoft Dynamics CRM Software Development Kit (SDK) and outlines the most common questions that developers might ask about developing within Microsoft Dynamics CRM.

Chapter 2, "Development Overview and Environment," provides information about the various software editions and looks at the unique Microsoft Dynamics CRM issues related to setting up a development environment.

Chapter 3, "Communicating with Microsoft CRM APIs," explains how to programmatically connect with the Microsoft Dynamics CRM APIs. This chapter also covers how you connect to the APIs in the various deployment options: on-premise, Internet-facing, and Microsoft Dynamics CRM Online.

Chapter 4, "Security," supplies information about how your custom code interacts with the Microsoft Dynamics CRM security model. This chapter also takes a look at using custom code to encrypt specific data attributes.

Chapter 5, "Plug-ins," offers a detailed look at the Microsoft Dynamics CRM plug-in model. This includes creating the project, registering the plug-in, deploying the plug-in, and then working with the *IPluginExecutionContext*.

Chapter 6, "Programming Workflow," examines the Microsoft Dynamics CRM workflow module and how it takes advantage of the Windows Workflow Foundation. More important, this chapter explains how you can create your own custom workflow activities that you can reference in Microsoft Dynamics CRM workflow rules.

Chapter 7, "Form Scripting," explains the client-side scripting model. The chapter also provides examples of how you can create custom client-side code that calls Web services, run scripts from ISV.Config buttons, and so on.

Chapter 8, "Developing with the Metadata Service," explains the Microsoft Dynamics CRM *MetadataService*, and how you can use this API to programmatically retrieve and modify data about the system schema.

Chapter 9, "Deployment," explains various topics related to deploying your Microsoft Dynamics CRM solution from one environment to another.

Chapter 10, "Developing Offline Solutions," outlines the nuances of writing custom code that works properly using Microsoft Dynamics CRM for Outlook with Offline Access.

Chapter 11, "Multilingual and Multi-Currency Applications," offers a look at how to use Microsoft Dynamics CRM's multilingual and multi-currency functionality within your custom code to support global deployments.

Chapter 12, "Advanced Workflow Programming," goes deeper into programming the Microsoft Dynamics CRM workflow functionality, and explains how you can create custom workflow activities with XAML.

Chapter 13, "Emulating User Interface with ASP.NET Development," shows how you can create custom Web pages and user interfaces that blend seamlessly into the out-of-the-box Microsoft Dynamics CRM user interface, which provides a better end-user experience for your organization.

Chapter 14, "Developing Custom Microsoft CRM Controls," provides examples of creating custom user controls that reference Microsoft Dynamics CRM data.

Chapter 15, "Additional Samples and Utilities," discusses some of the utility classes and code used in the previous chapters as well as providing additional examples using the Microsoft Dynamics CRM technologies.

Companion Content

This book features a companion Web site that makes available to you all the code used in the book. This code is organized by chapter, and you can download it from the companion site at the following URL: *http://www.microsoft.com/mspress/companion/9780735625945*.

System Requirements

We recommend that you refer to the Microsoft Dynamics CRM Implementation Guide for detailed system requirements. From a high level, you'll need the following hardware and software to run the code samples in this book:

Client

- Microsoft Windows XP with Service Pack 2 (SP2) or the Windows Vista operating system
- Microsoft Internet Explorer 6 SP1 or Internet Explorer 7
- Microsoft Visual Studio 2005 or Microsoft Visual Studio 2008 (for the code samples)
- Microsoft Office 2003 with SP3 or the 2007 Microsoft Office System with SP1 (if you want to use Microsoft Dynamics CRM for Microsoft Office Outlook)

Server

- Microsoft Windows Server 2003 or Microsoft Windows Small Business Server 2003
- Microsoft SQL Server 2005
- Microsoft Dynamics CRM 4.0 Server license (Workgroup, Professional, or Enterprise edition)
- Computer/processor: Dual 1.8-gigahertz (GHz) or higher Pentium (Xeon P4) or compatible CPU
- Memory: 1 gigabyte (GB) of RAM minimum, 2 GB or more of RAM recommended
- Hard disk: 400 megabytes (MB) free space
- Network card: 10/100 Mbps minimum, dual 10/100/1000 Mbps recommended

Find Additional Content Online

As new or updated material becomes available that complements your book, it will be posted online on the Microsoft Press Online Developer Tools Web site. The type of material you might find includes updates to book content, articles, links to companion content, errata, sample chapters, and more. This Web site is available at *www.microsoft.com/learning/books/online/developer*, and is updated periodically.

Support for This Book

Every effort has been made to ensure the accuracy of this book and the contents of the companion Web site. As corrections or changes are collected, they will be added to a Microsoft Knowledge Base article.

Microsoft Press provides support for books and companion content at the following Web site:

http://www.microsoft.com/learning/support/books/

Questions and Comments

If you have comments, questions, or ideas regarding the book or the companion Web site, or questions that are not answered by visiting the sites above, please send them to Microsoft Press via e-mail to

mspinput@microsoft.com

Or via postal mail to

Microsoft Press
Attn: *Programming Microsoft Dynamics CRM 4.0* Editor
One Microsoft Way
Redmond, WA 98052-6399

Please note that Microsoft software product support is not offered through the above addresses.

Part I

Overview

Chapter 1

Microsoft Dynamics CRM 4.0 SDK Overview

You are probably reading this book because your organization recently purchased Microsoft Dynamics CRM or because your organization is evaluating it. As a developer, you want to know what this new software application will mean to your day-to-day life. Will it cause you nightmares and sleepless nights? Or will it be a dream to work with and solve all your current development headaches? As you might guess, the true answer lies somewhere in between. However, we strongly believe that if you take the time to learn the Microsoft Dynamics CRM application, you will find yourself much closer to the latter. If you're new to Microsoft Dynamics CRM, your initial questions might include the following:

- Will the software limit what I can do?
- How do I customize and extend the software?
- What types of resources are available to help me with the software?

We wrote this book to explain how professional software developers can extend the Microsoft Dynamics CRM software application to meet their business needs. To create customizations and integrations outlined in this book, you must be comfortable developing Web-based applications using tools such as Microsoft Visual Studio. We assume you have working knowledge of Visual Studio and Web application configuration with Microsoft Internet Information Services (IIS). Even if you're not a developer, you might benefit from reading these chapters to understand the different types of customizations that the Microsoft Dynamics CRM programming model makes possible.

From a very high level, Microsoft Dynamics CRM is just a large and sophisticated Web application. The application serves Web pages through IIS while accessing data from a Microsoft SQL Server database. Consequently, users access data through a Web browser, in addition to having the option to install Microsoft Office Outlook integration software. For most developers, we recommend that they simply think of Microsoft Dynamics CRM as a typical Web application.

This chapter introduces three topics regarding programming Microsoft Dynamics CRM:

- The Software Development Kit
- A hitchhiker's guide to common questions
- Microsoft Dynamics CRM as a business-application platform

The subsequent chapters dive into the Microsoft Dynamics CRM software architecture and provide programming examples.

Software Development Kit Introduction

Like many commercial software applications, Microsoft Dynamics CRM offers a Software Development Kit (SDK) that documents how you can customize and extend the system. The SDK consists of many different components related to extending the software:

- A compiled Help file that documents the application's architecture and programming interfaces, provides a report writer's guide, and offers additional development information
- Microsoft Dynamics CRM 4.0 user interface style guide
- Code samples (walkthroughs)
- Helper classes and utilities
- Graphic images
- The SDKreadme.htm file, which documents any known issues

Sometimes people refer to just the compiled help file as the SDK, but you can see all of these documents when you download the SDK and extract the files.

Important Microsoft updates the SDK on a periodic basis (approximately once every two or three months), so be sure to obtain the latest version. You can download the Microsoft Dynamics CRM 4.0 Software Development Kit at *http://www.microsoft.com/downloads/details.aspx?FamilyID=82E632A7-FAF9-41E0-8EC1-A2662AAE9DFB*.

As part of the SDK, Microsoft documents all of the supported interaction points—also known as application programming interfaces (APIs)—that you can use when writing code that integrates with Microsoft Dynamics CRM. Using the APIs for your customizations provides several significant benefits:

- **Ease of use** The APIs include hundreds of pages of documentation complete with real-world examples, code samples, and helper classes to help you write code that works with Microsoft Dynamics CRM.
- **Supportability** If you encounter technical problems or issues using the APIs, you can contact Microsoft technical support or use the Microsoft Dynamics CRM public newsgroup for assistance.
- **Upgrade support** Microsoft makes every effort to ensure that the code you create for Microsoft Dynamics CRM using the APIs upgrades smoothly to future versions of

the product, even if the underlying Microsoft SQL Server database changes radically. This is also true for any updates and hotfixes that Microsoft might release for Microsoft Dynamics CRM.

- **Certification** By following the documented APIs, you can submit your customizations to a third-party testing vendor to certify that your application works within the confines of the SDK. This certification provides comfort and reassurance for people evaluating your customizations.

Hitchhiker's Guide to Common Questions

Throughout the years we've worked with Microsoft Dynamics CRM, we find that a common set of developer questions pop up again and again. This section lists some of these questions and points you to the chapters in this book where you can find additional details about what you're trying to accomplish.

Can we alter the CRM database structure to add our custom tables and columns?

Yes, you can extend the Microsoft Dynamics CRM database with new entities (tables), attributes (columns), and relationships (keys). You can also add new attributes to the out-of-box entities. However, you do not make these modifications to SQL Server directly. Instead you use one of two different tools to modify the database:

- A Web-based customization tool
- The metadata API

For more information about using the Web-based customization tool, please refer to the book *Working with Microsoft Dynamics CRM* by Mike Snyder and Jim Steger (Microsoft Press, 2008). That book includes several chapters on using the Web-based customization tools to modify the data structure.

The metadata API allows you to programmatically modify the database, including adding new attributes, entities, and so on. In this book, please refer to Chapter 8, "Developing with the Metadata Service," for more information about programmatically modifying the database.

Important Even though you can technically modify the database structure directly within SQL Server, you should not attempt to do so because the modifications might cause unintended consequences in your application, including possible data loss or system corruption. The Microsoft Dynamics CRM customization tools and the metadata API provide all of the resources you need to modify the database structure.

Another related question we frequently hear is "What does the database structure look like?" Although Microsoft Dynamics CRM does use a SQL Server database, theoretically you should not need to poke around the database structure or examine it. You can access data about the entities through the user interface or the metadata API. To further emphasize this idea, we want to point out that Microsoft released *logical* database diagrams for Microsoft Dynamics CRM 4.0. These logical database diagrams do not include the actual table structure; instead, they list the abstracted logical structure just as you utilize it through the user interface and API. You can download and view the Microsoft Dynamics CRM 4.0 logical database diagrams from *http://www.microsoft.com/downloads/details.aspx?FamilyID=b73912e8-861e-43ae-97b4-72b3e809f287&DisplayLang=en*. These database diagrams show the logical data relationships and the linked attributes between entities in Microsoft Office Visio format.

In addition to the logical database diagrams, you can also view information about the entities and entity relationships through the Metadata browser at *http://*<yourcrmserver>*/* <yourorganizationname>*/sdk/list.aspx* (see Figure 1-1).

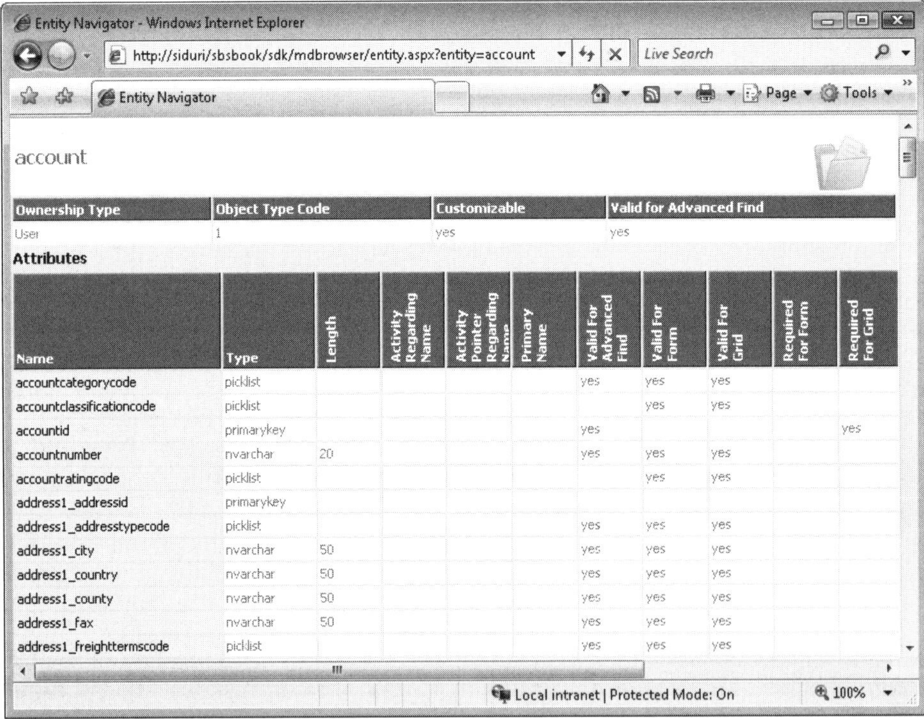

FIGURE 1-1 The Microsoft Dynamics CRM Metadata browser

Lastly, you can also use the metadata service API to programmatically view data about the database schema, attribute values, relationships, and so on.

If you're just dying to see the underlying database structure, of course you can simply open SQL Server and examine it for yourself. You will find that Microsoft Dynamics CRM uses a normalized underlying database structure with clearly named tables such as *account_base* and *account_extensionbase*.

How do we write custom code that gets data into and out of Microsoft Dynamics CRM?

When you create custom code that needs to interact with Microsoft Dynamics CRM data, you should use one of two techniques:

- ***CrmService* Web Service** An API that performs authentication and supports common data requests such as create, read, update, and delete. This API uses a Web service interface.
- **Filtered views** Filtered views are SQL Server database views that your custom application can query to obtain read-only information about records.

You should *avoid* creating custom code that accesses the SQL Server database tables directly—please stick to one of these two techniques. Both of these interfaces abstract the underlying database from your code so that if necessary Microsoft can modify the SQL Server database for hotfixes, new versions, and so on. If your custom code accesses a database table directly and then Microsoft needs to modify it, your custom code will probably break. However, if your code accesses the *CrmService* Web service or a filtered view, Microsoft updates these interfaces with the corresponding database changes so that your code continues to run as-is.

While the *CrmService* Web service provides access to data about records, Microsoft Dynamics CRM includes two additional Web services that you can utilize:

- ***MetadataService* Web Service** This Web service provides an API that allows you to query and manipulate the data structure.
- ***CrmDiscoveryService* Web Service** This Web service provides an API that allows you to query for information about the Microsoft Dynamics CRM installation.

Refer to Chapter 3, "Communicating with Microsoft Dynamics CRM APIs," for information about connecting to the APIs. Chapter 8 includes a deeper look at retrieving and modifying the database schema programmatically.

Can we change the current CRM form layouts and controls?

Yes, Microsoft Dynamics CRM offers multiple tools to modify the existing forms. The Web-based customization tools allow you to:

- Add, remove, and modify form fields.
- Add, remove, and move tabs.
- Change field and tab labels.

Figure 1-2 shows the form editor for the contact entity.

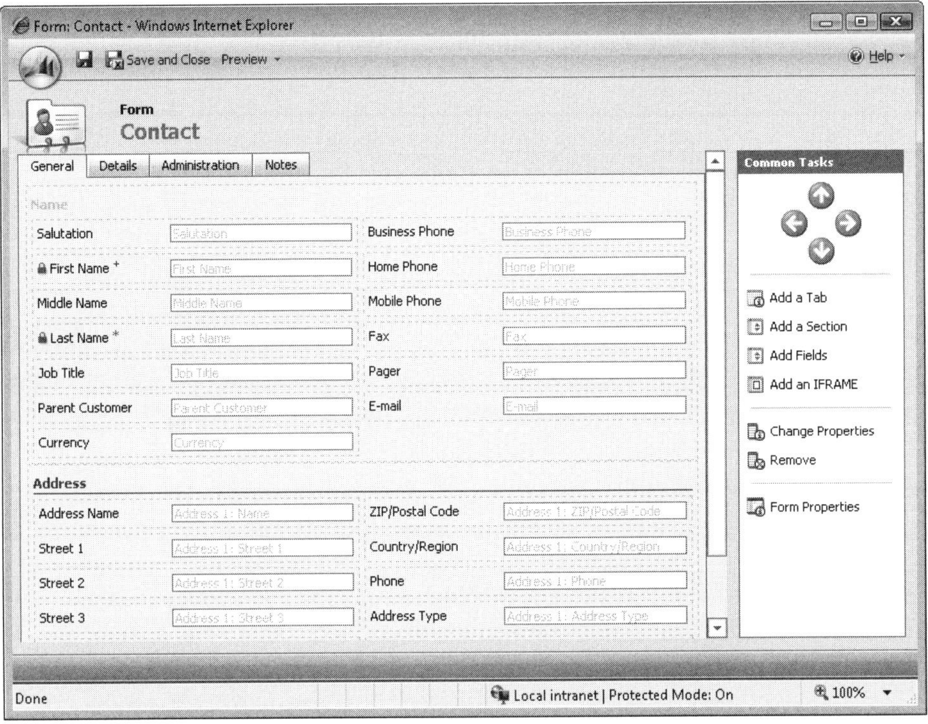

FIGURE 1-2 The contact form editor

Many of the attributes on the form include built-in controls such as a calendar for date fields, drop-down menus for picklist fields, check boxes for bit fields, and so on. Obviously this form editor provides great convenience for you to add and remove fields, in addition to changing the form layout. The book *Working with Microsoft Dynamics CRM* includes several chapters explaining how to modify form layouts.

However, if you want to use different controls than the ones included by default, Microsoft Dynamics CRM does not include a tool to swap out the default controls with your controls. However, you can implement your own custom controls by using a combination of IFrames and your own custom Web pages. An IFrame allows you to embed a custom Web page into a Microsoft Dynamics CRM form so that it appears in the context of other Microsoft Dynamics CRM fields. For more information on creating custom user controls, please refer to Chapter 14, "Developing Custom Microsoft Dynamics CRM Controls."

How do we implement our own custom business logic?

Microsoft Dynamics CRM includes several different options for implementing your custom business logic:

- **Form scripting events** Microsoft Dynamics CRM offers *onSave*, *onLoad*, and *onChange* form events that you can use to trigger form scripting code.
- **Server-side events** You can register Microsoft .NET assemblies that contain your custom code, and Microsoft Dynamics CRM will trigger these assemblies based on the user operations you configure, such as creating a record, deleting a record, assigning a record, and so on. These .NET assemblies are known as plug-ins in Microsoft Dynamics CRM, and you can run them either synchronously or asynchronously.
- **Microsoft Dynamics CRM Workflow** This option uses the Windows Workflow Foundation framework to create business automation processes triggered by the actions you configure. Sample workflow rules include e-mail alerts, task creation, record assignment, and so on.
- **Custom Web pages** You can embed your own custom Web pages directly within the Microsoft Dynamics CRM application and user interface. These pages can contain any type of business logic that you deem necessary.

As you would expect, you configure form scripting events on a record's form that Microsoft Dynamics CRM can trigger when a user saves a record, loads a form, or changes a field's data value. Form scripting events allow you to perform conditional form manipulation such as updating one field's value based on the value of a different field, or changing the form layout that a user sees based on the security role of the user viewing the record. You use JavaScript as your form scripting language. Figure 1-3 shows where you can load script onto a form. Please refer to Chapter 7, "Form Scripting," for a detailed look at the client script programming model. Microsoft Dynamics CRM executes form scripting both online and offline (within Microsoft Dynamics CRM for Outlook with Offline Access).

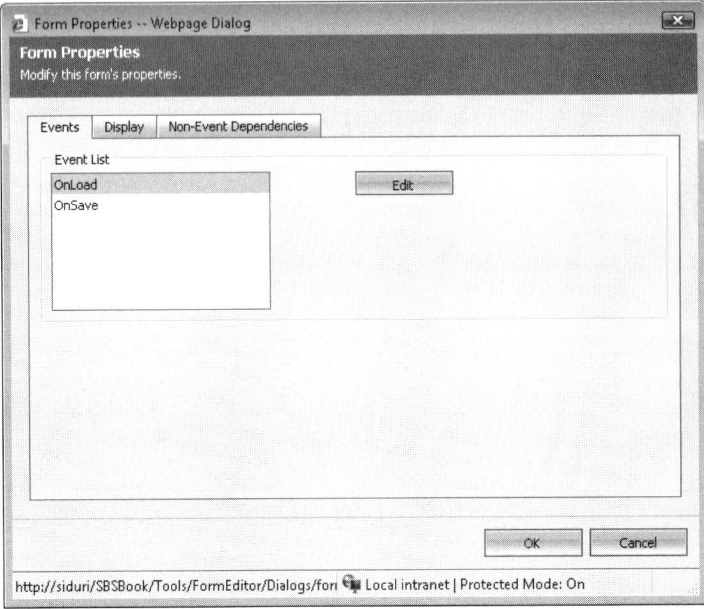

FIGURE 1-3 A dialog box for adding client-side scripts to a form

For server-side logic, Microsoft Dynamics CRM offers a plug-in model where you can create custom .NET assemblies that Microsoft Dynamics CRM executes based upon the defined trigger operations. For example, you can create an assembly that runs every time a user deactivates a lead or closes an opportunity. Because the plug-in model accepts .NET assemblies, developers can take advantage of the .NET Framework to accommodate almost any type of customization your organization might require. You can configure plug-ins to run either synchronously or asynchronously. In addition, you can even create plug-ins that run offline (disconnected from the server) in the Microsoft Dynamics CRM for Outlook software. Chapter 5, "Plug-ins," explains how to write plug-ins in exhaustive detail.

Microsoft Dynamics CRM Workflow offers another option for implementing your own business logic. Unlike form scripting events and plug-ins, Microsoft Dynamics CRM Workflow includes a user interface that nondevelopers can use to set up and create their own automation processes. As a developer, this frees you from simple and common requests such as creating e-mail alerts and notifications. Figure 1-4 shows an example of a workflow rule created in the Web interface. Please refer to *Working with Microsoft Dynamics CRM* for an explanation of the Workflow Web interface.

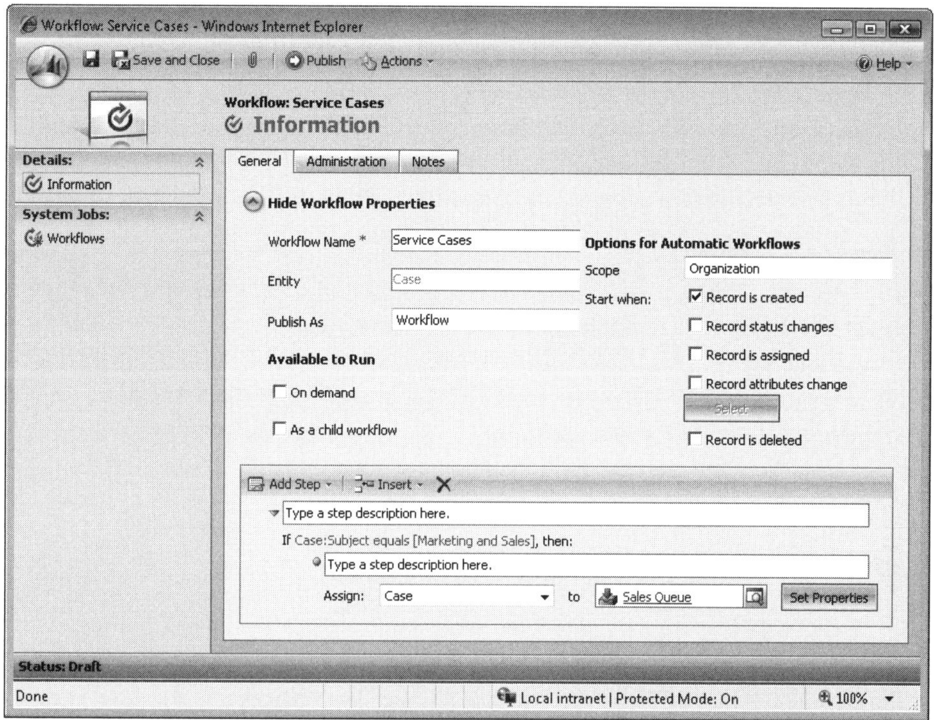

FIGURE 1-4 The Web-based workflow rule designer

Even though the Workflow Web interface is quite powerful, undoubtedly your users will encounter scenarios where they can't design their business logic within the existing Web-based tools. Fortunately, Microsoft Dynamics CRM allows you to create custom workflow assemblies that your users can reference in the Web workflow designer to utilize in their rules. Just like plug-ins, workflow assemblies are fully .NET-compliant so that you have almost unlimited programming options to create complex and sophisticated business logic within workflow. Chapter 6, "Programming Workflow," explains the process for creating workflow assemblies within Microsoft Dynamics CRM. Chapter 12, "Advanced Workflow Programming," contains additional information about more complex programming customizations within workflow.

Caution Many people assume that because Microsoft Dynamics CRM uses SQL Server, they can use database triggers for their business logic. This is not the case. If you want to create custom business logic related to database activity, you should plan to use one of the supported mechanisms such as form scripting events, plug-ins, or workflow instead of database triggers.

Another powerful option to implement your custom business logic in Microsoft Dynamics CRM is to create custom Web pages that you embed in the user interface. You can create these pages using any technology that you prefer—Microsoft Dynamics CRM simply references your pages.

How much control do we have over the user interface and branding?

As we already mentioned, Microsoft Dynamics CRM offers Web-based customization tools that allow you to modify the various forms with your custom attributes and relationships. This form-customization tool is nice because nondevelopers can use it to make modifications to your system.

However, you can perform more complex modifications to the user interface through the use of IFrames to implement your own custom user interface. While IFrames allow you to embed your custom Web pages within a Microsoft Dynamics CRM form, you can also modify the user interface by creating entirely new Web pages within the application. Users can access these custom Web pages through the primary navigation, or from buttons or links that you can add to existing records. Figure 1-5 shows the dialog to add an IFrame to a Microsoft Dynamics CRM form.

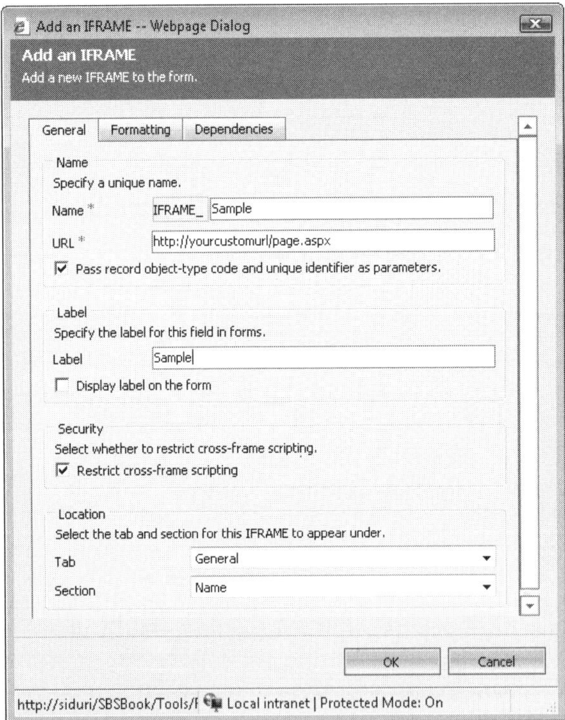

FIGURE 1-5 Adding an IFrame to a form

Please refer to Chapter 13, "Emulating the User Interface with ASP.NET Development," for information about creating new Web pages that work within Microsoft Dynamics CRM. Please refer to the book *Working with Microsoft Dynamics CRM* for an explanation of using the SiteMap and ISV.Config to modify the navigation model.

Warning Even though you can technically modify the .aspx Web pages and the .js files in the Microsoft Dynamics CRM Web application, Microsoft considers these types of modifications unsupported. Instead you should use the other techniques outlined above to implement your custom business logic and user interface. Modifying the .aspx or .js files will probably cause unexpected (bad) behavior within your system.

How do we deploy changes from one system to another?

Microsoft Dynamics CRM includes a customization import and export utility in the Web interface so that you can easily move customizations from one system to another (such as moving from development to staging to production). Figure 1-6 shows some of the customization import and export utilities.

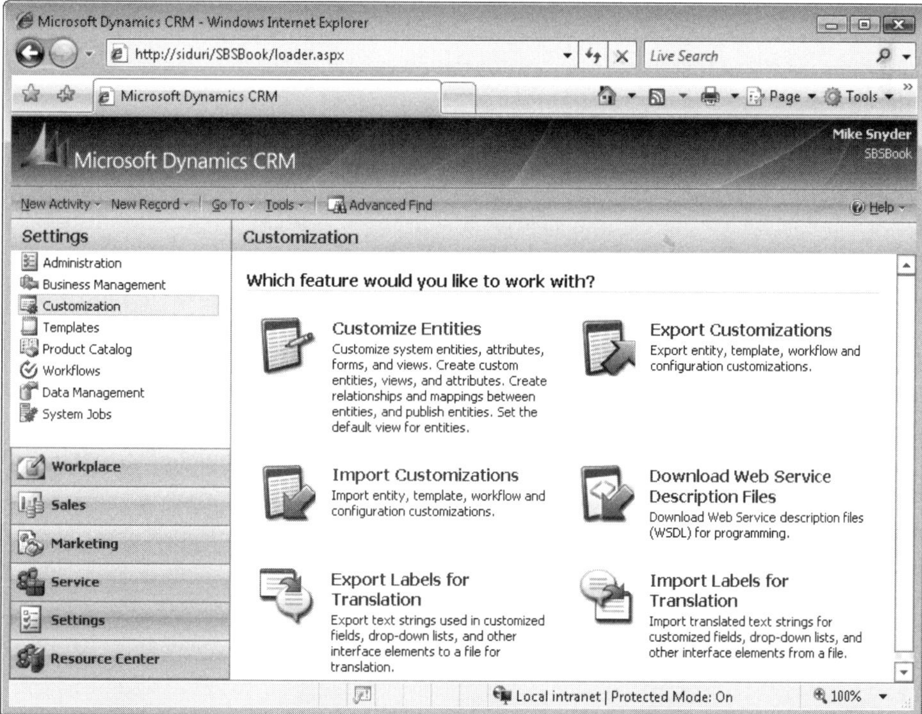

FIGURE 1-6 Import and export customizations in Microsoft Dynamics CRM

When you export customizations, Microsoft Dynamics CRM creates an XML file that contains all of the details of your entities. You can then take that customization file and import it into your target system. If you plan on frequent updates from one system to another, you can write code using the Microsoft Dynamics CRM Metadata API that will automatically export customizations from one system, import them into another system, and then publish those changes on the target system. If your system includes custom Web pages, you are responsible for deploying those files. Microsoft Dynamics CRM will not include your custom Web pages in the customizations import/export process. Chapter 9, "Deployment," takes a closer look at deploying your Microsoft Dynamics CRM customizations.

Will our customizations upgrade when Microsoft releases a new version of the software?

This question appears more frequently than probably all of the other questions combined, and understandably so! If you invest hundreds or thousands of hours customizing Microsoft Dynamics CRM, you want to know that you won't lose that investment when Microsoft releases the next version of the software. The key to answering this question is understanding what Microsoft means when they talk about "supported customizations." If Microsoft considers a customization supported, you can pretty safely assume that the customization will upgrade smoothly. We like to think of the SDK as the authoritative list of supported customizations, so if you follow the guidance outlined in that document you should not experience a problem.

Caution While most supported customizations upgrade to future versions, Microsoft cannot guarantee this. For example, upgrading from Microsoft Dynamics CRM 1.2 to Microsoft Dynamics CRM 3.0 included a few breaking changes related to activities. However, Microsoft only makes these types of changes when the benefit of the new functionality clearly outweighs the cost of re-creating a customization.

Having experienced multiple upgrades of Microsoft Dynamics CRM, we feel that Microsoft demonstrates a good track record of supporting customizations. For example, Microsoft completely revamped the asynchronous service for Microsoft Dynamics CRM 4.0, replacing 3.0 callouts with plug-ins in 4.0. The new 4.0 plug-in model included a large number of new benefits for developers and administrators, so plug-ins were a great architecture improvement over callouts. However, Microsoft included backward-compatibility support for Microsoft Dynamics CRM 3.0 callouts so that they can run in Microsoft Dynamics CRM 4.0 without any code changes.

More Info Microsoft stated that they plan to release a new major release of Microsoft Dynamics CRM once every two years. In the interim, Microsoft will release smaller updates, hotfixes, and security updates along the way. However, many customers find it comforting that the major updates follow a periodic update schedule at a reasonable interval.

Are role-based security permissions supported and configurable?

Microsoft Dynamics CRM uses a role-based security model to determine the various privileges with the system. Each user can possess one or more security roles, and each security role defines the various privileges within the system. Administrators can configure and assign security roles through a Web interface. Figure 1-7 shows how an administrator can configure a security role in the application.

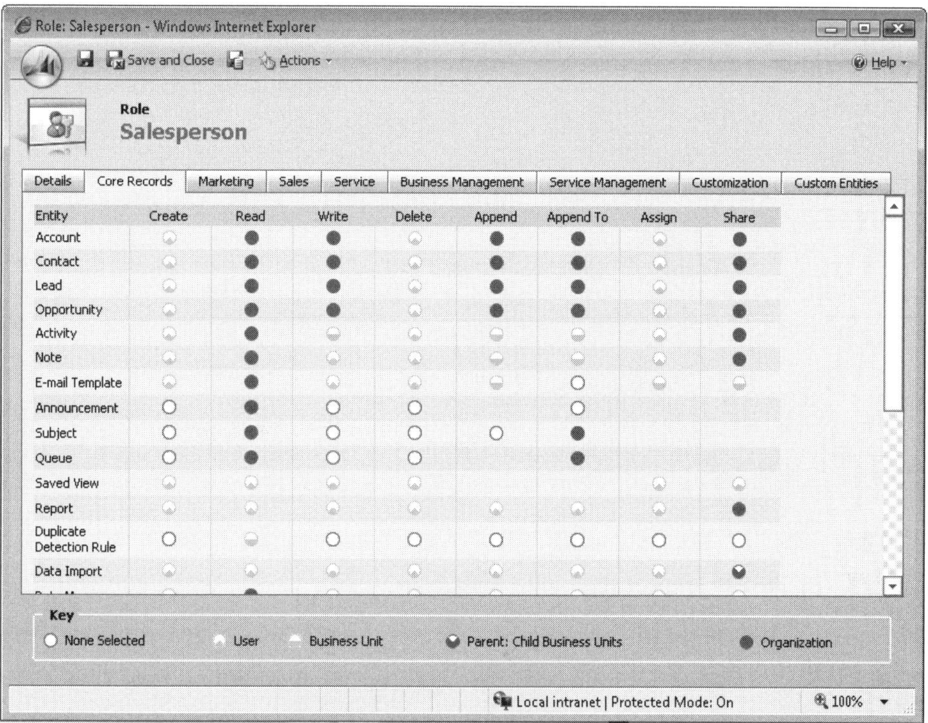

FIGURE 1-7 The security role editor in Microsoft Dynamics CRM

Please refer to *Working with Microsoft Dynamics CRM* for more information on setting up user security. For information about security within your programming customizations, please refer to Chapter 4, "Security," in this book.

Does Microsoft Dynamics CRM support multiple languages and currencies?

Yes, Microsoft Dynamics CRM is a truly global product that supports multiple languages and multiple currencies within a single deployment. Suppose that a sample organization has 500 users using Microsoft Dynamics CRM. That organization could theoretically set up their users as follows:

- 100 users with US English and US Dollars
- 100 users with Spanish and US Dollars
- 100 users with French and Euros
- 200 users with Spanish and Euros

As a developer, you must understand how your custom code needs to accommodate these types of multiple language and multiple currency scenarios. Chapter 11, "Multilingual and Multi-Currency Applications," takes a look at programming for these situations within Microsoft Dynamics CRM.

Will our programming customizations run offline?

As we previously mentioned, Microsoft Dynamics CRM includes optional add-in software for Microsoft Office Outlook. This add-in software comes in two different versions:

- Microsoft Dynamics CRM for Outlook
- Microsoft Dynamics CRM for Outlook with Offline Access

The offline-enabled version of this software allows your users to work while disconnected from the Microsoft Dynamics CRM server. As a developer, you have the option to create customizations that also run offline within Microsoft Dynamics CRM for Outlook. The SDK includes support for offline programming interfaces. Even if your customizations don't need to run offline, you should take some time to understand how users with the offline version of Microsoft Dynamics CRM for Outlook might interact with your server-based customizations. Please refer to Chapter 10, "Developing Offline Solutions," for more information on this topic.

How do you recommend we set up a Microsoft Dynamics CRM development environment?

When you're creating your Microsoft Dynamics CRM customizations, of course you don't want to develop and test your code in a production environment. You want to work in a sandbox system and then push your completed customizations to a different environment upon completion. Chapter 2, "Development Overview and Environment," examines different options for setting up a development system for your team of developers.

Microsoft Dynamics CRM as a Business Application Platform

If you're new to Microsoft Dynamics CRM, you might think of the application as just a sales, marketing, and service tool. However, we encourage you to think of new and creative ways to use your programming skills and the Microsoft Dynamics CRM platform to tackle new business challenges. We believe that Microsoft Dynamics CRM is an excellent development platform for many reasons, including:

- Metadata architecture that allows for easy extensions to the database model
- Web-based customization tools that allow nondevelopers to make application changes
- Built-in workflow capability
- Documented and easy-to-use software development kit
- Service-orientated architecture
- Native support for online and offline use
- Native support for multiple currencies and multiple languages
- Enterprise-class capabilities with SQL Server database
- Out–of-the-box integration with the common end-user applications Microsoft Office Outlook, Microsoft Office Excel, Microsoft Office Word, and Microsoft Office Communication Server
- Common user authentication with Microsoft Active Directory for single sign-on with Microsoft Office SharePoint Server

Having worked with many different customers implementing Microsoft Dynamics CRM, our company Sonoma Partners has helped many organizations use Microsoft Dynamics CRM as a business application platform to tackle nontraditional CRM business issues. Examples include:

- Helping a large national franchise to use Microsoft Dynamics CRM to scout, rank, and identify potential restaurant locations.
- Working with a national real-estate company to track condominium developments and condominium inventory in Microsoft Dynamics CRM. The company also tracked each buyer's preferences and upgrades such as appliances, paint color, furnishings, and so on.
- Developing a system for a nonprofit organization to qualify applicants of oil and heat subsidies, including tracking applications, receipts, and vendor payment status.

- Designing a database of hospitals and physicians for a long-term care management company to help them better understand the patient referral and new patient setup process.

Most people would not consider any of these examples as traditional CRM, yet all of them work excellently on the Microsoft Dynamics CRM platform! If your organization is considering building a custom software application from scratch, or if you have an existing home-grown custom application, we strongly urge you to consider using Microsoft Dynamics CRM as a platform to replace custom software applications. We hope that the chapters and examples in this book will give you the confidence that Microsoft Dynamics CRM is truly easy to program with, and offers an unbelievable amount of flexibility.

Tip Sometimes people use the term xRM to describe using a CRM software application as the business application platform to solve nontraditional business challenges. We've seen different definitions for the acronym xRM, but we like to think of the letter *X* as a variable just like you might remember from your algebra class. You can plug in almost any value for *X*, but it always includes the relationship management.

Summary

Microsoft Dynamics CRM includes many different software development tools that professional developers can use to create complex system customizations. The Microsoft Dynamics CRM SDK is the primary development documentation for developers, as the SDK includes architecture information, helper classes, and definitions of supported customizations. When developing Microsoft Dynamics CRM customizations, you should not access the SQL Server database directly. Instead you should connect to system data through the *CrmService* Web service or the *MetadataService* Web service. The *CrmService* provides basic create, read, update, and delete functionality, and the *MetadataService* provides a programmatic interface to the data schema. You can implement your own business logic in Microsoft Dynamics CRM using a combination of techniques, such as form scripting, server-side assemblies, workflow assemblies, and custom Web pages. Because of the flexibility of the Microsoft Dynamics CRM programming platform, the software offers an ideal development platform for tracking nontraditional CRM data beyond sales, marketing, and customer service.

Chapter 2

Development Overview and Environment

As you begin your development with Microsoft Dynamics CRM, you might be wondering how to best get started. Common questions include: How do I configure a development environment? What do I test? What hardware should I be considering?

This chapter focuses on the available options for your development and testing environments and also describes some useful development and deployment tools that can aid you in providing robust solutions on the Microsoft Dynamics CRM platform. We'll cover the following topics:

- Microsoft Dynamics CRM 4.0 system overview
- Hardware requirements
- Development environment considerations
- Testing environment considerations
- Migrating data
- Redeployment
- Development tools
- Additional development considerations

Microsoft Dynamics CRM 4.0 System Overview

Before preparing any development environment, you should first understand the primary components of Microsoft Dynamics CRM. At some point or another you will probably encounter each one of these components during customization and support of the application.

Please refer to the Microsoft Dynamics CRM Implementation Guide (available for download at *http://www.microsoft.com/downloads/details.aspx?FamilyID=1ceb5e01-de9f-48c0-8ce2-51633ebf4714&DisplayLang=en*) for more detailed information about the topics in this section.

Microsoft Dynamics CRM 4.0 Versions

You can purchase Microsoft Dynamics CRM in one of three editions as described in the following list. Each edition contains a full set of the CRM sales, marketing, and customer service features.

- **Microsoft Dynamics CRM 4.0 Workgroup Server** Allows a maximum of five users. This version also limits you to a single organization and can only be installed on a single server.
- **Microsoft Dynamics CRM 4.0 Professional Server** Allows unlimited users; also allows the Microsoft Dynamics CRM Web server to be installed on multiple computers, but is only available for a single organization.
- **Microsoft Dynamics CRM 4.0 Enterprise Server** Allows unlimited users and an unlimited number of organizations. Allows you to create role-based server instances, increasing scalability.

Microsoft Dynamics CRM Components

Microsoft Dynamics CRM 4.0 relies on several Microsoft technologies as part of its infrastructure, such as Active Directory, Microsoft SQL Server, and SQL Server Reporting Services. In addition to the required components, Microsoft Dynamics CRM 4.0 includes additional optional software components that your organization might want to use. Table 2-1 describes the common Microsoft Dynamics CRM 4.0 components.

TABLE 2-1 Microsoft Dynamics CRM Components

Component	Required	Description
Microsoft Active Directory	Yes	Used for initial user authentication and password management.
Microsoft Dynamics CRM Web Server	Yes	Core server software used with Internet Information Services (IIS) 6.0 or 7.0.
Microsoft SQL Server	Yes	Database server.
Microsoft SQL Server Reporting Services	Yes	Report server.
Microsoft Dynamics CRM 4.0 Connector for SQL Server Reporting Services	No	Service that connects the CRM Web server to the Reporting Services Web server. This connector eliminates the Kerberos double-hop authentication issue that can arise on multiple computer deployments. Although this component is not technically required for a basic on-premise deployment, you should consider installing it.

TABLE 2-1 Microsoft Dynamics CRM Components

Component	Required	Description
Microsoft Dynamics CRM E-mail Router	No	Provides integration to Microsoft Exchange.
Microsoft Dynamics CRM for Microsoft Office Outlook	No	Free add-in for Microsoft Office Outlook that provides integration to Microsoft Dynamics CRM.
Microsoft Dynamics CRM 4.0 Language Pack	No	Allows users to display the user interface in an alternate language from the base language.

Licensing

Microsoft Dynamics CRM requires two types of software licenses for each deployment: server licenses and Client Access Licenses (CALs). Every deployment must include at least one server license, and you must have one CAL for every active user in the system. Client Access Licenses are typically referred to as user licenses.

Customers can purchase CALs under one of two models:

- **Named User CALS** The number of user licenses that you need depends on the number of *named users* in your system. The CAL is tied to a specific user, and that user can access Microsoft Dynamics CRM from any computer.
- **Device CALs** Under this model, the CAL is tied to a specific device and different Microsoft Dynamics CRM users can access the system, as long as they access it from the same device. Device CALs fit best with multishift operations such as call centers and hospitals.

Important Named user licensing is different from many other software programs that base their licensing on the number of concurrent users. Every active user in Microsoft Dynamics CRM consumes a license, regardless of how often he or she accesses the system or how many users log on at the same time. But don't worry, when necessary a system administrator can easily transfer user licenses from one user to another such as when a user leaves the company or if an employee takes an extended leave of absence.

Table 2-2 lists the types of CALs available.

TABLE 2-2 Client Access License Types

CAL Type	Description
Full	Users with this license type have access to full functionality and are only limited by security roles and privileges. A user with the Full license type consumes a Microsoft Dynamics CRM CAL.
Read-Only	Users who have this license type can only view records and data in Microsoft Dynamics CRM 4.0. They cannot modify records or data. A user configured with the Read-Only license type consumes a Microsoft Dynamics CRM Limited CAL.
Administrative	This license type restricts a user to settings and configurations. A user with the Administrative license type does not consume a Microsoft Dynamics CRM CAL.

Microsoft also offers an external connector license to allow you to connect to Microsoft Dynamics CRM 4.0 data to external systems or users. The external connector is simply a license applied to a server and is available only for Microsoft Dynamics CRM Enterprise and Professional editions. Purchasing the external connector license does not include any additional software. Please review the Microsoft Product User Rights document located at *http://www.microsoftvolumelicensing.com/userights/PUR.aspx* for additional information.

Server Roles

Microsoft Dynamics CRM 4.0 Enterprise version includes two new server roles, which increase the flexibility and scalability of your deployment. With these roles, you can dedicate multiple computers to each specific type of service. You may hear about or use these roles during your development with Microsoft Dynamics CRM, so we wanted to be sure to briefly describe them for you.

The following server roles can be selected and installed during Setup:

- **Application Server Role** Provides deployment of the Microsoft Dynamics CRM 4.0 Web user interface and services
- **Platform Server Role** Allows for deployment of the asynchronous process service, such as the Workflow and Bulk E-mail services, and the Microsoft Dynamics CRM Web service APIs to a separate computer

The Application and Platform server roles provide the more common deployment models. However, you can also install specific services, such as the asynchronous processing service, deployment service, and SDK server individually to dedicated hardware as necessary.

Tip You should consider using a platform server to increase performance if your implementation relies heavily on a specific service. For instance, deploy the asynchronous processing service to dedicated hardware when your application requires a large amount of asynchronous or batch processing.

Hardware Requirements

Although the actual hardware you need depends on your own infrastructure and requirements, you can find the official hardware requirements on the Web at *http://www.microsoft.com/dynamics/crm/product/systemrequirements.mspx* and the suggested hardware for deployments up to 500 concurrent users at *http://www.microsoft.com/downloads/details.aspx?familyid=3BF7ECDA-7EAF-4F1C-BBFE-CAE19BC8BB78&displaylang=en*. The Microsoft Dynamics CRM Implementation Guide includes additional information about suggested hardware configurations.

Microsoft Dynamics CRM 4.0 Web Server Requirements

The Microsoft Dynamics CRM server component is a Web server component that requires use of IIS 6.0 or 7.0.

Table 2-3 lists Microsoft's minimum and recommended specifications for the Web server. Your deployment might demand different hardware requirements depending on the number of users accessing the system, the number of transactions, up-time requirements, and so on.

TABLE 2-3 Microsoft Dynamics CRM 4.0 Web Server Requirements

Requirement	Minimum	Recommended
Computer/processor	Dual 1.8-GHz Pentium (Xeon P4)	Dual 1.8-GHz Pentium (Xeon P4) or better
Memory (RAM)	1 gigabyte (GB) RAM	2 GB RAM or more
Hard disk	400 megabytes (MB) free hard-disk space	400 MB free hard-disk space
Network card	10/100 Mbps	Dual 10/100/1000 Mbps
Operating system	Microsoft Windows Server 2008, Standard, Enterprise, Datacenter, or Web Server editions Microsoft Windows Server 2003, Standard, Enterprise, or Web editions (with SP2 or R2 or later) Microsoft Windows Server 2003, Small Business R2 editions All with the latest service pack (SP)	Microsoft Windows Server 2008, Standard, Enterprise, Datacenter, or Web Server editions Microsoft Windows Server 2003, Standard, Enterprise, or Web editions (with SP2 or R2 or later) Microsoft Windows Server 2003, Small Business R2 editions All with the latest SP
Internet Information Services (IIS)	Version 6.0 (included with Windows Server 2003) or Version 7.0 (included with Windows Server 2008)	Version 6.0 or Version 7.0
Microsoft Data Access Components (MDAC)	Version 2.81 (included with Windows Server 2003) or later	Version 2.81 or later

The requirements for your development and test environment generally mirror or are slightly less powerful than your production environment. Note that more and more organizations are moving to a virtualized environment for their development and quality-assurance systems. The next section discusses further development environment options.

Virtualization

Virtualization refers to the ability to emulate a fully functioning computer on top of a physical host server. Microsoft supports Microsoft Dynamics CRM 4.0 on a computer using Microsoft Virtual Server 2005 in both production and development environments, as outlined in Knowledge Base article 946600 located at *http://support.microsoft.com/kb/946600.*

If your infrastructure utilizes virtualization, you have the ability to quickly bring up Microsoft Dynamics CRM environments for development and testing purposes at a fraction of the cost of using physical hardware.

Development Environment

Obviously, serious software developers use a development environment to build and test their programming changes before updating the production system. When setting up your Microsoft Dynamics CRM development environment, you should consider the following factors:

- The number of discrete projects or Microsoft Dynamics CRM organizations required
- The number of developers
- The types of customizations required
- Deployment configurations
- Available hardware
- Iteration frequency and deployment schedule

Considering that each organization has different needs based on these criteria, there is no "right way" to set up your development environment. The best option for your organization might not be appropriate for a different company.

The actual requirements of your production system dictate the environment you need to have in place for development (and testing). You should consider the following questions when beginning development on any Microsoft Dynamics CRM 4.0 project.

- Do you use the Windows 2003 or Windows 2008 operating system?
- Is your operating system 32-bit or 64-bit?

- Do your customizations need to be multi-tenant–capable?
- Will your application be accessed via the Outlook client?
- Do your customizations require offline capability?
- Do your customizations need to be SSL-compliant?
- Will your application be accessed with Internet Facing Deployment (IFD) or online deployments?
- Do your customizations need to be Web farm–compliant?
- Which version of Internet Explorer do your clients use?
- Will your customizations be accessed in multiple languages?
- What version of SQL Server is used, SQL Server 2005 or SQL Server 2008?
- Will your solution need to be accessed via a mobile client?

Next we will review different alternatives regarding how you might want to set up your server and Outlook client development environments.

Server Environment Development Options

Because Microsoft Dynamics CRM requires several infrastructure components such as Active Directory, Windows Server, and SQL Server, it's not convenient to set up different physical server environments for developing and testing. In addition to requiring more servers (either physical or virtual), it can be time-consuming just to set up these required components. Therefore, if you plan on having a team of developers working on Microsoft Dynamics CRM, you have a few other alternatives regarding how you set up your development server environment. The following sections explore four common development environment approaches:

- Using an isolated development environment
- Sharing a common Microsoft Dynamics CRM organization
- Using a hybrid environment
- Using different organizations in a single Microsoft Dynamics CRM deployment

Isolated Development Environment

An isolated development environment requires each developer to work from his or her individual (or isolated) copy of the Microsoft Dynamics CRM 4.0 application and database. This is most commonly done with a virtual image of Microsoft Dynamics CRM or when the base operating system of the developer's computer is Windows 2003 or Windows 2008 and Microsoft Dynamics CRM is installed directly on it.

This approach has the following advantages:

- Complete isolation of the development experience, allowing for the developer to maintain his or her environment as appropriate
- Simplified debugging of individual code
- Easier to develop custom Web pages with Microsoft Dynamics CRM because you can reference and debug the pages directly on the server

The isolated development environment does have a few disadvantages, including:

- You need to synchronize environment changes (customization changes) between multiple developers.
- Managing backups of the environment is more challenging because each developer has a full copy of the Microsoft Dynamics CRM system.
- Overall performance of the development computer may not be optimal because the developer's computer will be sharing resources with either the virtualization software or the Microsoft Dynamics CRM application.
- Since you are installing the Microsoft Dynamics CRM software to each developer's computer or using multiple Microsoft Dynamics CRM virtual images, additional software licenses, such as for SQL Server or the operating system software, may be required.
- Properly testing Web farm scenarios is more challenging.
- Large databases will take up more disk space and take longer to transfer between developer machines.

Figure 2-1 shows each developer's computer as a stand-alone Microsoft Dynamics CRM installation. You can (and should) share Active Directory and a development Exchange setup. The diagram also shows a build server used to aggregate Microsoft Dynamics CRM customizations and custom code from the development computers for deployment to a quality-assurance environment.

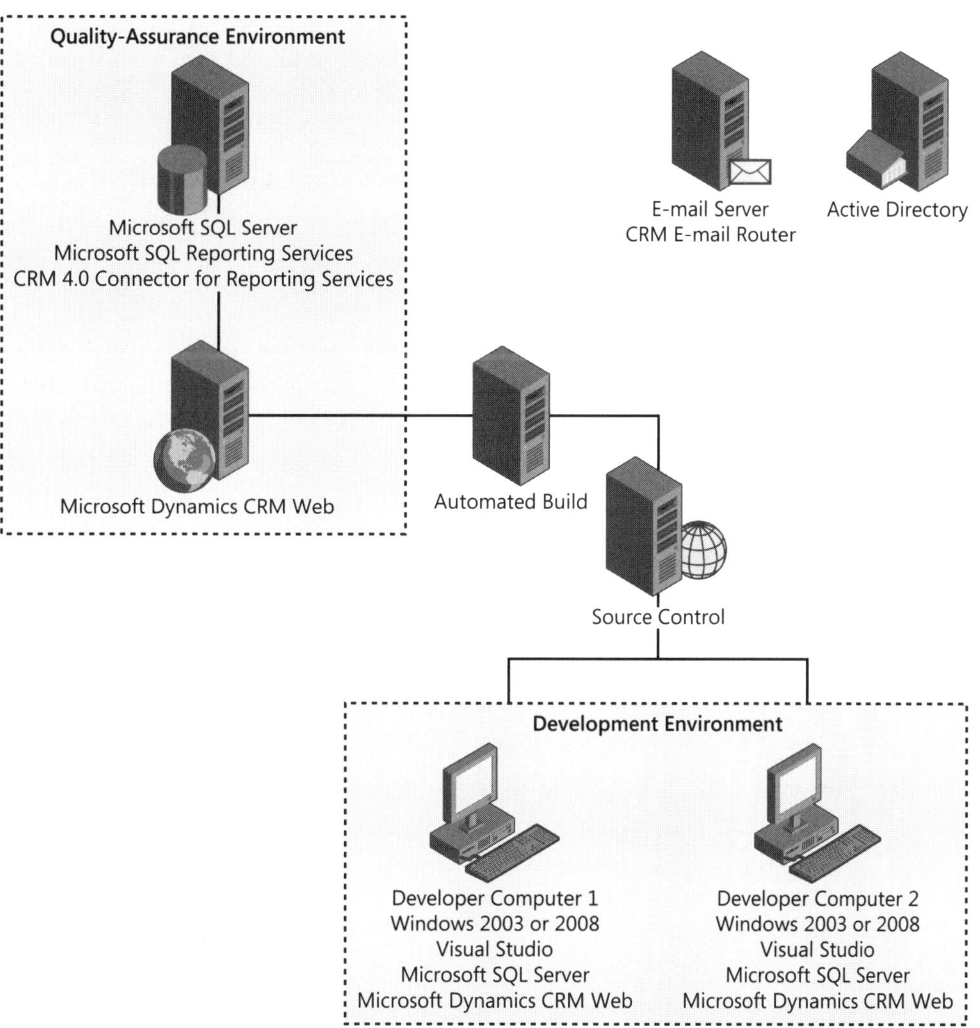

FIGURE 2-1 An example of an isolated Microsoft Dynamics CRM development environment

Although you should consider each of the disadvantages of the isolated approach, the most critical drawback that you should take into account is the merging of customization files. With multiple developers making schema and Microsoft Dynamics CRM customization changes on their discrete systems, you might have difficulty getting to a baseline set of final changes. It is possible to manually merge individual customization changes between environments, but that process is tricky and often would negatively impact the efficiency of your developers or quality-assurance team. If you plan to use this development environment approach, you should plan on including a programmatic approach to synchronize the environments between developers. Please refer to Chapter 8, "Developing with the Metadata Service," for more information on manipulating system customizations with code.

A hybrid environment approach, discussed later in the chapter, offers a possible solution to the problem of merging customizations. But let's first look at a different development environment option, sharing a common Microsoft Dynamics CRM environment.

Sharing a Common Microsoft Dynamics CRM Organization

The shared approach requires all of your developers to work from a common shared Microsoft Dynamics CRM deployment. They still develop their code on their individual computers, but they reference the customizations (i.e., schema) from a common installation.

This approach uses a common Web server or set of Web servers against a single database instance, so that each developer is always working on the most up-to-date schema and Microsoft Dynamics CRM customizations. You can also extend this approach by bringing up additional virtual servers pointed at the same Microsoft Dynamics CRM database, allowing you to use different server setups when developing and testing.

This approach has the following advantages:

- Schema and Microsoft Dynamics CRM customizations are accessed from a single location.
- Environment management is centralized for backups, storage space, and so on.
- No additional server software licensing is required.
- The load and specifications of each developer computer are reduced.
- Accommodating environment permutations (32-bit or 64-bit servers, Web farms, IFD, and so on) is easier.

The shared development environment also has the following disadvantages:

- The environment shares the asynchronous processing service and file system. This makes deploying and debugging changes more challenging for multiple developers working on any asynchronous logic (such as async plug-ins and workflow assemblies).
- Remote debugging must be used.
- Environment issues affect all developers.

Figure 2-2 shows a Microsoft Dynamics CRM installation shared by multiple developers. Each developer develops locally on his or her computer, but uses the schema and database from the shared Microsoft Dynamics CRM setup. The build server in this example merely compiles the custom code and extracts the customizations before applying to a quality-assurance environment.

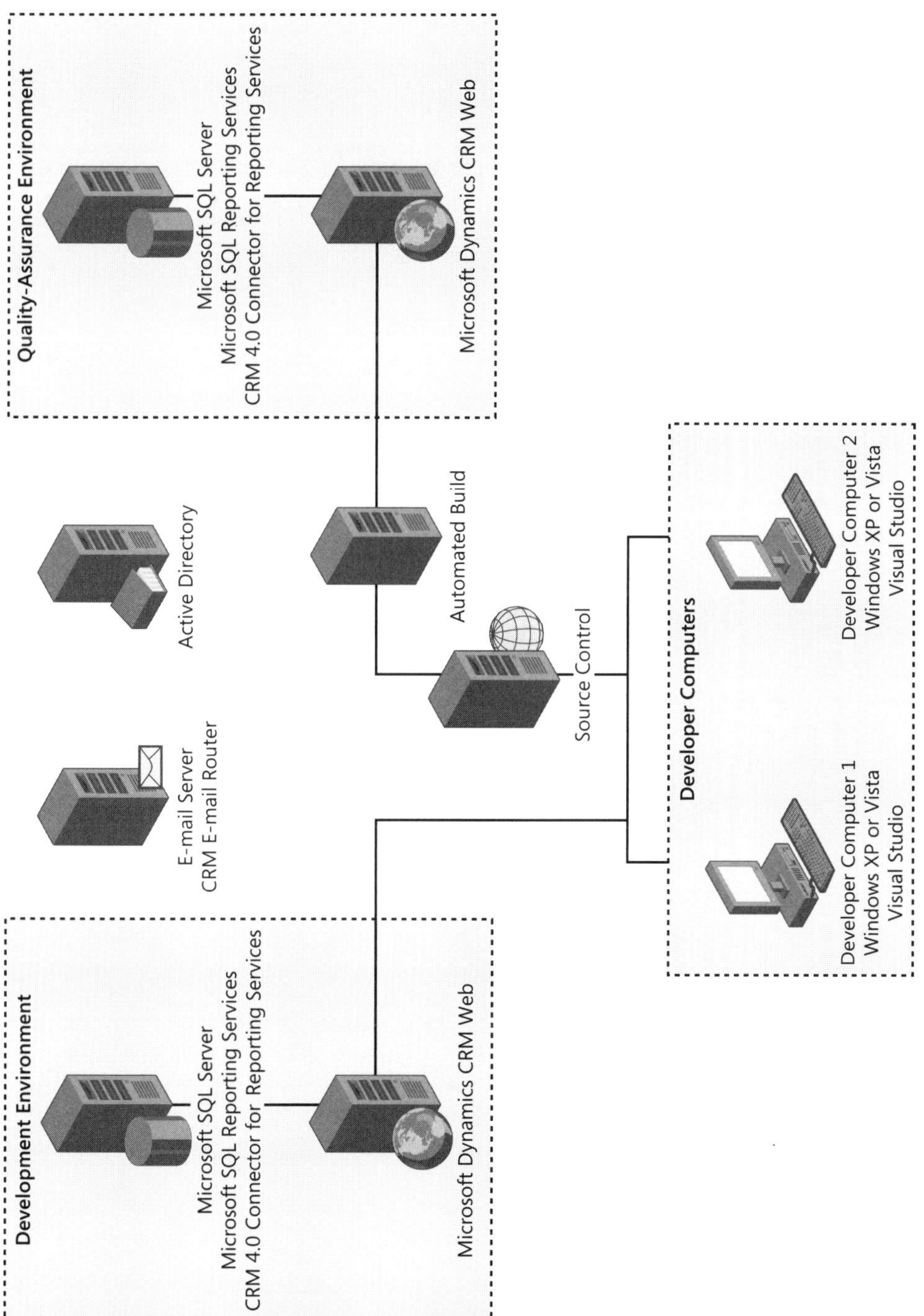

FIGURE 2-2 An example of using a shared Microsoft Dynamics CRM development environment

The key downside to the shared approach involves the Async service. Unfortunately, the Async service scans and executes against all organizations in the mscrm_config database. As you scale organizations to a centralized SQL Server computer, all of your developers are forced to use and debug against a single instance of the Async service.

Important Microsoft Dynamics CRM does not include an automated build server. You must set up your own if you want to leverage this functionality.

Using a Hybrid Environment

Now let's consider a third alternative that combines different facets of the first two environments. We start by assuming that you provide isolated Microsoft Dynamics CRM environments for each developer. That means each developer's computer requires a separate version of SQL Server 2005 and Microsoft Dynamics CRM 4.0 and that developers program their changes against their separate instance of Microsoft Dynamics CRM. Just as with the other approaches, you use the existing Active Directory infrastructure and a development Exchange environment. This provides all of the benefits described in the section titled "Isolated Development Environment" earlier in this chapter.

To help mitigate the main challenge of synchronizing Microsoft Dynamics CRM customizations between each development computer, you can create a shared customizations environment and force your team to make all Microsoft Dynamics CRM–related customization changes (such as schema updates) through that environment. Then you can automate a database backup/restore back to the individual developer environments either on a schedule or manually kicked off as needed. A disadvantage of this approach is that you will need to develop your own code and process to set up the automatic synchronizations of the database and customization changes, but that should be much easier than merging individual Microsoft Dynamics CRM customizations.

Figure 2-3 demonstrates a possible example of the hybrid development environment approach.

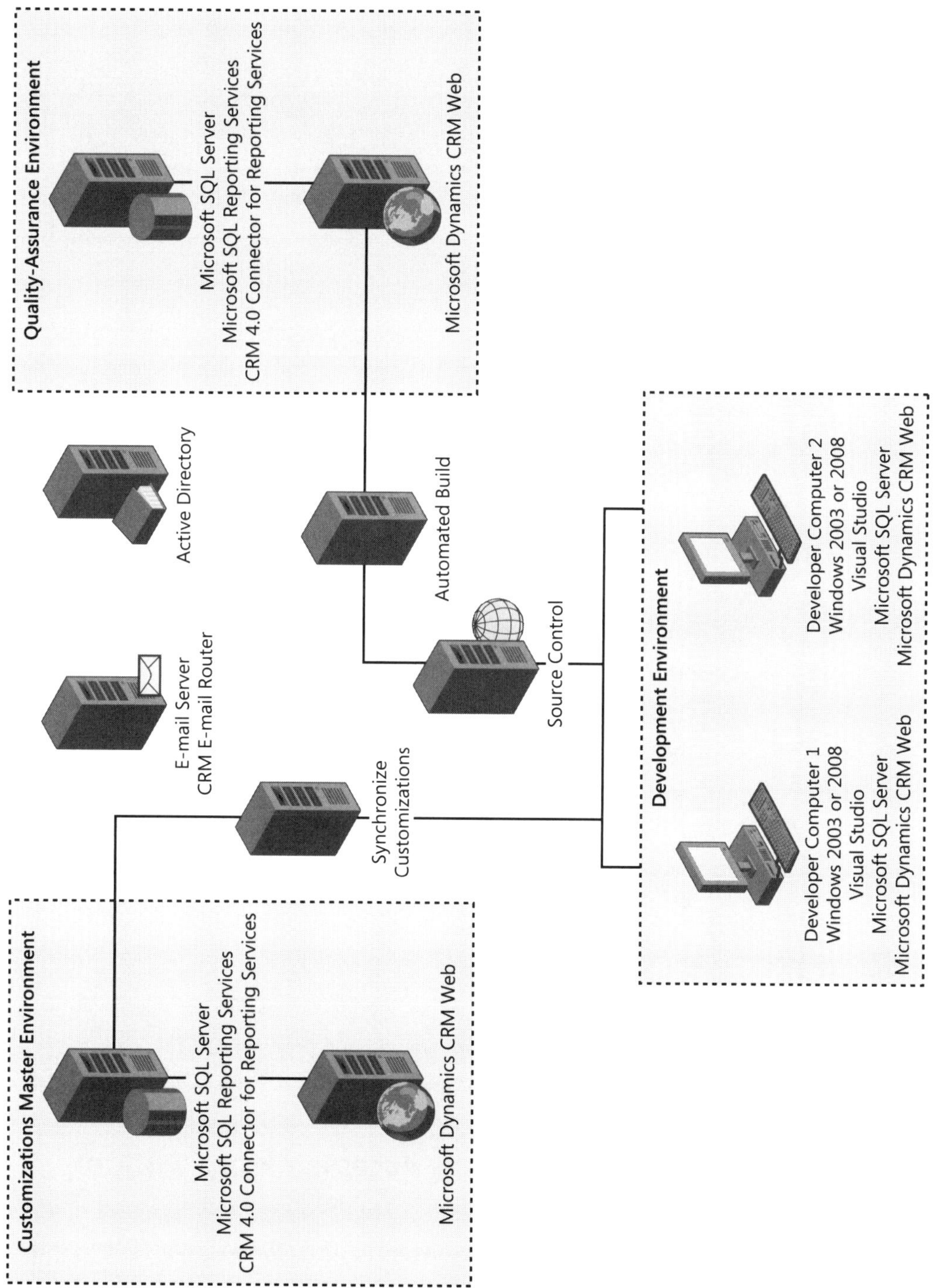

FIGURE 2-3 An example of a hybrid Dynamics CRM development environment

Using Different Organizations in a Single Microsoft Dynamics CRM Deployment

While the first three options provide the most flexibility for developers, another potential and simplified development environment option exists. By taking advantage of the multi-tenant functionality within the enterprise edition of Microsoft Dynamics CRM, you can simply create separate organizations for each environment (development, testing, etc.).

This approach has the following advantages:

- Provides development and testing environments that share a common set of hardware with no additional cost.
- You can be confident that the development system hardware specifications match the production system.

The multiple organization development environment has the following disadvantages:

- Server problems caused during development and testing will negatively impact production (or the other organizations on the server).
- Common development tasks such as resetting services or debugging code will affect production.
- Any custom Web page or Web service development becomes more challenging because you are sharing Web servers with production.
- Requires the enterprise edition of Microsoft Dynamics CRM.

Because the multi-tenant option reuses the same hardware as your production system, it works best when the configuration of Microsoft Dynamics CRM focuses mostly on native customizations and workflow. Native customization and workflow changes are contained within the Microsoft Dynamics CRM application and easily developed and deployed between organizations.

When possible, we recommend separating your development environment on its own set of hardware. However, if you are unable to use separate hardware for the development environment, consider the multi-tenant option over making programming or customization changes directly on the production organization.

Developing Customizations Accessed From Outlook

In addition to setting up your Microsoft Dynamics CRM development server, you should also think about how you will test your programming customizations within Microsoft Dynamics CRM for Outlook. In general, most of your customizations should execute equivalently from the Outlook interface, but if you have offline use as a requirement, you need to ensure that your logic works properly when disconnected from the server.

Microsoft Dynamics CRM for Outlook allows you to target only one Microsoft Dynamics CRM organization at a time. We recommend that you install the Outlook client on a separate desktop computer for testing and development. If you need to change your Outlook client from one organization to another, you can do so using the Outlook CRM client's Change Organization menu option.

Because Microsoft Dynamics CRM for Outlook client synchronizes contacts, activities, e-mail, and appointments into Outlook, you probably don't want to install this software on your normal Outlook profile. Therefore, it's a good idea to set up a separate test user and use that profile for testing. This way, you won't run the risk of accidentally contaminating your Outlook file with data from the test and development environments.

Tip You can only install Microsoft Dynamics CRM for Outlook with Offline Access for a single user on a computer. However if you're using the nonoffline version, you can log on to a computer with multiple users to access the software. Therefore, you could set up a single machine for testing the nonoffline version, and log on to the computer using different users (one for each organization).

Chapter 10, "Developing Offline Solutions," discusses developing with the Outlook client in greater detail.

Testing Environment Considerations

While this might seem obvious, you should make sure that your testing environment mirrors your production environment as closely as possible. For example, if you have a Web farm in production, you should have a Web farm in your testing environment. Pay attention to all of the details, such as operating system (Windows 2003 32-bit, Windows 2003 64-bit, and so on) as well as whether your users will be using Outlook to access your functionality. While you might not expect it, we have seen scenarios where code that works perfectly well on a 32-bit server does not work the same way on a 64-bit server. Therefore, please be sure you test all of the scenarios appropriately.

And of course, be sure that your test user has the same common permissions as your users. Often, developers use a system administrator account and inadvertently miss some potential defects when unit testing because of the privilege elevation of the account.

Migrating Data

Most of your implementations will contain a data migration component as part of your production deployment. Further, you need to import data when developing, testing, or providing a demo of the application. Given the importance of this task, you should understand your options for data migration within Microsoft Dynamics CRM.

The following approaches are common when importing data with Microsoft Dynamics CRM. They are listed starting from the easiest to accomplish to the most challenging:

- Native Microsoft Dynamics CRM import
- Data Migration Manager
- Third-party tools
- Custom code

Native Microsoft Dynamics CRM Import

Microsoft Dynamics CRM 4.0 allows for simple list imports to almost all entities, including custom entities. You access the native import functionality from the Tools menu and then proceed through a series of simple wizard screens to import your data. This approach works especially well when you have a 1-1 source-to-destination table mapping. Keep the following in mind when using the native Microsoft Dynamics CRM import tool:

- Be sure you have all required fields in your source data file.
- Save your source data file in the CSV format, and then run through the native import process.
- All records imported through the native Import functionality will be owned by you. If you need the records to be owned by someone else, you should either use an alternative method of import or simply reassign the records after you get them into the system (manually or with a workflow rule).
- To have relationships map, you need to have CRM automatically map the data for your import. To do this, ensure your import columns match EXACTLY the attribute display name. Further, you should also consider the following:
    - Be sure related records or picklist values exist in the system prior to import.
    - You can use the display value or the actual value of the lookup or picklist record. For lookup relationships, the display name will be the primary attribute and the record GUID will be its value. For picklist attributes, the display name will be the name shown to users and its value will be an integer.

- If your name (for either the lookup or the picklist) has duplicates, the record will not be imported. You will receive an error similar to "A duplicate lookup reference was found." You can avoid this by specifying the GUID (record ID of the referenced value) or integer (identifier for the picklist value) instead of the name. Keep in mind that only the record with the duplicate name will fail, not the entire import.

Data Migration Manager

Microsoft provides a more extensive data migration management tool called Microsoft Dynamics CRM 4.0 Data Migration Manager (DMM). The DMM includes sample data conversion maps from some common CRM systems. Further, the DMM overcomes the native import ownership limitation by allowing you to specify different owners for the records.

Caution A separate DMM exists for CRM Online. Be sure you use the correct version.

Download DMM for on-premise deployments at *http://www.microsoft.com/downloadS/details.aspx?FamilyID=6766880a-da8f-4336-a278-9a5367eb79ca&displaylang=en* and use *http://www.microsoft.com/downloads/details.aspx?FamilyId=2BBB3832-4B5F-4C2D-BFA8-2E74666F51DB&displaylang=en* for the CRM Online version.

Third-Party Tools

You can also find some useful third-party tools for data migration. A company called Scribe produces one of the more popular migration tools. The advantage of using a third-party tool would be to leverage existing templates and support from the import tool manufacturer. The downside is that these tools cost money and there is a learning curve to get your team up to speed on them.

Custom Code

When all else fails, you can always resort to writing your own import procedures, using the Microsoft Dynamics CRM API or directly with SQL. As you will learn throughout this book, you should have no trouble working with the Microsoft Dynamics CRM to load data into the application.

Caution Microsoft does not support inserting data directly to the SQL Server database.

When using the Microsoft Dynamics CRM API to insert data in bulk, you should pay attention to performance of the Web service. Because you will typically load data with a program running as a specific user, you can take advantage of connection sharing as shown below:

```
// Create the service
CrmService service = new CrmService();
service.Credentials = _crmService.Credentials;
service.Url = _crmService.Url;

// Enable unsafe connection sharing
service.UnsafeAuthenticatedConnectionSharing = true;
```

Enabling the *UnsafeAuthenticatedConnectionSharing* option will significantly increase performance of your migration.

Please review Chapter 3, "Communicating with the Microsoft CRM APIs" for more information regarding the *CrmService* Web service.

Redeployment

Often your developers or test team want real data to use in their development and testing environments. The process to move data from environment to environment depends on exactly what customizations and enhancements were made to the development system. It could consist of simply exporting and importing customizations, or it might contain more significant changes that warrant a full installation program. Fortunately, Microsoft Dynamics CRM 4.0 provides a simple process to redeploy an organization from one environment to another.

Microsoft Dynamics CRM 4.0 stores all of its transactional data and metadata in one database called <*organization*>_mscrm, where <*organization*> is the name of the organization you configured when you deployed. Therefore, to move transactional and metadata from one system to another, you simply need to restore the <*organization*>_mscrm database to your new environment and use the Microsoft Dynamics CRM Deployment Manager to import the new organization. This process includes customizations stored in the database, such as entity and attribute changes, security roles, native workflow rules, and any plug-in or workflow assembly deployed to the database. Custom Web pages or third-party integration still need to be deployed separately.

Important You need the Microsoft Dynamics CRM 4.0 Enterprise version to access multiple active organizations. Microsoft Dynamics CRM 4.0 Professional only permits one active organization at a time. You can import a new organization with Microsoft Dynamics CRM 4.0 Professional, but the import process will ask you to disable the current organization prior to proceeding with the import.

Let's step through a redeployment process on Microsoft Dynamics CRM Enterprise Server edition. In this example, we take a sample production system and redeploy it to our test environment.

Redeploying Microsoft Dynamics CRM

1. Back up the source Microsoft Dynamics CRM database. The database will be named *<organization>*_mscrm.
2. Restore the backup file on your new target SQL Server computer.
3. Log on to the Microsoft Dynamics CRM Web server and open the Microsoft Dynamics CRM Deployment Manager console from the Program Files menu.
4. Right-click Organizations and select Import Organization.

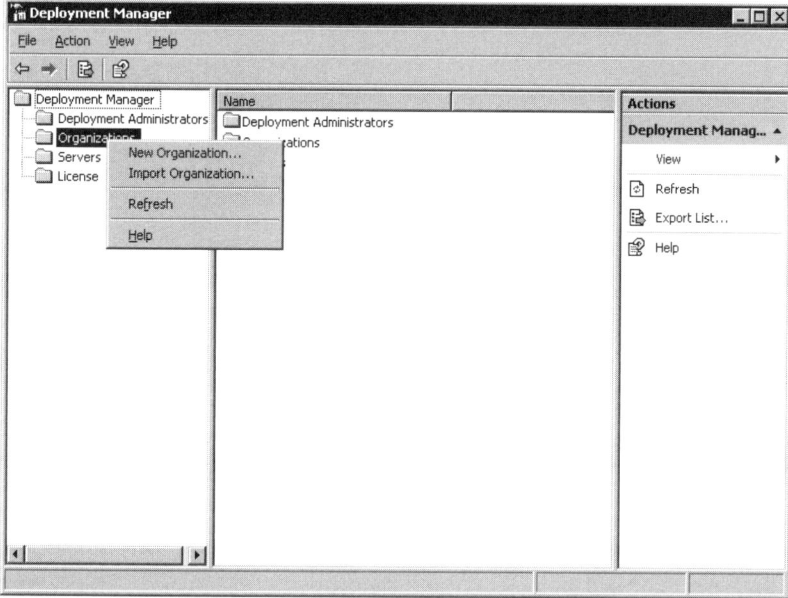

5. On the Import Organization Wizard page, select the target SQL Server and choose your newly restored database.

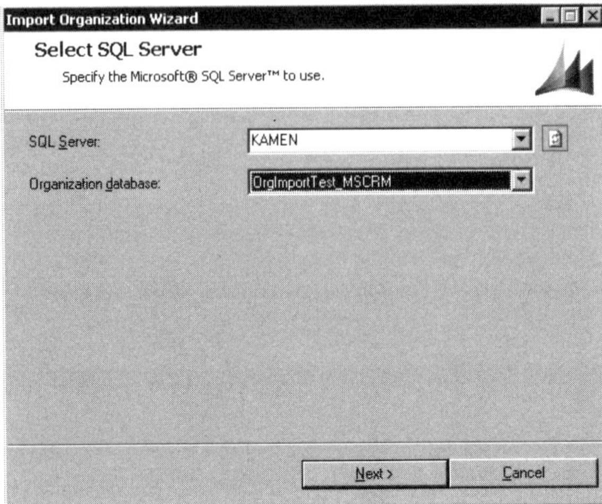

6. Enter the display name and name for your new organization and click Next.

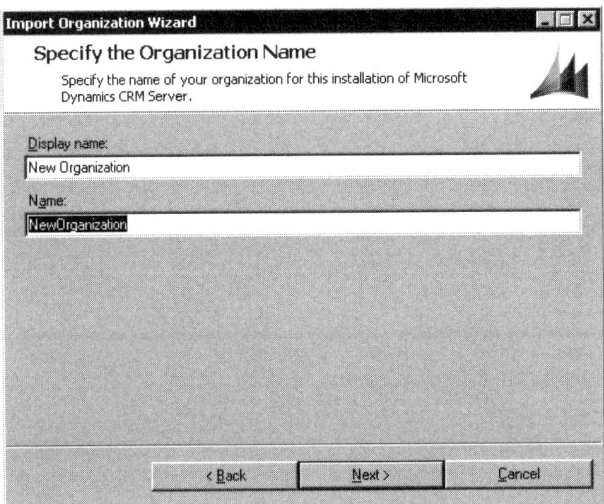

7. As with a brand-new Microsoft Dynamics CRM installation, you need an existing Reporting Services installation. In the Report Server URL field, enter a valid Reporting Services URL and click Next.

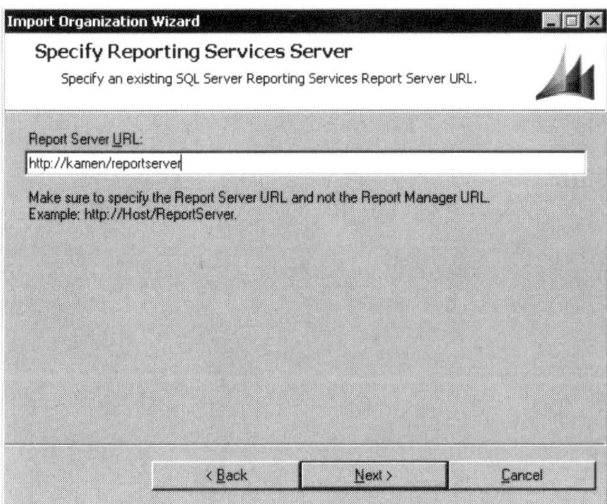

8. Now map the users from the source system to the users in the destination system. Remember that Microsoft Dynamics CRM uses Active Directory to authenticate users to the application. You have numerous options for mapping users. For our example, we will leave the default settings selected. Click Next.

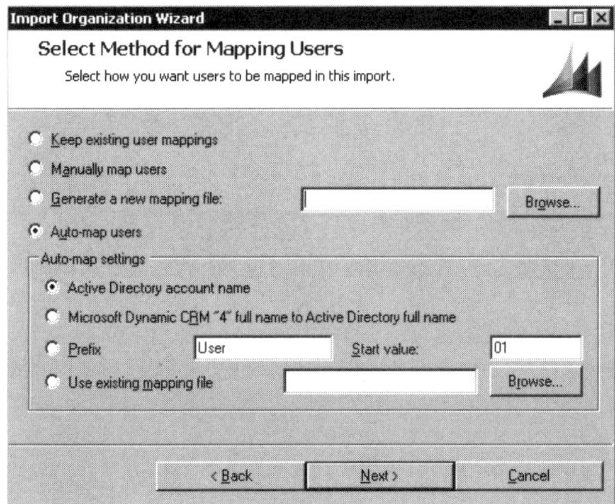

More Information Please review the Microsoft Dynamics CRM Operating Implementation Guide for additional details on mapping users.

9. Optionally, edit any user mappings. Click Next.

10. The Microsoft Dynamics CRM Import Organization Wizard now validates your entries. If the review screen returns no errors, click Next. Otherwise, correct the error and then try again.

11. On the Ready to Import page, review your sections. If you are satisfied with your selections, click Import to begin the import organization process.

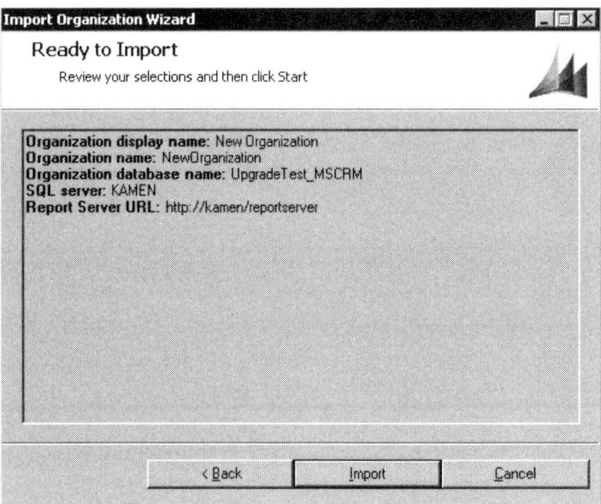

These simple steps allow you to quickly and easily move a Microsoft Dynamics CRM deployment between servers or within environments.

Development Tools

Every organization that develops software relies on development tools. One of the great benefits of Microsoft Dynamics CRM is that you use the same tools to develop solutions with Microsoft Dynamics CRM that you use when developing solutions for any Microsoft technology. Therefore, none of the tools discussed in this section is unique to working with Microsoft Dynamics CRM.

This section examines some of the common software development tools you should have in place when working with Microsoft Dynamics CRM, including:

- Integrated development environment (IDE)
- Source control
- Continuous integration
- Installer
- Additional development utilities

Integrated Development Environment (IDE)

Microsoft Visual Studio is most likely to be your primary integrated development environment (IDE). The examples in this book use Visual Studio 2008. Because Microsoft built Microsoft Dynamics CRM on the .NET architecture, you may use any .NET client tool for your development experience (including Notepad)! However, most developers working with Microsoft Dynamics CRM choose Visual Studio as their development tool.

Source Control

Source control defines the means of keeping track of changes and versions to all software files during a project. Numerous tools exist to perform this function and typically a source control system already exists within your environment, including Microsoft Visual Studio Team System, Microsoft Visual SourceSafe, CVS, ClearCase, Vault, and so on.

If you don't have a version control tool in place or you are investigating an alternative, we recommend a free, open-source tool call Subversion (SVN). SVN provides the core file control logic and integrates to most systems. Additional tools talk to SVN for actual file access; the most popular is Tortoise, as shown in Figure 2-4.

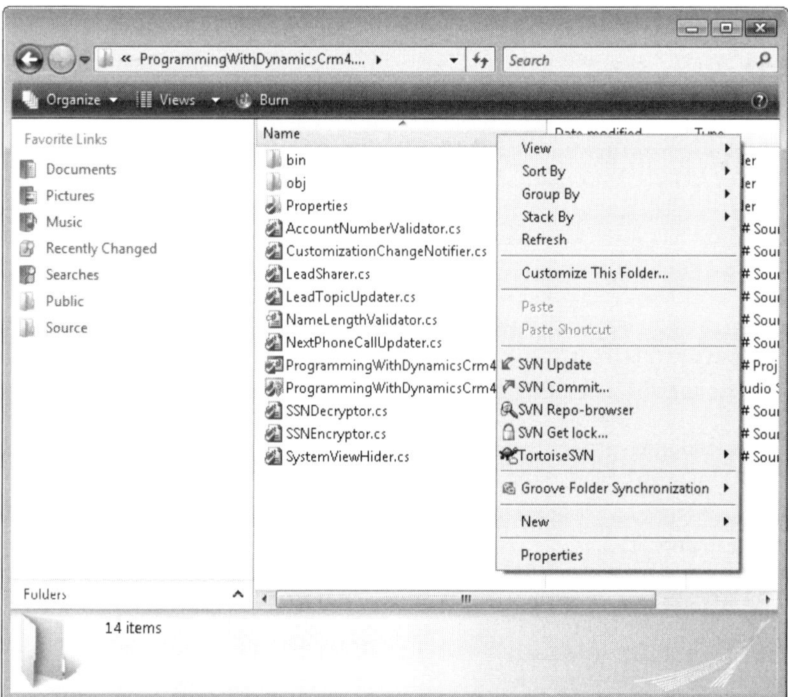

FIGURE 2-4 TortoiseSVN browser menu

More Information Learn more about SVN version control system and the TortoiseSVN browser at: *http://subversion.tigris.org* and *http://tortoisesvn.tigris.org*.

Continuous Integration Tool

Often as you bring up your development environment, setting up a continuous integration environment tends to get overlooked. However, a continuous integration system, especially automated builds, provides the following benefits:

- Ensures a more robust application during development by finding build defects quickly
- Simplifies deployments by ensuring a consistent set of files and steps
- Can include additional post-build steps and processes
- Labels source code at each build version, allowing you to branch and fix issues easily
- Can be used to export and store customizations as a backup file
- Can provide additional automated testing

SourceForge.NET provides an excellent free tool called CruiseControl.NET to manage automated builds for your code. You can use CruiseControl.NET in conjunction with MSBuild from Visual Studio or a free tool such as NAnt from SourceForge.NET.

More Information You may download and review more information regarding CruiseControl.NET at *http://sourceforge.net/projects/ccnet* and NAnt at *http://nant.sourceforge.net/*.

Installer

Some of your Microsoft Dynamics CRM customizations may not deploy with the Microsoft Dynamics CRM import/export customizations functionality, including:

- Custom Web pages
- Plug-in assemblies
- Workflow assemblies
- Custom reports
- Data migration

When you deploy files and changes that are not encapsulated within Microsoft Dynamics CRM's import/export customization functionality, you should consider whether you need to use an installer.

Multiple installer programs exist on the market, including one that comes with Visual Studio. Each installer program has its own set of features, functionality, and benefits. We use the NSIS system from SourceForge.NET.

NSIS provides robust Windows installers in a very easy, scriptable, and extensible framework. Using NSIS you can create common installation wizard pages that can take information from the user and use built-in or custom functions to properly deploy and provision your application.

NSIS contains a tool that allows you to compile NSI scripts into executables, as shown in Figure 2-5. Additionally, you can access numerous additional plug-ins, starter code, and help documentation to provide a solid start to your installation development.

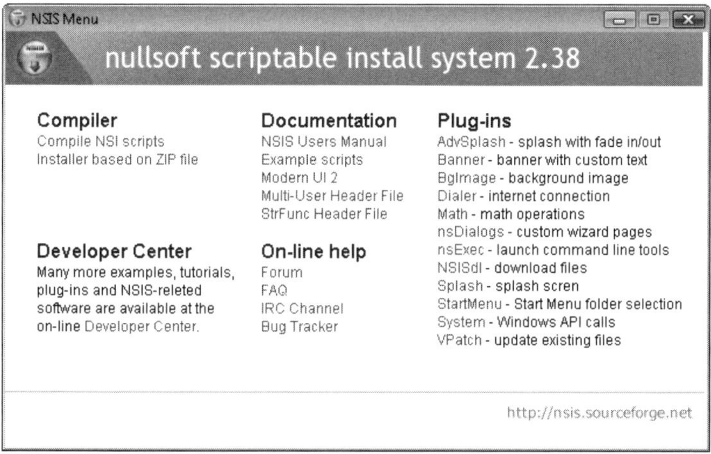

FIGURE 2-5 NSIS Menu

Tip You can also use a development tool such as Eclipse with an NSIS plug-in to author and build your installation scripts. You can learn more about EclipseNSIS at *http://nsis.sourceforge.net/EclipseNSIS_-_NSIS_plugin_for_Eclipse*.

Listing 2-1 shows a very simple script that generates an installer that copies a simple help file to a defined location.

LISTING 2-1 Sample NSIS installer script

```
Name "NSIS Test"

# Defines
!define REGKEY "SOFTWARE\$(^Name)"
!define TRUE 1

# MUI defines
```

```
!define MUI_ICON "${NSISDIR}\Contrib\Graphics\Icons\modern-install.ico"
!define MUI_FINISHPAGE_NOAUTOCLOSE

# Included files
!include Sections.nsh
!include MUI.nsh

# Installer pages
!insertmacro MUI_PAGE_WELCOME
!insertmacro MUI_PAGE_DIRECTORY
!insertmacro MUI_PAGE_INSTFILES
!insertmacro MUI_PAGE_FINISH

# Installer languages
!insertmacro MUI_LANGUAGE English

# Installer attributes
OutFile setup.exe
InstallDir "$PROGRAMFILES\NSIS Test"
CRCCheck on
XPStyle on
ShowInstDetails show

# Installer sections
Section "Help Sample" Main
    SetOutPath $INSTDIR
    SetOverwrite on
    # Copies HelpSample.htm to the path specified in the installation wizard.
     File "HelpSample.htm"
    WriteRegStr HKLM "${REGKEY}\Components" "Help Sample" 1
SectionEnd

# Installer functions
Function .onInit
    InitPluginsDir
FunctionEnd
```

Figure 2-6 displays one of the sample wizard pages for a Windows installer using the sample NSIS script in Listing 2-1.

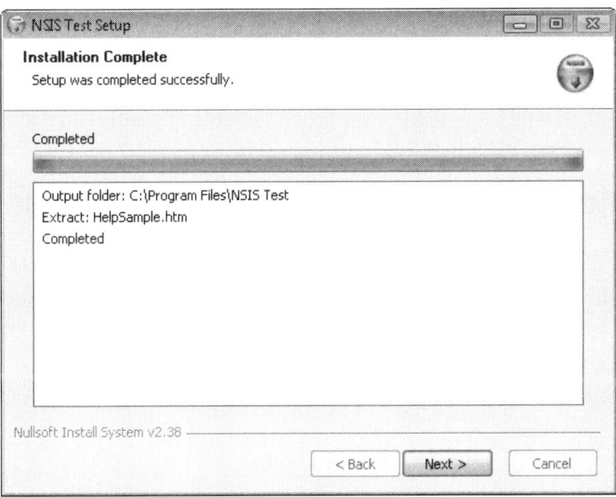

FIGURE 2-6 Sample Windows installer

More Information Please visit *http://nsis.sourceforge.net/Main_Page* for additional information regarding NSIS.

Additional Development Utilities

If you develop solutions with any Microsoft technology, including Microsoft Dynamics CRM, you definitely should consider having the tools listed in Table 2-4.

TABLE 2-4 Additional Development Utilities

Tool	Download
FxCop	*http://msdn.microsoft.com/en-us/library/bb429476(vs.80).aspx* A free code best practice analyzer. You can incorporate it into your automatic builds, and it is highly customizable.
ILMerge	*http://research.microsoft.com/~mbarnett/ILMerge.aspx* A free tool to merge multiple assemblies into a single assembly. Perfect for deploying referenced assemblies with a plug-in or workflow assembly.
.NET Reflector	*http://www.aisto.com/roeder/dotnet/* An excellent tool for analyzing .NET assemblies.
Fiddler	*http://www.fiddlertool.com* A free HTTP debugging proxy tool. Fiddler is essential for tracking and parsing the HTTP traffic between Microsoft Dynamics CRM both for development and debugging purposes.
DebugBar	*http://www.debugbar.com/* A licensed Web development tool that integrates directly within Internet Explorer. Allows you to quickly navigate the DOM of a Microsoft Dynamics CRM Web page.

TABLE 2-4 Additional Development Utilities

Tool	Download
IE Dev Toolbar	*http://www.microsoft.com/downloadS/details.aspx?familyid=E59C3964-672D-4511-BB3E-2D5E1DB91038&displaylang=en* A free Web development tool with functionality similar to the DebugBar tool.
NUnit	*http://www.nunit.org/index.php* A free, open-source unit-testing framework.
RhinoMocks	*http://www.ayende.com/projects/rhino-mocks.aspx* Another free, open-source unit-testing framework. See Chapter 5, "Plug-ins," for an example that uses the RhinoMocks framework.

Additional Development Considerations

In addition to the topics discussed in depth within this chapter, please keep the following items in mind as you prepare your environments.

- Thoroughly review the Implementation Guide for installation and configuration details about Microsoft Dynamics CRM deployment and environment options.
- Understand the business requirements for your Microsoft Dynamics CRM project and how they affect development and testing. You should have an environment for each configuration you plan to support that mirrors production.
- Create both a development and a staging environment. You can make use of virtualization to help mitigate hardware costs.
- Use a source control system (for example, Visual SourceSafe or Subversion) for your custom files and consider a continuous integration tool (such as CruiseControl.NET) as well.
- Back up your databases and any custom source files. You can use the Microsoft Dynamics CRM API to easily export your customizations and include that in your backup procedures.
- Multi-tenant deployments require Microsoft Dynamics CRM 4.0 Enterprise Edition.
- You can add and delete organizations only through the Deployment Manager installed on the Microsoft Dynamics CRM Web server.
- Microsoft Dynamics CRM 4.0 stores all of its transactional data and metadata in one database called <*organization*>_mscrm, where <*organization*> is the name of the organization you configured when you deployed. In addition to this database, Microsoft Dynamics CRM uses one configuration database (mscrm_config), which manages the different organizations and their settings installed on that SQL Server instance.

- Microsoft Dynamics CRM 4.0 allows only one installation per SQL Server instance. You need to install another brand-new Microsoft Dynamics CRM environment to another SQL Server instance or a completely separate SQL Server instance.
- You can share SQL Server, Reporting Services, and Exchange Server hardware between your staging and development environments, provided that you use multi-tenancy.
- You can use virtual servers to create complete instances of Microsoft Dynamics CRM or any of the components. Monitor performance and determine whether you need to apply more resources to the virtual image or possibly move to a physical server.
- Remember that each organization is an isolated environment of customizations and data. You cannot natively share data or records between organizations, although you can write tools (or find third-party tools) to synchronize the data.
- Create organizational units (OUs) in your development Active Directory domain for each separate installation so that it is easier to keep track of your installation groups in Active Directory.
- Use the new import organization feature of the Deployment tool to synchronize your data between Microsoft Dynamics CRM deployments in different domains. You cannot simply restore the databases to the new domain because the system GUIDs will not match.

Summary

You develop solutions for Microsoft Dynamics CRM in the same manner that you develop a solution on any Microsoft platform. Microsoft Dynamics CRM uses the same recommended architecture and frameworks that most Microsoft developers are accustomed to seeing. You should build your development environment and use the tools in the way that makes the most sense for your organization.

Chapter 3

Communicating with Microsoft CRM APIs

As a developer, you will spend a lot of time working with the Microsoft Dynamics CRM APIs because they provide the recommended access to the system data. The Microsoft Dynamics CRM APIs consist of a collection of Web services and assemblies that you can consume directly with your custom programming code or application.

Microsoft Dynamics CRM 4.0 provides multiple ways for you to enhance its native functionality with your own unique code. This chapter will examine how you can communicate with the APIs. Subsequent chapters explore the integration options in further detail. We'll cover the following topics in this chapter:

- Overview of the Microsoft Dynamics CRM 4.0 SDK
- Accessing the APIs in Microsoft Visual Studio 2008
- Using the *CrmService* Web Service
- Using the *MetadataService* Web Service
- Using the *CrmDiscoveryService* Web Service
- Connecting to Microsoft Dynamics CRM IFD
- Connecting to Microsoft Dynamics CRM Offline
- Connecting to Microsoft Dynamics CRM Online

Overview of the Microsoft Dynamics CRM 4.0 SDK

The Microsoft Dynamics CRM 4.0 SDK defines all the supported programming interaction points, also known as application programming interfaces (APIs), that you can access when writing code that integrates with Microsoft Dynamics CRM. Using the APIs for your customizations provides several significant benefits:

- **Ease of use** The APIs include hundreds of pages of documentation, complete with real-world examples, code samples, and helper classes to help you write code that works with Microsoft Dynamics CRM.
- **Supportability** If you encounter technical problems or issues using the APIs, you can contact Microsoft technical support or use the Microsoft Dynamics CRM public newsgroup for assistance.

- **Upgrade support** Microsoft makes every effort to ensure that code that you create for Microsoft Dynamics CRM using the APIs will upgrade smoothly with future versions of the product, even if the underlying Microsoft SQL Server database changes radically. This is also true for any updates or hotfixes that Microsoft might release for Microsoft Dynamics CRM.
- **Certification** By following the documented APIs, you can submit your customizations to a third-party testing vendor to certify that your application works within the confines of the SDK. This certification provides comfort and reassurance for people evaluating your customizations.

Accessing the APIs in Visual Studio 2008

Before you can programmatically use the methods and logic available in Microsoft Dynamics CRM, you must first add the API references to your project. You can add any of the APIs by using one of the following methods:

- Access the Web reference URL directly in Visual Studio 2008.
- Download the WSDL definition to the file system and add the Web reference locally.
- Reference the Microsoft.Crm.Sdk and Microsoft.Crm.SdkTypeProxy assemblies.

With the Web service APIs, you have a choice of referencing the service endpoint directly or connecting to an exported WSDL file. We discuss both approaches shortly. Table 3-1 lists the three Web service–based APIs available, the recommended namespace names, and where you can download the WSDL file. Even though we recommend that you use the same naming convention described in Table 3-1, you can choose whatever naming convention you prefer.

TABLE 3-1 Available Microsoft Dynamics CRM Web Service APIs

API Name	Namespace Name	WSDL Location
CrmService	*CrmSdk*	Download from Microsoft Dynamics CRM user interface for each organization
MetadataService	*MetadataSdk*	Download from Microsoft Dynamics CRM user interface for each organization
CrmDiscoveryService	*CrmSdk.Discovery*	Included in the WSDL folder of the Microsoft Dynamics CRM SDK

Table 3-2 lists the Microsoft Dynamics CRM Web service API URL locations for on-premise deployments.

TABLE 3-2 Available Microsoft Dynamics CRM Web Service API End Points

API name	On-premise deployment endpoint
CrmService	*http://*<crmserver>*/mscrmservices/2007/crmservice.asmx*
MetadataService	*http://*<crmserver>*/mscrmservices/2007/metadataservice.asmx*
DiscoveryService	*http://*<crmserver>*/mscrmservices/2007/ad/crmdiscoveryservice.asmx*

Note Microsoft Dynamics CRM Online uses a unique address for the DiscoveryService Web service: *https://dev.crm.dynamics.com/mscrmservices/2007/passport/crmdiscoveryservice.asmx*.

Microsoft also offers three assemblies that you can use to programmatically interact with Microsoft Dynamics CRM instead (with some benefits and constraints):

- Microsoft.Crm.Sdk.dll
- Microsoft.Crm.SdkTypeProxy.dll
- Microsoft.Crm.Outlook.Sdk.dll

The Web service APIs can provide a dynamic, strongly typed development reference for custom entities and attributes. This provides a more robust development experience. However, you must keep the Web references up to date to utilize your new customizations with strongly typed code at compile time.

On the other hand, the assembly references wrap the Web service functionality and provide most of the core functionality (and default entity access). Further, these assemblies provide additional helper functionality. However, your code will not be able to use the strongly typed references for any schema customizations made to the system. Also, when using the assembly references, you take advantage of the Microsoft Dynamics CRM's *DynamicEntity* concept (which we discuss in detail later in the chapter). By using this approach, you will have an easier time deploying common solutions across multiple and changing environments.

Tip Are your custom entities or new attributes not appearing in Microsoft IntelliSense in Visual Studio? Make sure that you have published your changes *and* updated your Web reference in Visual Studio 2008. Updating the reference depends on the technique you used to reference the WSDL. If you used the URL, you can update the reference directly from Visual Studio 2008. If you referenced the file, you need to first export a new WSDL and replace the existing one before you see the change.

When developing assembly-based solutions such as plug-ins and workflow assemblies, we recommend that you reference the API assemblies instead of using the Web references. For Web development applications, you can use either the WSDL or assembly reference approach.

Note You can access the *CrmDiscoveryService* functionality only as a Web-based WSDL reference.

Microsoft built Microsoft Dynamics CRM 4.0 against the Microsoft .NET Framework 3.0. Consequently, most developers will build their solutions with Visual Studio 2008 targeted at the .NET Framework 3.0. Technically, you could also build against the .NET Framework 3.5, but then you will need to make sure that the .NET 3.5 Framework is installed on the destination server. Note that the ASP.NET version configured in Internet Information Services (IIS) will probably be 2.0.50727, but this is the run-time version of .NET. The run-time versions of the .NET Framework 3.0 and 3.5 are identical to those of the .NET Framework 2.0, so any code developed with those versions of the .NET framework will run properly on the 2.0.50727 run-time engine.

More Info Please review the latest SDK for the most up-to-date information on support for .NET Framework versions.

The following example demonstrates how to add references for the *CrmService* and Microsoft.Crm.Sdk using each of the preceding techniques. You would use a similar technique for the other API references.

Adding the *CrmService* Web reference URL directly in your project

1. Create a new Console application project in Visual Studio 2008 and select the .NET 3.0 Framework.

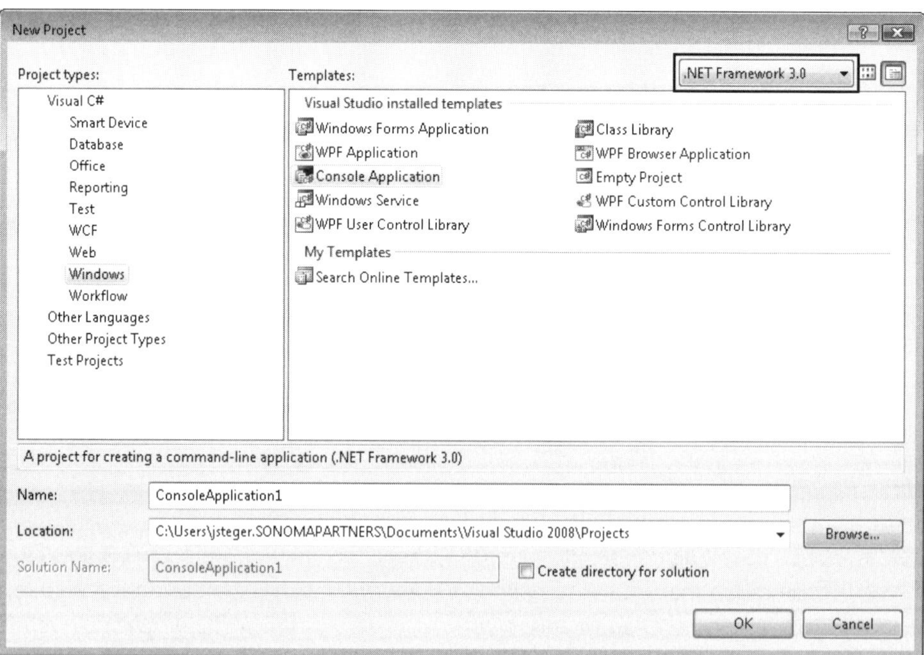

2. Right-click the project, and then click Add Service Reference.
3. Click the Advanced button in the Add Service Reference box.
4. In the Service Reference Settings box, click Add Web Reference.
5. In the Add Web Reference dialog box, add the *CrmService* reference:
    a. In the URL box, type **http://*<crmserver>*/mscrmservices/2007/crmservice.asmx**, and then click Go.
    b. In the Web reference name box, type **CrmSdk**. (Note that if you are using C#, this is case sensitive.)
    c. Click Add Reference.

Adding an on-premise *CrmService* service WSDL reference to your project

1. Open Microsoft Dynamics CRM in a Web browser, click Settings, click Customization, and then select Download Web Service Description Files.
2. Click the icon of the *CrmService.asmx* file to download. The file will open in a Web browser window.
3. In the Web browser, save the page to your file system as an XML file. (In Internet Explorer 7, click Page, and then click Save As.) Be sure to change the file name to end with the .xml or .wsdl extension (for example, *CrmServiceWsdl.xml*).
4. Create a new Console application project in Visual Studio 2008 and target the .NET 3.0 Framework.
5. Right-click the project, and then click Add Service Reference.
6. Click the Advanced button in the Add Service Reference box.
7. In the Service Reference Settings box, click Add Web Reference.
8. In the Add Web Reference dialog box, add the *CrmService* reference:
    a. In the URL box, type the location of your downloaded WSDL file (for example, **c:*CrmServiceWsdl.xml***), and then click Go.
    b. In the Web reference name box, type **CrmSdk**. (Note that if you are using C#, this is case sensitive.)
    c. Click Add Reference.

Note The Visual Studio 2005 Add Web Reference command automatically appears in Visual Studio 2008 when you target the .NET 2.0 Framework.

Adding the SDK assemblies references to your project

1. Create a new Console application project in Visual Studio 2008.
2. Right-click the project, and then click Add Reference.
3. In the Add Reference dialog box, click the Browse tab.
4. Navigate the file system and find the Microsoft.Crm.Sdk.dll assembly. The SDK assemblies reside in the SDK's bin folder or the GAC folder of the Microsoft Dynamics CRM server installation CD. Click OK to add.
5. Repeat steps 2-4, but now add the Microsoft.Crm.Sdk.TypeProxy.

After you add the references to your project, you are ready to begin development.

Caution Do not add both the WSDL-based reference and the Microsoft.Crm.* assemblies to your project. The references share the same namespace and many of the same properties and methods, which will force to you fully qualify all of your commands. We recommend you use one approach per project file.

Before we begin to code, let's review the key functionality contained in each of Web service APIs.

CrmService Web Service

The Web service is the core API mechanism for programmatically interacting with all entities in Microsoft Dynamics CRM. This service contains six common methods that work on all entities, and an *Execute* method that is available for all other needs. The service is strongly typed and WSDL compliant, and it can be updated with any changes to the schema directly through Visual Studio 2008.

Important Microsoft Dynamics CRM automatically updates its API interfaces as you add custom entities and custom attributes using the Web-based administration tools. For example, if you add multiple custom attributes to the Account entity, you can reference these new attributes programmatically through the API, and you can even use IntelliSense updates to reflect these new attributes in Visual Studio 2008 when using the WSDL-based API.

The *CrmService* Web service is located at *http://*<crmserver>*/mscrmservices/2007/crmservice.asmx*, where *<crmserver>* is the Microsoft Dynamics CRM Web server.

In addition, we recommend that you initialize the service *Url* property in your code, as shown in the following code example:

```
public static CrmService GetCrmService(string orgName, string server)
{
  // Standard CRM Service Setup
  CrmAuthenticationToken token = new CrmAuthenticationToken();
  token.AuthenticationType = 0; //AD (On-premise)
  token.OrganizationName = orgName;

  CrmService service = new CrmService();
  service.Credentials = System.Net.CredentialCache.DefaultCredentials;

  // If you know you are using the default credentials,
  // you can replace the service.Crendentials line with the following line
  // service.UseDefaultCredentials = true;

  service.CrmAuthenticationTokenValue = token;
  service.Url = string.Format("http://{0}/mscrmservices/2007/crmservice.asmx",server);

  return service;
}
```

Note We reuse the *GetCrmService()* method in some of the examples.

With the service's *Url* property, you can access the Web service URL, which might be different from the URL specified in your project's Web reference. Set the *Url* property of the service by using a configuration approach or by using the *CrmDiscoveryService* so that you can deploy to different environments without having to recompile your code. We demonstrate setting the service *Url* property using the *CrmDiscoveryService* later in the chapter.

Tip Specifying a valid organization name in the token for your service's URL is critical. If you receive a 401: Unauthorized error, first check to see whether you have the correct unique organization name for your service's endpoint.

Now that you have a little background on the *CrmService* Web service, we can review these additional topics related to the *CrmService*:

- Authentication
- Common methods
- *Execute* methods
- *Request* and *Response* classes
- *DynamicEntity* class
- Attributes

Authentication

When your code references the Microsoft Dynamics CRM APIs, of course you need to provide the appropriate authentication information so that you receive the appropriate security-related information. How you authenticate to the APIs depends on how your code will be deployed. From an authentication standpoint, Microsoft Dynamics CRM considers three different deployment models:

- On-premise (intranet via Active Directory)
- Internet-facing deployment (IFD)
- Microsoft Dynamics CRM Online

Note Microsoft Dynamics CRM Online uses Windows Live Id authentication. Please refer to the SDK for additional information.

We discuss the on-premise authentication in three areas:

- Authenticating to the API services
- Configuring the security token
- Understanding the security context of the method call

Authenticating to the API Services

With an on-premise deployment, your code needs to pass valid Active Directory credentials to communicate properly with the Microsoft Dynamics CRM Web service APIs. You commonly see this handled with the following *Credentials* line of code:

```
CrmService service = new CrmService();
service.Credentials = System.Net.CredentialCache.DefaultCredentials;
```

This code uses the logged-on user's credentials for validation. By default, the Microsoft Dynamics CRM APIs then translate the domain credentials to the proper CRM system user and uses the CRM user ID (usually referred to as the *systemuserid*) throughout the life of that service's instantiation.

Instead of using the logged-on user's credentials, you can also specify a user to authenticate by passing in a valid set of credentials as shown in the following line of code:

```
service.Credentials = new NetworkCredential("UserName","UserPassword","UserDomain");
```

Obviously, try to avoid hard-coding any credential set, but if you do have to use this approach, be sure to encrypt the information. We describe the hard-coded credential option so that you can understand that authenticating to the Web service is network-dependent, not Microsoft Dynamics CRM–dependent. As long as a user has a valid Active Directory credential set, the user can authenticate to the service APIs, even if that user is not a valid Microsoft Dynamics CRM user. However, to actually retrieve any data you must provide a valid Microsoft Dynamics CRM *systemuserid*. This concept is discussed further shortly.

Configuring the Security Token

In addition to the multiple deployment models, some editions of Microsoft Dynamics CRM include the option for a user to work with multiple organizations (multi-tenant). Therefore, you need to construct and pass an authentication token to the API as part of the SOAP header. The code for the token typically is the following:

```
CrmAuthenticationToken token = new CrmAuthenticationToken();
token.AuthenticationType = 0; //AD (On-premise)
token.OrganizationName = "<ValidOrganizationName>";
```

You need to set the authentication type and specify the unique name of the organization you want to access. Table 3-3 lists the possible values for the *AuthenticationType* property. Choose the type appropriate for your deployment.

TABLE 3-3 ***AuthenticationType*** **Values**

Description	Value
Active Directory	0
Microsoft Dynamics CRM Online	1
Internet-facing deployment (IFD)	2

Finally, you can set the service's *CrmAuthenticationTokenValue* property to your newly created token, as shown in the following code:

```
service.CrmAuthenticationTokenValue = token;
```

More Info You can learn more about the Web service security in Chapter 4, "Security."

Understanding the Security Context of a Method Call

Now that you have properly connected to the service, you need to understand the Microsoft Dynamics CRM security context under which the call is being made. This need is often overlooked because Microsoft Dynamics CRM implicitly defaults to the user set with the *Credentials* property.

The security context used by Microsoft Dynamics CRM determines which actions can be performed with the API. For instance, if you write logic that creates a new lead, the calling user must have rights to create a lead.

Important Context also varies depending on how you access the API. For example, plug-ins execute under the same identity as the Microsoft Dynamics CRM Web application pool. Workflow context execution varies depending on how the rule is initiated.

Microsoft Dynamics CRM recognizes that at times you might need to perform actions on behalf of a user whose rights in the Microsoft Dynamics CRM application differ from the user who triggered the logic. You can perform this type of authentication in your code by using a technique known as impersonation. Chapter 4 takes a closer look at impersonation and other security-related topics.

Common Methods

The following six methods provide the basic create, read, update, and delete (CRUD) operations for entities, including custom entities:

- ***Create*** Creates a new record for a given entity.
- ***Retrieve*** Returns a single record based on the entity ID passed in.
- ***RetrieveMultiple*** Returns multiple records based on a query expression.
- ***Update*** Edits an existing record.
- ***Delete*** Removes a record.
- ***Fetch*** Returns multiple records based on a FetchXML query. The FetchXML query syntax mirrors that of previous Microsoft Dynamics CRM versions.

Let's review how you would use one of the common methods in your code. This example retrieves the account name, main telephone number, and relationship type for a single Account record, and then displays the information. You will work with the Account record shown in Figure 3-1. For simplicity, this example runs in a console application.

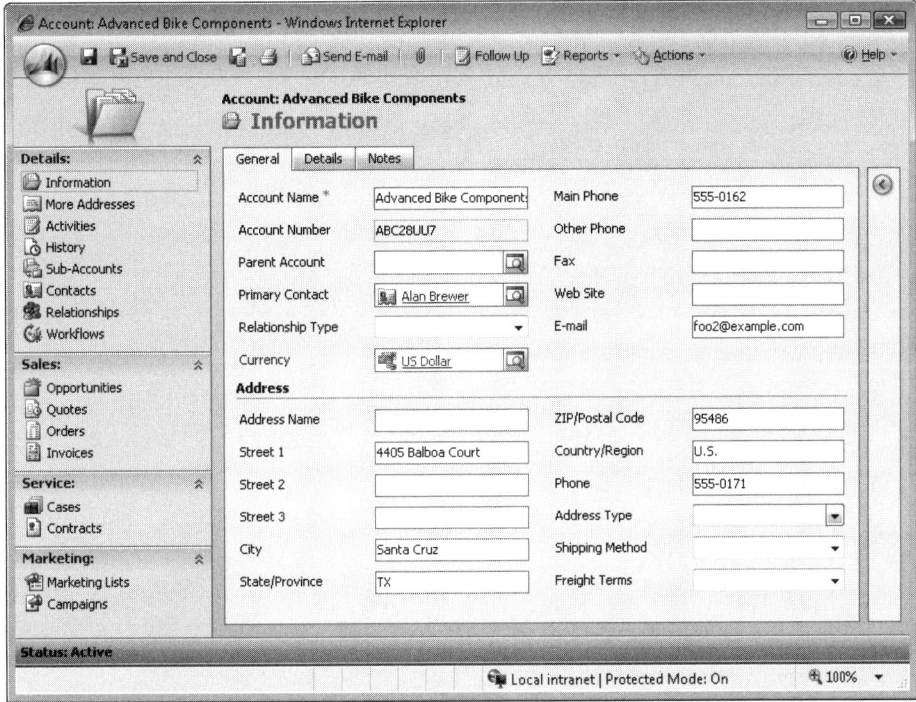

FIGURE 3-1 Account form

Because this is the first SDK example, we will walk you through the process of creating a basic console application in Visual Studio 2008.

Creating a new console project

1. Open Visual Studio 2008.
2. On the File menu, click New, and then click Project.
3. Under Project Types, select Visual C# Projects, and then click Console Application under Templates.
4. In the Name box, type **ProgrammingDynamicsCrm4.SdkExamples**.
5. Using either WSDL-based approach explained earlier in this chapter to add the service reference, add a Web reference to the *CrmService* Web service, calling it **CrmSdk**.

Now that you have the basic console application in place, add the logic to return values from an Account using the Microsoft Dynamics CRM *retrieve* method.

> **Note** The schema name for the relationship type attribute is *customertypecode*.

Retrieving an Account record from Microsoft Dynamics CRM

1. In the default Program.cs file, add the code shown in Listing 3-1.
2. Open an existing Account record in your Microsoft Dynamics CRM system. After you have the record open, press the F11 key to access the address bar in Internet Explorer. In the address bar, you can retrieve the Lead record's unique identifier. The ID will be the 32-character string between the braces after the *id=* parameter. In the following example, the Account record ID would be D7B3DC72-0E2C-DD11-8A81-0019D13DDA0E:

   `http://siduri/ProgBook/sfa/accts/edit.aspx?id={D7B3DC72-0E2C-DD11-8A81-0019D13DDA0E}#.`
3. Replace the *accountId* value with your own.
4. Update the organization name and server with the correct unique organization name and Web server of your Microsoft Dynamics CRM system.
5. Save the class file.
6. On the Build menu, click Build Solution.

Listing 3-1 shows the code for retrieving the Account record. If you run this example, you might have to update the namespace of your CrmSdk, depending on the name of your project.

LISTING 3-1 Retrieving an Account record

```
using System;
using System.Collections.Generic;
using System.Text;
using System.Net;
using ProgrammingDynamicsCrm4.SdkExamples.CrmSdk;

namespace ProgrammingDynamicsCrm4.SdkExamples
{
  class Program
  {

    static void Main(string[] args)
    {
      // Replace the default guid with a specific account from your system.
      Guid accountId = new Guid("3963176C-0E2C-DD11-8A81-0019D13DDA0E");
      RetriveAccount(accountId);
    }


    public static void RetriveAccount(Guid accountId)
    {
      // Use generic GetCrmService method from earlier
      // Replace <organization> and <server> with your values
      CrmService service = GetCrmService("<organization>", "<server>");

      // Set the columns to return.
      ColumnSet cols = new ColumnSet();
```

```
      cols.Attributes =
        new string[] { "name", "telephone1", "customertypecode" };

      try
      {
        // Retrieve the record, casting it as the correct entity.
        account oAccount =
          (account)service.Retrieve(EntityName.account.ToString(), accountId, cols);

        // Display the results.
        // Because you have a strongly typed response,
        //   you can access the properties directly from the object.
        Console.WriteLine("Account Name: {0}", oAccount.name);
        Console.WriteLine("Main Phone: {0}", oAccount.telephone1);
        Console.WriteLine("Relationship Type: {0}", Account.customertypecode.Value);
        Console.ReadLine();
      }
      catch (System.Web.Services.Protocols.SoapException ex)
      {
        Console.WriteLine(ex.Detail.InnerText);
      }
    }


    public static CrmService GetCrmService(string orgName, string server)
    {
      CrmAuthenticationToken token = new CrmAuthenticationToken();
      token.AuthenticationType = 0; //AD (On-premise)
      token.OrganizationName = orgName;

      CrmService service = new CrmService();
      service.UseDefaultCredentials = true;

      service.CrmAuthenticationTokenValue = token;
      service.Url =
        string.Format("http://{0}/mscrmservices/2007/crmservice.asmx", server);

      return service;
    }
  }
}
```

After you add this code, compile it, and run the project, you might receive the following error message:

```
Object reference not set to an instance of an object.
Console.WriteLine(oAccount.customertypecode.Value);
```

This error occurs because Microsoft Dynamics CRM does not return an object reference for any attribute that has a value of null. You receive this error because the sample Account does not have a *Relationship Type* value selected in the picklist, hence its value is null in the database. So, when your code tries to access the *customertypecode* value property, you get an exception.

Important Microsoft Dynamics CRM will not return a requested field if the field has a null value in the database.

To account for the possibility that Microsoft Dynamics CRM might not return a field that your code is expecting, you should ensure that the attribute you want to access is not null. The following code example shows one way to check for null values:

```
Console.Write("Relationship Type: ");
if (oAccount.customertypecode != null)
        Console.WriteLine(oAccount.customertypecode.Value);
```

After the code in Listing 3-1 is updated to check for a null value and refreshed, you'll receive output similar to that shown in Figure 3-2.

FIGURE 3-2 Account retrieval example

Even though the API contains the other methods *Create*, *RetrieveMultiple*, *Update*, *Delete*, and *Fetch*, we will not go through examples of using those methods in this book because they work in a similar fashion to the example we just completed. The SDK contains many more examples of the six common methods if you're looking for more information and samples.

Execute Method

The *Execute* method allows you to run any special commands or business logic not addressed by the common methods. Unlike the common methods, the *Execute* method works on *Request* and *Response* classes. You pass a *Request* class as a parameter to the *Execute* method, which then processes the request and returns a response message. Though the *Execute* method can perform all of the actions of the common methods, its real purpose is to provide you with the functionality that the common methods lack. Typical actions for which you might use the *Execute* method are to retrieve the current user, assign and route records, and send e-mail messages through Microsoft Dynamics CRM. For instance, the following code example shows how to use the *Execute* method to retrieve the current user:

```
// Use generic GetCrmService method from earlier
// Replace <organization> and <server> with your values
CrmService service = GetCrmService("<organization>","<server>");

// Get current user object.
WhoAmIRequest userRequest = new WhoAmIRequest();
WhoAmIResponse user = (WhoAmIResponse) service.Execute(userRequest);
```

Note You must always cast the returning message to the appropriate instance of the *Response* class.

Request and *Response* Classes

Microsoft Dynamics CRM uses a *Request* and *Response* message class model for the *Execute* method. You must create a *Request* class message and set the appropriate properties. You then send the *Request* object to the platform by using the *Execute* method. The platform runs the request and sends back an instance of a *Response* class message.

Microsoft Dynamics CRM *Request* and *Response* classes support generic, targeted, specialized, and dynamic entity requests. These *Request* classes always end in the word *Request*, such as *WhoAmIRequest*, *CreateRequest*, and *SendEmailRequest*. Generic requests are not dependent on a specific entity and do not contain an entity name in their class name. Generic requests can work across multiple entities (such as the *AssignRequest*) in addition to sometimes working with no entities (such as the *WhoAmIRequest*).

The following code sample demonstrates how you can use existing published duplicate detection rules within code by using the generic *RetrieveDuplicatesRequest*:

```
// Use generic GetCrmService method from earlier
// Replace <organization> and <server> with your values
CrmService service = GetCrmService("<organization> ", "<server>");

lead lead = new lead();
lead.emailaddress1 = "someone@example.com";

// Create a RetrieveDuplicates request
RetrieveDuplicatesRequest Request = new RetrieveDuplicatesRequest();
Request.BusinessEntity = lead;
Request.MatchingEntityName = EntityName.lead.ToString();
Request.PagingInfo = new PagingInfo();

try
{
  RetrieveDuplicatesResponse Response =
```

```
    (RetrieveDuplicatesResponse)service.Execute(Request);
   foreach (lead leadResult in Response.DuplicateCollection.BusinessEntities)
   {
     Console.Write(leadResult.leadid.Value.ToString());
     Console.WriteLine(leadResult.fullname);
   }
   Console.ReadLine();
 }
 catch (System.Web.Services.Protocols.SoapException ex)
 {
   // Handle error.
 }
```

Figure 3-3 shows the output.

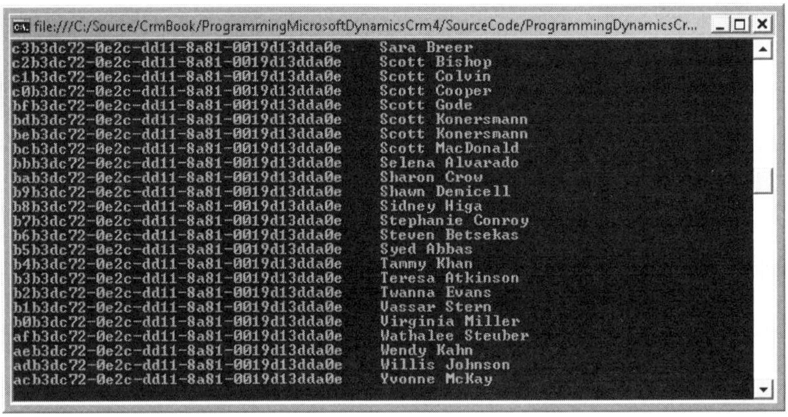

```
file:///C:/Source/CrmBook/ProgrammingMicrosoftDynamicsCrm4/SourceCode/ProgrammingDynamicsCr...
c3b3dc72-0e2c-dd11-8a81-0019d13dda0e    Sara Breer
c2b3dc72-0e2c-dd11-8a81-0019d13dda0e    Scott Bishop
c1b3dc72-0e2c-dd11-8a81-0019d13dda0e    Scott Colvin
c0b3dc72-0e2c-dd11-8a81-0019d13dda0e    Scott Cooper
bfb3dc72-0e2c-dd11-8a81-0019d13dda0e    Scott Gode
bdb3dc72-0e2c-dd11-8a81-0019d13dda0e    Scott Konersmann
beb3dc72-0e2c-dd11-8a81-0019d13dda0e    Scott Konersmann
bcb3dc72-0e2c-dd11-8a81-0019d13dda0e    Scott MacDonald
bbb3dc72-0e2c-dd11-8a81-0019d13dda0e    Selena Alvarado
bab3dc72-0e2c-dd11-8a81-0019d13dda0e    Sharon Crow
b9b3dc72-0e2c-dd11-8a81-0019d13dda0e    Shawn Demicell
b8b3dc72-0e2c-dd11-8a81-0019d13dda0e    Sidney Higa
b7b3dc72-0e2c-dd11-8a81-0019d13dda0e    Stephanie Conroy
b6b3dc72-0e2c-dd11-8a81-0019d13dda0e    Steven Betsekas
b5b3dc72-0e2c-dd11-8a81-0019d13dda0e    Syed Abbas
b4b3dc72-0e2c-dd11-8a81-0019d13dda0e    Tammy Khan
b3b3dc72-0e2c-dd11-8a81-0019d13dda0e    Teresa Atkinson
b2b3dc72-0e2c-dd11-8a81-0019d13dda0e    Twanna Evans
b1b3dc72-0e2c-dd11-8a81-0019d13dda0e    Vassar Stern
b0b3dc72-0e2c-dd11-8a81-0019d13dda0e    Virginia Miller
afb3dc72-0e2c-dd11-8a81-0019d13dda0e    Wathalee Steuber
aeb3dc72-0e2c-dd11-8a81-0019d13dda0e    Wendy Kahn
adb3dc72-0e2c-dd11-8a81-0019d13dda0e    Willis Johnson
acb3dc72-0e2c-dd11-8a81-0019d13dda0e    Yvonne McKay
```

FIGURE 3-3 Duplicate example

Generic requests that apply to entities require a target message class to specify which entity should receive the action. A target class name begins with the word *Target* and, once instantiated and configured, is then applied to the *target* property of a generic class.

Specialized requests are similar to targeted requests except that they work only on a specific entity to perform a distinct action. Their naming convention is *<Action><EntityName>Request*. Good examples of these requests are the *SendEmailRequest* and the *LoseOpportunityRequest*.

With the dynamic entity request, you can use requests at run time for any entity. By setting the parameter *ReturnDynamicEntities* to *True*, your results are returned as a *DynamicEntity* class instead of the *BusinessEntity* class. Not all requests permit the *DynamicEntity* option, and you should refer to the SDK for the complete list that does. We go into more detail about the *DynamicEntity* class next.

DynamicEntity Class

The *DynamicEntity* class, derived from the *BusinessEntity* class, provides run-time access to custom entities and custom attributes even if those entities and attributes did not exist when you compiled your assembly. The *DynamicEntity* class contains the logical name of the entity and a property-bag array of the entity's attributes. In programming terms, you can think of this as a loosely typed object. With the *DynamicEntity* class, you can access entities and attributes created in Microsoft Dynamics CRM even though you might not have the actual entity definition from the WSDL.

The *DynamicEntity* class must be used with the *Execute* method, and it contains the following properties:

- ***Name*** Sets the entity schema name
- ***Properties*** Array of type *Property* (which is a name/value pair)

Review the syntax of the *DynamicEntity* class to create a Lead. You create a *string* property to store the subject text, which you pass into the *DynamicEntity dynLead*. After you create the *DynamicEntity* object and set its name to *lead*, you create the *TargetCreateDynamic* class to serve as the target message for the *CreateRequest* call:

```
  // Use generic GetCrmService method from earlier
  // Replace <organization> and <server> with your values
  CrmService service = GetCrmService("<organization>","<server>");

  // Set up dynamic entity.
  DynamicEntity dynLead = new DynamicEntity();

  dynLead.Name = "lead";
  dynLead.Properties = new Property[] {
     CreateStringProperty("subject","New Lead Using Dynamic Entities"),
     CreateStringProperty("lastname","Steen"),
     CreateStringProperty("firstname","Heidi")
  };

  // Standard target request, passing in the dynamic entity.
  TargetCreateDynamic target = new TargetCreateDynamic();
  target.Entity = dynLead;
  CreateRequest create = new CreateRequest();
  create.Target = target;
  CreateResponse response = (CreateResponse)service.Execute(create);

// Helper method that creates a string property based on passed-in values
private Property CreateStringProperty(string Name, string Value)
{
  StringProperty prop = new StringProperty();
  prop.Name = Name;
  prop.Value = Value;
  return prop;
}
```

Obviously, you would not use the dynamic entity approach instead of the common *Create* method to create a Lead record if you have access at compile time to the *CrmService* Web service—the dynamic entity approach is not as efficient and requires more code. However, Microsoft Dynamics CRM provides this class for run-time situations in which you might not know the entity, or when new attributes might be added to an existing entity.

However, you will make heavy use of the *DynamicEntity* class with Microsoft Dynamics CRM because it is your primary entity class for writing plug-ins and workflow assemblies, as you will see later in this chapter.

We also want to highlight the helper method used in this example for creating the properties that you want to set. In this particular example, you know you are working with a *string* and *owner* properties, but in some scenarios, you might not know the property type. To address this, you should query the metabase and determine the data types of your desired attributes at run time. With Microsoft Dynamics CRM, you can do this with the *MetadataService* Web service, as you will see shortly.

More Info The SDK provides helper classes that contain many useful methods. Be sure to review them and add them to your projects to ease development.

Attributes

Remember that when you use an individual WSDL in your code, the Microsoft Dynamics CRM attributes will be strongly typed. Therefore, you must create a typed attribute when setting values for an entity, unless you are using the *DynamicEntity* class. The SDK documentation lists examples of each type and how to use them, so we won't list them here. However, you will see examples of this throughout the sample code.

MetadataService Web Service

In addition to the *CrmService* Web service, the Microsoft Dynamics CRM API includes a *MetadataService* Web service that you can use to programmatically access the metadata. You can perform the following types of actions with the *MetadataService* Web service:

- Retrieve the metadata for a specific entity, either system or custom.
- Retrieve the attributes for an entity.
- Retrieve the metadata for a specific attribute, such as the possible state names or picklist values for an attribute.
- Create a custom entity.

- Add or update an attribute for an entity, either system or custom.
- Create or delete a relationship between two entities.
- Retrieve all the metadata to create a metadata cache in a client application.
- Determine whether the metadata has changed since a previous retrieve.
- Retrieve all the entities and determine which ones are custom entities.
- Add or remove an option from a picklist attribute.
- Write an install and uninstall program for your custom solution.

The *MetadataService* Web service is located at *http://*<crmserver>*/mscrmservices/2007/metadataservice.asmx*, where *crmserver* is the Microsoft Dynamics CRM Web server. As with the *CrmService* Web service, you need to add a Web reference in your project to access the methods and properties available.

Please review Chapter 8, "Developing with the Metadata Service," for further information regarding the *MetadataService* Web service.

CrmDiscoveryService Web Service

The *CrmDiscoveryService* Web service can provide a list of organizations and their corresponding Web service endpoint URLs. You use this information to configure the *CrmService* and *MetadataService* Web service proxies and call Web service methods that access an organization's data. The discovery service URL is fixed per installation so that you can programmatically configure solutions for multiple organizations in a single environment.

The discovery Web service is most applicable for the following situations:

- Large-scale installations of Microsoft Dynamics CRM, where the installation may have the Web service APIs installed on a server different from the Microsoft Dynamics CRM Web server
- Independent software vendors (ISVs) solutions

More Info A multi-tenant installation is one in which multiple CRM organizations are configured against a common set of hardware. Remember that each organization contains a unique database that contains the custom configuration and all the business data. You need the Enterprise edition of Microsoft Dynamics CRM to setup and deploy a multi-tenant deployment.

The *CrmDiscoveryService* Web service for an on-premise installation is located at *http://*<crmserver>*/mscrmservices/2007/AD/CrmDiscoveryService.asmx*, where *crmserver* is the Microsoft Dynamics CRM Web server.

Note Microsoft Dynamics CRM Online uses a different URL for the discovery service. If you are working with a Microsoft Dynamics CRM Online implementation, use the following URL instead: *https://dev.crm.dynamics.com/MSCRMServices/2007/Passport/CrmDiscoveryService.asmx*.

Listing 3-2 shows some basic code using the *CrmDiscoveryService* to retrieve organizations and their API Web service URLs.

LISTING 3-2 Example using the *CrmDiscoveryService*

```
// Create and configure the CrmDiscoveryService Web service proxy.
CrmDiscoveryService discoveryService = new CrmDiscoveryService();
discoveryService.UseDefaultCredentials = true;
discoveryService.Url =
  "http://<servername>/MSCRMServices/2007/AD/CrmDiscoveryService.asmx";

// Retrieve the list of organizations to which the logged-on user belongs.
RetrieveOrganizationsRequest orgRequest = new RetrieveOrganizationsRequest();
RetrieveOrganizationsResponse orgResponse =
    (RetrieveOrganizationsResponse)discoveryService.Execute(orgRequest);

// Loop through list to locate the target organization.
OrganizationDetail orgInfo = null;
foreach (OrganizationDetail orgDetail in orgResponse.OrganizationDetails)
{
    if (orgDetail.OrganizationName.Equals("AdventureWorksCycle"))
    {
        orgInfo = orgDetail;
        break;
    }
}

// Check whether a matching organization was not found.
if (orgInfo == null)
    throw new Exception("The specified organization was not found.");
```

After you obtain the organization details, you can then access the *CrmService* and *MetadataService* Web services to perform your business logic using the following code:

```
CrmAuthenticationToken token = new CrmAuthenticationToken();
token.AuthenticationType = 0;     //AD authentication type
token.OrganizationName = orgInfo.OrganizationName;

CrmService crmService = new CrmService();
crmService.Url = orgInfo.CrmServiceUrl;
crmService.CrmAuthenticationTokenValue = token;
crmService.Credentials = System.Net.CredentialCache.DefaultCredentials;
```

Connecting to Microsoft Dynamics CRM IFD

Microsoft allows you to expose your Microsoft Dynamics CRM deployment to the cloud using the Internet-facing deployment (IFD) option. IFD still authenticates against Active Directory, but rather than using a Kerberos ticket, it uses forms-based authentication.

If you develop for IFD, you should use the *CrmImpersonator* class when instantiating your service objects. The *CrmImpersonator* class allows code to execute under the process credentials instead of the running thread's identity. When a *CrmImpersonator* object is used within a *using* statement, the block of code executes under the process until the end of the *using* statement, at which point execution returns to running under the thread ID.

Important You access the *CrmImpersonator* class from the Microsoft Dynamics CRM SDK assemblies. The class does not exist with the WSDL references.

By implementing your code within the *CrmImpersonator* using block, you can use the existing authentication process and prevent the user from having to explicitly re-authenticate to your custom page. Listing 3-3 provides some sample code using this technique.

More Info Please refer to Chapter 13, "Emulating User Interface with ASP.NET Development," for additional information regarding the *CrmImpersonator* class.

LISTING 3-3 Example using *CrmImpersonator* within a *Using* statement

```
using (new CrmImpersonator())
{
    CrmAuthenticationToken token;

    // Offline always requires Windows authentication
    if (offline == true)
    {
        token = new CrmAuthenticationToken();
        token.OrganizationName = orgname;
        token.AuthenticationType = 0;
    }
    else
    {
        token =
          CrmAuthenticationToken.ExtractCrmAuthenticationToken(Context, orgname);
    }

    //Create the Service
    CrmService service = new CrmService();
    service.Credentials = System.Net.CredentialCache.DefaultCredentials;
    service.CrmAuthenticationTokenValue = token;
    service.Url = <CrmServiceUrl>; //Pass in a valid CrmService URL

    // perform some action...
}
```

Connecting to Microsoft Dynamics CRM Offline

Microsoft Dynamics CRM also allows for offline access of its Web service APIs. Working with the offline APIs is no different from working with their online counterparts, except you will need to access the Web services from a local URL. Simply use the registry to construct the proper URL and to retrieve the organization name as shown in the following code:

```
//Retrieve the Port and Organization Name from the Registry
using (RegistryKey key = Registry.CurrentUser.OpenSubKey(
       "Software\\Microsoft\\MSCRMClient"))
{
    string orgName = key.GetValue("ClientAuthOrganizationName").ToString();
    string port = key.GetValue("CassiniPort").ToString();

    //Construct the URL
    UriBuilder uriBuilder = new UriBuilder("http", "localhost");
    uriBuilder.Port = int.Parse(port);
    uriBuilder.Path = "/mscrmservices/2007/";
    string crmServiceUrl = url.ToString() + "crmservice.asmx";
    string metadataServiceUrl = uriBuilder.ToString() + "metadataservice.asmx";

    //Connect to the service objects…
}
```

Note The Microsoft Dynamics CRM Outlook client only allows access to a single organization.

For more information regarding offline development, see Chapter 10, "Developing Offline Solutions."

Connecting to Microsoft Dynamics CRM Online

Microsoft Dynamics CRM Online provides the same service APIs as the on-premise and IFD deployments. However, because Microsoft Dynamics CRM Online uses Windows Live ID for authentication, you must first obtain a valid ticket before attempting to access the Web service methods.

In addition to using a different authentication method from the on-premise and IFD deployments, writing custom code for Microsoft Dynamics CRM contains some additional differences. At the time of this writing, Microsoft Dynamics CRM Online does not allow the following:

- You cannot upload custom Web pages, plug-ins, and workflow assemblies to the Microsoft Dynamics CRM Online server.
- You cannot upload custom report RDL files. You must use the Report Wizard when creating new reports.
- You cannot use impersonated or delegated API calls.

Despite these restrictions, a developer has ample opportunity to programmatically interact with the Microsoft Dynamics CRM Online with script (as described further in Chapter 7, "Form Scripting") and with the Web service APIs. We will now examine the options available for communicating with Microsoft Dynamics CRM Online's APIs.

Windows Live ID provides multiple methods for authenticating a user and retrieving a valid ticket for use with Microsoft Dynamics CRM Online. Some of the main options available are:

- Identity Client Run-Time Library (IDCRL) Ticket Service Library
- Federation

More Info At the time of printing, the Federation option was not yet available. Visit *http://dev.live.com/liveID/default.aspx* for more information regarding the Windows Live ID SDK and authentication options.

We will review using the Win32 IDCRL library to obtain a valid Windows Live ID ticket. The Microsoft Dynamics CRM SDK provides the source code to create a .NET wrapper to this library. The source for this can be found at SDK\Server\Helpers\CS\IdCrlWrapper. Using this wrapper, you can pass valid Live ID credentials to the *LogonManager* class and retrieve a ticket that can be used to authenticate Microsoft Dynamics CRM Online.

To get started, you need to perform the following steps:

1. Download the msidcrl40.dll assembly and install it in %windows%\system32 or the output directory of your client-side application.
2. Create a .NET wrapper around the IDCRL library using the source code provided in the Microsoft Dynamics CRM SDK, and reference the wrapper in your project.
3. Ensure that the identity of the user is not a network service account. For Web applications, you need to change the application pool's identity to Local System or a domain user.
4. For Web applications, ensure that the default proxy is configured.

The code in Listing 3-4 demonstrates how to create a *CrmService* object using the IDCRL library for Microsoft Dynamics CRM Online.

LISTING 3-4 Microsoft Dynamics CRM Online *CrmService* utility

```
public static CrmService GetOnlineCrmService(string userName, string password, string
partner, string environment, string orgName)
{
  CrmDiscoveryService discoveryService = new CrmDiscoveryService();
  discoveryService.Url = "https://dev.crm.dynamics.com/MSCRMServices/2007/Passport/
CrmDiscoveryService.asmx";
```

```
    RetrievePolicyRequest policyRequest = new RetrievePolicyRequest();
    RetrievePolicyResponse policyResponse =
     (RetrievePolicyResponse)discoveryService.Execute(policyRequest);

    using (LogonManager lm = new LogonManager())
    {
      string passportTicket = lm.Logon(_username, _password, _partner,
        policyResponse.Policy, _environment);

      RetrieveCrmTicketRequest crmTicketRequest = new RetrieveCrmTicketRequest();
      crmTicketRequest.OrganizationName = _orgname;
      crmTicketRequest.PassportTicket = passportTicket;

      RetrieveCrmTicketResponse crmTicketResponse =
        (RetrieveCrmTicketResponse)discoveryService.Execute(crmTicketRequest);

      // Create and configure an instance of the CrmService Web service.
      CrmAuthenticationToken token = new CrmAuthenticationToken();
      token.AuthenticationType = AuthenticationType.Passport;
      token.CrmTicket = crmTicketResponse.CrmTicket;
      token.OrganizationName = crmTicketResponse.OrganizationDetail.OrganizationName;

      CrmService crmService = new CrmService();
      crmService.Url = crmTicketResponse.OrganizationDetail.CrmServiceUrl;
      crmService.CrmAuthenticationTokenValue = token;
      return crmService;
    }
  }
```

Let's assume the following scenario: each week you need to retrieve the accounts created this current week to import the data into a custom application. Figure 3-4 displays sample output of all accounts opened in the current week from your CRM Online organization.

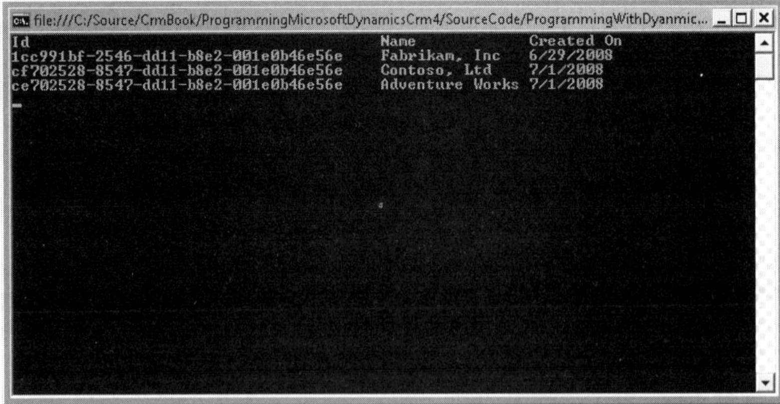

FIGURE 3-4 Retrieving recent accounts from CRM Online

For demonstration purposes, Listing 3-5 simply writes the results to a display but of course you could use this data in different formats or outputs. Be sure to update the *_username*, *_password*, and *_orgname* variables with valid information.

LISTING 3-5 Accessing Microsoft Dynamics CRM Online

```
using System;
using System.Xml;
using System.Text;
using System.Web.Services.Protocols;

using Microsoft.Crm.Passport.Sample;
using Microsoft.Crm.Sdk;
using Microsoft.Crm.Sdk.Query;
using Microsoft.Crm.SdkTypeProxy;
using ProgrammingWithDynamicsCrm4.CrmOnline.CrmSdk.Discovery;


namespace ProgrammingWithDynamicsCrm4.CrmOnline
{
  class Program
  {
    // Replace with valid values for your Online account
    static private string _username = "passport@hotmail.com";
    static private string _password = "password";
    static private string _orgname = "orgname";

    static private string _partner = "crm.dynamics.com";
    static private string _environment = "Production";
    static private string ExpiredAuthTicket = "8004A101";

    static void Main(string[] args)
    {
      try
      {
        CrmService crmService = GetOnlineCrmService(_username, _password, _partner,
         _environment, _orgname);

        try
        {
          QueryExpression query = new QueryExpression();

          // Set up standard query expression
          ColumnSet cols = new ColumnSet();
          cols.AddColumns(new string[] { "name", "createdon" });


          // Create the ConditionExpression.
          ConditionExpression condition = new ConditionExpression();
          condition.AttributeName = "createdon";
          condition.Operator = ConditionOperator.ThisWeek;
```

```
            // Builds the filter based on the condition
            FilterExpression filter = new FilterExpression();
            filter.FilterOperator = LogicalOperator.And;
            filter.AddCondition(condition);

            query.EntityName = EntityName.account.ToString();
            query.ColumnSet = cols;
            query.Criteria = filter;
            query.AddOrder("name", OrderType.Descending);

            // Retrieve the values from Microsoft CRM.
            BusinessEntityCollection retrieved = crmService.RetrieveMultiple(query);

            // Loop through results and display back to the user.
            foreach (account accountResult in retrieved.BusinessEntities)
            {
              Console.Write(accountResult.name.ToString() + "\t");
              Console.WriteLine(accountResult.createdon.date.ToString());
            }
            Console.ReadLine();
          }
          catch (System.Web.Services.Protocols.SoapException ex)
          {
            // Handle error.
          }
        }

       // Handle any Web service exceptions that might be thrown.
        catch (SoapException ex)
        {
          // Handle the exception thrown from an expired ticket condition.
          if (GetErrorCode(ex.Detail) == ExpiredAuthTicket)
          {
            throw new Exception("The Microsoft Dynamics CRM Online
              ticket has expired.", ex);
          }
          else
          {
            // Handle other exceptions.
            throw new Exception("An error occurred while attempting to authenticate.", ex);
          }
        }
      }

      private static string GetErrorCode(XmlNode errorInfo)
      {
        XmlNode code = errorInfo.SelectSingleNode("//code");
        return (code == null) ? string.Empty : code.InnerText;
      }
```

```
    public static CrmService GetOnlineCrmService(string userName, string password,
      string partner, string environment, string orgName)
    {
      //...Get online service code...
    }
  }
}
```

Summary

The Microsoft Dynamics CRM APIs provide the recommended methods for accessing entities and manipulating data in the system without requiring you to understand the underlying mechanisms of the platform. You access the APIs by using the Web Service WSDLs or with the proxy assemblies. By simply altering the authentication approach, you can easily use code across Microsoft Dynamics CRM's multiple deployment models.

Part II
Extending Microsoft CRM

Chapter 4
Security

Microsoft Dynamics CRM offers an extremely flexible security model that you can customize to meet your organization's security needs. By configuring security settings, you can construct a security and information access solution that will meet the needs of your organization. The process to customize the Microsoft Dynamics CRM security settings requires that you configure your organization structure, decide which security roles your system users (employees) will have, and then define the security privileges associated with each security role. Microsoft Dynamics CRM provides a granular level of security throughout the application. The security model even allows for ad hoc sharing and team-based collaboration on a record-by-record basis. Microsoft Dynamics CRM offers a Web interface for managing, editing, and assigning security roles, and that tool works fine for power users. However, as a developer within Microsoft Dynamics CRM you should understand additional security concepts and tools as you develop your programming customizations.

Chapter 3, "Communicating with Microsoft CRM APIs," showed you the different methods of authentication available when using the Microsoft Dynamics CRM SDK. After your code authenticates a user, the Microsoft Dynamics CRM security model controls the data the user can work with and the actions the user can perform. As a developer, this security model will save you a lot of time because you won't have to write custom code that manages the application security. The Microsoft Dynamics CRM platform defines each user's privileges and access to data automatically in the API.

Note This chapter will mainly focus on security-related programming for Microsoft Dynamics CRM. Refer to Chapter 3, "Managing Security and Information Access," in *Working with Dynamics CRM 4.0* (Microsoft Press, 2008) for a more in-depth discussion of the general Microsoft Dynamics CRM security model.

This chapter discusses the different security concepts that you need to understand to successfully develop custom applications and plug-ins for Microsoft Dynamics CRM, including:

- Role-based and object-based security
- Security principals
- Access rights
- Impersonation
- Using the Microsoft Dynamics CRM SDK to perform security-related operations
- Direct SQL access for Microsoft Dynamics CRM
- Encrypting Microsoft Dynamics CRM data

Role-Based and Object-Based Security

All users in Microsoft Dynamics CRM must have one or more security roles assigned to them. A *security role* describes a set of privileges and access levels within the system. Each privilege pertains to one of the following:

- An action against an entity (such as the ability to read or create Accounts)
- A more global action in the system (such as the ability to go offline with the Microsoft Dynamics CRM for Outlook with Offline Access client)

When a user logs on to the system, Microsoft Dynamics CRM looks at the privileges of the user's assigned security roles and uses that information to determine what the software will allow the user to do and see throughout the system. This is known as *role-based security.*

A user is considered to hold a privilege if he is assigned a security role with that privilege enabled, but this does not automatically grant the user access to every object the privilege pertains to. Each privilege within Microsoft Dynamics CRM also has associated with it a *privilege depth*. Whereas a privilege describes what actions can be taken in the system, a *privilege depth* indicates which specific objects that action can be taken on. Think of this as *object-based security.* For example, a user may hold the *prvReadAccount* privilege, allowing him to read accounts, but the *privilege depth* of the privilege determines which accounts he has read access to. Microsoft Dynamics CRM determines a user's access to a particular object by considering what the object's ownership type is, who or what the owner of the object is, and what business unit the user belongs to. Table 4-1 illustrates how privilege depths work.

TABLE 4-1 ***PrivilegeDepth* Enumeration**

Name	Value	Description
Basic	0	Grants user-level access. The user can only perform the privileged action on records he owns or records that are shared with him.
Local	1	Grants business-unit access. The user can only perform the privilege on records in his own business unit.
Deep	2	Grants parent and child business-unit access. The user can perform the privilege on records in her business unit or any business unit lower in the business unit hierarchy.
Global	3	Grants organization-level access. The user can perform the privilege on any record in the system.

Note Privileges that pertain to non-entity actions (such as Export to Excel) can only be granted with global depth, indicating that the action can be performed by that user if he or she possesses the privilege.

Security Principals

Security principals in Microsoft Dynamics CRM are users or groups that can own or access records. Table 4-2 describes the two types of security principals in Microsoft Dynamics CRM.

TABLE 4-2 Security Principals

Name	Description
User	A user in the system who has assigned security roles that determine his or her access.
Team	Teams do not have security roles, but you can share objects. The actual access to the record is determined by the share privileges

You might expect that a team can own a record, but only users can own a record in Microsoft Dynamics CRM. Instead of changing a record's owner to a team, you share a record with a team, and then define the privileges associated with the share. For example, you can share account record A with a team, granting the team members read and write privileges, but share account record B with the same team and grant the team members only read privileges.

Access Rights

Microsoft Dynamics CRM uses the term *access rights* to describe object-based security. When you develop custom code for Microsoft Dynamics CRM, you need to carefully consider how the system handles access rights. In particular, it's important to consider the privileges and access rights of the user that your code will run under. This factor can get a little tricky because most actions require multiple access rights to execute properly. Table 4-3 lists some common actions that require more than one access right that you might use in your custom code, along with the required access rights for each action.

TABLE 4-3 Common Actions and Required Access Rights

Action	Required Access Rights
Creating and owning an instance of an entity	Read, Create
Sharing an instance of an entity	Share (required by the user doing the sharing), Read (required by both the user doing the sharing and the user the instance is being shared with)
Assigning an instance of an entity	Assign, Write, Read
Appending to an instance of an entity	Read, AppendTo
Appending an instance of an entity	Read, Append

A security dependency exists with certain entities that require a relationship to another entity. For example, an Opportunity is always related to an Account or a Contact. In this case, to create a new instance of an Opportunity, a user needs AppendTo access on Account or Contact and Append access on Opportunity. In these instances, with related entities and required privileges, troubleshooting the exact privileges that the user needs can take some time because the required privileges aren't always obvious. For example, consider the privileges required to create an appointment with the *regardingobjectid* attribute set to a Contact record:

- *prvAppendActivity*
- *prvAppendQueueItem*
- *prvAppendToContact*
- *prvCreateActivity*
- *prvCreateQueueItem*
- *prvReadActivity*
- *prvReadContact*
- *prvReadUser*
- *prvShareActivity*

Some of these might jump out at you as surprising, such as needing Create Queue Item privileges to create an appointment. If you find yourself stuck trying to figure out the correct security settings, you can reference Appendix A of the SDK, which lists the privileges by Message.

Impersonation

Impersonation allows you to make *CrmService* or *MetadataService* API calls on behalf of another Microsoft Dynamics CRM system user. In this section we will discuss using impersonation in Web applications and also in plug-ins.

Impersonation for Web applications

In Chapter 3, you learned how to create an instance of *CrmService* that you can then use for actions such as creating or updating an entity. When used in the context of Web pages, code executes under the security credentials of the user browsing the Web page, so by default all of your *CrmService* calls execute as the browsing user. At times, you might want to execute code using security credentials different from those of the user browsing the Web page. In Microsoft Dynamics CRM, you can execute business logic on behalf of another user through a technique called *impersonation*.

Impersonation requires you to take the following steps:

- Explicitly set the authentication token's *CallerId* property using a valid Microsoft Dynamics CRM system user.
- Ensure that the network credentials of the user used to authenticate to the Web service are those of a member of the *PrivUserGroup* in the Active Directory directory service.

You can set the *CallerId* property very easily by adding the following line of code to your standard service setup.

```
token.CallerId = new Guid("00000000-0000-0000-0000-000000000000");
```

Replace the string of zeros (also referred to as an empty *Guid*) with the actual *systemuserid* globally unique identifier (*Guid*) of the Microsoft Dynamics CRM user whom you want to impersonate. Microsoft Dynamics CRM ignores an empty *Guid* and uses the security credentials of the user browsing the Web page. If you specify a *Guid* that does not exist, Microsoft Dynamics CRM throws an exception.

Also note that the authenticating user of the API Web service must be a member of the *PrivUserGroup* in Active Directory. These are the network credentials specified in the *service.Credentials* property. The *PrivUserGroup* is an Active Directory group added during the installation of Microsoft Dynamics CRM.

Important The user that corresponds to the *systemuserid* specified in the *CallerId* property is not the user who needs to be a member of the *PrivUserGroup*. The Active Directory user specified in the *service.Credentials* property is the user who must be added.

Although impersonation is a powerful technique, any time you impersonate you open a potential security risk and add configuration challenges to your implementation. We recommend that you try to avoid using impersonation whenever possible. In most cases, you can find an alternative way to execute the logic required by altering the user's Microsoft Dynamics CRM security permissions or by changing the logic's design.

Warning Impersonation is not supported with workflow assemblies, when the code is executed in offline mode, or with Microsoft Dynamics CRM Online.

Impersonation for Plug-ins

In addition to using impersonation with the *CrmService* API, you can use impersonation with custom plug-ins. The plug-in code runs under the user defined on the Identity tab of the CrmAppPool Properties dialog box. The CrmAppPool Properties dialog box can be found in Internet Information Services (IIS) Manager under the Application Pools folder.

Accessing the CrmAppPool identity

1. Open Internet Information Services (IIS) Manager.
2. Expand the Application Pools folder.
3. Right-click CrmAppPool and select Properties.
4. Click the Identity tab.

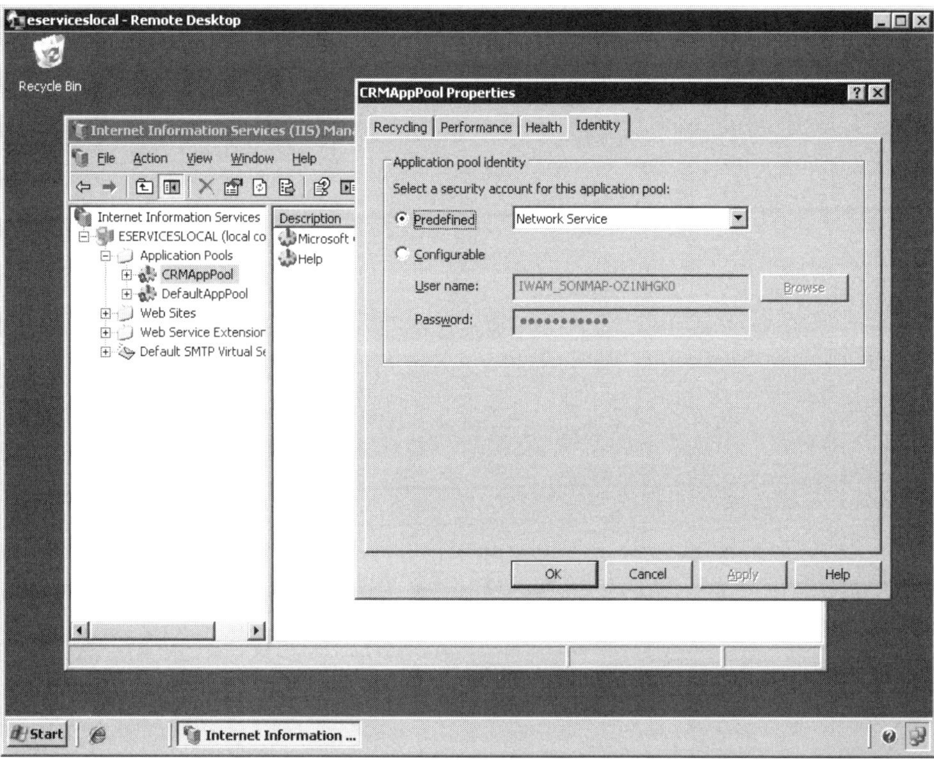

Note By default, CrmAppPool runs under the Network Service account. If this account is changed to another user account, that account must be added to the *PrivUserGroup* in Active Directory.

Setting up a *CrmService* instance for impersonation in a plug-in is pretty simple. To create an instance of the *CrmService* that will make its calls under the logged-on user, you would use the following line of code:

```
ICrmService crmService = context.CreateCrmService(true);
```

The preceding line provides the same functionality as the following line:

```
ICrmService crmService = context.CreateCrmService(context.UserId);
```

To avoid using impersonation when your plug-in executes, create the service by passing *false* into the *CreateCrmService* method:

```
ICrmService crmService = context.CreateCrmService(false);
```

Your calls will now run under the system account instead of the logged-on user's account. The system account is set up by default when Microsoft Dynamics CRM is installed. This user account will not be displayed in the system user views in the user interface. If you query the SystemUserBase table for *fullname* equal to "SYSTEM" in the Microsoft Dynamics CRM database, you can find this user record. The system user account has high-level access with a few caveats, such as not being able to create a Task.

Warning Impersonation does not work in plug-ins running offline. Offline plug-in code will always execute as the logged-on user.

More Info For more information on impersonation in plug-ins, see Chapter 5, "Plug-ins."

Using the Microsoft Dynamics CRM SDK to Perform Security-Related Operations

The Microsoft Dynamics CRM SDK provides methods for you to programmatically manage your security roles and privileges. It also exposes methods with which you can retrieve roles and privileges for a specific user. In this section, we will discuss how to execute this type of functionality and walk through a few examples.

Programmatically Creating a Security Role and Adding Privileges

If you plan to deploy custom security roles to multiple instances of Microsoft Dynamics CRM, or if you are an independent software vendor (ISV) developing a custom solution that integrates with Microsoft Dynamics CRM, it might make sense for you to create a utility that programmatically creates your custom security roles as part of the installation process.

Listing 4-1 shows code that creates a new security role named "My New Role" and then adds the Create privilege for the Account entity. The role is created in the currently logged-on user's business unit.

LISTING 4-1 Creating a role and adding privileges source code

```
const string accountCreatePriv = "D26FE964-230B-42DD-AD93-5CC879DE411E";

CrmService service = CrmServiceUtility.GetCrmService("server_name",
    "organization_name");

WhoAmIRequest whoAmIRequest = new WhoAmIRequest();
WhoAmIResponse currentUser = (WhoAmIResponse)service.Execute(whoAmIRequest);

role newRole = new role();

newRole.name = "My New Role";
newRole.businessunitid = new Lookup();
newRole.businessunitid.Value = currentUser.BusinessUnitId;
newRole.organizationid = new UniqueIdentifier();
newRole.organizationid.Value = currentUser.OrganizationId;

TargetCreateRole target = new TargetCreateRole();
target.Role = newRole;

CreateRequest newRoleRequest = new CreateRequest();
newRoleRequest.Target = target;

CreateResponse newRoleResponse = (CreateResponse)service.Execute(newRoleRequest);

RolePrivilege[] privileges = new RolePrivilege[1];

privileges[0] = new RolePrivilege();
privileges[0].PrivilegeId = new Guid(accountCreatePriv);
privileges[0].Depth = PrivilegeDepth.Global;

AddPrivilegesRoleRequest addPrivRequest = new AddPrivilegesRoleRequest();

addPrivRequest.Privileges = privileges;
addPrivRequest.RoleId = newRoleResponse.id;

AddPrivilegesRoleResponse addPrivResponse = (AddPrivilegesRoleResponse)service.
    Execute(addPrivRequest);
```

The listing shows creating a record in the same manner as any other entity, but it requires that you set a few fields. First we need to make a *WhoAmIRequest* to retrieve the currently logged-on user's ID, business unit, and organization. We then can create a new instance of the *role* class, populate the necessary attributes, and use the *CrmService* to create our new role.

Warning The user executing this code needs to have the Create and Read privileges set on the Role entity.

After we create the role, we can add all the necessary privileges. In our example we add the Create privilege on the Account entity. The *Guid* of the privilege we are adding is hard-coded in the *accountCreatePriv* variable. Notice that we set the *Depth* property of our privilege to *Global*. This gives our privilege organization-level rights.

After the code creates the role, it will show up like any other security role in the Microsoft Dynamics CRM user interface (UI). You can then edit the role through the UI. Figure 4-1 shows what the resulting role looks like in the UI.

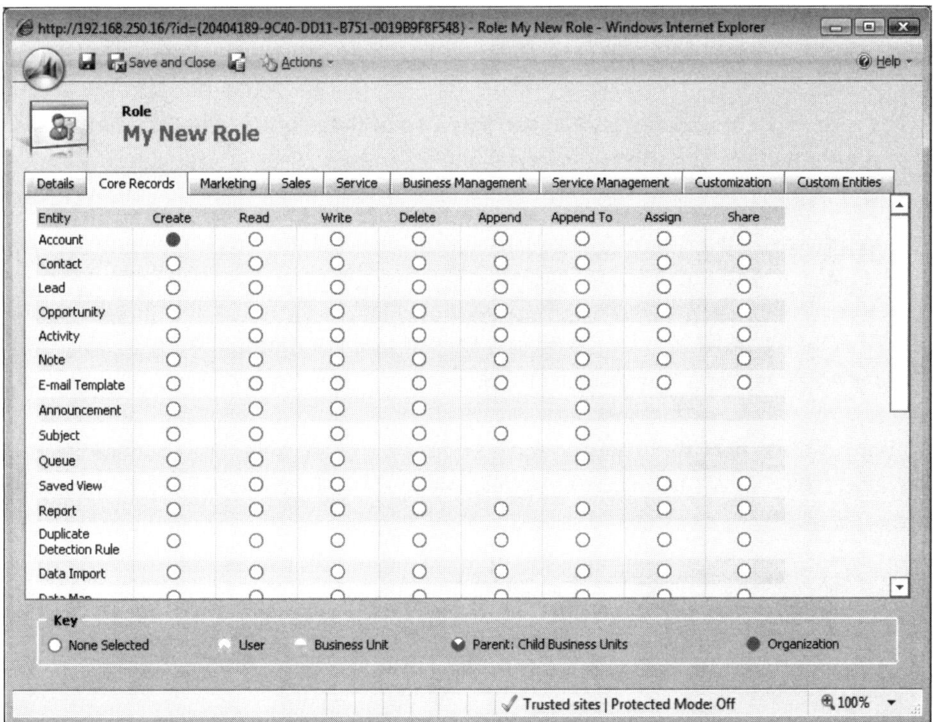

FIGURE 4-1 "My New Role" security role

Programmatically Assigning a Security Role

In addition to creating a role programmatically, we can also assign roles programmatically to users. Listing 4-2 shows sample code for assigning the sample security role that we just created to a user.

LISTING 4-2 Assigning a security role

```
CrmService service = CrmServiceUtility.GetCrmService("server_name", "organization");

// Guid of the user we want to add the role to
```

```
Guid userId = new Guid("DC8B2248-191D-DD11-8839-0019B9F8F548");

// Guid of the role we want to add to the user
Guid roleId = new Guid("20404189-9C40-DD11-B751-0019B9F8F548");

AssignUserRolesRoleRequest assign = new AssignUserRolesRoleRequest();

assign.UserId = userId;
assign.RoleIds = new Guid[] { roleId };

AssignUserRolesRoleResponse assigned = (AssignUserRolesRoleResponse)service.
    Execute(assign);
```

The code is pretty simple—just obtain the *Guid* of the user and the *Guid* of the role you want to assign the user, and then use the *AssignUserRolesRoleRequest* class.

Retrieving Roles and Privileges

At some point, you will probably want to build logic into your custom code that depends on the security roles and privileges of a specific use. For example, let's say you want a piece of logic to run only for users with the "Salesperson" role. To accomplish this, you can use the *CrmService* to retrieve security roles and privileges for a given user, and then use this information to determine how your custom code should react. The code for the *IsSalesPerson* method in Listing 4-3 demonstrates how to check the security role of a user to determine if she possesses the Salesperson security role using the Microsoft Dynamics CRM API.

LISTING 4-3 *IsSalesPerson* method

```
public bool IsSalesPerson(Guid systemUserId)
{
    bool isSalesPerson = false;

    CrmService service = CrmServiceUtility.GetCrmService("server_name",
        "organization");

    QueryExpression query = new QueryExpression();
    query.EntityName = "role";
    query.ColumnSet = new AllColumns();

    LinkEntity userRole = new LinkEntity();
    userRole.LinkFromEntityName = EntityName.role.ToString();
    userRole.LinkFromAttributeName = "roleid";
    userRole.LinkToEntityName = EntityName.systemuserroles.ToString();
    userRole.LinkToAttributeName = "roleid";

    ConditionExpression userCondition = new ConditionExpression();
    userCondition.AttributeName = "systemuserid";
    userCondition.Operator = ConditionOperator.Equal;
    userCondition.Values = new object[] { systemUserId };
```

```
    userRole.LinkCriteria = new FilterExpression();
    userRole.LinkCriteria.Conditions.Add(userCondition);

    query.LinkEntities.Add(userRole);

    BusinessEntityCollection roles = service.RetrieveMultiple(query);

    foreach (BusinessEntity be in roles.BusinessEntities)
    {
        role currentRole = (role)be;

        if (currentRole.name == "Salesperson")
        {
            isSalesPerson = true;
            break;
        }
    }

    return isSalesPerson;
}
```

The *QueryExpression* used in Listing 4-3 queries the Role entity. Because we are trying to determine whether the current user has a certain security role, we need to add a *LinkEntity* that links *role* to *systemuserrole* and a condition to return records only for the current user.

Tip During development you might want to quickly reference information stored in the Microsoft Dynamics CRM database. In the preceding example, it would be helpful to quickly query for all roles assigned to a specified user to verify that your code is functioning correctly. The roles for all system users are stored in the SystemUserRoles table.

You can retrieve the privileges for a user by using *RetrieveUserPrivilegesRequest*. By setting the *UserId* property and then executing the request, you can retrieve an array of *RolePrivilege* objects. Each *RolePrivilege* object contains the depth (see Table 4-1) and the *Guid* of the privilege. The following code provides a quick example of using *RetrieveUserPrivilegeRequest*:

```
CrmService service = CrmServiceUtility.GetCrmService("server_name", "organization");
WhoAmIRequest userRequest = new WhoAmIRequest();
WhoAmIResponse user = (WhoAmIResponse)service.Execute(userRequest);

RetrieveUserPrivilegesRequest retrieve = new RetrieveUserPrivilegesRequest();

retrieve.UserId = user.UserId;

RetrieveUserPrivilegesResponse retrieved = (RetrieveUserPrivilegesResponse)service.
    Execute(retrieve);
```

Sharing Records

If a system user possesses the Share privilege on an entity, she can then share records of that entity type with another system user or a team. The depth of the sharing privileges in the sharing user's security role determines which users and teams are available for her to share with. When you are sharing a record, you can specify what access rights you want to grant to the users participating in the share. For example, you may want to assign a Lead record to two users but give only one of them access to update the record.

Note You cannot give a user sharing rights that the user would not normally have based on his or her privileges. For example, if a user does not have Read privileges to Lead records and you share a Lead with him, he will still not be able to read the Lead record.

If your business requirements dictate that users frequently share records, manually sharing them can be a tedious process for users and prone to error if users forget to share their records. In this section we will demonstrate how to add a plug-in to automatically share Lead records with a team when those records are created. Listing 4-4 contains the source code for the plug-in.

Note See Chapter 5 for more details on adding the plug-in code file and deploying the plug-in.

LISTING 4-4 LeadSharer source code

```
using System;
using System.Collections.Generic;
using System.Text;
using Microsoft.Crm.Sdk;
using ProgrammingWithDynamicsCrm4.Plugins.Attributes;
using Microsoft.Crm.SdkTypeProxy;

namespace ProgrammingWithDynamicsCrm4.Plugins
{
    [PluginStep("Create",
                PluginStepStage.PostEvent,
                Description = "Shares the lead with a team",
                StepId = "LeadPostCreate",
                PrimaryEntityName = "lead",
                Mode = PluginStepMode.Synchronous,
                SupportedDeployment = PluginStepSupportedDeployment.ServerOnly)]

    public class LeadSharer : IPlugin
    {
        public void Execute(IPluginExecutionContext context)
        {
            // This Guid is the id of the team we will share the lead with
            Guid teamId = new Guid("376A5F7E-5341-DD11-B751-0019B9F8F548");
```

```
            ICrmService crmService = context.CreateCrmService(true);

            SecurityPrincipal principal = new SecurityPrincipal();
            principal.Type = SecurityPrincipalType.Team;
            principal.PrincipalId = teamId;

            PrincipalAccess principalAccess = new PrincipalAccess();
            principalAccess.Principal = principal;

            principalAccess.AccessMask = AccessRights.ReadAccess | AccessRights.
                WriteAccess;

            TargetOwnedLead target = new TargetOwnedLead();
            target.EntityId = new Guid(context.OutputParameters[ParameterName.Id].
                ToString());

            GrantAccessRequest grantAccessRequest = new GrantAccessRequest();
            grantAccessRequest.PrincipalAccess = principalAccess;
            grantAccessRequest.Target = target;

            GrantAccessResponse grantAccessResponse =
              (GrantAccessResponse)crmService.Execute(grantAccessRequest);
        }
    }
}
```

Notice that in the code we create an instance of the *SecurityPrincipal* class. The *Type* property on the *SecurityPrincipal* object can be set to a user or a team. Table 4-4 lists the values for the *SecurityPrincipalType* enumeration. Next we create a *PrincipalAccess* object and set its *Principal* property to our *SecurityPrincipal* object. The *PrincipalAccess* object's *AccessMask* property determines the access rights that are given to the team or user we are sharing the entity instance with. Table 4-5 describes the possible values for the *AccessMask* property.

TABLE 4-4 *SecurityPrincipalType* Enumeration

Name	Value	Description
Team	1	The security principal is a team.
User	0	The security principal is a system user.

TABLE 4-5 AccessRights Enumeration

Name	Value	Description
AppendAccess	4	Gives the security principal rights to append the entity instance to another entity instance
AppendToAccess	8	Gives the security principal rights to append another entity instance to the entity instance
AssignAccess	0x80	Gives the security principal rights to assign the entity instance to another security principal
CreateAccess	0x10	Gives the security principal rights to create an entity instance

TABLE 4-5 AccessRights Enumeration

Name	Value	Description
DeleteAccess	0x20	Gives the security principal rights to delete an entity instance
ReadAccess	1	Gives the security principal rights to read entity instances
ShareAccess	0x40	Gives the security principal rights to share an entity instance
WriteAccess	2	Gives the security principal rights to update an entity instance

A quick way to verify that your record has been shared is to check it against the Microsoft Dynamics CRM user interface.

Verifying that a record is shared

1. Open Microsoft Dynamics CRM in your Web browser.
2. Navigate to the entity grid view of the record.

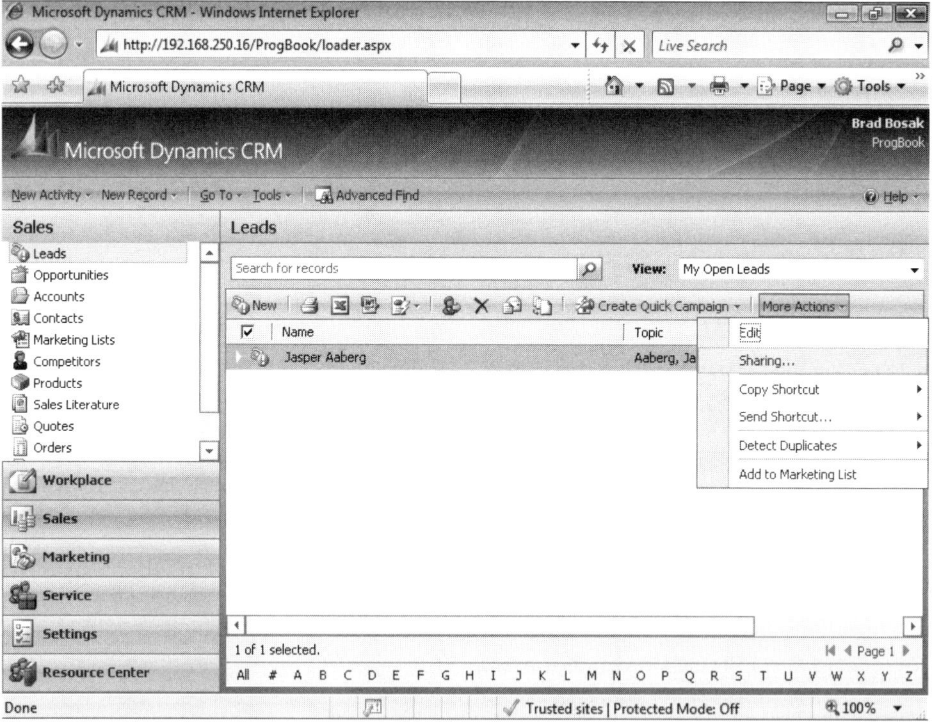

3. Click More Actions and select Sharing.

You will see a window containing all the users or teams that the record is shared with, along with their access writes on the instance (Figure 4-2).

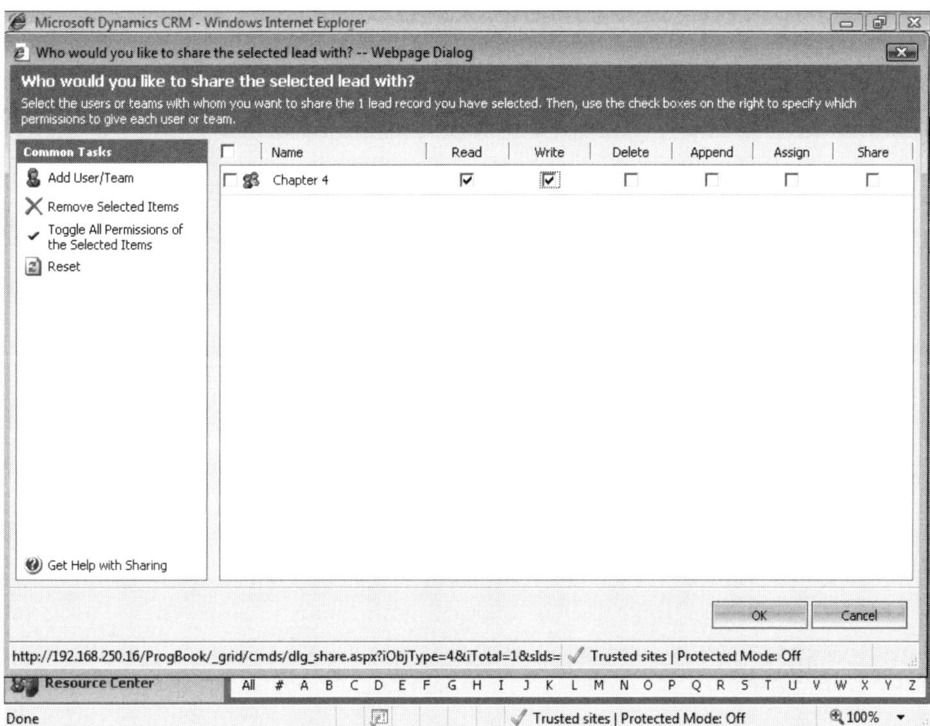

FIGURE 4-2 Shared Lead record.

Assigning Records

We talked about sharing records with teams and users, but sometimes you will want to actually change ownership of an entity instance. In these cases you need to use the Microsoft Dynamics CRM SDK's assign message. Programmatically assigning a record triggers the same functionality as assigning a record through the user interface. The *ownerid* attribute of the entity instance is updated to the *Guid* of the assignee. If *CascadeAssign* is turned on for the relationships between the assigned object and associated objects, any associated objects that have the same owner as the instance being assigned will also be assigned to the new owner. The user making the call needs the Assign privilege for the entity type and assign access rights for the entity being assigned. Listing 4-5 shows some sample code for assigning an Account instance to another system user.

LISTING 4-5 Assigning a record

```
CrmService service = CrmServiceUtility.GetCrmService("serverName", "orgName");

Guid accountId = new Guid("3963176C-0E2C-DD11-8A81-0019D13DDA0E");
```

```
// Guid of the user we are assigning the account to
Guid systemUserId = new Guid("237D2B4E-191D-DD11-8839-0019B9F8F548");

SecurityPrincipal assignee = new SecurityPrincipal();
assignee.Type = SecurityPrincipalType.User;
assignee.PrincipalId = systemUserId;

TargetOwnedAccount target = new TargetOwnedAccount();
target.EntityId = accountId;

AssignRequest assign = new AssignRequest();
assign.Assignee = assignee;
assign.Target = target;

AssignResponse assignResponse = (AssignResponse)service.Execute(assign);
```

When assigning a record, we create a new *SecurityPrincipal* object the same way we did when sharing a record. (See Table 4-4 for a description of the *SecurityPrincipalType* enumeration.) The next class we use is *TargetOwnedAccount*. Each entity type has its own target class. The naming convention is *TargetOwned* followed by the entity's name. (These class names all use Pascal case.) The target's *EntityId* property is then set to the *Guid* of the Account record we are assigning. Finally we create the *AssignRequest* and execute it.

Tip If you are using a dynamic entity, the target class is *TargetOwnedDynamic*.

Using Direct SQL for Accessing Microsoft Dynamics CRM Data

The Microsoft Dynamics CRM SDK provides a great deal of functionality to developers, but on certain occasions you may want to connect directly to the SQL Server database in your custom development.

Warning You should never use direct SQL to update or insert data in the Microsoft Dynamics CRM database because it sidesteps the security model and could cause severe damage to your Microsoft Dynamics CRM environment. The same warning applies to adding and altering tables. You should always create your entities and attributes through the Microsoft Dynamics CRM UI or by using *MetadataService*. For more information regarding Microsoft Dynamics CRM's *MetadataService*, see Chapter 8, "Developing with the Metadata Service."

Determining the Organization's Connection String

When you programmatically connect to the SQL Server, the first factor to consider is what connection string to use to connect to the Microsoft Dynamics CRM database. Previous versions of Microsoft Dynamics CRM stored the database connection string in the registry, but Microsoft Dynamics CRM 4.0 stores the connection string in the MSCRM_CONFIG database. This allows Microsoft Dynamics CRM to store multiple connection strings because each organization uses its own database. The connection strings stored in the MSCRM_CONFIG database use Windows Authentication to connect to SQL Server. This is very important to understand if you want to query against the filtered views and use the native security model, which we will discuss further in the next section. The following code shows a method named *GetConnectionString* that demonstrates how to retrieve the connection string by organization name.

Note The connection string is returned in the following format: Provider=SQLOLEDB;Data Source=[SQLSERVER];Initial Catalog=[CRMDATABASE];Integrated Security=SSPI.

```
public string GetConnectionString(string organizationName)
{
   string configurationDatabaseConnectionString;

   // grab the ms crm config database connection string from the crm server's registry
   using (RegistryKey mscrmKey = Registry.LocalMachine.OpenSubKey(@"SOFTWARE\Microsoft\
       MSCRM"))
   {
      if (mscrmKey == null)
      {
         throw new InvalidOperationException(
             @"Registry key 'HKEY_LOCAL_MACHINE\SOFTWARE\Microsoft\MSCRM' does not exist or
             is inaccessible.");
      }

      configurationDatabaseConnectionString = (string)mscrmKey.GetValue("configdb", String.
          Empty);
      if (String.IsNullOrEmpty(configurationDatabaseConnectionString))
      {
         throw new InvalidOperationException(
            @"Registry value 'HKEY_LOCAL_MACHINE\SOFTWARE\Microsoft\MSCRM\configdb' does not
            exist or is inaccessible.");
      }
   }

   // make a call to config database to get the connection string to the current
   // organization's database
   using (SqlConnection conn = new SqlConnection(configurationDatabaseConnectionString))
   {
      using (SqlCommand cmd = new SqlCommand(
                                  "SELECT ConnectionString FROM Organization WHERE
```

```
UniqueName=@orgName", conn))
      {
         cmd.Parameters.Add(new SqlParameter("orgName", organizationName));
         using (SqlDataAdapter adapter = new SqlDataAdapter(cmd))
         {
            DataTable organization = new DataTable();
            adapter.Fill(organization);

            if (organization.Rows.Count == 0)
            {
               throw new InvalidOperationException(String.Format("No organization with the
                   name '{0}' exists.", organizationName));
            }

            if (organization.Rows.Count > 1)
            {
               throw new InvalidOperationException(
                                        String.Format("More than one organization with the
                                            name '{0}' exists.", organizationName));
            }

            return (string)organization.Rows[0]["ConnectionString"];
         }
      }
   }

}
```

Note We discuss using the SQL authentication approach later in this chapter.

Filtered Views

The Microsoft Dynamics CRM database contains a list of SQL views referred to as filtered views. Each entity offers a corresponding filtered view, and they are convenient because they simplify the underlying table structure into a single entity view. Further, Microsoft Dynamics CRM automatically updates these views each time you make schema changes. The filtered views use the native security model to determine what data Microsoft Dynamics CRM should display to the user .

Note Filtered views are not available for Microsoft Dynamics CRM Online.

Built-in security is the biggest advantage of using filtered views, but they also provide some extra functionality. Querying against the base tables in the Microsoft Dynamics CRM database can lead to some pretty complex SQL statements. Using the filtered views will save you from having to add extra joins to retrieve the text values for some attribute types, such as *PickList*, *Lookup*, or *Customer*. Filtered views contain columns for the *name* field of certain attribute types. This saves you from having to do an extra join in your query. For example, if you need to retrieve your Account's primary contact's full name, you simply select the *primarycontactidname* field in your query, as shown here:

```
SELECT
    primarycontactidname
FROM
    FilteredAccount
WHERE
    accountid = '<insert Account Guid>'
```

To do this using the base tables requires a more complex query that joins on the ContactBase table:

```
SELECT
    c.fullname
FROM
    AccountBase a
INNER JOIN
    ContactBase c ON a.primarycontactid = c.contactid
WHERE
    accountid = '<insert Account Guid>'
```

The following attribute types will have a corresponding *name* field in the filtered views:

- *Boolean*
- *Customer*
- *Lookup*
- *Owner*
- *State*
- *Status*

To see a list of all available columns in the filtered views, access them using Microsoft SQL Server Management Studio.

Accessing filtered views in Management Studio

1. Open Microsoft SQL Server Management Studio and connect to your database server.
2. Expand your Microsoft Dynamics CRM database.
3. Expand the Views folder and look for views starting with Filtered.

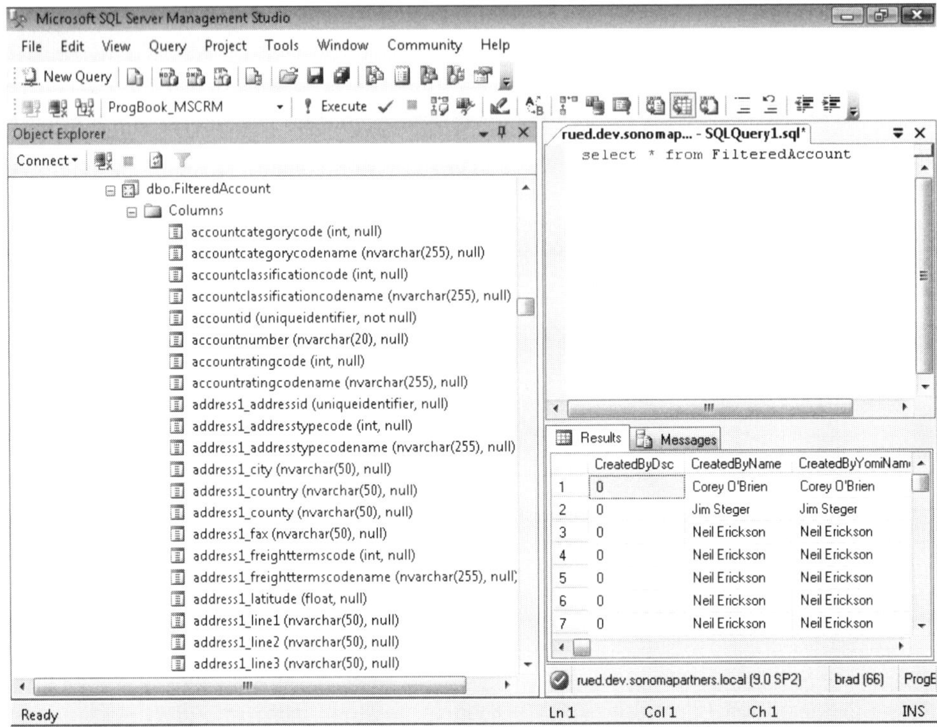

Additional Programming Considerations with Filtered Views

Microsoft Dynamics CRM uses a custom SQL function to determine the proper system user with which to enforce the proper security settings. This function requires authentication to SQL Server by using Windows authentication or it needs to be passed a valid user context for your queries to return data.

In most cases, you can simply connect to the database by using Windows authentication instead of SQL Server authentication.

More Info Remember that Microsoft doesn't support changes to the Microsoft Dynamics CRM databases, including adding your own routines or stored procedures. The preferred recommendation is to create your own database to store your custom routines.

This SSPI authentication approach presents numerous challenges in environments with multiple servers because it relies on Kerberos and delegation. What we have seen in practice is that these networking issues can be very problematic to maintain and troubleshoot.

An alternative to the Kerberos authentication approach is to authenticate to SQL Server using SQL authentication and then switch the user context programmatically in your query.

You can use the *content_info()* function to impersonate a user. First, create SQL Server authentication with an account that has access to any custom and Microsoft Dynamics CRM databases. Then, use this account when connecting to the database with a connection string such as the following:

```
server=databaseserver;database=yourcustomdatabase;uid=sqluser;pwd=sqlpwd
```

With SQL Server 2005, you can add synonyms to the Microsoft Dynamics CRM filtered views to query from your custom database. Synonyms provide a pointer (or alias) to its target, in this case the filtered views, so that you don't have to refresh the synonym when Microsoft Dynamics CRM updates the filtered views. Then, you can use the command in a routine such as the following:

```
create procedure MyStoredProcedure
(
  @userid uniqueidentifier
)
as

declare @original uniqueidentifier
set @original = context_info() -- store original value

set context_info @userid

/* Execute code with this new context value */
-- Example: This will pull only the accounts that the @userid has read access to
-- select name from filteredaccount

-- Set context back to original value
if @original is null
      set context_info 0x
else
      set context_info @original
end
```

Because *context_info()* persists for the entire session, you simply capture what it was before you changed it and then set it back after the query logic is complete.

Tip You won't be able to set the *context_info()* directly to null. If you wish to null out the context, use the following command: *set context_info 0x*.

Microsoft Dynamics CRM filtered views do have a potential drawback when it comes to performance. Because the views were designed to denormalize picklist and lookup relationships, the number of joins can be quite large. If your tables contain a large volume of data, you might find that these views seriously impact performance. If you find the performance of the filtered view lacking, you may need to query the base tables and provide your own security mechanism to filter the data.

Data Encryption

At times you might want to store sensitive information such as social security numbers or passwords in your Microsoft Dynamics CRM system. Information like this usually should not be stored as plain text in the database because anyone with administrator access to the database could view the information, and if a malicious user compromises your database, vital customer information is easy to steal. Out of the box, Microsoft Dynamics CRM does not provide a way for you to encrypt data stored in an attribute. However, you can use some custom coding techniques to implement data encryption. We will consider two different data encryption scenarios:

- One-way encryption
- Two-way encryption

One-Way Encryption

Let's assume we added a new custom attribute to the Contact entity to store passwords for a portal site. For this example, assume the portal site is using SSL to communicate with the server so that passwords aren't sent to the server in the clear. Because you'll be storing the passwords of external contacts, let's assume that your security requirements dictate that you cannot store passwords as plain text in the Microsoft Dynamics CRM database. By default, Microsoft Dynamics CRM stores attribute data in SQL Server as plain text. Fortunately, we can use an encryption algorithm and custom code to encrypt the contact's passwords in the database .

Note For the following example, two new custom attributes, named *new_username* and *new_password,* have been added to the Contact entity.

For this example, the portal users create their user accounts from an external Web site, and the application stores this data in the Microsoft Dynamics CRM database. Listing 4-6 shows the code to create the UI for our Create User Account page.

LISTING 4-6 CreateUserAccount.aspx

```
<%@ Page Language="C#"
    AutoEventWireup="true"
    CodeFile="CreateUserAccount.aspx.cs"
    Inherits="Security_CreateUserAccount" %>

<html xmlns="http://www.w3.org/1999/xhtml">
<head runat="server">
    <title>Untitled Page</title>
</head>
```

```
<body>
    <form id="form1" runat="server">
    <div>
        User Name: <asp:TextBox ID="username" runat="server" />
        <br />
        Password: <asp:TextBox ID="password" TextMode="Password" runat="server" />
        <br />
        First Name <asp:TextBox ID="firstname" runat="server" />
        <br />
        Last Name <asp:TextBox ID="lastname" runat="server" />
        <br />
        <input type="submit" value="Create Account" />
    </div>
    </form>
</body>
</html>
```

The *CreateUserAccount.aspx* page is pretty straightforward. We add a few text boxes to capture the information we need to create the new Contact record and a submit button. Listing 4-7 has the full source code for the code behind the page.

LISTING 4-7 CreateUserAccount.aspx.cs

```
using System;
using System.Collections;
using System.Configuration;
using System.Data;
using System.Web;
using System.Web.Security;
using System.Web.UI;
using System.Web.UI.HtmlControls;
using System.Web.UI.WebControls;
using System.Web.UI.WebControls.WebParts;
using Microsoft.Crm.SdkTypeProxy;
using Microsoft.Crm.Sdk;
using System.Security.Cryptography;
using System.Text;

public partial class Security_CreateUserAccount : System.Web.UI.Page
{
    protected void Page_Load(object sender, EventArgs e)
    {
        if (Page.IsPostBack)
        {
            string userName = this.username.Text;
            string password = this.password.Text;
            string firstName = this.firstname.Text;
            string lastName = this.lastname.Text;

            CrmService service =
                CrmServiceUtility.GetCrmService(ConfigurationManager.AppSettings
                  ["CrmServer"], ConfigurationManager.AppSettings["OrgName"]);
```

```
            DynamicEntity contact = new DynamicEntity();
            contact.Name = EntityName.contact.ToString();

            StringProperty userNameProp = new StringProperty();
            userNameProp.Name = "new_username";
            userNameProp.Value = userName;

            contact.Properties.Add(userNameProp);

            // encrypt the entered password

            MD5CryptoServiceProvider md5 = new MD5CryptoServiceProvider();

            byte[] encryptedPassword;

            UTF8Encoding textencoder = new UTF8Encoding();

            encryptedPassword = md5.ComputeHash(textencoder.GetBytes(password));

            md5.Clear();

            StringProperty passwordProp = new StringProperty();
            passwordProp.Name = "new_password";
            passwordProp.Value = Convert.ToBase64String(encryptedPassword);

            contact.Properties.Add(passwordProp);

            StringProperty firstNameProp = new StringProperty();
            firstNameProp.Name = "firstname";
            firstNameProp.Value = firstName;

            contact.Properties.Add(firstNameProp);

            StringProperty lastNameProp = new StringProperty();
            lastNameProp.Name = "lastname";
            lastNameProp.Value = lastName;

            contact.Properties.Add(lastNameProp);

            service.Create(contact);
        }
    }
}
```

Note This example uses the *Microsoft.Crm.Sdk.dll* and *Microsoft.Crm.Sdk.TypeProxy.dll* assemblies and *not* the direct Web references to the Microsoft Dynamics CRM SDK. Therefore, we need to use a *DynamicEntity* class to create the Contact record because of the two custom attributes we are populating.

The creation of the actual Contact in Microsoft Dynamics CRM is straightforward as well. We simply grab the values the user entered on our form, create an instance of the *DynamicEntity* class, populate its properties, and then call the *Create* method on the *CrmService*. For this example we use a fast and easy to implement encryption algorithm named Message-Digest Algorithm 5 (MD5). Because MD5 offers one-way encryption, after we encrypt and store the password, we will not be able to return it to its original plain text characters. MD5 always encrypts a given string to the same value. In the case of passwords this is not a problem because we can just encrypt the user's password at logon time and compare it to the encrypted value stored in the database.

The classes we need to implement MD5 encryption are located in the *System.Security.Cryptography* namespace. We first use the *UTF8Encoding* class to get a byte array from our password string. The *ComputeHash* method on the *MD5CryptoServiceProvider* instance is then called to encrypt our byte array. Microsoft Dynamics CRM does not provide us with an attribute type capable of storing binary data, so we need to convert our encrypted bytes into a string that can be stored in a *nvarchar* database field. To do this we use the *Convert.ToBase64String* method:

```
passwordProp.Value = Convert.ToBase64String(encryptedPassword);
```

Now that we are storing the encrypted passwords, let's briefly discuss how we can use them in our site's login page. When a user enters her credentials, we first have to run the entered password text through the same MD5 encryption. This encrypted value can then be used to query for a matching contact record. If a match is found, you can now direct the user to the home page of your portal.

Two-Way Encryption

One-way data encryption works well for information like passwords, but what happens when you need to retrieve the encrypted data and revert it back to its original plain text? In cases like these, you need to use two-way encryption. In this section we will create a plug-in to encrypt social security numbers being stored in the Contact entity. Listing 4-8 has the full source code for this plug-in.

Note For the following example, a new attribute named *new_ssn* has been added to the Contact entity.

LISTING 4-8 SSNEncryptor.cs source code

```
using System;
using System.Collections.Generic;
using System.Text;
using Microsoft.Crm.Sdk;
using ProgrammingWithDynamicsCrm4.Plugins.Attributes;
using System.Security.Cryptography;

namespace ProgrammingWithDynamicsCrm4.Plugins
{
    [PluginStep("Create",
            PluginStepStage.PreEvent,
            PrimaryEntityName = "contact",
            FilteringAttributes = "new_ssn")]

    [PluginStep("Update",
            PluginStepStage.PreEvent,
            PrimaryEntityName = "contact",
            FilteringAttributes = "new_ssn")]

    public class SSNEncryptor : IPlugin
    {
        public void Execute(IPluginExecutionContext context)
        {
            DynamicEntity target = (DynamicEntity)context.InputParameters[ParameterName.
                Target];

            if (target.Properties.Contains("new_ssn"))
            {
                string ssn = (string)target["new_ssn"];

                byte[] aInput = ASCIIEncoding.ASCII.GetBytes(ssn);

                TripleDESCryptoServiceProvider tripleDESCryptoServiceProvider =
                    new TripleDESCryptoServiceProvider();
                MD5CryptoServiceProvider MD5CryptoServiceProvider =
                    new MD5CryptoServiceProvider();

                tripleDESCryptoServiceProvider.Key =
                    MD5CryptoServiceProvider.ComputeHash(ASCIIEncoding.ASCII.
                        GetBytes("secretkey"));
                tripleDESCryptoServiceProvider.Mode = CipherMode.ECB;
                ICryptoTransform iCryptoTransform = tripleDESCryptoServiceProvider.
                    CreateEncryptor();

                target.Properties["new_ssn"] =
                Convert.ToBase64String(iCryptoTransform.TransformFinalBlock(aInput, 0,
                    aInput.Length));
            }
        }
    }
}
```

This plug-in runs whenever a Contact record is created or updated. If the *new_ssn* attribute is populated or changed, it takes the new value and encrypts it before saving the information in the database. Notice the string "secretkey" being passed into the *MD5CryptoServiceProvider* class's *ComputeHash* method. This same string is used later to decrypt the data. In a real-world application, you would want to use a larger random string of characters for your secret key.

Next we need a way for end users to update social security numbers. If we stopped here, end users would see a mess of characters displayed in our Contact form's social security number field (Figure 4-3).

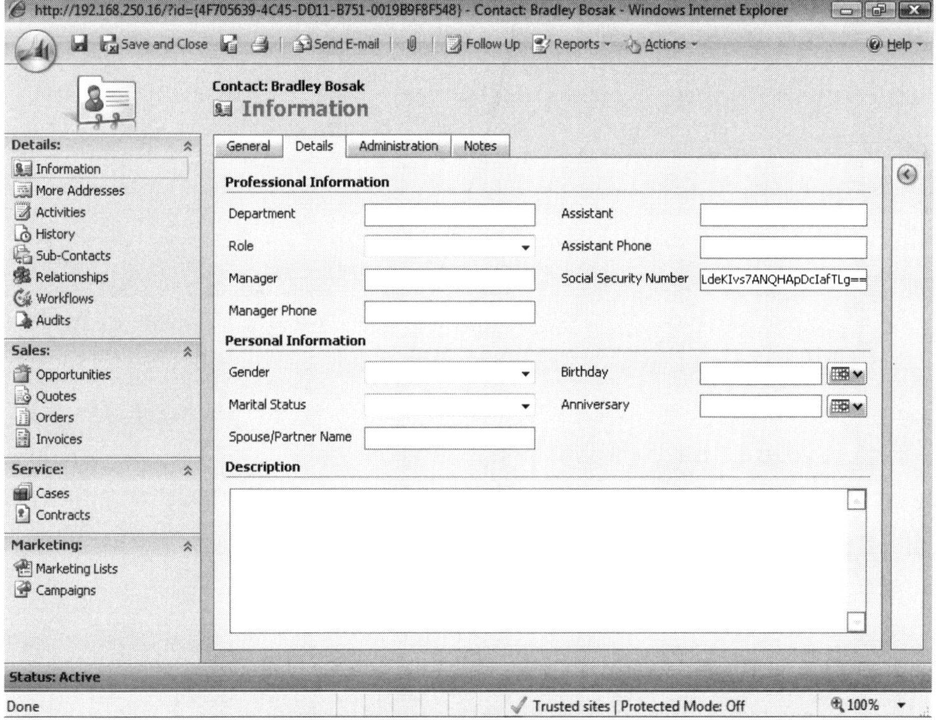

FIGURE 4-3 Encrypted Social Security Number display

Therefore, we need to decrypt our data prior to it being displayed on the form. One solution is to create a plug-in that fires on the *Retrieve* message for a Contact. The plug-in verifies that the *new_ssn* attribute is in the returned property collection, decrypts the data, and then updates the *new_ssn* property with the plain text. Listing 4-9 shows the full source code for this plug-in.

LISTING 4-9 SSNDecryptor.cs source code

```
using System;
using System.Collections.Generic;
using System.Text;
using Microsoft.Crm.Sdk;
using ProgrammingWithDynamicsCrm4.Plugins.Attributes;
using System.Security.Cryptography;

namespace ProgrammingWithDynamicsCrm4.Plugins
{
    [PluginStep("Retrieve",
            PluginStepStage.PostEvent,
            PrimaryEntityName = "contact")]
    [PluginStep("RetrieveMultiple",
            PluginStepStage.PostEvent,
            PrimaryEntityName = "contact")]
    public class SSNDecryptor : IPlugin
    {
        public void Execute(IPluginExecutionContext context)
        {
            if (context.MessageName == "Retrieve")
            {
                DynamicEntity contact =
                            (DynamicEntity)context.OutputParameters[ParameterName
                                .BusinessEntity];
                DecryptSSN(contact);
            }
            else
            {
                BusinessEntityCollection results =
            (BusinessEntityCollection)context.OutputParameters[ParameterName.
                BusinessEntityCollection];

                foreach (DynamicEntity result in results.BusinessEntities)
                {
                    DecryptSSN(result);
                }
            }
        }

        private static void DecryptSSN(DynamicEntity contact)
        {
            if (contact.Properties.Contains("new_ssn"))
            {
                string ssn = (string)contact.Properties["new_ssn"];
                byte[] aInput = Convert.FromBase64String(ssn);

                TripleDESCryptoServiceProvider tripleDESCryptoServiceProvider =
                    new TripleDESCryptoServiceProvider();
                MD5CryptoServiceProvider MD5CryptoServiceProvider =
                    new MD5CryptoServiceProvider();
```

```
                tripleDESCryptoServiceProvider.Key =
                    MD5CryptoServiceProvider.ComputeHash(ASCIIEncoding.ASCII.
                        GetBytes("secretkey"));
                tripleDESCryptoServiceProvider.Mode = CipherMode.ECB;
                ICryptoTransform iCryptoTransform = tripleDESCryptoServiceProvider.
                    CreateEncryptor();

                target.Properties["new_ssn"] =
                Convert.ToBase64String(iCryptoTransform.TransformFinalBlock(aInput, 0,
                    aInput.Length));
            }
        }
    }
}
```

After you deploy this plug-in, end users never even know that Microsoft Dynamics CRM encrypts the confidential information because users will see the plain text social security numbers on the Contact form. However, if you query for the *new_ssn* field in the Microsoft Dynamics CRM database, you get the encrypted value.

Summary

This chapter provided you with some key security concepts that developers should understand when creating custom code for Microsoft Dynamics CRM. You should now have a good understanding of Microsoft Dynamics CRM security principals and access rights. Microsoft Dynamics CRM allows developers to write code that programmatically performs many of the key security management activities, such as creating a role, assigning records, and sharing retrieving security roles. Everything you can configure security to do through the Microsoft Dynamics CRM UI, you can configure programmatically using the SDK. When you connect your code to Microsoft Dynamics CRM API, it automatically manages the record security for you, saving you the extra effort of writing code to determine the appropriate privileges. Microsoft Dynamics CRM also allows you to use impersonation to run code as a user different from the person browsing the Web application. For most programming requirements, you can perform all the data operations you need through the Microsoft Dynamics CRM API. However, sometimes you might need to access data in the SQL Server database directly. Microsoft offers filtered views within the SQL Server database as an alternative method for retrieving data. Even though Microsoft Dynamics CRM does not provide an out-of-the-box tool to encrypt data stored in an entity's attribute, this chapter showed examples and sample code of how to perform one-way and two-way encryption of your data.

Chapter 5
Plug-ins

Plug-ins provide one of the most powerful customization points within Microsoft Dynamics CRM. As users work in the application, their actions cause Microsoft Dynamics CRM to trigger events that developers can use to execute custom business logic through the use of plug-ins. For example, you can register plug-ins to run business logic every time a user creates an account or deletes an activity. You can create plug-ins to run in response to a vast number of events, including plug-ins for custom entities. You can use plug-ins for a variety of features, such as synchronizing data to an external database, tracking changes in an audit log, or simply creating follow-up tasks for a newly created account.

Note At the time this book went to press, Microsoft Dynamics CRM Online (the Microsoft hosted version of Microsoft Dynamics CRM) does not support custom plug-ins.

Some of the tasks you can accomplish with plug-ins—such as populating fields with default values or specific field formatting—you can also accomplish with form JavaScript. Plug-ins have the advantage of running on the server, so you are guaranteed that these types of tasks will run even if the entity is created or updated from a bulk import or through the Web service API.

Note If you are familiar with Microsoft Dynamics CRM 3.0, you are probably thinking that plug-ins sound very similar to callouts. Plug-ins are in fact the replacement for callouts, but they offer a much more robust programming model. Microsoft Dynamics 4.0 does support version 3.0 callouts if you still need to use them, but they access CRM via the version 3.0 endpoint and do not support version 4.0 features such as multi-tenancy.

In this chapter, we will explore the following topics in detail:

- Writing your first plug-in
- The event execution pipeline
- Details of the *IPluginExecutionContext* interface
- Impersonation
- Exception handling

- Deploying plug-ins
- Debugging plug-ins
- Unit testing plug-ins
- Real-world plug-in samples

Writing Your First Plug-in

When working with a new framework or technology, we find it easiest to start with a simple hands-on example and then dig deeper into real-world examples. We'll start by implementing a simple plug-in to provide a more concrete foundation for the remainder of the chapter. This plug-in verifies that an account's *accountnumber* follows a specific format. In this example, Microsoft Dynamics CRM executes the plug-in when a new account is created or modified to verify that the account number starts with two letters followed by six numbers.

As mentioned earlier, you could accomplish this same type of account validation through scripting with the form's *onsave* event. However, enforcing business logic on the form might not be ideal because modifications to the account number through workflow or through an external application would bypass the *onsave* event script and possibly allow an invalid account number format. By using a plug-in, we can guarantee that Microsoft Dynamics CRM enforces our business logic regardless of the method used to create the account.

Creating the Plug-in Project

Plug-ins are implemented as classes that implement a specific interface and are contained within a signed Microsoft .NET assembly. The assembly needs to target the Microsoft .NET runtime version 2.0, which can be accomplished by creating a class library in Microsoft Visual Studio 2008 targeting the .NET Framework 2.0, 3.0, or 3.5. However, installing Microsoft Dynamics CRM 4.0 only guarantees that Microsoft .NET Framework 3.0 is installed on the server. If you need assemblies included in the Microsoft .NET Framework 3.5, you have to install that version of the framework yourself. Before we can create our first plug-in, we need to create a class library project. Follow these steps to set up your first plug-in project.

Creating the plug-in project in Microsoft Visual Studio 2008

1. Open Microsoft Visual Studio 2008.
2. On the File Menu, select New and then click Project.
3. In the New Project dialog box, select the Other Project Types > Visual Studio Solutions type, and then select the Blank Solution template.
4. Type the name **ProgrammingWithDynamicsCrm4** in the Name box. Click OK.

5. On the File Menu, select Add and then click New Project.
6. In the New Project dialog box, select the Visual C# project type targeting the .NET Framework 3.0 and then select the Class Library template.
7. Type the name **ProgrammingWithDynamicsCrm4.Plugins** in the Name box. Click OK.
8. Delete the default Class.cs file.
9. Right-click the ProgrammingWithDynamicsCrm4.Plugins project in Solution Explorer and then click Add Reference.
10. On the Browse tab, navigate to the CRM SDK's bin folder and select microsoft.crm.sdk.dll and microsoft.crm.sdktypeproxy.dll. Click OK.
11. Right-click the ProgrammingWithDynamicsCrm4.Plugins project in Solution Explorer and then click Add Reference.
12. On the .NET tab, select System.Web.Services. Click OK.
13. Right-click the ProgrammingWithDynamicsCrm4.Plugins project in Solution Explorer and then click Properties.
14. On the Signing tab, select the Sign The Assembly box and then select <New...> from the list below it.
15. Type the key file name ProgrammingWithDynamicsCrm4.Plugins, and then clear the Protect My Key File With A Password check box. Click OK.
16. Close the project properties window.

Implementing the Plug-in Class

After setting up our project, we are ready to implement our first plug-in. Let's start by adding a class to our newly created project.

Adding the AccountNumberValidator class

1. Right-click the ProgrammingWithDynamicsCrm4.Plugins project in Solution Explorer. Under Add, click Class.
2. Type **AccountNumberValidator.cs** in the Name box. Click Add.

Replace the generated code in the *AccountNumberValidator* class with the code displayed in Listing 5-1.

LISTING 5-1 The *AccountNumberValidator* plug-in source code

```
using System;
using Microsoft.Crm.Sdk;
using System.Text.RegularExpressions;

namespace ProgrammingWithDynamicsCrm4.Plugins
{
    public class AccountNumberValidator: IPlugin
    {
        public void Execute(IPluginExecutionContext context)
        {
            DynamicEntity target =
                (DynamicEntity)context.InputParameters[ParameterName.Target];

            if (target.Properties.Contains("accountnumber"))
            {
                string accountNumber = (string)target["accountnumber"];
                Regex validFormat = new Regex("[A-Z]{2}-[0-9]{6}");

                if (!validFormat.IsMatch(accountNumber))
                {
                    string message =
                        "Account number does not follow the required format. " +
                        "(AA-######)";

                    throw new InvalidPluginExecutionException(message);
                }
            }

        }

    }
}
```

AccountNumberValidator, a very simple plug-in, extracts the target account as a *DynamicEntity* and validates that the *accountnumber* property follows a specific pattern (two capital letters followed by a dash and then six numbers). We know the target input parameter will be a *DynamicEntity* representing the account because we will be registering this plug-in with the Create and Update messages for the account entity.

Notice that the only requirement at the class level for a plug-in is that it must implement the *Microsft.Crm.Sdk.IPlugin* interface. *IPlugin* has only a single method, named *Execute*, which takes a single argument of type *IPluginExecutionContext*. We will be exploring the *IPluginExecutionContext* interface in detail—as well as how Microsoft Dynamics CRM 4.0 handles exceptions thrown by plug-ins—later in this chapter. For more information on the *DynamicEntity* class and its use, refer to Chapter 3, "Using the Web Service APIs."

Building the Registration Tool

Unlike for workflows, form changes, and other customizations to Microsoft Dynamics CRM, no Web-based interface is included to register plug-ins. However, the Microsoft Dynamics CRM SDK includes two utilities to help you register plug-ins, and you can also register plug-ins using the API.

Later in the chapter we will explore using the API to write your own plug-in registration tools, but for this first example we will use one of the CRM SDK's registration tools, PluginRegistration. PluginRegistration is a Windows desktop application that has an intuitive graphical user interface for registering plug-ins and configuring which messages cause the plug-in to execute. You can find the PluginRegistration tool in the Tools folder within the CRM SDK.

The Microsoft Dynamics CRM SDK distributes PluginRegistration as source code only, so you will need to compile it before you can run it. Follow the guidelines in the readme.doc included in the tools\PluginRegistration folder to compile the application. PluginRegistration is distributed as a Visual Studio 2005 project, but Visual Studio 2008 can automatically upgrade it without problems.

Deploying the Plug-in

After compiling our plug-in registration tool, we are ready to register our first plug-in. During registration you specify which messages for specific entities will cause the plug-in to execute. Depending on the message, you can specify additional filtering or request more information to be provided to your plug-in during execution.

Important To register a plug-in you must be listed as a Deployment Administrator on the CRM server. To verify that you are a Deployment Administrator, log on to the CRM server and launch the Deployment Manager tool, which is located in the Microsoft Dynamics CRM group on the Start menu. If you are not a Deployment Administrator, the tool will show an error indicating so and then exit. If this is the case, you need to have a Deployment Administrator use this tool and add you to the list of Deployment Administrators.

When you register a plug-in, Microsoft Dynamics CRM offers you multiple registration properties:

- **Mode** A plug-in can execute either synchronously or asynchronously.
- **Stage** This option specifies whether the plug-in will respond to pre-events or post-events.
- **Deployment** A plug-in can execute only on the server, within the Outlook client, or both.

- **Messages** This option determines which Microsoft Dynamics CRM events should trigger your logic, such as *Create*, *Update*, and even *Retrieve*.
- **Entity** A plug-in can execute against most of the entities, including custom entities.
- **Rank** This option is an integer that specifies the order in which all plug-in steps should be executed.
- **Assembly Location** This option tells Microsoft Dynamics CRM whether the assemblies are stored in the database or on the Web server's file system.
- **Images** You can pass attribute values from the record as either pre-images or post-images for certain message types.

You configure these plug-in properties when you register the plug-in with Microsoft Dynamics CRM.

Mode

Microsoft Dynamics CRM allows you to execute plug-ins synchronously or asynchronously. Asynchronous plug-ins are loaded into the Microsoft CRM Asynchronous Service and executed at some point after the main event processing is complete. Asynchronous plug-ins are ideal for handling situations that are not critical to complete immediately, such as audit logging. Because the plug-in executes asynchronously, it does not negatively affect the response time for an end user who initiates the core operation.

Real World In practice, most plug-ins perform tasks that users expect to see feedback on as soon as they save their changes within the CRM application. Because of this, you will probably find that most plug-ins are registered to execute synchronously. When it is determined that a plug-in can be registered to execute asynchronously, implementing a custom workflow step instead is frequently more beneficial because business users can more easily maintain the workflow. Scenarios still exist in which an asynchronous plug-in is the right answer, but they are not very common. Microsoft Dynamics CRM does not support pre-event plug-ins configured for asynchronous operation.

Stage

When you register a plug-in, you can configure the plug-in to run before or after the core operation takes place. A plug-in that executes before the core operation is referred to as a *pre-event* plug-in, while a plug-in that executes after the core operation is a *post-event* plug-in. Pre-event plug-ins are useful when you want to validate or alter data prior to submission. With post-event plug-ins, you can execute additional logic or integration after the data has been safely stored in the database.

Important How do you know which stage to register for? If a plug-in needs to interrupt or modify values before they are committed to the database, you should register it as a pre-event plug-in. Otherwise, you end up needing to execute an additional message to apply your change when you could have accomplished this by just modifying the data before the original message's core operation executed. On the other hand, if your plug-in needs to create a child entity whenever the parent entity type is created, you need to register it to execute during the post-event stage to have access to the newly created parent's ID.

Deployment

One of the great new features of Microsoft Dynamics CRM 4.0 is the ability to have your plug-in logic execute offline with the Outlook client, further extending your existing solution. You can choose to have the plug-in execute only against the server, run offline with the Outlook client, or both.

Remember that when a client goes offline and then returns online, any plug-in calls are executed after the data synchronizes with the server. If you choose to have your logic execute both with the server and offline, be prepared for Microsoft Dynamics CRM to execute your plug-in code twice.

Caution Microsoft Dynamics CRM does not support an asynchronous implementation of a plug-in with offline deployment. If you want to have your plug-in work offline, you need to register it in synchronous mode.

For more information about developing offline solutions and using plug-ins offline, please refer to Chapter 10, "Developing Offline Solutions."

Messages

In the documentation, Microsoft Dynamics CRM 4.0 refers to server-based trigger events as *messages*. The Microsoft Dynamics CRM 4.0 SDK also supports all the events from Microsoft Dynamics CRM 3.0, such as *Create*, *Update*, *Delete*, and *Merge*. In addition, Microsoft Dynamics CRM 4.0 includes some new messages such as *Route*, *Retrieve*, and *RetrieveMultiple*.

See the "Supported Messages and Entities" section later in this chapter for more information about the available messages. You can also use the API to write code to see whether Microsoft Dynamics CRM supports a particular message.

Entities

Most system and all custom entities are available for plug-in execution. Please refer to the "Supported Messages and Entities" section for more information on the supported entities.

Rank

Rank merely denotes the order in which a plug-in should fire. Rank is simply an integer, and Microsoft Dynamics CRM starts with the plug-in with the lowest rank and then cycles through all available plug-ins. You should definitely consider the order of plug-ins, depending on the logic they perform.

Assembly Location

You can deploy plug-in assemblies to the database, to a folder on the Microsoft Dynamics CRM server, or to the Global Assembly Cache (GAC) on the server. Typically the database is the best option because you do not need to manually copy the file to the server before registering the plug-in. Unless you have a specific need to do otherwise, we recommend that you leave the default option and deploy your plug-ins to the database.

Images

Images provide you with the record attribute values. Images exist as pre-values (before the core platform operation) and post-values. Not all messages allow images.

Now that you understand a little more background about the plug-in registration process, use the following steps to register the *AccountNumberValidator* plug-in.

Connecting to the server with the PluginRegistration tool

1. Launch the PluginRegistration tool that you compiled in the previous section. You will see the New Connection screen first (Figure 5-1).
2. Type any name you want for the Label. It is only used for display purposes in the PluginRegistration tool.
3. Type the name of your CRM server for the Discovery Server.
4. Optionally, specify the port your CRM server is running on if it is not port 80.
5. Optionally, specify the domain and user name you want to use to connect to the CRM server. If you specify a domain and user name, you will be prompted for a password when you connect. If you leave these fields blank, the tool connects as the currently logged on user.
6. Click Connect. You should now see a list of organizations under your connection.
7. Double-click the organization you want to register the plug-in with.

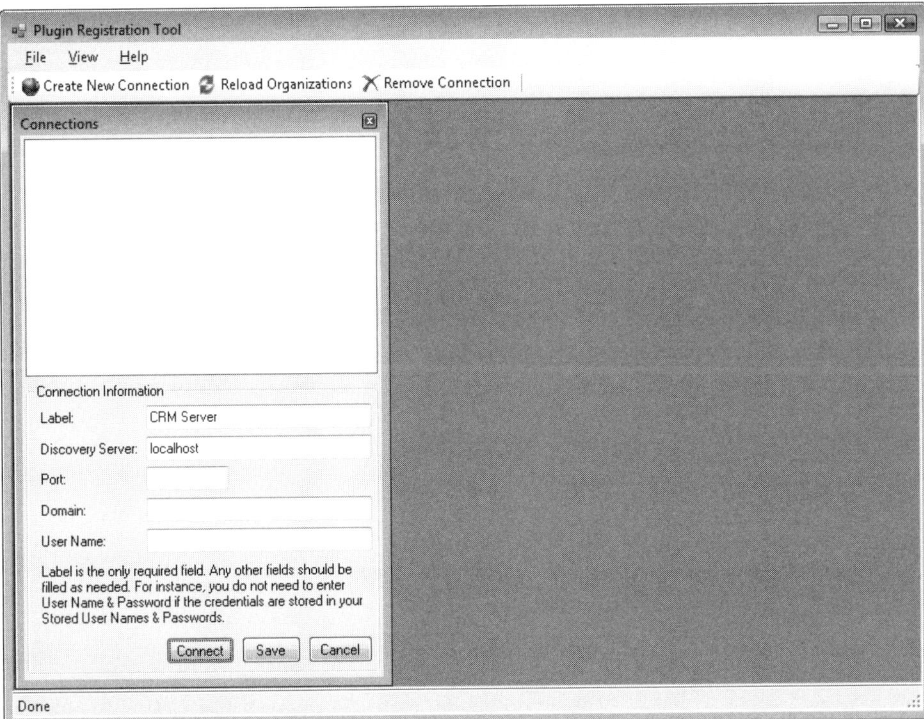

FIGURE 5-1 The New Connection screen

Now that you are connected to the server, next you will register the assembly on the server.

Registering the assembly

1. Select Register New Assembly from the Register toolbar drop-down list to open the Register New Assembly dialog box (Figure 5-2).
2. Click the ellipsis button to browse and select the plug-in DLL. Note that the assembly and plug-in classes are selected by default in the selection tree.
3. Leave Database selected as the deployment location.

   While you can deploy plug-ins to a folder or to the GAC on the Microsoft Dynamics CRM server, it is typically better to deploy to the database because you do not need to manually set up the assembly on the server. This point becomes even more valid if you are dealing with a web farm environment because you would need to copy the assembly to each server if you don't specify database deployment.
4. Click Register Selected Plugins.

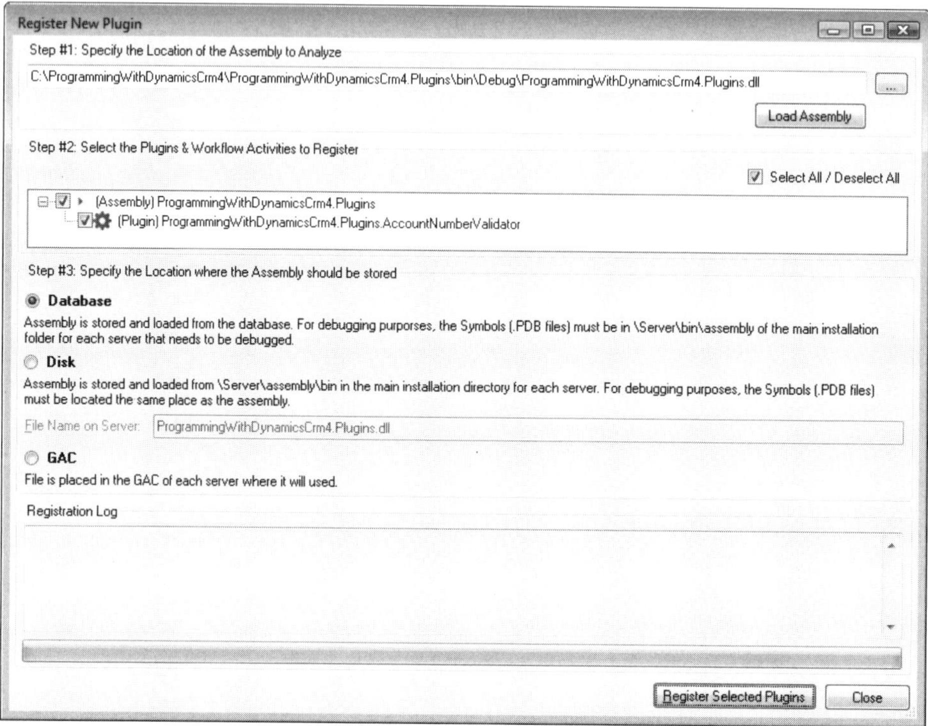

FIGURE 5-2 The Register New Assembly dialog box

After this step you should see a series of messages in the Registration log. If all goes well, a confirmation dialog box will pop up to tell you that one assembly and one plug-in were registered.

Last you need to configure when the plug-in should run. You do this by registering steps with the PluginRegistration tool. Steps contain information such as the entity and message that will cause a plug-in to execute, as well as the stage it will execute in. Each plug-in can have multiple steps, allowing it to execute for different entities and messages.

Registering plug-in steps

1. Right-click the *AccountNumberValidator* plug-in in the Registered Plugins & Custom Workflow Activities tree, and then select Register New Step to open the Register New Step dialog box (Figure 5-3).
2. Type **Create** in the Message box.
3. Type **account** in the Primary Entity box.
4. Specify **accountnumber** for the Filtering Attributes by clicking on the ellipsis button and then clearing all but the Account Number check box in the resulting dialog box.

5. Select the Pre Stage option.
6. Leave the rest of the settings at their default values.
7. Click Register New Step.
8. Repeat steps 1 through 7, but type **Update** in the Message box.

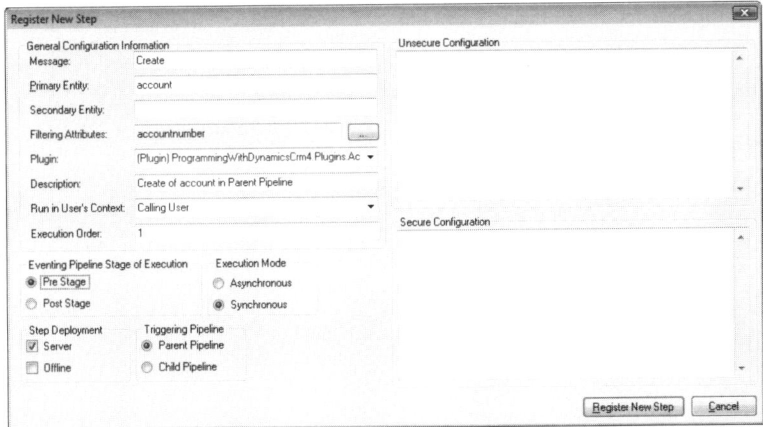

FIGURE 5-3 The Register New Step dialog box

Now that you've registered the plug-in, it will verify that all newly created or modified account numbers match the specified format. If a user tries to create or update an account using an invalid account number, the error shown in Figure 5-4 appears. Likewise, if a workflow or service call tries to create or modify an account with an invalid account number, Microsoft Dynamics CRM will not update the account and will bubble up an exception to the caller.

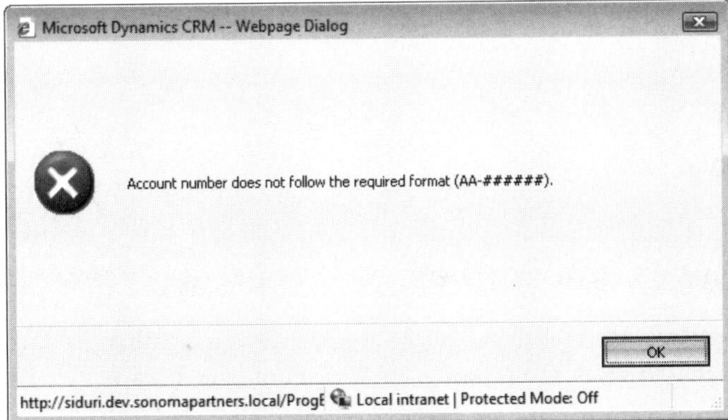

FIGURE 5-4 An error presented to the user by the *AccountNumberValidator* plug-in

The Event Execution Pipeline

Now that we implemented a basic plug-in, let's step back and look at the bigger picture. Plug-ins run within an execution pipeline specific to the message being executed. Also executing within the pipeline is the core operation, which is implemented by Microsoft Dynamics CRM 4.0. The core operation typically consists of a database operation—either retrieving, updating, inserting, or deleting records. For example, when a RetrieveMultiple request is executed, the core operation is the selection of data from the database. Figure 5-5 illustrates the various stages of the event execution pipeline.

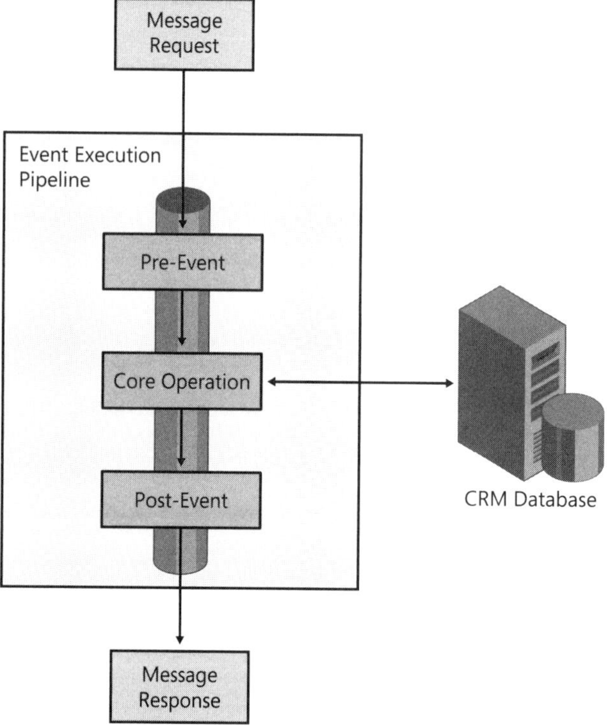

FIGURE 5-5 The event execution pipeline

Supported Messages and Entities

When trying to determine how to register a plug-in or even what is possible to hook into, you often find yourself wondering which messages exist for any given entity. The CRM SDK includes a Microsoft Office Excel spreadsheet that lists all the events that can be registered for and their corresponding entities. The file is named Plug-in Message-Entity Table.xls and is located in the Tools subfolder of the SDK.

This spreadsheet includes filterable columns and can be an excellent tool when you are trying to determine which messages an entity supports—or when you are just trying to brainstorm creative solutions. From this list you can see that several messages, such as Import, Export, and Publish, are not even tied to an entity. Figure 5-6 shows the spreadsheet filtered to only display messages supported by the Account entity.

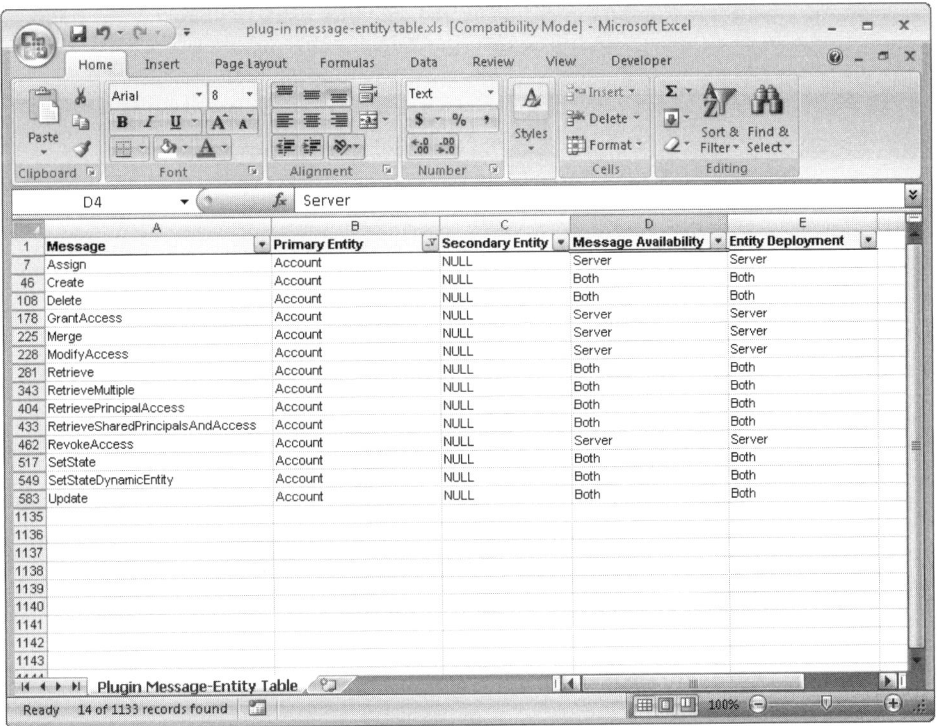

	Message	Primary Entity	Secondary Entity	Message Availability	Entity Deployment
7	Assign	Account	NULL	Server	Server
46	Create	Account	NULL	Both	Both
108	Delete	Account	NULL	Both	Both
178	GrantAccess	Account	NULL	Server	Server
225	Merge	Account	NULL	Server	Server
228	ModifyAccess	Account	NULL	Server	Server
281	Retrieve	Account	NULL	Both	Both
343	RetrieveMultiple	Account	NULL	Both	Both
404	RetrievePrincipalAccess	Account	NULL	Both	Both
433	RetrieveSharedPrincipalsAndAccess	Account	NULL	Both	Both
462	RevokeAccess	Account	NULL	Server	Server
517	SetState	Account	NULL	Both	Both
549	SetStateDynamicEntity	Account	NULL	Both	Both
583	Update	Account	NULL	Both	Both

FIGURE 5-6 The plug-in message entity spreadsheet

Parent and Child Pipelines

Some events will in turn cause other events to be executed. When this happens, a secondary pipeline is created for this event and is referred to as a child pipeline. For example, when an Opportunity is converted to an Account, the Create event is executed in a child pipeline. If you want to handle the creation of an account in this scenario, you need to specify Child as the *InvocationSource* when registering your plug-in step.

Typically, plug-ins only execute outside the main database transaction and cannot cause a rollback to occur. However, when a plug-in is running inside a child pipeline, it is executing inside the parent pipeline's transaction, and if the plug-in throws an exception, the parent's transaction will be rolled back.

Caution One additional point to be aware of is that when you run a plug-in inside a child pipeline, you cannot use the *IPluginExecutionContext* interface's *CreateCrmService* method. If you do, an exception is thrown. The use of the *CreateCrmService* method was intentionally disabled in child pipelines because it would be too easy to cause an infinite loop or a database deadlock if it were enabled. If you absolutely need to talk back to the CRM services inside a child pipeline, you can manually create a *CrmService*, but be sure to use it with caution. Additionally, any calls you make with your own *CrmService* run within their own thread and are outside transactions in which the plug-in executes. This means that if the transaction is rolled back for any reason, changes made with your instance of *CrmService* will not be undone.

IPluginExecutionContext

As stated earlier, every plug-in must implement the *IPlugin* interface, which includes the *Execute* method in its definition. The *Execute* method takes a single argument of type *IPluginExecutionContext*, which provides the plug-in with the state of the current execution pipeline and a means to communicate with the Microsoft Dynamics CRM Web service API. *IPluginExecutionContext* has twenty-two properties and two methods, all of which are described in the following list.

- ***BusinessUnitId* property** *BusinessUnitId* is a *Guid* that represents the business unit that the primary entity belongs to.
- ***CallerOrigin* property** *CallerOrigin* is an in*stance of o*ne of the following classes: *ApplicationOrigin, AsyncServiceOrigin, OfflineOrigin, or WebServiceApiOrigin*. You can use this property to determine who initiated the pipeline. The following code determines whether the pipeline was initiated from the CRM Web service.

```
public bool IsOriginatingFromWebServiceApi(IPluginExecutionContext context)
{
    return context.CallerOrigin is WebServiceApiOrigin;
}
```

- ***CorrelationId, CorrelationUpdatedTime, and Depth* properties** These three properties are combined to detect infinite loops in plug-ins. If you only use the *IPluginExecutionContext* interface's *CreateCrmService* method *to create CrmService* instances, you don't need to worry about these three properties, as they will be set on the returned *CrmService* for you. However, if you need to create your own instance of a *CrmService* class, you can use these properties to initialize its *CorrelationTokenValue* property, which ensures safety from infinite loops. The code shown here demonstrates how to use the correlation properties when creating your own *CrmService* instances.

```
public CrmService GetSafeCrmService(IPluginExecutionContext context)
{
    CrmService crmService = new CrmService();
```

```
    crmService.CorrelationTokenValue = new CorrelationToken(
        context.CorrelationId,
        context.CorrelationUpdatedTime,
        context.Depth
    );

    // finish initializing crmService here...

    return crmService;
}
```

More Info One additional use for *CorrelationId* is as a unique value for logging. In a production environment you will likely have multiple plug-ins executing at the same time, and the unique ID can be useful in determining which plug-in instance is generating the log messages.

- ***InitiatingUserId* property** This property is always the *Guid* of the user that caused the event to execute, regardless of whether the plug-in was registered to impersonate another user. See the *UserId* property later in this section for more information.
- **InputParameters property** This property is an instance of *Microsoft.Crm.Sdk.PropertyBag*. Each value contained in *PropertyBag* corresponds with a property on the *Request* that caused this event to execute. For example, *CreateRequest* has a property named *Target*, so you would find a value in *InputParameters* with a key of "*Target*".

Tip When accessing the values in *InputParameters*, you should use the *ParameterNames* static class, instead of typing keys, to avoid run-time errors caused by typos.

```
if (context.InputParameters.Contains(ParameterName.Target))
{
    DynamicEntity target = (DynamicEntity)
        context.InputParameters[ParameterName.Target];
    // ...
}
```

- ***InvocationSource* property** The *InvocationSource* property is an integer value that you can use to determine whether the current plug-in is running in a child pipeline. Table 5-1 lists the valid values as defined by the *MessageInvocationSource* class.

TABLE 5-1 *MessageInvocationSource* Values

Field	Value	Description
Child	1	Specifies a child pipeline
Parent	0	Specifies a parent pipeline

- ***IsExecutingInOfflineMode* property** You can register plug-ins to run offline with Microsoft CRM for Outlook with Offline Access. If a plug-in is running in such a state, this Boolean property is set to true. See Chapter 10 for more information on offline plug-ins.

- ***MesssageName* property** *MessageName* is a string property that allows the current plug-in to know the name of the message that is being executed (*Create*, *Update*, *Assign*, and so on).
- ***Mode* property** *Mode* is an integer property that you can use to determine whether the plug-in is executing synchronously or asynchronously. The valid values are from the *MesssageProcessingMode* class, as listed in Table 5-2.

TABLE 5-2 *MessageProcessingMode* Values

Field	Value	Description
Asynchronous	1	Specifies asynchronous processing
Synchronous	0	Specifies synchronous processing

- ***OrganizationId* and *OrganizationName* properties** These properties contain information about the organization that the current entity belongs to and that the current pipeline is executing within.

Caution The initial release of Microsoft Dynamics CRM 4.0 had a bug that caused the friendly organization name to be passed into the plug-in execution context instead of the actual name. When you create an organization, these two values are the same by default, but if they are different you can run into issues quickly. The main problem is that when you use the *CreateCrmService* method, an invalid organization is specified for the *ICrmService* proxy and any calls you make with it result in an unauthorized exception. At the time this book went to press, Microsoft was aware of the defect and was implementing a fix, but until the fix is released you can just keep the organization name and the friendly name identical.

- ***OutputParameters* property** Similar to the *InputParameters* property, this property is an instance of a *PropertyBag*. The values in the *OutputParameters* property correspond with the properties on the *Response* for the message being executed. For example, a *CreateResponse* has an *Id* property, so a post-event plug-in could expect the corresponding value in the *OutputParameters* property using a key value of "Id".

Tip Using the static *ParameterNames* class instead of string keys is encouraged so that you'll discover errors at compile time instead of at run time.

```
// Getting the entity id in a Post-Event for a Create message
Guid contactId = (Guid)context.OutputParameters[ParameterName.Id];
```

- ***ParentContext* property** *ParentContext* is another instance of *IPluginExecutionContext*. If the current plug-in is executing in a child pipeline,

ParentContext will contain the context of the parent pipeline; otherwise, *ParentContext* will be null.

- ***PreEntityImages* and *PostEntityImages* properties** *PreEntityImages* and *PostEntityImages* are both *PropertyBag* properties. When registering a plug-in, you can specify for certain messages that you want a snapshot of the entity before or after the core operation has completed. You also specify the alias you would like to give that snapshot. Those snapshots, or images, show up in these two collections with the alias as the key. *PreEntityImages* contains the images from before the core operation, and *PostEntityImages* contains the images from after the core operation.
- ***PrimaryEntityName* property** *PrimaryEntityName* is a string property that contains the name of the primary entity for which the pipeline is executing.
- ***SecondaryEntityName* property** *SecondaryEntityName* is a string property that contains the name of the secondary entity for which the pipeline is executing, if one exists. A majority of the messages deal with a single entity, so this property will almost always be set to "none". However some messages, like SetRelated, refer to two entities. In this case, you can use *SecondEntityName* to find out the type of the second entity.
- ***SharedVariables* property** *SharedVariables* is a *PropertyBag* property that is meant to be used by plug-in developers to pass information between plug-ins. Using *SharedVariables*, a pre-event plug-in can pass along information to a post-event plug-in. Another potential use is to look up data in a parent pipeline step and then later access it in a child pipeline through the child's *ParentContext* property's *SharedVariables* property.
- ***Stage* property** *Stage* is an integer property that a plug-in can use to determine whether it is running as a pre-event or a post-event plug-in. The valid values are from the *MessageProcessingStage* class, as listed in Table 5-3.

TABLE 5-3 *MessageProcessingStage* Values

Field	Value	Description
AfterMainOperationOutsideTransaction	50	Specifies to process after the main operation, outside the transaction
BeforeMainOperationOutsideTransaction	10	Specifies to process before the main operation, outside the transaction

More Info There are, in fact, three other values for Stage, but they are for internal use only by Microsoft Dynamics CRM and you will receive an error if you try to register your plug-in to run in one of these stages. Just in case you run into one of these values while trying to debug an issue, they are BeforeMainOperationInsideTransaction (20), MainOperation (30), and AfterMainOperationInsideTransaction (40).

- ***UserId* property** *UserId* is a *Guid* property that represents the user that the plug-in is running as for any *CrmService* calls. This value is typically the user that initiated the event, but if a plug-in is registered to impersonate another user, this value contains the impersonated user's ID. See the *InitiatingUserId* property for more information.
- ***CreateCrmService* method** This is an overloaded method that you can use to create an instance of an *ICrmService* interface that has the same methods as the *CrmService* class, which is explained in detail in Chapter 3. The arguments control impersonation within the plug-in and are explored in more depth in the "Impersonation" section later in this chapter.
- ***CreateMetadataService* method** You use the *CreateMetadataService* method to get an instance of the *IMetadataService* interface that has the same methods as the *MetadataService* class, which is explained in detail in Chapter 3. The method accepts a single Boolean named *useCurrentUserId* and is used for impersonation within the plug-in. See the next section, "Impersonation," for more details.

Impersonation

Impersonation in Microsoft Dynamics CRM occurs when a *CrmService* or *MetadataService* call is made on behalf of another user. Plug-ins have two options for impersonation. First, they can be registered to impersonate a specific user by default. Second, they can specify a user ID to impersonate on the fly during execution.

Important Plug-in impersonation does not work offline. Actions offline are always taken by the logged-on user.

Impersonation During Registration

When you register a plug-in, you can specify an *impersonatinguserid* value. In this situation, any calls to the *IPluginExecutionContext* interface's *CreateCrmService* or *CreateMetadataService* methods with a value of *true* for the *useCurrentUser* argument result in a service that is impersonating the user specified at registration. Passing *false* for the *useCurrentUser* argument results in a service that is executing as the "system" user. In addition, the *IPluginExecutionContext* interface's *UserId* property contains the user ID specified during registration.

Impersonation During Execution

A plug-in's second option for impersonation is to specify a user ID when calling the *IPluginExecutionContext* interface's *CreateCrmService* method. This allows the plug-in to determine on the fly which user to impersonate, possibly pulling a value from a registry setting or configuration file.

Best Practices You may be wondering which method of impersonation you should use. Unless you know that you need to impersonate another user, you should simply pass in *true* to the *useCurrentUser* argument and create service instances that will behave as determined by the plug-in registration. Most often, plug-ins will be registered without an *impersonatinguserid* specified and you will run as the user that initiated the event. If at a later point it is determined that you need a plug-in to run with impersonation, you can change the plug-in step without needing to recompile the plug-in assembly. Avoid passing in *false* for *useCurrentUser* unless you need to because this value means that calls into the *CrmService* effectively run as an administrator, possibly elevating the privilege of the user who caused the plug-in to execute.

Exception Handling

We frequently receive questions regarding exceptions when writing plug-ins. How are exceptions handled? Should all inner exceptions be handled by the plug-in? Does Microsoft Dynamics CRM automatically log exceptions? What does an end user see when an exception goes unhandled? Fortunately these questions have fairly straightforward answers, as detailed in the following sections.

Exceptions and the Event Processing Pipeline

The impact of an unhandled exception within a plug-in on the event processing pipeline is fairly intuitive. If you registered your plug-in as a pre-event plug-in and it throws an exception or lets an exception go unhandled, no further plug-ins will execute and the core operation will not occur. If you registered your plug-in as a post-event and it throws an exception, no further plug-ins will execute, and since the core operation already occurred Microsoft Dynamics CRM will not roll it back. However, if the plug-in is executing in a child pipeline, an unhandled exception results in the parent pipeline's core operation being rolled back.

Exception Feedback

Microsoft Dynamics CRM logs all unhandled exceptions in the Event Viewer on the server where they occurred. In addition, if the exception generating event was initiated by the user through the Microsoft Dynamics CRM user interface, the user is presented with an error message. To control the message that the user sees, you should throw an *InvalidPluginExecutionException*. In this case, the *Message* property for the exception is displayed. If you let an exception of another type go unhandled, a generic error message may be used.

Deployment

At the beginning of the chapter we briefly touched on one of the tools used to deploy plug-ins. In this section we'll take a deeper look at what happens during plug-in registration and how you can write your own registration tools.

Plug-in Entities

Microsoft Dynamics CRM stores plug-in information in a series of entities as listed in Table 5-4.

TABLE 5-4 Plug-in Entities

Entity Name	Description
pluginassembly	Represents the registered plug-in assembly. Can have multiple *plugintype* entities associated with it.
plugintype	Represents the class in the plug-in assembly that implements *IPlugin*. Can have multiple steps associated with it.
sdkmessageprocessingstep	Represents a step in the event execution pipeline when a plug-in type should be executed. Can have multiple *sdkmessageprocessingimage* entities and multiple *sdkmessageprocessingstepsecureconfig* entities associated with it.
sdkmessageprocessingstepimage	Represents the definition of which types of images should be provided to a plug-in for a particular step. Images are essentially snapshots of the entity before or after the core operation has taken place.
sdkmessageprocessingstepsecure-config	Represents secure configuration information for a particular plug-in step. Passed to the plug-in constructor if provided.

Programmatic Plug-in Registration

You can register and deploy plug-ins programmatically through the API, which allows you to implement your own deployment tools without a lot of code. To demonstrate this, we will implement a plug-in registration tool that uses custom .NET attributes to specify how to register our plug-ins. This approach offers the benefit of letting the developer implement the plug-in to specify its use as he codes it.

Because both the plug-in assembly and our installation tool reference our custom .NET attributes, we need to put them in their own class library. Follow these steps to add the project to our existing solution.

Adding the custom attribute project

1. On the File Menu, select Add and then click New Project.
2. In the New Project dialog box, select the Visual C# project type targeting the .NET Framework 3.0, and then select the Class Library template.
3. Type the name **ProgrammingWithDynamicsCrm4.Plugins.Attributes** in the Name box, and then click OK.
4. Delete the default Class.cs file.
5. Right-click the ProgrammingWithDynamicsCrm4.Plugins.Attributes project in Solution Explorer and then click Properties.
6. On the Signing tab, select the Sign The Assembly box and select <New...> from the drop-down list below it.
7. Type the key file name **ProgrammingWithDynamicsCrm4.Plugins.Attributes** and then clear the Protect My Key File With A Password check box. Click OK.
8. Close the project properties window.

Adding the PluginStepAttribute class

Next we need to define the custom attribute class.

1. Right-click the ProgrammingWithDynamicsCrm4.Plugins.Attributes project in Solution Explorer. Under Add, click Class.
2. Type **PluginStepAttribute.cs** in the Name box and click Add.

Listing 5-2 shows the full source code for the *PluginStepAttribute* class.

LISTING 5-2 *PluginStepAttribute* source code

```
using System;

namespace ProgrammingWithDynamicsCrm4.Plugins.Attributes
{
    [AttributeUsage(AttributeTargets.Class, AllowMultiple=true)]
    public class PluginStepAttribute: Attribute
    {
        public PluginStepAttribute(string message, PluginStepStage stage)
        {
            this.Message = message;
            this.Stage = stage;
        }

        public PluginStepStage Stage { get; private set; }
        public string Message { get; private set; }

        public string PrimaryEntityName { get; set; }
```

```
        public string SecondaryEntityName { get; set; }

        public PluginStepMode Mode { get; set; }
        public int Rank { get; set; }
        public string Description { get; set; }
        public string FilteringAttributes { get; set; }
        public PluginStepInvocationSource InvocationSource { get; set; }
        public PluginStepSupportedDeployment SupportedDeployment { get; set; }
    }
}
```

Custom attributes like the one we have defined here allow us to embed extra information into our compiled types and assemblies. We can use this attribute to attach information about our plug-in registration to the plug-in class itself. The following example demonstrates how this attribute might be applied to a plug-in class.

```
[PluginStep("Update", PluginStepStage.PreEvent, PrimaryEntityName = "account")]
public class MyPluginClass: IPlugin
{
    ...
}
```

Notice that even though the class name is *PluginStepAttribute*, we can omit the trailing *Attribute*—which is just a shortcut supplied by .NET—when applying it to a class. Also worth noticing is that we've exposed some of the arguments as constructor arguments and others as public properties. In general, when you work with custom attributes you want to make anything required a constructor argument and anything optional a public property. You might argue that *PrimaryEntityName* should have been in the list of required attributes, but you can register for a few messages that do not have an entity associated with them.

If you have a sharp eye, you probably noticed that we still need to define the types for a few properties in *PluginStepAttribute*. These four types are all defined as enums so that you will receive IntelliSense in Visual Studio 2008 when you apply this attribute to a plug-in class. The enums are defined as shown in Listing 5-3.

LISTING 5-3 Enum type definitions

```
namespace ProgrammingWithDynamicsCrm4.Plugins.Attributes
{
    public enum PluginStepInvocationSource
    {
        ParentPipeline = 0,
        ChildPipeline = 1,
    }

    public enum PluginStepMode
    {
        Synchronous = 0,
```

```
            Asynchronous = 1,
        }

        public enum PluginStepStage
        {
            PreEvent = 10,
            PostEvent = 50,
        }

        public enum PluginStepSupportedDeployment
        {
            ServerOnly=0,
            OutlookClientOnly=1,
            Both=2,
        }
    }
```

You can place these definitions in their own files or just after the *PluginStepAttribute* class in PluginStepAttribute.cs.

Now we should be able to go back to our original ProgrammingWithDynamicsCrm4.Plugins project and add a reference to our new attributes project.

Adding a reference to the attributes project

1. Right-click the ProgrammingWithDynamicsCrm4.Plugins project in Solution Explorer and then click Add Reference.
2. On the Projects tab, select ProgrammingWithDynamicsCrm4.Plugins.Attributes. Click OK.

Now we can add our attribute to the *AccountNumberValidator* plug-in. You will need to add the following using statement at the top of AccountNumberValidator.cs:

```
using ProgrammingWithDynamicsCrm4.Plugins.Attributes;
```

Then you can add the following two attributes to the class definition:

```
[PluginStep("Create", PluginStepStage.PreEvent, PrimaryEntityName = "account",
    FilteringAttributes = "accountnumber")]
[PluginStep("Update", PluginStepStage.PreEvent, PrimaryEntityName = "account",
    FilteringAttributes = "accountnumber")]
public class AccountNumberValidator: IPlugin
{
    ...
}
```

At this point, the only remaining step is creating the actual tool to register the plug-in.

Creating the ProgrammingWithDynamicsCrm4.PluginDeploy project

1. On the File Menu, select Add and then click New Project.
2. In the New Project dialog box, select the Visual C# project type targeting the .NET Framework 3.0 and then select the Console Application template.
3. Type the name **ProgrammingWithDynamicsCrm4.PluginDeploy** in the Name box and click OK.
4. Right-click the ProgrammingWithDynamicsCrm4.PluginDeploy project in Solution Explorer and then click Add Reference.
5. On the Browse tab, navigate to the CRM SDK's bin folder and select microsoft.crm.sdk.dll and microsoft.crm.sdktypeproxy.dll. Click OK.
6. Right-click the ProgrammingWithDynamicsCrm4.PluginDeploy project in Solution Explorer and then click Add Reference.
7. On the .NET tab, select System.Web.Services and System.Configuration. Click OK.
8. Right-click the ProgrammingWithDynamicsCrm4.PluginDeploy project in Solution Explorer and then click Add Reference.
9. On the Projects tab, select ProgrammingWithDynamicsCrm4.Plugins.Attributes and click OK.

Now we can proceed to the *Main* method. Replace the generated code in Program.cs with the code shown in Listing 5-4.

LISTING 5-4 PluginDeploy's *Main* method

```
using System;
using System.Collections.Generic;
using System.Configuration;
using System.IO;
using System.Net;
using System.Reflection;
using System.Text;
using System.Web.Services.Protocols;
using Microsoft.Crm.Sdk;
using Microsoft.Crm.Sdk.Query;
using Microsoft.Crm.SdkTypeProxy;
using ProgrammingWithDynamicsCrm4.Plugins.Attributes;

namespace ProgrammingWithDynamicsCrm4.PluginDeploy
{
    static void Main(string[] args)
    {
        if (args.Length != 3)
        {
            string exeName = Path.GetFileName(Environment.GetCommandLineArgs()[0]);
```

```
                Console.WriteLine(
                    "Usage: {0} <pluginAssembly> <crmServerUrl> <organizationName>",
                    exeName);
                Environment.Exit(1);
            }

            try
            {
                string pluginAssemblyPath = args[0];
                string crmServer = args[1];
                string organizationName = args[2];

                DeployPlugin(pluginAssemblyPath, crmServer, organizationName);
            }
            catch (SoapException e)
            {
                Console.WriteLine(e.Detail.InnerText);
            }
            catch (Exception e)
            {
                Console.WriteLine(e.Message);
            }
        }
}
```

The *Main* method doesn't do much more than look for simple usage errors and display unhandled exceptions to the user. All of the real work is left to the *DeployPlugin* method, which is shown in Listing 5-5.

LISTING 5-5 The *DeployPlugin* method

```
private static void DeployPlugin(
    string pluginAssemblyPath,
    string crmServer,
    string organizationName)
{
    Console.Write("Initializing CrmService... ");
    CrmService crmService = CreateCrmService(crmServer, organizationName);
    Console.WriteLine("Complete");

    pluginassembly pluginAssembly = LoadPluginAssembly(pluginAssemblyPath);

    UnregisterExistingSolution(crmService, pluginAssembly.name);

    SdkMessageProcessingStepRegistration[] steps =
        LoadPluginSteps(pluginAssemblyPath);

    RegisterSolution(crmService, pluginAssembly, steps);
}
```

The first thing *DeployPlugin* does is create an instance of the *CrmService*. *CreateCrmService* is a helper method that creates a *CrmService* in a fairly straightforward way. Listing 5-6 shows the implementation of *CreateCrmService*.

LISTING 5-6 The *CreateCrmService* method

```
private static CrmService CreateCrmService(
    string crmServer, string organizationName)
{
    UriBuilder crmServerUri = new UriBuilder(crmServer);
    crmServerUri.Path = "/MSCRMServices/2007/CrmService.asmx";

    string userName = ConfigurationManager.AppSettings["crmUserName"];
    string password = ConfigurationManager.AppSettings["crmPassword"];
    string domain = ConfigurationManager.AppSettings["crmDomain"];

    CrmService crmService = new CrmService();
    if (String.IsNullOrEmpty(userName))
    {
        crmService.UseDefaultCredentials = true;
    }
    else
    {
        crmService.Credentials = new NetworkCredential(userName, password, domain);
    }

    crmService.Url = crmServerUri.ToString();
    crmService.CrmAuthenticationTokenValue = new CrmAuthenticationToken();
    crmService.CrmAuthenticationTokenValue.AuthenticationType =
        AuthenticationType.AD;
    crmService.CrmAuthenticationTokenValue.OrganizationName = organizationName;

    return crmService;
}
```

CreateCrmService checks in the application configuration file to see whether any credentials are specified to use when communicating with Microsoft Dynamics CRM. If it does not find any, it uses the credentials of the user that started the process.

After *DeployPlugin* aquires a *CrmService*, it calls *LoadPluginAssembly* to load an instance of the *pluginassembly* class from the plug-in DLL. The source for *LoadPluginAssembly* is shown in Listing 5-7.

LISTING 5-7 The *LoadPluginAssembly* method

```
private static pluginassembly LoadPluginAssembly(string pluginAssemblyPath)
{
    Assembly assembly = Assembly.LoadFile(pluginAssemblyPath);
    pluginassembly pluginAssembly = new pluginassembly();
    pluginAssembly.name = assembly.GetName().Name;
    pluginAssembly.sourcetype = new Picklist(AssemblySourceType.Database);
    pluginAssembly.culture = assembly.GetName().CultureInfo.ToString();
```

```
    pluginAssembly.version = assembly.GetName().Version.ToString();

    if (String.IsNullOrEmpty(pluginAssembly.culture))
    {
        pluginAssembly.culture = "neutral";
    }

    byte[] publicKeyToken = assembly.GetName().GetPublicKeyToken();
    StringBuilder tokenBuilder = new StringBuilder();
    foreach (byte b in publicKeyToken)
    {
        tokenBuilder.Append(b.ToString("x").PadLeft(2, '0'));
    }
    pluginAssembly.publickeytoken = tokenBuilder.ToString();

    pluginAssembly.content = Convert.ToBase64String(
        File.ReadAllBytes(pluginAssemblyPath));

    return pluginAssembly;
}
```

Most of the *pluginassembly* class's properties are populated using reflection on the assembly after it is loaded. The *publickeytoken* property is a little bit more work because we need to convert the byte array to a hexadecimal string. The *content* property is a Base64-formatted string that contains the raw bytes from the assembly DLL. Also note that we have just hard-coded *sourcetype* to be a database deployment.

After *PluginDeploy* receives *pluginassembly*, it calls *UnregisterExistingSolution* to make sure that no pre-existing version of this assembly is registered on the CRM server. The *Unregister-ExistingSolution* source code is shown in Listing 5-8.

LISTING 5-8 The *UnregisterExistingSolution* method

```
private static void UnregisterExistingSolution(
    CrmService crmService,
    string assemblyName)
{
    QueryByAttribute query = new QueryByAttribute();
    query.EntityName = EntityName.pluginassembly.ToString();
    query.ColumnSet = new ColumnSet(new string[] { "pluginassemblyid" });
    query.Attributes = new string[] { "name" };
    query.Values = new object[] { assemblyName };

    RetrieveMultipleRequest request = new RetrieveMultipleRequest();
    request.Query = query;

    RetrieveMultipleResponse response;
    Console.Write("Searching for existing solution... ");
    response = (RetrieveMultipleResponse)crmService.Execute(request);
    Console.WriteLine("Complete");
```

```
    if (response.BusinessEntityCollection.BusinessEntities.Count > 0)
    {
        pluginassembly pluginAssembly = (pluginassembly)
            response.BusinessEntityCollection.BusinessEntities[0];
        Console.Write("Unregistering existing solution {0}... ",
            pluginAssembly.pluginassemblyid.Value);

        UnregisterSolutionRequest unregisterRequest =
            new UnregisterSolutionRequest();
        unregisterRequest.PluginAssemblyId = pluginAssembly.pluginassemblyid.Value;

        crmService.Execute(unregisterRequest);
        Console.WriteLine("Complete");
    }
}
```

The *UnregisterExistingSolution* method starts by querying *CrmService* to see whether any *pluginassembly* entities are already registered with the same name. If it finds one, it executes an *UnregisterSolutionRequest*, passing in the *Guid* of the assembly that was determined to be a match.

DeployPlugin is now ready to use our custom attribute and create an array of *SdkMessageProcessingStepRegistration* instances. *SdkMessageProcessingStepRegistration* is a part of the *Microsoft.Crm.Sdk* namespace and is used to simplify the registration of plug-ins. Listing 5-9 shows the source code for *LoadPluginSteps*.

LISTING 5-9 The *LoadPluginSteps* method

```
private static SdkMessageProcessingStepRegistration[] LoadPluginSteps(string
pluginAssemblyPath)
{
    List<SdkMessageProcessingStepRegistration> steps =
        new List<SdkMessageProcessingStepRegistration>();

    Assembly assembly = Assembly.LoadFile(pluginAssemblyPath);
    foreach (Type pluginType in assembly.GetTypes())
    {
        if (typeof(IPlugin).IsAssignableFrom(pluginType) && !pluginType.IsAbstract)
        {
            object[] stepAttributes =
                pluginType.GetCustomAttributes(typeof(PluginStepAttribute), false);

            foreach (PluginStepAttribute stepAttribute in stepAttributes)
            {
                steps.Add(CreateStepFromAttribute(pluginType, stepAttribute));
            }
        }
    }

    return steps.ToArray();
}
```

LoadPluginSteps loads the assembly from the disk and then uses reflection to iterate through all the types defined in the assembly. If it finds a concrete implementation of *IPlugin*, it determines whether our *PluginStepAttribute* is associated with that type. For each *PluginStepAttribute* associated with the *plugin* type, it calls *CreateStepFromAttribute* to create an instance of *SdkMessageProcessingStepRegistration*. The *CreateStepFromAttribute* source code is shown in Listing 5-10.

LISTING 5-10 The *CreateStepFromAttribute* method

```
private static SdkMessageProcessingStepRegistration CreateStepFromAttribute(
    Type pluginType,
    PluginStepAttribute stepAttribute)
{
    SdkMessageProcessingStepRegistration step =
        new SdkMessageProcessingStepRegistration();
    step.Description = stepAttribute.Description;
    step.FilteringAttributes = stepAttribute.FilteringAttributes;
    step.InvocationSource = (int)stepAttribute.InvocationSource;
    step.MessageName = stepAttribute.Message;
    step.Mode = (int)stepAttribute.Mode;
    step.PluginTypeName = pluginType.FullName;
    step.PluginTypeFriendlyName = pluginType.FullName;
    step.PrimaryEntityName = stepAttribute.PrimaryEntityName;
    step.SecondaryEntityName = stepAttribute.SecondaryEntityName;
    step.Stage = (int)stepAttribute.Stage;
    step.SupportedDeployment = (int)stepAttribute.SupportedDeployment;

    if (String.IsNullOrEmpty(step.Description))
    {
        step.Description = String.Format("{0} {1} {2}",
            step.PrimaryEntityName, step.MessageName, stepAttribute.Stage);
    }

    return step;
}
```

Almost all the *SdkMessageProcessingStepRegistration* values are assigned directly from corresponding values on our *PluginStepAttribute* class. The *PluginTypeName* property comes from the actual plug-in type (and we use that for the *PluginTypeFriendlyName* too). If no *Description* is provided, we derive one from the *PrimaryEntityName*, *MessageName*, and *Stage* properties.

Finally, *DeployPlugin* is ready to send all this information over to the CRM server. *RegisterSolution* is called, passing our previously loaded *pluginassembly* and our newly initialized array of *SdkMessageProcessingStepRegistrations*. The *RegisterSolution* source code is shown in Listing 5-11.

LISTING 5-11 The *RegisterSolution* method

```
private static void RegisterSolution(CrmService crmService, pluginassembly
pluginAssembly, SdkMessageProcessingStepRegistration[] steps)
{
    RegisterSolutionRequest registerRequest = new RegisterSolutionRequest();
    registerRequest.PluginAssembly = pluginAssembly;
    registerRequest.Steps = steps;
    Console.Write("Registering solution... ");
    crmService.Execute(registerRequest);
    Console.WriteLine("Complete");
}
```

RegisterSolution is a straightforward method that simply creates a *RegisterSolutionRequest* and executes it with the *CrmService*.

At this point you should be able to compile the solution and use ProgrammingWithDynamicsCrm4.PluginDeploy.exe to deploy ProgrammingWithDynamicsCrm4.Plugins to your CRM server. The command line used to deploy a plug-in is:

```
ProgrammingWithDynamicsCrm4.PluginDeploy.exe <pathToAssembly> <crmServerUrl>
<organizationName>
```

Images

One concept that our previous example did not touch on is the ability to request entity images during registration. An image is essentially a snapshot of an entity and it can be taken either before or after the core operation is performed. Images allow a plug-in access to attribute values that would otherwise not be available. For example, an audit log plug-in could be provided with an image that contains the original attribute values for an entity that has just been modified. Using this image, the plug-in could record both the new and old attribute values in a log. Another example of using images would be a plug-in that needs to keep a calculated value on a parent entity up to date. When the child entity is associated with a new parent, a plug-in can use a pre-image to retrieve the previous parent and ensure that both the new and the old parent are kept up to date.

We refer to images that are taken before the core operation as *pre-images* and images taken after the core operation as *post-images*. These images are then passed to a plug-in through the *IPluginExecutionContext* interface's *PreEntityImages* and *PostEntityImages* properties.

When your plug-in requires an image, you need to specify the type of image and the name of the message property that contains the entity you want an image of. In addition, not all messages can produce images. Table 5-5 lists all supported messages and their corresponding message property names.

TABLE 5-5 Messages That Support Images

Message	Message Property Name	Notes
Assign	Target	
Create	Id	Does not support pre-images
Delete	Target	Does not support post-images
DeliverIncoming	EmailId	
DeliverPromote	EmailId	
Merge	Target	
Merge	SubordinateId	
Route	Target	
Send	EmailId	
SetState	EntityMoniker	
SetStateDynamicEntity	EntityMoniker	
Update	Target	

Programmatic Image Registration

To add image support to ProgrammingWithDynamicsCrm4.PluginDeploy, we need an additional attribute class. Using the steps outlined earlier, add a new class to the ProgrammingWithDynamicsCrm4.Plugins.Attributes project named *PluginImageAttribute*. The source code for this class is shown in listing 5-12.

LISTING 5-12 *PluginImageAttribute* source code

```
using System;

namespace ProgrammingWithDynamicsCrm4.Plugins.Attributes
{
    [AttributeUsage(AttributeTargets.Class, AllowMultiple=true)]
    public class PluginImageAttribute: Attribute
    {
        public PluginImageAttribute(
            ImageType imageType,
            string stepId,
            string messagePropertyName,
            string entityAlias)
        {
            this.ImageType = imageType;
            this.StepId = stepId;
            this.MessagePropertyName = messagePropertyName;
            this.EntityAlias = entityAlias;
        }

        public ImageType ImageType { get; private set; }
        public string StepId { get; private set; }
```

```
        public string MessagePropertyName { get; private set; }
        public string EntityAlias { get; private set; }
        public string Attributes { get; set; }
    }

    public enum ImageType
    {
        PreImage = 0,
        PostImage = 1,
        Both = 2,
    }
}
```

All the properties except *Attributes* are required for *PluginImageAttribute*, so they are all passed in to the constructor. If no attributes are specified for an image, it is populated with all of the entity's attributes that have values.

One property that might not have a readily apparent use is *StepId*. Because an image is associated with a particular step and we can have multiple steps per plug-in, we need a way to tie the two attributes together. To do this, we assign a unique value to the *StepId* property on both the *PluginStepAttribute* and *PluginImageAttribute* classes. We need to modify the *PluginStepAttribute* class to include the following new property:

```
public string StepId { get; set; }
```

Notice that *StepId* is optional on the *PluginStepAttribute* class because it is only needed if the developer wants to specify an image for that step.

Now a developer can register for an image on her plug-in class by using two attributes together:

```
[PluginStep("Update", PluginStepStage.PreEvent, PrimaryEntityName = "account",
    StepId="AccountPreUpdate")]
[PluginImage(ImageType.PreImage, "AccountPreUpdate", "Target", "Account")]
public class MyPlugin: IPlugin
{
    ...
}
```

Notice that the *StepId* for this example is arbitrarily set to *AccountPreUpdate*. It doesn't matter what value you use as long as the values for the step and the image match.

Finally, we need to modify our console application to use the new *PluginImageAttribute* type. We need to insert the code from Listing 5-13 into the *CreateStepFromAttribute* method just before the *return* statement.

LISTING 5-13 Modifications to the *CreateStepFromAttribute* method

```
if (!String.IsNullOrEmpty(stepAttribute.StepId))
{
    List<SdkMessageProcessingStepImageRegistration> images =
        new List<SdkMessageProcessingStepImageRegistration>();
    object[] imageAttributes = pluginType.GetCustomAttributes(
        typeof(PluginImageAttribute), false);

    foreach (PluginImageAttribute imageAttribute in imageAttributes)
    {
        if (imageAttribute.StepId == stepAttribute.StepId)
        {
            images.Add(CreateImageFromAttribute(imageAttribute));
        }
    }

    if (images.Count > 0)
    {
        step.Images = images.ToArray();
    }
}
```

This change checks whether the current step attribute has a step ID assigned. If it does, the method looks for image attributes on the plugin type. If it finds any image attributes, it calls the *CreateImageFromAttribute* method, which is shown in Listing 5-14.

LISTING 5-14 The *CreateImageFromAttribute* method

```
private static SdkMessageProcessingStepImageRegistration
CreateImageFromAttribute(PluginImageAttribute imageAttribute)
{
    SdkMessageProcessingStepImageRegistration image =
            new SdkMessageProcessingStepImageRegistration();

    if (!String.IsNullOrEmpty(imageAttribute.Attributes))
    {
        image.Attributes = imageAttribute.Attributes.Split(',');
    }

    image.EntityAlias = imageAttribute.EntityAlias;
    image.ImageType = (int)imageAttribute.ImageType;
    image.MessagePropertyName = imageAttribute.MessagePropertyName;

    return image;
}
```

CreateImageFromAttribute creates a new instance of the *SdkMessageProcessingStepImage-Registration* class and populates it from the image attribute. The appropriate images are assigned back to the step's *Images* property and are automatically registered when the call to *RegisterSolution* is made.

The final code for Program.cs is shown in Listing 5-15.

LISTING 5-15 Source code for ProgrammingWithDynamicsCrm4.PluginDeploy's Program.cs

```
using System;
using System.Collections.Generic;
using System.Configuration;
using System.IO;
using System.Net;
using System.Reflection;
using System.Text;
using System.Web.Services.Protocols;
using Microsoft.Crm.Sdk;
using Microsoft.Crm.Sdk.Query;
using Microsoft.Crm.SdkTypeProxy;
using ProgrammingWithDynamicsCrm4.Plugins.Attributes;

namespace ProgrammingWithDynamicsCrm4.PluginDeploy
{
    class Program
    {
        static void Main(string[] args)
        {
            if (args.Length != 3)
            {
                string exeName = Path.GetFileName(
                    Environment.GetCommandLineArgs()[0]);
                Console.WriteLine(
                    "Usage: {0} <pluginAssembly> <crmServerUrl> <organizationName>",
                    exeName);
                Environment.Exit(1);
            }

            try
            {
                string pluginAssemblyPath = args[0];
                string crmServer = args[1];
                string organizationName = args[2];

                DeployPlugin(pluginAssemblyPath, crmServer, organizationName);
            }
            catch (SoapException e)
            {
                Console.WriteLine(e.Detail.InnerText);
            }
            catch (Exception e)
            {
                Console.WriteLine(e.Message);
            }
        }

        private static void DeployPlugin(
            string pluginAssemblyPath,
            string crmServer,
            string organizationName)
```

```
{
    Console.Write("Initializing CrmService... ");
    CrmService crmService = CreateCrmService(crmServer, organizationName);
    Console.WriteLine("Complete");

    pluginassembly pluginAssembly = LoadPluginAssembly(pluginAssemblyPath);

    UnregisterExistingSolution(crmService, pluginAssembly.name);

    SdkMessageProcessingStepRegistration[] steps =
        LoadPluginSteps(pluginAssemblyPath);

    RegisterSolution(crmService, pluginAssembly, steps);
}

private static pluginassembly LoadPluginAssembly(string pluginAssemblyPath)
{
    Assembly assembly = Assembly.LoadFile(pluginAssemblyPath);
    pluginassembly pluginAssembly = new pluginassembly();
    pluginAssembly.name = assembly.GetName().Name;
    pluginAssembly.sourcetype = new Picklist(AssemblySourceType.Database);
    pluginAssembly.culture = assembly.GetName().CultureInfo.ToString();
    pluginAssembly.version = assembly.GetName().Version.ToString();

    if (String.IsNullOrEmpty(pluginAssembly.culture))
    {
        pluginAssembly.culture = "neutral";
    }

    byte[] publicKeyToken = assembly.GetName().GetPublicKeyToken();
    StringBuilder tokenBuilder = new StringBuilder();
    foreach (byte b in publicKeyToken)
    {
        tokenBuilder.Append(b.ToString("x").PadLeft(2, '0'));
    }
    pluginAssembly.publickeytoken = tokenBuilder.ToString();

    pluginAssembly.content =
        Convert.ToBase64String(File.ReadAllBytes(pluginAssemblyPath));

    return pluginAssembly;
}

private static void UnregisterExistingSolution(
    CrmService crmService,
    string assemblyName)
{
    QueryByAttribute query = new QueryByAttribute();
    query.EntityName = EntityName.pluginassembly.ToString();
    query.ColumnSet = new ColumnSet(new string[] { "pluginassemblyid" });
    query.Attributes = new string[] { "name" };
    query.Values = new object[] { assemblyName };
```

```
    RetrieveMultipleRequest request = new RetrieveMultipleRequest();
    request.Query = query;

    RetrieveMultipleResponse response;
    Console.Write("Searching for existing solution... ");
    response = (RetrieveMultipleResponse)crmService.Execute(request);
    Console.WriteLine("Complete");

    if (response.BusinessEntityCollection.BusinessEntities.Count > 0)
    {
        pluginassembly pluginAssembly = (pluginassembly)
            response.BusinessEntityCollection.BusinessEntities[0];
        Console.Write("Unregistering existing solution {0}... ",
            pluginAssembly.pluginassemblyid.Value);

        UnregisterSolutionRequest unregisterRequest =
            new UnregisterSolutionRequest();
        unregisterRequest.PluginAssemblyId =
            pluginAssembly.pluginassemblyid.Value;

        crmService.Execute(unregisterRequest);
        Console.WriteLine("Complete");
    }
}

private static SdkMessageProcessingStepRegistration[] LoadPluginSteps(
    string pluginAssemblyPath)
{
    List<SdkMessageProcessingStepRegistration> steps =
        new List<SdkMessageProcessingStepRegistration>();

    Assembly assembly = Assembly.LoadFile(pluginAssemblyPath);
    foreach (Type pluginType in assembly.GetTypes())
    {
        if (typeof(IPlugin).IsAssignableFrom(pluginType)
            && !pluginType.IsAbstract)
        {
            object[] stepAttributes = pluginType.GetCustomAttributes(
                typeof(PluginStepAttribute), false);
            foreach (PluginStepAttribute stepAttribute in stepAttributes)
            {
                steps.Add(CreateStepFromAttribute(pluginType,
                    stepAttribute));
            }
        }
    }

    return steps.ToArray();
}

private static SdkMessageProcessingStepRegistration CreateStepFromAttribute(
    Type pluginType,
    PluginStepAttribute stepAttribute)
```

```
{
    SdkMessageProcessingStepRegistration step =
        new SdkMessageProcessingStepRegistration();
    step.Description = stepAttribute.Description;
    step.FilteringAttributes = stepAttribute.FilteringAttributes;
    step.InvocationSource = (int)stepAttribute.InvocationSource;
    step.MessageName = stepAttribute.Message;
    step.Mode = (int)stepAttribute.Mode;
    step.PluginTypeName = pluginType.FullName;
    step.PluginTypeFriendlyName = pluginType.FullName;
    step.PrimaryEntityName = stepAttribute.PrimaryEntityName;
    step.SecondaryEntityName = stepAttribute.SecondaryEntityName;
    step.Stage = (int)stepAttribute.Stage;

    if (String.IsNullOrEmpty(step.Description))
    {
        step.Description = String.Format("{0} {1} {2}",
            step.PrimaryEntityName, step.MessageName, stepAttribute.Stage);
    }

if (!String.IsNullOrEmpty(stepAttribute.StepId))
{
    List<SdkMessageProcessingStepImageRegistration> images =
        new List<SdkMessageProcessingStepImageRegistration>();
    object[] imageAttributes = pluginType.GetCustomAttributes(
        typeof(PluginImageAttribute), false);
    foreach (PluginImageAttribute imageAttribute in imageAttributes)
    {
        if (imageAttribute.StepId == stepAttribute.StepId)
        {
            images.Add(CreateImageFromAttribute(imageAttribute));
        }
    }

    if (images.Count > 0)
    {
        step.Images = images.ToArray();
    }
}

    return step;
}

private static SdkMessageProcessingStepImageRegistration
    CreateImageFromAttribute(PluginImageAttribute imageAttribute)
{
    SdkMessageProcessingStepImageRegistration image =
        new SdkMessageProcessingStepImageRegistration();

    if (!String.IsNullOrEmpty(imageAttribute.Attributes))
    {
        image.Attributes = imageAttribute.Attributes.Split(',');
    }
```

```
            image.EntityAlias = imageAttribute.EntityAlias;
            image.ImageType = (int)imageAttribute.ImageType;
            image.MessagePropertyName = imageAttribute.MessagePropertyName;

            return image;
        }

        private static void RegisterSolution(
            CrmService crmService,
            pluginassembly pluginAssembly,
            SdkMessageProcessingStepRegistration[] steps)
        {
            RegisterSolutionRequest registerRequest = new RegisterSolutionRequest();
            registerRequest.PluginAssembly = pluginAssembly;
            registerRequest.Steps = steps;
            Console.Write("Registering solution... ");
            crmService.Execute(registerRequest);
            Console.WriteLine("Complete");
        }

        private static CrmService CreateCrmService(
            string crmServer,
            string organizationName)
        {
            UriBuilder crmServerUri = new UriBuilder(crmServer);
            crmServerUri.Path = "/MSCRMServices/2007/CrmService.asmx";

            string userName = ConfigurationManager.AppSettings["crmUserName"];
            string password = ConfigurationManager.AppSettings["crmPassword"];
            string domain = ConfigurationManager.AppSettings["crmDomain"];

            CrmService crmService = new CrmService();
            if (String.IsNullOrEmpty(userName))
            {
                crmService.UseDefaultCredentials = true;
            }
            else
            {
                crmService.Credentials = new NetworkCredential(
                    userName, password, domain);
            }

            crmService.Url = crmServerUri.ToString();
            crmService.CrmAuthenticationTokenValue = new CrmAuthenticationToken();
            crmService.CrmAuthenticationTokenValue.AuthenticationType =
                AuthenticationType.AD;
            crmService.CrmAuthenticationTokenValue.OrganizationName =
                organizationName;

            return crmService;
        }
    }
}
```

Custom Configuration

We have not yet touched on one entity tied to plug-in registration: *sdkmessageprocessing-stepsecureconfig*. You use this entity to pass a step-specific configuration value to the plug-in. The data in these entities is secure because only users with high security roles (for example, System Administrator or System Customizer) have permission to read these entities; therefore, you can safely use them to store sensitive information such as database connection strings. If you don't need the security, you can also specify a value to the *sdkmessageprocessingstep* class's *configuration* property. In our previous example you would specify the value to the *CustomConfiguration* property on the *SdkMessageProcessingStepRegistration* class.

For a plug-in to get the custom configuration value that you registered it with it must implement a constructor that takes one or two string arguments. If the version that takes two arguments exists, it will be called with the nonsecure configuration and the secure configuration as the two values. If the single argument version is implemented, it will be called with the nonsecure configuration value. Listing 5-16 shows an example of the two argument version.

LISTING 5-16 A plug-in constructor accepting custom configuration values

```
public class MyPlugin: IPlugin
{
    private string _connectionString;
    private Guid _defaultAccount;

    public MyPlugin(string unsecureConfig, string secureConfig)
    {
        if (!String.IsNullOrEmpty(unsecureConfig))
        {
            _defaultAccount = new Guid(unsecureConfig);
        }
        _connectionString = secureConfig;
    }

    ...
}
```

Deploying Referenced Assemblies

Frequently a plug-in includes dependencies on other assemblies. If those assemblies are not a part of the .NET Framework or the CRM SDK, you need to consider how to deploy them. The simplest option is to deploy them into the GAC on the CRM server. Depending on how frequently those referenced assemblies change, keeping the server's GAC up to date can be a hassle. The GAC is not easily maintained remotely, and you usually end up using Remote Desktop or something equivalent to manually copy the files into the GAC.

Tip You might recall the reference to our custom attribute class library that we added to our plug-in assembly. Because the plug-in does not reference any of the classes in the custom attribute assembly at run time, you don't need to deploy the custom attribute DLL to the Microsoft Dynamics CRM server at all!

An alternative is to use a tool called ILMerge. You use ILMerge to combine multiple .NET assemblies into a single one. This allows you to merge your plug-in DLL with any of the DLLs it references and then deploy the single DLL to the CRM database. We frequently create a post-build step on our plug-in class library project to merge the output with the dependencies.

To add a post-build step in Visual Studio, right-click the project in Solution Explorer and select Properties. Then click the Build Events tab. You can then enter command-line commands into the post-build event command line.

Here is an example of what the post-build command line might look like:

```
if not exist PreMerge mkdir PreMerge
del /Q PreMerge\*.*

move ProgrammingWithDynamicsCrm4.Plugins.dll PreMerge
move ProgrammingWithDynamicsCrm4.Plugins.pdb PreMerge
move <referencedDll> PreMerge

$(SolutionDir)Tools\ILMerge.exe /keyfile:$(ProjectDir)
ProgrammingWithDynamicsCrm4.Plugins.snk /lib:PreMerge /out:
ProgrammingWithDynamicsCrm4.Plugins.dll ProgrammingWithDynamicsCrm4.Plugins.dll
<referencedDll>
```

In this example, we want the final DLL to be in the same folder and have the same name as the original DLL, so we create a subfolder called PreMerge within the output folder. We then proceed to copy the recently compiled DLL and its dependencies into the PreMerge folder. Notice that we do not include Microsoft.Crm.Sdk.dll or Microsoft.Crm.SdkTypeProxy.dll. Because those files will be on the server, we do not need to merge them into our DLL. The final step is to execute ILMerge.exe specifying the keyfile to use to sign the assembly, the folder where it can find the DLLs to include, the name of the output file, and the list of DLLs to include in the merge.

More Info For more information on ILMerge, see *http://research.microsoft.com/~mbarnett/ILMerge.aspx*.

Debugging Plug-ins

The first thing you will probably do after deploying a plug-in is attempt to execute it to see whether it works. If you are greeted with a vague error message, you can check the Event Viewer on the CRM server for more information, but eventually you will find that you need more information, especially for more advanced plug-ins. Remote debugging and logging are two common techniques used to chase down errors in plug-ins.

Remote Debugging

By far the most powerful option, remote debugging allows you to set breakpoints in your plug-in code and step through the process in Visual Studio. The steps for setting up remote debugging are detailed in Chapter 9 in the companion book to this one: *Working With Microsoft Dynamics CRM 4.0* by Mike Snyder and Jim Steger. The CRM SDK also has information to help you set up remote debugging.

The downside to remote debugging is that it blocks other calls to the CRM application while you are stepping through your code. This can be a problem if you have multiple developers working with the same environment at the same time, and it will definitely be a problem if you are trying to debug something in a production environment.

Logging

The next-best option to discovering errors is to include extensive logging code in your plug-ins. Plug-ins typically execute in a process that is running as the Network Service user and should have rights to access the file system. You could then write some simple logging logic to output to a text file. Listing 5-17 demonstrates some simple logging code.

LISTING 5-17 Simple logging code

```
private static readonly object _logLock = new Object();
protected static void LogMessage(string message)
{
    try
    {
        if (IsLoggingEnabled)
        {
            lock (_logLock)
            {
                File.AppendAllText(LogFilePath, String.Format("[{0}] {1} {2}",
                    DateTime.Now, message, Environment.NewLine));
            }
        }
    }
    catch
    {
    }
}
```

The *IsLoggingEnabled* and *LogFilePath* properties could be initialized once at startup or be implemented to check the registry at a certain frequency to determine whether logging should occur and where the log file should be created. With this method implemented, you can add logging messages to your plug-ins to help chase down those hard-to-interpret errors:

```
if (IsLoggingEnabled)
{
    StringBuilder message = new StringBuilder();
    message.Append("InputParameters: ");
    foreach (PropertyBagEntry entry in context.InputParameters.Properties)
    {
        message.Append(entry.Name);
        message.Append(" ");
    }

    LogMessage(message.ToString());
}
```

Warning Be sure that you restrict directory access to only those users who need access to the log data, especially if the logs might contain sensitive customer data. Plug-ins execute as the user who the Microsoft Dynamics CRM Web application pool is configured to run as. By default this is the special Network Service user. This user will, of course, need write access to the log folder.

Unit Testing

Automated unit testing, used to validate the individual units of functionality in a program, continues to gain momentum and popularity in the software development community. Unit testing can improve the quality of an application and reduce the risk of breaking functionality when changes are made to the code.

Taken a step further, you can use unit tests as a design tool. Test-driven design (TDD) is a methodology that dictates that unit tests should be written before implementing the feature. The developer then implements the functionality in the simplest way possible to satisfy the unit test.

Mock Objects

Writing unit tests that depend on an external data source, such as the CRM Web Services, introduces additional challenges. Every time a test runs, the state of the server impacts the test results, causing tests that previously passed to unexpectedly fail. Because tests should only start to fail when the code changes, this server dependency needs to be removed.

Fortunately, nothing in the plug-in definition dictates that it must communicate with a live server. A plug-in only references a single type in its definition, *IPluginExecutionContext*. Because *IPluginExecutionContext* is an interface, we can provide our own implementation during testing and remove the dependency on the server. This concept of providing a "fake" implementation of an abstract type is commonly called *mocking* in automated unit testing.

Test Frameworks

In our sample test, we will take advantage of two testing frameworks. The Microsoft Unit Testing Framework, commonly referred to as MSTest, is now included in all editions of Visual Studio 2008, with the exception of the Express edition. This framework provides custom attributes used to decorate test classes and a library of assertions that you can use within your tests to validate the actual results against the expected results. In addition, MSTest integrates with the Visual Studio 2008 user interface and allows you to execute your tests without leaving the development environment.

A framework called Rhino Mocks provides our mock *IPluginExecutionContext* implementation. Rhino Mocks works by generating classes on the fly that can implement a specific interface or extend a base class. As the test authors, we define which methods the tested functionality will call and what should be returned when those calls are made.

More Info You can find more information and download instructions for Rhino Mocks at *http://www.ayende.com/projects/rhino-mocks.aspx.*

Sample Test

Now we will walk through the implementation of an automated unit test that verifies that our *AccountNumberValidator* plug-in is implemented correctly. Before we can write our first test, we need to include a test project in our solution.

Adding the test project

1. On the File Menu, select Add and then click New Project.
2. In the New Project dialog box, within the Visual C# > Test project types, select the Test Project template targeting the .Net Framework 3.0.
3. Type the name **ProgrammingWithDynamicsCrm4.PluginTests** into the Name box and click OK.
4. Delete the default UnitTest1.cs file.
5. Right-click the ProgrammingWithDynamicsCrm4.PluginTests project in Solution Explorer and then click Add Reference.

6. On the Browse tab, navigate to the CRM SDK's bin folder and select microsoft.crm.sdk.dll and microsoft.crm.sdktypeproxy.dll. Click OK.
7. Right-click the ProgrammingWithDynamicsCrm4.PluginTests project in Solution Explorer and then click Add Reference.
8. On the Project tab, select the ProgrammingWithDynamicsCrm4.Plugins project and click OK.

Now we can add our test class. Typically you would add a unit test to your project, which already contains sample code, but to introduce things one at a time, we will build the class from scratch. Create a class named *AccountNumberValidatorTests* and enter the code from Listing 5-18.

LISTING 5-18 The empty *AccountNumberValidatorTests* class

```
using System;
using Microsoft.Crm.Sdk;
using Microsoft.VisualStudio.TestTools.UnitTesting;
using ProgrammingWithDynamicsCrm4.Plugins;

namespace ProgrammingWithDynamicsCrm4.PluginTests
{
    [TestClass]
    public class AccountNumberValidatorTests
    {
    }
}
```

Note the inclusion of the *TestClass* attribute on the *AccountNumberValidatorTests* class. This attribute, defined by the MSTest framework, indicates that the *AccountNumberValidatorTests* class contains tests and should be included when tests are run.

To define our first test, add the following code to the *AccountNumberValidatorTests* class:

```
[TestMethod]
public void TestInvalidFormat()
{
    AccountNumberValidator validator = new AccountNumberValidator();
    validator.Execute(null);
}
```

Similar to the *TestClass* attribute previously discussed, the *TestMethod* attribute identifies a method that represents a test within the test class. When all tests are run, MSTest will iterate through all the classes marked with a *TestClass* attribute and execute the methods marked with a *TestMethod* attribute individually.

You can run this test by selecting Test > Run > Tests in Current Context from the menu, but at this point it will always fail with the message "Test method ProgrammingWith-

DynamicsCrm4.PluginTests.AccountNumberValidatorTests.TestInvalidFormat threw exception: System.NullReferenceException: Object reference not set to an instance of an object." This makes sense because the *AccountNumberValidator* plug-in expects a valid (non-null) *IPluginExecutionContext* to be passed in to the *Execute* method.

To provide an implementation of the *IPluginExecutionContext* interface to the *AccountNumberValidator* class, we need to add a reference to the Rhino Mocks framework.

Adding the Rhino Mocks Reference

1. Download and extract the latest stable build of the Rhino Mocks framework that targets .NET 2.0 from *http://www.ayende.com/projects/rhino-mocks/downloads.aspx.*
2. Right-click the ProgrammingWithDynamicsCrm4.PluginTests project in Solution Explorer and then click Add Reference.
3. On the Browse tab, navigate to the Rhino Mocks framework folder and select Rhino.Mocks.dll. Click OK.

Before we define our mock implementation, we should add a using statement to the top of the AccountNumberValidatorTests.cs file to make references to the framework easier:

```
using Rhino.Mocks;
```

With the Rhino Mocks framework properly referenced, we can modify the *TestInvalidFormat* method to match Listing 5-19.

LISTING 5-19 The *TestInvalidFormat* method updated with a mock *IPluginExecutionContext*

```
[TestMethod]
public void TestInvalidFormat()
{
    MockRepository mocks = new MockRepository();
    IPluginExecutionContext context = mocks.CreateMock<IPluginExecutionContext>();

    PropertyBag inputParameters = new PropertyBag();

    DynamicEntity account = new DynamicEntity();
    account["accountnumber"] = "123456";
    inputParameters[ParameterName.Target] = account;

    using (mocks.Record())
    {
        Expect.On(context).Call(context.InputParameters).Return(inputParameters);
    }

    using (mocks.Playback())
    {
        AccountNumberValidator validator = new AccountNumberValidator();
        validator.Execute(context);
    }
}
```

The first difference we notice is the inclusion of the *mocks* variable. This instance of the *MockRepository* class is responsible for creating instances of our mock classes, as well as switching between record and playback modes, which we will discuss shortly. Creating an instance of a mock object is as simple as calling the *CreateMock* method and passing in the type you want to mock in the generics argument.

The next steps revolve around defining the expected use of the mock object. The *AccountNumberValidator* plug-in only accesses the *InputParameters* property on the *IPluginExecutionContext*. To avoid an error during test execution, we need to let Rhino Mocks know how it should respond when the *InputParameters* property is accessed. We begin by creating an instance of a *PropertyBag* and setting up the target property in it to contain a simple instance of a *DynamicEntity* with a short name.

With the local version of *inputParameters* set up and ready to go, we tell our *MockRepository* to switch to record mode. Record mode allows us to define our expectations on any mock objects. The next line might look a little odd if you are not used to dealing with mock frameworks. It reads more like English than typical C# code and tells the *MockRepository* to expect a call for the *InputParameters* property on the mock *IPluginExecutionContext*. It goes on to say that when this call is made, return our local *inputParameters* variable.

Implementing a Simple Mock Object

Looking at the overhead involved with setting up a mock framework you might find yourself wondering if it would be easier to implement the *IPluginExecutionContext* interface in your own test class. Such a class might look like this:

```
public class MockPluginExecutionContext : IPluginExecutionContext
{
    private PropertyBag _inputParameters;
    public PropertyBag InputParameters
    {
        get { return _inputParameters; }
        set { _inputParameters = value; }
    }

    // remaining IPluginExecutionContext members here...
}
```

This would allow the previous *TestShortName* method shown in Listing 5-19 to be simplified to this:

```
public void TestShortName()
{
    MockPluginExecutionContext context = new MockPluginExecutionContext();
    context.InputParameters = new PropertyBag();

    DynamicEntity account = new DynamicEntity();
    account["name"] = "ABC";
```

```
        context.InputParameters[ParameterName.Target] = account;

        AccountNumberValidator validator = new AccountNumberValidator();
        validator.Execute(context);
    }
```

For simple tests such as *TestInvalidFormat*, this is a perfectly valid and simple choice for implementing a mock object. The challenges arrive when the plug-ins become more complex and start to use the *CreateCrmService* and *CreateMetadataService* methods exposed on the *IPluginExecutionContext* interface. With a mock framework you can specify that the context should return another mock implementation of *ICrmService* or *IMetadataService* when these methods are called and then further define your expectations on those mock implementations. Using your own library of mock classes, you will find it increasingly difficult to specify the expected behavior for the functionality being tested.

With the expectations defined on our mock object, we switch the *MockRepository* to playback mode, in which all the expectations must be met as defined during the record mode.

Finally, we pass our mock *IPluginExecutionContext* in to the *AccountNumberValidator*'s *Execute* method. If we run our test at this point, however, we still get a failure with the message: "Test method ProgrammingWithDynamicsCrm4.PluginTests.AccountNumberValidatorTests.TestShortName threw exception: Microsoft.Crm.Sdk.InvalidPluginExecutionException: Account number does not follow the required format (AA-######)." This, of course, is the expected behavior for our plug-in and means that it is validating as expected.

Tests that require an exception to be thrown in order for the test to pass have an additional attribute at their disposal. The *ExpectedException* attribute is applied at the method level and notifies MSTest that for this test to pass, the specific exception must be thrown. An example of the *ExpectedException* attribute applied to our *TestInvalidFormat* method can be seen here:

```
[TestMethod]
[ExpectedException(typeof(InvalidPluginExecutionException),
    "Account number does not follow the required format (AA-######).")]
public void TestInvalidFormat()
{
    ...
}
```

With this addition our test will run and pass every time, unless the *AccountNumberValidator* code is modified to change the behavior. If the test fails, it is up to the developer to modify the test accordingly—to include the new functionality or determine whether the new code has inadvertently broken something that was previously working.

For this test class to be complete, it should minimally test account numbers that are in a valid format as well. It could additionally test for a null *IPluginExecutionContext* or an *InputParameters* property that does not include a value for the "target" key. All these scenarios would be simple to include using the techniques already demonstrated.

Sample Plug-ins

Now that you have a good understanding of how plug-ins work, let's dig into some real-world examples. We will cover three different plug-in examples:

- Rolling up child entity attributes to a parent entity
- System view hider
- Customization change notifier

All these examples include source code that you can examine and use in your Microsoft Dynamics CRM deployment.

Rolling Up Child Entity Attributes to a Parent Entity

Frequently you will encounter a request to include some information in a view, such as the number of active contacts for a particular account or the next activity due date on a lead. You can accomplish this by writing a plug-in in a generic way so that it can handle all the messages involved in modifying a child record. The next example keeps track of the next scheduled phone call's *scheduledstart* value and stores it in a custom attribute on the related lead.

Start by adding a new class named *NextPhoneCallUpdater* to the ProgrammingWithDynamics-Crm4.Plugins project. Then stub out the class to match Listing 5-20.

LISTING 5-20 The start of the *NextPhoneCallUpdater* plug-in

```
using System;
using Microsoft.Crm.Sdk;
using Microsoft.Crm.Sdk.Query;
using Microsoft.Crm.SdkTypeProxy;
using ProgrammingWithDynamicsCrm4.Plugins.Attributes;

namespace ProgrammingWithDynamicsCrm4.Plugins
{
    public class NextPhoneCallUpdater : IPlugin
    {
        public void Execute(IPluginExecutionContext context)
        {
        }
    }
}
```

The first thing we need to think about is which messages our plug-in needs to register for. It needs to listen to Create and Delete messages for a *phonecall*. It also needs to listen to Update messages in case the *scheduledstart* attribute is changed or the *regardingobjectid* is changed. Finally, it needs to listen to the SetState and SetStateDynamicEntity messages to detect when the *phonecall* is marked as Complete or Cancelled. SetState and SetStateDynamicEntity are two different messages that accomplish the same thing, but you need to listen for both if you want to handle updates from the Web service API and from the CRM application. Based on this information we can add our *PluginStep* and *PluginImage* attributes to our class definition as shown in Listing 5-21.

LISTING 5-21 The *PluginStep* and *PluginImage* attributes for the *NextPhoneCallUpdater* plug-in

```
[PluginStep("Create", PluginStepStage.PostEvent,
    PrimaryEntityName = "phonecall", StepId = "PhoneCallPostCreate")]
[PluginImage(ImageType.PostImage, "PhoneCallPostCreate", "Id", "PhoneCall")]

[PluginStep("Update", PluginStepStage.PostEvent,
    PrimaryEntityName = "phonecall", StepId = "PhoneCallPostUpdate")]
[PluginImage(ImageType.Both, "PhoneCallPostUpdate", "Target", "PhoneCall")]

[PluginStep("Delete", PluginStepStage.PostEvent,
     PrimaryEntityName = "phonecall", StepId = "PhoneCallPostDelete")]
[PluginImage(ImageType.PreImage, "PhoneCallPostDelete", "Target", "PhoneCall")]

[PluginStep("SetState", PluginStepStage.PostEvent,
     PrimaryEntityName = "phonecall", StepId = "PhoneCallPostSetState")]
[PluginImage(ImageType.Both, "PhoneCallPostSetState", "EntityMoniker", "PhoneCall")]

[PluginStep("SetStateDynamicEntity", PluginStepStage.PostEvent,
    PrimaryEntityName = "phonecall", StepId = "PhoneCallPostSetStateDynamicEntity")]
[PluginImage(ImageType.Both, "PhoneCallPostSetStateDynamicEntity", "EntityMoniker",
"PhoneCall")]
public class NextPhoneCallUpdater : IPlugin
{
    ...
}
```

This probably looks like a lot of code to register for the appropriate messages, and it is. However, when you are keeping track of information on a child entity you need to account for all of the scenarios that could change your calculated value, and register messages accordingly. Therefore, you often register for these same messages whenever you need to populate one of these rolled-up attributes.

Also note the images that we set up for each step. Create gets a post-image, Delete gets a pre-image, and the rest get both types of images. The values we pass in for *MessagePropertyName* on the images come from Table 5-5.

The *Execute* method needs to determine which lead the *phonecall* is associated with in the pre-image and which it is associated with in the post-image. If they are different, both need to be updated. If they are the same, only that single lead will be updated. The *Execute* method source code is shown in Listing 5-22.

LISTING 5-22 *NextPhoneCallUpdater's Execute* method

```
public void Execute(IPluginExecutionContext context)
{
    Guid preLeadId = GetRegardingLeadId(context.PreEntityImages, "PhoneCall");
    Guid postLeadId = GetRegardingLeadId(context.PostEntityImages, "PhoneCall");

    ICrmService crmService = context.CreateCrmService(true);
    UpdateNextCallDueDate(crmService, preLeadId);

    if (preLeadId != postLeadId)
    {
        UpdateNextCallDueDate(crmService, postLeadId);
    }
}
```

The *Execute* method is fairly easy to understand, but it passes off most of the work to two additional methods, *GetRegardingLeadId* and *UpdateNextCallDueDate*. Let's start by taking a look at *GetRegardingLeadId* in Listing 5-23.

LISTING 5-23 The *GetRegardingLeadId* method

```
private Guid GetRegardingLeadId(PropertyBag images, string entityAlias)
{
    Guid regardingLeadId = Guid.Empty;

    if (images.Contains(entityAlias))
    {
        DynamicEntity entity = (DynamicEntity)images[entityAlias];

        if (entity.Properties.Contains("regardingobjectid"))
        {
            Lookup regardingObjectId = (Lookup)entity["regardingobjectid"];
            if (regardingObjectId.type == "lead")
            {
                regardingLeadId = regardingObjectId.Value;
            }
        }
    }

    return regardingLeadId;
}
```

Because not all messages have a pre-image and a post-image, we wrote this method to be forgiving if the image is not found. If the phone call image is found and the *regardingobjectid* attribute is associated with a lead, the method returns the *Guid* from *regardingobjectid*. Otherwise, it returns an empty *Guid*.

Once the lead IDs are identified, we need to update the attribute on the corresponding leads. *UpdateNextCallDueDate* is responsible for performing this functionality. Listing 5-24 is the full source code for the *UpdateNextCallDueDate* method.

LISTING 5-24 The *UpdateNextCallDueDate* method

```
private void UpdateNextCallDueDate(ICrmService crmService, Guid leadId)
{
    if (leadId != Guid.Empty)
    {
        DynamicEntity lead = new DynamicEntity("lead");
        lead["leadid"] = new Key(leadId);

        DynamicEntity phoneCall = GetNextScheduledPhoneCallForLead(crmService,
            leadId);
        if (phoneCall != null)
        {
            lead["new_nextphonecallscheduledat"] = phoneCall["scheduledstart"];
        }
        else
        {
            lead["new_nextphonecallscheduledat"] = CrmDateTime.Null;
        }

        crmService.Update(lead);

    }
}
```

UpdateNextCallDueDate is responsible for updating the custom *new_nextphonecallesched-uledat* attribute on the lead. It sets it to the earliest *scheduledstart* value for phone calls associated with this lead. If no phone calls are associated with the lead (or they do not have *scheduledstart* values), it nulls out the *new_nextphonecallscheduledat* attribute on the lead.

UpdateNextCallDueDate calls one additional method, *GetNextScheduledPhoneCallForLead*, to determine which phone call it should use. The source code for *GetNextScheduledPhoneCall-ForLead* is displayed in Listing 5-25.

LISTING 5-25 The *GetNextScheduledPhoneCallForLead* method

```
private DynamicEntity GetNextScheduledPhoneCallForLead(
    ICrmService crmService, Guid leadId)
{
    QueryExpression query = new QueryExpression();
    query.EntityName = EntityName.phonecall.ToString();

    ColumnSet cols = new ColumnSet(new string[] { "scheduledstart" });
```

```
    query.ColumnSet = cols;

    FilterExpression filter = new FilterExpression();
    query.Criteria = filter;

    ConditionExpression regardingCondition = new ConditionExpression();
    regardingCondition.AttributeName = "regardingobjectid";
    regardingCondition.Operator = ConditionOperator.Equal;
    regardingCondition.Values = new object[] { leadId };
    filter.Conditions.Add(regardingCondition);

    ConditionExpression activeCondition = new ConditionExpression();
    activeCondition.AttributeName = "statecode";
    activeCondition.Operator = ConditionOperator.Equal;
    activeCondition.Values = new object[] { "Open" };
    filter.Conditions.Add(activeCondition);

    ConditionExpression scheduledCondition = new ConditionExpression();
    scheduledCondition.AttributeName = "scheduledstart";
    scheduledCondition.Operator = ConditionOperator.NotNull;
    filter.Conditions.Add(scheduledCondition);

    query.PageInfo = new PagingInfo();
    query.PageInfo.Count = 1;
    query.PageInfo.PageNumber = 1;
    query.AddOrder("scheduledstart", OrderType.Ascending);

    RetrieveMultipleRequest request = new RetrieveMultipleRequest();
    request.Query = query;
    request.ReturnDynamicEntities = true;

    RetrieveMultipleResponse response;
    response = (RetrieveMultipleResponse)crmService.Execute(request);

    DynamicEntity phoneCall = null;
    if (response.BusinessEntityCollection.BusinessEntities.Count == 1)
    {
        phoneCall = (DynamicEntity)
            response.BusinessEntityCollection.BusinessEntities[0];
    }
    return phoneCall;
}
```

GetNextScheduledPhoneCallForLead constructs a *QueryExpression* that filters for active *phonecall* entities that are associated with the specified lead and have a *scheduledstart* value. The query is set to return only one record and is sorted by the *scheduledstart* attribute in ascending order. If no matching *phonecall* is found, it returns *null*.

The end result is that regardless of how a *phonecall* entity is created, updated, or deleted, the parent entity's attribute will always be recalculated.

System View Hider

Microsoft Dynamics CRM includes default system views for entities such as accounts, contacts, and others. You might find that your organization does not want to use all these system views, and therefore you'd like to remove one or more of them. Unfortunately, if you try to customize the entity with the Web interface to delete a system view, you will receive an error message stating that you cannot remove a system view.

Fortunately, however, you can use a plug-in to hide specific system views from your users. For this sample, let's assume we want to hide the No Orders in Last 6 Months system view on both the account and contact entities. The plug-in can do this because CRM queries for the list of *systemview* entities associated with a particular entity when displaying the picklist of views. This plug-in example is fairly straightforward to implement, so let's start by looking at the completed code in Listing 5-26.

LISTING 5-26 *SystemViewHider* plug-in source code

```
using System;
using Microsoft.Crm.Sdk;
using Microsoft.Crm.Sdk.Query;
using Microsoft.Crm.SdkTypeProxy;
using ProgrammingWithDynamicsCrm4.Plugins.Attributes;

namespace ProgrammingWithDynamicsCrm4.Plugins
{
    [PluginStep("RetrieveMultiple", PluginStepStage.PreEvent,
        PrimaryEntityName="savedquery")]
    public class SystemViewHider : IPlugin
    {
        public void Execute(IPluginExecutionContext context)
        {
            object[] systemViews = new object[]
            {
                //Contacts: No Orders in Last 6 Months
                new Guid("9818766E-7172-4D59-9279-013835C3DECD"),

                //Accounts: No Orders in Last 6 Months
                new Guid("C147F1F7-1D78-4D10-85BF-7E03B79F74FA"),
            };

            if (context.InputParameters != null && systemViews.Length > 0)
            {
                if (context.InputParameters.Properties.Contains(
                    ParameterName.Query))
                {
                    QueryExpression query;
                    query = (QueryExpression)
                        context.InputParameters[ParameterName.Query];
```

```
                        if (query.EntityName == EntityName.savedquery.ToString())
                        {
                            if (query.Criteria != null)
                            {
                                if (query.Criteria.Conditions != null)
                                {
                                    ConditionExpression condition =
                                        new ConditionExpression();
                                    condition.AttributeName = "savedqueryid";
                                    condition.Operator = ConditionOperator.NotIn;
                                    condition.Values = systemViews;

                                    query.Criteria.Conditions.Add(condition);

                                    context.InputParameters[ParameterName.Query] =
                                        query;
                                }
                            }
                        }
                    }
                }
            }
        }
    }
```

The first thing to notice is this plug-in takes advantage of a message that might not be as obvious as some that we have dealt with in the past. The RetrieveMultiple message is a valid message to register for, and as is shown here you can manipulate the *QueryExpression* being passed to it before the core operation is executed.

The other factor that allows this plug-in to work is that the system view IDs for native entities are always the same across CRM installations. If this were not the case, we would need to specify the view IDs during registration in the *customconfiguration* attribute for the plug-in step or perform a query within the plug-in to find the right view ID to exclude.

Customization Change Notifier

Customers often ask how they can keep track of customization changes in a development environment, or even for auditing in a production environment. If multiple people possess system administrator privileges, they could be making customization changes to the system at the same time. This might cause confusion or problems, especially if multiple users work with the same entity at the same time.

Obviously a good software development process dictates that developers and system administrators should communicate and follow a strict process when making changes to any environment. However, we created a sample plug-in that records customization changes. The plug-in presented in this sample doesn't prevent two users from working on the same records at the same time, but you can use it in conjunction with your development process as a safety net.

The *CustomizationChangeNotifier* plug-in listens for the Publish and PublishAll messages. To specify which users to notify of customization changes, we have added a custom Boolean attribute named *new_receivecustomizationnotifications* on the *systemuser* entity. By checking the corresponding check box on the *systemuser* form, the user is included in the notification e-mails. This plug-in differs from previous samples because it subscribes to both the pre-event and post-event steps and passes information between the two steps. Listing 5-27 shows the start of the *CustomizationChangeNotifier* code.

LISTING 5-27 *CustomizationChangeNotifier*

```
using System;
using System.Collections.Generic;
using System.IO;
using System.Text;
using System.Xml;
using System.Xml.Xsl;
using Microsoft.Crm.Sdk;
using Microsoft.Crm.Sdk.Query;
using Microsoft.Crm.SdkTypeProxy;
using ProgrammingWithDynamicsCrm4.Plugins.Attributes;

namespace ProgrammingWithDynamicsCrm4.Plugins
{
    [PluginStep("Publish", PluginStepStage.PreEvent)]
    [PluginStep("Publish", PluginStepStage.PostEvent)]
    [PluginStep("PublishAll", PluginStepStage.PreEvent)]
    [PluginStep("PublishAll", PluginStepStage.PostEvent)]
    public class CustomizationChangeNotifier : IPlugin
    {
        public void Execute(IPluginExecutionContext context)
        {
        }
    }
}
```

So far everything looks pretty normal, with the exception of the already mentioned fact that we registered this plug-in for both the pre-event and post-event steps. Listing 5-28 fills out the *Execute* method, and things start to get interesting.

LISTING 5-28 *CustomizationChangeNotifier's Execute* method

```
public void Execute(IPluginExecutionContext context)
{
    if (context.Stage ==
        MessageProcessingStage.BeforeMainOperationOutsideTransaction)
    {
        byte[] preXml = GetCustomizationSnapshot(context);
```

```
            context.SharedVariables["CustomizationChangeNotifier.PreXml"] = preXml;
        }
        else
        {
            SendNotification(context,
                (byte[])context.SharedVariables["CustomizationChangeNotifier.PreXml"]);
        }

    }
```

Because this plug-in executes in two different steps it needs to determine which step it is executing in right away and call the appropriate method. During the pre-event step, this plug-in grabs a snapshot of the customizations and stores them in the context's *SharedVariables PropertyBag*. Then, during the post-event step, it gets that customization snapshot out of *SharedVariables* and passes it on to the *SendNotification* method.

SharedVariables is shared by all plug-ins within a pipeline. Because of this, you should be sure the keys you use are likely to be unique. The only reason we use a byte array here is to deal with the compressed version of the customization data. It is also worth mentioning that we could have implemented this plug-in as two different plug-ins, each registered for its own step, but both steps have enough shared functionality that it made sense to use a single plug-in class. Let's examine the source code for *GetCustomizationSnapshot* in Listing 5-29.

LISTING 5-29 *GetCustomizationSnapshot*

```
private byte[] GetCustomizationSnapshot(IPluginExecutionContext context)
{
    ICrmService crmService = context.CreateCrmService(true);

    if (context.MessageName == "Publish")
    {
        ExportCompressedXmlRequest request = new ExportCompressedXmlRequest();
        string parameterXml = (string)context.InputParameters["ParameterXml"];
        request.ParameterXml = TransformParameterXmlToExportXml(parameterXml);
        request.EmbeddedFileName = "customizations.xml";

        ExportCompressedXmlResponse response =
            (ExportCompressedXmlResponse)crmService.Execute(request);
        return response.ExportCompressedXml;
    }
    else
    {
        ExportCompressedAllXmlRequest request =
            new ExportCompressedAllXmlRequest();
        request.EmbeddedFileName = "customizations.xml";
        ExportCompressedAllXmlResponse response =
            (ExportCompressedAllXmlResponse)crmService.Execute(request);
        return response.ExportCompressedXml;
    }
}
```

If you recall, not only did we register this plug-in for two steps, but we also registered it for two messages. Depending on whether the message is Publish or PublishAll, the plug-in will either get a subset of the current customizations or all of them. The two messages, ExportCompressedXml and ExportCompressedAllXml, are used to get the customization changes from CRM. The *EmbeddedFileName* property is used to specify the name of the file that is embedded in the zip file that is returned.

Unfortunately, the *ParameterXml* passed in through the context's *InputParameters PropertyBag* is not quite the same as what is required by the ExportCompressedXml message. ExportCompressedXml requires all of the root node's children (entities, nodes, security roles, workflows, and settings) even if you are not asking for any of those customization types. The *ParameterXml* only contains the customizations that are being published. Because of this slight difference, we need to do a transformation on the XML as shown in Listing 5-30.

LISTING 5-30 The *TransformParameterXmlToExportXml* method

```
private string TransformParameterXmlToExportXml(string parameterXml)
{
    string xsl = @"
        <xsl:transform version='1.0'
          xmlns:xsl='http://www.w3.org/1999/XSL/Transform'>
          <xsl:template match='/'>
            <importexportxml>
              <entities>
                <xsl:apply-templates select='publish/entities/entity' />
              </entities>
              <nodes>
                <xsl:apply-templates select='publish/nodes/node' />
              </nodes>
              <securityroles>
                <xsl:apply-templates select='publish/securityroles/securityrole' />
              </securityroles>
              <workflows>
                <xsl:apply-templates select='publish/workflows/workflow' />
              </workflows>
              <settings>
                <xsl:apply-templates select='publish/settings/setting' />
              </settings>
            </importexportxml>
          </xsl:template>

          <xsl:template match='@*|node()'>
            <xsl:copy>
              <xsl:apply-templates select='@*|node()'/>
            </xsl:copy>
          </xsl:template>

        </xsl:transform>";

    XslCompiledTransform transform = new XslCompiledTransform();
    transform.Load(XmlReader.Create(new StringReader(xsl)));
```

```
        XmlTextReader publishXmlReader =
            new XmlTextReader(new StringReader(parameterXml));
        publishXmlReader.Namespaces = false;

        StringBuilder results = new StringBuilder();
        XmlWriter resultsWriter = XmlWriter.Create(results);
        transform.Transform(publishXmlReader, null, resultsWriter);

        return results.ToString();
    }
```

Most of this method is just the declaration of the XSLT. While the specific details of the XSLT are outside the scope of this book, an abundance of information is available about XSLT both in books and on the Internet. The rest of the code in this method is simply using the XSLT to transform the *ParameterXml* passed in to the return value, which is passed to the *ExportCompressedXmlRequest*.

As shown back in Listing 5-28, when the *Execute* method is called for the post-event step, it passes along the plug-in context and the compressed XML from the pre-event step to the *SendNotification* method. The source code for the *SendNotification* method is displayed in Listing 5-31.

LISTING 5-31 The *SendNotification* method

```
private void SendNotification(IPluginExecutionContext context, byte[] preXml)
{
    ICrmService crmService = context.CreateCrmService(true);
    activityparty[] recipients = GetNotifcationRecipients(crmService);

    if (recipients.Length > 0)
    {
        byte[] postXml = GetCustomizationSnapshot(context);

        email email = new email();
        email.from = new activityparty[1];
        email.from[0] = new activityparty();
        email.from[0].partyid = new Lookup("systemuser", context.UserId);
        email.subject = "Customization Notification";
        email.description = @"You are receiving this email
            because a customization change has been published.";
        email.to = recipients;

        Guid emailId = crmService.Create(email);

        emailId = CreateEmailAttachment(crmService, emailId, preXml,
            "PreCustomizations.zip", "application/zip", 1);
        emailId = CreateEmailAttachment(crmService, emailId, postXml,
            "PostCustomizations.zip", "application/zip", 2);
```

```
        SendEmailRequest sendRequest = new SendEmailRequest();
        sendRequest.EmailId = emailId;
        sendRequest.IssueSend = true;
        sendRequest.TrackingToken = String.Empty;
        crmService.Execute(sendRequest);
    }
}
```

SendNotification starts by getting a list of recipients that have indicated they want to be notified of customization changes. As long as at least one user has indicated that he or she would like to receive change notifications, another snapshot of the customizations is taken that can be used to compare against the customizations that are captured in the pre-event step. An e-mail message is then prepared, including both snapshots of the customization files as attachments, and sent to the list of recipients.

GetNotificationRecipients, as shown in Listing 5-32, queries to find which system users have the custom attribute *new_receivecustomizationnotifications* set to true and returns an array of *activityparty* instances that reference them.

LISTING 5-32 The *GetNotificationRecipients* method

```
private activityparty[] GetNotifcationRecipients(ICrmService crmService)
{
    QueryByAttribute query = new QueryByAttribute();
    query.EntityName = "systemuser";
    query.ColumnSet = new ColumnSet(new string[] { "systemuserid" });
    query.Attributes = new string[] { "new_receivecustomizationnotifications" };
    query.Values = new object[] { true };

    RetrieveMultipleRequest request = new RetrieveMultipleRequest();
    request.Query = query;
    request.ReturnDynamicEntities = true;

    RetrieveMultipleResponse response;
    response = (RetrieveMultipleResponse)crmService.Execute(request);
    List<BusinessEntity> systemUsers =
        response.BusinessEntityCollection.BusinessEntities;

    List<activityparty> recipients = new List<activityparty>();
    foreach (DynamicEntity systemUser in systemUsers)
    {
        activityparty recipient = new activityparty();
        Guid systemUserId = ((Key)systemUser["systemuserid"]).Value;
        recipient.partyid = new Lookup("systemuser", systemUserId);
        recipients.Add(recipient);
    }

    return recipients.ToArray();
}
```

The last remaining piece of code is the *CreateEmailAttachment* method, which is displayed in Listing 5-33. As the name implies, this method creates an attachment for an e-mail message in CRM.

LISTING 5-33 The *CreateEmailAttachment* method

```
private static Guid CreateEmailAttachment(ICrmService crmService, Guid emailId,
    byte[] data, string filename, string mimeType, int attachmentNumber )
{
    activitymimeattachment emailAttachment = new activitymimeattachment();
    emailAttachment.activityid = new Lookup("email", emailId);
    emailAttachment.attachmentnumber = new CrmNumber(attachmentNumber);
    emailAttachment.mimetype = mimeType;
    emailAttachment.body = Convert.ToBase64String(data);
    emailAttachment.filename = filename;

    crmService.Create(emailAttachment);
    return emailId;
}
```

This sample demonstrates some of the more creative and powerful uses of plug-ins and *SharedVariables* as well as illustrating how to send an e-mail message with attachments using the CRM service.

Summary

Microsoft Dynamics CRM 4.0 offers a powerful means of extensibility through plug-ins, which you can register directly into the event execution pipeline. You can register and deploy plug-ins by using existing tools or by implementing your own deployment tools using an API. Because Microsoft Dynamics CRM implements plug-ins with no dependencies on specific class implementations, they are a good target for automated unit tests. The number of messages that can be registered for is significantly larger than any previous version of Microsoft Dynamics CRM and allows developers to extend CRM much further than was possible in the past.

Chapter 6

Programming Workflow

Microsoft Dynamics CRM includes a workflow module that allows you to create a set of rules that the software will run automatically based on trigger actions that you configure in the system. Some of the potential workflow rule triggers include creating a new record, updating a record status, assigning a record, and modifying a data field. Using workflow allows you to create automation processes, including:

- Assigning leads based on geography
- Creating e-mail alerts if a particular data field changes
- Updating record values or creating new records
- Implementing a sales process

Because every organization has unique business automation needs, Microsoft designed the workflow module to accommodate a wide range of functionality. And because business needs change frequently over time, Microsoft Dynamics CRM designed the workflow module so that power users (nondevelopers) can create, modify, and publish workflow rules through a Web-based workflow designer.

While the Web-based workflow designer offers great functionality and flexibility to create complex business processes, you will undoubtedly encounter requirements that you simply can't accommodate within the workflow designer. Fortunately, Microsoft Dynamics CRM allows you to create custom programming code that you can reference in a workflow rule as a workflow assembly. Similar to plug-ins, workflow assemblies support .NET-compliant languages so that you have the option to create your workflow assemblies with your preferred tools. Once you create and register a workflow assembly, your power users can reference and utilize these assemblies within the workflow designer. Therefore, they don't need to understand the details of the workflow assembly code, but they can take advantage of the assemblies you created.

In this chapter, we will briefly recap how to create, publish, run, and test a workflow rule in the workflow designer, and then we'll explore how Microsoft Dynamics CRM workflow utilizes Windows Workflow Foundation. Then we'll go deep into the specifics of creating a workflow assembly and registering it with Microsoft Dynamics CRM. We'll wrap up the chapter with several real-world sample workflow assemblies.

Chapter 12, "Advanced Workflow Programming," takes an even deeper look at workflow programming by exploring using workflow as entities and creating declarative workflows with XAML.

More Information For a comprehensive review of workflow basics and how to use the workflow designer, please refer to *Working with Microsoft Dynamics CRM 4.0* by Mike Snyder and Jim Steger (Microsoft Press, 2008). This book goes into more detail about creating workflow rules with the workflow designer, setting security on workflow, and troubleshooting.

Overview

In this chapter we cover the following topics:

- The workflow designer
- Windows Workflow Foundation
- Custom workflow activities

We conclude this chapter with three workflow programming examples: math building blocks, retrieve most available user, and calculate related aggregate.

Important At the time this book went to press, you could not deploy your workflow assemblies to Microsoft Dynamics CRM Online deployments. Therefore, this chapter only applies to on-premise or partner-hosted deployments.

The Workflow Designer

Before we get into the specifics of custom programming in Microsoft Dynamics CRM workflow, let's briefly review creating and running workflow rules through the Web interface.

First, we will create a workflow rule that automatically creates and schedules a follow-up phone call for a newly created account. Microsoft Dynamics CRM will run this workflow rule whenever you create a new account. We will also design the workflow rule to dynamically populate values in the phone call activity using values from the newly created account.

Creating a native workflow in Microsoft Dynamics CRM

1. Open Microsoft Dynamics CRM in your Web browser.
2. Navigate to the Workflows view by clicking Go To in the top menu and then selecting Workflows within Settings.

   You will see a list of workflows you own (or an empty list if this is the first time you have visited this area).

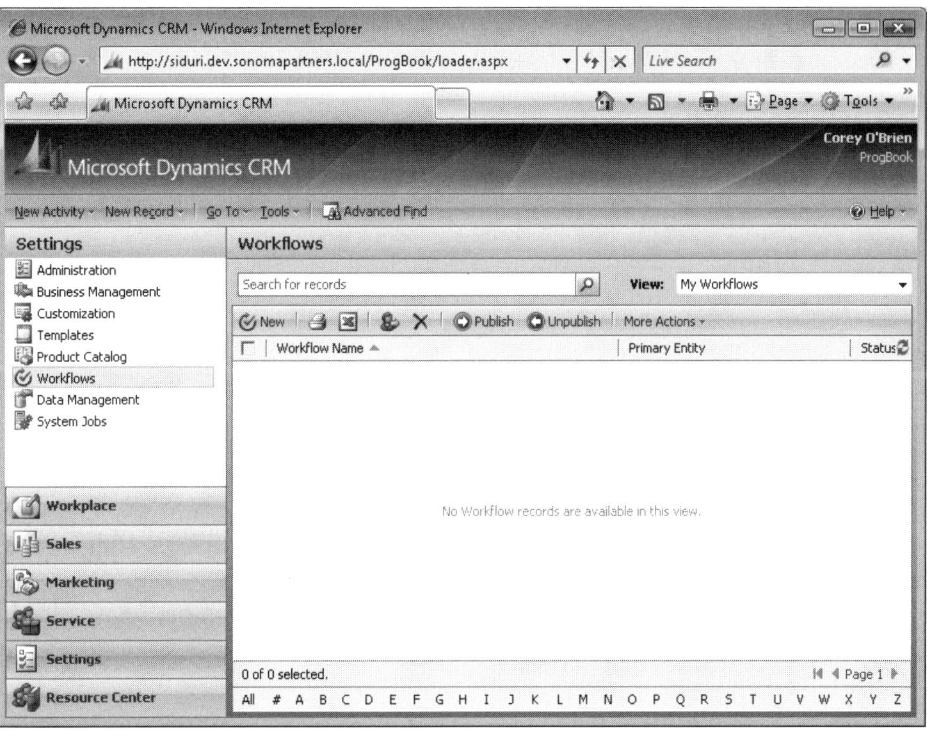

3. Click New on the Workflow toolbar.
4. Type **New Account Telephone Workflow** in the Workflow name field and click OK. You will be presented with the Microsoft Dynamics CRM native workflow designer.

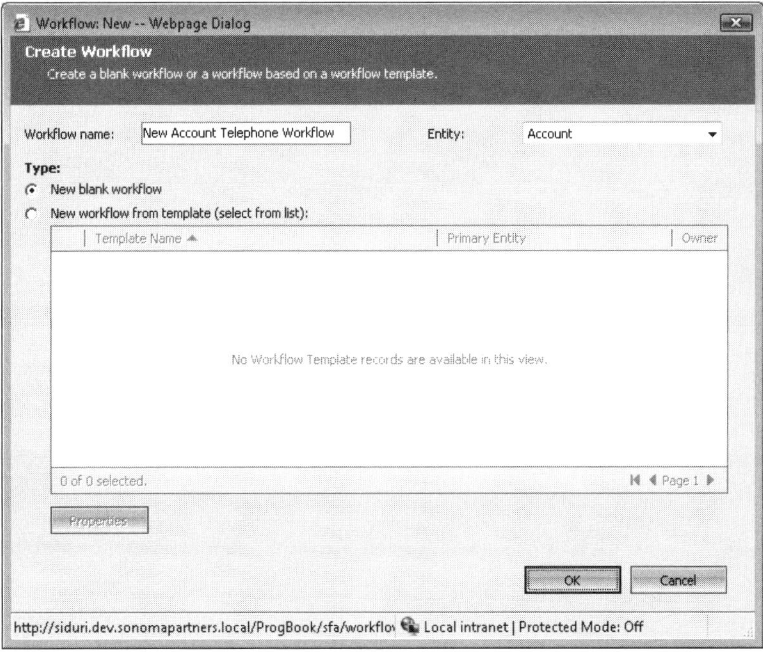

5. We want the workflow to run whenever an account is created and only for those accounts that you own, so leave all the properties in the top half of the screen at their default values.

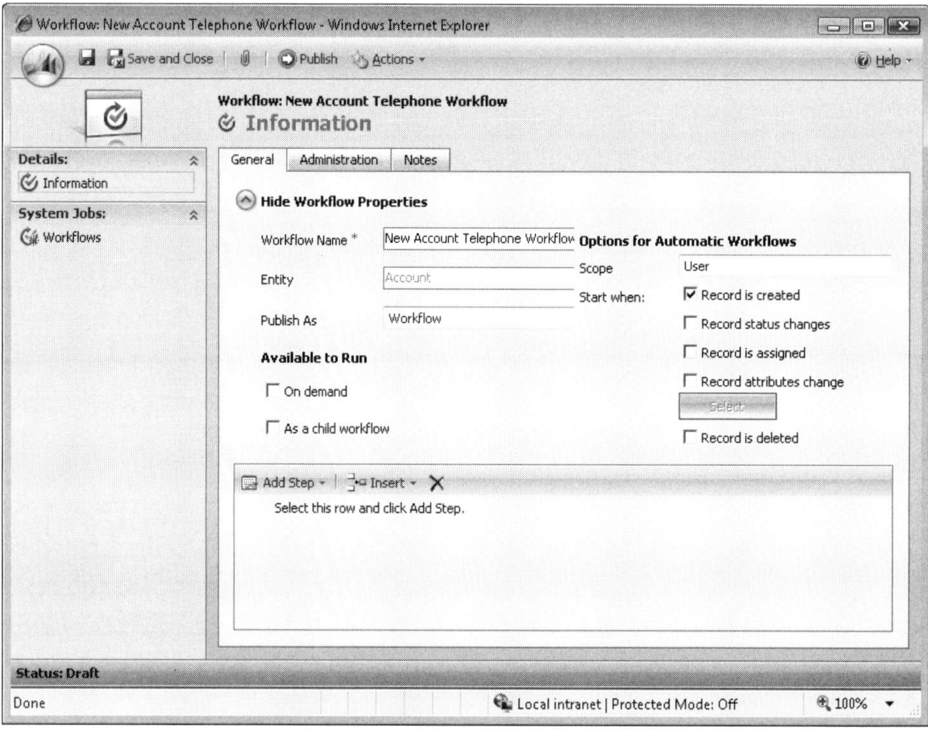

6. Click Add Step at the bottom of the workflow designer, and then select Create Record.
7. Type **Create a Follow Up Phone Call** as the description and then select Phone Call as the record type to create.

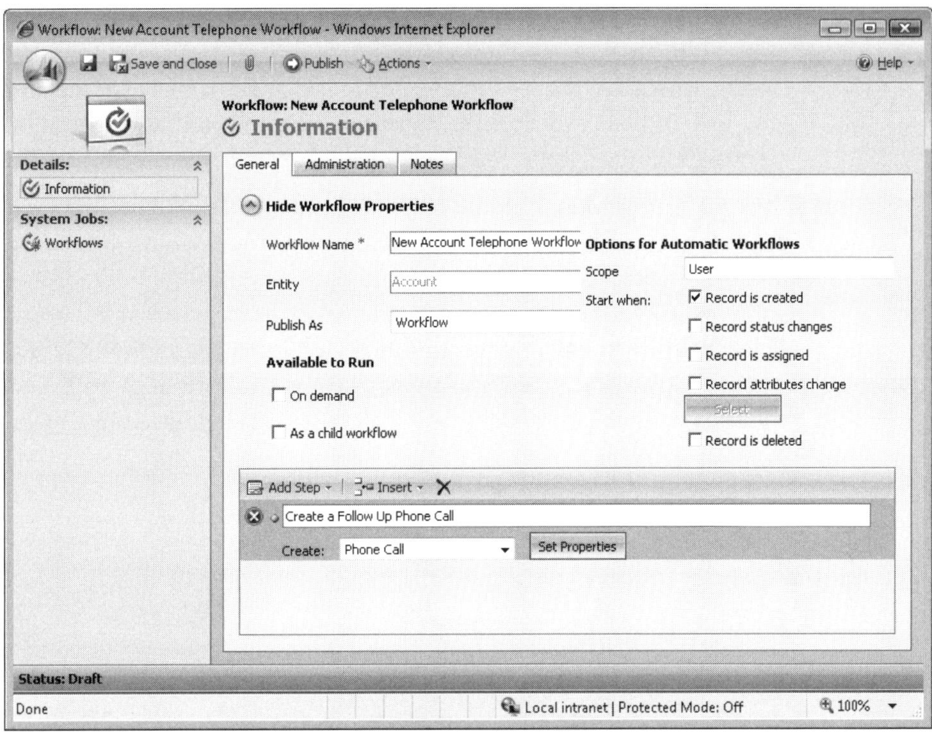

8. Click Set Properties to open the Create Phone Call dialog box.

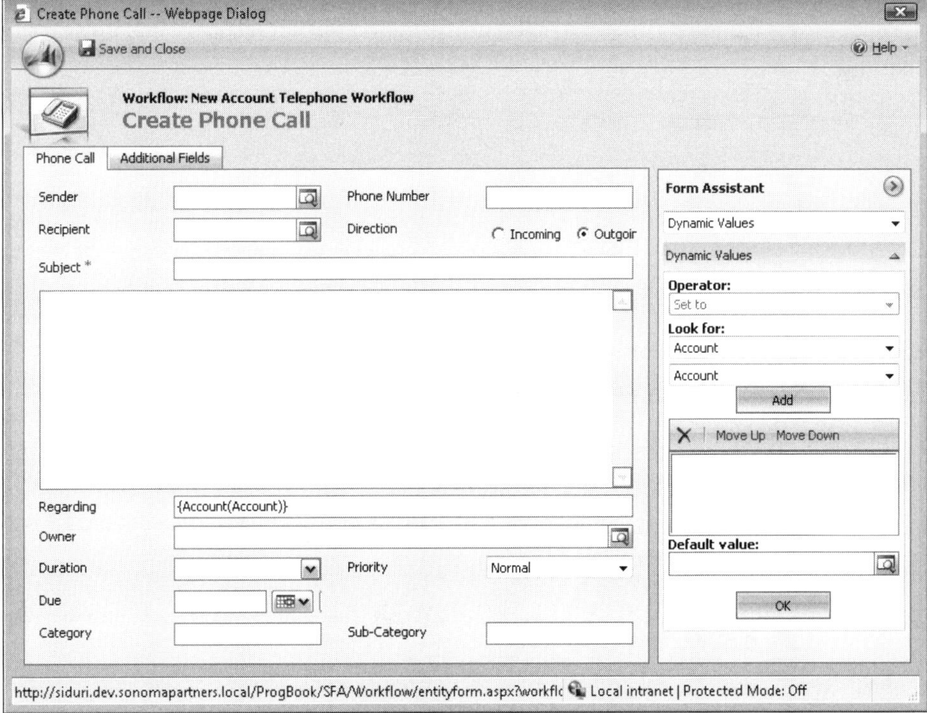

9. Next we will specify dynamic values for the phone call record so that it includes information from the account record. To do this, set focus in the Sender field, and then select Owner from the second drop-down list under Look For in the Form Assistant. (You use the first drop-down list to select the entity you want a value from; you use the second drop-down list to select the attribute from that entity.)
10. Click Add in the Form Assistant to add the selected attribute to the list of values that appears near the bottom of the Form Assistant. The Form Assistant enables you to assign form fields to properties of the current workflow, its steps, or the primary entity. When you specify multiple dynamic values to the list at the bottom of the Form Assistant, the first one that has a non-null value will be assigned to the target field. In addition, you can use the Default Value field at the bottom of the Form Assistant to specify a value that should be used if all of the dynamic values are null.
11. Click OK to populate the Sender field with the dynamic values.

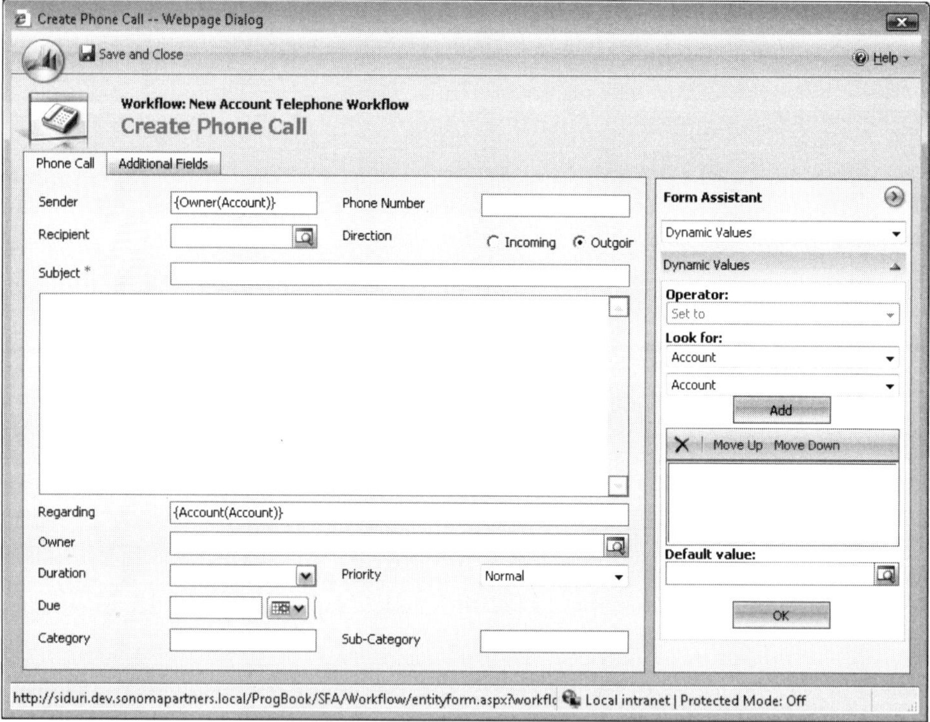

12. Repeat steps 9 through 11 to set the Recipient field. In this case we want to specify the Account as the recipient of the phone call. To specify an entity instead of an attribute for a dynamic value, select the entity name from the second drop-down list. So for this example, choose the Account option in the second picklist.
13. Type **Welcome call for new account:** in the Subject field and keep the focus at the end of the text.

14. Once again, repeat steps 9 through 11 to append the Account Name attribute from the Account entity to the end of the Subject field.
15. Click Add and then click OK.
16. Set focus in the Due field and select 3 from the Days drop-down list in the Form Assistant. Select After from the Operator drop-down list and then select the Created On attribute from the Account entity.
17. Click Add and then click OK.

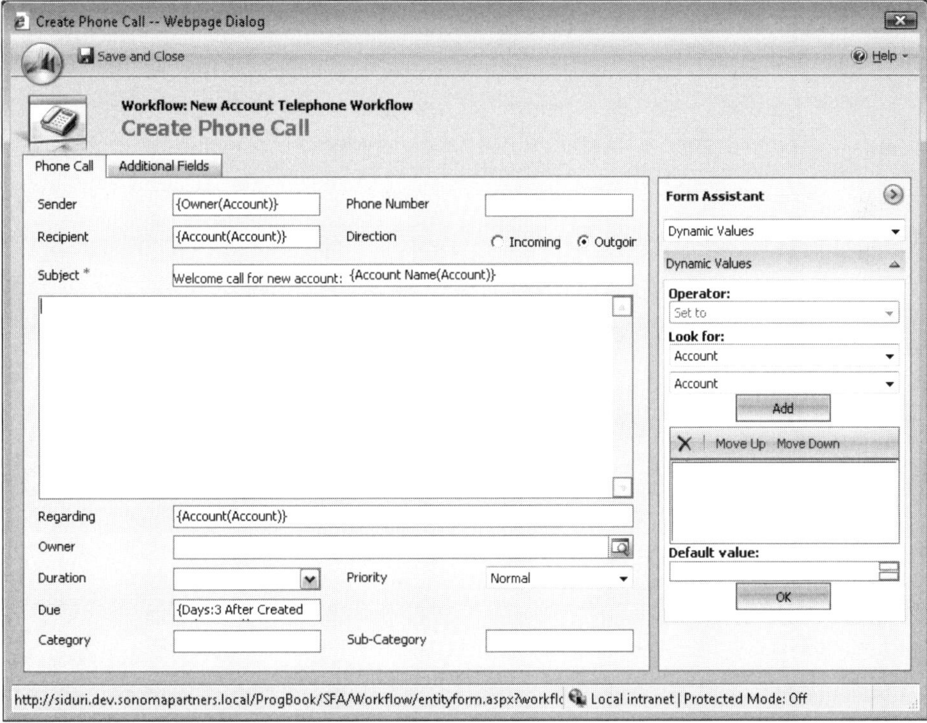

18. Click Save And Close on the top menu bar.
19. Click Publish on the menu bar of the workflow screen, and then click OK in the Workflow Publish Confirmation dialog box to publish the workflow.

While this is a fairly simple workflow rule, it demonstrates some of the powerful workflow capabilities natively available within Microsoft Dynamics CRM. We specified how to trigger the workflow rule, defined the scope of the workflow rule (which records it should run against), created the steps to take when the workflow runs, and dynamically assigned values to the newly created phone call record.

Testing the Workflow

Now that we've configured and published the workflow, you can test the rule by simply creating an account and confirming that it creates the appropriate phone call activity.

Creating an account and verifying the workflow results

1. On the Microsoft Dynamics CRM top menu, click New Record and then select Account.
2. Type a name in the Account Name field.
3. Click Save on the top menu bar.

   After the page reloads, click Activities in the left navigation pane. Depending on how quickly you clicked, you might not see a phone call activity yet. Since workflow runs asynchronously, it might not have completed processing the workflow rule yet.
4. If no phone call activity appears, wait a few seconds and click the Activities grid's refresh icon until the new phone call activity appears.

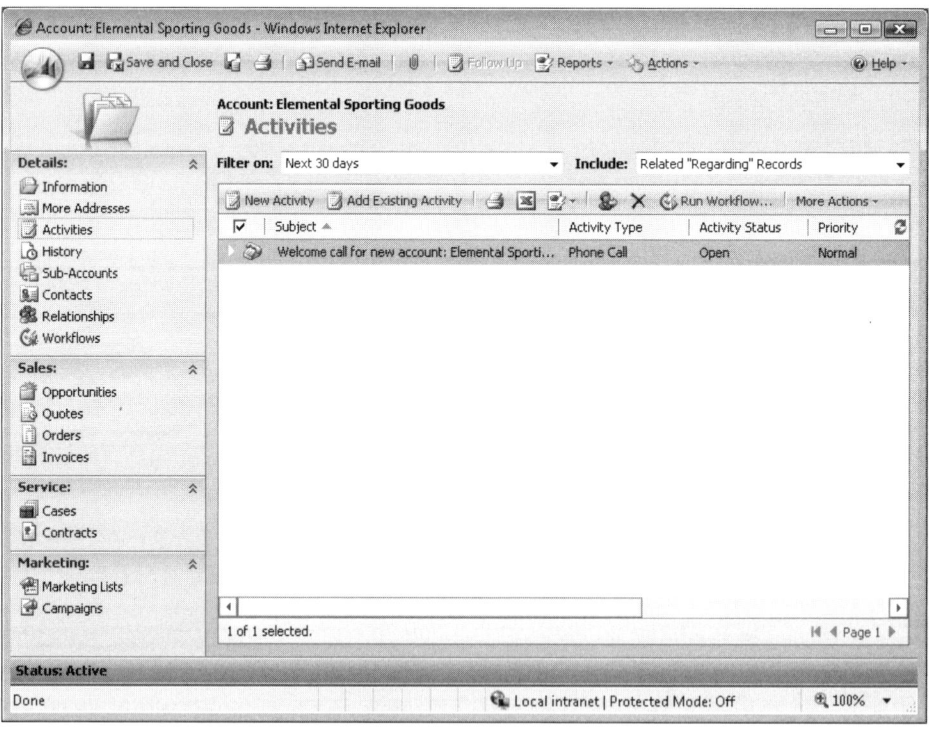

5. Open the phone call activity and verify that Microsoft Dynamics CRM correctly populated the Sender, Recipient, Subject, and Due fields with the dynamic data values we configured in the workflow rule.

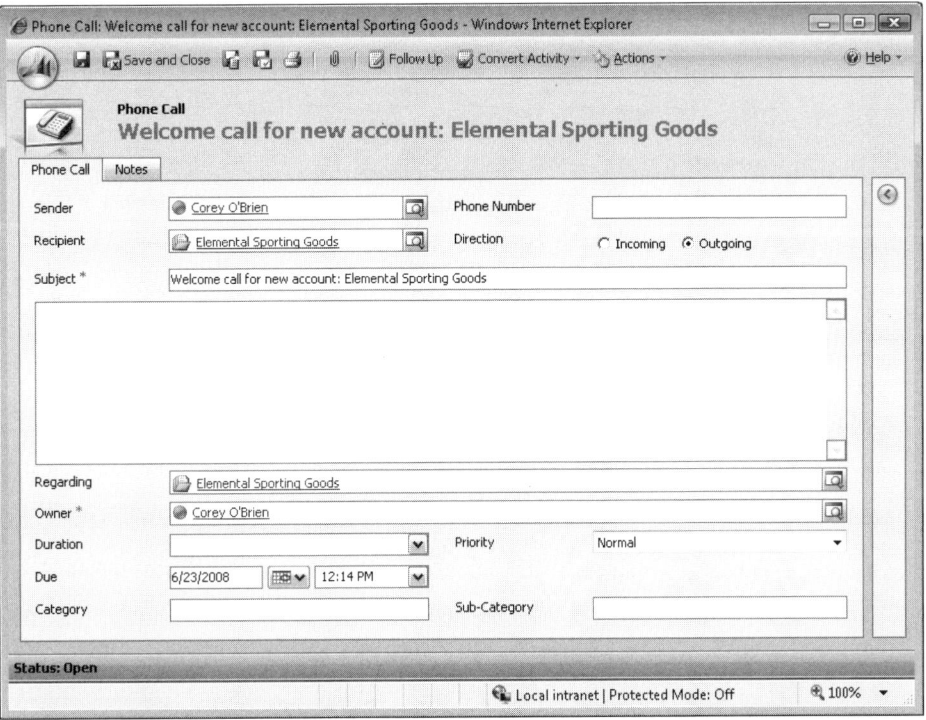

6. Close the phone call window.

7. On the account form, click Workflows in the left navigation pane and verify that you see the New Account Telephone Workflow successfully completed.

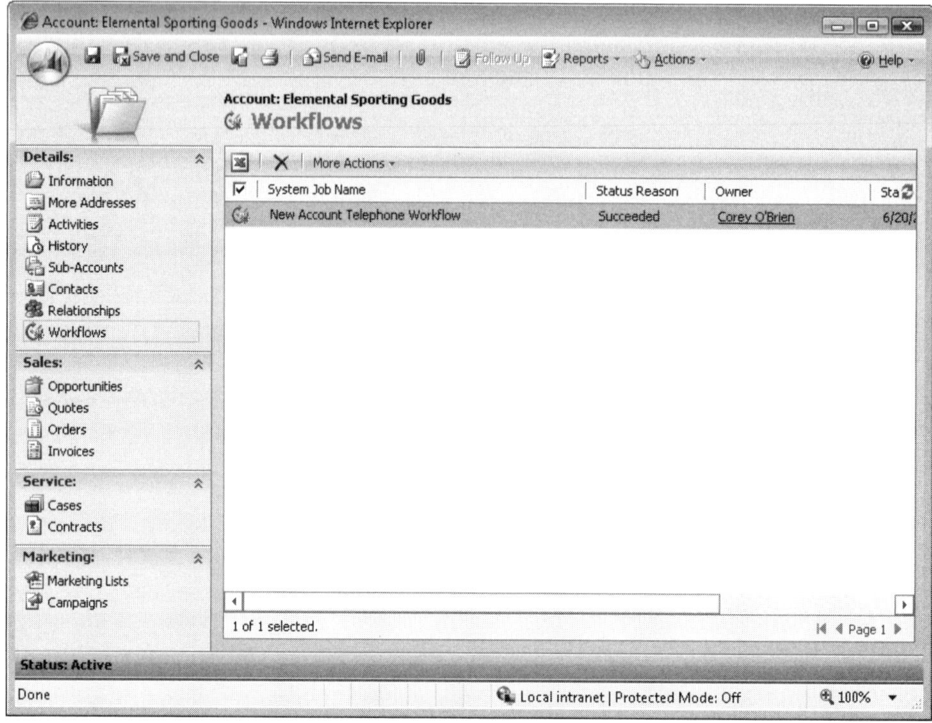

Workflow Definitions

Now that we have executed a workflow rule successfully, let's take a step back and examine workflow definitions in a little more detail. One of the first things we did when creating the phone call workflow was specify a name and select which entity to associate it with. The associated entity is passed in to the executing workflow instance and is also used to determine when the workflow is executed. Specifying the workflow trigger is the next key part of a workflow definition. Microsoft Dynamics CRM can trigger workflow using one of three primary techniques: automatically in response to system events, manually, or as child workflows.

Automatic Workflows

You will often want workflows to execute automatically in response to a system event. The workflow dialog allows you to define automatic workflows by selecting events to automatically trigger the workflow. Table 6-1 shows the system events that can be used to trigger an automatic workflow.

TABLE 6-1 Automatic Workflow Trigger Events

Event	Description
Record is created	The workflow executes whenever an instance of the associated entity is created.
Record status changes	The workflow executes whenever an associated entity's state changes (typically moving from Active to Inactive).
Record is assigned	The workflow executes whenever an instance of the associated entity is assigned to a new user.
Record attributes change	The workflow executes whenever an instance of the associated entity is modified. When this trigger is included, you can further specify which attributes must be modified for the workflow to execute.
Record is deleted	The workflow executes whenever an instance of the associated entity is deleted.

In addition to specifying the events for an automatic workflow, you can define a scope for the automatic triggers. Scope is used to limit which records automatically trigger the workflow. Table 6-2 lists the scope values and their meanings.

TABLE 6-2 Automatic Workflow Scope Values

Scope Name	Description
User	The associated entity will trigger the workflow only if that entity's owner is the same as the workflow's owner.
Business Unit	The associated entity will trigger the workflow only if that entity's owner is in the same business unit as the workflow's owner.
Parent: Child Business Units	The associated entity will trigger the workflow only if that entity's owner is in the same business unit as the workflow's owner or a child of that business unit.
Organization	The associated entity will trigger the workflow regardless of who owns it.

Manual Workflows

You can specify that a workflow run on demand in the workflow dialog to create a manual workflow. Manual workflows can be started by the user whenever they want to execute them. For instance, you could create a workflow that will e-mail a contact using a specific e-mail template. After the workflow is published, you can simply select the contact you want to e-mail from the contact grid, click the Run Workflow button from the toolbar, and then select your workflow from the window that opens.

Child Workflows

Child workflows are executed by a Start Child Workflow step in another workflow. A workflow can also start a child instance of itself this way.

Tip The only native support for looping in workflows is to have a workflow recursively create an instance of itself by using the Start Child Workflow step. Other techniques for implementing looping are available, but they require custom coding. We will explore these techniques later in this chapter.

Workflow Steps

The next part of a workflow definition is also the most important. For a workflow to actually do anything, you must include one or more steps in its definition. Microsoft Dynamics CRM exposes several steps natively and also allows you to develop your own custom steps that you can include in the native workflow designer. We will discuss custom steps later in this chapter. Table 6-3 lists the native steps.

TABLE 6-3 Natively Supported Workflow Steps

Step Name	Description
Stage	A stage is simply used to group other steps together to keep more complicated workflow definitions organized and maintainable.
Check condition	Check condition acts like an *if* statement in C# or other programming languages. If the configured condition evaluates to *true*, the child steps are executed.
Conditional branch	Conditional branch steps can only follow a check condition step and provide behavior similar to an *else if* statement in programming languages. They provide an alternate condition and child steps that can be checked and executed if the preceding check condition step evaluates to *false*.
Default action	Default action steps must either follow a check condition step or a conditional branch step and are similar to an *else* statement found in programming languages. If none of the preceding conditions is found to be true, the child steps of the default action step are executed.
Wait condition	Wait condition steps are similar to check condition steps, but they suspend the workflow until the condition evaluates to *true*.
Parallel wait branch	Parallel wait branch steps must follow a wait condition step and are used to provide an alternate condition to wait for. Whichever condition evaluates to *true* first determines which child steps are executed.
Create record	Create record steps are used to create a new instance of an entity.
Update record	Update record steps are used to update existing entities. The entity being updated must be the main associated entity or one of the entities related to it.
Assign record	Assign record steps are used to assign an entity to a new owner. Only the main associated entity or one of the entities related to it can be reassigned.
Send e-mail	The send e-mail step is used to send an e-mail message. The e-mail can be custom and completely defined in the step properties, or it can be based on an e-mail template.

TABLE 6-3 Natively Supported Workflow Steps

Step Name	Description
Start child workflow	Start child workflow steps are used to create instances of a workflow. The child workflow must include "Available to run as a child workflow" in its definition.
Change status	The change status step allows you to change the status of an entity. The entity being updated must be the main associated entity or one of its related entities.
Stop workflow	The stop workflow step allows you to stop the currently executing workflow with a status of either Succeeded or Canceled.

Dynamic Values in Workflow

One of the most important workflow features that you will use (probably in every single rule that you create) is *dynamic values*. As you saw in the earlier example, you can use dynamic values in your workflow rules to populate your conditions, actions, and so on with data specific to the workflow entity or its related entities.

When you're designing your workflow rule, you access dynamic values in workflow from the Form Assistant. You will notice that Microsoft Dynamics CRM automatically changes the dynamic values choices based on the field your cursor focuses on. To insert a dynamic value in workflow, select a field on the form where you want the dynamic value to appear, use the Form Assistant to select the value, and then click OK.

Tip Because the dynamic values Form Assistant automatically updates the options depending on your context, we must admit it can cause a little confusion when you initially start working with workflow rules. However, you can rest assured that you will quickly become comfortable using dynamic values in workflow rules.

In addition to including dynamic values in the form, you can also use dynamic values to update data fields even if the attribute does not appear on the entity form. To access and dynamically update a data field that does not appear on the form, click the Additional Fields tab.

In the Form Assistant pane, you can see the following aspects of dynamic values:

- Operator
- Look for options
- Dynamic Values box
- Default value

Operator

Microsoft Dynamics CRM automatically updates the operator values based on the form field with the current focus. So, if you select a numeric field on the form, Microsoft Dynamics CRM shows you operator options specific to numeric fields; when you select a date field, Microsoft Dynamics CRM shows you options specific to date fields. Table 6-4 shows the operator options and when you can apply them.

TABLE 6-4 Operator Options

Operator	Description
Set to	The default operator. Simply assigns the dynamic value to the field. For *DateTime* fields, additional time options are displayed.
Increment by	Can be used to increase the current value by the selected dynamic value. Available only for numeric fields for the Update Record action.
Decrement by	Can be used to reduce the current value by the selected dynamic value. Available only for numeric fields for the Update Record action.
Multiply by	Used to multiply the current value by the selected dynamic value. Available only for numeric fields for the Update Record action.
Clear	Removes the current value from the field. Available only with the Update Record action.

Important The *Set to* operator is the only option displayed unless you are using the Update Record step.

As mentioned, when you select a date field, Microsoft Dynamics CRM displays different operator options, as shown in Figure 6-1. By using the date-specific options, you can define the dynamic value for dates to be a certain amount of time before or after a custom date field.

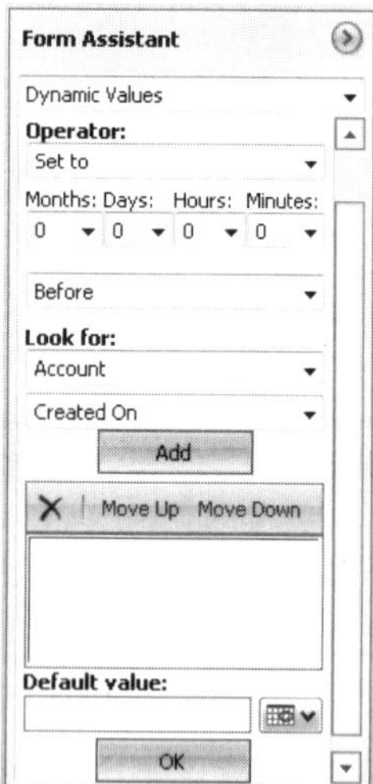

FIGURE 6-1 Additional date-based dynamic values options

Look for Options

Microsoft Dynamics CRM splits the Look for options into entity and attribute lists. The entity list displays the current primary entity, all related entities, a workflow option, and any custom assembly steps configured in the workflow rule (Figure 6-2). Workflow automatically updates the attribute list based on the selected entity, and it only displays attributes of the data type available for the field currently in focus. For example, if your cursor is in a date field, you can't select a non-date field attribute with dynamic values. Microsoft Dynamics CRM even allows you to populate dynamics values using custom attributes and custom entities that you create.

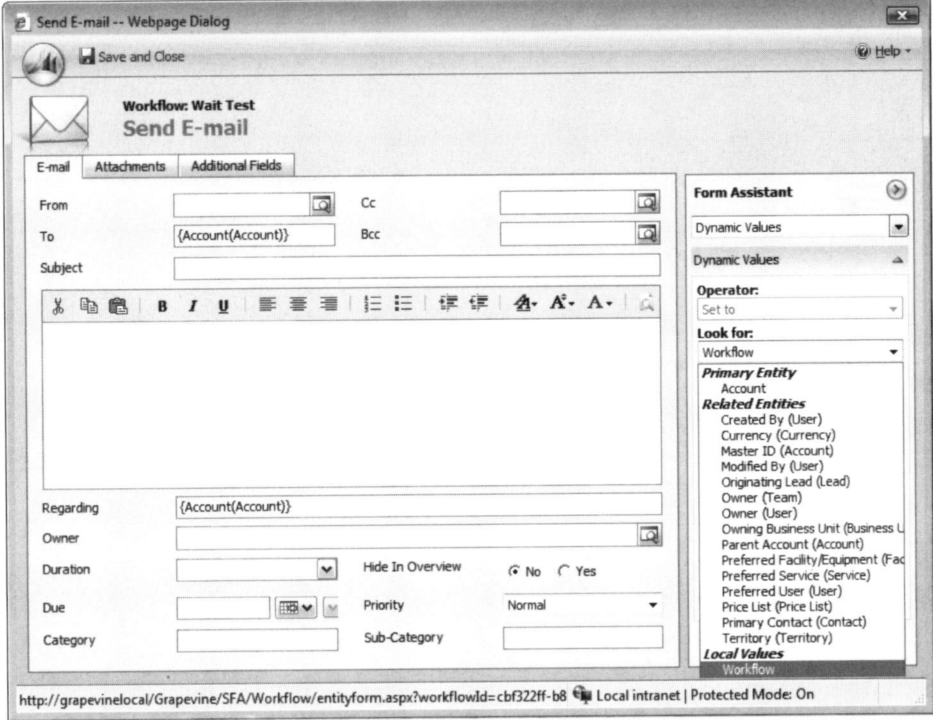

FIGURE 6-2 Accessing primary entity, related entity, and local values in dynamic values Look for

If you select the Workflow option in the Look for picklist as shown in Figure 6-2, the user interface displays these special attribute choices (depending on the field with focus):

- ***Activity Count*** The current number of activities associated with the primary entity excluding any created by the workflow rule.
- ***Activity Count Including Workflow*** The current number of activities associated with the primary entity plus any activities specifically created by the workflow rule.
- ***Execution Time*** The amount of time elapsed on the current workflow step. The execution time value resets each time a step is taken.

If you configure a wait condition and select the Workflow option, Microsoft Dynamics CRM gives you a fourth option, Timeout. If you select Timeout, you can also access a special Duration dynamic value in addition to the typical Before and After values (Figure 6-3). By using the Duration option, you can specify an amount of time that the workflow rule should wait before it proceeds to the next step.

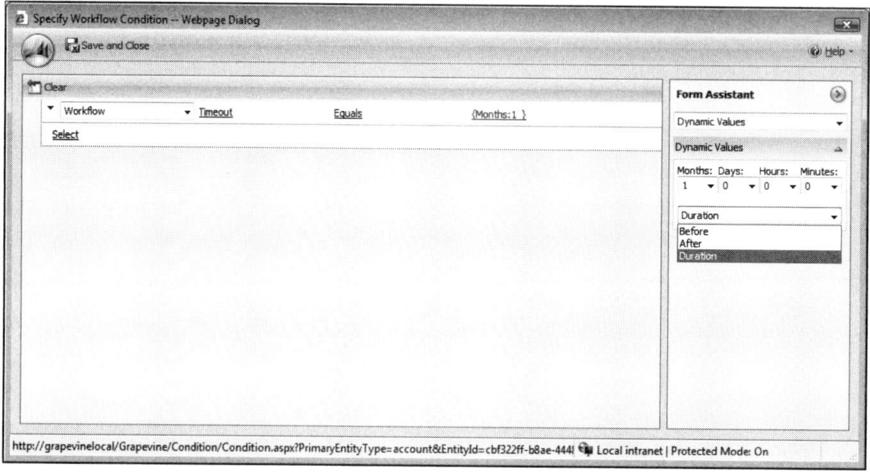

FIGURE 6-3 Accessing the Duration option for a time-out wait condition

> **Tip** For wait conditions, you will almost always want to use the Timeout option to ensure that the workflow rule waits the correct amount of time before proceeding to the next step.

Dynamic Values Box

The Dynamic Values box stores values as you select them in the picklists and click the Add button. Most of the time, you will have only one value; however, the design allows for multiple values if one of them is null. A common use for this technique is choosing a customer value for an Opportunity or Case. Because the customer of an Opportunity can either be an Account or a Contact, you may want to configure dynamic values to accommodate either scenario (Figure 6-4). In this example, Microsoft Dynamics CRM will try to populate the top value in the box (Account Name) as the dynamic value. If no account name value exists because the customer of the Opportunity is a Contact, Microsoft Dynamics CRM will try to populate the dynamic value with the next value in the box. If that value doesn't exist either, workflow will populate the dynamic value using the default value that you specify.

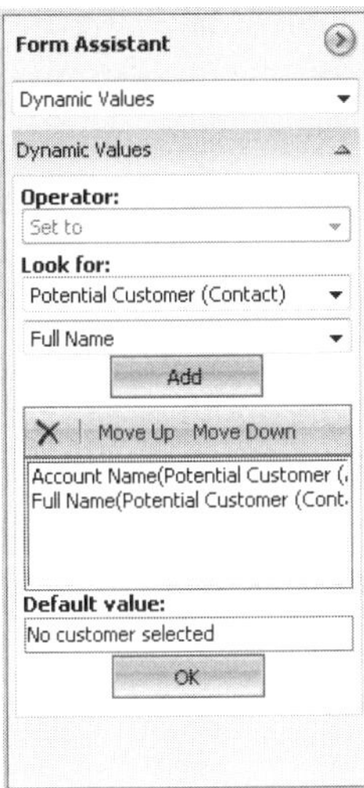

FIGURE 6-4 Multiple values selected in the Dynamic Values box

Default Value

If your dynamic value doesn't return any data from the database, you can use the default value to ensure that the value contains some data. You should strongly consider specifying a default value unless you are certain the data field chosen will always have a value. Default values do not apply to workflow wait conditions.

By now you have probably noticed that the out-of-the-box workflow functionality in Microsoft Dynamics CRM is quite powerful. Next we'll look at how Microsoft Dynamics CRM implements this functionality and then move on to how you can extend it.

Windows Workflow Foundation

Windows Workflow Foundation provides a comprehensive programming model, run-time engine, and tools to manage workflow logic and applications. Microsoft Dynamics CRM workflow uses the Windows Workflow Foundation framework for its core infrastructure. The Microsoft Dynamics CRM workflow designer is unique to Microsoft Dynamics CRM, but it creates workflows for execution with Windows Workflow Foundation. Consequently, as users design workflow rules in Microsoft Dynamics CRM, they might never know that Windows Workflow Foundation is running behind the scenes. Windows Workflow Foundation, or WF for short, has been part of the Microsoft .NET Framework since version 3.0. WF is not a stand-alone application; instead it is a collection of extensible services and base classes that you can use to add workflow functionality quickly and consistently to an application.

One of the main advantages of using a standard framework like WF is that it provides a common toolset and functionality across multiple software applications. Microsoft currently uses WF in several different solutions, such as Microsoft Office SharePoint Server and, of course, Microsoft Dynamics CRM. WF will also take over the workflow services in the next version of Microsoft BizTalk Server. At this point, the main WF development tools are Microsoft Visual Studio or application-specific designers like the one found in Microsoft Dynamics CRM. However, we expect that the widespread use of WF will increase the demand for additional workflow designer tools intended for business users to create more complex workflow processes.

Activities

A workflow in WF is composed of a collection of activities. The activities included out of the box with WF are not application specific, they can apply to many different types of applications. For example, *SequenceActivity* is a simple activity that contains a collection of child activities that are always executed in order. The *IfElseActivity* is used to branch code based on a condition evaluated at run time. You might be thinking that WF activities sound very similar to the steps we defined in the Microsoft Dynamics CRM workflow designer, and for good reason. Microsoft Dynamics CRM steps map directly to Windows Workflow Foundation activities. Table 6-5 lists the steps and their corresponding activity classes.

TABLE 6-5 Workflow Steps and Activity Classes

Step Name	Activity Class
Stage	*Microsoft.Crm.Workflow.Activities.StageActivity*
Check condition	*System.Workflow.Activities.IfElseActivity*
Conditional branch	*System.Workflow.Activities.IfElseBranchActivity*
Default action	*System.Workflow.Activities.IfElseBranchActivity*
Wait condition	A combination of *System.Workflow.Activities.WaitLoopActivity*, *System.Workflow.IfElseActivity*, and *System.Workflow.Activities.IfElseBranchActivity*
Parallel wait branch	A combination of *System.Workflow.Activities.WaitLoopActivity*, *System.Workflow.IfElseActivity*, and *System.Workflow.Activities.IfElseBranchActivity*
Create record	*Microsoft.Crm.Workflow.Activities.CreateActivity*
Update record	*Microsoft.Crm.Workflow.Activities.UpdateActivity*
Assign record	*Microsoft.Crm.Workflow.Activities.AssignActivity*
Send e-mail	*Microsoft.Crm.Workflow.Activities.SendEmailActivity* or *Microsoft.Crm.Workflow.Activities.SendEmailFromTemplateActivity*
Start child workflow	*Microsoft.Crm.Workflow.Activities.ChildWorkflowActivity*
Change status	*Microsoft.Crm.Workflow.Activities.SetStateActivity*
Stop workflow	*Microsoft.Crm.Workflow.Activities.StopWorkflowActivity*

Any of the classes in the *System.Workflow.Activities* namespace are native to Windows Workflow Foundation. Classes found in the *Microsoft.Crm.Workflow.Activities* namespace are domain-specific classes implemented by Microsoft Dynamics CRM. As you can see, many of the steps map to custom activities that are specific to Microsoft Dynamics CRM, but all of the custom activity classes inherit from either *Activity* or *SequenceActivity*, which are exposed as public classes by Windows Workflow Foundation.

More Info Microsoft Dynamics CRM wraps the activities listed in Table 6-5 in a custom activity called *StepActivity* to allow a user to assign descriptions to each step and to track the status of each step after it has executed. Although *StepActivity* inherits from *SequenceActivity*, it will typically only have a single child activity.

Dynamic Value Binding

Now that we understand activities and how they map to steps in a Microsoft Dynamics CRM workflow, the next logical topic is how the workflow designer implements dynamic value assignment across workflow steps. Once again, Windows Workflow Foundation provides a solution. As we'll see in the next section, you can implement custom activities that can be configured in the native workflow designer. You can implement the properties on your custom activities in a special fashion to expose them for activity binding within WF and the Microsoft Dynamics CRM workflow designer. Activity binding allows properties from one activity to be bound to properties of another activity during workflow execution. We'll explore the steps required to expose your activity's properties to the workflow designer in the section "Custom Workflow Activities" later in this chapter.

You may have noticed that many of the dynamic values used in the workflow designer are not associated with a particular step, but instead with entities associated with the workflow in general. When you bind one of these values to an activity, the workflow designer inserts a special *PolicyActivity* just before the entity you are assigning a value to. *PolicyActivity* is a native WF class that can perform actions based on evaluating conditions. In this case the condition is generated to always evaluate to *true* because the *PolicyActivity* is only being used to populate the entity-based values immediately before the workflow step is executed and does not need to evaluate a real condition.

More Info Windows Workflow Foundation is a complex topic to which many books are entirely dedicated. If you would like a better understanding of how WF works and how you can take advantage of the built-in classes, read *Microsoft Windows Workflow Foundation Step by Step* by Kenn Scribner (Microsoft Press, 2007).

Custom Workflow Activities

With a rudimentary understanding of Windows Workflow Foundation, we are now equipped to dive into ways that you can extend the native workflow functionality within Microsoft Dynamics CRM. The most common method for extending workflow functionality is by registering your own custom activities with Microsoft Dynamics CRM. This lets you reference them as custom steps in the workflow designer.

Implementing a Custom Activity

Because this is our first activity, we'll keep it simple. We'll create an activity that calculates the difference between two times and displays this difference as text, such as "5 months" or "12 minutes".

To get started, we'll need an assembly to hold our custom activities.

Creating a custom activity assembly

1. Start Visual Studio 2008.
2. If you've already created the ProgrammingWithMicrosoftDynamicsCrm4 solution in a previous chapter, you can open it now and skip ahead to step 6.
3. On the File Menu, select New and then click Project.
4. In the New Project dialog box, select Other Project Types and then select the Blank Solution template.
5. Type the name **ProgrammingWithDynamicsCrm4** in the Name box and click OK.
6. On the File Menu, select Add and then click New Project.
7. In the New Project dialog box, select the Visual C# project type targeting the .NET Framework 3.0 and then select the Class Library template.

Note Project templates that are preconfigured for Windows Workflow Foundation are included with Visual Studio 2008, but to demystify the assembly contents we will build a class library by hand.

8. Type the name **ProgrammingWithDynamicsCrm4.Workflow** in the Name box and click OK.
9. Delete the default Class.cs file.
10. Right-click the ProgrammingWithDynamicsCrm4.Workflow project in Solution Explorer and then click Add Reference.

11. On the Browse tab, navigate to the CRM SDK's bin folder and select microsoft.crm.sdk.dll and microsoft.crm.sdktypeproxy.dll. Click OK.
12. Right-click the ProgrammingWithDynamicsCrm4.Workflow project in Solution Explorer and then click Add Reference.
13. On the .NET tab, select System.Workflow.Activities and System.Workflow.ComponentModel. Click OK.
14. Right-click the ProgrammingWithDynamicsCrm4.Workflow project in Solution Explorer and then click Properties.
15. On the Signing tab, select the Sign The Assembly check box and then select New from the drop-down list.

Important To be registered with Microsoft Dynamics CRM, the assembly must be strongly named.

16. Type **ProgrammingWithDynamicsCrm4.Workflow** in the Key File name box, clear the Protect My Key File With A Password check box and then click OK.
17. Close the Project Properties window.

At this point you can compile the project, but of course without any classes the assembly isn't too valuable. We'll remedy that by adding our first custom activity class.

Creating your first custom activity

1. Right-click the ProgrammingWithDynamicsCrm4.Workflow project in Solution Explorer and select Class from the Add menu.
2. Specify **CalculateAgeActivity** as the class name and click Add.

Best Practice It is an unwritten rule that custom activity class names should end with the word *Activity*. Also, it is very common for the class name to start with a verb like Calculate, followed by a noun like Age.

3. Delete the predefined contents of the CalculateAgeActivity.cs file after it opens.

Now that we have a blank file ready to go, let's start by including the following *using* statements at the top of the file:

```
using System;
using System.Workflow.ComponentModel;
using Microsoft.Crm.Sdk;
using Microsoft.Crm.Workflow;
```

Now we need to add the class definition. Note two items of interest here. First, we inherit from *System.Workflow.ComponentModel.Activity* the way that all activities are required to do (either directly or indirectly). Second, we apply the *CrmWorkflowActivity* attribute to our class, which tells the Microsoft Dynamics CRM workflow designer how to display our custom activity in the user interface. Listing 6-1 shows the simple, stubbed-out *CalculateAgeActivity* class definition.

LISTING 6-1 *CalculateAgeActivity* class definition

```
namespace ProgrammingWithDynamicsCrm4.Workflow
{
    [CrmWorkflowActivity("Calculate Age",
        "Programming Microsoft CRM 4")]
    public class CalculateAgeActivity: Activity
    {
    }
}
```

The next thing we need to do is define the properties for our class. We need two *CrmDateTime* properties that we can compare and a string property to contain our human-readable age output value. Normally you would implement them like this:

```
private CrmDateTime _earlierDate;
public CrmDateTime EarlierDate
{
    get { return _earlierDate; }
    set { _earlierDate = value; }
}
```

However, this implementation would not expose your properties to be bound to the values of other activities. To achieve this, we need to use a *DependencyProperty* for the backing store of the property. You can achieve this by implementing your properties as follows:

```
public static DependencyProperty EarlierDateProperty = DependencyProperty.Register(
    "EarlierDate", typeof(CrmDateTime), typeof(CalculateAgeActivity));

[CrmInput("Earlier Date")]
public CrmDateTime EarlierDate
{
    get { return (CrmDateTime)GetValue(EarlierDateProperty); }
    set { SetValue(EarlierDateProperty, value); }
}
```

Wow! That seems like quite a bit of code for a simple property. The first thing you probably noticed is that you no longer have a private field. It is replaced by a static public *DependencyProperty*. This *DependencyProperty* is used like a key for getting and setting the value of the property. The *DependencyProperty* is created by calling the static *DependencyProperty.Register* method, which takes arguments of the property name as a string, the property type, and the activity class type.

The addition of the *CrmInput* attribute on the property definition is also new. This attribute tells the workflow designer that the property is meant to be used as an input and also provides the label that should be presented in the designer's user interface.

Finally, the property getter and setter use the *GetValue* and *SetValue* methods, which are defined on *DependencyObject* (*Activity*'s base class). Both *GetValue* and *SetValue* take a *DependencyProperty* as an argument to determine which property value should be retrieved or assigned.

Although these steps might seem like a burden, they allow Windows Workflow Foundation to efficiently bind activities together without those activities having any knowledge of each other.

Tip You can use a snippet in Visual Studio 2008 to insert properties that use a *DependencyProperty* as the backing store by typing in **propdp** and then pressing the Tab key twice. As with all snippets, you can specify the different values, such as the property type and name, and then just press Tab to jump to the next input field. When you are done entering input fields, press Enter and you'll return to the normal text input mode.

Unfortunately, the snippet was designed for use with Windows Presentation Foundation (WPF), which also uses dependency properties. Because of this, the snippet calls an overloaded version of *DependencyProperty.Register* passing in a *System.Windows.UIPropertyMetadata*, which is used to specify a default value for the property. You can just delete this last argument and it will work fine—it's just an additional step.

Armed with this understanding of dependency properties, we can define the remaining two properties like this:

```
public static DependencyProperty LaterDateProperty = DependencyProperty.Register(
    "LaterDate", typeof(CrmDateTime), typeof(CalculateAgeActivity));

[CrmInput("Later Date")]
public CrmDateTime LaterDate
{
    get { return (CrmDateTime)GetValue(LaterDateProperty); }
    set { SetValue(LaterDateProperty, value); }
}

public static DependencyProperty AgeProperty = DependencyProperty.Register(
    "Age", typeof(string), typeof(CalculateAgeActivity));

[CrmOutput("Age")]
public string Age
{
    get { return (string)GetValue(AgeProperty); }
    set { SetValue(AgeProperty, value); }
}
```

The only thing worth noting here is that our *Age* property has been marked with the *CrmOutput* attribute, which tells the workflow designer that the property should be used for output and given the label "Age" in the user interface.

Now that our properties have been defined, we just need to implement the part of the activity that actually does something. The base *Activity* class defines an *Execute* method that is called by the workflow run time whenever the activity needs to be executed. Listing 6-2 shows *CalculateAgeActivity*'s implementation of *Execute*.

LISTING 6-2 *CalculateAgeActivity's Execute* method

```
protected override ActivityExecutionStatus Execute(
    ActivityExecutionContext executionContext)
{
    CrmDateTime earlierDate = this.EarlierDate;

    if (earlierDate != null)
    {
        CrmDateTime laterDate = this.LaterDate ?? CrmDateTime.Now;
        this.Age = GenerateHumanReadableAge(
            laterDate.UniversalTime - earlierDate.UniversalTime);
    }

    return ActivityExecutionStatus.Closed;
}
```

This method simply gets the values from our two input *CrmDateTime* parameters and passes their difference into the *GenerateHumanReadableAge* method, which does all the work. The return value is assigned to our output *Age* parameter. Also, if the *LaterDate* property is null, it uses the current date and time for that value. Notice that we use the UTC version of both dates through the *UniversalTime* property. We are not using the *ActivityExecutionContext* object that is passed in at this point, but we'll cover it later in the chapter.

More Info The return value for the *Execute* method is of type *ActivityExecutionStatus*. You almost always want to return *ActivityExecutionStatus.Closed*, which indicates to the workflow run time that this activity is complete and the next activity can begin executing. However, you can use several other states to indicate that either something has gone wrong or that your activity is temporarily suspended. See *http://msdn.microsoft.com/en-us/library/system.workflow.componentmodel.activityexecutionstatus.aspx* for more information on the *ActivityExecutionStatus* enumeration.

Listing 6-3 shows the implementation of the *GenerateHumanReadableAge* method, which is actually not specific to WF or Microsoft Dynamics CRM in any way.

LISTING 6-3 The *GenerateHumanReadableAge* method

```
private string GenerateHumanReadableAge(TimeSpan age)
{
    string result;
    int years = age.Days / 365;
    int months = age.Days / 30;
    int weeks = age.Days / 7;

    if (years > 1)
    {
        result = String.Format("{0} years", years);
    }
    else if (months > 1)
    {
        result = String.Format("{0} months", months);
    }
    else if (weeks > 1)
    {
        result = String.Format("{0} weeks", weeks);
    }
    else if (age.Days > 1)
    {
        result = String.Format("{0} days", age.Days);
    }
    else if (age.Hours > 1)
    {
        result = String.Format("{0} hours", age.Hours);
    }
    else if (age.Minutes > 1)
    {
        result = String.Format("{0} minutes", age.Minutes);
    }
    else
    {
        result = String.Format("{0} seconds", age.Seconds);
    }

    return result;
}
```

This method follows a fairly simple algorithm to convert a *TimeSpan* into some text that gives an approximate age that is more human-readable.

Deploying the Custom Assembly

Now that our custom activity is implemented (and should compile without errors), we need to register the assembly with the Microsoft Dynamics CRM server. Registering a custom workflow assembly is very similar to registering a plug-in assembly. In fact, the *plugintype* and *pluginassembly* entities are used to store information about custom workflow activities and their assemblies, respectively.

We will take a look at registering assemblies both by using the PluginRegistration tool from the CRM SDK and by extending the ProgrammingWithDynamicsCrm4.PluginDeploy tool we implemented in Chapter 5, "Plug-ins."

Registration with the PluginRegistration Tool

If you want to get this sample up and running quickly, you can follow these steps to use the PluginRegistration tool from the CRM SDK. See the section "Building the Registration Tool" in Chapter 5 for instructions on how to compile the PluginRegistration tool.

Registering your custom workflow assembly

1. Launch the PluginRegistration tool.
2. Connect to your Microsoft Dynamics CRM server. (See Chapter 5 for information on setting up the connection.)
3. Select Register New Assembly from the Register toolbar button.
4. Click the ellipsis button to navigate to and select your compiled ProgrammingWith-DynamicsCrm4.Workflow.dll.

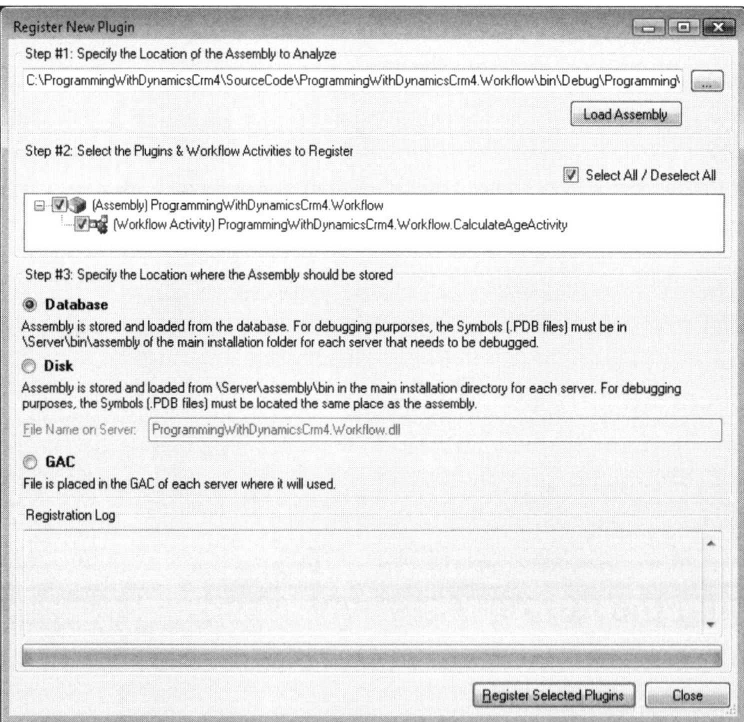

5. Click the Register Selected Plugins button at the bottom of the dialog box. (Yes, it does say "Plugins," but it is for both plug-ins and workflow assemblies.)

   You should receive a message that your assembly was successfully registered.

That's all it takes to use the PluginRegistration tool, which is the quickest way to get your custom assemblies up and running on your Microsoft Dynamics CRM server.

Programmatic Custom Activity Registration

To demonstrate how to programmatically register custom activities, we'll just enhance the ProgrammingWithDynamicsCrm4.PluginDeploy project that we created in Chapter 5. Because of the overlap in entities used to contain plug-in and workflow activity registration data, our changes will be minimal.

Extending ProgrammingWithDynamicsCrm4.PluginDeploy to register activities

1. First add a reference to the System.Workflow.ComponentModel assembly: right-click the ProgrammingWithDynamicsCrm4.PluginDeploy project in Solution Explorer and then click Add Reference.
2. On the .NET tab, select System.Workflow.ComponentModel and click OK.
3. Open the Program.cs file in the ProgrammingWithDynamicsCrm4.PluginDeploy project.
4. To keep the code as concise as possible, add the following two using statements near the top of the file after the pre-existing using statements:

```
using System.Workflow.ComponentModel;
using Microsoft.Crm.Workflow;
```

5. Because the workflow activity types are not included in *RegisterSolutionRequest*, we need to update the *RegisterSolution* method to return the *pluginassemblyid* for the assembly it registers. Change *RegisterSolution* to match the following implementation:

```
private static Guid RegisterSolution(CrmService crmService, pluginassembly
    pluginAssembly, SdkMessageProcessingStepRegistration[] steps)
{
    RegisterSolutionRequest registerRequest = new RegisterSolutionRequest();
    registerRequest.PluginAssembly = pluginAssembly;
    registerRequest.Steps = steps;
    Console.Write("Registering solution... ");
    RegisterSolutionResponse registerResponse =
        (RegisterSolutionResponse)crmService.Execute(registerRequest);
    Console.WriteLine("Complete");

    return registerResponse.PluginAssemblyId;
}
```

6. To now add the new functionality, replace the last line of the *DeployPlugin* method with the following lines that just call two new methods:

```
Guid pluginAssemblyId = RegisterSolution(crmService, pluginAssembly,
    steps);

plugintype[] workflowActivities =
    LoadWorkflowActivities(pluginAssemblyPath, pluginAssemblyId);
RegisterWorkflowActivities(crmService, workflowActivities);
```

7. Next, define the *LoadWorkflowActivities* method. *LoadWorkflowActivities* iterates through all the types in the specified assembly and finds any that inherit from *Activity* and are decorated with a *CrmWorkflowActivity* attribute. Any matches are packaged into *plugintype* classes and returned. The method is implemented as shown here:

```
private static plugintype[] LoadWorkflowActivities(string pluginAssemblyPath,
    Guid pluginAssemblyId)
{
    List<plugintype> workflowActivities = new List<plugintype>();
    Assembly assembly = Assembly.LoadFile(pluginAssemblyPath);

    foreach (Type activityType in assembly.GetTypes())
    {
        CrmWorkflowActivityAttribute activityAttribute =
            (CrmWorkflowActivityAttribute)Attribute.GetCustomAttribute(
            activityType, typeof(CrmWorkflowActivityAttribute));

        if (activityType.IsSubclassOf(typeof(Activity)) && activityAttribute != null)
        {
            plugintype workflowActivity = new plugintype();
            workflowActivity.typename = activityType.FullName;
            workflowActivity.pluginassemblyid =
                new Lookup("pluginassembly", pluginAssemblyId);
            workflowActivity.isworkflowactivity = new CrmBoolean(true);
            workflowActivity.friendlyname = activityAttribute.Name;
            workflowActivities.Add(workflowActivity);
        }
    }

    return workflowActivities.ToArray();
}
```

8. Now define the *RegisterWorkflowActivities* method, which simply iterates through the *plugintype* entities returned from *LoadWorkflowActivities* and passes them to the *Create* method on the *CrmService*. The code for *RegisterWorkflowActivities* is shown here:

```
private static void RegisterWorkflowActivities(CrmService crmService, plugintype[]
    workflowActivities)
{
    foreach (plugintype workflowActivity in workflowActivities)
    {
        crmService.Create(workflowActivity);
    }
}
```

After these changes, you can use ProgrammingWithDynamicsCrm4.PluginDeploy to register both plug-ins and custom workflow activities. In fact, you can put custom workflow activities and plug-ins within the same assembly and ProgrammingWithDynamicsCrm4.PluginDeploy will properly detect and register both of them with the Microsoft Dynamics CRM server.

Testing the Custom Activity

Now that our assembly is registered with the server, we can create a new workflow to test it. Our new workflow will be triggered by a case changing to the resolved state. It will then send an e-mail to the manager of the case's owner, letting her know how long the case was open.

Creating the case age notifier workflow

1. Open Microsoft Dynamics CRM in your Web browser.
2. Navigate to the Workflows view by clicking Go To in the top menu and then selecting Workflows in the Settings section.
3. Click New on the Workflow toolbar.
4. Type **Case Age Notifier** for the workflow name.
5. Select Case for the workflow entity. Click OK.
6. In the workflow designer, change the Scope to Organization and make sure the only Start When value is Record Status Changes.
7. Click Add Step on the step menu bar and then select Check Condition.
8. Click the <condition> (click to configure) link in the newly added step.
9. Configure the condition to check whether the case status equals Resolved.
10. Click the Select This Row and then click Add Step Line under the condition, and then click Add Step on the step menu bar. Select Calculate Age from the Programming Microsoft CRM 4 submenu.

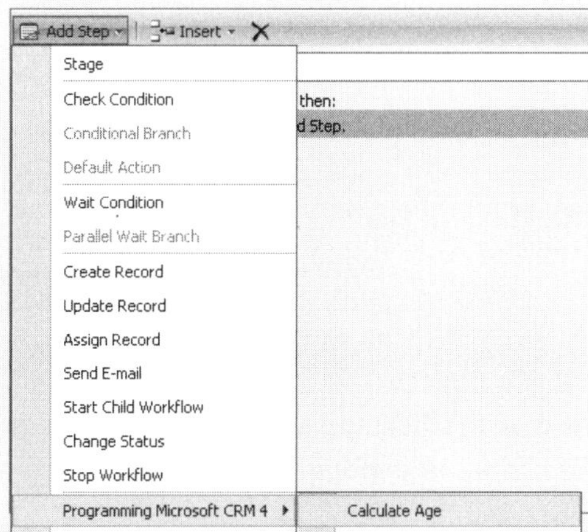

11. Click Set Properties for the Calculate Age step.

12. Use the Form Assistant to specify the Created On attribute for the Case entity in the Earlier Date field. Leave the Later Date field blank. (It will default to the current system time.)

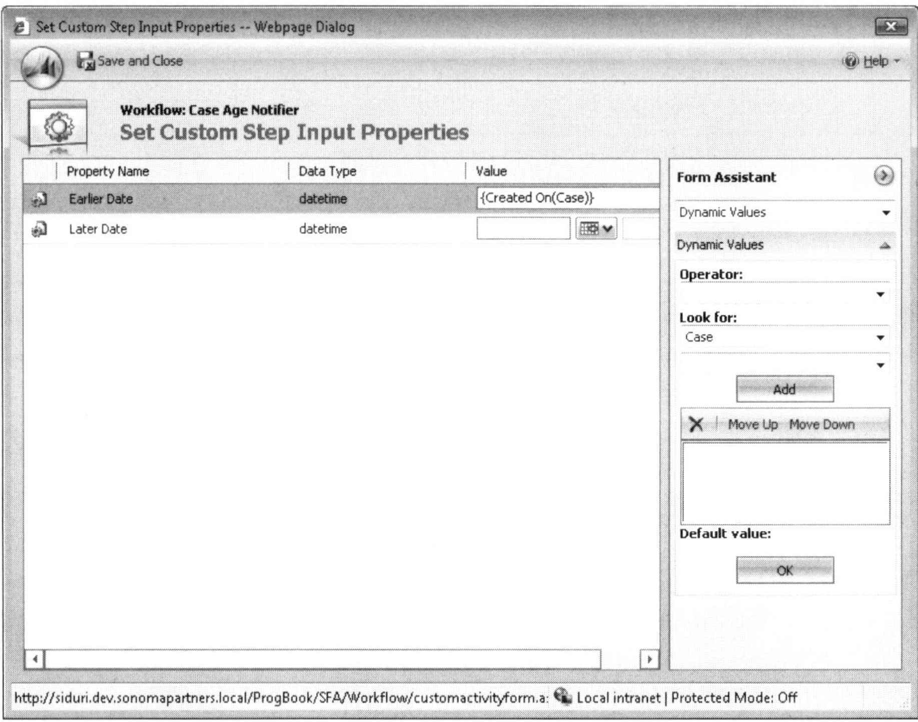

13. Click Save And Close.

14. Click Add Step on the step menu bar and then select Send E-mail.

15. Click Set Properties on the Send E-mail step.

16. Using the Form Assistant, set the From field to be the case's owner.

17. Specify both the owner's manager and the case's owner as values in the To field by adding them to the list in the Form Assistant. To add the owner's manager, you need to select Owner (User) in the first Look For picklist and Manager in the second picklist. This is because the manager is actually an attribute on a related entity. You add the case's owner to the list by selecting Case in the first picklist and Owner in the second picklist. By specifying both the owner's manager and the case's owner, you are indicating to e-mail the owner directly if he or she does not have a manager assigned.

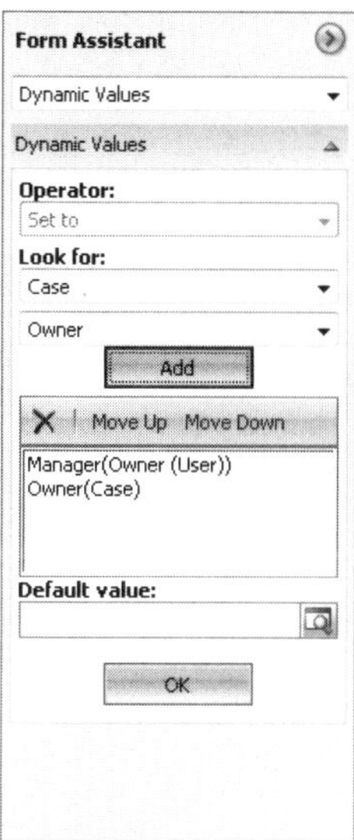

18. In the Subject box, type **Case closed after**, and be sure to leave a space at the end of the text for the dynamic value.

19. Next add the *Age* property from the Calculate Age step to the end of the subject box. You do this using a similar method to specifying dynamic values from related entities. Start by selecting Calculate Age from the first Look For picklist and Age for the second and then click Add.

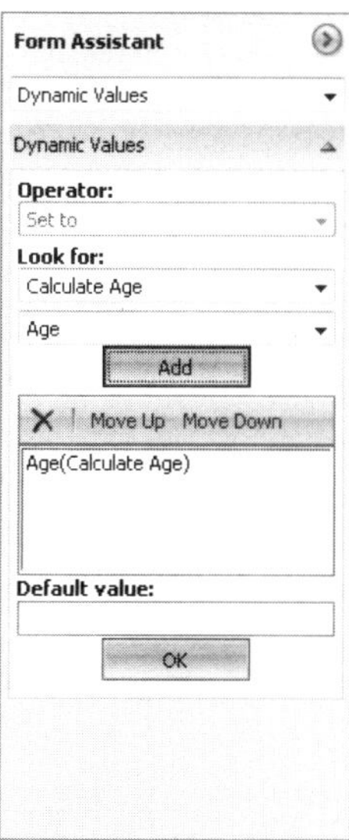

20. Click OK at the bottom of the Form Assistant to add the dynamic value to the subject box. Your Send E-mail properties window should look like this when you are complete:

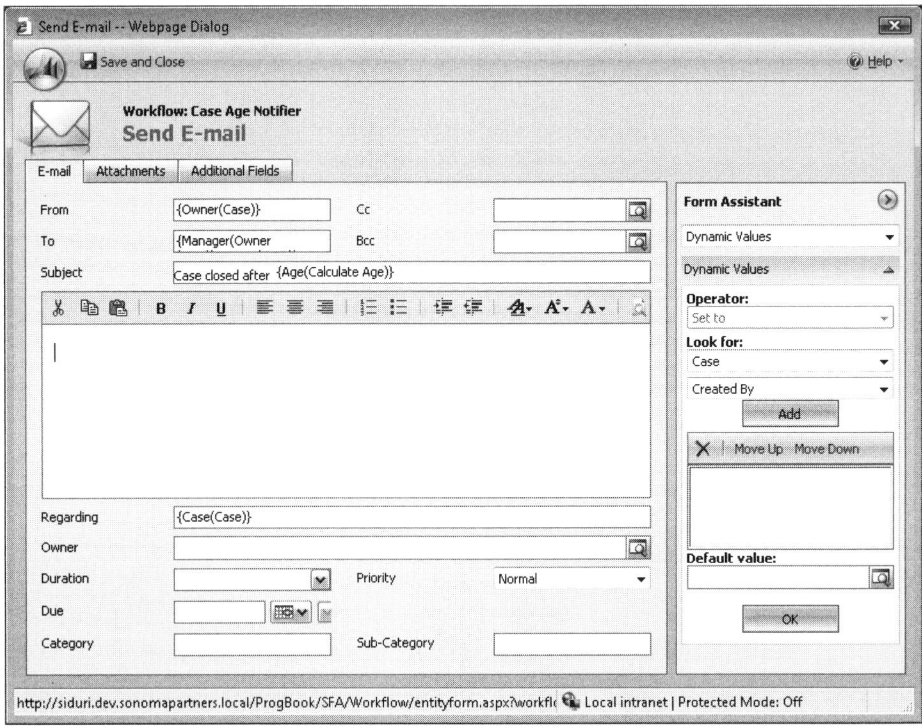

21. Click Save And Close.

Your completed workflow should look like this:

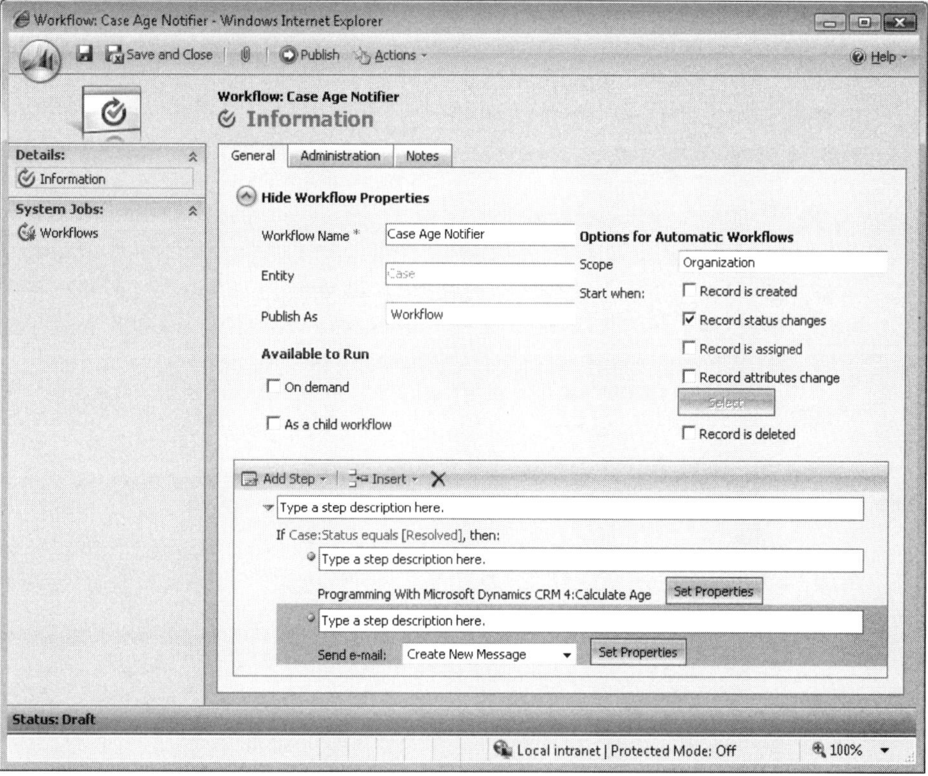

22. Click Publish to publish your workflow.

At this point you should be able to create a test case in the Service area. After resolving it, you (or your manager if you have one set up) should receive an e-mail with the case's age in the subject line.

This sample, although simple, demonstrates some of the flexibility available to you when extending the native workflow functionality within Microsoft Dynamics CRM. In the "CRM Workflow Attributes" section, we'll take a look back at some of the attributes and classes we used to implement this sample and explore them in more detail.

Investigating Custom Activity Errors

When implementing custom activities, you will inevitably come across a workflow that has a status of "Waiting" in the workflow grids. If you open the workflow, you will see a generic error message like this:

> *"An error has occurred. Try this action again. If the problem continues, check the Microsoft Dynamics CRM Community for solutions or contact your organization's Microsoft Dynamics CRM Administrator. Finally, you can contact Microsoft Support."*

A message such as this typically means that an exception has not been handled in your custom activity and the workflow instance has been suspended so that a system administrator can deal with it appropriately. You can use three fairly straightforward techniques to retrieve the exception information from a suspended workflow: Advanced Find, a SQL query, and a *CrmService* query

- Advanced Find is the quickest way to get the additional error information because you can set it up within Microsoft Dynamics CRM itself. Start by basing your Advanced Find view on the Suspended System Jobs view. Next add the *Message* attribute to the columns. You can optionally filter the system jobs to show only workflows. When you run the Advanced Find, the Message column displays the exception information. The only downside to using the Advanced Find technique is that the message information is typically long and not ideal for displaying in a grid column.

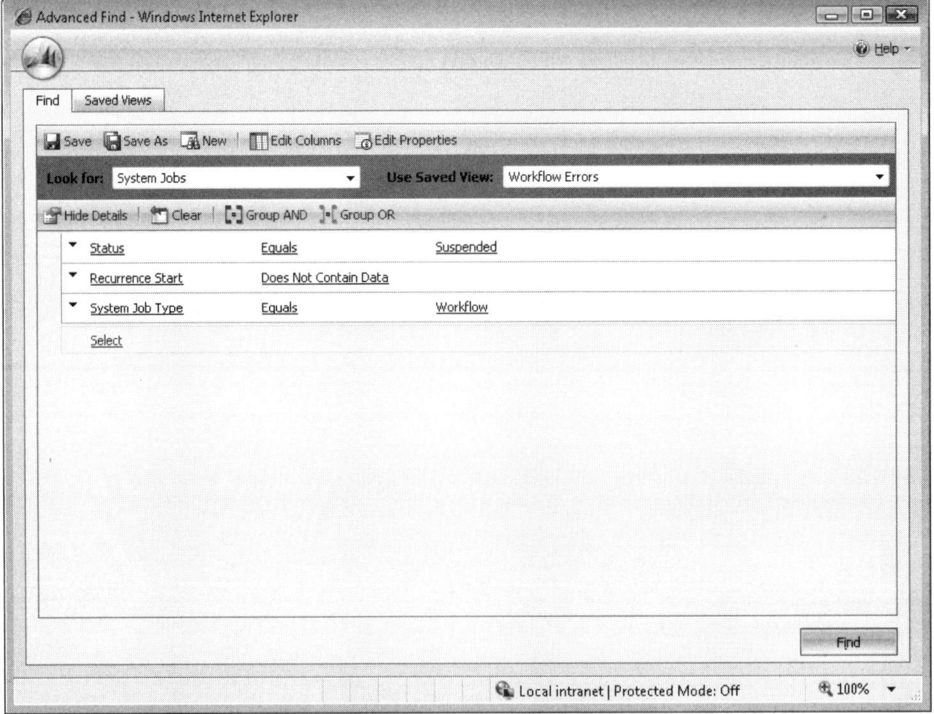

- A SQL query can be a more robust method of retrieving the exception information if you have database access. The following SQL script returns the same information as the Advanced Find query in the first example:

```
SELECT AsyncOperationIdName, ActivityName, Message
FROM WorkflowLog
WHERE status=3
ORDER BY CreatedOn DESC
```

- A CRM query provides a third option for retrieving the exception details. This option might be useful if you are developing a support tool for diagnosing suspended workflows. The following *Query* returns the same error information as the first two methods:

```
QueryByAttribute query = new QueryByAttribute();
query.EntityName = EntityName.workflowlog.ToString();

ColumnSet cols = new ColumnSet();
cols.AddColumns("asyncoperationid", "activityname", "message");
query.ColumnSet = cols;

query.Attributes = new string[] { "status" };
query.Values = new object[] { 3 };
```

All these techniques are valid ways to retrieve the exception information from a workflow instance. Determining which is best suited to your situation is up to you.

CRM Workflow Attributes

As you have seen in the preceding samples, you can apply several attributes to your custom activity classes and dependency properties. Understanding these attributes is critical if you want your custom activities to work correctly the first time they are deployed. The full list of custom workflow attributes is shown in Table 6-6.

TABLE 6-6 CRM-Related Workflow Attributes

Attribute	Applied To	Description
CrmAttributeTarget	*Picklist* or *Status* dependency properties	Used to specify which entity type and attribute can be assigned to the property. This will be used to filter the dynamic values in the Form Assistant and also provide an option to select a specific picklist or status value in the workflow designer for this property.
CrmDefault	Dependency property	Specifies a default value that should be assigned to the property if none is set in the workflow designer.
CrmInput	Dependency property	Used to designate a property that should be used for input. Also used to set the label for the property that will be shown in the workflow designer.
CrmOutput	Dependency property	Used to designate a property that should be used for output. Also used to set the label for the property that will be shown in the workflow designer.
CrmReferenceTarget	Required for *Lookup*, *Customer*, or *Owner* dependency properties	This attribute dictates which type of entity can be assigned to the property. Only the appropriate entity types will be shown in the list of dynamic values in the Form Assistant.
CrmWorkflowActivity	Custom *Activity*-derived classes	This attribute is required for custom activities to be displayed in the workflow designer. Also used to specify the name of the step displayed in the designer's user interface.

Workflow Context

When your custom activity executes, you frequently need information about the current state of the workflow that your dependency properties cannot provide. For example, if you need to know the type of entity the current workflow is executing for, or the message that triggered the workflow, you need something more than the dependency properties. This is where the *ActivityExecutionContext* argument comes in. Passed in to the *Execute* method as an argument, *ActivityExecutionContext* can be used to retrieve information about the workflow or request additional services provided by the host application.

More Info *ActivityExecutionContext* is a class provided by Windows Workflow Foundation that has many capabilities. For more information on the *ActivityExecutionContext* class, please see *http://msdn.microsoft.com/en-us/library/system.workflow.componentmodel.activityexecutioncontext.aspx.*

Because our workflows are going to be specifically for Microsoft Dynamics CRM, we frequently just want to get to the *IWorkflowContext* service, which provides access to the *ICrmService* and *IMetadataService* services as well as details about the primary entity for the workflow. Listing 6-4 shows how to retrieve *IWorkflowContext* within the *Execute* method.

LISTING 6-4 Retrieving the *IWorkflowContext* interface

```
protected override ActivityExecutionStatus Execute(ActivityExecutionContext
    executionContext)
{
    IContextService contextService = executionContext.GetService<IContextService>();
    IWorkflowContext workflowContext = contextService.Context;

    ...

    return ActivityExecutionStatus.Closed;
}
```

As shown, the first step is to retrieve the *IContextService* from the *ActivityExecutionContext* and then access the *IWorkflowContext* from the *IContextService*'s *Context* property. *IWorkflowContext* exposes several methods, most of which are only used by Microsoft Dynamics CRM internally. The six methods and their descriptions are listed in Table 6-7.

TABLE 6-7 *IWorkflowContext's* Methods

Method Name	Description
CreateCrmService	Creates an instance of *ICrmService* that the activity can use to communicate back to CRM
CreateMetadataService	Creates an instance of *IMetadataService* that the activity can use to access CRM's metadata information

TABLE 6-7 ***IWorkflowContext's* Methods**

Method Name	Description
EvaluateCondition	Evaluates a condition based on a primary value, an operator, and a list of values as arguments. Returns a *bool* that represents the result of the evaluation. Typically only used by Microsoft Dynamics CRM.
EvaluateExpression	Evaluates an expression that consists of an operator and a list of values. Returns an *object* that represents the result of the evaluation. Typically only used by Microsoft Dynamics CRM.
PopulateEntitiesFrom	Used internally by Microsoft Dynamics CRM.
RetrieveActivityCount	Retrieves the current number of activities for the primary entity. Typically only used by Microsoft Dynamics CRM.

Of these methods, you will likely only use *CreateCrmService* and *CreateMetadataService*. Both methods come in two flavors: one without any arguments, and one that takes a Boolean argument specifying whether the service should run as the admin user. If you use the parameterless version or pass in *false* to the overloaded version, you will be provided with a service that runs as the current user. By specifying *true* to the overloaded version, you can get a service that runs as the admin user. This allows your custom workflow activities to access data that the workflow owner may not typically have access to.

IWorkflowContext also exposes many properties. Although you may not use several of them frequently or at all, it is good to have a basic understanding of them. Table 6-8 lists the *IWorkflowContext* properties available to custom activities.

TABLE 6-8 ***IWorkflowContext's* Properties**

Property Name	Type	Description
ActivationId	*Guid*	The workflow ID for the currently executing workflow.
AsyncOperationId	*Guid*	The ID for the system job that started the workflow.
EntityDependencies	*Collection<EntityDependency>*	A list of workflow entity dependencies. For more information on workflow dependencies, see Chapter 12.
InputParameters	*PropertyBag*	The input parameters specified by the message that triggered the workflow.
MessageName	*String*	The name of the message that triggered the workflow.
OrganizationId	*Guid*	The ID for the organization the current workflow belongs to.
OutputParameters	*PropertyBag*	The output parameters returned by the core operation from the original execution pipeline.
PluginTypeId	*Guid*	The ID for the compiled workflow type. For more information on the workflow compilation process during publication, see Chapter 12.

TABLE 6-8 *IWorkflowContext's* Properties

Property Name	Type	Description
PrimaryEntityId	*Guid*	The ID for the primary entity instance that triggered the workflow.
PrimaryEntityImage	*DynamicEntity*	A snapshot of the primary entity instance that triggered the workflow. The attributes included in the image are based on the attributes you reference in your workflow steps.
PrimaryEntityName	*String*	The entity name for the primary entity that triggered the workflow.
PrimaryEntityPostImage	*DynamicEntity*	A snapshot of the primary entity instance after the core operation was completed. The attributes included in the image are based on the attributes you reference in your workflow steps.
PrimaryEntityPreImage	*DynamicEntity*	A snapshot of the primary entity instance before the core operation was completed. The attributes included in the image are based on the attributes you reference in your workflow steps.
SharedVariables	*PropertyBag*	A collection that can be used to pass values between custom activities within the same workflow instance.
StageName	*String*	The name of the stage as defined in the native workflow designer.
UserId	*Guid*	The ID of the system user under which the current workflow is executing. In addition, this is the user that will be passed to the Microsoft Dynamics CRM Web service API when calls are made within the workflow.

Although many of these properties have straightforward definitions, the image properties are worth taking a closer look at.

Entity Images in Custom Workflow Activities

In Chapter 5 we discussed entity images as they pertain to plug-ins. You use entity images with plug-ins to get attribute values from an entity that would otherwise not be available. For instance, you can get attribute values on an entity that has already been deleted by registering for a pre-image in a plug-in. When registering a plug-in, you specify which images you want and which attributes should be included within it.

However, with workflows you cannot specify which images and entities to include when using the native workflow designer. The image registration information is determined by the messages that can trigger a workflow as well as which attributes are referenced within the various workflow steps.

More Info The images and attributes to include are stored in an entity named *workflowdependency*. See Chapter 12 for a full explanation of this entity.

Creating an Entity Image Debugging Activity

To understand which entities and attributes are included in a workflow, it can be useful to implement a debugging activity. We will create the *DebugEntityImagesActivity* to demonstrate this concept.

Use the steps previously outlined in this chapter to add a class named *DebugEntityImagesActivity* to the ProgrammingWithDynamicsCrm4.Workflow project. Replace the code in the newly added DebugEntityImagesActivity.cs with the contents of Listing 6-5.

LISTING 6-5 Start of the *DebugEntityImagesActivity* class

```
using System;
using System.IO;
using System.Reflection;
using System.Workflow.ComponentModel;
using Microsoft.Crm.Sdk;
using Microsoft.Crm.Workflow;

namespace ProgrammingWithDynamicsCrm4.Workflow
{
    [CrmWorkflowActivity("Debug Entity Images", "Debug")]
    public class DebugEntityImagesActivity: Activity
    {
    }
}
```

Similar to our previous example, we start with a class that inherits from *Activity* and apply the *CrmWorkflowActivity* attribute to provide a suitable display name and folder for our custom activity. Next we'll add a single dependency property to allow the user to specify an output text file to capture the information we extract from the entity images. Listing 6-6 shows the *OutputFileName* property implementation.

LISTING 6-6 *DebugEntityImagesActivity's OutputFileName* property

```
public static DependencyProperty OutputFileNameProperty =
    DependencyProperty.Register("OutputFileName", typeof(string),
    typeof(DebugEntityImagesActivity));

[CrmInput("Ouput File Name")]
public string OutputFileName
{
    get { return (string)GetValue(OutputFileNameProperty); }
    set { SetValue(OutputFileNameProperty, value); }
}
```

By this point, this should be nothing new. *OutputFileName* is a simple dependency property that is marked to be used as an input property within the Microsoft Dynamics CRM workflow designer. Next, we'll override the *Execute* method as shown in Listing 6-7.

LISTING 6-7 *DebugEntityImagesActivity's Execute* method

```
protected override ActivityExecutionStatus Execute(
    ActivityExecutionContext executionContext)
{
    if (!String.IsNullOrEmpty(this.OutputFileName))
    {
        IContextService contextService =
            executionContext.GetService<IContextService>();
        IWorkflowContext workflowContext = contextService.Context;

        using (StreamWriter output = File.AppendText(this.OutputFileName))
        {
            output.WriteLine(DateTime.Now);

            SerializeDynamicEntity(output,
                "PrimaryEntityImage", workflowContext.PrimaryEntityImage);

            SerializeDynamicEntity(output,
                "PrimaryEntityPreImage", workflowContext.PrimaryEntityPreImage);

            SerializeDynamicEntity(output,
                "PrimaryEntityPostImage", workflowContext.PrimaryEntityPostImage);
        }
    }

    return ActivityExecutionStatus.Closed;
}
```

The *Execute* method opens a text file for appending and serializes the current date and time into it. The method continues by calling *SerializeDynamicEntity* for each of the three entity image properties on the workflow context. Listing 6-8 shows the source code for the *SerializeDynamicEntity* method.

LISTING 6-8 The *SerializeDynamicEntity* method

```
private void SerializeDynamicEntity(
    TextWriter output, string title, DynamicEntity dynamicEntity)
{
    if (dynamicEntity == null)
    {
        output.WriteLine("{0}: (null)", title);
    }
    else
    {
        output.WriteLine("{0}:", title);
        output.WriteLine("{");
```

```
        foreach (Property prop in dynamicEntity.Properties)
        {
            output.Write("    {0}: ", prop.Name);
            SerializePropertyValue(output, dynamicEntity[prop.Name]);
            output.WriteLine();
        }

        output.WriteLine("}");
    }
}
```

SerializeDynamicEntity is responsible for converting a *DynamicEntity* to text and serializing it to the output stream. This fairly straightforward implementation is dependent on the *SerializePropertyValue* method to convert the various property values to a string. The implementation of *SerializePropertyValue* is shown in Listing 6-9.

LISTING 6-9 The *SerializePropertyValue* method

```
private void SerializePropertyValue(TextWriter output, object value)
{
    if (value == null)
    {
        output.Write("(null)");
    }
    else
    {
        PropertyInfo nameProperty = value.GetType().GetProperty("name");

        if (nameProperty != null && nameProperty.PropertyType == typeof(string))
        {
            output.Write("{0} ", nameProperty.GetValue(value, null));
        }

        PropertyInfo valueProperty = value.GetType().GetProperty("Value");
        if (valueProperty != null)
        {
            output.Write(valueProperty.GetValue(value, null));
        }
        else
        {
            output.Write(value);
        }
    }
}
```

SerializePropertyValue uses reflection to transform the property values into a string. Because most of the Microsoft Dynamics CRM types (such as *CrmNumber, CrmDateTime,* and *CrmBoolean*) have a *Value* property, we can use reflection to get the property by name without having to know the actual property type. Likewise, we look for a *name* property to output as well, because types such as *Picklist*, *Lookup*, and *Customer* include the display name of the referenced entity instance in addition to the ID. Finally, in case the value is a standard Microsoft .NET Framework type and does not have a *Value* property, we output it directly. This will most commonly cover string values.

At this point you should be able to compile and deploy the activity assembly using the steps previously outlined in this chapter. Next we will create a workflow to determine how the entity images are populated based on the message and workflow steps.

Using the *DebugEntityImagesActivity*

To use the *DebugEntityImagesActivity*, we'll need to create a new workflow that includes a step for our custom activity. Using the steps previously defined in this chapter, create a workflow definition named Debug Images for the account entity that runs automatically whenever an account is created. Add our custom step, Debug Entity Images, as the only step in the workflow. Update the properties for the step to specify a file where the debug information will be written. The file does not need to exist, but the Microsoft CRM Asynchronous Processing Service must have write access to the folder. By default, the service runs as the Network Service user. When you are finished, your workflow should resemble Figure 6-5.

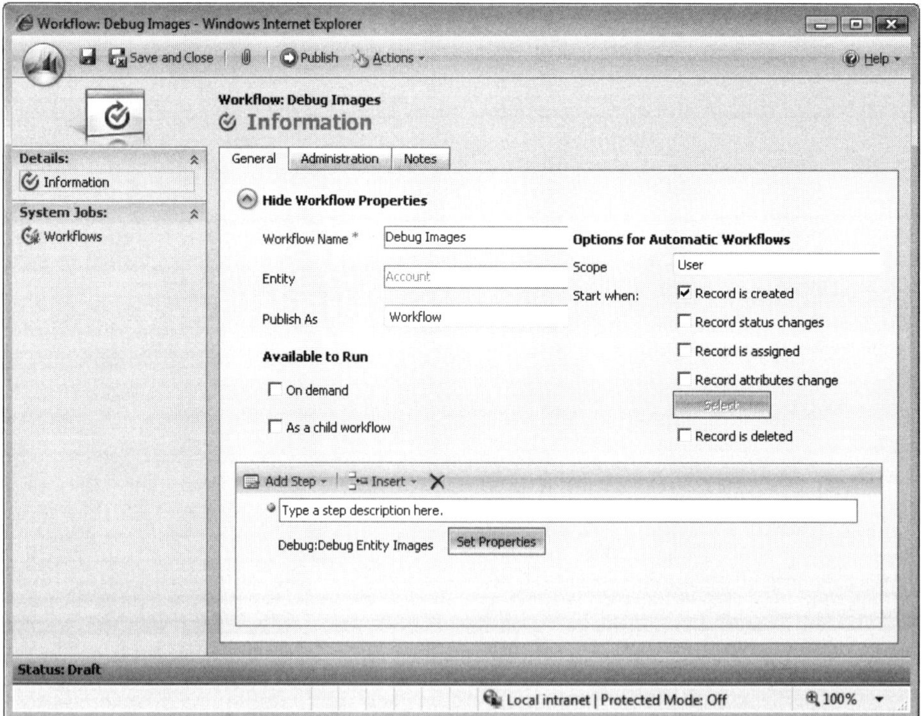

FIGURE 6-5 A workflow to test the *DebugEntityImagesActivity*

Once you publish the workflow, create an account, specifying **Test** as the account name. After you save the account, the output file you specified on the custom workflow step should be updated within a few seconds. Once it is updated, you will likely see something like the following upon opening it:

```
7/22/2008 8:28:50 PM
PrimaryEntityImage:
{
    name: Test
    accountid: c6a6b6ab-5658-dd11-b751-0019b9f8f548
    owningbusinessunit:  23da3575-181d-dd11-8839-0019b9f8f548
}
PrimaryEntityPreImage: (null)
PrimaryEntityPostImage:
{
    accountid: c6a6b6ab-5658-dd11-b751-0019b9f8f548
    ownerid: Corey O'Brien 237d2b4e-191d-dd11-8839-0019b9f8f548
    owningbusinessunit:  23da3575-181d-dd11-8839-0019b9f8f548
}
```

Although the details will be different in your output file, you should have the exact same attributes included. Based on this output, it would appear that for the Create message, Microsoft Dynamics CRM is including a post-image and minimal attributes. It makes sense that the pre-image is null, because as we learned in Chapter 5, the Create message cannot supply a pre-image.

Let's take a look at what happens when we handle an Update message. Unpublish your workflow and change it to also run automatically when the record attributes change. Specify Account Name and Account Number as the attributes to monitor. Once you publish the workflow, open the Test account that you created previously. Change the name to **Test 2**, specify an account number of **IL-123456**, and then save the account. Once your workflow runs, you should have a new entry at the bottom of your output file similar to the following:

```
7/22/2008 9:42:08 PM
PrimaryEntityImage:
{
    name: Test
    accountid: c6a6b6ab-5658-dd11-b751-0019b9f8f548
    owningbusinessunit:  23da3575-181d-dd11-8839-0019b9f8f548
}
PrimaryEntityPreImage:
{
    accountid: c6a6b6ab-5658-dd11-b751-0019b9f8f548
    ownerid: Corey O'Brien 237d2b4e-191d-dd11-8839-0019b9f8f548
    owningbusinessunit:  23da3575-181d-dd11-8839-0019b9f8f548
    name: Test 2
}
PrimaryEntityPostImage:
{
    accountid: c6a6b6ab-5658-dd11-b751-0019b9f8f548
    ownerid: Corey O'Brien 237d2b4e-191d-dd11-8839-0019b9f8f548
    owningbusinessunit:  23da3575-181d-dd11-8839-0019b9f8f548
}
```

Now we have a pre-image, but why isn't the *accountnumber* attribute included in any of the images? The *accountnumber* attribute isn't included because Microsoft Dynamics CRM examines the workflow steps to determine which attributes are accessed by the workflow. Because it does not see a reference to *accountnumber*, it does not create a workflow dependency to include it in the image.

To prove this point, let's edit the workflow one more time and reference *accountnumber*. Unpublish the workflow and add a Check Condition step after the existing Debug Entity Images step. Specify the condition to simply check that the account number contains data. The condition page should look like Figure 6-6 when you are finished.

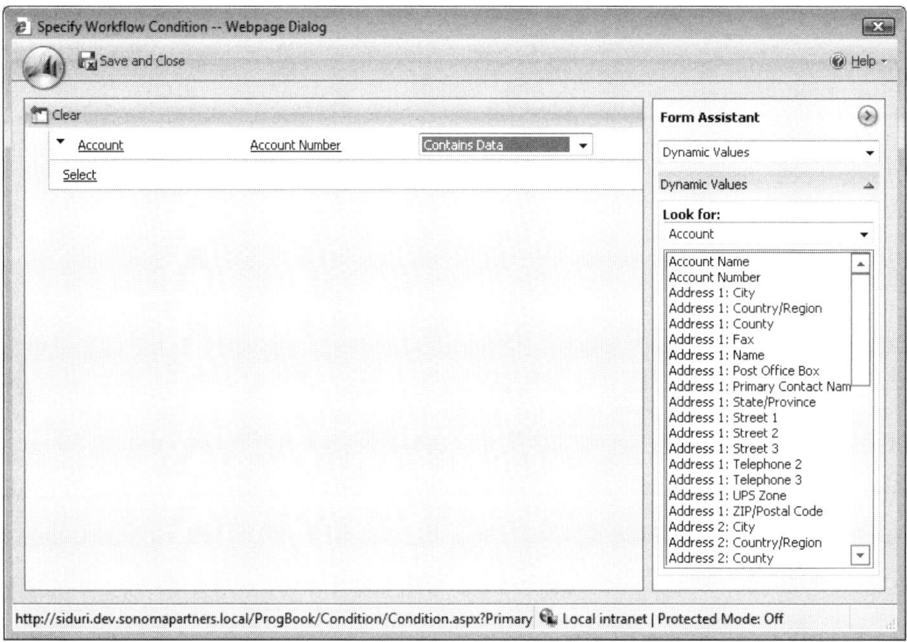

FIGURE 6-6 Referencing the account number attribute

Save the condition and then publish the workflow. Notice that we did not specify a step to execute if the condition evaluates to true. Next, edit the Test 2 account and change the account number to **MI-654321**. After you save the account and the workflow runs, open your output file and examine the results. You should see a new entry at the bottom similar to the following:

```
7/22/2008 9:56:56 PM
PrimaryEntityImage:
{
    name: Test 2
    accountnumber: MI-654321
    accountid: c6a6b6ab-5658-dd11-b751-0019b9f8f548
    owningbusinessunit:  23da3575-181d-dd11-8839-0019b9f8f548
}
```

```
PrimaryEntityPreImage:
{
    accountid: c6a6b6ab-5658-dd11-b751-0019b9f8f548
    ownerid: Corey O'Brien 237d2b4e-191d-dd11-8839-0019b9f8f548
    owningbusinessunit:  23da3575-181d-dd11-8839-0019b9f8f548
    name: Test 2
    accountnumber: IL-123456
}
PrimaryEntityPostImage:
{
    accountid: c6a6b6ab-5658-dd11-b751-0019b9f8f548
    ownerid: Corey O'Brien 237d2b4e-191d-dd11-8839-0019b9f8f548
    owningbusinessunit:  23da3575-181d-dd11-8839-0019b9f8f548
}
```

Now we can see that the *accountnumber* attribute is included in the images even though we didn't do anything more than add a step to see if it contained data. By referencing a property in a condition or as a dynamic value within a workflow, you can guarantee it will be included in the entity images and therefore available to your custom activities. In Chapter 12 we will examine setting up your own workflows and workflow dependencies from scratch without the Microsoft Dynamics CRM workflow designer. If, however, you prefer to design your workflows natively, you can use the *DebugEntityImagesActivity* to discover how Microsoft Dynamics CRM registers for images based on the message and workflow steps defined.

Workflow Designer Limitations

As powerful and flexible as the Microsoft Dynamics CRM workflow designer is, it does have a few limitations. For example, only the following preset list of property types can be assigned values in the designer:

- *CrmBoolean*
- *CrmDateTime*
- *CrmDecimal*
- *CrmFloat*
- *CrmMoney*
- *CrmNumber*
- *Customer*
- *Lookup*
- *Owner*
- *Picklist*
- *Status*
- *String*

In addition, although you can create composite activities—activities that can contain one or more child activities—the designer does not allow you to add child activities to them. For example, if you want to make a custom activity that continues to execute a list of child activities until an input parameter evaluates to true, you have to define the list of child activities at compile time, because the designer does not allow you to add child steps within a custom activity.

Example Activities: Math Building Blocks

When designing custom workflow activities, you will find that they tend to fall into one of two categories. Either they are generic building blocks that can be used by a variety of workflows, or they are extremely specialized and only suited to the task they were originally designed for. Whenever possible, try to design your custom activities to be reusable across workflows. This may mean that you end up implementing multiple smaller activities, but the users that take advantage of your activities will thank you for the flexibility.

In this example, we will demonstrate how a series of simple activities can provide a more flexible workflow design environment. Listing 6-10 shows the full definition of the *AddValuesActivity*.

LISTING 6-10 *AddValuesActivity* source

```
using System.Workflow.ComponentModel;
using Microsoft.Crm.Sdk;
using Microsoft.Crm.Workflow;

namespace ProgrammingWithDynamicsCrm4.Workflow
{
    [CrmWorkflowActivity("Add Values", "Math")]
    public class AddValuesActivity: Activity
    {
        public static DependencyProperty ValueAProperty =
           DependencyProperty.Register(
           "ValueA", typeof(CrmFloat), typeof(AddValuesActivity));

        [CrmInput("Value A")]
        [CrmDefault("0")]
        public CrmFloat ValueA
        {
            get { return (CrmFloat)GetValue(ValueAProperty); }
            set { SetValue(ValueAProperty, value); }
        }

        public static DependencyProperty ValueBProperty =
            DependencyProperty.Register(
            "ValueB", typeof(CrmFloat), typeof(AddValuesActivity));

        [CrmInput("Value B")]
        [CrmDefault("0")]
```

```
        public CrmFloat ValueB
        {
            get { return (CrmFloat)GetValue(ValueBProperty); }
            set { SetValue(ValueBProperty, value); }
        }

        public static DependencyProperty ResultProperty =
            DependencyProperty.Register(
            "Result", typeof(CrmFloat), typeof(AddValuesActivity));

        [CrmOutput("Result")]
        public CrmFloat Result
        {
            get { return (CrmFloat)GetValue(ResultProperty); }
            set { SetValue(ResultProperty, value); }
        }

        protected override ActivityExecutionStatus Execute(
            ActivityExecutionContext executionContext)
        {
            double a = 0;

            if (this.ValueA != null)
            {
                a = this.ValueA.Value;
            }

            double b = 0;
            if (this.ValueB != null)
            {
                b = this.ValueB.Value;
            }

            this.Result = new CrmFloat(a + b);

            return ActivityExecutionStatus.Closed;
        }
    }
}
```

This sample uses techniques discussed throughout the chapter to build a simple activity that can be used to add two numbers together and expose the result through an output property. Even though this example uses *CrmFloat* as the input and output properties, the native workflow designer is smart enough to convert other numerical types such as integers and currency into and out of the *CrmFloat* correctly.

Using this example, you could easily build a series of activities to perform various mathematical operations. At that point, you could configure a workflow to pass the results of one math activity in as the input values to another math activity. By chaining these activities together, you can perform complex accounting formulas to update an attribute on an entity. By keeping the scope of your custom workflow activities simple, you can provide the users that design workflows with a powerful toolset.

Example Activity: Retrieve Most Available User

Now that you have a better understanding of some of the more advanced concepts in custom activity development, we can look at a real-world example that comes up frequently. Often, business users define a process that is used to assign leads to salespeople or cases to support staff. The process varies from organization to organization, but regardless of what it is, it can usually be accomplished using a custom workflow activity.

To demonstrate, we'll create an activity called *RetrieveMostAvailableUserActivity*. Our implementation focuses on retrieving the most available user based on the user's current case load. These concepts could just as easily be applied to the user with the fewest leads assigned or any other entity for that matter. In addition, we'll allow the person designing the workflow to optionally specify a Team to constrain the list of users examined to a smaller set. To start, add a new class named *RetrieveMostAvailableUserActivity* to the ProgrammingWithDynamicsCrm4.Workflow project. Stub out the contents of this new class to match Listing 6-11.

LISTING 6-11 Start of the *RetrieveMostAvailableUserActivity* class

```
using System;
using System.Collections.Generic;
using System.Workflow.ComponentModel;
using System.Xml;
using Microsoft.Crm.Sdk;
using Microsoft.Crm.Sdk.Query;
using Microsoft.Crm.SdkTypeProxy;
using Microsoft.Crm.Workflow;

namespace ProgrammingWithDynamicsCrm4.Workflow
{
    [CrmWorkflowActivity("Retrieve Most Available User",
        "Programming Microsoft CRM 4")]
    public class RetrieveMostAvailableUserActivity : Activity
    {

    }
}
```

By now you should be familiar with this starting point. We have a class derived from *Activity* that is decorated with the *CrmWorkflowActivity* attribute to define the human-readable name of the activity.

Next, we define the dependency properties we need. Insert the code shown in Listing 6-12 into *RetrieveMostAvailableUserActivity*'s definition.

LISTING 6-12 *RetrieveMostAvailableUserActivity*'s dependency properties

```
public static DependencyProperty TeamProperty =
    DependencyProperty.Register("Team", typeof(Lookup),
    typeof(RetrieveMostAvailableUserActivity));

[CrmInput("Team")]
[CrmReferenceTarget("team")]
public Lookup Team
{
    get { return (Lookup)GetValue(TeamProperty); }
    set { SetValue(TeamProperty, value); }
}

public static DependencyProperty MostAvailableUserProperty =
    DependencyProperty.Register("MostAvailableUser", typeof(Lookup),
    typeof(RetrieveMostAvailableUserActivity));

[CrmOutput("Most Available User")]
[CrmReferenceTarget("systemuser")]
public Lookup MostAvailableUser
{
    get { return (Lookup)GetValue(MostAvailableUserProperty); }
    set { SetValue(MostAvailableUserProperty, value); }
}
```

Here we're adding two properties, *Team* and *MostAvailableUser*. *Team* is an input property and is optionally used to limit the set of users evaluated. The *CrmInput* attribute specifies that the property is used for input and defines the human-readable name for it, while the *CrmReferenceTarget* attribute tells Microsoft Dynamics CRM that this *Lookup* property only accepts references to the *team* entity. Similarly, we specify that the *MostAvailableUser* property is used for output and that it only references *systemuser* entities.

With our dependency properties in place, we are ready to move on and define the *Execute* method. Place the code shown in Listing 6-13 beneath the dependency properties, but still within the *RetrieveMostAvailableUserActivity* definition.

LISTING 6-13 *RetrieveMostAvailableUserActivity*'s *Execute* method

```
protected override ActivityExecutionStatus Execute(
    ActivityExecutionContext executionContext)
{
    IContextService contextService = executionContext.GetService<IContextService>();
    IWorkflowContext workflowContext = contextService.Context;
    ICrmService crmService = workflowContext.CreateCrmService(true);
```

```
        List<systemuser> users = RetrieveSystemUsers(crmService);
        systemuser mostAvailableUser = RetrieveMostAvailableUser(crmService, users);

        if (mostAvailableUser != null)
        {
            this.MostAvailableUser = new Lookup(
                EntityName.systemuser.ToString(),
                mostAvailableUser.systemuserid.Value);
        }

        return ActivityExecutionStatus.Closed;
    }
```

Our *Execute* method starts by obtaining an *IWorkflowContext* using the technique shown earlier in the chapter. However, notice that it passes in *true* for the *runAsAdmin* argument. Because we are accessing records that the workflow user may not have access to in order to determine the most available user, we need to elevate the *CrmService* calls to run as the admin user. We then proceed to call two methods to first retrieve the list of potential users and then determine which of those users is the most available to take on an additional case. Finally, if a user is found, we assign that user to our *MostAvailableUser* output property.

Let's continue by looking at the *RetrieveSystemUsers* method. Listing 6-14 displays the implementation.

LISTING 6-14 The *RetrieveSystemUsers* method

```
    private List<systemuser> RetrieveSystemUsers(ICrmService crmService)
    {
        QueryExpression query = new QueryExpression();

        ColumnSet cols = new ColumnSet();
        cols.AddColumns("systemuserid", "fullname");
        query.ColumnSet = cols;

        query.EntityName = EntityName.systemuser.ToString();

        if (this.Team != null)
        {
            LinkEntity teamMembershipLink = query.AddLink(
                "teammembership", "systemuserid", "systemuserid");

            teamMembershipLink.LinkCriteria.AddCondition(
                "teamid", ConditionOperator.Equal, this.Team.Value);
        }

        RetrieveMultipleRequest request = new RetrieveMultipleRequest();
        request.Query = query;

        RetrieveMultipleResponse response =
            (RetrieveMultipleResponse)crmService.Execute(request);
```

```
    List<systemuser> users = new List<systemuser>();
    foreach (systemuser user in response.BusinessEntityCollection.BusinessEntities)
    {
        users.Add(user);
    }

    return users;
}
```

RetrieveSystemUsers is fairly straightforward. It sets up a *RetrieveMultipleRequest* and executes it using the *ICrmService* passed in to it. It then extracts the *systemuser* entities from the response and puts them into a list, which is returned. The only part of this method that might warrant a little more explanation is the filtering by team. If the *Team* input property is defined, the query is joined to the *teammembership* intersect table, which has a *teamid* attribute that can be used to return only the users who belong to a particular team.

Now that we have our list of potential users, we need to determine which of them has the lightest case load. This is what the *RetrieveMostAvailableUser* method is designed to accomplish. Listing 6-15 shows its definition.

LISTING 6-15 The *RetrieveMostAvailableUser* method

```
private systemuser RetrieveMostAvailableUser(
    ICrmService crmService, List<systemuser> users)
{
    systemuser mostAvailableUser = null;

    int leastCases = int.MaxValue;

    foreach (systemuser user in users)
    {
        int count = RetrieveCaseCountForUser(crmService, user.systemuserid.Value);

        if (count == 0)
        {
            mostAvailableUser = user;
            break;
        }
        else if (count < leastCases)
        {
            mostAvailableUser = user;
            leastCases = count;
        }
    }

    return mostAvailableUser;
}
```

RetrieveMostAvailableUser simply iterates through the list of potential users and calls *RetrieveCaseCountForUser* for each of them. As it loops through the users, it keeps track of the user with the lowest case count and returns that user at the end. If at any point a user with zero cases is found, the method stops looping through the users because there cannot be a user with fewer than zero cases.

Real World If you are a seasoned relational database veteran, you are no doubt groaning at this point about the use of multiple queries to calculate the user with the lowest case load. While this would be trivial to achieve using *GROUP BY* and *COUNT* statements in SQL, part of the purpose of this example is to demonstrate how to interact with *ICrmService* within a custom workflow activity. Unfortunately, *ICrmService* has very limited access to any sort of aggregate functionality. As an alternative to an aggregate function, you could retrieve all cases that belong to any of the users on the team using a *QueryExpression* with *ConditionOperator.In* and the array of user IDs. This would reduce the number of service calls, but would potentially retrieve a lot of records that you would need to iterate through to calculate the case count per user.

If you want to write an activity that accesses the filtered views in CRM, you certainly can. Take a look at the Filtered Views Sample Code topic within the CRM SDK for an example of how to connect to the CRM database.

The only method left to look at now is *RetrieveCaseCountForUser*. Listing 6-16 shows the definition of *RetrieveCaseCountForUser*.

LISTING 6-16 The *RetrieveCaseCountForUser* method

```
private int RetrieveCaseCountForUser(ICrmService crmService, Guid userId)
{
    string fetchXml = String.Format(@"
            <fetch mapping='logical' aggregate='true'>
                <entity name='incident'>
                    <attribute name='incidentid' aggregate='count' alias='count' />
                    <filter type='and'>
                        <condition attribute='ownerid' operator='eq' value='{0}' />
                        <condition attribute='statecode' operator='eq' value='0' />
                    </filter>
                </entity>
            </fetch>",
        userId);

    XmlDocument resultsDoc = new XmlDocument();
    resultsDoc.LoadXml(crmService.Fetch(fetchXml));

    XmlNode countNode = resultsDoc.SelectSingleNode("//count/text()");
    int count = int.Parse(countNode.Value);
    return count;
}
```

The limited aggregate functionality supported by the CRM services is exposed through the *Fetch* method of *ICrmService*. We prepare our fetch statement by initializing a string with XML that filters cases based on the user's ID and an active *statecode* attribute. By specifying *aggregate='true'* on the fetch node and *aggregate='count'* on the attribute node, we tell

CRM to return the count of entities that match the given criteria. The *Fetch* method returns a string containing something like the following:

```
<resultset morerecords="0"><result><count>71</count></result></resultset>
```

We can now use a simple XPath statement to return the text of the *count* node, which is the number of active cases assigned to the specified user.

After compiling and deploying this example, you should be able to configure a workflow to automatically assign newly created cases to the user with the lightest case load. It might also be a good idea to mark the workflow as available to run on demand, so that a case could easily be reassigned using the workflow's logic manually as well as automatically. Although the logic used to determine the user to assign a case or lead to may differ, by using the techniques shown in this example you can create a flexible activity that you can use in multiple workflows.

Example Activity: Calculate Related Aggregate

Our last example tackles a more complicated real-world request. Eventually you will be asked to store a value on a parent entity that is calculated from values in the related child entities. Frequently these calculated values are simple aggregates, such as the count of child entities or perhaps a sum of some attribute on the child entities. For example, you might be asked to populate a custom attribute named *new_assignedleadcount* on the *systemuser* entity with the number of leads owned by that user. In addition, you might need to keep track of the average revenue of those leads in another custom attribute on the *systemuser* named *new_averageleadrevenue*.

Because these aggregate values typically do not need to be calculated synchronously, they are good candidates to be updated in a workflow. We'll implement a custom activity called *CalculateRelatedAggregateActivity* that can iterate through related entities and expose the aggregate values in output properties. We'll start by preparing the now-familiar custom activity class template as shown in Listing 6-17.

LISTING 6-17 The beginning of the *CalculateRelatedAggregateActivity* class

```
using System;
using System.Collections.Generic;
using System.Reflection;
using System.Workflow.ComponentModel;
using Microsoft.Crm.Sdk;
using Microsoft.Crm.Sdk.Metadata;
using Microsoft.Crm.Sdk.Query;
using Microsoft.Crm.SdkTypeProxy;
using Microsoft.Crm.SdkTypeProxy.Metadata;
using Microsoft.Crm.Workflow;
```

```
namespace ProgrammingWithDynamicsCrm4.Workflow
{
    [CrmWorkflowActivity("Calculate Related Aggregate",
        "Programming Microsoft CRM 4")]
    public class CalculateRelatedAggregateActivity: Activity
    {
    }
}
```

At this point, there is nothing new. As usual, we'll continue by adding our dependency properties. Because *CalculateRelatedAggregateActivity* has a lot of dependency properties and their use is more complex, we'll start by just adding the input properties as shown in Listing 6-18.

LISTING 6-18 *CalculateRelatedAggregateActivity*'s input properties

```
public static DependencyProperty RelationshipNameProperty =
    DependencyProperty.Register("RelationshipName", typeof(string),
    typeof(CalculateRelatedAggregateActivity));

[CrmInput("Relationship Name")]
public string RelationshipName
{
    get { return (string)GetValue(RelationshipNameProperty); }
    set { SetValue(RelationshipNameProperty, value); }
}

public static DependencyProperty IncludeInactiveRecordsProperty =
    DependencyProperty.Register("IncludeInactiveRecords", typeof(CrmBoolean),
    typeof(CalculateRelatedAggregateActivity));

[CrmDefault("false")]
[CrmInput("Include Inactive Records")]
public CrmBoolean IncludeInactiveRecords
{
    get { return (CrmBoolean)GetValue(IncludeInactiveRecordsProperty); }
    set { SetValue(IncludeInactiveRecordsProperty, value); }
}

public static readonly DependencyProperty PrimaryEntityIsParentProperty =
    DependencyProperty.Register("PrimaryEntityIsParent", typeof(CrmBoolean),
    typeof(CalculateRelatedAggregateActivity));

[CrmDefault("false")]
[CrmInput("Primary Entity Is Parent")]
public CrmBoolean PrimaryEntityIsParent
{
    get { return (CrmBoolean)GetValue(PrimaryEntityIsParentProperty); }
    set { SetValue(PrimaryEntityIsParentProperty, value); }
}
```

```
public static readonly DependencyProperty UsePreImageProperty =
    DependencyProperty.Register("UsePreImage", typeof(CrmBoolean),
    typeof(CalculateRelatedAggregateActivity));

public CrmBoolean UsePreImage
{
    get { return (CrmBoolean)GetValue(UsePreImageProperty); }
    set { SetValue(UsePreImageProperty, value); }
}

public static readonly DependencyProperty SumAttributeProperty =
    DependencyProperty.Register("SumAttribute", typeof(string),
    typeof(CalculateRelatedAggregateActivity));

[CrmInput("Sum Attribute")]
public string SumAttribute
{
    get { return (string)GetValue(SumAttributeProperty); }
    set { SetValue(SumAttributeProperty, value); }
}

public static readonly DependencyProperty AverageAttributeProperty =
    DependencyProperty.Register("AverageAttribute", typeof(string),
    typeof(CalculateRelatedAggregateActivity));

[CrmInput("Average Attribute")]
public string AverageAttribute
{
    get { return (string)GetValue(AverageAttributeProperty); }
    set { SetValue(AverageAttributeProperty, value); }
}
```

We added six input properties: *RelationshipName*, *IncludeInactiveRecords*, *PrimaryEntityIsParent*, *UsePreImage*, *SumAttribute*, and *AverageAttribute*.

- *RelationshipName* is the schema name for the relationship that ties the two entities together. You can get the relationship's schema name by opening the parent entity definition from the Customize Entities view in Microsoft Dynamics CRM and clicking the 1:N Relationships area. For the example mentioned earlier, *systemuser* is related to *lead* through the relationship with a schema name of lead_owning_user.
- *IncludeInactiveRecords* is a Boolean property used to indicate whether inactive records should be included in the calculation.
- *PrimaryEntityIsParent* is also a Boolean property, but it is used to indicate whether the workflow's primary entity is the parent or child in the relationship. This property is necessary because an entity can be self-referential in Microsoft Dynamics CRM 4.0. Most often, your workflows will be associated with the child entity in the relationship, so you will be able to leave this set at the default value of false.

- *UsePreImage* is a Boolean property that can be used to indicate that the parent ID should be retrieved from the pre-image instead of the current entity instance. You set this property to true if you need to update a parent entity that just had a child associated with a new parent. You could then include two *CalculateRelatedAggregateActivity* steps: one to update the old parent entity and one to update the new parent. This property is ignored if *PrimaryEntityIsParent* is true.
- *SumAttribute* can be used to indicate the name of the child attribute that should be summed.
- *AverageAttribute* can be used to indicate the name of the child attribute that should be averaged.

Next we'll define the output properties, which are shown in Listing 6-19.

LISTING 6-19 *CalculateRelatedAggregateActivity*'s output properties

```
public static DependencyProperty CountProperty = DependencyProperty.Register(
    "Count", typeof(CrmNumber), typeof(CalculateRelatedAggregateActivity));

[CrmOutput("Count")]
public CrmNumber Count
{
    get { return (CrmNumber)GetValue(CountProperty); }
    set { SetValue(CountProperty, value); }
}

public static DependencyProperty SumProperty = DependencyProperty.Register(
    "Sum", typeof(CrmFloat), typeof(CalculateRelatedAggregateActivity));

[CrmOutput("Sum")]
public CrmFloat Sum
{
    get { return (CrmFloat)GetValue(SumProperty); }
    set { SetValue(SumProperty, value); }
}

public static DependencyProperty AverageProperty = DependencyProperty.Register(
    "Average", typeof(CrmFloat), typeof(CalculateRelatedAggregateActivity));

[CrmOutput("Average")]
public CrmFloat Average
{
    get { return (CrmFloat)GetValue(AverageProperty); }
    set { SetValue(AverageProperty, value); }
}
```

All three of the output properties are used to return the aggregate results. As you might guess, *Count* is set to the number of child entities, while *Sum* contains the sum of the attribute specified by *SumAttribute*, and *Average* contains the average of the attribute specified by *AverageAttribute*. *Count* will always be populated, but *Sum* and *Average* are only populated if the corresponding input property was set to specify an attribute name. Next we'll take a look at the *Execute* method, shown in Listing 6-20.

LISTING 6-20 *CalculateRelatedAggregateActivity's Execute* method

```
protected override ActivityExecutionStatus Execute(
    ActivityExecutionContext executionContext)
{
    if (!String.IsNullOrEmpty(this.RelationshipName))
    {
        if (this.PrimaryEntityIsParent == null)
        {
            this.PrimaryEntityIsParent = new CrmBoolean(false);
        }

        if (this.IncludeInactiveRecords == null)
        {
            this.IncludeInactiveRecords = new CrmBoolean(false);
        }

        if (this.UsePreImage == null)
        {
            this.UsePreImage = new CrmBoolean(false);
        }

        IContextService contextService =
            executionContext.GetService<IContextService>();
        IWorkflowContext workflowContext = contextService.Context;

        List<DynamicEntity> relatedEntities = GetRelatedEntities(workflowContext);
        RollUpEntities(relatedEntities);

    }
    return ActivityExecutionStatus.Closed;
}
```

Execute starts by setting up some simple defaults for properties, and then calls *GetRelatedEntities* to get a list of the child entities. It passes this list to *RollUpEntities*, which is responsible for calculating the aggregates. We'll take a look at *GetRelatedEntities* first, which is shown in Listing 6-21.

LISTING 6-21 The *GetRelatedEntities* method

```
private List<DynamicEntity> GetRelatedEntities(IWorkflowContext workflowContext)
{
    OneToManyMetadata relationship = GetRelationship(workflowContext);

    if (relationship == null)
    {
        throw new InvalidOperationException(String.Format(
            "Could not find relationship with name '{0}' and {1} as {2}.",
            this.RelationshipName,
```

```
                workflowContext.PrimaryEntityName,
                this.PrimaryEntityIsParent.Value ? "parent" : "child"));
        }

        Guid parentEntityId = GetParentEntityId(workflowContext, relationship);

        List<DynamicEntity> relatedEntities = new List<DynamicEntity>();
        if (parentEntityId != Guid.Empty)
        {

            RetrieveMultipleRequest retrieveRequest = new RetrieveMultipleRequest();
            retrieveRequest.ReturnDynamicEntities = true;
            retrieveRequest.Query = CreateQueryForRelatedEntities(
                workflowContext, parentEntityId, relationship);

            ICrmService crmService = workflowContext.CreateCrmService(true);
            RetrieveMultipleResponse retrieveResponse =
                (RetrieveMultipleResponse)crmService.Execute(retrieveRequest);

            foreach (DynamicEntity relatedEntity in
                retrieveResponse.BusinessEntityCollection.BusinessEntities)
            {
                relatedEntities.Add(relatedEntity);
            }
        }

        return relatedEntities;
    }
```

GetRelatedEntities starts by calling *GetRelationship* to retrieve the relationship metadata. After validating that the correct relationship was found, *GetParentEntityId* is called to retrieve the parent entity ID. As long as a valid parent entity ID exists, *GetRelatedEntities* continues by calling *CreateQueryForRelatedEntities* to build a query, and then executes it against the *CrmService*. The resulting dynamic entities are bundled into a list and returned. Next we'll take a look at the *GetRelationship* method, shown in Listing 6-22.

LISTING 6-22 The *GetRelationship* method

```
private OneToManyMetadata GetRelationship(IWorkflowContext workflowContext)
{
    IMetadataService metadataService = workflowContext.CreateMetadataService(true);

    RetrieveRelationshipRequest relationshipRequest = new
        RetrieveRelationshipRequest();
    relationshipRequest.Name = this.RelationshipName;

    RetrieveRelationshipResponse relationshipResponse =
        (RetrieveRelationshipResponse)metadataService.Execute(relationshipRequest);

    if (relationshipResponse.RelationshipMetadata.RelationshipType !=
        EntityRelationshipType.OneToMany)
```

```
    {
        return null;
    }

    OneToManyMetadata relationship =
        (OneToManyMetadata)relationshipResponse.RelationshipMetadata;

    if (this.PrimaryEntityIsParent.Value &&
        relationship.ReferencedEntity != workflowContext.PrimaryEntityName)
    {
        return null;
    }

    if(!this.PrimaryEntityIsParent.Value &&
        relationship.ReferencingEntity != workflowContext.PrimaryEntityName)
    {
        return null;
    }

    if (relationship.ReferencingAttribute == "owninguser" ||
        relationship.ReferencingAttribute == "owningteam")
    {
        relationship.ReferencingAttribute = "ownerid";
    }

    return relationship;
}
```

GetRelationship executes a fairly straightforward metadata request to retrieve the relationship information. In addition, it validates that the workflow's primary entity is either the child or parent in the relationship, based on the value of *PrimaryEntityIsParent*. It also maps the internal attribute names *owninguser* and *owningteam* to the publicly visible *ownerid* attribute. Internally, Microsoft Dynamics CRM uses the *owninguser* and *owningteam* attributes to associate an entity owner to either a team or user, but by the time the end users see these attributes, they are combined into the *ownerid* attribute.

Next let's examine the *GetParentEntityId* method, which is called by *GetRelatedEntities* after it retrieves the relationship metadata from *GetRelationship*. *GetParentEntityId* is shown in Listing 6-23.

LISTING 6-23 The *GetParentEntityId* method

```
private Guid GetParentEntityId(
    IWorkflowContext workflowContext, OneToManyMetadata relationship)
{
    Guid parentEntityId = Guid.Empty;
    if (this.PrimaryEntityIsParent.Value)
    {
        parentEntityId = workflowContext.PrimaryEntityId;
    }
```

```
        else if (this.UsePreImage.Value)
        {
            DynamicEntity preImage = workflowContext.PrimaryEntityPreImage;
            parentEntityId = GetReferenceValue(
                preImage, relationship.ReferencingAttribute);
        }
        else
        {
            DynamicEntity image = workflowContext.PrimaryEntityImage;
            parentEntityId = GetReferenceValue(
                image, relationship.ReferencingAttribute);

            if (parentEntityId == Guid.Empty)
            {
                image = RetrievePrimaryEntity(
                    workflowContext, relationship.ReferencingAttribute);
                parentEntityId = GetReferenceValue(
                    image, relationship.ReferencingAttribute);
            }
        }

        return parentEntityId;
    }
```

GetParentEntityId is responsible for retrieving the ID of the parent entity. If *PrimaryEntityIsParent* is true, the parent entity ID is simply the ID of the workflow's primary entity. Otherwise, if *UsePreImage* is true, the parent ID is retrieved from the pre-image. Finally, if both of these properties are false, the parent ID is retrieved from the primary entity. The method first checks in the primary entity image, and if it doesn't find the entity there, the method calls *RetrievePrimaryEntity* to fetch a copy of the entity from the *CrmService*. The *GetReferenceValue* helper method is called throughout to help extract the parent entity ID from the *DynamicEntity* instances. *GetReferenceValue* and *RetrievePrimaryEntity* are both straightforward methods and as such are both shown in Listing 6-24.

LISTING 6-24 The *RetrievePrimaryEntity* and *GetReferenceValue* methods

```
    private DynamicEntity RetrievePrimaryEntity(
        IWorkflowContext workflowContext, params string[] attributeNames)
    {
        ICrmService crmService = workflowContext.CreateCrmService(true);
        RetrieveRequest retrievePrimaryEntityRequest = new RetrieveRequest();
        retrievePrimaryEntityRequest.ReturnDynamicEntities = true;
        retrievePrimaryEntityRequest.ColumnSet = new ColumnSet(attributeNames);
        retrievePrimaryEntityRequest.Target = new TargetRetrieveDynamic
        {
            EntityName = workflowContext.PrimaryEntityName,
            EntityId = workflowContext.PrimaryEntityId
        };
```

```
    RetrieveResponse retrievePrimaryEntityResponse =
        (RetrieveResponse)crmService.Execute(retrievePrimaryEntityRequest);

    return (DynamicEntity)retrievePrimaryEntityResponse.BusinessEntity;
}

private static Guid GetReferenceValue(DynamicEntity entity, string attributeName)
{
    if (entity != null && entity.Properties.Contains(attributeName))
    {
        CrmReference reference = entity[attributeName] as CrmReference;
        if (reference != null)
        {
            return reference.Value;
        }
    }

    return Guid.Empty;
}
```

RetrievePrimaryEntity creates a simple *RetrieveRequest* to get the primary entity from the *CrmService*, while *GetReferenceValue* safely extracts a *Guid* from a *DynamicEntity*. After the parent entity ID is determined, *RetrieveRelatedEntities* calls *CreateQueryForRelatedEntities* to build a *QueryExpression* that can retrieve the child entities. Listing 6-25 shows the source code for *CreateQueryForRelatedEntities*.

LISTING 6-25 The *CreateQueryForRelatedEntities* method

```
private QueryExpression CreateQueryForRelatedEntities(
    IWorkflowContext workflowContext, Guid parentEntityId,
    OneToManyMetadata relationship)
{
    QueryExpression query = new QueryExpression();
    query.EntityName = relationship.ReferencingEntity;

    ColumnSet cols = new ColumnSet();
    if (!String.IsNullOrEmpty(this.SumAttribute))
    {
        cols.AddColumn(this.SumAttribute);
    }

    if (!String.IsNullOrEmpty(this.AverageAttribute))
    {
        cols.AddColumn(this.AverageAttribute);
    }
    query.ColumnSet = cols;

    query.Criteria.AddCondition(
        relationship.ReferencingAttribute,
        ConditionOperator.Equal,
        parentEntityId);
```

```
    if (this.IncludeInactiveRecords == null || !this.IncludeInactiveRecords.Value)
    {
        query.Criteria.AddCondition("statecode", ConditionOperator.Equal, 0);
    }
    return query;
}
```

If the *SumAttribute* and *AverageAttribute* properties have values, those columns are included in the results. The only condition that is guaranteed to be added is that the relationship's *ReferencingAttribute* is equal to the parent entity's ID. If *IncludeInactiveRecords* is not true, the query also filters on the *statecode* attribute.

Once the query is executed, all of the related entities are passed back to the *Execute* method, which calls *RollUpEntities* to calculate the aggregate values. *RollUpEntities* is shown in Listing 6-26.

LISTING 6-26 The *RollUpEntities* method

```
private void RollUpEntities(List<DynamicEntity> entities)
{
    this.Count = new CrmNumber(entities.Count);

    if (!String.IsNullOrEmpty(this.SumAttribute))
    {
        double value = 0.0;
        foreach (DynamicEntity entity in entities)
        {
            if (entity.Properties.Contains(this.SumAttribute))
            {
                value += ConvertValueToDouble(entity[this.SumAttribute]);
            }
        }
        this.Sum = new CrmFloat(value);
    }

    if (!String.IsNullOrEmpty(this.AverageAttribute))
    {
        double value = 0.0;
        double averageCount = 0.0;
        foreach (DynamicEntity entity in entities)
        {
            if (entity.Properties.Contains(this.AverageAttribute))
            {
                value += ConvertValueToDouble(entity[this.AverageAttribute]);
                averageCount++;
            }
        }

        if (averageCount > 0)
        {
            this.Average = new CrmFloat(value / averageCount);
        }
    }
}
```

RollUpEntities starts by capturing the number of related entities in the *Count* property. It then loops through the related entities and calculates the *Sum* and *Average* properties if *SumAttribute* and *AverageAttribute* values were specified. *RollUpEntities* only depends on one other method, *ConvertValueToDouble*, which is shown in Listing 6-27.

LISTING 6-27 The *ConvertValueToDouble* method

```
private double ConvertValueToDouble(object property)
{
    if (property != null)
    {
        PropertyInfo valueProperty = property.GetType().GetProperty("Value");
        if (valueProperty != null)
        {
            return Convert.ToDouble(valueProperty.GetValue(property, null));
        }
    }

    return 0.0;
}
```

ConvertValueToDouble uses reflection to extract a value from the *DynamicEntity* value passed in and then converts that value to a *double*. And with that, we are done!

CalculateRelatedAggregateActivity demonstrates some of the powerful reusable functionality that you can provide by implementing your own custom workflow activities within Microsoft Dynamics CRM. Using this activity, you can maintain calculated values on parent entities based on attributes found on related child entities.

Summary

In this chapter we've taken a look at the powerful native workflow support in Microsoft Dynamics CRM, including its use of Windows Workflow Foundation. We learned how to create custom workflow activities to extend the native workflow functionality, as well as how to register them both with pre-existing tools and programmatically. We then explored the workflow context and how we can use it to communicate back to the Microsoft Dynamics CRM services. This chapter concluded with three different workflow programming examples that show how to implement workflow assemblies to fulfill real-world business requirements.

Chapter 7

Form Scripting

You probably already know how to perform basic form customizations for each entity in Microsoft Dynamics CRM. You can easily add fields, tabs, and sections to a form by using the Web-based administration tool without having to do any programming. However, if you want to set up more complex form customizations than the Web-based administration tool allows, Microsoft Dynamics CRM offers a rich form scripting and extension programming model.

In the context of Web-based applications, the term *client-side* typically refers to code that executes on the user's Web browser. Microsoft Dynamics CRM allows for form scripting code to work offline and on the client, expanding the notion of client-side code. The three supported methods you can use to create custom scripts tie into form and field events–*onLoad*, *onSave*, and *onChange*. This chapter examines these form scripting programming techniques. We also supply multiple examples of how you might implement some customizations that these powerful form scripting and extensions allow and provide a brief discussion on the development and deployment strategies you should consider when you work with form scripting.

Because of the nature of the form scripting programming model, this chapter contains a significant amount of dynamic HTML (DHTML) and scripting code. Even if you're not an expert with these technologies, this chapter can help you understand the types of customizations possible in Microsoft Dynamics CRM.

In this chapter, we'll cover the following topics:

- Form scripting overview
- Calling Web services from script
- Using the CRM API SOAP request from script
- Testing and deployment
- Scripting from ISV.Config buttons
- Advanced topics, including form type considerations, cross-site scripting, using script for validation, and loading external script files
- Script examples

Form Scripting Overview

The previous chapters discussed application programming interfaces (APIs) and server-side event options for Microsoft Dynamics CRM. In this chapter we will focus on the many events and programmatic possibilities available to you by using form scripting techniques.

As you would expect, the Microsoft Dynamics CRM SDK acts as an excellent reference, and you can always consult it for additional detail and sample code options. We reference some of the SDK information here for convenience but add to the information in the SDK to cover additional topics and samples.

We cover the following topics in this section:

- Understanding scripting with Microsoft Dynamics CRM
- Referencing Microsoft Dynamics CRM elements
- Available Microsoft Dynamics CRM form events

Understanding Client-Side Scripting with Microsoft Dynamics CRM

Client-side scripting helps distribute the application processing load between the client computer and the Web server. Because Microsoft Dynamics CRM uses a Web-based architecture, it displays all its data on Web pages. However, Microsoft Dynamics CRM pages don't appear as typical Web pages that users see when browsing the Internet. Rather, Microsoft Dynamics CRM relies heavily on DHTML to achieve a more advanced and functional user interface. Because the DOM treats each HTML element as an object, a developer can use traditional DHTML programming techniques to access Microsoft Dynamics CRM forms to create even more customized and sophisticated Web pages in Microsoft Dynamics CRM.

Microsoft Dynamics CRM supports a specialized subset of DOM methods and events as defined in the client-side SDK. We examine many of the available properties and methods here, but you can refer to the Microsoft Dynamics CRM SDK for a complete list of supported methods.

Referencing Microsoft Dynamics CRM Elements

The "Client Extensions and Scripting" section of the Microsoft Dynamics CRM SDK provides information regarding client methods, properties, and events available to a programmer. In Tables 7-1 through 7-9, we highlight a few that you will probably use frequently in your own scripts.

Note Pay special attention to the new global variables available to you. These variables are important for multilingual and multi-tenant deployments.

TABLE 7-1 Global Variables

Name	Description
SERVER_URL	Returns the URL of the CRM Web server
USER_LANGUAGE_CODE	Provides the language code set by the user in Microsoft Dynamics CRM
ORG_LANGUAGE_CODE	Returns the base language for the organization
ORG_UNIQUE_NAME	Returns the organization name

TABLE 7-2 Global Methods

Method	Description
IsOnline	Gets a Boolean value indicating whether the form is currently online
IsOutlookClient	Gets a Boolean value indicating whether the form is currently being displayed in one of the Microsoft Office Outlook clients
IsOutlookLaptopClient	Gets a Boolean value indicating whether the form is currently being displayed in Microsoft Dynamics CRM for Outlook with Offline Access
IsOutlookWorkstationClient	Gets a Boolean value indicating whether the form is currently being displayed in Microsoft Dynamics CRM for Outlook

TABLE 7-3 *crmForm* Properties

Property	Description
All	A collection of CRM attributes on the form.
IsDirty	Gets or sets a value indicating whether any of the fields on the form have been modified.
FormType	Gets an integer value designating the mode of the form. Possible values are: 0 = Undefined Form Type 1 = Create Form 2 = Update Form 3 = Read-Only Form 4 = Disabled Form 5 = Quick Create Form 6 = Bulk Edit Form Please review more information regarding form types in the "Advanced Topics" section of this chapter.
ObjectId	Gets the entity GUID that the form is displaying. This property returns null if the form is in Create mode.
ObjectTypeName	Gets the entity name of the displayed form.

TABLE 7-4 *crmForm* Methods

Method	Description
Save()	Executes the save function (simulates a user clicking *Save*).
SaveAndClose()	Executes the save and close function (simulates a user clicking *Save and Close*).
SetFieldReqLevel(sField, bRequired)	Sets a field as required. Note that this method might change or might not be available in future releases.

TABLE 7-5 *crmForm.all* Field Collection Properties

Property	Description
Precision	Gets the number of digits to display for *currency* and *float* data types.
DataValue	Gets or sets the value of the field. Additional parameters are available for *picklist* and *lookup* field types.
Disabled	Gets or sets a value indicating whether the field is available for user entry.
ForceSubmit	Gets or sets a value indicating whether the field should be submitted to the database on a save. By default, any enabled, modified field will be submitted. This property is useful when you need to submit a disabled field.
IsDirty	Gets a value indicating whether the field has been modified.
Min	Gets the minimum allowable value for *currency*, *float*, and *integer* data types.
Max	Gets the maximum allowable value for *currency*, *float*, and *integer* data types.
MaxLength	Gets the maximum length of a string or memo field.
RequiredLevel	Gets the required status of the field. Possible values are: 0 = No Constraint 1 = Business Recommended 2 = Business Required

TABLE 7-6 *crmForm.all* Field Collection Methods

Method	Description
SetFocus()	Moves the mouse cursor to the field, making it active on the form
FireOnChange()	Executes the Microsoft Dynamics CRM *OnChange* event for the attribute specified

The *lookup* and *picklist* field types differ from the other fields because they act as arrays (a collection of name/value pairs). The value that Microsoft Dynamics CRM stores in the database (a GUID for lookup fields and an integer for picklist fields) is not the value that the user sees on the form. Microsoft Dynamics CRM includes the following additional attributes for displaying the translated value as shown in the next three tables.

Note Don't forget that the *lookup* and *picklist* field types have access to most of the methods contained in the *crmForm.all* collection as described in Table 7-6. For example, a *lookup* or *picklist* field also has the *Disabled* and *ForceSubmit* properties.

TABLE 7-7 ***crmForm.all.<lookupfield>* Attributes**

Attribute	Description
Id	Gets or sets the GUID identifier. Required for set.
TypeName	Gets or sets the referenced entity name. Required for set.
Name	Gets or sets the name of the record to be displayed in the lookup field on the form. Required for set.

Note You should plan to use only the *TypeName* attribute. For backward compatibility, Microsoft Dynamics CRM also exposes the *Type* attribute, which is based on a unique integer assigned to every native entity and to custom entities when they are created in a new deployment. You cannot rely on these integers in your code because they can differ for custom entities between deployments.

The attributes listed in Table 7-7 are available for each item within the array returned when you access *crmForm.all.<lookupfield>.DataValue*. For standard lookup attributes, there will only be one item returned. For *PartyList* attributes, such as the To field on an e-mail activity form, you could have multiple items returned. The code below loops through a *PartyList* attribute and displays the various attribute values for each record.

```
var lookupItem = new Array;
lookupItem = crmForm.all.to.DataValue;

var i;
var result;

// Loop through displaying the data
for (i in lookupItem)
{
  if (lookupItem[i] != null)
  {
    // Text value of the lookup.record
    result = lookupItem[i].name + " | ";

    // GUID of the lookup.record
    result += lookupItem[i].id + " | ";

    // Entity name of the lookup.record
    result += lookupItem[i].typename;

    alert(result);
  }
}
```

TABLE 7-8 ***crmForm.all.<picklistfield>*** **Properties and Methods**

Syntax	Description
DataValue	Gets or sets the currently selected option, returning an integer.
SelectedText	Gets the text displayed with the currently selected option.
GetSelectedOption	Gets a picklist.
Options	Returns an array of picklist objects and sets new options for a drop-down list by specifying an array of picklist objects.
AddOption(Name, DataValue)	Adds a new option at the end of the picklist collection. *Name* and *DataValue* must have valid values.
DeleteOption(value)	Removes a picklist option based on the passed in integer value.

TABLE 7-9 ***crmForm.all.<picklistfield>*** **Attributes**

Attribute	Description
Text	Gets or sets the text displayed for the option
DataValue	Gets or sets the index value of the selected option

Available Events

Microsoft Dynamics CRM supports three client-side events that you can use for your custom scripts:

- **Form *onLoad* event** Executes immediately after the form loads in the browser. By using this event, you can manipulate the form before Microsoft Dynamics CRM displays it to the user.
- **Form *onSave* event** Triggers when the user clicks the Save, Save and Close, or Save and New buttons. This event occurs before the form is submitted to the server and can be used to cancel the save operation. Also, this event always fires, even if the user did not change any of the fields on the form.
- **Field *onChange* events** Fires when the user navigates away from a form field (clicks elsewhere or presses the Tab key) in which he or she has changed the value.

Tip If you want to cancel the save operation, use the following syntax within the *onSave* event: *event.returnValue = false;*.

You can add your client-side script to an entity form, in addition to adding scripts with the ISV.Config file by using the JavaScript attribute. Here's a quick refresher on adding client-side scripts with the entity form. We'll cover adding form scripting through ISV.Config later in this chapter.

Adding event code

1. Using the System Administrator or System Customizer role, navigate to the Settings section, click Customizations, and then click Customize Entities.
2. In the Customize Entities section, double-click the entity that you want to customize.
3. In the navigation pane, click Forms and Views.
4. Double-click Form from the resulting list.

The form editor page is displayed and shows all the tabs and fields that the form will display to the user.

Customizing form events

To customize the form events (*onLoad* and *onSave*), follow these steps:

1. Click Form Properties in the Common Tasks area. A dialog box appears that lists the *onLoad* and *onSave* events.
2. Select the event to which you want to add code, and then click Edit.
3. Enter your custom script in the Event Detail Properties dialog box, select the Event Is Enabled check box, and then click OK.

Adding scripts to the field event

Adding scripts to the field event (*onChange*) works the same way as it does for form events:

1. In the form editor, double-click the field where you will add your code. Or you can select a field and then click Change Properties.
2. The Field Properties dialog box opens. Click the Events tab.
3. Click Edit. You will see the Event Detail Properties dialog box, as shown in Figure 7-1.

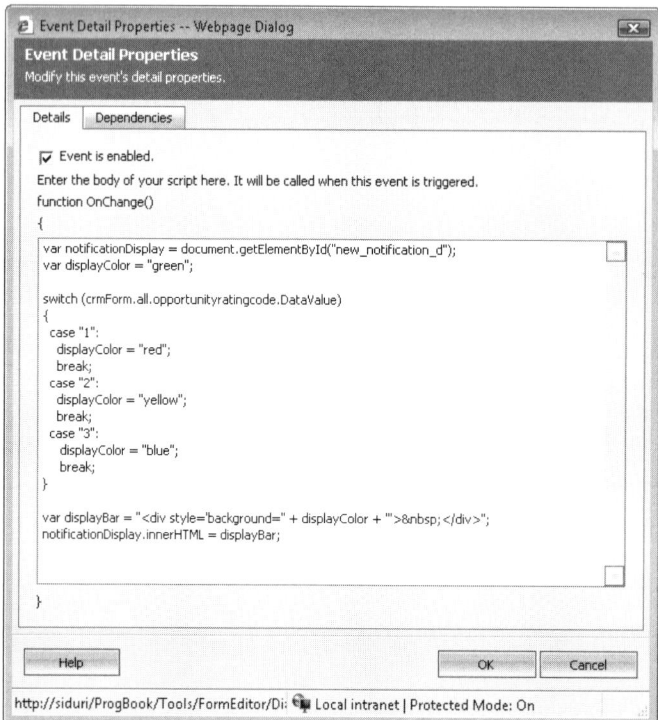

FIGURE 7-1 The Event Detail Properties dialog box

Remember the following key points related to configuring your client-side scripts on the entity forms:

- You must enable your script by selecting the Event Is Enabled check box in the Event Detail Properties dialog box. This check box tells Microsoft Dynamics CRM to run the script the next time the event is triggered.
- Although not required, it's a good practice to specify the fields your script uses on the Dependencies tab. Specifying dependent fields blocks users from accidentally removing fields from the form that your script requires.
- You can test and debug your scripts prior to publishing the form to production by using one of the form preview options: Create, Update, or Read-Only.
- Microsoft Dynamics CRM provides a Simulate Form Save button on the preview of a form that triggers the *onSave* event. You can use this button to test your *onSave* custom scripts.
- Remember to publish your customizations when you have finished.

Warning Microsoft Dynamics CRM disables fields with an *onChange* event enabled in the bulk edit form, preventing a user from entering any text.

We show additional scripting examples later in this chapter; we just wanted to quickly introduce you to the customization process and terminology.

Calling Web Services from Script

At some point, you will want to call Web services from script to compute more complex business logic and then possibly return a result back to the script. You can call Web services from script in a variety of ways. The most common way is to create an *XmlHTTP* object and pass in the appropriate parameters, as shown in the following code:

```
var url = "/ISV/SonomaPartners/Webservices/TestService.asmx/RetrieveAccount";

var oXmlHTTP = new ActiveXObject("Msxml2.XMLHTTP");
oXmlHTTP.Open("POST", url, false);
oXmlHTTP.setRequestHeader("Content-Type", "application/x-www-form-urlencoded")
oXmlHTTP.Send("OrgName=" + ORG_UNIQUE_NAME + "&Id=" + id);

var results = "";
if ((oXmlHTTP.responseXML.xml) != null && (oXmlHTTP.responseXML.xml.toString().length > 0))
  results = oXmlHTTP.responseXML.selectSingleNode("string").text;
```

The response is specific to the return type of the Web service you call.

Note Remember that Microsoft Dynamics CRM 4.0 is a multi-tenant–capable application, which means that your custom Web services need to know the organization name if making any calls back to the Microsoft Dynamics CRM Web services.

Using the CRM API SOAP Request from Script

You can use JavaScript to execute CRM Web service methods by constructing a SOAP message. By using this handy technique, you can perform rather interesting and complex logic in JavaScript. For example, the following code shows the full SOAP XML used to retrieve the full name of an existing contact record.

```
<?xml version="1.0" encoding="utf-8"?>
<soap:Envelope xmlns:soap="http://schemas.xmlsoap.org/soap/envelope/" xmlns:xsi=
"http://www.w3.org/2001/XMLSchema-instance" xmlns:xsd="http://www.w3.org/2001/XMLSchema">
  <soap:Header>
    <CrmAuthenticationToken xmlns="http://schemas.microsoft.com/crm/2007/WebServices">
      <AuthenticationType
```

```
xmlns="http://schemas.microsoft.com/crm/2007/CoreTypes">0</AuthenticationType>
      <OrganizationName
xmlns="http://schemas.microsoft.com/crm/2007/CoreTypes">OrganizationName</OrganizationName>
      <CallerId xmlns="http://schemas.microsoft.com/crm/2007/CoreTypes">00000000-0000-0000-
        0000-000000000000</CallerId>
    </CrmAuthenticationToken>
  </soap:Header>
  <soap:Body>
    <Retrieve xmlns="http://schemas.microsoft.com/crm/2007/WebServices">
      <entityName>contact</entityName>
      <id>b07be4aa-f87b-dc11-8276-0003ff8a2b47</id>
      <columnSet xmlns:q1="http://schemas.microsoft.com/crm/2006/Query" xsi:type="q1:
        ColumnSet">
        <q1:Attributes>
          <q1:Attribute>fullname</q1:Attribute>
        </q1:Attributes>
      </columnSet>
    </Retrieve>
  </soap:Body>
</soap:Envelope>
```

Note In the previous script, you need to provide the correct *OrganizationName* and *CallerId* values. Microsoft Dynamics CRM provides a helper method named *GenerateAuthenticationHeader* that can be used to simplify construction of the *CrmAuthenticationToken* node. We discuss the *GenerateAuthenticationHeader* method later in the chapter.

You can call any Web service using this technique, including the Microsoft Dynamics CRM *CrmService* and *MetadataService*. The Microsoft Dynamics CRM SDK has examples of the SOAP XML for most of the common methods. However, you can always use a tool such as Fiddler to capture the HTTP requests and determine the SOAP request you need to construct.

Note Both the Microsoft Dynamics CRM SDK and *Working with Microsoft Dynamics CRM 4.0* (Microsoft Press, 2008) discuss in depth how to use Fiddler to capture Microsoft Dynamics CRM Web service requests.

Rather than building the *CrmAuthenticationToken* manually each time, Microsoft Dynamics CRM provides the *GenerateAuthenticationHeader* method to do this for you. Using the *GenerateAuthenticationHeader* method not only saves you lines of code but also provides the proper organization, so be sure to use it.

The following script function shows the SOAP required to query the *MetadataService* for information about a specific attribute.

```
function RetrieveAttributeInfomration(entity, attributeName)
{
  var serverUrl = "/MSCrmServices/2007/MetadataService.asmx";
```

```
  var xmlhttp = new ActiveXObject("Microsoft.XMLHTTP");
  xmlhttp.open("POST", serverUrl, false);
  xmlhttp.setRequestHeader("Content-Type", "text/xml; charset=utf-8")
  xmlhttp.setRequestHeader("SOAPAction", "http://schemas.microsoft.com/crm/2007/WebServices/
    Execute")

  // Define the retrieve message
  var message =
  [
    "<?xml version='1.0' encoding='utf-8'?>",
    "<soap:Envelope xmlns:soap=\"http://schemas.xmlsoap.org/soap/envelope/\" ",
    "xmlns:xsi=\"http://www.w3.org/2001/XMLSchema-instance\" ",
    "xmlns:xsd=\"http://www.w3.org/2001/XMLSchema\">",
    GenerateAuthenticationHeader(),
    "<soap:Body>",
    "<Execute xmlns='http://schemas.microsoft.com/crm/2007/WebServices'>",
    "<Request xsi:type='RetrieveAttributeRequest'>",
    "<MetadataId>00000000-0000-0000-0000-000000000000</MetadataId>",
    "<EntityLogicalName>",
    entity,
    "</EntityLogicalName>",
    "<LogicalName>",
    attributeName,
    "</LogicalName>",
    "<RetrieveAsIfPublished>true</RetrieveAsIfPublished>",
    "</Request></Execute>",
    "</soap:Body>",
    "</soap:Envelope>"
  ].join("");

  xmlhttp.send(message);
  return xmlhttp.responseXML.xml;
}
```

Tip Be sure that you have the correct URL for the the *SOAPAction* header.

By creating the SOAP call directly with script, you enjoy the following benefits:

- You can use the same script with either a Microsoft Dynamics CRM Online or an on-premise deployment.
- You can easily deploy the script logic by using Microsoft Dynamics CRM export/import customizations.
- The script works in offline mode without additional deployment requirements.

These benefits can be useful in certain circumstances, but you should also consider the following drawbacks:

- More effort is required for development and maintenance because you need to determine the SOAP envelope for each message in the SDK.

- Because your code is not compiled, it is more fragile, and errors in development can manifest themselves more easily.
- You lose some reusability. You need to copy common functionality between multiple entities.
- You cannot protect any important business logic from being viewed by others.

Testing and Deployment

If you're new to form scripting in Microsoft Dynamics CRM, you might wonder what's the best approach for testing and debugging your scripts. We recommend that you use the Microsoft Visual Studio integrated debugger attached to Internet Explorer when testing form scripting in Microsoft Dynamics CRM.

Debugging JavaScript

Even though Microsoft Dynamics CRM supports different scripting languages, most developers use JavaScript for their scripting. JavaScript offers a *debugger* statement, and we recommend utilizing it as part of your script debugging. To use this helpful statement in conjunction with Internet Explorer to achieve an integrated script debugging experience, follow the procedures described in this section.

First you need to configure Internet Explorer to allow for script debugging.

Configuring Internet Explorer

1. Open Internet Explorer, click Tools, and then click Internet Options.
2. On the Advanced tab, clear the Disable Script Debugging (Internet Explorer) option.

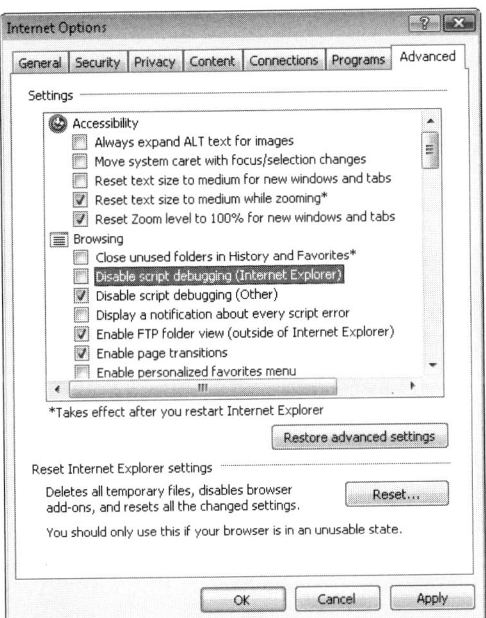

Now you just need to add the *debugger* command in the JavaScript code and refresh the page in the browser to start the debugging process.

Listing 7-1 offers a quick example of how this works. Add the simple JavaScript e-mail validation code shown in the listing to the *onChange* event of an account's e-mail address and check the Event Is Enabled box. Notice that we added the *debugger* statement in the first line.

LISTING 7-1 JavaScript debugging example

```
debugger;
var oEmailAddress1 = document.crmForm.all.emailaddress1;
var sCleanedEmailAddress = oEmailAddress1.DataValue.replace(/[^0-9,A-Z,a-z,\@,\.]/g,
"");
var regexEmail = /^.+@.+\..{2,3}$/;

// Test the cleaned e-mail string against the e-mail regular expression
if ( (regexEmail.test(sCleanedEmailAddress)) )
{
 oEmailAddress1.DataValue = sCleanedEmailAddress;
}
else
{
 alert("The E-mail Address appears to be invalid. Please correct.");
}
```

Preview the account form and type an e-mail address in the E-mail field, as shown in Figure 7-2.

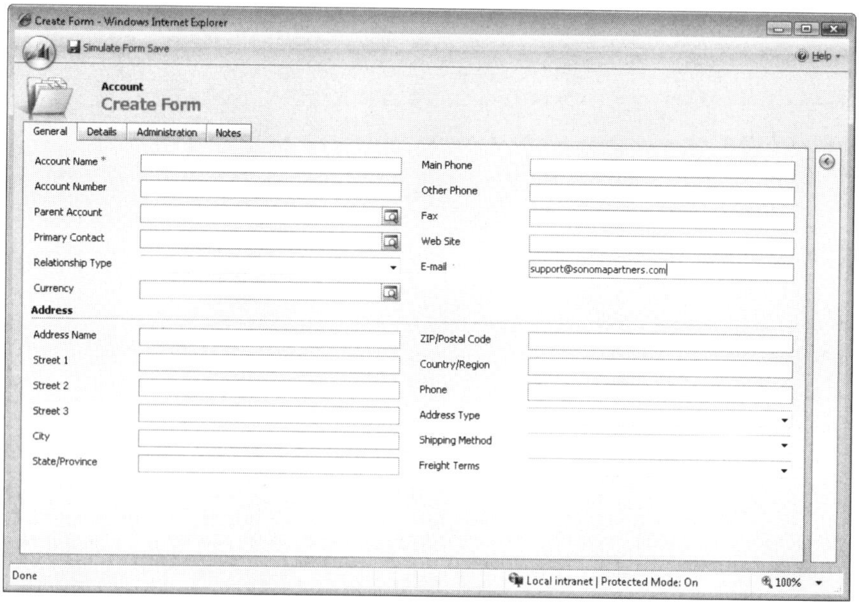

FIGURE 7-2 Typing in an e-mail address to test JavaScript debugging

After you leave the field, the *onChange* code executes and your debugger statement displays the Visual Studio dialog box shown in Figure 7-3.

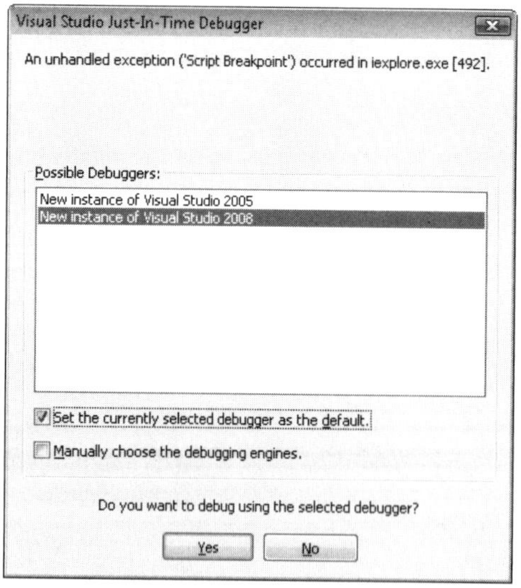

FIGURE 7-3 JavaScript debugging dialog box

You can start a new instance of Visual Studio 2008 and then perform real-time debugging of the JavaScript code, as shown in Figure 7-4.

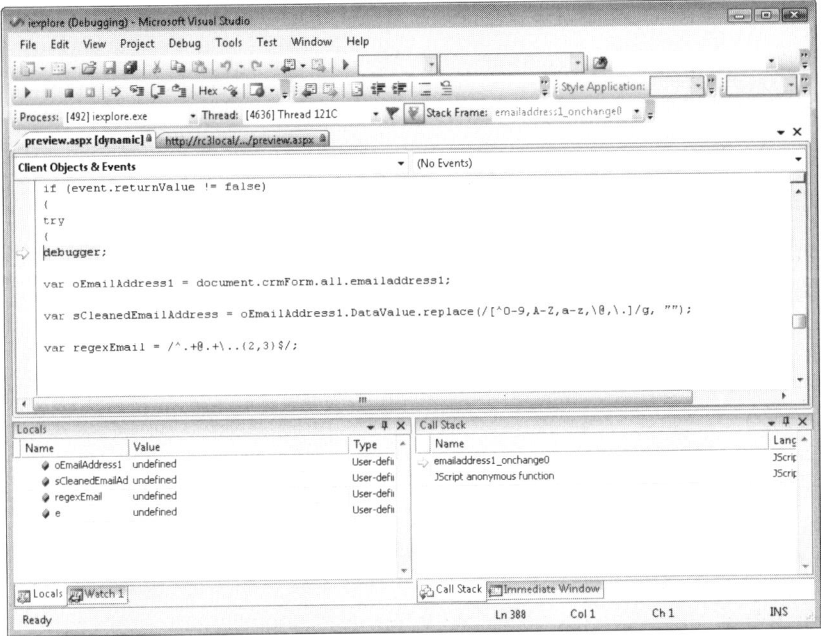

FIGURE 7-4 Debugging JavaScript in Visual Studio 2008

Additional Testing and Debugging Tips

We recommend the following additional testing and debugging techniques when developing your custom scripts:

- Always test your scripts in a Microsoft Dynamics CRM development environment and not on production servers.
- When possible, set up a simple Web page with a test form, and test your JavaScript outside Microsoft Dynamics CRM. This approach provides for faster development and debugging. Then, copy and paste the final code into the appropriate Microsoft Dynamics CRM event.
- Use the *Preview* command to test your client-side scripts before publishing.
- If it appears that your code doesn't work as expected, first ensure that you enabled your event. You should then use the JavaScript integrated debugging technique described earlier. If you have trouble getting integrated debugging to work, you can always use the *alert()* method to output various logic points and try to eliminate the interaction with Microsoft Dynamics CRM first. In many cases, the flaw may be contained in the code logic itself, independent of the integrated properties of Microsoft Dynamics CRM.

Scripting from ISV.Config Buttons

Microsoft Dynamics CRM permits you to add custom buttons by using the ISV.Config file. Typically these buttons reference a Web page, but Microsoft Dynamics CRM also allows for script to execute directly from the button.

Using script directly from the ISV.Config buttons offers the following advantages:

- You can execute simple logic without having to deploy a custom Web page, which proves very effective with Microsoft Dynamics CRM Online.
- You can provide additional script logic prior to launching a custom Web page.
- Deployment is simplified because the code is installed as part of the Microsoft Dynamics CRM import customizations process.

However, use caution with this approach, because you are embedding your script logic within an XML attribute tag. As such, you need to conform to XML standards (escaping special characters, using tick marks instead of quotation marks, and so on), and your script will be more difficult to read and debug.

To better understand a real-world example of scripting from the ISV.Config button, consider the following scenario. You need to create a button on the Case entity that creates a child Case record, duplicates some key properties of a Case record for a Microsoft Dynamics CRM Online deployment, and then links that child case back to the original case. Because the scenario requires you to deploy to Microsoft Dynamics CRM Online, you should keep the business logic contained within the button.

You can address this business scenario by performing the following steps:

- Configure a hierarchical relationship with the case entity by using the Web-based configuration tools
- Add a button (with custom script in the ISV.Config) to the case record

Let's start by creating a new relationship from the Case entity. This new relationship allows you to link two different cases to each other in a hierarchical relationship.

Create the child case relationship

1. Open Microsoft Dynamics CRM in a Web browser, and then click Settings from the Application Area.
2. Click Customizations, and then click Customize Entities.
3. Double-click the Case entity.
4. After the form loads, click 1:N Relationships.
5. Click the New 1-to-Many Relationship button to open the Relationship Form.

6. Create the 1:N relationship from case to case, as shown here:

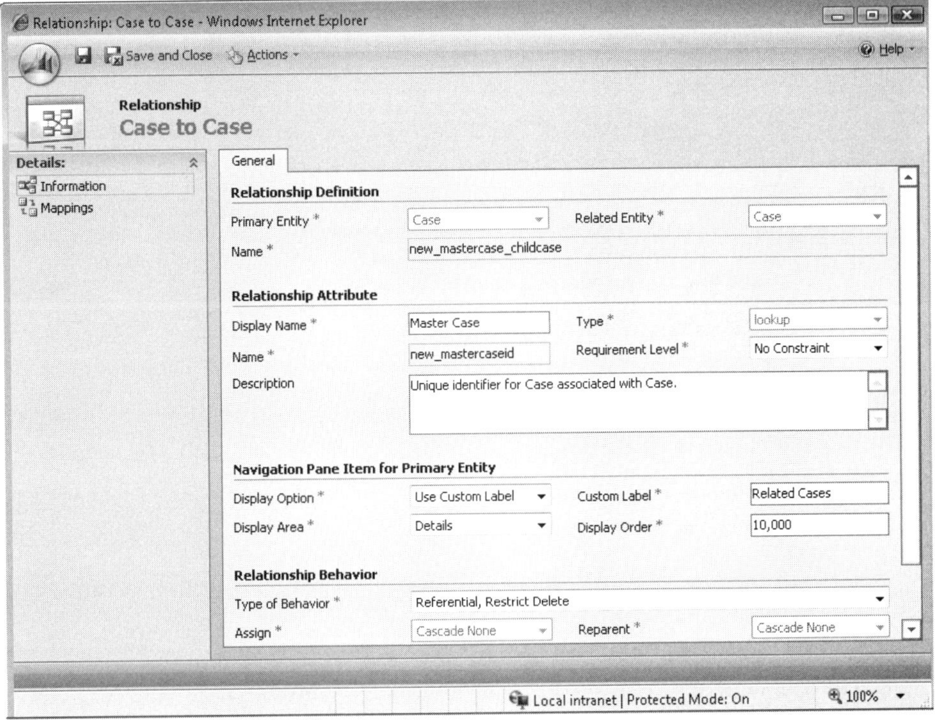

7. Click Save and Close on the Relationship: New Web form.
8. On the Case entity form, click Forms and Views, and then double-click Form.
9. Add the new Master Case lookup attribute to the Case form.
10. Save and close the form.
11. On the Case entity form, click Actions and then select Publish. Then click Save and Close for the entity.

Now that you have added the relationship and attribute to the form, you need to add your custom button and logic to Microsoft Dynamics CRM.

Add the New Child Case button

1. In the Settings area, click Customization, and then click Export Customizations.
2. Select the ISV.Config record, and then click Export Selected Customizations.
3. Save the zip file to your computer.
4. Unzip the downloaded file, and then open the resulting file in your favorite XML editor.

5. Add the following XML within the *<Entities>* node. Be sure to check that an existing incident entity node doesn't already exist.

```
<Entity name="incident">
  <ToolBar ValidForCreate="0" ValidForUpdate="1">
    <Button Icon="/_imgs/ico_16_112.gif" JavaScript="
var url = '/cs/cases/edit.aspx?';
var params =
[
'customerid=',crmForm.all.customerid.DataValue[0].id,
'&amp;customeridname=',crmForm.all.customerid.DataValue[0].name,
'&amp;customeridtype=',crmForm.all.customerid.DataValue[0].typename,
'&amp;new_mastercaseid=',crmForm.ObjectId,
'&amp;new_mastercaseidname=',crmForm.all.title.DataValue,
'&amp;subjectid=',crmForm.all.subjectid.DataValue[0].id,
'&amp;subjectidname=',crmForm.all.subjectid.DataValue[0].name,
'&amp;casetypecode=',crmForm.all.casetypecode.DataValue,
'&amp;caseorigincode=',crmForm.all.caseorigincode.DataValue,
'&amp;customersatisfactioncode=',crmForm.all.customersatisfactioncode.DataValue
].join('');
openStdWin(url+params);">
      <Titles>
        <Title LCID="1033" Text="New Child Case" />
      </Titles>
      <ToolTips>
        <ToolTip LCID="1033" Text="Create new child Case record." />
      </ToolTips>
    </Button>
  </ToolBar>
</Entity>
```

6. Import your updated ISV.Config file.

7. Publish the ISV.Config.

Tip To make development easier, consider developing your code independently of the ISV.Config file by using a stubbed page with the same form/data. This allows you to more quickly troubleshoot your script logic without the overhead of importing the ISV.Config file repeatedly.

Figure 7-5 shows the new button that you just added to the toolbar of the Case form. You can also see the new Master Case field that you added to the Case form.

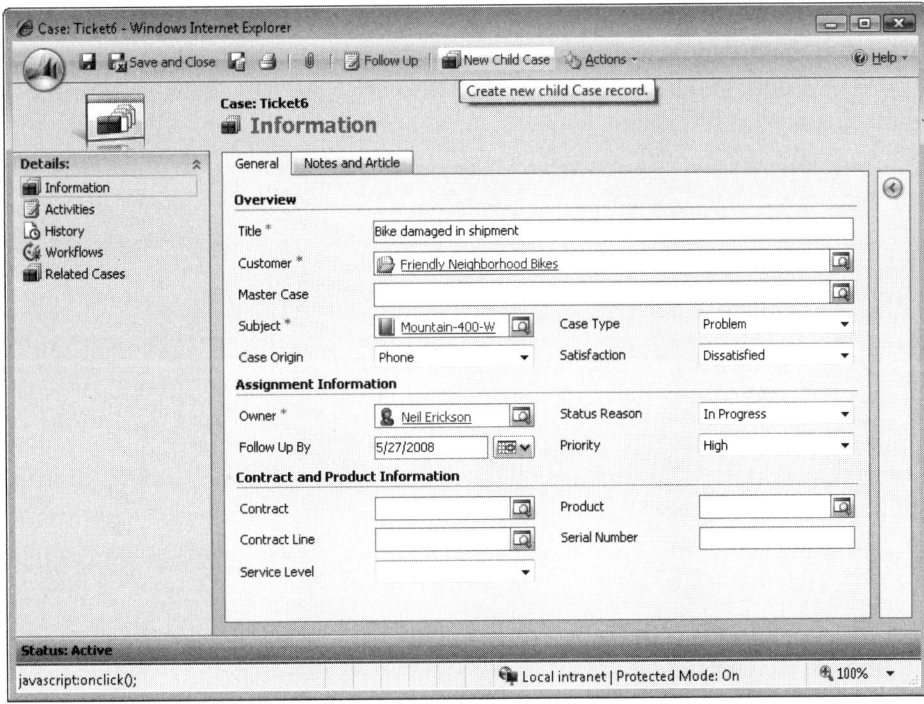

FIGURE 7-5 New Child Case button

The script in this example takes advantage of the ability of Microsoft Dynamics CRM to provide default values using the query string. The next section explores this query string technique in more detail. Keep in mind the following points with this sample code:

- You need to use single quotation marks instead of double quotation marks.
- You need to escape the ampersand (&) with *&*.
- The master case ID will be the *ObjectId* of the current Case record. You also need to set the name for the lookup value. The lookup name is always the primary attribute of the entity, which is Case's title in this example.
- Customer lookup attributes are a special case of the lookup and require the *type* attribute to define whether the record is an account or a contact. Be sure to pass the entity name instead of the type code for the *type* value.
- The JavaScript attribute allows for line breaks within your code. Although this increases the overall size of the file, it definitely allows for more readable code.
- Any errors with this approach will be suppressed and the button will not function.
- The code does not contain any error handling. If the lookup values for customer and subject do not contain any values, the page will not open. You can add additional checking for null lookup values if you want.

- The code reuses the CRM *openStdWin* method. If you prefer, you can use JavaScript's *window.open* method and pass it the proper parameters to ensure that your code can be properly upgraded. However, you will need to be sure to escape your query string parameters yourself.

Note Both the Microsoft Dynamics CRM SDK and *Working with Microsoft Dynamics CRM 4.0* discuss the ISV.Config file and functionality in depth.

Default Values Using the Query String

Microsoft Dynamics CRM provides a useful but little-known feature to programmatically pre-populate default values on a form when you create a new record. This technique works on most entities, including custom entities. Conceptually it works very simply. If you pass in additional, specially named query string parameters, the Microsoft Dynamics CRM form takes those parameters and provides default values for the form.

Note The Microsoft Dynamics CRM SDK contains additional information regarding this approach, as well as the URLs for the entity forms.

Keep in mind the following considerations when using the query string to provide default form values:

- Activity forms do not support default values from the query string.
- When providing default values for lookup and picklist values, you need to specify the additional values to properly construct those attributes:
  - Lookups include a name and ID. The ID will always be the attribute name, and the name will always be in the format *attributename*-name. (For instance, the *Subject* attribute on a Case form is *subjectid*.) Therefore, you need to pass the GUID to *subjectid* and the subject name as *subjectidname*.
  - Customer lookups require an extra attribute to define whether the record is an account or a contact. The name of the parameter will be *attributename*type. Be sure to pass the entity name as the value, instead of the type code.
  - For picklists, you only need to pass the integer data value.
  - Boolean values can either be 0/1 or true/false. Consider always using 0/1, which takes up fewer characters in the query string.

- In Internet Explorer, query strings have a maximum length of 2,083 characters. Be aware of this limitation when you need to include a long list of default attributes.
- Be cautious of passing *textarea* attributes in the query string, because the data stored in these values can contain carriage returns and new line characters.
- Passing an invalid parameter generates a hard error.
- You must pass valid static values for each attribute (for example, no script or variables).

Advanced Topics

So far you have seen how to use script to accomplish a variety of functions within the Microsoft Dynamics CRM Web form as well as how to include form scripting with custom buttons. The following section describes additional topics that you should consider when using script within the Microsoft Dynamics CRM application, including:

- Form type considerations
- Cross-site scripting
- Using script for validation
- Loading external script files

Form Type Considerations

Microsoft Dynamics CRM includes numerous form types that you have access to from the *crmForm.FormType* property. Table 7-10 lists the possible form types with Microsoft Dynamics CRM.

TABLE 7-10 Microsoft Dynamics CRM Form Types

Form Type Code	Form	Description
0	Undefined	Internal use only.
1	Create	Displayed when a record is created. User must have the Create privilege.
2	Update	Displayed when an existing active record is opened by someone who has the Update privilege.
3	Read-only	Displayed when an existing active record is opened by someone who does not have the Update privilege.

TABLE 7-10 Microsoft Dynamics CRM Form Types

Form Type Code	Form	Description
4	Disabled	Form is displayed when the record is in the inactive state. No user will be able to edit the values on the record, although a user with the Update privilege will be able to reactivate the record.
5	Quick create	Form is displayed for any user with the Create privilege. The form only shows the business required and business recommended fields.
6	Bulk edit	Special form that allows for editing multiple existing active records. User needs the Update privilege. Note: Custom script does not execute on this form.

Figure 7-6 shows an example of the account form in read-only mode.

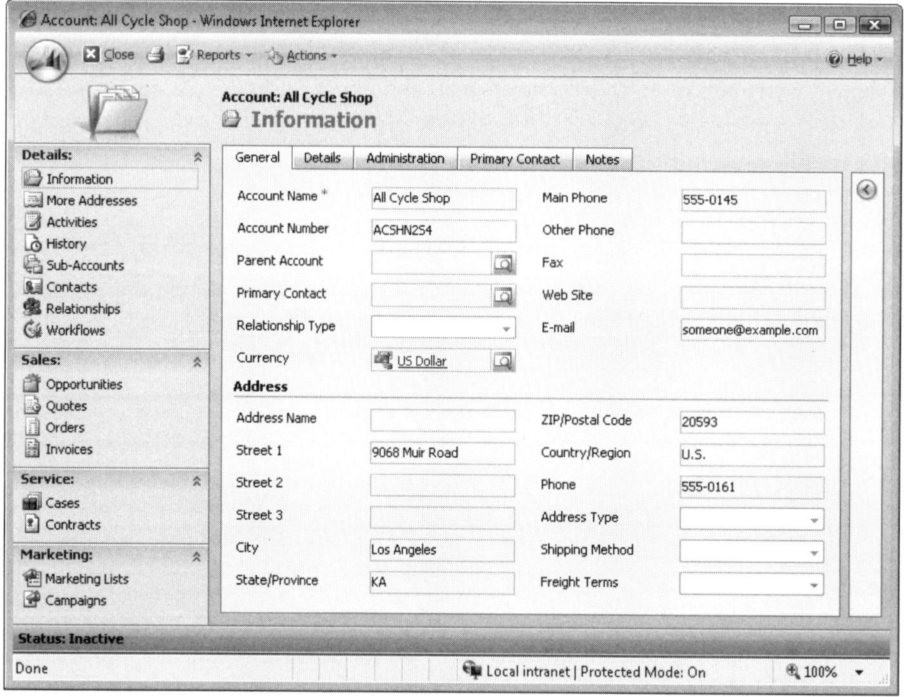

FIGURE 7-6 Account form in read-only mode

Note Workflow uses a form similar to the create form. However, the workflow form does not have a FormTypeCode.

When you develop scripts for Microsoft Dynamics CRM, you need to be sure to address how your script should run within each form type; otherwise you might have script that works with one form type but throws an error with a different form type. The most overlooked form is the quick-create form type. The quick-create form only displays required fields, and as a result some fields might not be available on that page for your script.

As you have probably noticed in the examples in this chapter (as well as in the SDK), you see the form type constants listed, and either a *switch* or *if* statement is used to determine when to execute the logic contained within the script. Here is an example:

```
var CRM_FORM_TYPE_CREATE      = 1;
var CRM_FORM_TYPE_UPDATE      = 2;
var CRM_FORM_TYPE_READONLY    = 3;
var CRM_FORM_TYPE_DISABLED    = 4;
var CRM_FORM_TYPE_QUICKCREATE = 5;
var CRM_FORM_TYPE_BULKEDIT    = 6;

switch (crmForm.FormType)
{
  case CRM_FORM_TYPE_CREATE :
  case CRM_FORM_TYPE_UPDATE :
  case CRM_FORM_TYPE_READONLY :
    // Your logic here
    break;
  case CRM_FORM_TYPE_QUICKCREATE :
    // Your logic for quick create here
    break;
}
```

Important The bulk edit and workflow forms do not execute any custom script.

Cross-Site Scripting (XSS)

We couldn't possibly provide a comprehensive analysis of Web application security in the scope of this book, but we want to touch on the notion of Microsoft Dynamics CRM cross-site scripting and its IFrame-related security issues. Cross-site scripting provides a powerful (and potentially dangerous) feature in Web applications, including Microsoft Dynamics CRM.

Cross-site scripting, also known as XSS, refers to the technique of using script to access elements between parent and child Web pages. With Microsoft Dynamics CRM, XSS provides powerful opportunities to interact with the native Microsoft Dynamics CRM form and its data from IFrames and Web pages launched from custom buttons or menu items.

For instance, suppose you have a button located on the toolbar of the Case grid. Your target page requires that the unique identifier of each record be selected when a user clicks the button. The following code demonstrates an example of using XSS to retrieve the selected record ids.

```
<!DOCTYPE HTML PUBLIC "-//W3C//DTD HTML 4.0 Transitional//EN">
<html>
<head>
<title>Custom Grid Page</title>
<script language="javascript" type="text/javascript">
function window.onload()
```

```
{
  document.write("<div style='font-size:10pt;'>Requested Ids<br><br>");
  // Determine if the window has dialog arguments passed to it
  if(window.dialogArguments)  {
    // If so, retrieve the arguments into an array
    var arr = new Array(window.dialogArguments.length -1);
    arr = window.dialogArguments;
    var selectedIds = '';
    // Loop through arguments and display back to user
    for(i=0; i< arr.length; i++)
    {
      selectedIds += arr[i] + "<br>";
    }
    document.write(selectedIds);
  }
  else {
    document.write("No records were selected.");
  }
  document.write("</div>");
}
</script>
</head>
<body>
</body>
</html>
```

Figure 7-7 displays the result of running the Web page from a modal button from the Case grid.

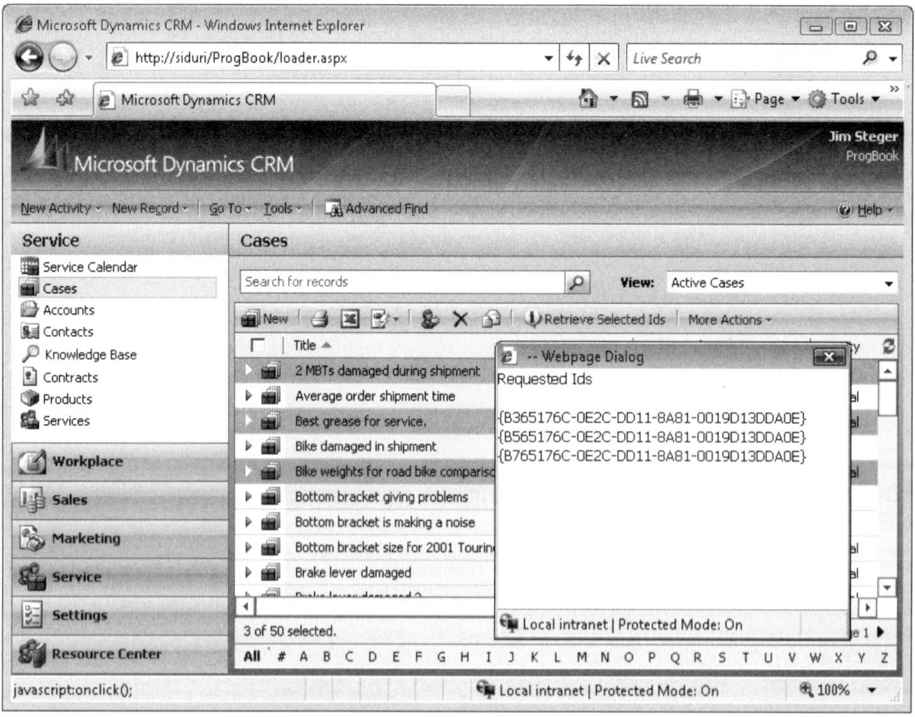

FIGURE 7-7 Retrieving record IDs from the grid to your custom page

In most cases, DHTML and the user's browser settings permit scripting access to and from IFrame documents that reside on the same domain and reference matching protocols (such as FTP, HTTP, or HTTPS).

More Info *Working with Microsoft Dynamics CRM 4.0* contains more information about IFrame security and XSS functionality.

XSS also poses a security risk to your application. All Web sites and Web applications need to account for the possibility of XSS and decide the impact it might have on your application. Microsoft provides a way to disable all script on the IFrame by checking the Restrict Cross-Frame Scripting option when creating a new IFrame. Checking this option prevents any script from executing on the child page.

More Info For additional information about the IFrame *security* attribute, visit *http://msdn2.microsoft.com/en-us/library/ms534622.aspx.*

Using Script for Validation

You have seen examples in this chapter of using form scripting to address different types of business requirements, including the ability to call Web service within your script. Consequently, you can use form scripting to meet all sorts of scenarios. One place where you might find that scripting techniques really come in handy is when you need to validate or format form entries. Using form scripts for validation offers numerous advantages, such as the following:

- Easy to implement and test
- Simple to deploy with the customization import and export options
- Provides instant feedback to the user
- Improves performance by preventing a round-trip to the server to evaluate logic

For example, let's validate the account number using script instead of the plug-in described in Chapter 5, "Plug-ins." Recall that you need to ensure that any entered account number conforms to the format *AA-######*; otherwise, the application should prevent the form from saving.

Add the following code to the *onChange* event of the Account's *accountnumber* attribute.

```
var accountNumber = crmForm.all.accountnumber.DataValue;
var regexFormat = /[A-Z]{2}-[0-9]{6}/;

// Validate the format of the account number
```

```
if ( ! regexFormat.test(accountNumber) ) {
 alert("The account number must match the following format: AA-######.");
}
```

Now, instead of waiting for the user to save and find out from the plug-in that he has the wrong format for the entered account number, the user can be alerted immediately to the mistake upon leaving the account number field, as shown in Figure 7-8.

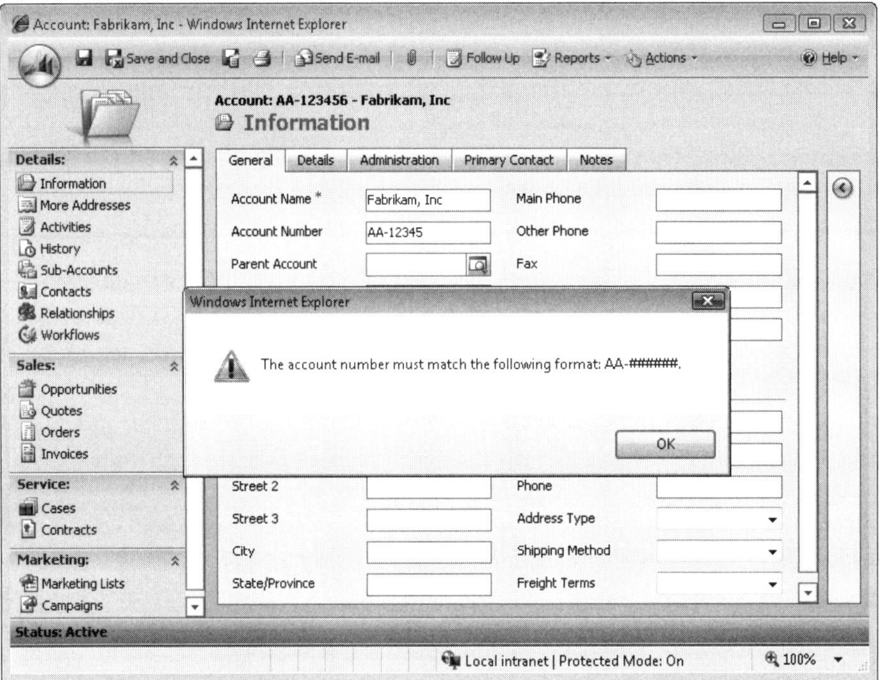

FIGURE 7-8 Client script validation

However, using client script exclusively for validation does come with some important disadvantages:

- Script validation works only when a user enters data from the form. It does not validate data added to the system via other means (such as bulk imports, workflow, or server-based integrations).
- Script validation requires JavaScript to be enabled on the user's browser; some mobile devices might not allow JavaScript.
- Validation code is accessible if the Web site's source is viewed.

When choosing whether to use client-side or server-side programming techniques for your validation needs, you need to consider all the situations by which data might be inserted, overall performance and user experience, as well as the type of validation required. Often a combination of both client-side and server-side validation should be employed to maximize the benefits of both approaches. However, if you do use both client-side and server-side techniques, you should obviously try to avoid duplicating the validation logic in multiple places because it might become out of sync and increase programming effort. In this case, consider moving the validation logic to a Web service that both the client-side and server-side code can reference.

Loading External JavaScript Files

After you start developing a large number of form scripts, you might find that you want to reuse some of your code for different entities and fields. One technique to accommodate this is to add code on a form's *onLoad* event that references an external script file. The main reason to do this is for ease of script administration and code reuse. For example, let's assume you have an *onChange* phone number formatting script on the 15 or 20 phone number fields for the Lead, Account, and Contact entities. Now, if you decide to update your script, you would have to update the script manually in each *onChange* location. However, if you had referenced an external script you could simply update the phone number formatting code in one location and save yourself the time and hassle of performing multiple updates. However, while this technique is definitely convenient, you might find that it's not appropriate for all circumstances. You should consider the following when referencing an external script:

- **Deployment overhead** Script code added directly to events can be deployed with the built-in import/export mechanisms. However, by referencing an external file, you are responsible for deploying and updating the references in the Microsoft Dynamics CRM form events, including the offline clients.
- **Microsoft Dynamics CRM Online script access** You will experience more challenges implementing this technique with Microsoft Dynamics CRM Online because you need to load any external files from another hosted site. You cannot upload a custom script file to the Microsoft Dynamics CRM Online server.
- **Access issues** When referencing a file on an external Web site, if that site is not available or if there is a delay in loading the file, the required methods might not be available to your code and might cause errors.
- **Web browser caching** The Web browser can cache external files. After you deploy a modification to an external file, users might need to delete their browser's cache to load the updated file's changes.

With the code in Listing 7-2, you can add an external script reference using the DOM. You should update the *url* variable with the proper path to your script file and then add the script to the form's *onLoad* event.

LISTING 7-2 Referencing a basic external script file using the DOM

```
// Define your script URL
var url = "/ISV/SonomaPartners/custom/scripts/script.js";

// Create the script element
var scriptElement =
document.createElement("<script src='" + url + "' language='javascript'>");
document.getElementsByTagName("head")[0].insertAdjacentElement("beforeEnd",
scriptElement);
```

Note Adding the following code directly to the *onLoad* event will not work:

```
<script language="JavaScript"
src="http://<crmserver>/ISV/SonomaPartners/custom/scripts/script.js"></script>
```

The manner by which Microsoft Dynamics CRM injects the *onLoad* script code into the form's output prevents this line from executing properly.

As mentioned previously, one of the drawbacks to using a file reference is that the browser will load the JavaScript files asynchronously. As such, if you need to execute logic in the form's *onLoad* event that relies on a method residing in your external script, you could end up with an error if that script hasn't been loaded in time.

You can help mitigate the asynchronous loading concern in a couple of ways. One approach is to take advantage of the fact that the Web browser reads the files sequentially (that is, from top to bottom). Place any logic that requires a method from the external JavaScript file at the bottom of that file. This ensures that the dependent logic loads correctly.

Another option is to use the *onreadystatechange* event when you load your script. The *onreadystatechange* event fires after the script has fully loaded, allowing you to execute additional code safely. The following code sample shows how you can use a custom *Script_OnLoad* function in conjunction with the *onreadystatechange* event.

```
// Create the script element
var scriptElement = document.createElement("<script type='text/javascript'>");
scriptElement.src = "/ISV/SonomaPartners/custom/scripts/script.js";
scriptElement.attachEvent("onreadystatechange", Script_OnLoad);
document.getElementsByTagName("head")[0].insertAdjacentElement("beforeEnd", scriptElement);

function Script_OnLoad()
{
  if (event.srcElement.readyState == "loaded" || event.srcElement.readyState == "complete")
  {
    // Safely call functions defined in your external script file.
  }
}
```

You might also consider using *XmlHttp* to load the external file and then use the JavaScript *eval* method to load the resulting script. This approach allows you to quickly and easily load script files. In Listing 7-3, simply update the *url* variable with the proper path to your script file, and then add the script to the form's *onLoad* event.

LISTING 7-3 Referencing a basic external script file using the JavaScript *eval* method

```
var url = "/ISV/SonomaPartners/scripts/global.js";

// Create an http request
var xmlhttp = new ActiveXObject("Microsoft.XMLHTTP");
xmlhttp.open("GET", url, false);
xmlhttp.send();

// Use the JavaScript eval method on the resulting script
eval(xmlhttp.responseText);
```

Warning The *eval* method opens the possibility for injection and cross-site scripting attacks. Please consider the security vulnerabilities as they pertain to your application prior to implementing.

Scripting Examples

Now that you understand the framework and the details of the Microsoft Dynamics CRM scripting SDK, we want to get into the fun of coding examples and real-world uses of these features. We included a variety of script samples for reference and to provide a starting point for your own customization needs. The following examples offer just a sampling of the many ways in which you can integrate custom logic by using scripting:

- Display customer information in a tooltip.
- Set the form's title at run time.
- Enhance the form's display.

You can use each of the examples discussed with any deployment of Microsoft Dynamics CRM, including CRM Online. Chapter 15, "Additional Samples and Utilities," contains more scripting samples and utilities for your use.

Caution Most of the sample scripts use DOM properties or methods not available with the CRM SDK and therefore might not upgrade to future versions of Microsoft Dynamics CRM.

Display Customer Information in a ToolTip

The first example demonstrates a simple technique for displaying related information about a customer by using Internet Explorer's tooltip functionality. An element's tooltip displays information when a user places the mouse over it. Figure 7-9 shows an example of what the user sees when she hovers her mouse over the Potential Customer label on an Opportunity form after you apply the code in Listing 7-4.

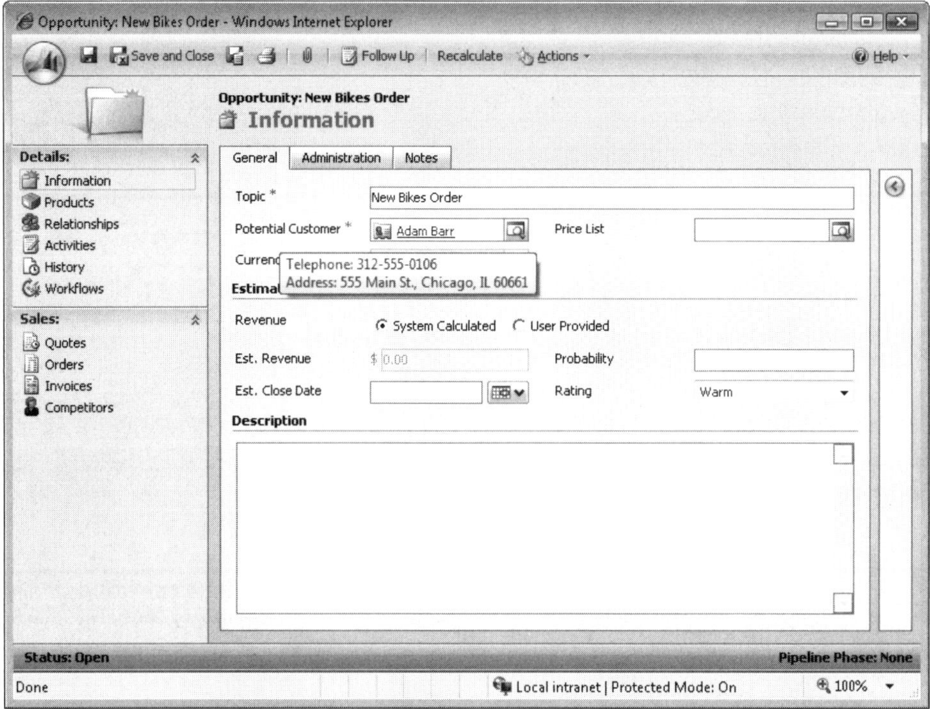

FIGURE 7-9 Customer detail displayed from an Opportunity form

The script in Listing 7-4 retrieves some information about the customer by constructing a SOAP message. It then concatenates the result to a string to be applied to the *title* property of the potential customer label (*customerid_c*).

The script can be immediately used on an Opportunity or a Case form because both entities use a Customer field. Remember to apply the script to both the *onLoad* event as well as the *onChange* event of the *Customer* attribute. You can also use this approach with any related field, including custom relationships, or extend it to display additional information.

Caution Remember that script doesn't render when you open the form in bulk edit mode.

LISTING 7-4 Display customer information from a customer label

```
var CRM_FORM_TYPE_CREATE         = 1;
var CRM_FORM_TYPE_UPDATE         = 2;
var CRM_FORM_TYPE_READONLY       = 3;

switch (crmForm.FormType)
{
  case CRM_FORM_TYPE_CREATE :
  case CRM_FORM_TYPE_UPDATE :
  case CRM_FORM_TYPE_READONLY :

  var customer = new Array;
  customer = crmForm.all.customerid.DataValue;

  if (customer != null)
  {
    var customerId = customer[0].id;
    var typeName = customer[0].typename;

    var details = RetrieveCustomerDetails(customerId, typeName);
    if (details != null)
    {
      crmForm.all.customerid_c.title = BuildCustomerDetails(details);
    }
  }
}

function BuildCustomerDetails(customerDetails)
{
  // Create a new DOM document and load the response XML
  var doc = new ActiveXObject("MSXML2.DOMDocument");
  doc.async = false;
  doc.loadXML(customerDetails);

  var result = "";

  // Return the q1:telephone1 node
  var telephone1Node = doc.selectSingleNode("//q1:telephone1");
  if( telephone1Node != null )
    result += "Telephone: " + telephone1Node.text + "\n";

  // Return the q1:address1_line1 node
  var address_line1Node =
        doc.selectSingleNode("//q1:address1_line1");
  if( address_line1Node != null )
    result += "Address: " + address_line1Node.text;

  // Return the q1:address1_city node
  var address_cityNode = doc.selectSingleNode("//q1:address1_city");
  if( address_cityNode != null )
    result += ", " + address_cityNode.text;
```

```
  // Return the q1:address1_stateorprovince node
  var address_stateorprovinceNode =
        doc.selectSingleNode("//q1:address1_stateorprovince");
  if( address_stateorprovinceNode != null )
    result += ", " + address_stateorprovinceNode.text;

  // Return the q1:address1_postalcode node
  var address_postalcodeNode =
        doc.selectSingleNode("//q1:address1_postalcode");
  if( address_postalcodeNode != null )
    result += " " + address_postalcodeNode.text;

  return result;
}

// Return additional customer details for a record
function RetrieveCustomerDetails(customerId, typeName)
{
  // Define URL to CRM API service
  var serverUrl = "/MSCrmServices/2007/CrmService.asmx";

  // Set up XMLHTTP request
  var xmlhttp = new ActiveXObject("Microsoft.XMLHTTP");
  xmlhttp.open("POST", serverUrl, false);
  xmlhttp.setRequestHeader("Content-Type", "text/xml; charset=utf-8")
  xmlhttp.setRequestHeader("SOAPAction",
"http://schemas.microsoft.com/crm/2007/WebServices/Retrieve")

  // Define the retrieve message
  var message =
  [
    "<?xml version='1.0' encoding='utf-8'?>",
    "<soap:Envelope xmlns:soap=\"http://schemas.xmlsoap.org/soap/envelope/\" ",
    "xmlns:xsi=\"http://www.w3.org/2001/XMLSchema-instance\" ",
    "xmlns:xsd=\"http://www.w3.org/2001/XMLSchema\">",
    GenerateAuthenticationHeader(),
    "<soap:Body>",
    "<Retrieve xmlns='http://schemas.microsoft.com/crm/2007/WebServices'>",
    "<entityName>",
    typeName,
    "</entityName>",
    "<id>",
    customerId,
    "</id>",
    "<columnSet xmlns:q1='http://schemas.microsoft.com/crm/2006/Query' xsi:type='q1:
      ColumnSet'>",
    "<q1:Attributes><q1:Attribute>address1_line1</q1:Attribute>",
    "<q1:Attribute>address1_city</q1:Attribute>",
    "<q1:Attribute>address1_stateorprovince</q1:Attribute>",
    "<q1:Attribute>address1_postalcode</q1:Attribute>",
    "<q1:Attribute>telephone1</q1:Attribute></q1:Attributes>",
    "</columnSet>",
    "</Retrieve>",
    "</soap:Body>",
```

```
    "</soap:Envelope>"
  ].join("");

  xmlhttp.send(message);
  return xmlhttp.responseXML.xml;
}
```

Setting the Form's Title at Run Time

An entity's form title is always in the format *Entity: [Primary Attribute Value]*. While this format works fine in most situations, you might find that you want a more descriptive title based on information gathered at run time. Figure 7-10 shows an example of changing the title of an account record to include the account number.

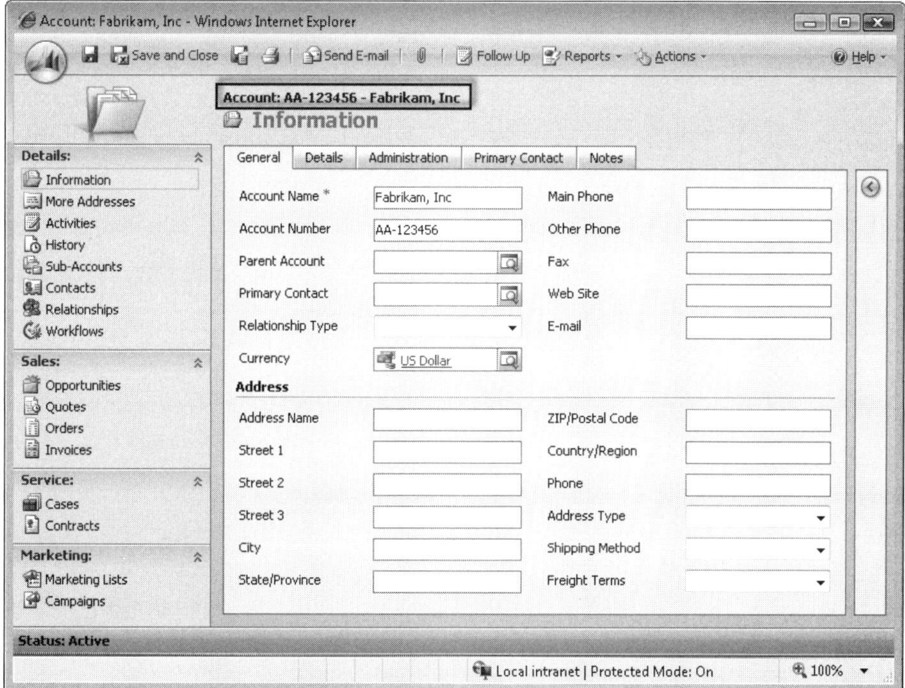

FIGURE 7-10 Account title

To use this example, add the code in Listing 7-5 to the *onLoad* event of the Account form.

Caution This code may not be upgradeable in future releases of Microsoft Dynamics CRM.

LISTING 7-5 Setting the Account form's title at run time

```
var CRM_FORM_TYPE_UPDATE     = 2;
var CRM_FORM_TYPE_UPDATE     = 2;
var CRM_FORM_TYPE_READ_ONLY  = 3;

// Only set the title if the form is in update or read-only mode
if ( (crmForm.FormType == CRM_FORM_TYPE_UPDATE)
      || (crmForm.FormType == CRM_FORM_TYPE_READ_ONLY) ) {
  var cells = document.getElementsByTagName("span");

  // Only continue if the account number has a value
  if (crmForm.all.accountnumber.DataValue != null)
  {
  // Loop through the span elements for the ms-crm-Form-Title class style
    for (var i = 0; i < cells.length; i++) {
      if (cells[i].className == "ms-crm-Form-Title") {
        cells[i].innerText = "Account: " +
          crmForm.all.accountnumber.DataValue + " - " + crmForm.all.name.DataValue;
        break;
      }
    }
  }
}
```

Enhancing the Form's Display

Microsoft Dynamics CRM forms provide a standard way to display data to users. A system administrator has the ability to alter the form's layout, including adding tabs, sections, and fields. However, the Microsoft Dynamics CRM form editor does not permit you to change the color or graphical design. But because you have full access to the form's DOM, you can alter various elements on the form to provide a more visually appealing display.

In this next sample, you will add a color-coded bar across the opportunity entity to quickly inform the user of the Opportunity's rating. The script changes the bar's color based on the selected Rating value of the Opportunity. As you will quickly see, the code can easily be extended for many useful scenarios. Figure 7-11 shows the colored bar across the top of the General tab. The bar is displayed in red when the Rating value equals Hot.

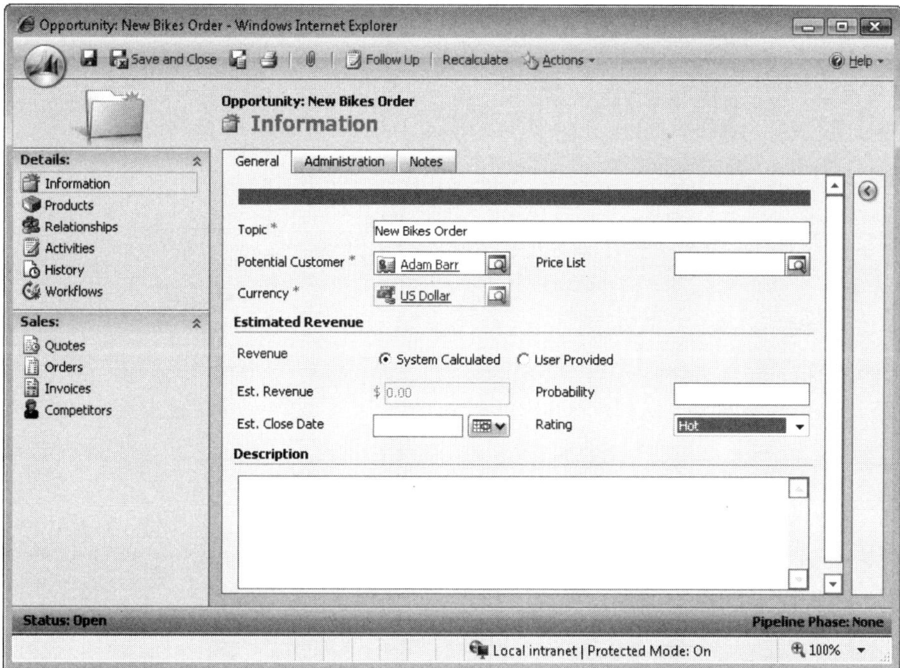

FIGURE 7-11 Opportunity rating display

To complete this sample, follow these straightforward steps:

Add a notification bar to the Opportunity form

1. On the Opportunity entity, create a new one-character *nvarchar* attribute called **Notification**.

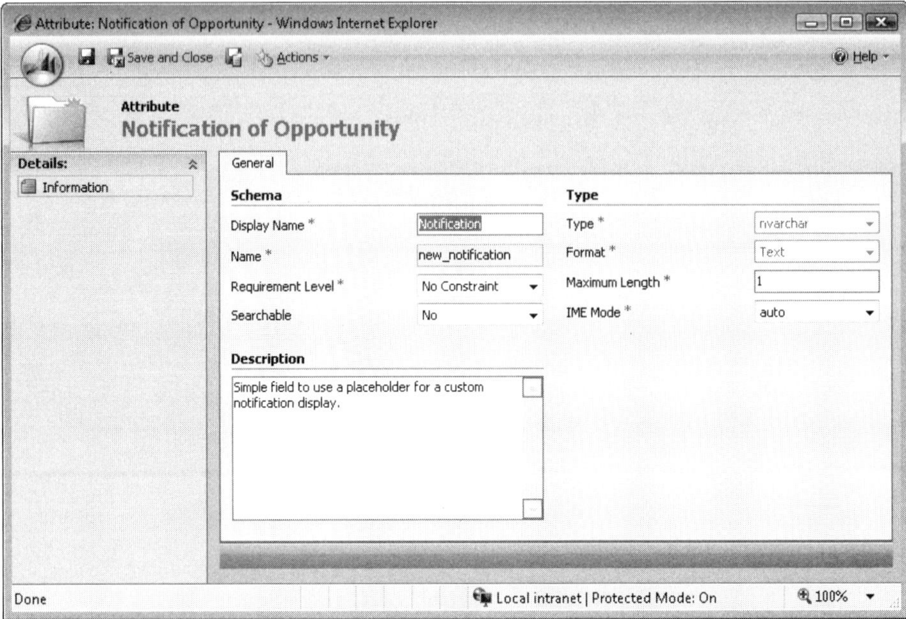

2. Add the Notification attribute to the top of the Opportunity form on the first tab.
3. Update the Notification attribute properties on the form by turning off the label display and have the attribute span two columns.
4. Add the following script to the form's *onLoad* event and the *customerratingcode* attribute's *onChange* event.

```
UpdateDisplayBar();

function UpdateDisplayBar()
{
  var notificationDisplay = document.getElementById("new_notification_d");
  var displayColor = "#EAF3FF";

  switch (crmForm.all.opportunityratingcode.DataValue)
  {
    case "1":
      displayColor = "red";
      break;
    case "2":
      displayColor = "yellow";
      break;
    case "3":
      displayColor = "blue";
      break;
  }

  var displayBar = "<div style='background=" + displayColor + "'> </div>";
  notificationDisplay.innerHTML = displayBar;
}
```

5. Save and publish your changes.

Summary

This chapter discusses some of the methods and options available to a script developer who wants to enhance and extend the Microsoft Dynamics CRM application. By using scripts and the application extensions enabled by Microsoft Dynamics CRM, you can easily create user-friendly and complex application integration that can span the multiple deployment models of Microsoft Dynamics CRM.

Chapter 8

Developing with the Metadata Service

As you learned earlier in this book, Microsoft Dynamics CRM includes a *MetadataService* Web service that allows you to programmatically read and modify the system schema. The *MetadataService* Web service exposes the same functionality that system customizers can access through the Web-based customization tools. The Microsoft Dynamics CRM metadata repository is effectively a stand-alone, middle-tier application. It stores and manages the metadata for the CRM application itself.

By working with the *MetadataService*, you can perform the following types of actions:

- Retrieve the metadata for a specific entity, either system or custom.
- Retrieve the attributes for an entity.
- Retrieve the metadata for a specific attribute, such as the possible state names or picklist values for an attribute.
- Create a custom entity.
- Add or update an attribute for an entity, either system or custom.
- Create or delete a relationship between two entities.
- Retrieve all the metadata to create a metadata cache in a client application.
- Determine whether metadata has changed since it was previously retrieved.
- Retrieve all the entities and determine which ones are custom entities.
- Add or remove an option from a picklist attribute.
- Write an install and uninstall program for your custom solution.
- Add and remove schemas for the purposes of deploying a solution. (Chapter 9, "Deployment," covers this scenario in specific detail.)

The prior version of Microsoft Dynamics CRM (version 3.0) also included a *MetadataService* Web service, but that version of the API allowed you only to read metadata; you could not modify the metadata. The ability to modify the schema through the *MetadataService* endpoint was added in Microsoft Dynamics CRM 4.0. (You might hear people refer to the Microsoft Dynamics CRM 3.0 *MetadataService* Web service as the 2006 endpoint.)

As listed above, the editable metadata service opens up all sorts of new and interesting programming options. For example, one tool that makes heavy use of the *MetadataService* is the Microsoft Dynamics CRM Data Migration Manager (DMM). As a stand-alone application, the DMM uses the metadata APIs to conduct its schema manipulation (used to extend the schema during data import). Figure 8-1 shows the Data Migration Manager and how to create a custom entity in its user interface. As a developer, you can use the metadata to develop your own unique Microsoft Dynamics CRM solutions.

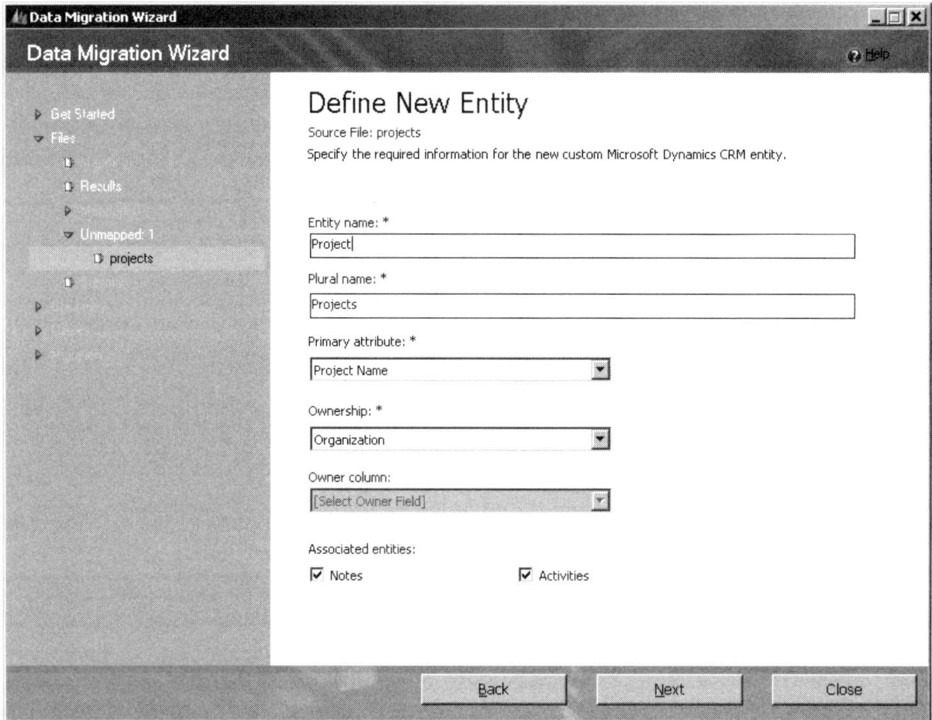

FIGURE 8-1 Data Migration Manager performing remote customization

In this chapter, we'll cover the following topics:

- Connecting to the *MetadataService*
- Retrieving metadata
- Remote customization
- Caching metadata
- Handling errors

Connecting to the *MetadataService*

The first step to work with the *MetadataService* is to connect to the API. Chapter 3, "Communicating with Microsoft CRM APIs," includes a detailed look at the various approaches related to connecting to the Microsoft Dynamics CRM APIs, but we will quickly review some of the key concepts here.

Referencing the *MetadataService*

The *MetadataService* supports all three deployment models: on-premise, Internet-facing deployment (IFD), and Windows Live ID (for Microsoft Dynamics CRM Online). You have the same options when accessing the *MetadataService* Web service as with the *CrmService*. To refresh the information provided earlier, you can include a reference to the service by one of the following approaches:

- Access the Web reference URL directly in Visual Studio 2008.
- Download the WSDL definition to the file system and add the Web reference locally.
- Reference the Microsoft.Crm.Sdk and Microsoft.Crm.SdkTypeProxy assemblies.

Because the *MetadataService* schema does not change, you should consider using the proxy assemblies to access the *MetadataService* functionality.

Be sure that you have the following namespaces included in your code:

- Microsoft.Crm.Sdk
- Microsoft.Crm.Sdk.Metadata
- Microsoft.Crm.SdkTypeProxy.Metadata

After you have the metadata service referenced in your code and are able to compile it, you still need to provide a valid endpoint for run-time use. We will now discuss the options available to configure the *MetadataService* endpoint.

Locating the Endpoints

You can locate the *MetadataService*'s endpoint (metadataservice.asmx) using several different techniques, and each option offers its own benefits and constraints, as discussed in Chapter 3. You should use caution before assuming that you know a Web service endpoint based on the URL of the user interface. Because the Enterprise edition of Microsoft Dynamics CRM supports role-based server deployments, it is possible that the server (or servers) hosting the API is different from the server hosting the Web user interface. Always use the appropriate mechanisms, detailed in the following section, to locate this URL. The main options to locate the *MetadataService* endpoints are:

- Use a setting within your application to specify the endpoint.
- Use the Microsoft Dynamics CRM *DiscoveryService* Web service to locate the *MetadataService* URL.
- Access *IMetadataService* through a plug-in.
- Connect to the offline *MetadataService* URL.

Application Settings

Commonly, you will want to write applications that allow the *MetadataService* endpoint to be specified in a configuration file or registry entry. This allows the most control over the endpoint location and still permits it to be specified at deployment. If your application is located on the Microsoft Dynamics CRM 4.0 server, it can access a registry key maintained by Microsoft Dynamics CRM 4.0 itself. The following code demonstrates the simplest way to access the service endpoint.

```
public static MetadataService GetMetadataService(string organizationName)
  {
    CrmAuthenticationToken token = new CrmAuthenticationToken();
    token.OrganizationName = organizationName;

    MetadataService service = new MetadataService();
    // Replace <crmserver> with your own value
    service.Url = "http://<crmserver>/MSCRMServices/2007/MetadataService.asmx";
    service.UseDefaultCredentials = true;
    service.CrmAuthenticationTokenValue = token;

    return service;
  }
```

For the sake of brevity, we will use the *GetMetadataService* method throughout the sample code in the remainder of this chapter.

Discovery Service

You use the *CrmMetadataServiceUrl* property of the *OrganizationDetail* object to determine the URL of the *MetadataService*, as demonstrated in the following code sample:

```
string orgName = "contoso";
string metadataServiceUrl;

CrmDiscoveryService discoveryService = new CrmDiscoveryService();
discoveryService.Credentials = CredentialCache.DefaultCredentials;
```

```
// Replace localhost with the correct URL for your application
discoveryService.Url = "http://localhost/MSCRMServices/2007/AD/CrmDiscoveryService.asmx";

RetrieveOrganizationsRequest retrieveOrgRequest = new RetrieveOrganizationsRequest();
RetrieveOrganizationsResponse retrieveOrgResponse =
    (RetrieveOrganizationsResponse)discoveryService.Execute(retrieveOrgRequest);

foreach (OrganizationDetail orgDetail in retrieveOrgResponse.OrganizationDetails)
{
    if (orgDetail.OrganizationName == orgName)
    {
        metadataServiceUrl = orgDetail.CrmMetadataServiceUrl;
        break;
    }
}
```

You should consider using the Discovery service option when you are unsure of the actual endpoints of your final deployment or when you are using Microsoft Dynamics CRM Online.

Plug-ins

Just as the *ICrmService* interface is provided to plug-ins for accessing the *CrmService* Web service API from within a plug-in, an interface is also exposed for the *MetadataService*. This interface is called *IMetadataService* and is generated using the *CreateMetadataService* method on the *IPluginExecutionContext* object, as shown in the following code:

```
using System;
using System.Collections.Generic;
using System.Text;
using Microsoft.Crm.Sdk;
using Microsoft.Crm.SdkTypeProxy;

namespace MetadataPluginSample
{
    public class MyPlugin : IPlugin
    {
        public void Execute(IPluginExecutionContext context)
        {
            IMetadataService metadataService = context.CreateMetadataService(true);
        }
    }
}
```

More Info Please review Chapter 5, "Plug-ins," for more information regarding plug-ins and the *IPluginExecutionContext* object.

Offline

The *MetadataService* is also available in Microsoft Dynamics CRM for Outlook with Offline Access. Chapter 3 details how to locate and configure the URL endpoint and offline development is covered extensively in Chapter 10, "Developing Offline Solutions."

The offline client's middle tier does not support customization, and subsequently not all *MetadataService* messages are available while offline. Only the following messages are available:

- RetrieveAllEntitiesRequest
- RetrieveAllEntitiesResponse
- RetrieveEntityRequest
- RetrieveEntityResponse
- RetrieveAttributeRequest
- RetrieveAttributeResponse
- RetrieveRelationshipRequest
- RetrieveRelationshipResponse
- RetrieveTimestampRequest
- RetrieveTimestampResponse

Using the *MetadataService* with the *CrmImpersonator* Class

Chapter 3 introduced the *CrmImpersonator* class as a way to seamlessly authenticate with IFD deployments. Take special care when using the *MetadataService* with the *CrmImpersonator* class. Because of the way the *CrmImpersonator* class operates, you should avoid using the discovery service for locating the endpoint. Either manually set the endpoint from a configuration setting or use the registry.

The following sample code shows how to access the *MetadataService* Web service from the registry when using the impersonation pattern with the metadata service:

```
//Retrieve Server URL from the Registry
string metadataServiceUrl;
using (RegistryKey key = Registry.LocalMachine.OpenSubKey("Software\\Microsoft\\MSCRM"))
{
    metadataServiceUrl =
        key.GetValue("ServerUrl").ToString() + "/2007/metadataservice.asmx";
}
```

```
//Wrap Code in Using statement
using (new CrmImpersonator())
{
    CrmAuthenticationToken token =
     CrmAuthenticationToken.ExtractCrmAuthenticationToken(Context,"MyOrganizationName");
    token.AuthenticationType = 0;
    token.OrganizationName = "MyOrganizationName";
    MetadataService metadataService = new MetadataService();
    metadataService.CrmAuthenticationTokenValue = token;
    metadataService.Credentials = CredentialCache.DefaultCredentials;
    metadataService.Url = metadataServiceUrl;
}
```

2006 Endpoint

As we mentioned earlier, the 3.0 version of Microsoft Dynamics CRM included a *MetadataService* Web service. The URL of this Web service is *http://<crmserver>/mscrm-services/2006/metadataservice.asmx*. Even though Microsoft Dynamics CRM 4.0 includes a new *MetadataService*, you can still access the 3.0 service. Some developers refer to this Web service as the 2006 endpoint (because of the 2006 in its URL) and the 4.0 Web service is known as the 2007 endpoint.

The capabilities of the 2006 endpoint service differ significantly from the 2007 endpoint. The 2006 endpoint is only capable of reading the metadata, and you can only connect to the default organization. When writing new code, you should only use the 2007 endpoint. Microsoft included the 2006 endpoint in Microsoft Dynamics CRM 4.0 for backward compatibility for customers upgrading from Microsoft Dynamics CRM 3.0 to 4.0.

Microsoft Dynamics CRM Security

As with core entities, Microsoft Dynamics CRM 4.0 also contains a set of security privileges for many of the common metadata components, such as entities, attributes, and relationships. At a minimum, the user executing the *MetadataService* call will need to have read privileges for the specific metadata being operated on. Figure 8-2 shows a sample Microsoft Dynamics CRM security role listing the metadata privileges.

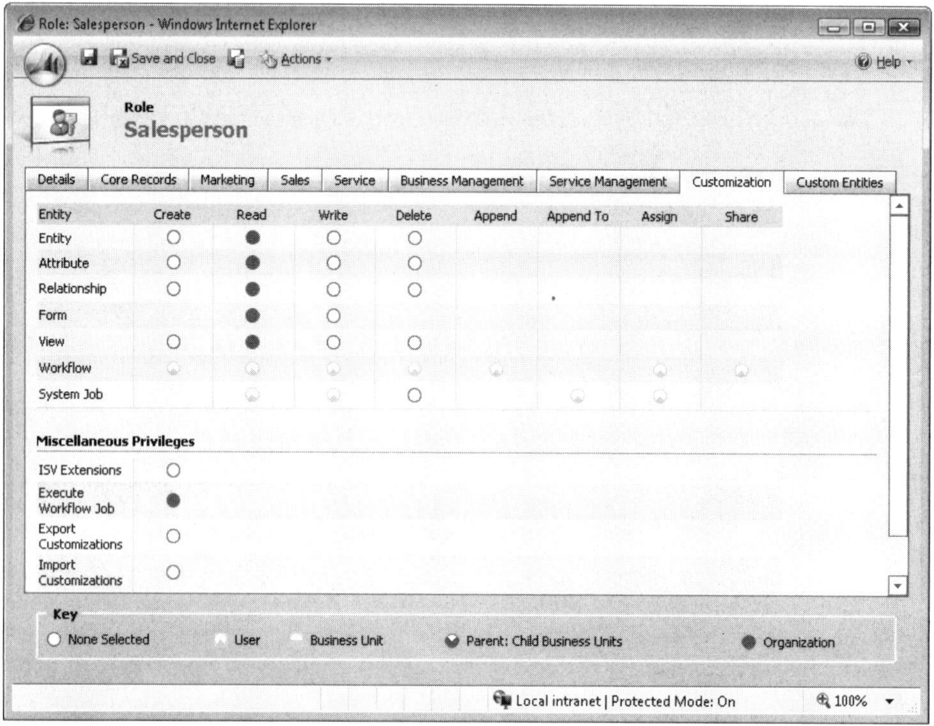

FIGURE 8-2 Metadata privileges

Note Microsoft Dynamics CRM 3.0 did not enforce privileges for *MetadataService* calls. When upgrading your code to Microsoft Dynamics CRM 4.0, be sure to appropriately update the security roles of your users for any *MetadataService* interaction.

Retrieving Metadata

The *MetadataService* uses an object structure that differs from the *CrmService*. All metadata objects inherit from the *CrmMetadata* object. A number of objects are also shared by the *MetadataService* and the *CrmService* Web Service (for example, CRM data types).

Warning Watch out for type name collisions when using both the *MetadataService* and the regular Web service inside a class. You might need to partition your code better or use namespace aliasing to prevent compilation issues.

Names Used in the *MetadataService*

It's important to understand the difference between the logical names and schema names used by the *MetadataService*. In most cases these names are identical (with some variation for case differences). Be alert when comparing values; you may need to adjust your casing appropriately.

- **Logical name** The unique property name or class name of an object. The logical name is always lowercase. In the user interface, the logical name is simply referred to as Name.
- **Schema name** The unique name used by CRM to store the object in the database. The schema name often uses Pascal casing.

New schema names and logical names must conform to a naming convention and have a customization prefix (between two and eight characters with an underscore). Examples include: *new_* and *contoso_*.

Retrieving Entities

CRM's metadata essentially consists of a collection of entities. All other pieces of metadata (attributes, relationships, and so on) are linked by an entity. The *EntityMetadata* object describes the schema information for a CRM entity. Most of the *EntityMetadata's* properties are normal CRM types (for example, *CrmBoolean*) that describe the characteristics of the entity. Each entity has five important collections of related objects, which we will discuss in detail later in the chapter:

- Privileges
- Attributes
- ManyToManyRelationships
- ManyToOneRelationships
- OneToManyRelationships

RetrieveEntityRequest

You use *RetrieveEntityRequest*—with its corresponding response message *RetrieveEntityResponse*—to retrieve a single *EntityMetadata* object from CRM. The *RetrieveEntityRequest* object has three properties that should always be set:

- EntityItems
- RetrieveAsIfPublished
- LogicalName

The *EntityItems* property determines whether the five important collections (*Privileges, Attributes, ManyToManyRelationships, ManyToOneRelationships,* and *OneToManyRelationships*) are populated when the entity data is retrieved. Retrieving these collections is a heavyweight task, and for performance reasons a developer might choose to retrieve only some of the entity's related data. Because *EntityItems* is marked with *FlagsAttribute,* multiple values can be combined using a bitwise *OR* (the | operator in C#). The *EntityItems* enum has the following values:

- *EntityItems.All* Retrieves privileges, attributes, ManyToManyRelationships, ManyToOneRelationships, and OneToManyRelationships.
- *EntityItems.EntityOnly* Used when you only want the basic entity metadata returned and none of the related collections populated. All the other *EntityItems* values will include the entity metadata as well, so while it will not cause an error, this value never needs to be combined with the other *EntityItems* values.
- *EntityItems.IncludeAttributes* Specifies that the *Attribute* collection should be populated.
- *EntityItems.IncludePrivileges* Specifies that the *Privileges* collection should be populated.
- *EntityItems.IncludeRelationships* Specifies that the ManyToManyRelationships, ManyToOneRelationships, and OneToManyRelationships collections should be populated.

The *RetrieveAsIfPublished* property determines whether unpublished metadata is shown. When this property is set to *true*, CRM simulates an entity publish operation when retrieving the metadata. If you want to retrieve metadata as experienced by end users, set this property to *false*. If you want to retrieve metadata as experienced by customizers (in the customization user interface of the application), set this property to *true*.

The *LogicalName* property determines which entity is retrieved.

More Info Refer to the following article in the Microsoft Dynamics CRM 4.0 Software Development Kit (SDK), which provides additional information regarding logical names: *http://msdn.microsoft.com/en-us/library/cc151044.aspx*.

The following code shows how to retrieve a single entity from CRM:

```
MetadataService metadataService = GetMetadataService("contoso");

RetrieveEntityRequest request = new RetrieveEntityRequest();
request.EntityItems = EntityItems.All;
request.RetrieveAsIfPublished = true;
request.LogicalName = "account";
RetrieveEntityResponse response = (RetrieveEntityResponse)metadataService.Execute(request);
```

RetrieveAllEntitiesRequest

RetrieveAllEntitiesRequest retrieves all entities in CRM (System, Custom, and Customizable). You also need to set the *RetriveAsIfPublished* property and determine the depth and detail of the related entity collections using the *MetadataItems* property. *RetrieveAllEntitiesRequest* uses the *MetadataItems* property to govern the level of detail returned by the request. The *MetadataItems* property is an enum type that is also named *MetadataItems*. Similar to the *EntityItems* enum, multiple values can be combined to control the retrieval behavior as follows:

- *MetadataItems.All* Retrieve *Privileges, Attributes, ManyToManyRelationships, ManyToOneRelationships*, and *OneToManyRelationships*. Because this value already returns everything, it should not be combined with other values.
- *MetadataItems.EntitiesOnly* Return only the entity metadata and not the related collections. All the other *MetadataItems* values include the entity metadata as well, so you never need to combine *EntitiesOnly* with the other values.
- *MetadataItems.IncludeAttributes* Specifies to populate the *Attribute* collection.
- *MetadataItems.IncludePrivileges* Specifies to populate the *Privileges* collection.
- *MetadataItems.IncludeRelationships* Specifies to populate the *ManyToManyRelationships*, *ManyToOneRelationships*, and *OneToManyRelationships* collections.

Notice that *RetrieveAllEntitiesResponse* contains an array of *CrmMetadata* objects. This array will only ever contain *EntityMetadata* objects (which inherit from *CrmMetadata*).

The following code retrieves all entities from CRM and writes their logical names to the console. Figure 8-3 displays the resulting output.

```
MetadataService metadataService = GetMetadataService("contoso");

RetrieveAllEntitiesRequest request = new RetrieveAllEntitiesRequest();
request.MetadataItems = MetadataItems.EntitiesOnly;
request.RetrieveAsIfPublished = false;
RetrieveAllEntitiesResponse response =
  (RetrieveAllEntitiesResponse)metadataService.Execute(request);

foreach (EntityMetadata entity in response.CrmMetadata)
{
    Console.WriteLine(entity.LogicalName);
}
```

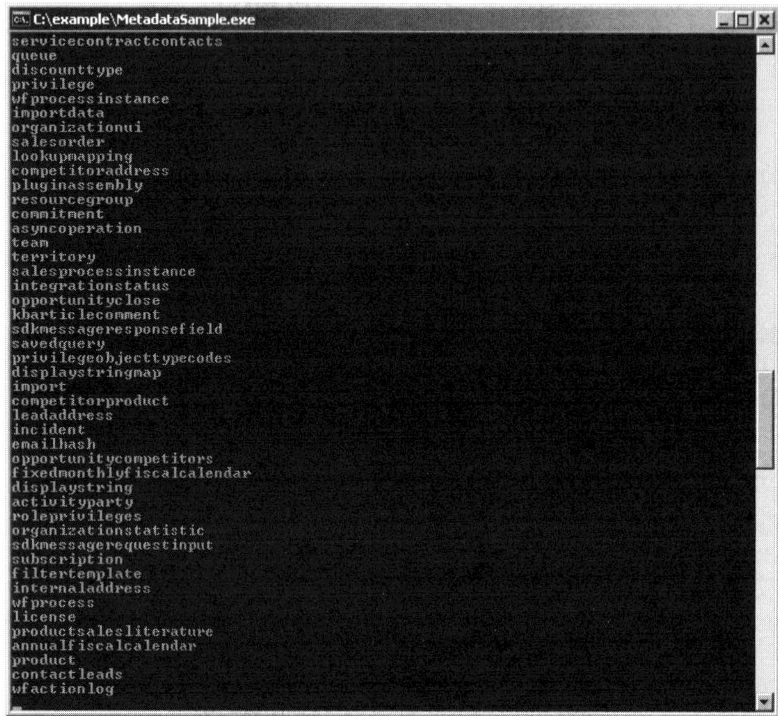

FIGURE 8-3 *RetrieveAllEntities* sample code output

Retrieving Attributes and Relationships

You can retrieve attributes and relationships in one of two ways: individually, by using the appropriate *Retrieve* message specifying their unique logical names, or as part of a collection in the *RetrieveEntityRequest* or *RetrieveAllEntities* request. The *MetadataService* does not offer a message to retrieve all of an organization's attributes or relationships. Both requests also make use of the *RetrieveAsIfPublished* property, which you should always set. (See the section "Retrieving Entities" earlier in the chapter for more information on this topic.)

Attribute Considerations

When retrieving an attribute with *RetriveAttributeRequest* you simply provide the logical names of the attribute and its parent entity. You can also use the attribute's unique *MetadataId* (a GUID) if known.

Tip You can often substitute the *MetadataId* for logical names of entities, attributes, and relationships. Note that these IDs are not consistent between organizations.

Relationship Considerations

When retrieving a relationship with *RetrieveRelationshipRequest*, you simply provide the logical name of the relationship or its *MetadataId* (a GUID). You do not need to specify any parent entity information. *RetrieveRelationshipRequest* returns a *RelationshipMetadata* object. However, you need to cast this object to one of its child types: *OneToManyMetadata* or *ManyToManyMetadata*. *ManyToOneMetadata* does not exist—a many-to-one relationship is simply a one-to-many relationship viewed from a different perspective.

Two properties often cause confusion with the *OneToManyMetadata* object: *ReferencedEntity* and *ReferencingEntity*. Table 8-1 lists how the user interface describes each property.

TABLE 8-1 Reference Entity Labels

Object Property	Label in the Customization User Interface
ReferencedEntity	Primary Entity
ReferencingEntity	Related Entity

RetrieveAllEntitiesResponse contains a copy of each one-to-many relationship in the appropriate arrays (*OneToManyRelationships* and *ManyToOneRelationships*) for both the *Referenced* and *Referencing* entities, as shown in Table 8-2.

TABLE 8-2 Reference Entity Array Relationship

Entity	Array Relationship Is Found In
ReferencedEntity	*OneToManyRelationships*
ReferencingEntity	*ManyToOneRelationships*

You can locate a relationship's logical name in the customization user interface. Figure 8-4 shows the relationship's logical name in the Name field of the relationship customization form.

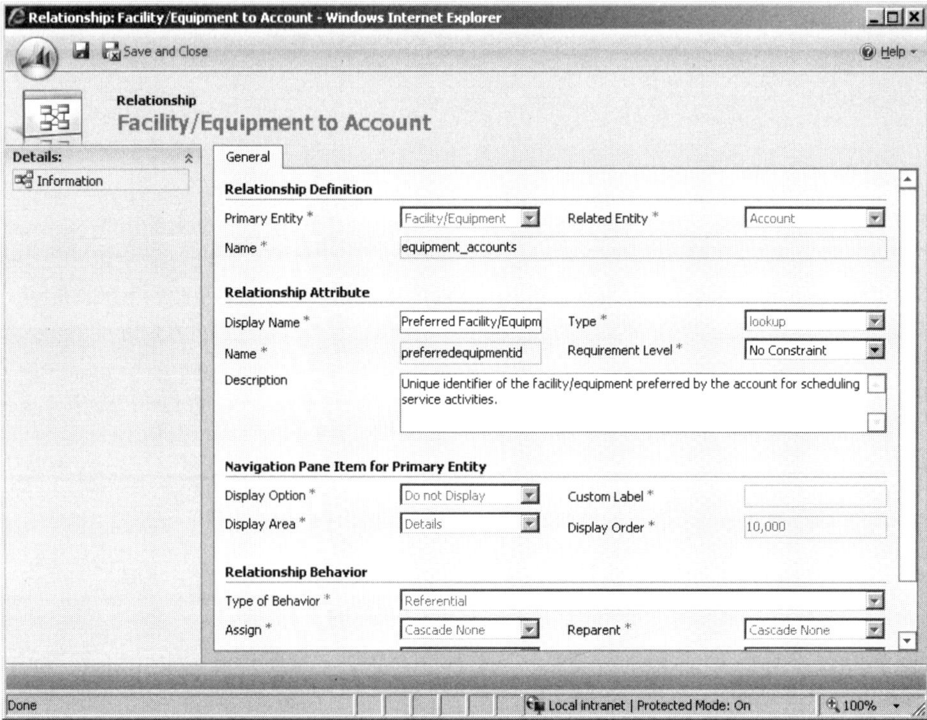

FIGURE 8-4 One-to-many relationship customization form

The following code sample demonstrates how to retrieve the *equipment_accounts* relationship shown in Figure 8-4 and display the *Referencing* and *Referenced* entity information.

```
MetadataService metadataService = GetMetadataService("contoso");

RetrieveRelationshipRequest request = new RetrieveRelationshipRequest();
request.Name = "equipment_accounts";
request.RetrieveAsIfPublished = true;
RetrieveRelationshipResponse response =
    (RetrieveRelationshipResponse)metadataService.Execute(request);

if (response.RelationshipMetadata is OneToManyMetadata)
{
    OneToManyMetadata equipmentAccounts =
     (OneToManyMetadata)response.RelationshipMetadata;

    Console.Write("Referenced Entity: ");
    Console.WriteLine(equipmentAccounts.ReferencedEntity);

    Console.Write("Referencing Entity: ");
    Console.WriteLine(equipmentAccounts.ReferencingEntity);
}
```

This relationship creates a lookup attribute on the account to the equipment entity. Therefore, the Account entity is referencing the Equipment entity, and the Equipment entity is being referenced by the Account entity. Figure 8-5 shows console output for the sample.

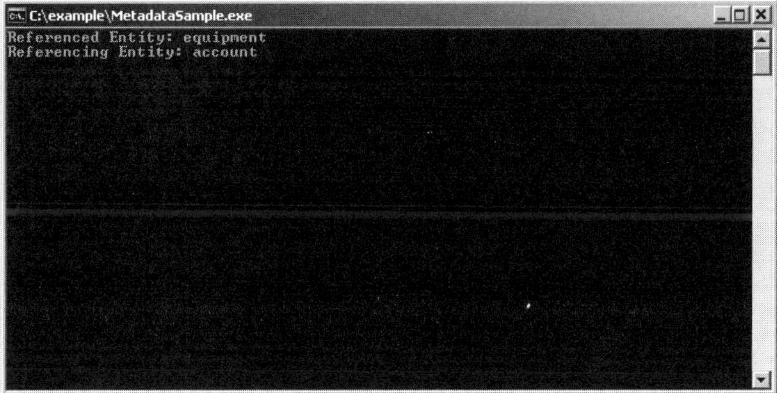

FIGURE 8-5 Console output for relationship retrieval sample

Multilingual Strings

Many of the properties of the objects in the *MetadataService* make use of multilingual strings. The *CrmLabel* object facilitates the storage of such items. In Microsoft Dynamics CRM 3.0, properties such as the Display Name of an entity (Account, Contact, Lead, Project, and so on) were stored as a simple string in the metadata. With the introduction of multilingual user interface features in Microsoft Dynamics CRM 4.0, this is no longer practical given the normalization of this information.

Tip We recommend that you install and activate at least one additional language on all your development servers, even if you don't need multiple languages right now. Installing multiple languages will expose new defects or scenarios that you would not experience with only one language installed. Microsoft provides the various language packs at no cost. You can download them from *http://www.microsoft.com/downloads*.

The *CrmLabel* object stores the strings for a particular property inside an array of *LocLabel* objects. A *LocLabel* object consists of a string property (for the actual string user by the user interface) and an *int* property (the LCID). LCIDs (Locale IDs) indicates the Language and Culture/Region of the string.

More Info A full list of LCIDs is available from Microsoft's Web site: *http://www.microsoft.com/globaldev/reference/lcid-all.mspx*.

The following code is a useful helper method that creates an instance of *CrmLabel* and initializes it with a *LocLabel* value for a single locale. We will take advantage of this helper method in later code samples in this chapter.

```
public static CrmLabel CreateLabel(string label, int languageCode)
{
    CrmLabel crmLabel = new CrmLabel();
    crmLabel.LocLabels = new LocLabel[1];
    crmLabel.LocLabels[0].Label = label;
    crmLabel.LocLabels[0].LanguageCode = new CrmNumber();
    crmLabel.LocLabels[0].LanguageCode.Value = languageCode;
    return crmLabel;
}
```

We recommend that metadata developers always assume that CRM may have multiple languages installed. Table 8-3 lists the language packs that Microsoft Dynamics CRM offered at the time this book went to press.

TABLE 8-3 Microsoft Dynamics CRM 4.0 language packs

Arabic	French	Norwegian
Chinese (Hong Kong)	German	Polish
Chinese (Simplified)	Greek	Portuguese (Brazil)
Chinese (Traditional)	Hebrew	Portuguese (Iberian)
Czech	Hungarian	Russian
Danish	Italian	Spanish
Dutch	Japanese	Swedish
English	Korean	Turkish
Finnish		

More Info Please refer to the Microsoft Dynamics CRM 4.0 Implementation Guide for details on downloading, installing, and activating language packs.

CRM also provides a handy helper property, *UserLocLabel*, which is a property of the *CrmLabel* object. This string property is set to the string of the *LocLabel* for the LCID of the user making the call. For example, if my language is set to French (LCID 1036), the string value of the *UserLocLabel* will be the 1036 string.

Tip Never try to set the *UserLocLabel* property. It is read-only!

In the following example the code displays the strings for the *DisplayCollectionName* property (the entity plural name) in the console. This code assumes you have already retrieved the *EntityMetadata* object (called entity here) from the *MetadataService*. Figure 8-6 shows the console output.

```
//Assumes that an EntityMetadata object called entity was created and retrieved from CRM

Console.WriteLine("Entity Plural Name Strings");
Console.WriteLine();

Console.WriteLine("User LocLabel");
Console.WriteLine(entity.DisplayCollectionName.UserLocLabel.LanguageCode.Value);
Console.WriteLine(entity.DisplayCollectionName.UserLocLabel.Label);
Console.WriteLine();

Console.WriteLine("LocLabel Collection");
foreach (LocLabel loclabel in entity.DisplayCollectionName.LocLabels)
{
    Console.WriteLine(loclabel.LanguageCode.Value);
    Console.WriteLine(loclabel.Label);
    Console.WriteLine();
}
```

FIGURE 8-6 Language strings console application

As Figure 8-6 shows, the organization had U.S. English (1033) and French (1036) installed and activated.

Available Languages

You should only use LCIDs for languages installed on the Microsoft Dynamics CRM server. Attempts to use LCIDs for unavailable languages will silently fail. Use *RetrieveAvailable-LanguagesRequest* with the *CrmService* to retrieve an array of LCIDs in the *LocaleIds* property of the *RetrieveAvailableLanguagesResponse* object.

The following code shows how to retrieve the available languages and display them in the console:

```
//Connect to the regular CRM Service
CrmAuthenticationToken token = new CrmAuthenticationToken();
token.AuthenticationType = 0;
token.OrganizationName = "contoso";
```

```
CrmService crmService = new CrmService();
crmService.CrmAuthenticationTokenValue = token;
crmService.Credentials = CredentialCache.DefaultCredentials;
crmService.Url = "http://crm/mscrmservices/2007/crmservice.asmx";

RetrieveAvailableLanguagesRequest request = new RetrieveAvailableLanguagesRequest();
RetrieveAvailableLanguagesResponse response =
    (RetrieveAvailableLanguagesResponse) crmService.Execute(request)

Console.WriteLine("Available Languages");
foreach (int i in response.LocaleIds)
{
    Console.WriteLine(i);
}
```

Remote Customization

In addition to retrieving data about the entities and data schema, the Microsoft Dynamics CRM *MetadataService* allows you to programmatically modify schema changes. This section will explore the structure of *CrmMetadata's* objects in more detail and show how you can programmatically create, update, and delete objects.

Entities

Working with entities in the *MetadataService* closely mirrors the experience found in CRM's customization user interface. Consequently, you cannot perform actions with the *MetadataService* that users can't perform in the user interface. Developers typically use *MetadataService* messages to manipulate metadata on remote systems to facilitate the deployment of their solutions.

Creating Entities

Unfortunately creating an entity with the *MetadataService* is not as straightforward as creating a data record with the *CrmService*. To create an entity, you use *CreateEntityRequest* and set the following properties: *Entity* (*EntityMetadata*), *PrimaryAttribute* (*StringAttributeMetadata*), *HasNotes* (*bool*), and *HasActivities* (*bool*). Once you create an entity's Primary Attribute, Notes, and Activity settings, you cannot change them.

When you set the schema name it must be unique among all entities and *ManyToManyRelationships* because a unique database table is created using this name (hence the term *schema*). The lowercase version of the schema name is the entity's resulting logical name.

Best Practice To avoid confusion with case-sensitive code, use lowercase letters for the schema name.

Creating an entity using the *MetadataService* has the same consequences as creating one with the customization user interface. Microsoft Dynamics CRM automatically creates a number of standard attributes (for example, Created On, Modified On) in addition to creating forms and views for the entity. In addition, Microsoft Dynamics CRM create relationships to the System User entity (for example, Created By, Modified By, Owner).

The following code sample demonstrates how to create a custom entity named "project" using the *MetadataService*:

```
MetadataService metadataService = GetMetadataService("contoso");

EntityMetadata projectMetadata = new EntityMetadata();

projectMetadata.SchemaName = "new_project";
projectMetadata.DisplayName = CreateLabel("Project", 1033);
projectMetadata.DisplayCollectionName = CreateLabel("Projects", 1033);
projectMetadata.Description = CreateLabel(
    "Describes a Project. A time bound collection of work.", 1033);
projectMetadata.OwnershipType = new CrmOwnershipTypes();
projectMetadata.OwnershipType.Value = OwnershipTypes.UserOwned;

StringAttributeMetadata nameMetadata = new StringAttributeMetadata();

nameMetadata.SchemaName = "new_name";
nameMetadata.DisplayName = CreateLabel("Project Name", 1033);
nameMetadata.Description = CreateLabel("The Name of the Project", 1033);
nameMetadata.MaxLength = new CrmNumber();
nameMetadata.MaxLength.Value = 200;
nameMetadata.RequiredLevel = new CrmAttributeRequiredLevel();
nameMetadata.RequiredLevel.Value = AttributeRequiredLevel.Required;

CreateEntityRequest request = new CreateEntityRequest();
request.Entity = projectMetadata;
request.PrimaryAttribute = nameMetadata;
request.HasActivities = true;
request.HasNotes = true;

metadataService.Execute(request);
```

Figure 8-7 shows the new entity through the user interface.

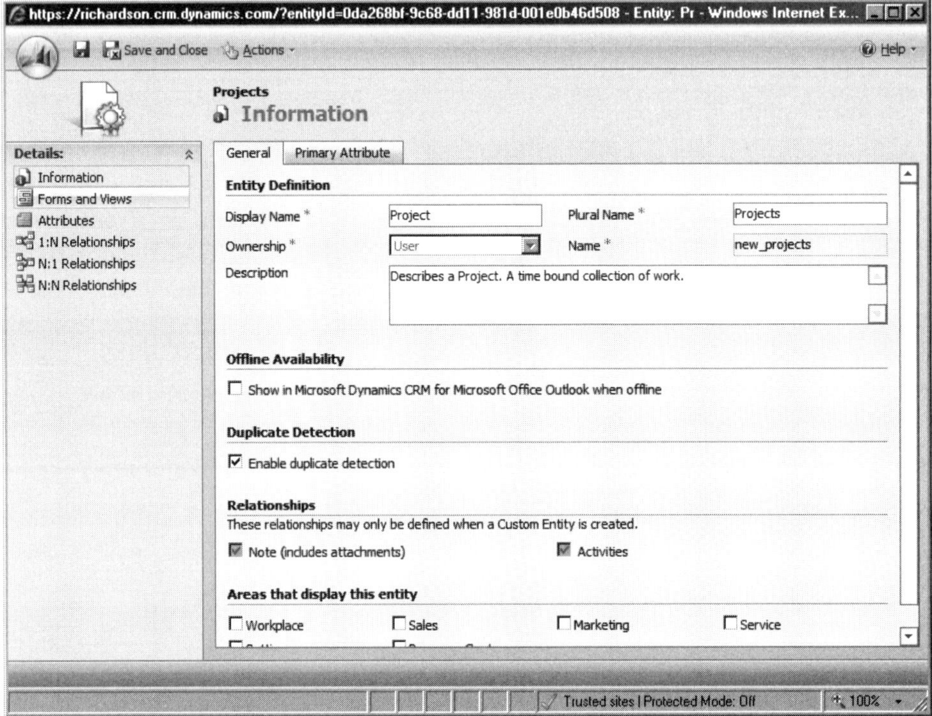

FIGURE 8-7 Entity form

If you don't provide explicit values in the organization's base language for the entity *DisplayName*, *DisplayCollectionName*, and attribute's *DisplayName*, an error results. You must always populate these values in the organization's base language.

Once you create an entity, the *CreateEntityResponse* has GUID properties that you can use with *RetrieveEntityRequest* and *RetrieveAttributeRequest* as a means of locating these objects. You can take advantage of these metadata identifiers in your own code. For example:

```
//Execute the Request
CreateEntityResponse createResponse =
    (CreateEntityResponse)metadataService.Execute(createRequest);
Guid entityId = createResponse.EntityId.Value;

//Retrieve New Entity
RetrieveEntityRequest retrieveRequest = new RetrieveEntityRequest();
retrieveRequest.EntityItems = EntityItems.EntityOnly;
retrieveRequest.MetadataId = entityId;
retrieveRequest.RetrieveAsIfPublished = true;
RetrieveEntityResponse retrieveResponse =
    (RetrieveEntityResponse)metadataService.Execute(retrieveRequest);
string entityLogicalName = retrieveResponse.EntityMetadata.LogicalName;

//Write Logical Name to Console
Console.WriteLine(entityLogicalName);
```

Updating Entities

Only a relatively small number of entity properties are valid for updating. To update related attributes and relationships you need to use their own unique update messages.

You can only update the following properties:

- Description
- DisplayCollectionName
- DisplayName
- DuplicateDetection
- IsAvailableOffline

Similar to updates using the *CrmService* Web service, you simply instantiate an object—in this case an *EntityMetadata* object—set the properties you want to change, and add the unique identity (*LogicalName*). The following code sample demonstrates this technique to change the Display Name and Duplicate Detection settings of the entity:

```
MetadataService metadataService = GetMetadataService("contoso");

EntityMetadata entity = new EntityMetadata();
entity.LogicalName = "new_project";

entity.DisplayName = CreateLabel("Technical Project", 1033);
entity.DuplicateDetection = new CrmBoolean();
entity.DuplicateDetection.Value = true;

UpdateEntityRequest updateRequest = new UpdateEntityRequest();
updateRequest.Entity = entity;
updateRequest.MergeLabels = true;

metadataService.Execute(updateRequest);
```

Notice the *MergeLabels* property on the *UpdateEntityRequest*. When this property is set to false, all *LocLabels* in the *CrmLabel* objects being updated will be overwritten. When this property is set to true, CRM merges the array of *LocLabels with the labels that currently exist for the entity*. This allows developers to update a string for a single language without having to restate all the strings for all the other languages available in the organization.

Deleting Entities

Deleting an entity through the *MetadataService* is very straightforward. Simply use the *DeleteEntityRequest* message and supply the entity's logical name. All related records, forms, views, attributes, and relationships will also be deleted. This functionality is identical to deleting an entity using the customization user interface. Only custom entities can be deleted from CRM.

Note Similar to the user interface experience, Microsoft Dynamics CRM prevents you from deleting an entity referenced on a published form or view.

The following code shows how to delete an entity:

```
MetadataService metadataService = GetMetadataService("contoso");

DeleteEntityRequest deleteRequest = new DeleteEntityRequest();
deleteRequest.LogicalName = "new_project";

metadataService.Execute(deleteRequest);
```

Attributes

Each attribute type in CRM has a unique object type that inherits from the *AttributeMetadata* object, which in turn inherits from *CrmMetadata*. It is important to understand the data type of each attribute because each one has unique properties and behaviors. If you're not familiar with the various Microsoft Dynamics CRM data types and their properties, you might want to open the customization user interface to view more information about the various attributes. Getting comfortable with all of the different attributes will save you time when you develop your code.

Creating an attribute simply requires a reference to the logical name of the parent entity and an *AttributeMetadata* object. The following example shows how to create a custom attribute named Project Cost with a *Money* data type for our project entity, that we created in earlier examples:

```
MetadataService metadataService = GetMetadataService("contoso");

MoneyAttributeMetadata cost = new MoneyAttributeMetadata();
cost.SchemaName = "new_cost";
cost.RequiredLevel = new CrmAttributeRequiredLevel();
cost.RequiredLevel.Value = AttributeRequiredLevel.Recommended;
cost.MinValue = new CrmDouble();
cost.MinValue.Value = 0;
cost.MaxValue = new CrmDouble();
cost.MaxValue.Value = 10000000;
cost.DisplayName = CreateLabel("Project Cost", 1033);

CreateAttributeRequest createRequest = new CreateAttributeRequest();
createRequest.EntityName = "new_project";
createRequest.Attribute = cost;
metadataService.Execute(createRequest);
```

You can directly retrieve attributes using *RetrieveAttributeMetadata* by specifying the logical names of the attribute and its parent entity or by retrieving the entity and parsing collection of attributes on its attribute property. You can update and delete attributes by simply providing the entity and attribute names.

Display Masks

Most of the properties of *AttributeMetadata* objects are self-explanatory and very easy for a developer to interpret, so we won't spend a lot of time explaining them. However, one property does require more explanation: *DisplayMask*. This is a bit-level setting property used to conserve space in the database. It is an older piece of metadata brought forward from previous versions. Developers will typically only modify this property to change the *Searchable* property of an attribute. *Searchable* (also known as Valid For Advanced Find) determines whether an attribute can be visible in the Advanced Find user interface. Figure 8-8 shows the attribute form with the *Searchable* attribute's value set to Yes.

Caution Incorrectly formatting *DisplayMask* can cause unexpected behavior in the application. Proceed with caution and thoroughly test any code that interacts with this property.

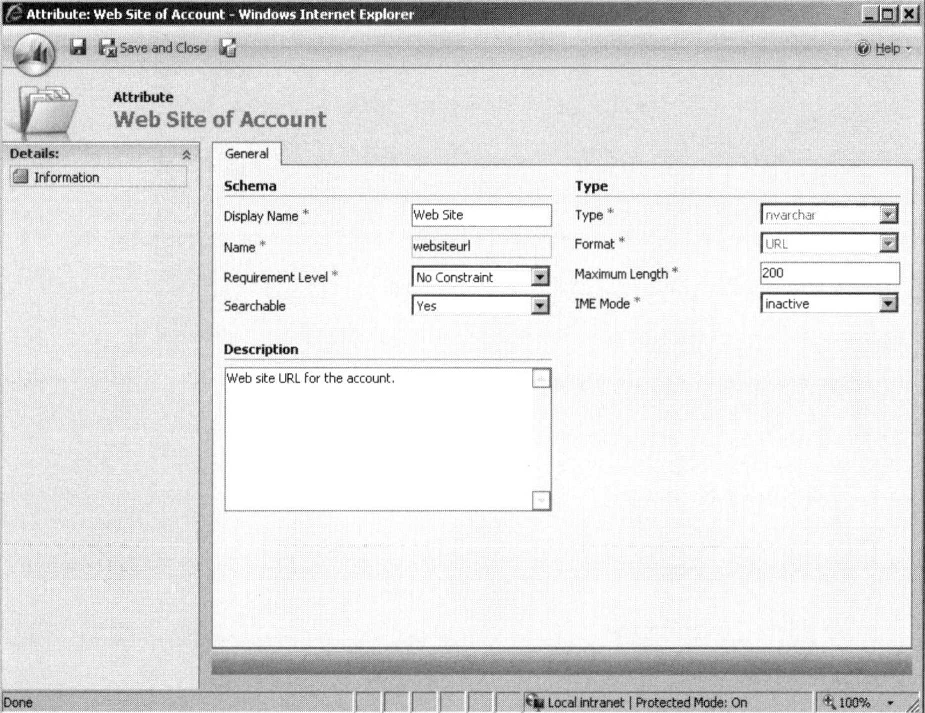

FIGURE 8-8 The Searchable select box set to Yes

First let's retrieve the *DisplayMask* value for this attribute and display it in the console, as shown in Figure 8-9.

Tip When doing a retrieve in anticipation of then updating the metadata, it is a good idea to use *RetrieveAsIfPublished = true*. This returns the data as shown in the customization user interface.

```
MetadataService metadataService = GetMetadataService("contoso");

RetrieveAttributeRequest request = new RetrieveAttributeRequest();
request.LogicalName = "websiteurl";
request.EntityLogicalName = "account";
request.RetrieveAsIfPublished = true;

RetrieveAttributeResponse response =
    (RetrieveAttributeResponse)metadataService.Execute(request);

StringAttributeMetadata websiteUrl =
    (StringAttributeMetadata)response.AttributeMetadata;

Console.WriteLine(websiteUrl.DisplayMask.Value);
```

FIGURE 8-9 *DisplayMask* values displayed in the console

The following values are returned:

- ValidForAdvancedFind
- ValidForForm
- ValidForGrid

Let's now remove the *ValidForAdvancedFind* value so that it is no longer available in the Advanced Find user interface. Notice that we also need to set the other two values in the *DisplayMasks* property.

```
MetadataService metadataService = GetMetadataService("contoso");

StringAttributeMetadata websiteUrl = new StringAttributeMetadata();
```

```
websiteUrl.DisplayMask = new CrmDisplayMasks();
websiteUrl.DisplayMask.Value = DisplayMasks.RequiredForForm | DisplayMasks.RequiredForGrid;
websiteUrl.LogicalName = "websiteurl";

UpdateAttributeRequest request = new UpdateAttributeRequest();
request.Attribute = websiteUrl;
request.EntityName = "account";
request.MergeLabels = false;
metadataService.Execute(request);
```

If we now refer back to the customization user interface, we can see that the Searchable property has now been set to No, as shown in Figure 8-10.

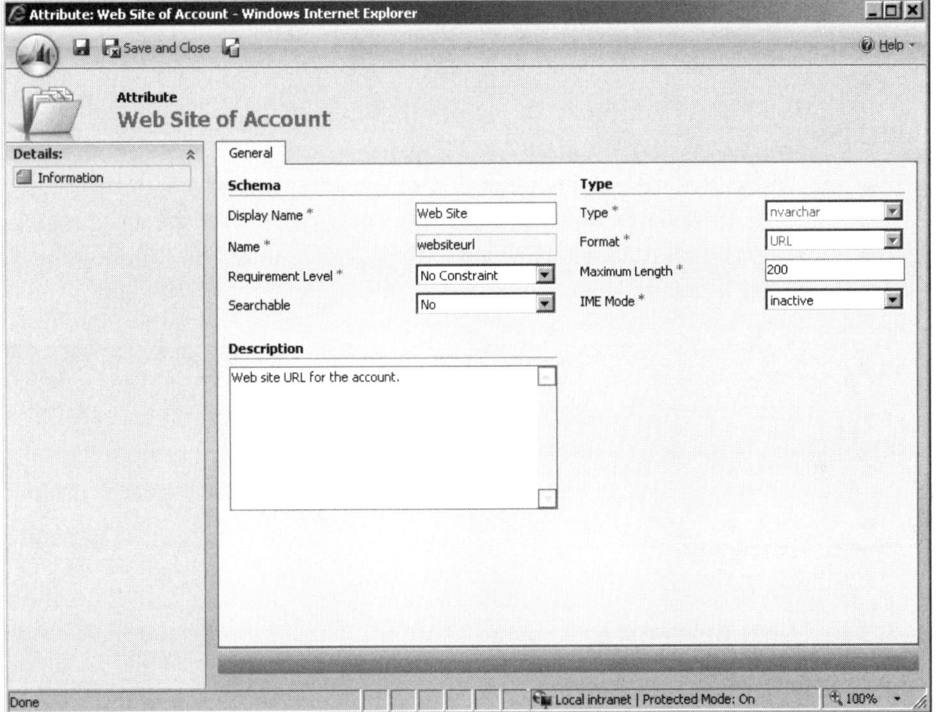

FIGURE 8-10 The Searchable value set to No

If we re-run the Console sample that reads the *DisplayMask* values, we will get the result shown in Figure 8-11.

FIGURE 8-11 Updated *DisplayMask* values displayed in console

Picklists

The Picklist attribute type has a number of special messages available to it in the *MetadataService*. The following code sample demonstrates how to create a new Picklist attribute. The various picklist values are found in the Options Array. You need to specify each one and provide the appropriate multilingual values using the *CrmLabel* object.

Tip The Picklist default value is set using an *Int*, not a *CrmNumber*. You do need to set the values of each *Option* object with a *CrmNumber*, but always use an *Int* when setting the default value.

```
MetadataService metadataService = GetMetadataService("contoso");

//Create Attribute object
PicklistAttributeMetadata picklist = new PicklistAttributeMetadata();

string[] labels = new string[]
{
    "Gold",
    "Silver",
    "Bronze"
};

//Set number of Options
picklist.Options = new Option[labels.Length];

for (int i = 0; i < labels.Length; i++)
{
    picklist.Options[i] = new Option();
    picklist.Options[i].Value = new CrmNumber();
```

```
    picklist.Options[i].Value.Value = i + 1;
    picklist.Options[i].Label = CreateLabel(labels[i], 1033);
}


//Set the Default Value to Gold using an Int and not a CrmNumber
picklist.DefaultValue = 1;

//Set the Requirement Level
picklist.RequiredLevel = new CrmAttributeRequiredLevel();
picklist.RequiredLevel.Value = AttributeRequiredLevel.None;

//Set the Schema Name
picklist.SchemaName = "new_medalrating";

//Set the Display Name
picklist.DisplayName = CreateLabel("Medal Rating", 1033);

//Execute the CreateAttributeRequest
CreateAttributeRequest request = new CreateAttributeRequest();
request.Attribute = picklist;
request.EntityName = "account";
metadataService.Execute(request);
```

Manipulating the arrays of picklist options can be time-consuming. The *MetadataService* provides some special messages to ease this burden: *InsertOptionValue*, *UpdateOptionValue*, *DeleteOptionValue*, and *OrderOptionValue*.

The *InsertOptionValueRequest* allows you to simply "inject" a new option into the picklist without calling *UpdateAttributeRequest* and specifying the entity array. In the following example we add a new option called *Copper* into the Medal Rating Attribute we created in the previous example:

```
MetadataService metadataService = GetMetadataService("contoso");

InsertOptionValueRequest request = new InsertOptionValueRequest();
request.AttributeLogicalName = "new_medalrating";
request.EntityLogicalName = "account";

request.Value = new CrmNumber();
request.Value.Value = 4;

request.Label = CreateLabel("Copper", 1033);

metadataService.Execute(request);
```

In the next example we use *UpdateOptionValueRequest* to change the U.S. English (1033) value of *Gold* (Option 1) to *Platinum*. The *MergeLabels* property is set to true so that only the strings for the languages provided are updated.

Tip The *UpdateOptionValueRequest* value must be an integer, not a *CrmNumber*. This differs from *CreateOptionValueRequest*, where a *CrmNumber* is used.

```
MetadataService metadataService = GetMetadataService("contoso");

UpdateOptionValueRequest request = new UpdateOptionValueRequest();
request.AttributeLogicalName = "new_medalrating";
request.EntityLogicalName = "account";
request.Value = 1;
request.Label = CreateLabel("Platinum", 1033);
request.MergeLabels = true;

metadataService.Execute(request);
```

The *OrderOptionRequest* request allows you to reorder the picklist values as they are displayed by the user interface. Note that this order is independent of the language selected. You simply create an ordered array of integers to represent the new display order, as shown in the following example:

```
MetadataService metadataService = GetMetadataService("contoso");

OrderOptionRequest request = new OrderOptionRequest();
request.AttributeLogicalName = "new_medalrating";
request.EntityLogicalName = "account";
request.Values = new int[] { 4, 3, 1, 2 };

metadataService.Execute(request);
```

The *DeleteOptionValueRequest* is very straightforward. Simply provide the logical names of the attribute, entity, and integer for the item you want to delete.

Relationships

It's important to understand the relationship capabilities of Microsoft Dynamics CRM 4.0 before embarking on programming the various relationship-specific messages of the metadata service. You can find a good primer on the relationship capabilities in your CRM server's online help: *http://<servername>/help*. Figure 8-12 shows the help screen for entity relationships.

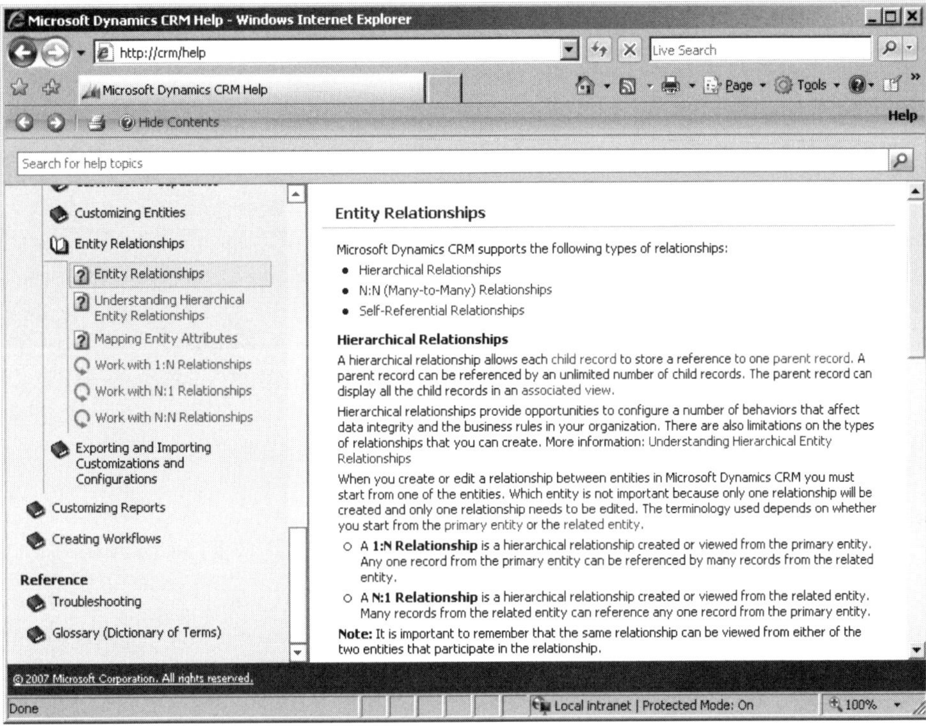

FIGURE 8-12 Online help for relationships

Tip If you don't have a CRM server installed you can also reach the help provided by CRM Online at *http://help.crm.dynamics.com/help*. Better still, you don't need a CRM Online account to access it!

One-to-Many Relationships

Modifying one-to-many relationships is relatively straightforward. Simply set all the appropriate properties and execute the correct request:

- CreateOneToManyRequest
- UpdateRelationshipRequest
- DeleteRelationshipRequest

Remember that one-to-many and many-to-one relationships are the same thing. The important thing to remember is the Referenced and Referencing entities.

One major difference between the customization user interface and the *MetadataService* when creating and updating relationships is the way cascading properties are handled. The user interface does have three "helper" settings (Parental, Referential Restrict Delete, and

Referential) that preconfigure the cascading rules. This often causes confusion with developers who believe these to be actual settings. In reality they are just templates that are applied to the Cascading properties. In the *MetadataService* you should set each value manually and ensure that you understand the consequences of each (clearly documented in the online help).

When creating a one-to-many relationship you need to supply a Lookup attribute for the referencing entity. In the following example we create a relationship from Project to Account. In other words, the Account entity is the referenced (the "one") entity and the Project entity is the referencing (the "many") entity. In the Microsoft Dynamics CRM user interface, you can add an Account Lookup attribute on the Project form. And, since an account can have many projects, you will see a link to Projects in the Account form's left navigation area.

```
MetadataService metadataService = GetMetadataService("contoso");

//Create the Relationship object
OneToManyMetadata relationship = new OneToManyMetadata();
relationship.ReferencingEntity = "new_project";
relationship.ReferencedEntity = "account";
relationship.SchemaName = "new_project_account";

//Define the Associate Menu Behavior. This will appear on the Account Form
relationship.AssociatedMenuBehavior = new CrmAssociatedMenuBehavior();
relationship.AssociatedMenuBehavior.Value = AssociatedMenuBehavior.UseCollectionName;

relationship.AssociatedMenuGroup = new CrmAssociatedMenuGroup();
relationship.AssociatedMenuGroup.Value = AssociatedMenuGroup.Marketing;

relationship.AssociatedMenuOrder = new CrmNumber();
relationship.AssociatedMenuOrder.Value = 10001;

//Define each Cascading Behavior
relationship.CascadeAssign = new CrmCascadeType();
relationship.CascadeAssign.Value = CascadeType.NoCascade;

relationship.CascadeDelete = new CrmCascadeType();
relationship.CascadeDelete.Value = CascadeType.RemoveLink;

relationship.CascadeMerge = new CrmCascadeType();
relationship.CascadeMerge.Value = CascadeType.NoCascade;

relationship.CascadeReparent = new CrmCascadeType();
relationship.CascadeReparent.Value = CascadeType.NoCascade;

relationship.CascadeShare = new CrmCascadeType();
relationship.CascadeShare.Value = CascadeType.UserOwned;

relationship.CascadeUnshare = new CrmCascadeType();
relationship.CascadeUnshare.Value = CascadeType.NoCascade;
```

```
//Create the Lookup Attribute
LookupAttributeMetadata lookup = new LookupAttributeMetadata();
lookup.SchemaName = "new_account";
lookup.DisplayName = CreateLabel("Account", 1033);
lookup.RequiredLevel = new CrmAttributeRequiredLevel();
lookup.RequiredLevel.Value = AttributeRequiredLevel.Recommended;

//Create and Execute the Request
CreateOneToManyRequest request = new CreateOneToManyRequest();
request.OneToManyRelationship = relationship;
request.Lookup = lookup;

metadataService.Execute(request);
```

Four menu groups exist on each record's left navigation area, and you can decide when you create a relationship where the resulting link will be displayed. By default, these groups are named

- Details
- Sales
- Marketing
- Service

AssociatedMenuGroup is a noncustomizable enum that has the same values. However, you can actually rename the labels for these groups within the ISV.Config. After you export the ISV.config file, you need to search for the *NavBarAreas* element. Listing 8-1 shows a sample element included and commented out in the default ISV.config file.

LISTING 8-1 Sample update to NavBarAreas element

```
<NavBarAreas>
  <NavBarArea Id="Marketing">
    <Titles>
      <Title LCID="1033" Text="Project Management"/>
    </Titles>
  </NavBarArea>
</NavBarAreas>
```

Modify these values using any text editor, and import the file back into Microsoft Dynamics CRM using the Import Customizations mechanism. You can see the results in Figure 8-13.

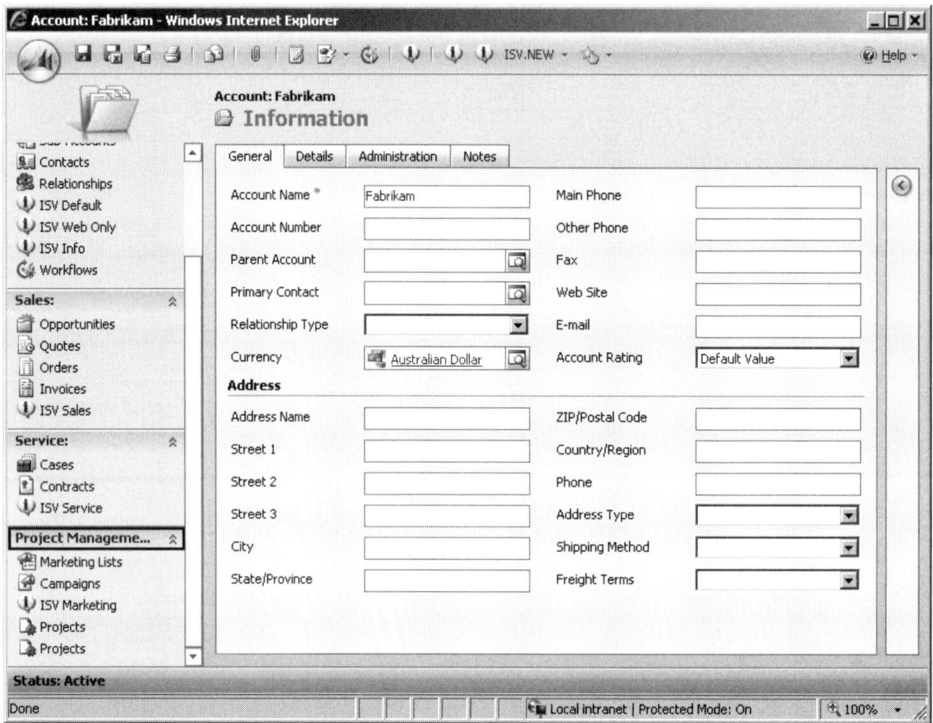

FIGURE 8-13 The renamed area on the Account Form

Many-to-Many Relationships

Many-to-many relationships are peer relationships between two entities. Microsoft Dynamics CRM creates an intersect entity to store the intersect data for each many-to-many relationship. When you create a many-to-many relationship, you need to specify the schema name of the relationship and the schema name of the Intersect entity. The relationship schema name must be unique among all other relationships (including one-to-many relationships), while the schema name of the Intersect entity must be unique among all entities.

The following code sample demonstrates how to create a many-to-many relationship:

```
MetadataService metadataService = GetMetadataService("contoso");

//Create the Relationship Object
ManyToManyMetadata relationship = new ManyToManyMetadata();
relationship.SchemaName = "new_account_project";

//Set Values for One Side of the Relationship
relationship.Entity1LogicalName = "account";

relationship.Entity1AssociatedMenuBehavior = new CrmAssociatedMenuBehavior();
```

```
relationship.Entity1AssociatedMenuBehavior.Value = AssociatedMenuBehavior.UseCollectionName;

relationship.Entity1AssociatedMenuGroup = new CrmAssociatedMenuGroup();
relationship.Entity1AssociatedMenuGroup.Value = AssociatedMenuGroup.Marketing;

relationship.Entity1AssociatedMenuOrder = new CrmNumber();
relationship.Entity1AssociatedMenuOrder.Value = 10002;

//Set Values for the Other Side of the Relationship
relationship.Entity2LogicalName = "new_project";

relationship.Entity2AssociatedMenuBehavior = new CrmAssociatedMenuBehavior();
relationship.Entity2AssociatedMenuBehavior.Value = AssociatedMenuBehavior.UseCollectionName;

relationship.Entity2AssociatedMenuGroup = new CrmAssociatedMenuGroup();
relationship.Entity2AssociatedMenuGroup.Value = AssociatedMenuGroup.Marketing;

relationship.Entity2AssociatedMenuOrder = new CrmNumber();
relationship.Entity2AssociatedMenuOrder.Value = 10001;

//Create and Execute the Request
CreateManyToManyRequest request = new CreateManyToManyRequest();
request.IntersectEntitySchemaName = "new_account_project";
request.ManyToManyRelationship = relationship;
metadataService.Execute(request);
```

Relationship Eligibility Messages

Unfortunately, you cannot create relationships between all the entities because some of the out-of-the-box entities contain special behaviors. You can use the following six special messages in the *MetadataService* to determine whether a relationship is valid. Usually these messages are only used if an alternative customization user interface is being developed (similar to the Data Migration Manager mentioned at the start of this chapter).

- *CanBeReferencedRequest* Returns a *Boolean* if an entity can be a Referenced entity in a one-to-many relationship.
- *GetValidReferencedEntitiesRequest* Returns an array of entity logical names that can be Referenced entities in a one-to-many relationship.
- *CanBeReferencingRequest* Returns a Boolean if an entity can be a Referencing entity in a one-to-many relationship.
- *GetValidReferencingEntitiesRequest* Returns an array of entity logical names that can be a Referencing entity in a one-to-many relationship.
- *CanBeManyToManyRequest* Returns a Boolean if an entity can participate (as either Entity1 or Entity2) in a many-to-many relationship.
- *GetValidManyToManyRequest* Returns an array of entity logical names that can participate (as either Entity1 or Entity2) in a many-to-many relationship.

You can set an optional property referencing an entity for the *GetValidReferencedEntities*, *GetValidReferencingEntities*, and *GetValidManyToMany* messages. The *MetadataService* will filter the returned results to the entities that are valid references.

Real World Developers typically use these messages to populate drop-down lists when implementing a Create Relationship User Interface.

Publishing Metadata

Just like modifying the data schema through the Web interface, you must publish your customization changes before users will see the changes you made. You might expect that you can publish customizations using the *MetadataService*, but you need to use the *CrmService* API to publish customizations. Use the *PublishAllXml* and *PublishXml* messages in the *CrmService* Web service to accomplish this.

As you learned in Chapter 5, both the *Publish* and *PublishAll* messages are eligible for plug-in registration. This enables developers to monitor the publish action and act accordingly. With the *MetadataService* also available inside plug-ins (see "Connecting to the *MetadataService*" earlier in this chapter), you can build plug-ins that can manage the metadata process. Please note that Microsoft Dynamics CRM does not execute *MetadataService* operations through the standard pipeline, and therefore you cannot register plug-ins against its operations.

More Info See an example of how to use the *Publish* and *PublishAll* messages for capturing customization changes in Chapter 5.

Caching the Metadata

Making repetitive requests to the *MetadataService* Web service can have a negative impact on performance. Further, the metadata information does not change frequently. As such, many developers create a cache of the data retrieved from *MetadataService* inside their own applications.

Using the Timestamp

The *RetrieveAllEntitiesResponse* class has a *Timestamp* property that indicates the last time the metadata was updated. When building a cache you should compare the current timestamp with the one stored with your cache and refresh your cache appropriately. The timestamp can also be queried on the server using the *RetrieveTimestampRequest*. Developers should retrieve metadata using *RetrieveAllEntitiesRequest* and cache the

RetrieveAllEntitiesResponse in their application. Periodically the application should then use *RetrieveTimestampRequest* to check for metadata updates. If the timestamp retrieved doesn't match the timestamp in the cache, the cache can be invalidated and refreshed from CRM.

You will see a vast performance difference in retrieving the timestamp versus retrieving all entities in terms of operation time and server load. You should execute *RetrieveAllEntities-Request* sparingly.

Tip Judiciously use the *MetadataItems* property of *RetrieveAllEntitiesRequest*. If your cache doesn't require additional information, don't retrieve it!

Example File System Cache

In this scenario, a basic console application has been programmed to store a cache of metadata on the disk. Each time the application runs, it checks CRM to see whether the cache needs to be updated.

This basic example uses XML object serialization to store the metadata cache. The cache, in this example, is all entities in the organization. When the cache is first generated, it is saved to the disk. Each time the application checks the cache it first retrieves the timestamp from CRM and compares this to the timestamp in the cache. If the timestamps don't match, the application retrieves the entity metadata from CRM and writes a new cache to the file system.

Listing 8-2 displays the complete code for this application. The application will require appropriate Web Service WSDLs for the *MetadataService* and the Crm*DiscoveryService*.

More Info See Chapter 15, "Additional Samples and Utilities," for another sample of metadata caching.

LISTING 8-2 Sample metadata file system cache

```
using System;using System.IO;
using System.Xml;
using System.Xml.Serialization;
using Example23.CrmDisco;
using Example23.CrmMeta;

namespace MetadataSample
{
    class Program
    {
        static void Main(string[] args)
```

```
{
    #region Set Sample App Variables
    string orgName = "contoso";
    string discoveryServiceUrl =
        "http://crm/mscrmservices/2007/ad/crmdiscoveryservice.asmx";
    string metadataServiceUrl = string.Empty;
    string cachePath = "cache.xml";
    #endregion

    #region Check Metadata URL with the Discovery Service
    CrmDiscoveryService discoveryService = new CrmDiscoveryService();
    discoveryService.UseDefaultCredentials = true;
    discoveryService.Url = discoveryServiceUrl;
    RetrieveOrganizationsRequest retrieveOrgRequest = new
        RetrieveOrganizationsRequest();

    RetrieveOrganizationsResponse retrieveOrgResponse;
    retrieveOrgResponse = (RetrieveOrganizationsResponse)
        discoveryService.Execute(retrieveOrgRequest);

    foreach (OrganizationDetail orgDetail in
            retrieveOrgResponse.OrganizationDetails)
    {
        if (orgDetail.OrganizationName == orgName)
        {
            metadataServiceUrl = orgDetail.CrmMetadataServiceUrl;
            break;
        }
    }
    #endregion

    #region Create Metadata Service Object
    CrmAuthenticationToken token = new CrmAuthenticationToken();
    token.AuthenticationType = 0;
    token.OrganizationName = orgName;
    MetadataService metadataService = new MetadataService();
    metadataService.CrmAuthenticationTokenValue = token;
    metadataService.UseDefaultCredentials = true;
    metadataService.Url = metadataServiceUrl;
    #endregion

    #region Creating Your Own Cache
    //Check the TimeStamp
    RetrieveTimestampRequest timestampRequest =
        new RetrieveTimestampRequest();
    RetrieveTimestampResponse timestampResponse;
    timestampResponse = (RetrieveTimestampResponse)
        metadataService.Execute(timestampRequest);

    //This object represents the Cache in memory
    RetrieveAllEntitiesResponse metadataCache =
        new RetrieveAllEntitiesResponse();

    //Does the Cache Exist?
    if (File.Exists(cachePath))
```

```
    {
        //Retrieve Cache the Cache
        metadataCache = RetrieveCache(cachePath);

        //Check Freshness of the Cache
        if (metadataCache.Timestamp != timestampResponse.Timestamp)
        {
            File.Delete(cachePath);
            metadataCache = CreateCache(cachePath, metadataService);
        }
    }
    else
    {
        //Create a New Cache
        metadataCache = CreateCache(cachePath, metadataService);
    }

    //Write the Logical Name of each entity to the Console
    foreach (EntityMetadata entity in metadataCache.CrmMetadata)
    {
        Console.WriteLine(entity.LogicalName);
    }
    #endregion

}

//Private Method to Retrieve the Metadata from CRM and Cache It
private static RetrieveAllEntitiesResponse CreateCache(
    string cachePath, MetadataService metadataService)
{
    RetrieveAllEntitiesRequest retrieveAllRequest =
        new RetrieveAllEntitiesRequest();
    retrieveAllRequest.RetrieveAsIfPublished = false;
    retrieveAllRequest.MetadataItems = MetadataItems.All;
    RetrieveAllEntitiesResponse retrieveAllResponse;
    retrieveAllResponse = (RetrieveAllEntitiesResponse)
        metadataService.Execute(retrieveAllRequest);

    Console.WriteLine("Retrieved from CRM");
    using (XmlWriter writer = XmlWriter.Create(cachePath))
    {
        XmlSerializer serializer =
            new XmlSerializer(typeof(RetrieveAllEntitiesResponse));
        serializer.Serialize(writer, retrieveAllResponse);
    }
    return retrieveAllResponse;
}

//Private Method to Retrieve the Metadata from the Cache
private static RetrieveAllEntitiesResponse RetrieveCache(string cachePath)
{
    using (XmlReader reader = XmlReader.Create(cachePath))
    {
        XmlSerializer deserializer =
            new XmlSerializer(typeof(RetrieveAllEntitiesResponse));
```

```
                    return (RetrieveAllEntitiesResponse)
                        deserializer.Deserialize(reader);
                }
            }
        }
    }
```

Handling Errors

The *MetadataService* is not immune to the myriad of error conditions that may arise while you are customizing the schema in the user interface. Developers need to ensure that their applications can respond gracefully to errors issued by the *MetadataService*. As a SOAP Web service, the *MetadataService* returns errors as *System.Web.Services.Protocols.SoapException*, as shown in the following code. Figure 8-14 shows the console output.

```
MetadataService metadataService = GetMetadataService("contoso");

//Create Request
DeleteAttributeRequest request = new DeleteAttributeRequest();
request.EntityLogicalName = "new_project";
request.LogicalName = "new_cost";

//Attempt the Execute the Request
try
{
    metadataService.Execute(request);
}
catch (System.Web.Services.Protocols.SoapException ex)
{
    XmlDocument doc = new XmlDocument();
    doc.LoadXml(ex.Detail.InnerXml);

    Console.WriteLine("Error XML: " + doc.OuterXml);
    Console.WriteLine();

    string code = doc["error"]["code"].InnerText;
    string description = doc["error"]["description"].InnerText;
    string type = doc["error"]["type"].InnerText;

    Console.WriteLine("Error Code: " + code);
    Console.WriteLine();
    Console.WriteLine("Error Description: " + description);
    Console.WriteLine();
    Console.WriteLine("Error Type: " + type);
}
```

```
C:\example\MetadataSample.exe
Error XML: <error><code>0x80048418</code><description>The attribute cannot be de
leted because it is referenced by the following objects Forms:Published Technica
l Project Form</description><type>Platform</type></error>

Error Code: 0x80048418

Error Description: The attribute cannot be deleted because it is referenced by t
he following objects Forms:Published Technical Project Form

Error Type: Platform
```

FIGURE 8-14 Error codes displayed in the console

Tip CRM's error codes are published in the SDK. You can view a complete list of codes at *http://msdn.microsoft.com/en-us/library/bb930493.aspx*. These codes include those for the *MetadataService*.

Summary

The *MetadataService* offers a powerful tool with which developers can read and manipulate the schema of a CRM organization. The *MetadataService* allows you to programmatically perform the same operations that system customizers can perform in the user interface. This includes creating custom entities, creating and updating attributes, reading data about the various objects in the system, and manipulating multilingual capabilities. Developers should always thoroughly test their *MetadataService* code, because with this additional power comes more responsibility. The ability to delete a custom entity (and all its related data) in a single message is an example of *MetadataService* power.

Part III

Advanced Topics

Chapter 9

Deployment

So far you've learned a lot about how to create programming customizations to Microsoft Dynamics CRM. Now we want to share some thoughts and ideas about deploying your custom solutions from one environment to another. Once you have created your solution and tested it within your development environment, you next need to package and deploy the solution to environments such as production.

This chapter discusses common deployment steps and then focuses on the various options and considerations of installing and testing Microsoft Dynamics CRM solutions between environments. We'll cover the following topics in this chapter:

- Common deployment steps
- Deploying Microsoft Dynamics CRM components
- Offline application deployment
- Testing strategies
- Additional deployment considerations
- An example of a deployment sequence

Common Deployment Steps

Assuming you have successfully developed and tested a solution on your development environment, you need to deploy the solution to your test environment and then ultimately to production. The following steps describe a common software deployment sequence you might follow:

- **Build** Compiling the code into an executable and distributable form
- **Install** Placing the solution files on target computer(s)
- **Configure** Configuring the installed solution to work with a specific Microsoft Dynamics CRM organization
- **Uninstall** Removing the solution

We highly recommend that you carefully consider each of these four steps when creating deployment packages for your solutions.

Note Because Microsoft Dynamics CRM is a multi-tenant application (multiple organizations can use the same programming customizations), be sure not to overlook the difference between the installation and configuration phases.

Let's review each of these steps in more detail.

Build

Developers commonly perform regular builds to their development environments. With Microsoft Dynamics CRM, each type of application extension, such as a plug-in or customization change, has its own set of steps required to compile the solution. We will not review each of those aspects again, as they are covered in depth in the other chapters of this book.

From an overall deployment perspective, be mindful of the additional requirements that your solution needs for a successful testing or production deployment. In each of these cases, not only do you need to have the additional components available during the build process, but they also must be available on the destination environment. For instance, Microsoft Dynamics CRM only requires the Microsoft .NET Framework 3.0, but you can't always be sure that the .NET Framework 3.5 is present on the server or the client. If you decide to include references to .NET Framework 3.5 libraries, your installation process should perform a dependency check.

Tip Be sure to include any dependencies required during the build phase in your installation process.

When building plug-in or workflow assemblies, those assemblies must be strongly typed. Also, you should use fully qualified assembly names for any Web site code. Typically this is done by including the full namespace of your project in the assembly name. These assemblies will be placed in the bin folder of the Microsoft Dynamics CRM Web site (see Figure 9-1) and therefore require unique names.

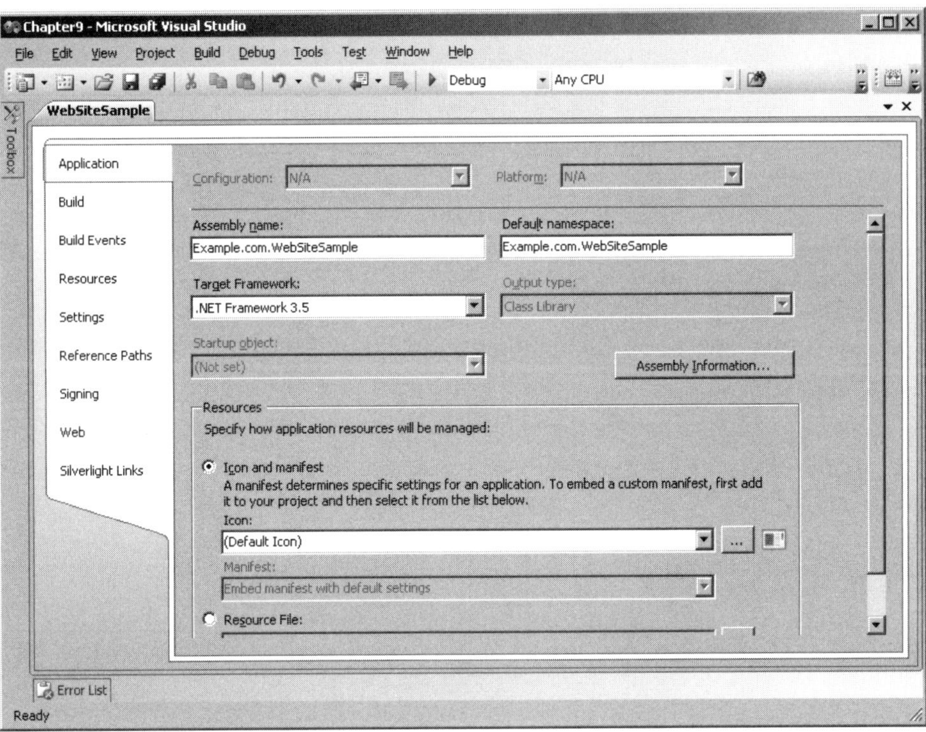

FIGURE 9-1 Visual Studio 2008 Web site properties

If you prefer the ASP.NET Web site approach, you need to download the Visual Studio 2008 Web Deployment Projects add-in for Visual Studio. This is a fully supported add-in released by Microsoft that offers additional and advanced build capabilities for Web sites. You can download it here: *http://www.microsoft.com/downloads/details.aspx?FamilyId=0AA30AE8-C73B-4BDD-BB1B-FE697256C459&displaylang=en.*

Important Your Web application (project or site) should not rely on a Web.config. Your application will inherit the settings of Microsoft Dynamics CRM's Web.config. Microsoft does not support modifying Microsoft Dynamics CRM's Web.config (to prevent developers from breaking other solutions), so your code should never rely on any settings in this file.

Install

Once you have built your application, you are now ready to install it to another environment. As part of the build process, you decide on and document the actions required to deploy the solution. We define installation as the process of applying the files, keys, and scripts that comprise your solution to target computers or servers. The installation process typically consists of the following two options:

- **Automated** Creating an installation program
- **Manual** Perform each task in a series of manual steps

More often, you might end up using a combination of these options for your final deployment package. Consider the following factors when choosing an installation process:

- How frequently will you be deploying the solution or updates to the solution? More frequent updates lend themselves to creating an automated installer.
- The complexity of the steps required for installation. If the installation is very complex, you might find it more cost effective to manually list the steps, given the time and testing required to automate the process.
- The number of steps or number of environments involved. Numerous steps lead to errors and are a better case for automation.
- The skill of the individual performing the installation. For less technical individuals or those who may have limited access, an automated installer can prove to be easier to distribute.

If possible, we recommend creating an installer program to help minimize the potential for error. Your installer program will bundle your plug-ins, workflow activities, and custom Web pages. As discussed in Chapter 2, "Development Overview and Environment," you have numerous options and tools available to create an installation program. While we prefer to use NSIS from SourceForge, you can also use Visual Studio 2008, which has support for creating installers for Windows and Web applications, as shown in Figure 9-2.

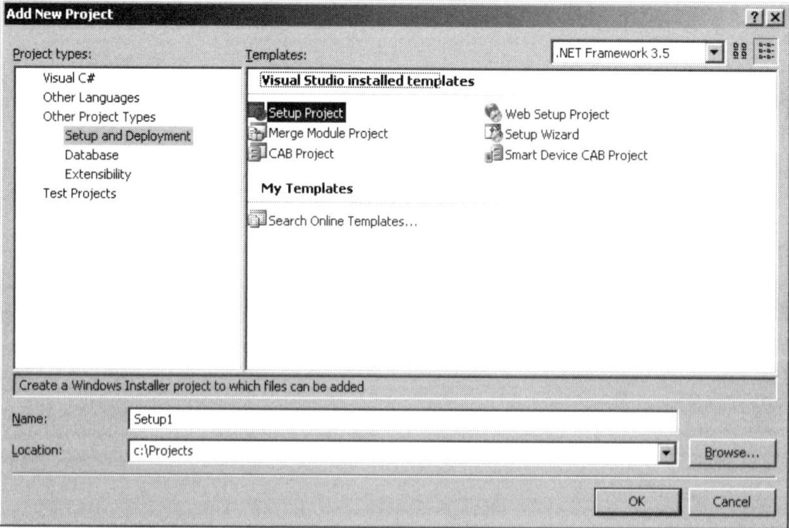

FIGURE 9-2 Visual Studio 2008 Add New Project dialog box

Note that the installation step takes place at the overall deployment level. This means that the assemblies and files are potentially accessible by *all* organizations within a given deployment. You should handle organization-specific settings during the configuration step, which we describe next.

During the install process, you should not configure any information about a specific Microsoft Dynamics CRM organization for your solution. Instead, we recommend that you separate the installation from the configuration as much as possible. The various Microsoft Dynamics CRM clients (Microsoft Dynamics CRM for Outlook, Data Migration Manager, and E-mail Router) are all excellent examples of this pattern. Each has a Microsoft Installer Package (MSI) that copies files, adds standard registry settings, adds assemblies to the Global Assembly Cache (GAC), and registers the program with Add-Remove Programs (ARP). During installation of these clients, absolutely no organizational information is collected or stored. A separate configuration process covers this. The reason for this approach is simple: If users want to reconfigure the application, they don't require the installer to do any action. It also allows for lower-privilege users to conduct configuration while still requiring administrators to install the solution.

It's also important to remember that multiple Microsoft Dynamics CRM servers may be used in a deployment. You should run your installer on each Microsoft Dynamics CRM server separately, which is another good reason to separate the install step from the configuration step.

Configure

The configuration step of a deployment solution involves collecting organization-specific information and then storing or using those values for your solution to use. Assuming you are using the Microsoft Dynamics CRM Web services, your application may require such information as:

- **Authentication Type** Windows, Internet Facing Deployment (IFD), or Windows Live ID
- **Organization Name** The friendly name and unique name of the organization
- **Microsoft Dynamics CRM Web Server** Used to complete the URL of the *CrmDiscoveryService* Web service

As we mentioned, Microsoft Dynamics CRM for Outlook uses a stand-alone configuration tool called the Microsoft Dynamics CRM Configuration Wizard to bind the client to an organization, as shown in Figure 9-3. When you configure Microsoft Dynamics CRM for Outlook, you will need to enter your Microsoft Dynamics CRM Web server and select an organization (if you have access to more than one).

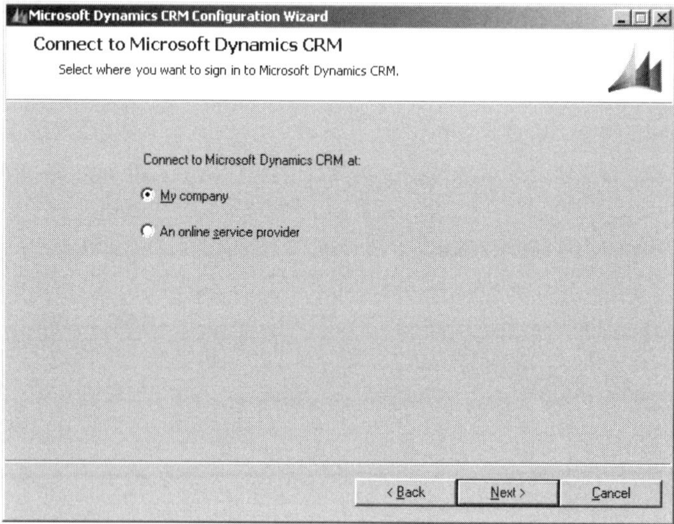

FIGURE 9-3 Microsoft CRM 4.0 Outlook Client Configuration Wizard

As part of your installer, you may want to cache information you retrieve from the Discovery Service (for example, the URLs of the *CrmService* Web service, *MetadataService* Web service, application user interface, and so on) to prevent having to make multiple calls to the service. However, it is important that you not treat this information as static because it is subject to change.

If your custom application uses Microsoft Dynamics CRM filtered views or any database scripts, you should also collect the Microsoft SQL Server connection string information during the configuration process (authentication, server name, database name). As a reminder we highly recommend that you use Integrated Windows Authentication to connect your custom code to the filtered views in the SQL Server database.

Tip If end users are conducting the configuration, it's ideal to use a wizard-style experience to guide them through the process. If your application is configured by IT professionals, you may want to use an XML file of configuration settings.

If you decide to create a stand-alone configuration application for your solution per our suggestion, the following steps demonstrate how this wizard application might function:

1. Prompt the user to enter the Microsoft Dynamics CRM URL.
2. Collect authentication credentials depending on authentication type.
3. Connect to the *CrmDiscoveryService*.
4. Display a list of organizations for a user to select.
5. Add any new entities with import customizations.

6. Modify the schema with the *MetadataService*.
7. Modify the user interface with import and export customizations.
8. Publish customizations.
9. Register plug-ins and workflow activities.
10. Add any custom security roles, workflow rules, or templates with import customizations.
11. Configure organization-specific settings.
12. Assign security roles.

Tip Be careful when using IFD for your configuration wizard. Plug-ins and workflow activities cannot be registered using the IFD authentication method.

As soon as you configure your application it should be ready for use. Your application should also allow users or administrators (whichever is appropriate for your scenario) to reconfigure the application at any time.

Uninstall

While many developers spend a lot of time worrying about the software installation process, uninstalling an application is often overlooked. However, providing a good uninstall process is a good practice for your organization. In some cases, the uninstall process can be relatively straightforward if you choose an automated installer approach such as MSI. Be sure that your uninstall process also cleans up any installation files or components as well as any configuration information (registry settings, XML files, and so on) added by your application.

During uninstall, you must decide whether or not to change any Microsoft Dynamics CRM modifications made to the organization. You should carefully examine the usage scenarios for your application and determine whether these modifications (for example, new custom entities and data) might be required after the solution is uninstalled. For example, when a user uninstalls a word processor, he doesn't expect all his documents to be deleted.

Tip Create a separate cleanup package to remove any organization modifications. Allow users and administrators to run this package separately. This ensures that critical data is not accidentally deleted during uninstall.

The uninstall process of a Microsoft Dynamics CRM solution has two primary components:

- Removing the solution components, such as static files, registry keys, and assemblies in the GAC
- Deleting any metadata and transactional data from an organization

Removing the Solution Components

An MSI is the best way to remove your static files, registry keys, and assemblies from the GAC. When you create your MSI with most installer programs, the uninstall process is automatically included. Simply run the MSI executable again or select Uninstall from Add/Remove Programs in Control Panel.

Caution You need to be sure that items (such as registry keys, common files, etc.) required by other programs aren't accidentally removed by your uninstall process. Be careful to review and test what parts of your solution will be removed.

Deleting Metadata and Transactional Data

The removal of organization-specific data can be more challenging. You should be mindful of scenarios where deleting the data is unacceptable (for example, when you uninstall Microsoft Dynamics CRM it never deletes the Microsoft Dynamics CRM databases to avoid the accidental loss of critical information).

The simplest approach would be to restore the database from a previous backup. This approach works fine for some development and testing environments (such as to facilitate rollback scenarios when testing an installer), but does not work in a live production environment. For the production environment, consider creating a cleanup program, similar to the Configuration Wizard described earlier, that gives an administrator the choice to remove some or all of the metadata and data related to the solution on the system.

For deleting entities, use the *DeleteEntity* message located within the *MetadataService* Web service. For modifying the user interface, use the same techniques that you used to add this data (export, modify the XML schema, and then re-import). You can use the *UnregisterSolution* message to remove plug-ins and workflow activities.

Tip Encourage your customers to make a database backup before uninstalling your solution. This simple step can save big headaches later on if the decision to uninstall was the wrong one!

Deploying Microsoft Dynamics CRM Components

As you know, Microsoft Dynamics CRM offers many different programming and customization options. Most solutions typically have one or more of the following Microsoft Dynamics CRM components to deploy:

- Customizations (entities, attributes, relationships)
- Workflow rules, templates, and security roles

- User interface changes (forms, ISV.Config, and site map)
- Custom Web pages
- Plug-in and workflow assemblies
- Online help
- Configuration settings
- Custom reports

Let's review each component in more detail.

Customizations

Customizations refer to changes made to the Microsoft Dynamics CRM data schema, such as adding entities, attributes, relationships, and views.

The options for deploying customizations from one environment to another include:

- Export and import customizations
- Using the *MetadataService*
- Importing the organization

Importing Customizations

Importing customizations is relatively straightforward. You can manually use the Microsoft Dynamics CRM user interface to both export and import customizations. However, if developing an automated installation program, you should use the *ImportCompressedXml* message. Always use the compressed (zip) versions of the customization files to avoid exceeding the 4-megabyte (MB) default file size limit.

We recommend using the import process for the following pieces of metadata:

- New entities
- New templates
- New security roles
- New workflows

The following code shows how to import a zip file:

```
static void ImportZip(CrmService service)
{
    //Get the Byte[] for the Customization File
    //Assume it is in the same directory as this application
    Byte[] bytes = System.IO.File.ReadAllBytes("customizations.zip");
```

```
        //Import the Customizations
        ImportCompressedAllXmlRequest request = new ImportCompressedAllXmlRequest();
        request.CompressedCustomizationXml = bytes;
        service.Execute(request);
    }
```

Tip The Import Customizations feature of Microsoft Dynamics CRM is designed to allow exporting from one organization and importing into another even if neither organization shares a common language. If your import file is missing language strings for a language provisioned on the system, it will simply leave them null. Certain strings, however, may never be null in the base language (for example, entity display names). The value from the base language of the exporting system will be substituted in this case and loaded into the base language on the importing system.

Do not use the Import Customization messages (*ImportAllXml*, *ImportXml*, *ImportCompressedAllXml*, *ImportCompressedXml*) to update schema metadata. Use the *MetadataService* instead, as described next.

Using the *MetadataService*

The *MetadataService* Web service provides excellent resources for configuring solutions. Chapter 8, "Developing with the Metadata Service," has extensive details on how to use this API. For deployment applications, use the *MetadataService* to:

- Add new attributes.
- Add new relationships.
- Modify existing entities.
- Modify existing attributes.
- Modify existing relationships.

Warning The *MetadataService* is language-sensitive. If the Locale ID (LCID) is hard-coded into your *MetadataService* code, it will fail if that language is not installed on the system. Keep in mind the multilingual capabilities of Microsoft CRM. Chapter 8 has more details regarding the *MetadataService* and multiple languages.

You can create new entities using the *MetadataService* as well. However, when a new entity is created, Microsoft Dynamics CRM creates unique GUIDs for some of the underlying metadata. Microsoft Dynamics CRM will synchronize some of these GUIDs when using the export/import process to ensure that duplicate schema entries are not processed. However, if you were to use the *MetadataService* to create the entities with an installer on two separate environments, each of those environments would contain unique GUIDs and Microsoft Dynamics CRM would interpret those entities as unique. Therefore, you would no longer be able to export and import customizations changes between those environments.

Publish Customizations

It's extremely easy to publish your customizations using the *CrmService* Web service. You should ensure that your customizations are published before you begin registering any plug-ins and workflow activities.

To publish all customizations on the server, use the *PublishAllXml* message (as shown in the following code). If you want to limit the scope of your publishing, you can use the more precise *PublishXml* message, which is documented in the Microsoft Dynamics CRM SDK.

```
static void PublishAll(CrmService service)
{
    PublishAllXmlRequest request = new PublishAllXmlRequest();
    service.Execute(request);
}
```

Note The publish messages are located with the *CrmService* API, not the *MetadataService* API.

Importing the Organization

Another approach would be to back up and restore the entire Microsoft Dynamics CRM database to a new environment. This technique installs all solution components stored within the database, including schema customizations. To do this, you would use the Microsoft Dynamics CRM Import process.

This approach has the advantage of easily moving all aspects of the deployed solution to another environment in a few simple steps. However, you will completely overwrite any existing data and changes to the new environment, so it clearly will not apply in all scenarios. Consider using this approach when doing a clean deployment in a new environment or when you need to synchronize two environments (such as synchronizing your user acceptance testing or development environments with production data).

Remember that this option will not redeploy any custom Web files, registry settings, third-party applications, etc. It deploys only those components and changes that are contained with the Microsoft Dynamics CRM database.

Chapter 2 describes this process in more detail.

Workflow Rules, Templates, and Security Roles

Assigning permissions should be the last step in your configuration. This helps to prevent (but may not eliminate) the chances of a user using your solution while configuration is taking place. You can use import customizations to easily add new security roles to the organization. You may also want to assign these roles to users during configuration. You can use the *AssignUserRolesRole* message to add roles to a particular user.

Warning Do not modify existing security roles. Doing so may compromise the operational security of the organization. Don't assume that any of the default security roles (except System Administrator) will be present on the system. Many customers delete all unused roles when they set up their systems for additional security.

User Interface Changes (Forms, ISV.Config, and Sitemap)

You should use caution when your solution needs to modify the user interface, such as updating existing forms or adding additional application menu items or left navigation links. You should expect that the destination Microsoft Dynamics CRM system has already been modified, and you need to inject your updates safely into the application.

As you already know, you can first export the item, modify its XML, and then re-import it. This is critical for preventing one developer from overwriting the customizations made by another developer. Schemas for each of these user interface constructs are available in the SDK and can be manipulated with normal XML programming techniques.

The following example shows how to append XML to any part of the customizations XML file:

```
static void ModifyUserInterface(CrmService service, string exportParameters,
 string path, string fragmentXml)
{
    //Export the current Customizations
    //Use the export parameters specified
    ExportXmlRequest exportRequest = new ExportXmlRequest();
    exportRequest.ParameterXml = exportParameters;
    ExportXmlResponse exportResponse =
      (ExportXmlResponse)service.Execute(exportRequest);

    //Add the XML fragment at the specified XPath location
    XmlDocument doc = new XmlDocument();
    doc.LoadXml(exportResponse.ExportXml);
    XmlDocumentFragment fragment = doc.CreateDocumentFragment();
    fragment.InnerXml = fragmentXml;
    XmlNodeList nodes = doc.SelectNodes(path);
    nodes[0].AppendChild(fragment);

    //Import the Customizations back into CRM
    ImportAllXmlRequest import = new ImportAllXmlRequest();
    import.CustomizationXml = doc.OuterXml;
    service.Execute(import);
}
```

For example, you could use this code to add a menu item to the settings area of the site map. To achieve this we would call the preceding method as follows:

```
static void ModifySiteMap(CrmService service)
{
    string exportParameters = "
        <importexportxml>
            <entities/>
            <nodes>
                <node>sitemap</node>
            </nodes>
            <securityroles/>
            <workflows/>
            <settings/>
        </importexportxml>";

    string path =
      "ImportExportXml/SiteMap/SiteMap/Area[@Id='Settings']/Group[@Id='Settings']";

    string fragmentXml =
      @"<SubArea Id='example_menu_item' Entity='example_entityname' />";

    ModifyUserInterface(service, exportParameters, path, fragmentXml);
}
```

Custom Web Pages

When installing your ASP.NET Web application on the Microsoft Dynamics CRM server, you have a limited set of choices for where to place files and what configuration options to use. You should place the compiled assemblies for your Web site in the bin folder of the Microsoft Dynamics CRM Web site. You should place all other files (ASPXs, ASMXs, resources, and so on) inside the ISV folder. Microsoft recommends that you use your company's name (or customization namespace) and then the name of your solution as your folder structure in the ISV folder, as shown in Figure 9-4. Consequently, you will deploy your custom Web files to two locations:

- Assemblies: bin\
- Web Files: \ISV\[Company]\[Solution]

> **Warning** If you find the restrictions for an integrated ASP.NET Web application too severe, you may want to consider creating your own virtual directory. However, if you choose this method, you will not be able to take advantage of the *CrmImpersonator* class, which is critical to authentication using IFD.

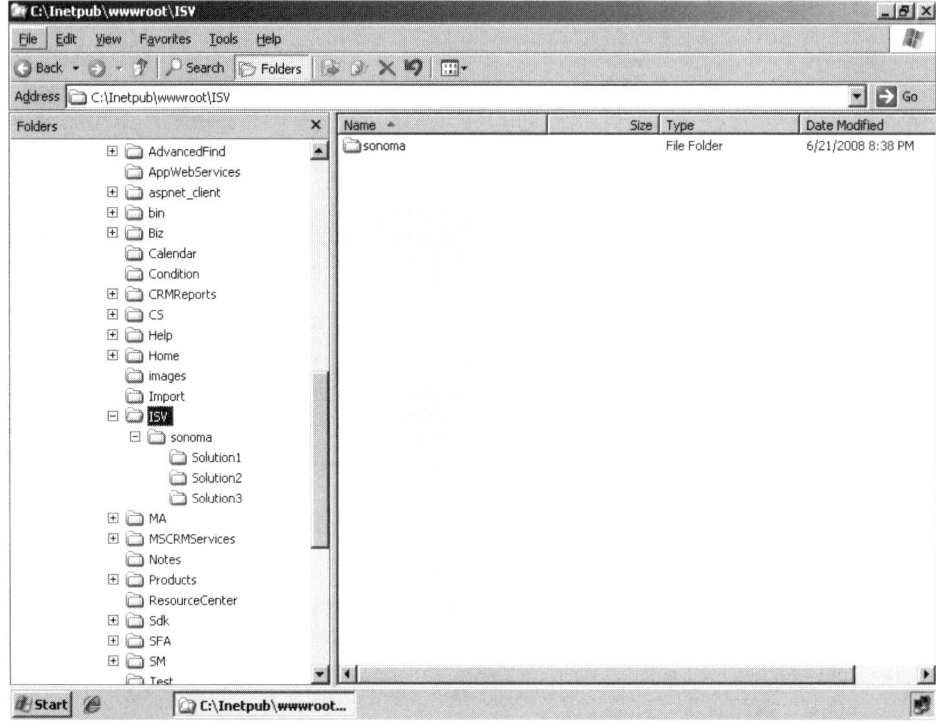

FIGURE 9-4 ISV folder in the Microsoft Dynamics CRM Web site

Under no circumstances should you modify any file in Microsoft Dynamics CRM's Web folder, including the Web.config. Modifying the files in the Microsoft Dynamics CRM Web folder will lead to unexpected system behavior and potential loss of your data.

> **Tip** Never assume that the Microsoft Dynamics CRM Web site will always be located at C:\inetpub\wwwroot. Many Web server administrators like to store the Inetpub folder on different drives than the operating system. You can find the file system location of the Microsoft Dynamics CRM Web site in the registry. Look for the value called WebSitePath in the registry key HKEY_LOCAL_MACHINE\SOFTWARE\Microsoft\MSCRM

Plug-in and Workflow Assemblies

Microsoft Dynamics CRM offers three different storage locations for deploying plug-ins and workflow activities:

- Global Assembly Cache (GAC)
- Database
- Disk

When deploying to production, developers should not use the disk deployment option —that option is intended for debugging purposes only.

The GAC deployment option is the most complex because you must not only place your assemblies in the GAC (usually achieved with an MSI), but you must also register the plug-ins and activities with each organization (in the configuration step). The advantage of GAC deployment is that you can easily replace the DLLs in the GAC for all organizations on the deployment. Developers will need to balance the desire for a central location for their assemblies (database) with the ability to share assemblies across organizations (GAC).

You should not handle database deployment during installation. Register the plug-ins and activities during the configuration step. Unless you have a need for regularly servicing the assemblies by updating the GAC and restarting IIS, it is recommended that you opt for the database route.

During the configuration step you should register any plug-ins and workflow activities. Use the API messages outlined in Chapter 5, "Plug-ins," to achieve this. Remember that a user who registers plug-ins and workflow activities must be a Deployment Administrator, as shown in Figure 9-5.

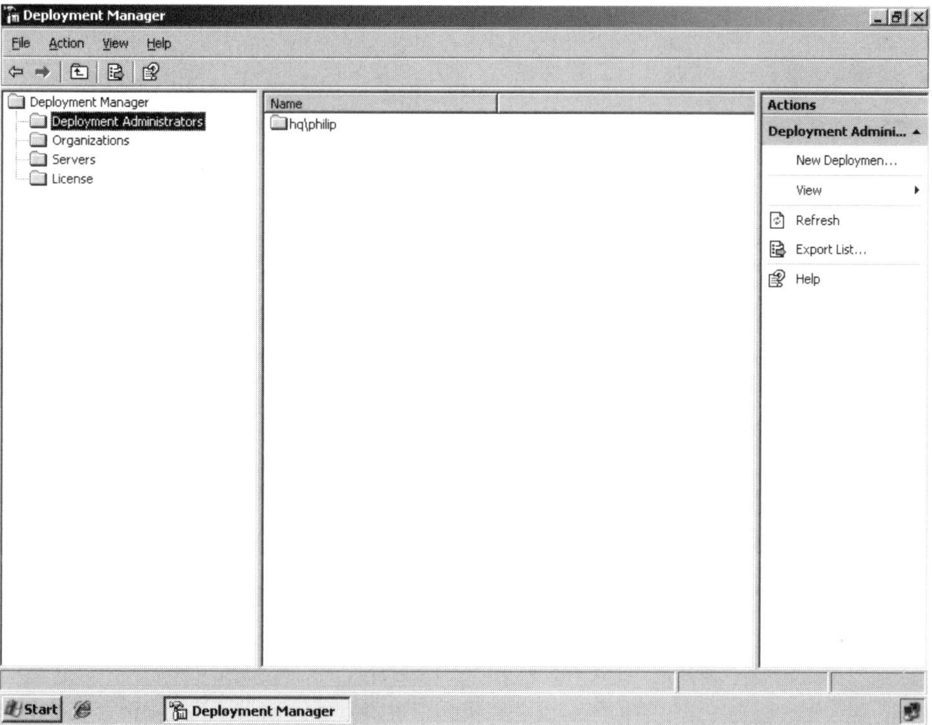

FIGURE 9-5 Microsoft Dynamics CRM 4.0 Deployment Manager

We also recommend that you use the plug-in's custom configuration and secure configuration capabilities during deployment. These special properties of a plug-in enable the storage of organization-specific configuration information conveniently with the plug-in registration. For instance, if you wanted to store a custom database connection string that your plug-in requires for integration purposes, you can store this information securely during the registration of the plug-in. Please refer to Chapter 5 for additional information.

Tip The source code for Microsoft's Plug-in registration tool is freely available and licensed with the Microsoft Permissive License (Ms-PL). You can use all or some of this code in your own solutions. More information can be found here: *http://code.msdn.microsoft.com/crmplugin*.

Online Help

Developers can also customize Microsoft Dynamics CRM's online Help files. The Online Help is the same for all organizations on the deployment. Because online Help is deployment-wide, you should modify it during the installation step.

You can find the help content in the Help folder of the Microsoft Dynamics CRM Web site. Each installed language has its own separate help content found in a folder corresponding to its Locale ID (LCID).

It's important to remember that the indexing catalog doesn't update immediately. You don't need to write code to force the refresh because it will happen automatically. However, when debugging your help content, you may want an immediate refresh. To do this, you need to stop and restart the Help catalog located by navigating to Computer Management > Services and Applications > Indexing Service, as shown in Figure 9-6.

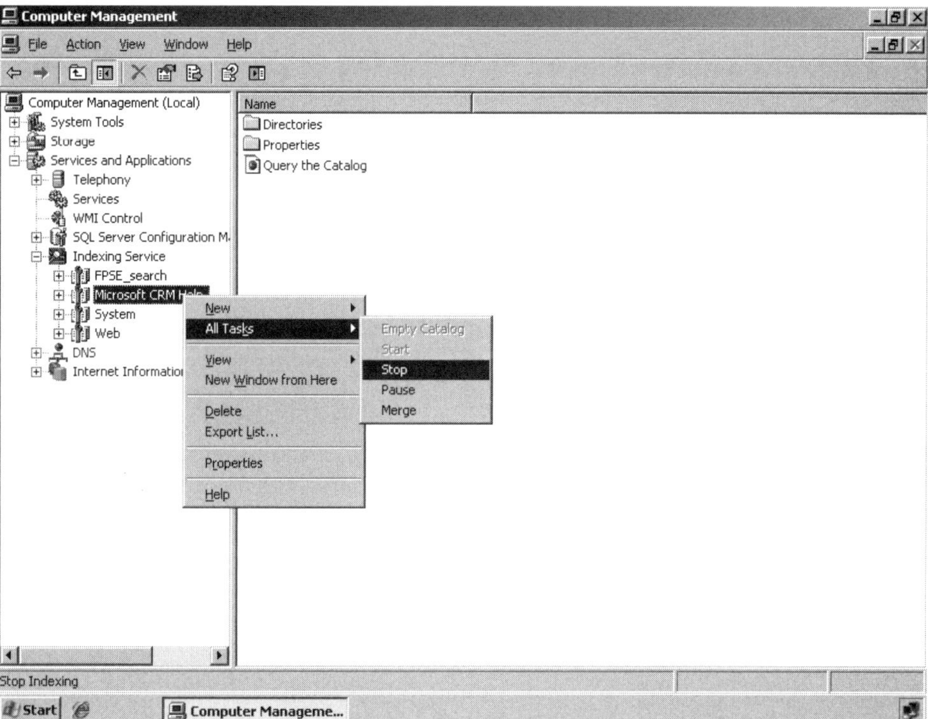

FIGURE 9-6 Stopping the Microsoft CRM Help index catalog

Please refer to the Microsoft Dynamics CRM SDK for more information regarding the online Help customization.

Custom Reports

Deploying custom reports to an environment can be done manually through the Microsoft Dynamics CRM user interface. However, Microsoft Dynamics CRM 4.0 now treats reports as a first-class entity. As such, you can create and update reports directly through the *CrmService* Web service. The code below shows an example of how to create a new report in Microsoft Dynamics CRM:

```
private Guid CreateReport(string reportFileName)
{
    FileInfo reportInfo = new FileInfo(reportFileName);

    report newReport = new report();
    newReport.name = Path.GetFileNameWithoutExtension(reportFileName);
    newReport.filename = reportFileName;
    newReport.filesize = new CrmNumber(reportInfo.Length);
    newReport.bodytext = File.ReadAllText(reportFileName);
    newReport.languagecode = new CrmNumber(1033);
```

```
    newReport.reporttypecode = new Picklist(1);

    CrmService crmService = CreateCrmService();
    crmService.Create(newReport);
}
```

You can use this approach within a custom installer or simple application to easily deploy a list of custom reports between environments.

Configuration Settings

Your application may require certain settings to be stored and configured in order to function properly. Systemwide settings that may apply to any organization in the deployment should be stored in the registry or custom database and completed during the installation step.

Caution Remember that in Web farm scenarios, you will need to change any systemwide settings stored in the registry on each Web server in the deployment.

Configuration settings unique to each deployment can be stored in a custom entity located within each organization. As such, you should use the configure step to populate these values. When using a configuration program, simply use the *Create* message from the *CrmService* Web service to insert the data.

Offline Application Deployment

Microsoft Dynamics CRM supports an offline API, allowing you to develop solutions that work when disconnected from the Microsoft Dynamics CRM Web server. When deploying an integrated solution that runs using the Microsoft Dynamics CRM for Outlook with Offline Access, you need to take additional considerations into account.

We recommend that you create a separate installer for offline applications, even if the contents of the installers are symmetrical between the server and the client. The client installer typically requires less overhead, and you should find it easier to manage as a separate executable.

Offline Web Applications

Remember that any custom Web pages that you load on the Microsoft Dynamics CRM server will not be accessible when the user works in a disconnected (offline) state. Microsoft Dynamics CRM uses a locally installed Cassini Web server to serve its Web pages. As discussed further in Chapter 10, "Developing Offline Solutions," your custom Web pages need to be accessible from the client's computer, which means you must deploy versions of your Web pages to the Cassini Web server.

You will use the same techniques to deploy your custom Web files to the Offline Client that you use for the Microsoft Dynamics CRM server. However, the file location of the Offline Client Web site is slightly different. You can locate the Web site directory from the following registry value:

HKEY_CURRENT_USER\Software\Microsoft\MSCRMClient\InstallPath

The InstallPath value will typically be C:\Program Files\Microsoft Dynamics CRM\Client\. The Web site is stored in the res\web folders underneath this directory. For example, the Web site path might be C:\Program Files\Microsoft Dynamics CRM\Client\res\web.

Tip Ensure that you test your offline install MSI on both Windows XP SP2 and Windows Vista. Both operating systems are supported by the Offline Client and enhanced security features in Windows Vista might cause some issues in environments where users do not have administrative access.

Plug-in Allow List

As you learned in Chapter 5, plug-ins can execute when a user is offline. Each plug-in used by the Offline Client must have its public key token placed in the registry of the local computer. Microsoft Dynamics CRM instituted this requirement to prevent a "man-in-the-middle" attack during offline synchronization. This type of attack involves the interception of the plug-in assembly (which is stored as a Base64-encoded string) during offline synchronization. The assembly is then changed to a malicious assembly. The Offline Client then runs that assembly when the plug-in is triggered while in the offline state. However, an attacker cannot easily forge the public key token on the assembly (you require the original certificate file) when compiling the malicious assembly. So Microsoft Dynamics CRM compares all offline plug-in assemblies to a *allow list* stored in the client computer's registry. The registry is used because it must be updated via a mechanism separate from offline synchronization. (Otherwise the attacker would simply change the allow list as well.)

Because the registry key used to store the allow list is user-specific, you may want to place the key in the registry during the configuration step.

The code sample in Listing 9-1 shows how to read your public key token from your plug-in assemblies:

LISTING 9-1 Reading a registry key

```
using System;
using System.IO;
using System.Reflection;

namespace ReadPublicKey
{
    class Program
    {
        static void Main(string[] args)
        {
            //Get the paths from the Console Applications Arguments
            //Eg. ReadPublicKey.exe c:\myplugin.dll
            //Ensure absolute paths are provided.
            string path = args[0];

            //Load the Assembly
            Assembly assembly = Assembly.LoadFile(path);
            string[] properties =
              assembly.GetName().FullName.Split(",= ".ToCharArray(),
              StringSplitOptions.RemoveEmptyEntries);
            string publicKeyToken = properties[6];

            //Write the Key to the Console
            Console.WriteLine(publicKeyToken);
            Console.ReadLine();
        }
    }
}
```

You should ensure that this value is added as a registry key in the following registry location: HKEY_CURRENT_USER\Software\Microsoft\MSCRMClient\AllowList.

The code in Listing 9-2 demonstrates how to add this key to the registry:

LISTING 9-2 Creating a registry key

```
using System;
using System.Text;
using Microsoft.Win32;

namespace AddPublicKey
{
    class Program
    {
        static void Main(string[] args)
        {
            //Get PublicKey Token from Args
            //eg. AddPublicKey.exe 84d2d3539f7d7390
```

```
            string publicKey = args[0];
            string path = @"Software\Microsoft\MSCRMClient\AllowList\" + publicKey;

            RegistryKey registrykey = Registry.CurrentUser.CreateSubKey(path);
            registrykey.Close();
        }
    }
}
```

Figure 9-7 shows the registry key after being added.

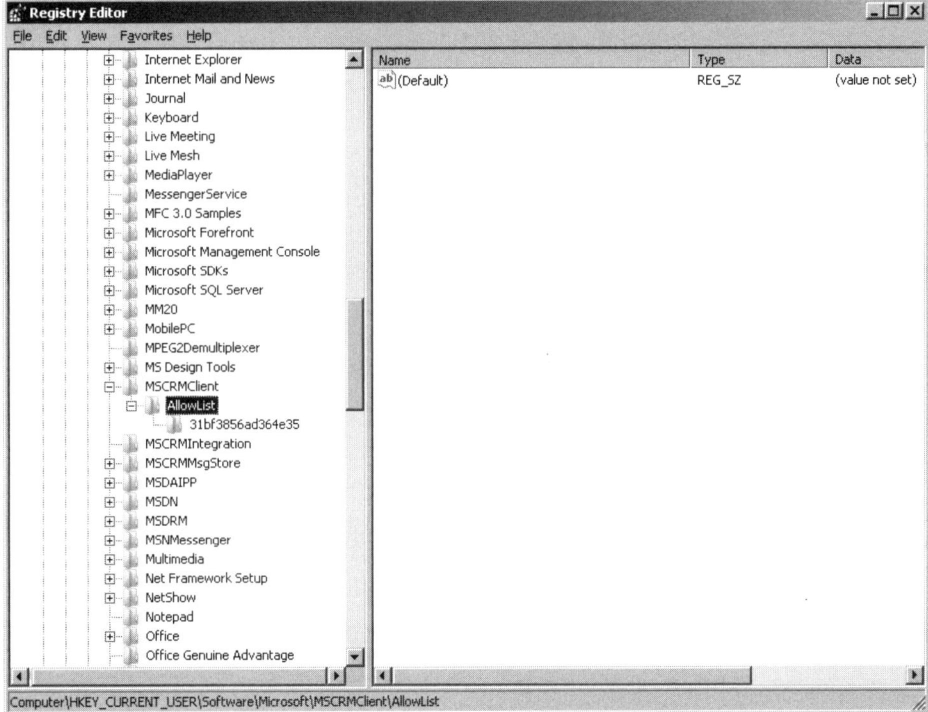

FIGURE 9-7 Editing the Plug-in Allow List with the Windows Registry Editor

Testing Strategies

Chapter 2 briefly discusses setting up and testing your application across different environments. The same testing strategy holds true for your deployment scenarios. You should always test and validate your solutions against the supported configurations that Microsoft CRM customers might be running. If you don't test your solution against one of these configurations, you need to communicate that caveat to your customers.

Server Topologies

Never assume that Microsoft Dynamics CRM and its dependent services will be set up on a single computer. Always assume scale-out and multirole deployments. Use the following checklist for testing the topological compatibility of your application:

- **Single-box deployment** Microsoft Dynamics CRM and SQL Server are on the same computer.
- **Two-box deployment** Microsoft Dynamics CRM and SQL Server are on separate computers.
- **Three (or more) box deployment** Microsoft Dynamics CRM servers are network load balanced (NLB) and SQL Server is on a separate computer.
- **Multi-role** Load-balance the Microsoft Dynamics CRM Web servers on multiple computers. Further separate the API server, the Microsoft Dynamics CRM asynchronous processing server, and SQL Server onto different computers.
- **Reporting server** Test reports with a Reporting Services computer separate from the SQL Server computer and the Microsoft Dynamics CRM server.

Operating Systems

Microsoft Dynamics CRM supports four different operating systems (two for the Outlook client and two for the server). All operating systems also come in 32-bit and 64-bit versions. Use the following checklist to ensure that your solution works with the correct operating systems:

- **Client** Windows XP-SP2 32-bit
- **Client** Windows XP-SP2 64-bit
- **Client** Windows Vista 32-bit
- **Client** Windows Vista 64-bit
- **Server** Windows Server 2003 32-bit
- **Server** Windows Server 2003 64-bit
- **Server** Windows Server 2008 32-bit
- **Server** Windows Server 2008 64-bit

Web Browsers

Microsoft Dynamics CRM supports two Web browsers: Internet Explorer 6.0 and Internet Explorer 7.0. You may want to have your custom code detect the *HTTP_USER_AGENT* of a user's browser and redirect to an error page if an unsupported browser is used.

Database Servers

Microsoft Dynamics CRM 4.0 supports both Microsoft SQL Server 2005 and SQL Server 2008 as its database and reporting catalog (SQL Server Reporting Services). You need to test against specific database servers only if you implement your own database or queries. If you build custom reports, you may want to test compatibility with SQL Server 2008 Reporting Services in addition to SQL Server 2005 Reporting Services.

Authentication

It's easy to cut corners and write your custom code so that it only supports Integrated Windows Authentication. However, many customers deploy Microsoft Dynamics CRM in an IFD environment, and your code should accommodate both authentication scenarios, especially if you are developing a third-party solution or add-on. Also, if your organization isn't using IFD today, don't assume that it won't want to deploy it in the future.

For plug-ins, you should be using the *ICrmService* interface for all calls back to CRM. This interface is already authenticated and shouldn't present any issues with Windows or IFD.

Multi-Tenant

If you're using the Enterprise edition of Microsoft Dynamics CRM, you can configure multiple organizations for a single deployment (multi-tenant). When you create your custom code and deploy it, you must carefully consider the security between organizations in a single deployment. As a general rule one tenant should never have access to the data managed by another. This is to protect the data of customers in shared hosting situations (Microsoft Dynamics CRM Online, Hosting Providers, or IT departments). Be sure that you test the following two situations with your solution:

- Solution is configured for the Default Organization only. Other tenants are present on the system.
- Solution is configured for the non-Default Organization. Other tenants are present on the system.

Warning The Microsoft Dynamics CRM 3.0 Web Service endpoints (also known as the 2006 endpoints) that ship with Microsoft Dynamics CRM 4.0 for backward compatibility only connect to the default organization. This is one reason why it is important to test on the non-default tenant.

Multilingual

You may choose to mandate one or more languages for your solution. If this is the case, your configuration code should check for these with the *RetrieveAvailableLanguages* message.

The following suggested test scenarios will help ensure that your solution is functional in multilingual configurations:

- Solution Base Language = Organization Base Language.
- Solution Base Language <> Organization Base Language. However, the Solution Base Language is provisioned and active on the organization.
- Solution Base Language is not installed on the organization.

Accessibility

If appropriate, you should also test your solution for accessibility. Just as you test for environmental compatibilities, you should examine the strengths of your application with respect to accessibility. Many companies and government agencies mandate certain accessibility features in the software products they buy. Work with your customers to understand these requirements in detail.

Windows High-Contrast mode is a special mode used by visually impaired users. It can be activated using the accessibility features in Windows. Windows users operating in this mode will also modify their Microsoft Dynamics CRM user profiles to optimize Microsoft Dynamics CRM's Web pages for high contrast. It's easy to overlook the high-contrast performance of your application because—many developers don't even know the setting exists!

High-contrast mode for Microsoft Dynamics CRM is turned on on the User Settings page, as shown in Figure 9-8.

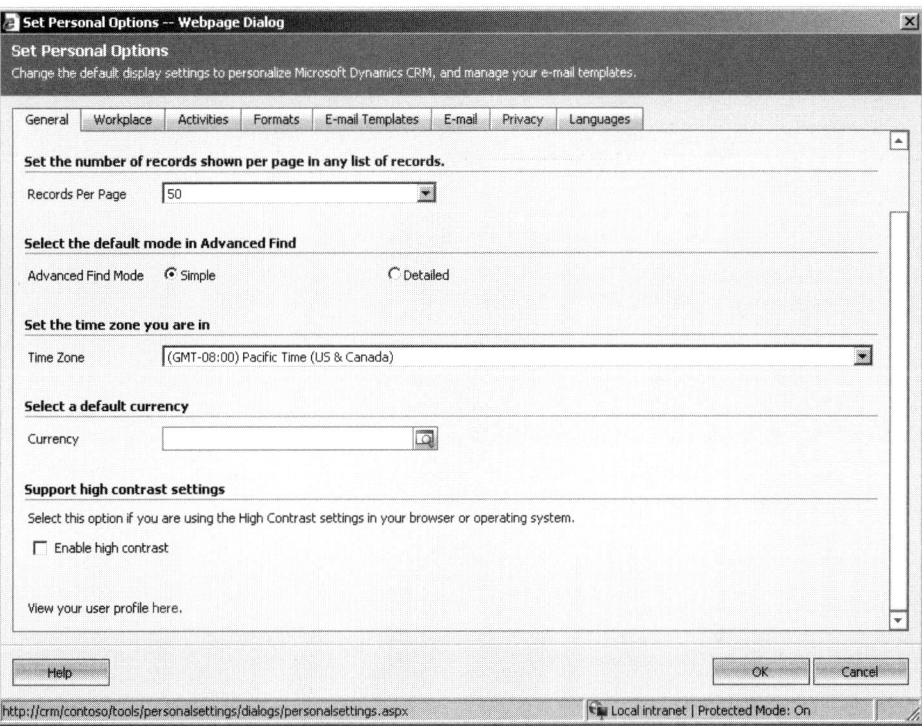

FIGURE 9-8 Set Personal Options dialog box

In Windows Vista, turn on High-Contrast mode in Control Panel and then activate it using left Alt+left Shift+Print Screen, as shown in Figure 9-9.

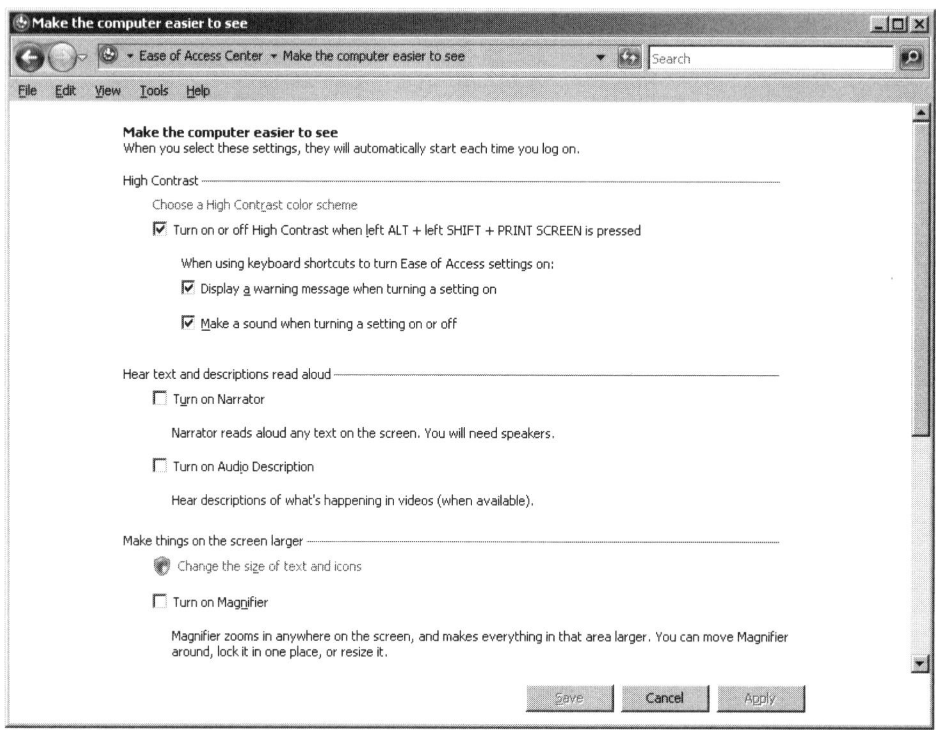

FIGURE 9-9 Windows Vista Ease of Access Center

Figure 9-10 shows Microsoft Dynamics CRM on High-Contrast Windows without optimizations. As you can see, not all of the icons appear on the screen.

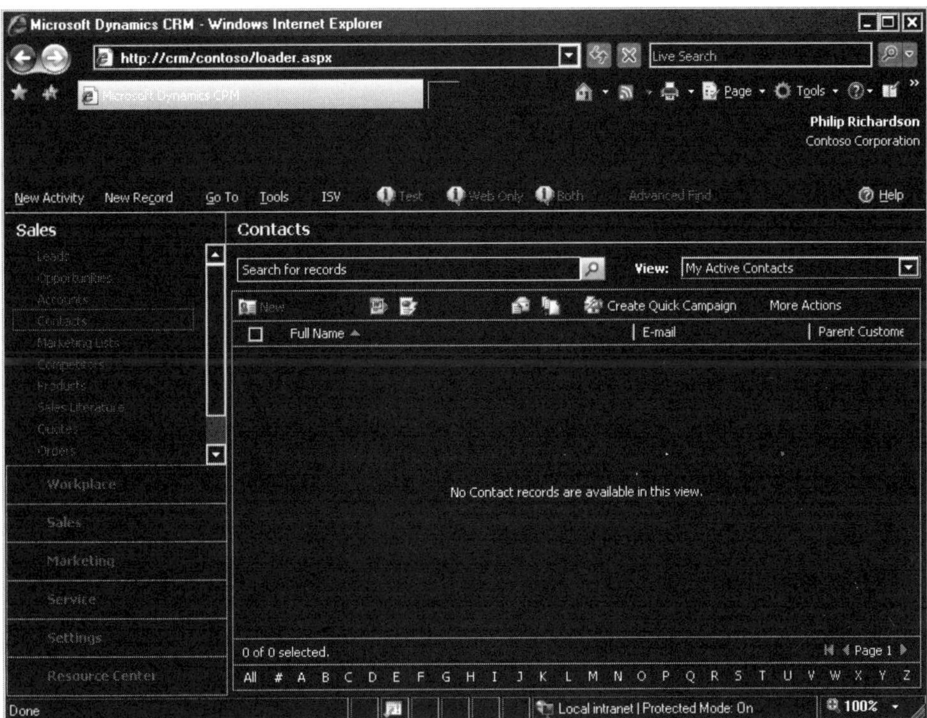

FIGURE 9-10 Windows High-Contrast On and Microsoft Dynamics CRM High-Contrast Off

Figure 9-11 shows Microsoft Dynamics CRM on High-Contrast Windows with optimizations.

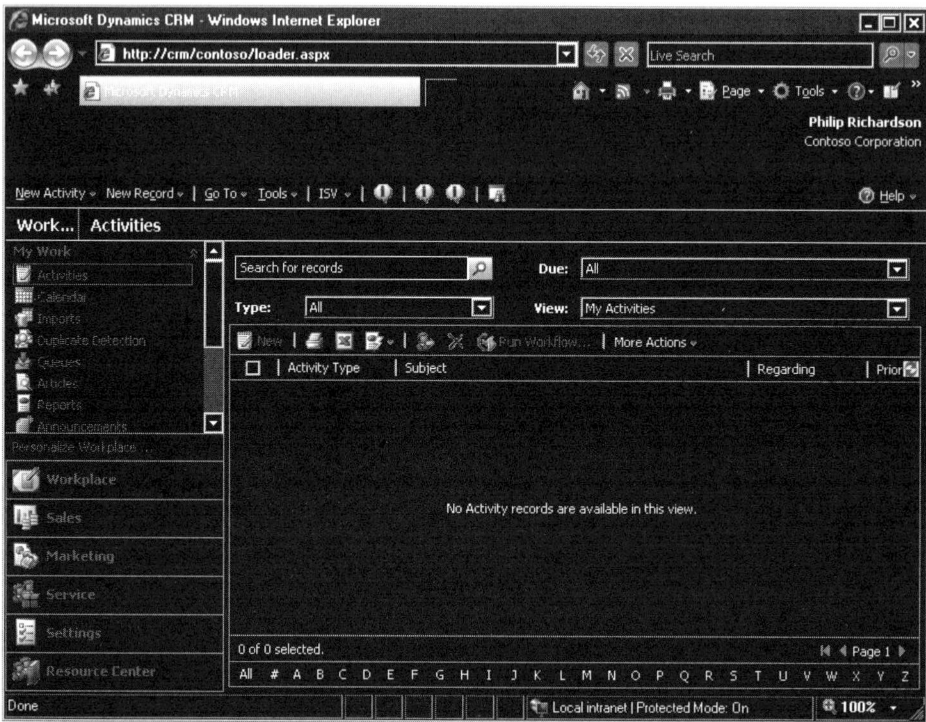

FIGURE 9-11 Windows High-Contrast On and Microsoft Dynamics CRM High-Contrast On

As you can see, all the elements appear in the Web user interface when it is aware of high contrast. Be sure to test your custom solution in these modes and fix any portions of your user interface that aren't displaying correctly.

Additional Deployment Considerations

Just as with developing custom solutions, the implementation of your deployment package may also contain errors. You should also consider the following when deploying Microsoft Dynamics CRM solutions:

- Missing prerequisites
- Resetting IIS
- Customizations management

Missing Prerequisites

Your solution's installation procedure needs to check for any prerequisites. You should never assume that a customer's environment possesses anything beyond the minimum prerequisites required by Microsoft Dynamics CRM itself.

The most common missing prerequisite when installing a solution is the .NET Framework. Three versions of the framework are typically encountered in customer Microsoft Dynamics CRM 4.0 environments: 3.0, 3.5, and 3.5 SP1. If you use Visual Studio 2008 or Visual Studio 2005 to create your MSI, you can specify a .NET Framework Launch Condition. Figure 9-12 shows how you can select a .NET Framework Launch Condition from your setup project, and Figure 9-13 shows how you select the version you want to enforce.

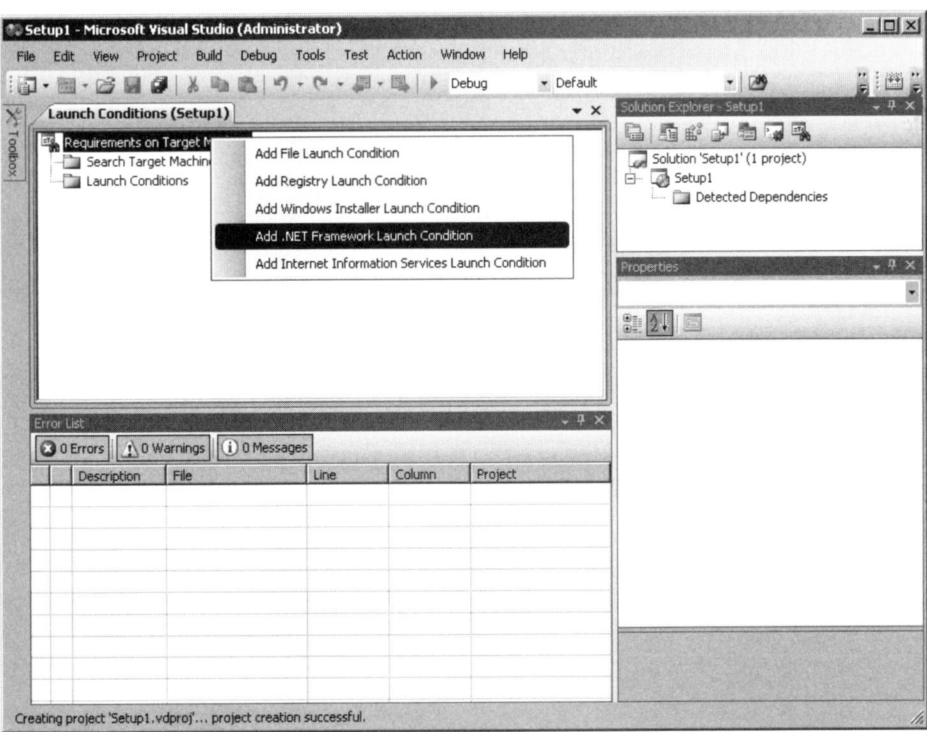

FIGURE 9-12 Adding .NET Framework Launch Condition

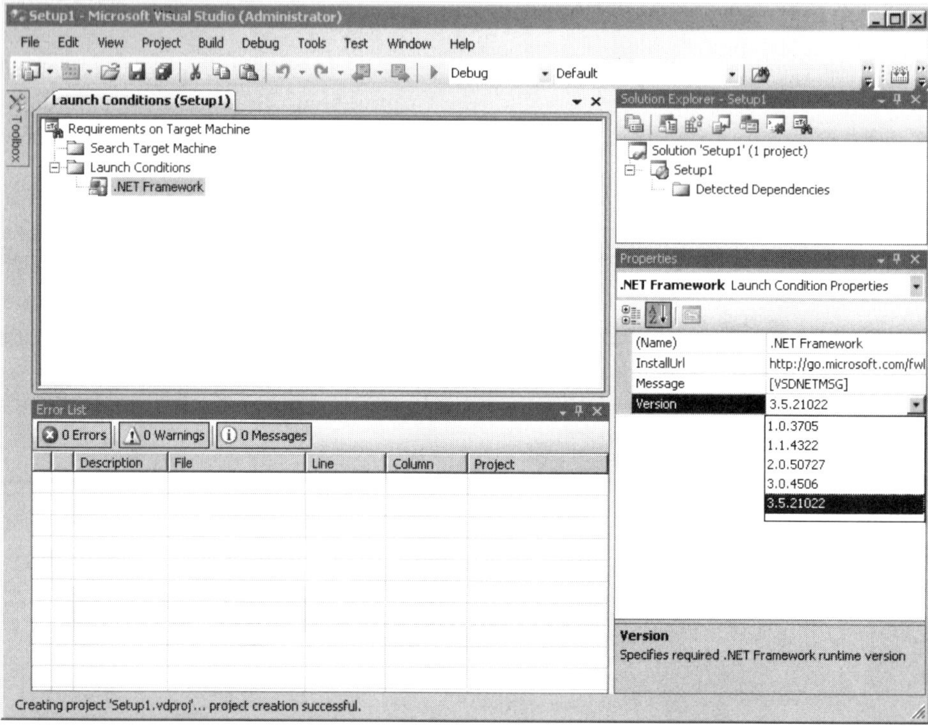

FIGURE 9-13 Selecting the required .NET version.

The following are additional prerequisites checks you may want to consider for your solutions:

- Operating system version
- RAM
- CPU
- Local disk space
- Database space
- Network latency
- Network bandwidth
- Languages spoken by end users
- Other Microsoft Dynamics CRM solutions produced by third-parties that are already installed

In most cases you may want to warn customers about your prerequisites using documentation (much like the Microsoft Dynamics CRM Implementation Guide). In other cases your installer should perform any dependency checking and provide the user with the opportunity to correct missing dependencies prior to continuing.

Resetting IIS

When attempting to update plug-ins and workflow assemblies, you may need to reset IIS because Microsoft Dynamics CRM caches instances of these assemblies in memory. You can choose to have customers do this manually or have your installer and configuration applications do this automatically. The best way to restart IIS using .NET is to use the *Process.Start* method. For more information regarding the *Process.Start* command, please review *http://msdn.microsoft.com/en-us/library/h6ak8zt5.aspx.*

Customizations Management

You generally use the native import/export customizations functionality of Microsoft Dynamics CRM when deploying customizations between environments. However, this process can also be found to cause deployment errors. In order to help minimize errors, always make customizations changes to a master Microsoft Dynamics CRM deployment and then import those changes to new environments.

Sometimes a large number of customizations create a server timeout, which will fail the import. You can attempt to import a few entities at a time or try some of the registry changes listed in the following Microsoft Knowledge Base article: *http://support.microsoft.com/kb/918609.*

Finally, you can use the *MetadataService* Web service to create attributes and relationships or automate the import and export process with the *CrmService* Web service.

Example Deployment Sequence

To conclude, we want to discuss a sample deployment sequence. In this example, we discuss the deployment steps of a simple and hypothetical application built by our favorite fictional company, Contoso.

We will install an application that provides enhanced privacy functionality in the form of a Do Not Email (DNE) list. Many companies maintain such lists to ensure that they do not violate privacy policies when conducting outbound sales and marketing activities.

Component Inventory

The hypothetical DNE application maintains the list of e-mail addresses in a custom entity. Plug-ins assist with intercepting any outbound e-mail sent by Microsoft Dynamics CRM and validates the e-mail address against the DNE list. A custom Web page, shown in an IFRAME on the Account, Contact, and Lead forms shows the user if a record is in the DNE list.

We list an inventory of a solution's components to analyze the various techniques that will be required to install, configure, and uninstall our solution. For our sample application, we need the following:

- Custom DNE entity
- IFrame configured on the Account, Contact, and Lead forms
- Custom Web page
- Plug-in

Now that we have our components, let's review each of the deployment steps.

Build

The DNE application consists of two components to build: the plug-in and the Web form. In this case, both will be compiled using Visual Studio 2008. They will use CLR 2.0 and require the .NET Framework 3.5 SP1.

Install

Our common set of files in the DNE application will be the Web files. As such, we want to ensure that this application is multi-tenant friendly and only deployed one time to each of the Web servers in our deployment. The Web page will be installed using a custom installer to deploy the files to each Web server used by the Microsoft Dynamics CRM environment. The installer follows the Microsoft Dynamics CRM recommendation and copies the files to the following locations:

- wwwroot$\bin: the compiled Web application assembly for the Web site will be placed here. Note that the assembly has a strong name such as Contoso.DoNotEmail.WebSite.dll.
- wwwroot$\ISV\Contoso\DoNotEmail: Any ASPX, CSS, and image files for the solution will be placed here.
- The installer should also check for the .NET Framework 3.5 SP1 to be present on all the Web servers.

Configuration

The configuration of the DNE application deploys all of the components unique to the organization. In this example, we perform the following steps during the configuration step:

- Import the DNE entity
- Update security roles to allow access to the DNE entity
- Modify entity forms to add IFrames
- Publish customizations
- Register the plug-in

The configuration steps are packaged using a configuration application called DNE Provisioning Utility. The DNE Provisioning Utility can be a simple console application, a Windows Presentation Foundation (WPF) application, or client executable. The tool requires the following information and then begins configuring the application:

- URL of the Microsoft Dynamics CRM server
- Organization name
- Authentication information

Since this solution contains a plug-in, the DNE Provisioning Utility will use the *RegisterSolution* message from the *CrmService* Web service. Therefore, use Windows Authentication to authenticate to the *CrmService*, and the user must be a member of the Microsoft Dynamics CRM deployment group.

Uninstall

The removal of the DNE application can be achieved by uninstalling the Web files from each Microsoft Dynamics CRM Web server (from Add/Remove Programs or by re-running the installer) and by manually deleting the customizations in the CRM organization.

Alternatively, you could augment the DNE Provisioning Utility to remove the components provisioned during the configuration step. Manual removal of customizations is often preferable for customers to avoid unintended removal of data or if other customizations are dependent on the new entity. You need to provide a programmatic way to remove the plug-in, or use the plug-in registration tool provided by Microsoft.

Summary

The process of solution packaging and deployment is often time-consuming and fraught with configuration issues. Having a strong understanding of your usage scenarios and being able to correctly categorize your applications (connected versus integrated) allows you to overcome these issues with relative ease.

Comprehensive testing of a solution deployment is another area where you might make dangerous assumptions. The testing section in this chapter offered guidance on how to approach your deployment test strategy. If you are unable to test for a particular scenario (or decide to explicitly disallow it), it's important that you make this known to your end customer.

Finally, it's important that your solution interacts well with other solutions. Customers of Microsoft Dynamics CRM often want to use solutions from multiple providers. If you follow the guidance in this chapter, your solution shouldn't interfere with others. If, for some reason, you need to make unsupported changes to Microsoft Dynamics CRM (for example, modifying Microsoft Dynamics CRM's Web.config), it's important to notify your customers.

Chapter 10

Developing Offline Solutions

One of the unique benefits of Microsoft Dynamics CRM is that your users can use Microsoft Dynamics CRM for Outlook with Offline Access to work with customer data while they are disconnected from the server. This feature can come in handy if your users need to work someplace without an Internet connection, such as on an airplane, at a trade show, or onsite at a customer's office. Microsoft Dynamics CRM refers to the concept of working disconnected from the server as working offline. When the user reconnects to the server again (known as going online), Microsoft Dynamics CRM for Outlook with Offline Access will automatically perform a bidirectional update of data changes with the server. Therefore, records created or modified while offline update to the CRM server.

As a developer, you should know how your programming customizations will behave if your company deploys Microsoft Dynamics CRM for Outlook with Offline Access. Fortunately, Microsoft Dynamics CRM includes an offline API so that most of your programming customizations can run offline in addition to online. Of course, you should learn about a few unique nuances to developing offline solutions. One of the most significant constraints of offline development is that workflow rules and asynchronous plug-ins do not execute offline.

In this chapter we will talk about communicating with the Microsoft Dynamics CRM SDK offline and then guide you through creating custom IFrame pages and plug-ins that function both online and offline. The chapter covers the following topics:

- Overview of developing with Microsoft Dynamics CRM for Outlook with Offline Access
- Offline development environment
- Offline navigation
- Communicating with the Microsoft Dynamics CRM SDK API offline
- Scripting for offline
- Developing IFrames for offline
- Developing an offline plug-in
- Offline development considerations

Overview

When you install Microsoft Dynamics CRM for Outlook with Offline Access, the software automatically installs all of the components your users need to work offline, including:

- Microsoft ASP.NET Cassini, the same Web server used by Microsoft Visual Studio 2008
- Microsoft Dynamics CRM Web files
- Microsoft SQL Server 2005 Express Edition, used to store the local copy of the Microsoft Dynamics CRM database

The Web files are installed to the same location that was selected during the install of Microsoft Dynamics CRM for Outlook. You can also find this location by looking at *InstallPath* value in the following registry key: *HKEY_LOCAL_MACHINE\SOFTWARE\Microsoft\MSCRMCLIENT*. That folder contains a folder named Client, and under the Client folder is another directory named res that contains the Web files.

Tip The default location of the offline Web files is C:\Program Files\Microsoft Dynamics CRM\Client\res\web, and the offline database files are installed to C:\Program Files\Microsoft Dynamics CRM\sql\4.0.

When the user is offline, Microsoft Dynamics CRM references data in the local database instead of the data on the CRM server. By default, Microsoft Dynamics CRM for Outlook does not copy the entire server database to the local database. Instead, Microsoft Dynamics CRM for Outlook uses local data groups to determine which subset of the data it should copy to the client computer. Users can modify their local data group within the CRM menu in Microsoft Dynamics CRM for Outlook.

Tip The MSDN Code Gallery offers a tool that you can use to automate the local data group creation for multiple users. You can find this tool at *http://code.msdn.microsoft.com/mscrmlocaldatagroup*.

During your offline development, you may want to query or manipulate your test data in the offline database. You can do this easily by using Microsoft SQL Server Management Studio Express to connect to the offline database. You can download SQL Server Management Studio Express for free from the Microsoft Web site: *http://www.microsoft.com/downloads/*.

Offline Development Environment

Because the offline API functions very similarly to the online API, you won't have much trouble understanding how it works. Therefore, one of the trickiest parts of developing an offline solution for Microsoft Dynamics CRM might be configuring your offline development environment. To develop for the offline client, you need an install of the offline client configured and pointed at your Microsoft Dynamics CRM install and organization. When you setup your offline development environment, you do have a few other options for deploying and testing:

- Workstation
- Laptop
- Virtual PC

Workstation

Deploying and testing your offline code on your workstation is the simplest and quickest method of the three. If you are currently not using the Microsoft Dynamics CRM for Outlook client on your workstation, you can install and configure it to point at your Microsoft Dynamics CRM development server.

This approach does have a few drawbacks. You can only configure Microsoft Dynamics CRM for Outlook with Offline Access for one user per computer, so it's not ideal if your testing requires multiple users or users in different roles. If another user logs on to your workstation and tries to configure the Outlook Client, she receives an error message stating that Microsoft Dynamics CRM for Outlook with Offline Access can only be configured for one user (Figure 10-1).

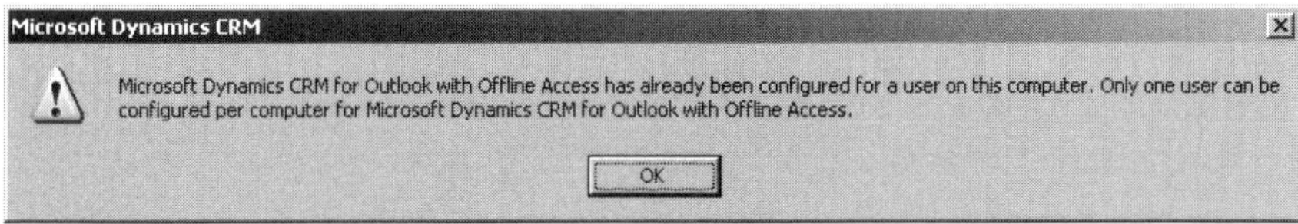

FIGURE 10-1 Microsoft Dynamics CRM for Outlook with Offline Access configuration error

In addition, if you install Microsoft Dynamics CRM for Outlook on your personal workstation, you run the risk of mixing up your regular Outlook information with contacts, appointments, and tasks from the development system.

Laptop

Another option is to install the offline client on a laptop. Although this option still only allows for the offline client to be configured for one user account, you have the option to share the computer with other developers or testers by simply moving the laptop from office to office.

Virtual PC

If you need to test your offline code with multiple user accounts or can't use the workstation or laptop option, you can create a Virtual PC with Microsoft Outlook installed on it. Then you can install and configure the Microsoft Dynamics CRM Outlook client on the Virtual PC and create a new Virtual PC for each user account you test with. You can then share the Virtual PC with multiple developers and testers.

Offline Navigation

While customizing Microsoft Dynamics CRM, you may add your own navigation and menu items through the ISV Config and the SiteMap. By default these custom elements are displayed in Microsoft Dynamics CRM for Outlook with Offline Access.

The ISV.Config allows you to add links to the left navigation area of an entity, custom menus, and items to an entity's toolbar, and custom buttons to an entity's grid. The SiteMap allows you to customize the Microsoft Dynamics CRM main navigation. Just as with the ISV Config, the SiteMap allows you to specify which clients your customizations are displayed in and also whether they are displayed in offline mode.

Client Attribute

You can use the *Client* attribute on an ISV Config or SiteMap node to configure which Microsoft Dynamics CRM clients display the customization. This is useful if you only want your custom navigation element to show in the Web interface or only in the Microsoft Dynamics CRM for Outlook client. The default value for this attribute is set to display in all clients. The ISV Config *Client* attributes can be set to either Web or Outlook. The following ISV Config elements implement the *Client* attribute:

- *Button*
- *Entity*
- *MenuItem*
- *NavBarItem*

The *SubArea* element of the SiteMap also has the *Client* attribute. It also defaults to display in all clients and can be updated to any of the following values:

- *All*
- *Outlook*
- *OutlookLaptopClient*
- *OutlookWorkstationClient*
- *Web*

The *OutlookLaptopClient* value refers to Microsoft Dynamics CRM for Outlook with Offline Access. The *OutlookWorkstationClient* value refers to the non-offline enabled version of Microsoft Dynamics CRM for Outlook. You can set multiple values by entering them as a comma-separated list. The following code sample shows a SiteMap *SubArea* that only appears in the Web client:

```
<SubArea Id="nav_calendar"
         Icon="/_imgs/area/18_calendar.gif"
         ResourceId="Homepage_Calendar"
         Url="/workplace/home_calendar.aspx"
         Client="Web">
    <Privilege Entity="activitypointer" Privilege="Read" />
</SubArea>
```

AvailableOffline Attribute

If you want to disable your custom navigation or buttons when the user is offline, you need to specifically set the *AvailableOffline* attribute of your element to false. This optional attribute defaults to true unless otherwise specified. The *AvailableOffline* attribute is available on the following ISV Config elements:

- *Button*
- *Entity*
- *MenuItem*
- *NavBarItem*

The *AvailableOffline* attribute is also available on the *SubArea* element of the SiteMap. The following code sample shows a button added to the ISV Config that is only available in the Outlook client and shows up in offline mode:

```
<Button Icon="/_imgs/ico_18_debug.gif"
        JavaScript="alert('test');"
        Client="Outlook" AvailableOffline="true">
    <Titles>
        <Title LCID="1033" Text="Outlook Only" />
    </Titles>
    <ToolTips>
        <ToolTip LCID="1033" Text="Outlook Only - This is available offline also." />
    </ToolTips>
</Button>
```

Communicating with the Microsoft Dynamics CRM SDK API Offline

Both the *CrmService* and *MetadataService* provided by the Microsoft Dynamics CRM SDK contain functionality that you can use in your offline programming. You can further extend the Microsoft Dynamics CRM for Outlook client using the Microsoft Dynamics CRM Outlook SDK.

Note In offline mode the Microsoft Dynamics CRM Web services will always use integrated authentication to authenticate the user. You cannot use impersonation while offline.

CrmService Offline

You can use the *CrmService* offline in the same way you use it online. Any data manipulation done in offline mode is stored in the user's local database and Microsoft Dynamics CRM will automatically synchronize with the main database the next time the user goes online.

Warning The synchronization process does not merge field-level changes with existing data. If you update a record offline, the sync process will update the entire record on the server. It's possible to encounter a scenario where an offline user modifies a record, and an online user modified that same record during the time the user was offline. In this scenario, the user who modified the record last wins and his changes survive on the server. This is true even if the two users modified different fields on the record.

Offline Message and Entity Availability

You can check whether a *CrmService* message is available offline by checking its availability, which you can do by querying the *sdkmessage* entity and checking its *availability* attribute. Table 10-1 contains a list of the possible *availability* values and what they mean. If the message can be used for more than one entity, you should also query the *sdkmessagefilter* entity's *availability* attribute to make sure the message works for the entity you are trying to use it with. For example, the *Create* message works both online and offline, but the *AddMemberList* message only works online.

TABLE 10-1 Message Availability Values

Value	Description
0	Message is only available on the server (online).
1	Message is only available on the client (offline).
2	Message is available both on the server and the client (online and offline).

The Microsoft Dynamics CRM 4.0 SDK contains a list of entities that are available for offline use. You can also check this programmatically by retrieving the entity's *EntityMetadata* and checking its *EntityMetadata.IsAvailableOffline* property. The *IsAvailableOffline* property is a *CrmBoolean* data type. The following code sample shows an example of checking an *EntityMetadata's* offline availability:

```
// entityMetadata is an instance of the EntityMetadata class
if (entityMetadata.IsAvailableOffline.Value)
{
    // custom offline logic here
}
```

Creating a *CrmService* Instance Offline

To create an instance of the *CrmService* offline, you need to extract a few values from the registry. Because the offline Web site is running on the local Cassini Web server we can use "localhost" as the server name. As you can see from the following code sample, we then need to grab the port number from the *CassiniPort* registry entry and the organization name from the *ClientAuthOrganizationName* registry entry. We can then construct our server as we normally would.

```
RegistryKey regkey = Registry.CurrentUser.OpenSubKey("Software\\Microsoft\\MSCRMClient");
string orgName = regkey.GetValue("ClientAuthOrganizationName").ToString();
string portNumber = regkey.GetValue("CassiniPort").ToString();

string baseUrl = "http://localhost:" + portNumber + "/mscrmservices/2007/";
crmUrl = baseUrl + "crmservice.asmx";

CrmAuthenticationToken token = new CrmAuthenticationToken();
token.OrganizationName = orgName;
token.AuthenticationType = 0;

CrmService service = new CrmService();
service.Credentials = System.Net.CredentialCache.DefaultCredentials;
service.CrmAuthenticationTokenValue = token;
service.Url = crmUrl;
```

Tip You can find the Microsoft Dynamics CRM for Outlook with Offline Access registry values at HKEY_CURRENT_USER\Software\Microsoft\MSCRMClient.

MetadataService Offline

When using the *MetadataService* offline, only the retrieve messages are available. You cannot manipulate entities—such as programmatically adding an attribute—while offline. This restriction is in place to prevent a conflict when the user goes online and the databases are synchronized. Chapter 8, "Developing with the Metadata Service," contains sample code for creating the *MetadataService* while running in offline mode.

Microsoft Dynamics Outlook SDK

You can use the *Microsoft.Crm.Outlook.Sdk* assembly to customize Microsoft Dynamics CRM for Outlook. The assembly contains a class named *CrmOutlookService* that has a few useful methods for programming for offline. To use the *CrmOutlookService* you create an instance the same way you do with the *CrmService* class. Table 10-2 lists the methods available for you to use from the *CrmOutlookService* instance, and Table 10-4 lists all of its properties. The *State* property of the *CrmOutlookService* has a value with the type of *ClientState*. Table 10-5 lists all of the possible *ClientState* values.

TABLE 10-2 *CrmOutlookService* Methods

Name	Description
GoOffline	Executes the same functionality as the Go Offline button. The online database data and customizations are synchronized to the user's local database.
GoOnline	Executes the same functionality as the Go Online button. The user's local database with be synchronized with the online database.
SetOffline	Sets Microsoft Dynamics CRM for Outlook with Offline Access to offline mode without synchronizing the online database with the local offline database.
Sync	Executes the synchronization between the online Microsoft Dynamics CRM database and Microsoft Dynamics CRM for Outlook.

The *Sync* method on the *CrmOutlookService* takes one argument of the type *OutlookSyncType*. This determines whether the online data will be synchronized with the client computer's Outlook store (for example, contacts, tasks, and appointments), the offline database, or the client computer's Outlook address book. Table 10-3 contains possible values for the *OutlookSyncType* enumeration.

TABLE 10-3 *OutlookSyncType* Members

Name	Description
Outlook	The synchronization occurs between Microsoft Dynamics CRM and the client computer's Outlook store.
AddressBook	The synchronization occurs between Microsoft Dynamics CRM and the client computer's Outlook address book.
Offline	The synchronization occurs between Microsoft Dynamics CRM and the local offline database.

TABLE 10-4 *CrmOutlookService* Properties

Name	Type	Description
IsCrmClientLoaded	*Boolean*	Returns true if the Microsoft Dynamics CRM for Outlook client has been loaded by Microsoft Outlook.
IsCrmClientOffline	*Boolean*	Returns true if Microsoft Dynamics CRM for Outlook with Offline Access is currently in offline mode.

TABLE 10-4 ***CrmOutlookService* Properties**

Name	Type	Description
IsCrmDesktopClient	*Boolean*	Returns true if Microsoft Dynamics CRM for Outlook has been installed. Returns false if Microsoft Dynamics CRM for Outlook with Offline Access has been installed.
ServerUri	*Uri*	Returns the Uri to connect to the Microsoft Dynamics CRM SDK. The return value differs depending on whether the client is online or offline.
State	*ClientState*	Returns the current state of the client.

TABLE 10-5 ***ClientState* Members**

Field	Description
Online	The client is online.
Offline	The client is offline.
SyncToOutlook	The client is currently in the synchronization process between the online server and Outlook.
SyncToOutlookError	An error has occurred during the synchronization with Outlook.
GoingOffline	The client is currently in the process of going into offline mode.
GoingOnline	The client is currently in the process of going into online mode.
ClientLoadFailure	Microsoft Outlook failed to load the Microsoft Dynamics CRM for Outlook client.
ClientVersionLower	The client version is lower than the version of Microsoft Dynamics CRM installed on the server.
ClientVersionHigher	The client version is higher than the version of Microsoft Dynamics CRM installed on the server.
PostOfflineUpgrade	The client has been upgraded while in offline mode.
OnlineCrmNotAvailable	The online Microsoft Dynamics CRM server is currently unavailable.
GoingOfflineCanceled	The user canceled the process of going offline.
BackgroundGoingOffline	The process of synchronizing the offline database is currently running in the background.

Scripting for Offline

In Chapter 7, "Form Scripting," you learned about adding custom JavaScript code to the Microsoft Dynamics CRM entity forms and attributes. Microsoft Dynamics CRM will automatically take all custom scripts offline to the client computer—you cannot specify some scripts to run offline or online only. Therefore, you need to make sure that your scripts will not encounter errors when they run offline disconnected from the server. Table 7-2 from Chapter 7 lists global functions available to you for detecting which client the user is on and whether the user is online or offline. You will see an example of this when we create our offline IFrame in the following section.

Developing IFrames for Offline

If you have developed custom IFrame or Web pages for your Microsoft Dynamics CRM system, you most likely want them to function for your users when they go offline with the Microsoft Dynamics CRM for Outlook with Offline Access. By planning ahead of time for offline usage, you can easily create custom Web pages and IFrames that will work both offline and online. However, some scenarios might exist where your custom Web pages cannot function offline because the Internet connection is absent:

- When it requires access to an external Web Service
- When it displays content from an external Web site
- When it retrieves or updates data from an external database

Of course, these scenarios are not caused by a Microsoft Dynamics CRM constraint. Instead, they are simply a limitation because no connectivity to these external systems exists. In cases where you know your IFrame cannot function offline, it is best to display a message explaining this to the user, or have your IFrame detect whether the user is offline and redirect the user to an offline friendly page.

Programming the IFrame

In this section we will develop an IFrame page that functions both online and offline. We will add the IFrame to the native Account entity's form and display contact information from the Account's selected primary contact. If the user views the page while in offline mode, we alert the user to let her know the information she is viewing may not be up to date. If you want to peek ahead to see what the finished output looks like, please refer to Figure 10-3.

Adding the AccountPrimaryContactInfo.aspx page

1. Open the ProgrammingWithDynamicsCrm4 solution with Microsoft Visual Studio 2008.
2. If you have not created the ProgrammingMicrosoftDynamicsCrm4.Web project in a previous chapter, right-click the solution name, add a new Web Site project named **ProgrammingMicrosoftDynamicsCrm4.Web** and add references to these Microsoft Dynamics CRM SDK assemblies: Microsoft.Crm.Sdk.dll and Microsoft.Crm.SdkProxy.dll.
3. Right-click the ProgrammingWithDynamicsCrm4.Web project and select Add New Item.
4. Select the Web Form template and type **AccountPrimaryContactInfo** in the Name box.
5. Click Add.

The preceding steps add two new files to the Web project: AccountPrimaryContactInfo.aspx and AccountPrimaryContactInfo.aspx.cs. Listing 10-1 shows the source code for our user interface page.

LISTING 10-1 AccountPrimaryContactInfo.aspx source code

```
<%@ Page Language="C#" AutoEventWireup="true"
         CodeFile="AccountPrimaryContactInfo.aspx.cs"
         Inherits="IFrames_AccountPrimaryContactInfo" %>

<!DOCTYPE html PUBLIC "-//W3C//DTD XHTML 1.0 Transitional//EN"
         "http://www.w3.org/TR/xhtml1/DTD/xhtml1-transitional.dtd">
<html xmlns="http://www.w3.org/1999/xhtml">
<head runat="server">
    <title>Untitled Page</title>

    <script type="text/javascript">

        function window.onload()
        {
            if ( !parent.IsOnline() )
            {
                document.getElementById("message").innerHTML =
                "Warning: You are currently offline. The contact information
                 displayed on this page may be out of date.";
            }
        }

    </script>

</head>
<body style="font-size: 11px;
             font-family: Tahoma;
             margin: 0px;
             border: 0px;
             background-color: #eaf3ff;">
    <form id="form1" runat="server">
    <table cellpadding="1"
           cellspacing="0"
           style="width: 100%; height: 100%; table-layout: fixed;"
           border="0">
        <colgroup>
            <col style="width: 111;" />
            <col />
            <col style="width: 115; padding-left: 23px;" />
            <col />
        </colgroup>
        <tr>
            <td colspan="4">
                <div id="message" style="color: Red" />
            </td>
        </tr>
        <tr>
```

```
                <td>
                    Full Name
                </td>
                <td>
                    <asp:Label ID="fullname" runat="server" />
                </td>
                <td>
                     
                </td>
                <td>
                     
                </td>
            </tr>
            <tr>
                <td>
                    Business Phone
                </td>
                <td>
                    <asp:Label ID="phone" runat="server" />
                </td>
                <td>
                    E-mail
                </td>
                <td>
                    <asp:Label ID="email" runat="server" />
                </td>
            </tr>
            <tr>
                <td>
                    City
                </td>
                <td>
                    <asp:Label ID="city" runat="server" />
                </td>
                <td>
                    State
                </td>
                <td>
                    <asp:Label ID="state" runat="server" />
                </td>
            </tr>
        </table>
        </form>
</body>
</html>
```

The display is a simple HTML table laid out similarly to the four-column layout used on the Microsoft Dynamics CRM entity forms. You will also notice that styles were added to the page to help blend it into the Account entity form. The end user will most likely not even realize that he is looking at custom IFrame page. You can find the styles used in the Microsoft Dynamics UI Style Guide included in the Microsoft Dynamics CRM SDK.

The code in the JavaScript block at the top of the aspx page is used to alert the user when the IFrame is being displayed in offline mode. The code calls the *IsOnline* method of the entity form:

```
if ( !parent.IsOnline() )
{
    document.getElementById("message").innerHTML = "Warning: You are currently offline.
The contact information displayed on this page may be out of date.";
}
```

The code to actually retrieve our Contact data is located in the code-behind file. Listing 10-2 shows the source code for this file.

LISTING 10-2 AccountPrimaryContactInfo.aspx.cs source code

```
using System;
using System.Collections;
using System.Configuration;
using System.Data;
using System.Web;
using System.Web.Security;
using System.Web.UI;
using System.Web.UI.HtmlControls;
using System.Web.UI.WebControls;
using System.Web.UI.WebControls.WebParts;
using Microsoft.Crm.Sdk;
using Microsoft.Win32;
using Microsoft.Crm.Sdk.Query;
using Microsoft.Crm.SdkTypeProxy;

public partial class IFrames_AccountPrimaryContactInfo : System.Web.UI.Page
{
    protected void Page_Load(object sender, EventArgs e)
    {
        string id = Request.QueryString["id"];

        if (string.IsNullOrEmpty(id))
            throw new Exception("The required query string parameter \"id\" was not
                                 found.");

        CrmService crmService = GetCrmService();

        // First retrieve the primary contact for the account
        ColumnSet accountCols = new ColumnSet();
        accountCols.AddColumn("primarycontactid");

        account crmAccount = (account)crmService.Retrieve("account",
                                                          new Guid(id),
                                                          accountCols);

        if (crmAccount.primarycontactid != null)
        {
            Guid primaryContactId = crmAccount.primarycontactid.Value;
```

```
            ColumnSet contactCols = new ColumnSet();
            contactCols.AddColumns("fullname",
                                   "telephone1",
                                   "emailaddress1",
                                   "address1_city",
                                   "address1_stateorprovince");

            contact crmContact = (contact)crmService.Retrieve("contact",
                                                              primaryContactId,
                                                              contactCols);

            this.fullname.Text = crmContact.fullname;
            this.phone.Text = crmContact.telephone1;
            this.city.Text = crmContact.address1_city;
            this.state.Text = crmContact.address1_stateorprovince;
            this.email.Text = crmContact.emailaddress1;
        }
    }


    private CrmService GetCrmService()
    {
        CrmAuthenticationToken token = new CrmAuthenticationToken();
        string crmUrl;
        string orgName = String.Empty;
        bool online = true;

        if (Request.Url.Host.ToString() == "127.0.0.1")
        {
            online = false;
        }

        if (online)
        {
            RegistryKey regkey =
               Registry.LocalMachine.OpenSubKey("SOFTWARE\\Microsoft\\MSCRM");
            string serverUrl = regkey.GetValue("ServerUrl").ToString();
            crmUrl = serverUrl + "/2007/crmservice.asmx";

            if (Request.QueryString["orgname"] != null)
            {
                orgName = Request.QueryString["orgname"];
            }
        }
        else
        {
            RegistryKey regkey =
               Registry.CurrentUser.OpenSubKey("Software\\Microsoft\\MSCRMClient");
            orgName = regkey.GetValue("ClientAuthOrganizationName").ToString();
            string portNumber = regkey.GetValue("CassiniPort").ToString();

            string baseUrl = "http://localhost:"
                             + portNumber
                             + "/mscrmservices/2007/";
```

```
            crmUrl = baseUrl + "crmservice.asmx";
        }

        token.OrganizationName = orgName;
        token.AuthenticationType = 0;

        CrmService service = new CrmService();
        service.Credentials = System.Net.CredentialCache.DefaultCredentials;
        service.CrmAuthenticationTokenValue = token;
        service.Url = crmUrl;

        return service;
    }
}
```

Because this page needs to function both online and offline, we need to accommodate the different locations of the Microsoft Dynamics CRM SDK services. We used the *GetCrmService* method in Listing 10-2 to accomplish this. As we discussed earlier in the section "Communicating with the Microsoft Dynamics CRM SDK API Offline," if the page is being run offline, the values needed by the *CrmService*, such as port number and organization name, are pulled from the client computer's registry.

After the *CrmService* has been created, the rest of the functionality is pretty straightforward. First we attempt to retrieve the primary contact *Guid* from the Account. If a value is returned, we then retrieve the necessary fields from that Contact record and populate our *Label* controls.

Deploying the IFrame Page

Now that we have completed our IFrame development, we need to update the Account form and deploy our Web files to the Microsoft Dynamics CRM server and client computer.

Microsoft Dynamics CRM Customizations

The first thing we need to do is add our IFrame to the Account entity's form. To accomplish this, we add a new tab named Primary Contact that contains an IFrame pointed at our aspx page.

Adding the IFrame to the Account Form

1. Open Microsoft Dynamics CRM in a Web browser and navigate to the Account entity's form customizations screen.
2. Click Add A Tab in the Common Tasks menu.
3. Type **Primary Contact** into the Name field and click OK.

4. An IFrame must be housed in a section, so click Add A Section from the Common Tasks menu.
5. Type **Contact Information** into the Name field.
6. Select both the Show The Name Of This Section On The Form and the Show Divider Line Below The Section Name check boxes and verify that the tab is set to our new Primary Contact tab. Click OK.

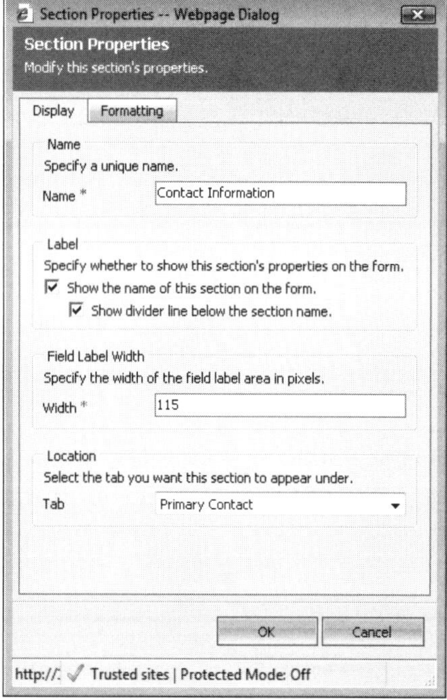

7. Select our new section and click Add An IFrame in the Common Tasks menu.
8. Enter **accountprimarycontactinfo** in the Name field.
9. Later we will deploy our Web files under the ISV folder of Microsoft Dynamics CRM, so type **/ISV/ProgrammingWithDynamicsCrm4/AccountPrimaryContactInfo.aspx** in the URL field.
10. Select the Pass Record Object-Type Code And Unique Identifier As Parameters check box.

11. Clear the Restrict Cross-Frame Scripting check box.

12. Verify that Tab is set to Primary Contact and Section is set to Contact Information.

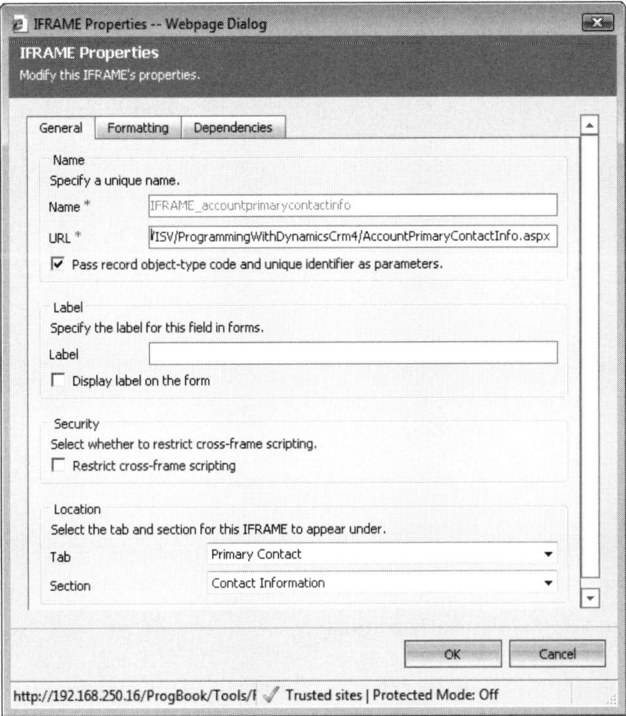

13. In the Formatting tab's Row Layout section, select the Automatically Expand To Use Available Space check box.

14. In the Formatting tab's Border section, clear the Display Border check box. This makes our IFrame integrate seamlessly into the form. Click OK.

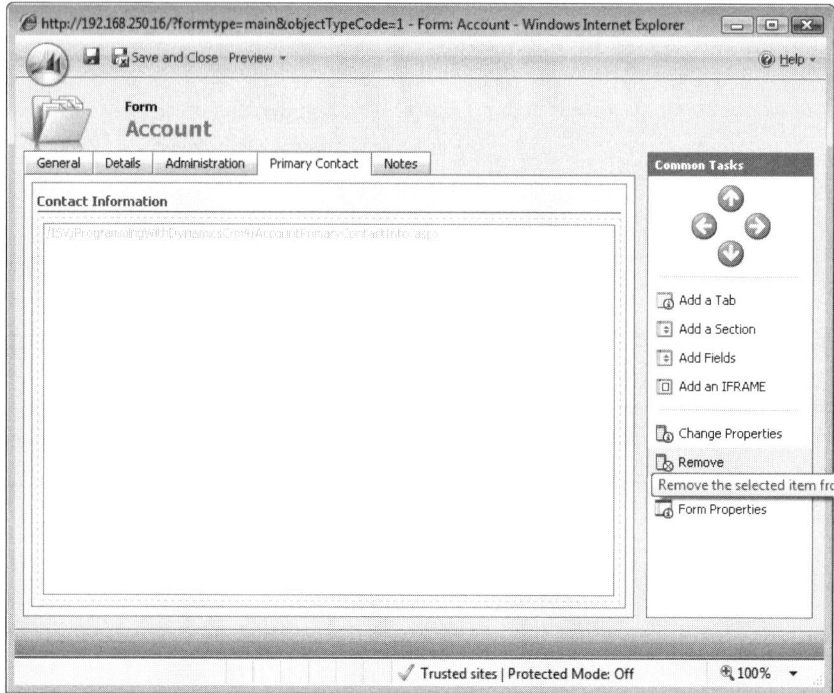

15. Save the form and publish your customizations.

After these changes are published, they are synced with the offline customizations in Microsoft Dynamics CRM for Outlook with Offline Access the next time the user goes offline.

Microsoft Dynamics CRM Web Server

For our IFrame to function while the user is online, we need to deploy our files to the CRM Web server. You can find a more detailed look at deployment in Chapter 9, "Deployment."

Deploying the Web files

1. On the Microsoft Dynamics CRM server, create a new folder named **Programming-WithDynamicsCRM4** under the ISV folder in the directory with your Microsoft Dynamics CRM Web files.
2. Copy the AccountPrimaryContactInfo.aspx and AccountPrimaryContactInfo.aspx.cs files into the newly created folder.

Microsoft Dynamics CRM for Outlook with Offline Access

Because Microsoft Dynamics CRM for Outlook with Offline Access uses its own set of Web files in offline mode, you also need to deploy the Web files to each client computer under the ISV folder in the directory with the offline Web files. You can do this using the same steps in the previous section.

> **Tip** The default location for the Web files for Microsoft Dynamics CRM for Outlook with Offline Access is C:\Program Files\Microsoft Dynamics CRM\Client\res\web\.

Testing the IFrame Page Offline

Now we will test our new IFrame when working offline. Open your instance of Microsoft Outlook that has Microsoft Dynamics CRM for Outlook with Offline Access installed and configured. Click the Go Offline button. When the synchronization process completes and the Go Offline button has been replaced with a Go Online button, navigate to the Accounts grid (Figure 10-2).

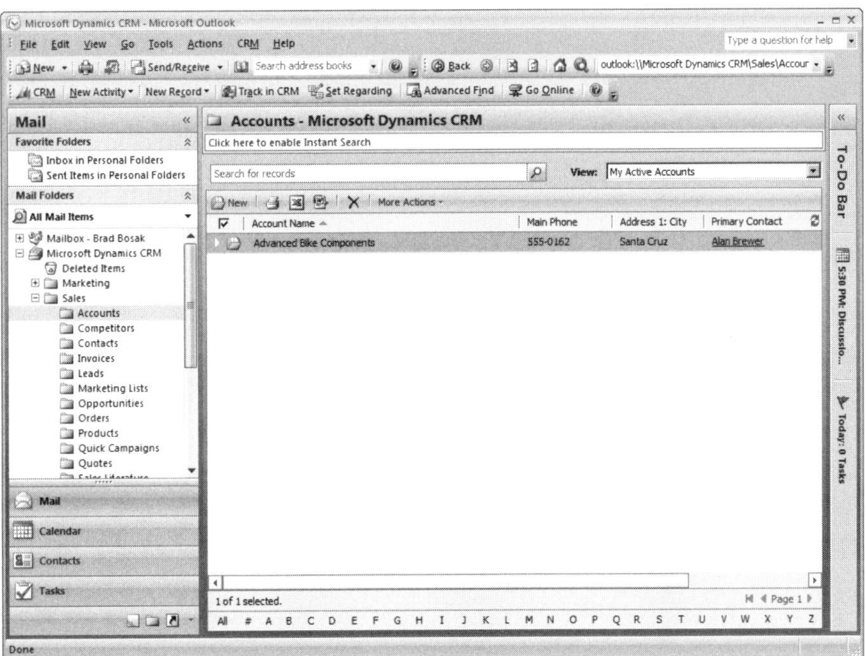

FIGURE 10-2 Offline Accounts view

Open an Account record that has the Primary Contact field populated, or open an Account, populate the Primary Contact field, and click Save. Click the Primary Contact tab we added. You should see the Primary Contact information along with our warning message (Figure 10-3).

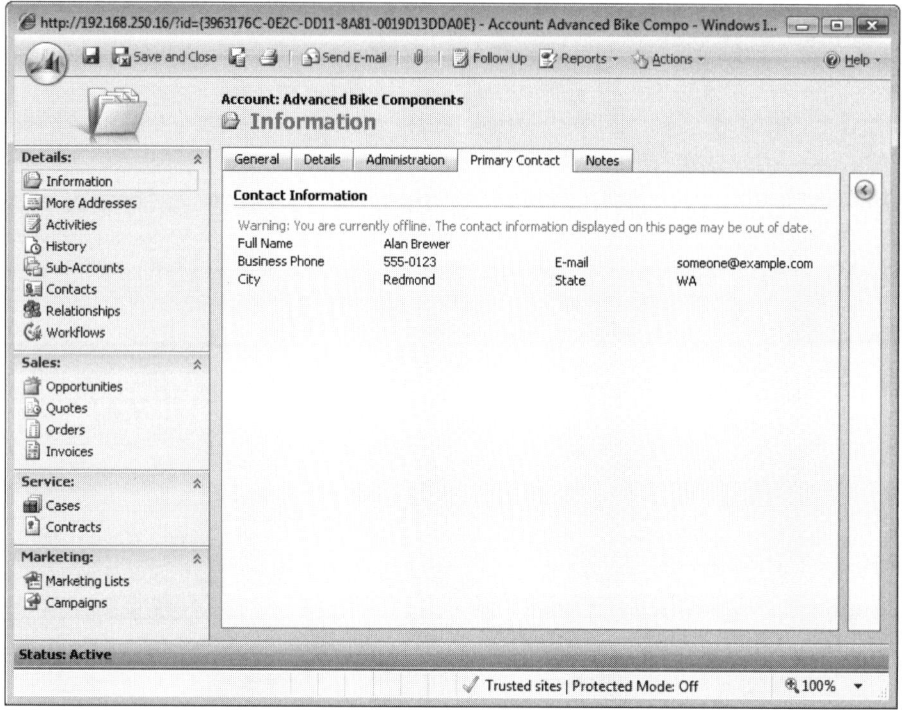

FIGURE 10-3 IFrame displayed in offline mode

Close the Account window and click the Go Online button. When the synchronization process is complete and you no longer see the Go Online button, reopen the same Account record and click the Primary Contact tab. You can now see the Primary Contact Information, but the warning message is gone because you are viewing the actual online form (Figure 10-4).

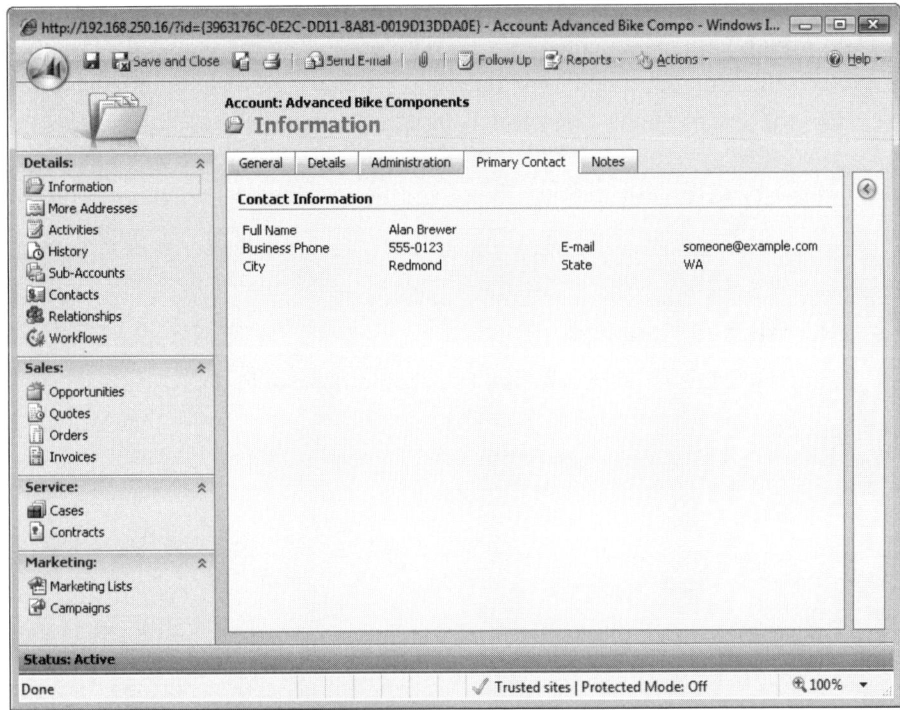

FIGURE 10-4 IFrame displayed in online mode

Developing an Offline Plug-in

Chapter 5, "Plug-ins," gave some examples of creating and deploying plug-ins for Microsoft Dynamics CRM. In this section we expand on this by creating a simple plug-in that functions while running Microsoft Dynamics CRM for Outlook in offline mode.

Programming the Plug-in

We'll develop the offline-capable plug-in in a similar manner as the other plug-ins we have developed, but we need to add logic to determine when the client computer is in offline mode. Our plug-in will update the subject of a Lead record when it is created. We will update the subject to the Lead's last name followed by its first name and the current date. When you create plug-ins, you want to be careful that Microsoft Dynamics CRM doesn't execute them twice (once offline and once online). In a situation where the user is offline and creates a lead and then returns online at a later date, our plug-in would be run both when the lead was created offline and when the user returned online. As you will see later in this section, we add a condition to the plug-in to prevent this from happening. Listing 10-3 shows the entire source code for the LeadTopicUpdater plug-in. Before we start coding, let's talk briefly about the Microsoft Dynamics CRM customizations that we need for this example to function properly. Because the plug-in automatically updates the subject attribute on the Lead entity, we disabled this attribute on the Lead form and set its requirement level to No Constraint. This allows the user to create a new lead without entering a subject.

Adding the LeadTopicUpdater.cs file

1. Open the ProgrammingWithDynamicsCrm4 solution with Microsoft Visual Studio 2008.
2. Right-click the ProgrammingWithDynamicsCrm4.Plugins project we created in Chapter 5 and select Add New Item.
3. Select the Class template and type **LeadTopicUpdater** in the Name box.
4. Click Add.

LISTING 10-3 LeadTopicUpdater.cs source code

```
using System;
using System.Collections.Generic;
using System.Text;
using ProgrammingWithDynamicsCrm4.Plugins.Attributes;
using Microsoft.Crm.Sdk;
using System.Xml;
using Microsoft.Crm.SdkTypeProxy;

namespace ProgrammingWithDynamicsCrm4.Plugins
{
    [PluginStep("Create",
                PluginStepStage.PostEvent,
                Description = "Updates the lead's topic",
                StepId = "LeadPostCreate",
                PrimaryEntityName = "lead",
                Mode = PluginStepMode.Synchronous,
                SupportedDeployment = PluginStepSupportedDeployment.Both)]

    public class LeadTopicUpdater : IPlugin
    {
        public void Execute(IPluginExecutionContext context)
        {
            DynamicEntity target =
                        (DynamicEntity)context.InputParameters[ParameterName.Target];

            if (!target.Properties.Contains("subject") ||
                string.IsNullOrEmpty(target.Properties["subject"].ToString()))
            {
                ICrmService crmService = context.CreateCrmService(true);

                lead crmLead = new lead();
                crmLead.leadid = new Key();
                crmLead.leadid.Value =
                    new Guid(context.OutputParameters[ParameterName.Id].ToString());
```

```
                // we will create a new topic with the format:
                // Last Name, First Name - Created Date
                string firstName = String.Empty;
                string lastName = String.Empty;
                string date = String.Empty;

                if (target.Properties.Contains("firstname"))
                    firstName = target.Properties["firstname"].ToString();
                if (target.Properties.Contains("lastname"))
                    lastName = target.Properties["lastname"].ToString();


                // get the user's date format
                string fetch = String.Format(@"<fetch mapping='logical'>
                                            <entity name='usersettings'>
                                               <attribute name='dateformatstring' />
                                               <filter type='and'>
                                                    <condition
                                                       attribute='systemuserid'
                                                       operator='eq'
                                                       value='{0}' />
                                                </filter>
                                            </entity>
                                           </fetch>", context.UserId.ToString());

                string fetchResults = crmService.Fetch(fetch);

                XmlDocument resultDoc = new XmlDocument();
                resultDoc.LoadXml(fetchResults);

                string dateFormat =
resultDoc.DocumentElement.FirstChild.SelectSingleNode("dateformatstring").InnerText;

                date = DateTime.Now.ToString(dateFormat);

                crmLead.subject = String.Format("{0}, {1} - {2}",
                                                lastName,
                                                firstName,
                                                date);

                crmService.Update(crmLead);
            }
        }
    }
}
```

We want to register the plug-in for both the Web and Outlook clients, so note that we set the *SupportedDeployment* of the *PluginStep* attribute to *Both*. You can find the *PluginStep-SupportedDeployment* enum in the ProgrammingWithDynamicsCrm4.Plugins.Attributes project we created in Chapter 5. Table 10-6 lists the fields of the *PluginStepSupportedDeployment* enum along with a description. Another thing to note is that the *Mode* is set to Synchronous. Asynchronous plug-ins do not run in offline mode.

Note The *PluginStep* attribute is discussed in detail in Chapter 5.

TABLE 10-6 *SupportedDeployment* Members

Field	Value	Description
Both	2	Registers the plug-in for both the Web server and the Outlook Client
OutlookClientOnly	1	Registers the plug-in for only the Outlook Client
ServerOnly	0	Registers the plug-in for only the Web server

The logic in our plug-in is pretty simple. We first check to see whether the lead currently has the subject field populated. If it doesn't have a subject, we then create an instance of the lead object, update its subject to our specified format, and call the *Update* method of the *CrmService*. Because we are checking to see whether a subject already exists, we are safe if the Plug-in is run more than once. This prevents the date from being incorrectly updated if the user created the lead offline. If the check is not in place, the next time the user goes online, the subject is updated with the current date instead of keeping the actual date the lead was created.

Another way to prevent a plug-in from running twice is to check the *CallerOrigin* property of the *IPluginExecutionContext* argument that is passed into the plug-in's *Execute* method. If the origin is of the type *OfflineOrigin*, the plug-in was fired when the offline client went into online mode. This concept is demonstrated in the following code snippet:

```
using System;
using Microsoft.Crm.Sdk;
using Microsoft.Crm.SdkTypeProxy;

public class OnlinePlugin : IPlugin
{
   public void Execute(IPluginExecutionContext context)
   {
      // Check to see if the plug-in was executed when going back online.
      CallerOrigin callerOrigin = context.CallerOrigin;
      if (callerOrigin is OfflineOrigin)
      {
         // The plug-in was excuted when the user clicked the go online button
         return;
      }
      else
      {
         // add the plug-in logic here
      }
   }
}
```

Tip If you want a piece of code to only run online or offline, you can check the value of the *IsExecutingInOfflineMode* property on the *IPluginExecutionContext* argument that is passed into your plug-in's *Execute* method.

Deploying the Plug-in

The "Deployment" section of Chapter 5 has all of the necessary steps for deploying the plug-in. You should deploy the plug-in to the database instead of the file system so that Microsoft Dynamics CRM automatically registers the plug-in on the client's computer the next time the client goes offline.

After we register the plug-in, we have one more step before it can run in offline mode. Microsoft Dynamics CRM for Outlook with Offline Access has another layer of security for offline plug-ins. When Microsoft Dynamics CRM for Outlook with Offline Access is installed it creates a registry key called *AllowList*. We need to add the public token key guid of our plug-in assembly as a new key under the *AllowList* key.

Note See the "Offline Applications" section of Chapter 9 for detailed instructions on adding the Plug-in assembly's public token key guid to the *AllowList* registry key.

Testing the Plug-in

To test our lead plug-in, open your instance of Microsoft Outlook that has Microsoft Dynamics CRM for Outlook with Offline Access installed and configured. Click the Go Offline button. When the synchronization process is complete and the Go Offline button has been replaced with a Go Online button, navigate to the Leads grid. Click New, and fill out the new Lead form. Click the Save button or the Save And Close button. Our plug-in should have executed and you can now see the subject updated with the Lead's name followed by the current date (Figure 10-5).

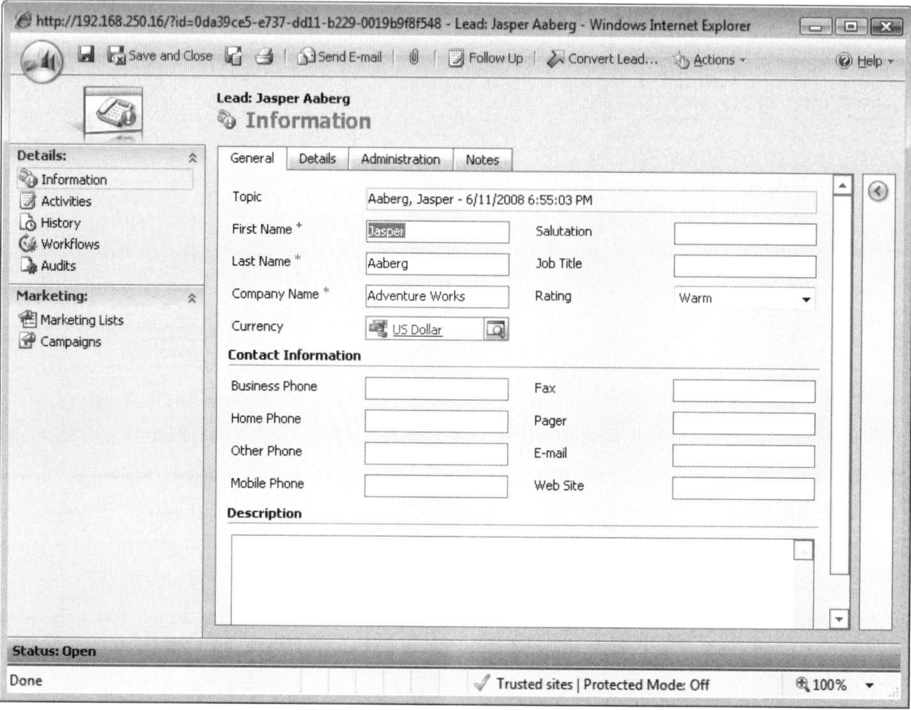

FIGURE 10-5 Updated lead topic

Offline Development Considerations

While developing for Microsoft CRM Dynamics for Outlook with Offline Access, remember to consider these factors unique to offline development:

- Not all *CrmService* messages are available for all entities while in offline mode.
- Only *Retrieve* messages are available on the *MetadataService* while in offline mode.
- Workflows do not work in offline mode.
- All offline plug-ins must be registered to run synchronously.
- Plug-ins can potentially run twice, once while offline and once on the server when going back online. You can add a check to your plug-in to avoid this scenario.
- You must also add the public key token of your plug-in assembly to the *AllowList* registry key so that it can run offline.
- You must deploy custom .aspx pages to each client computer. Microsoft Dynamics CRM does not automatically deploy the custom Web pages for you.

Summary

This chapter has provided you with an overview of developing for Microsoft Dynamics CRM for Outlook with Offline Access. The topics and examples in this chapter have given you good foundation knowledge and ideas for coding custom pages and plug-ins to run offline or in both online and offline mode. You should also now have a better idea of what to watch out for when architecting your offline solutions.

Chapter 11

Multilingual and Multi-Currency Applications

As a global product, Microsoft Dynamics CRM supports the needs of companies that have users located in multiple countries throughout the world. Microsoft Dynamics CRM offers both multi-currency and multilingual functionality so that users can view and work with records using the language and currency of their choice.

Out of the box, Microsoft Dynamics CRM 4.0 includes more than 20 different language packs that you can download and install in your system. Once you install and activate multiple language packs in your Microsoft Dynamics CRM deployment, each user can specify which language he or she prefers to see in the user interface.

For multiple currency support, Microsoft Dynamics CRM allows you to set up and record conversion rates between the system's base currency and other currencies. Just like multilingual support, users can configure their default currency. However, in addition they can also specify a currency on a record-by-record basis. For example, a user could create one opportunity using U.S. dollars and then create a different opportunity using euros.

As a developer, you should understand how to incorporate the multilingual and multi-currency functionality in your custom code. As you would expect, of course you can interact and manipulate the multilingual and multi-currency functionality using the Microsoft Dynamics CRM API. In this chapter, we will discuss extending Microsoft Dynamics CRM by creating custom code that works with multiple languages and currencies. The *CrmService* and *MetadataService* classes provided in the Microsoft Dynamics CRM SDK both provide messages and methods to assist you in localizing your applications. We will also discuss the usage of resource files in your custom code.

Programming for Multilingual Applications

As you learned, you can download, install, and enable one or more language packs for your Microsoft Dynamics CRM system. These language packs include translations for all of the user interface components that ship with the system. However, your system will most likely include custom attributes, custom views, and other areas that won't be included in the Microsoft-supplied language packs. Conveniently, the customization section of Microsoft Dynamics CRM allows you to export and import language labels for translation of your custom elements. However, you should also consider how multilingual deployments will impact your custom IFrames, dialog boxes, ISV pages, and so on. In this section, we will discuss using the *CrmService* to update translations and a few ways to make your custom code multilingual-capable and also easy to update with more languages in the future.

CrmService Messages for Multilingual Support

The Microsoft Dynamics CRM SDK contains messages that allow developers to work with the installed language packs. Table 11-1 lists all of these messages along with a description of each.

Note All of these messages are used with the *CrmService Execute* method.

TABLE 11-1 *CrmService* Messages for Multiple Language Packs

Name	Description
ExportCompressedTranslationsXml	Exports translations for all the installed language packs to an XML file and compresses it into a .zip file
ExportTranslationsXml	Exports translations for all the installed languages packs to an XML file
ImportTranslationsXmlWithProgress	Asynchronously imports translations for the installed language packs and allows you to retrieve data about the import job's progress
RetrieveAvailableLanguages	Retrieves a list of enabled languages, including the base language.
RetrieveDeprovisionedLanguages	Retrieves a list of disabled language packs
RetrieveInstalledLanguagePacks	Retrieves an integer array of the installed language pack Locale ID (LCID) values
RetrieveLocLabels	Retrieves the available labels for a specified attribute
RetrieveProvisionedLanguages	Retrieves a list of provisioned language packs
SetLocLabels	Sets the labels for a specified attribute

Now that we know what multilingual messages Microsoft Dynamics CRM offers, let's discuss how to programmatically export and import translations using the *CrmService*.

Exporting and Importing Translations

The *ExportCompressedTranslationsXml* and *ExportTranslationsXml* messages basically do the same thing, except that the *ExportCompressedTranslationsXml* message will compress the exported XML file in a .zip archive file. Using this message is a programmatic way to accomplish the same functionality as a user clicking the Export Labels For Translation link on the Settings Customization screen in the Microsoft Dynamics CRM UI. The exported file will contain translations for drop-down lists and other text UI elements. You can then alter the XML file with any new translations or change existing text. The *ImportTranslationsXml-WithProgress* message can then be used to take the exported and updated translation XML file and import the changes into Microsoft Dynamics CRM.

To help illustrate how to work with these messages, we will create a simple console application for demonstration purposes.

Creating the Translation Import/Export Console project

1. Open the ProgrammingWithDynamicsCrm4 solution in Microsoft Visual Studio 2008.
2. Right-click the solution name in Solution Explorer, select Add, and then click New Project.
3. In the New Project dialog box, select the Visual C# project type targeting the Microsoft .NET Framework 3.0 and then select the Console Application template.
4. Type **ProgrammingWithDynamicsCrm4.TranslationUtil** in the Name box and click OK.
5. Right-click the TranslationImportExport Project in Solution Explorer and click Add Reference.
6. On the Browse tab of the Add Reference dialog box, navigate to the Microsoft.Crm.Sdk.dll and Microsoft.Crm.Sdk.TypeProxy.dll assemblies and click OK.
7. We need to add two more references. Right-click the TranslationImportExport project in Solution Explorer and click Add Reference.
8. On the .NET tab of the Add Reference dialog box, select System.Web.Services and System.Configuration. Click OK.

Now that we've created our project, we can add the code. Listing 11-1 contains the full source code for our application.

LISTING 11-1 ProgrammingWithDynamicsCrm4.TranslationUtil source code

```
using System;
using System.Collections.Generic;
using System.Text;
using Microsoft.Crm.Sdk;
using Microsoft.Crm.SdkTypeProxy;
using System.IO;
using System.Xml;
using System.Web.Services.Protocols;
using Microsoft.Crm.Sdk.Query;
using System.Configuration;
using System.Net;

namespace ProgrammingWithDynamicsCrm4.TranslationUtil
{
    class Program
    {
```

```
static void Main(string[] args)
{
    if (args.Length != 4)
    {
        string exeName =
                Path.GetFileName(Environment.GetCommandLineArgs()[0]);
        Console.WriteLine("Usage: {0} <import/export> <file path>
                                      <crmServerUrl> <organizationName>",
                           exeName);
        Environment.Exit(1);
    }

    try
    {
        string commandType = args[0];
        string filePath = args[1];
        string crmServerUrl = args[2];
        string orgName = args[3];

        switch (commandType)
        {
            case "export":
                {
                    ExportTranslations(filePath, crmServerUrl, orgName);
                }
                break;
            case "import":
                {
                    ImportTranslations(filePath, crmServerUrl, orgName);
                }
                break;
            default:
                {
                    Console.WriteLine(
                String.Format( "{0}: unhandled command type", commandType));
                }
                break;
        }
    }
    catch (SoapException e)
    {
        Console.WriteLine(e.Detail.InnerText);
    }
    catch (Exception e)
    {
        Console.WriteLine(e.Message);
    }
}

private static void ExportTranslations(string exportFilePath,
                                        string crmServerUrl,
                                        string orgName)
{
    Console.WriteLine("Initializing CrmService...");
```

```
    CrmService service = CreateCrmService(crmServerUrl, orgName);

    Console.WriteLine("Complete");

    ExportCompressedTranslationsXmlRequest request =
                             new ExportCompressedTranslationsXmlRequest();

    request.EmbeddedFileName = "translations.xml";

    Console.WriteLine("Exporting Translations...");

    ExportCompressedTranslationsXmlResponse response =
         (ExportCompressedTranslationsXmlResponse)service.Execute(request);

    byte[] compressedXML = response.ExportCompressedXml;

    using (FileStream fs = new FileStream(
       String.Format(@"{0}\Translations.zip", exportFilePath.TrimEnd('\\')),
                        FileMode.Create))
    {
        fs.Write(compressedXML, 0, compressedXML.Length);
        fs.Close();
    }

    Console.WriteLine("The Translation Export Completed Successfully!");
}

private static void ImportTranslations(string importFilePath,
                                        string crmServerUrl,
                                        string orgName)
{
    Console.WriteLine("Initializing CrmService...");

    CrmService service = CreateCrmService(crmServerUrl, orgName);

    Console.WriteLine("Complete");

    XmlDocument translationXmlDoc = new XmlDocument();
    translationXmlDoc.Load(importFilePath);

    String translationXML = translationXmlDoc.OuterXml;

    ImportTranslationsXmlWithProgressRequest request =
                             new ImportTranslationsXmlWithProgressRequest();

    Guid tmpJobId = Guid.NewGuid();

    request.ImportJobId = tmpJobId;
    request.ImportXml = translationXML;

    Console.Write("Importing Translations...");

    service.ExecuteAsync(request);

    importjob job = new importjob();
```

```
            XmlDocument doc = new XmlDocument();

            String progress = String.Empty;

            bool incrementProgress = false;

            while (progress != "Succeeded")
            {
                System.Threading.Thread.Sleep(1000);

                try
                {
                    ColumnSet jobColumns = new ColumnSet();
                    jobColumns.AddColumn("data");

                    job =
(importjob)service.Retrieve(EntityName.importjob.ToString(), tmpJobId, jobColumns);

                    doc.LoadXml(job.data);

                    progress = doc.GetElementsByTagName("status").Item(0).InnerText;

                    incrementProgress = true;

                }
                catch { }

                if (incrementProgress)
                {
                    Console.Write("...");
                    incrementProgress = false;
                }
            }

            Console.WriteLine();
            Console.WriteLine("The Translation Import Completed Successfully!");
        }

        private static CrmService CreateCrmService(string crmServer,
                                                   string organizationName)
        {
            UriBuilder crmServerUri = new UriBuilder(crmServer);
            crmServerUri.Path = "/MSCRMServices/2007/CrmService.asmx";

            string userName = ConfigurationManager.AppSettings["crmUserName"];
            string password = ConfigurationManager.AppSettings["crmPassword"];
            string domain = ConfigurationManager.AppSettings["crmDomain"];

            CrmService crmService = new CrmService();
            if (String.IsNullOrEmpty(userName))
            {
                crmService.UseDefaultCredentials = true;
            }
            else
```

```
            {
                crmService.Credentials = new NetworkCredential(userName,
                                                               password,
                                                               domain);
            }

            crmService.Url = crmServerUri.ToString();
            crmService.CrmAuthenticationTokenValue = new CrmAuthenticationToken();
            crmService.CrmAuthenticationTokenValue.AuthenticationType =
                                                        AuthenticationType.AD;
            crmService.CrmAuthenticationTokenValue.OrganizationName =
                                                            organizationName;

            return crmService;
        }
    }
}
```

You will run this application from the command line and you can specify whether to import or export translations using the command-line arguments. Table 11-2 lists and describes the four command-line arguments. The command-line usage to import or export the translations is:

```
ProgrammingWithDynamicsCrm4.TranslationUtil.exe <commandType> <filePath> <serverUrl>
    <orgName>
```

TABLE 11-2 ProgrammingWithDynamicsCrm4.TranslationUtil Command-Line Arguments

Name	Description
Command Type	Determines whether to import or export translations. Possible values are import and export.
File Path	For exports this argument determines where the exported file will be saved. For imports this argument specifies where the updated translation XML file is located.
Microsoft Dynamics CRM server URL	Specifies the URL of the Microsoft Dynamics CRM server.
Organization Name	Specifies the name of the organization to export or import the translations from.

The *Main* method of our application contains a *switch* statement that determines whether to call the *ExportTranslations* method or the *ImportTranslations* method. If the incorrect number of arguments are given at the command line, we display a message to the user with the proper usage instructions. Now let's take a look at the source code behind the export and import functionality. The first method we will discuss is a helper method used to create an instance of *CrmService*.

The *CreateCrmService* method The *CreateCrmService* method creates an instance of the *CrmService* class using Active Directory authentication. By default it will use the credentials of the user running the application. However, if you want to export or import the translations under a different user account, you can add an app.config file to the project and add keys for the credentials you would like to make the calls under. The keys are added to the *AppSettings* node of the config file. Table 11-3 lists the keys along with a description of each.

TABLE 11-3 App.config *AppSettings*

Name	Description
crmUserName	User name of the Microsoft Dynamics CRM system user
crmPassword	Password of the Microsoft Dynamics CRM system user
crmDomain	Domain of the Microsoft Dynamics CRM system user

The *ExportTranslations* method First we create an instance of *CrmService* using our *CreateCrmService* method. Next we create an instance of the *ExportCompressedTranslationsXmlRequest*. Note that you specify the name of the XML file by setting the *EmbeddedFileName* property on the *ExportCompressedTranslationsXmlRequest* object, and you also specify a path to save the .zip file in the constructor of the *FileStream* object. In our application the name of our file is set to *translations.xml* and it will be saved to the path specified in the command line arguments as a .zip file named "Translations.zip".

Note You need to install and provision at least one language besides the base language before running the application.

Now, compile the application and run it. Use "export" for the type in the command-line arguments. The resulting output should look like Figure 11-1.

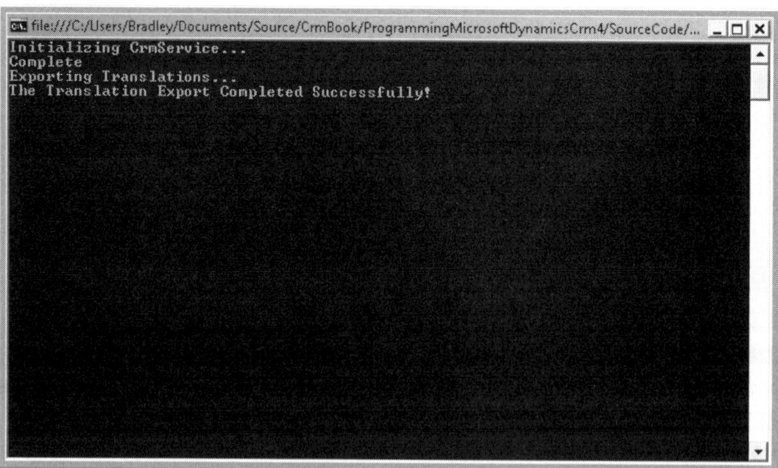

FIGURE 11-1 Export output

The resulting XML file is actually a Microsoft Office Excel XML document that you can open and edit in Excel (Figure 11-2). In this figure, columns B, C, and D display the translated text for three different languages:

- **1033 English – United States**
- **1036 French – France**
- **3082 Spanish - Spain (Modern Sort)**

To update the translation, simply type the new text in the appropriate cell.

Tip Although it's possible to determine the language by examining the text, you can also look up the language by cross-referencing the locale IDs (1033, 1036, 3082, and so on) with the published Microsoft list. For a list of locale ID values assigned by Microsoft, you can reference the Web page *http://www.microsoft.com/globaldev/reference/lcid-all.mspx*.

Once you update your translations, you can import the final values back into Microsoft Dynamics CRM using the next message we will discuss, *ImportXmlTranslationsWithProgress*.

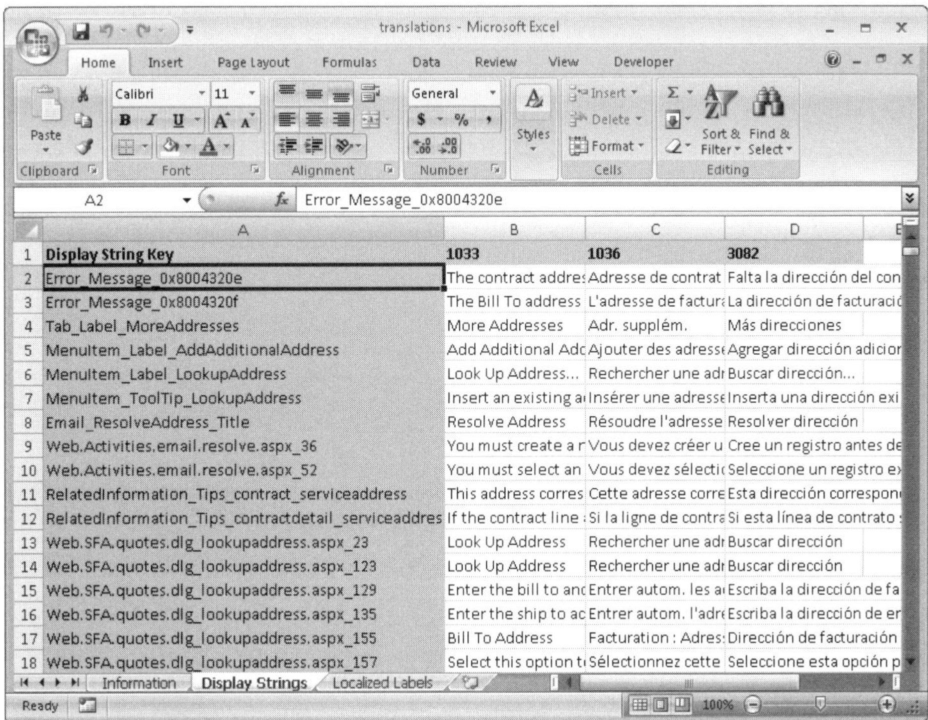

FIGURE 11-2 Translations XML file opened in Excel

The *ImportTranslations* method The *ImportTranslationsXmlWithProgress* message takes the exported and updated translation XML file and imports the changes into Microsoft Dynamics CRM. This method begins in the same way our export method did: by creating an instance of *CrmService*. Next we read our translations XML file specified in the file path command-line argument into an *XMLDocument* object. Once we have our XML, we can create the *ImportTranslationsXmlWithProgressRequest* object. Notice that we create a new *Guid* and use it to set the value of the request object's *ImportJobId* property:

```
ImportTranslationsXmlWithProgressRequest request =
                                    new ImportTranslationsXmlWithProgressRequest();

Guid tmpJobId = Guid.NewGuid();

request.ImportJobId = tmpJobId;
request.ImportXml = translationXML;
```

Creating the new *Guid* value is an important step because we will use this *Guid* to track the progress of our import job. Notice that we use the *ExecuteAsync* method this time instead of the normal *Execute* method on the *CrmService*. This kicks off an asynchronous job for our import. The *while* loop toward the end of the method is used to track the progress of our job. We use the *Retrieve* method of the *CrmService* to retrieve an instance of the Import Job entity. The try-catch block is in place because our job may not exist at the time we first make the retrieve call. If the catch block is hit, we simply continue the loop. Once the job exists in Microsoft Dynamics CRM, the loop continues until the job's status reads "Succeeded". During the loop, we continue to write out "..." to the user as a means of letting the user know that the import is still processing. Once everything is finished, we write out another message to the user. If you run our application again, this time using "import" as the first command-line argument, your output should look like Figure 11-3.

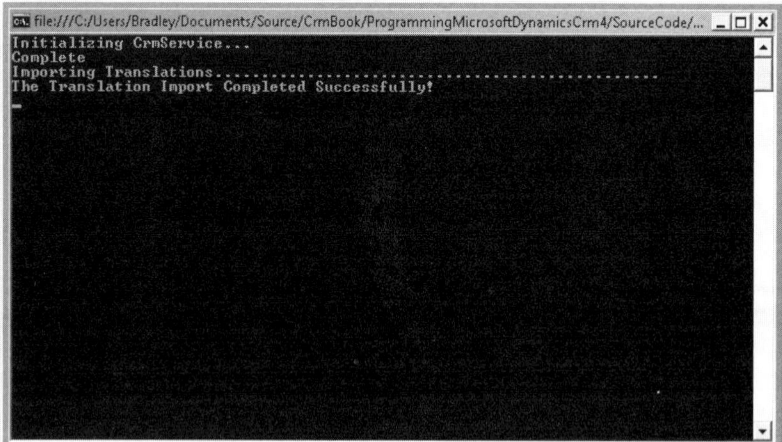

FIGURE 11-3 Import output

Using the Metadata Service for Multilingual Applications

Now that you understand how to programmatically export and import multilingual translations, let's examine using multilingual functionality in a custom Web page embedded in a Microsoft Dynamics CRM IFrame.

As you learned in Chapter 8, "Developing with the Metadata Service," the Metadata Service gives you the ability to retrieve information from entities and attributes such as attribute labels for the base language and all of the installed language packs. In this section, we will create an IFrame on the Contact entity that displays information from the Contact's selected parent customer record. We will code this custom IFrame Web page to automatically display the label text using the preferred language selected by the user. Therefore, different users viewing this custom IFrame see different label languages if they've selected two different preferred languages. To see the final output, you can skip ahead to view Figure 11-4.

Tip Microsoft Dynamics CRM users can set their preferred language for the UI and Help documentation on the Language tab of the Set Personal Options screen.

Programming the Multilingual IFrame

Now we will add a new Web Form to the ProgrammingMicrosoftDynamicsCrm4.Web project.

Adding the ContactParentCustomerInfo.aspx page

1. Open the ProgrammingWithDynamicsCrm4 solution in Visual Studio 2008.
2. If you have not created the ProgrammingMicrosoftDynamicsCrm4.Web project in a previous chapter, right-click the solution name, select Add, and then click New Web Site. Change the name of the Web site to **ProgrammingMicrosoftDynamicsCrm4.Web** and click OK. Add references to the Microsoft Dynamics CRM SDK assemblies: Microsoft.Crm.Sdk.dll and Microsoft.Crm.SdkProxy.dll.
3. If a folder named IFrames does not already exist, create one under the new Web site. Right-click the IFrames folder and then click Add New Item.
4. Select the Web Form template and type **ContactPrimaryCustomerInfo.aspx** in the Name field.
5. Click Add.

We start by setting up our form. Listing 11-2 contains the source code for the ContactParent CustomerInfo.aspx page.

LISTING 11-2 ContactParentCustomerInfo.aspx source code

```
<%@ Page Language="C#"
        AutoEventWireup="true"
        CodeFile="ContactParentCustomerInfo.aspx.cs"
        Inherits="IFrames_ContactParentCustomerInfo" %>

<!DOCTYPE html PUBLIC "-//W3C//DTD XHTML 1.0 Transitional//EN"
                        "http://www.w3.org/TR/xhtml1/DTD/xhtml1-transitional.dtd">

<html xmlns="http://www.w3.org/1999/xhtml">
<head runat="server">
    <title>Untitled Page</title>
</head>
<body style="font-size: 11px;
            font-family: Tahoma;
            margin: 0px;
            border: 0px;
            background-color: #eaf3ff;">
    <form id="form1" runat="server">
    <div id="warning"
        visible="false"
        style="background-color: #FFFFAE;height: 26px;border: 1px solid
                                                #C5C5C5;font-size: 11px;" runat="server">
        The record must be saved before you can view the customer information.
    </div>
    <div id="main" runat="server">
        <table cellspacing="1"
            cellpadding="0"
            border="0"
            style="width: 100%;table-layout: fixed;">
            <colgroup>
                <col style="width: 111px;" />
                <col />
                <col style="width: 115px; padding-left: 23px;" />
                <col />
            </colgroup>
            <tr>
                <td>
                    <asp:Label ID="street1Label" runat="server" />
                </td>
                <td>
                    <asp:Label ID="street1" runat="server" />
                </td>
                <td>
                    <asp:Label ID="stateLabel" runat="server" />
                </td>
                <td>
                    <asp:Label ID="state" runat="server" />
                </td>
            </tr>
            <tr>
                <td>
                    <asp:Label ID="street2Label" runat="server" />
                </td>
```

```
                <td>
                    <asp:Label ID="street2" runat="server" />
                </td>
                <td>
                    <asp:Label ID="zipLabel" runat="server" />
                </td>
                <td>
                    <asp:Label ID="zip" runat="server" />
                </td>
            </tr>
            <tr>
                <td>
                    <asp:Label ID="cityLabel" runat="server" />
                </td>
                <td>
                    <asp:Label ID="city" runat="server" />
                </td>
                <td>
                    <asp:Label ID="countryLabel" runat="server" />
                </td>
                <td>
                    <asp:Label ID="country" runat="server" />
                </td>
            </tr>
        </table>
    </div>
    </form>
</body>
</html>
```

You can see that we divided our page into two *div* tags. The first *div* contains a warning message. Notice that this message is hard-coded in English. We will discuss updating this warning for multiple languages using a resource file in the next section. The second *div* contains our form elements. Because this will be a read-only display, each field we want to show has two ASP.NET *Label* controls associated with it. The first *Label* control is populated with the attribute's Display Name translated into the user's preferred language, and the second *Label* control contains the attribute's data. Our form also contains some styles to make it blend in with the native Contact entity form, but we won't go into detail about that now because it is discussed in more detail in Chapter 13, "Emulating User Interface with ASP.NET Development." Now that our form is set, let's discuss the code to populate it. Listing 11-3 contains the source code for our IFrame's code behind.

LISTING 11-3 ContactParentCusomterInfo.aspx.cs

```
using System;
using System.Collections;
using System.Configuration;
using System.Data;
using System.Web;
using System.Web.Security;
```

```
using System.Web.UI;
using System.Web.UI.HtmlControls;
using System.Web.UI.WebControls;
using System.Web.UI.WebControls.WebParts;
using Microsoft.Crm.Sdk;
using Microsoft.Crm.SdkTypeProxy;
using Microsoft.Crm.Sdk.Query;
using Microsoft.Crm.SdkTypeProxy.Metadata;
using Microsoft.Crm.Sdk.Metadata;
using ProgrammingWithDynamicsCrm4.Utilities;

public partial class IFrames_ContactParentCustomerInfo : System.Web.UI.Page
{
    protected void Page_Load(object sender, EventArgs e)
    {
        string contactId = Request.QueryString["id"];
        string orgName = Request.QueryString["orgname"];

        if (!string.IsNullOrEmpty(contactId))
        {
            CrmService crmService =
       CrmServiceUtility.GetCrmService(CrmServiceUtility.GetServerURLFromRegistry(),
                                        orgName);

            MetadataService metadataService =
  CrmServiceUtility.GetMetadataService(CrmServiceUtility.GetServerURLFromRegistry(),
                                        orgName);

            ColumnSet contactColumns = new ColumnSet();
            contactColumns.AddColumn("parentcustomerid");

            contact crmContact =
                  (contact)crmService.Retrieve(EntityName.contact.ToString(),
                                               new Guid(contactId),
                                               contactColumns);

            if (crmContact.parentcustomerid != null)
            {
                string customerEntityName = crmContact.parentcustomerid.type;

                // set up labels using metadata
                AttributeMetadata addressLine1Metadata =
                      MetadataUtility.RetrieveAttributeMetadata(metadataService,
                                                          customerEntityName,
                                                          "address1_line1");
                this.street1Label.Text =
                          addressLine1Metadata.DisplayName.UserLocLabel.Label;

                AttributeMetadata addressLine2Metadata =
                          MetadataUtility.RetrieveAttributeMetadata(metadataService,
                                                          customerEntityName,
                                                           "address1_line2");
                this.street2Label.Text =
                          addressLine2Metadata.DisplayName.UserLocLabel.Label;
```

```
AttributeMetadata cityMetadata =
          MetadataUtility.RetrieveAttributeMetadata(metadataService,
                                                    customerEntityName,
                                                    "address1_city");
this.cityLabel.Text =
                        cityMetadata.DisplayName.UserLocLabel.Label;

AttributeMetadata stateMetadata =
          MetadataUtility.RetrieveAttributeMetadata(metadataService,
                                                    customerEntityName,
                                           "address1_stateorprovince");
this.stateLabel.Text =
                       stateMetadata.DisplayName.UserLocLabel.Label;

AttributeMetadata zipMetadata =
          MetadataUtility.RetrieveAttributeMetadata(metadataService,
                                                    customerEntityName,
                                                "address1_postalcode");

this.zipLabel.Text = zipMetadata.DisplayName.UserLocLabel.Label;

AttributeMetadata countryMetadata =
          MetadataUtility.RetrieveAttributeMetadata(metadataService,
                                                    customerEntityName,
                                                   "address1_country");
this.countryLabel.Text =
                     countryMetadata.DisplayName.UserLocLabel.Label;

// populate the form
TargetRetrieveDynamic targetRetrieve =
                                        new TargetRetrieveDynamic();

targetRetrieve.EntityName = crmContact.parentcustomerid.type;
    targetRetrieve.EntityId = crmContact.parentcustomerid.Value;

ColumnSet customerColumns = new ColumnSet();
    customerColumns.AddColumns("address1_line1",
                               "address1_line2",
                               "address1_city",
                               "address1_stateorprovince",
                               "address1_postalcode",
                               "address1_country");

RetrieveRequest retrieve = new RetrieveRequest();
retrieve.Target = targetRetrieve;
retrieve.ColumnSet = customerColumns;
retrieve.ReturnDynamicEntities = true;

RetrieveResponse retrieved =
                    (RetrieveResponse)crmService.Execute(retrieve);

DynamicEntity entity = (DynamicEntity)retrieved.BusinessEntity;
```

```
                if (entity.Properties.Contains("address1_line1"))
                    this.street1.Text =
                                    entity.Properties["address1_line1"].ToString();
                if (entity.Properties.Contains("address1_line2"))
                    this.street2.Text =
                                    entity.Properties["address1_line2"].ToString();
                if (entity.Properties.Contains("address1_city"))
                    this.city.Text =
                                     entity.Properties["address1_city"].ToString();
                if (entity.Properties.Contains("address1_stateorprovince"))
                    this.state.Text =
                           entity.Properties["address1_stateorprovince"].ToString();
                if (entity.Properties.Contains("address1_postalcode"))
                    this.zip.Text =
                                entity.Properties["address1_postalcode"].ToString();
                if (entity.Properties.Contains("address1_country"))
                    this.country.Text =
                                   entity.Properties["address1_country"].ToString();
            }
        }
        else
        {
            this.warning.Visible = true;
            this.main.Visible = false;
        }
    }
}
```

The first thing we do in the *Page_Load* method is check to see whether an ID was passed to us in the query string. If not, we can then turn on our message *div* to tell the user that the record must be saved before she can view the information. If an ID was passed to our IFrame, we can then retrieve the information we need from the Contact record's parent customer.

Note The *MetadataUtility* class used in this example is discussed in detail in Chapter 15, "Additional Samples and Utilities." This utility is used to retrieve and cache Microsoft Dynamics CRM metadata.

If the Contact record has a parent customer selected, we can then retrieve each attribute's metadata. Because the customer can be either an Account or a Contact, we create the *customerEntityName* variable and set it to the *parentcustomerid* attribute's *type*. This will store the logical name of the customer entity, so we can use it to retrieve the correct metadata. To populate our field labels, we use the *AttributeMetadata* class's *DisplayName* property. The *DisplayName* property is of the type *CrmLabel*. As we learned in Chapter 8, the *CrmLabel* class has a *LocLabels* property that contains a collection of all available translations for this label. For example, if English is your base language and you have the Spanish and French language packs installed and enabled in your Microsoft Dynamics CRM environment, the

LocLabels collection would contain three items, one for each enabled language. Each item in the *LocLabels* collection contains a *LanguageCode* property, so it would be possible for us to retrieve the user's preferred language's language code and then loop through the collection and pull out the appropriate label. Luckily, achieving this result is much simpler. The *CrmLabel* object also has a *UserLocLabel* property that contains the label already translated into the user's preferred language. This ensures that our label always shows the correct translation.

```
AttributeMetadata addressLine1Metadata =
                        MetadataUtility.RetrieveAttributeMetadata(metadataService,
                                                                  customerEntityName,
                                                                  "address1_line1");

this.street1Label.Text = addressLine1Metadata.DisplayName.UserLocLabel.Label;
```

After our field labels have been populated, we can retrieve the data we need from Microsoft Dynamics CRM and populate the fields. Because our customer can be an Account or a Contact, we can use *TargetRetrieveDynamic* as the *Target* property on our *RetrieveRequest* message. Once our *DynamicEntity* has been retrieved, we can use its *Properties* collection to populate our fields.

Deploying and Testing the Multilingual IFrame

Now that we have finished development of our page, we can deploy it to the Microsoft Dynamics CRM server and test it. We will start by adding our IFrame to the Contact entity.

Note This example assumes you have the English and Spanish language packs installed and enabled.

Adding the IFrame to the Contact form

1. Open Microsoft Dynamics CRM in a Web browser and navigate to the Contact entity's form customization screen.
2. Click Add A Section on the Common Tasks menu.
3. Type **Parent Customer Information** in the Name box.
4. Select both the Show The Name Of This Section On The Form and Show Divider Line Below The Section Name check boxes and verify that the Tab is set to General. Click OK.

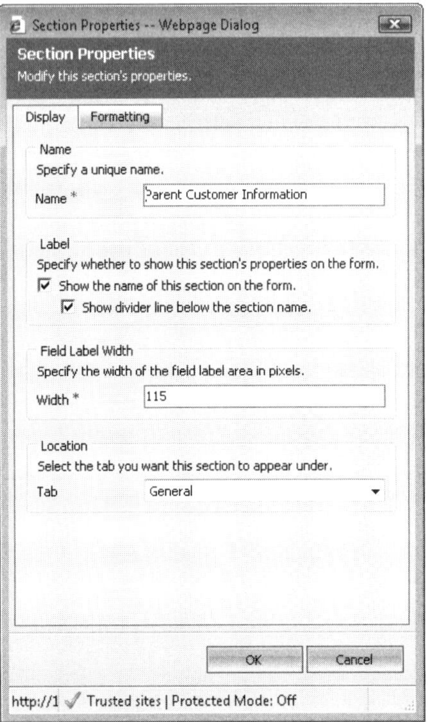

5. Select our new section and then click Add An IFrame on the Common Tasks menu.
6. Type **contactparentcusomterinfo** in the Name box.
7. Type **/ISV/ProgrammingWithDynamicsCRM4/ContactParentCustomerInfo.aspx** in the URL box.
8. Select the Pass Record Object-Type Code And Unique Identifier As Parameters check box.
9. Clear the Restrict Cross-Frame Scripting check box.
10. Verify that the Tab is set to General and the Section is set to Parent Customer Information.

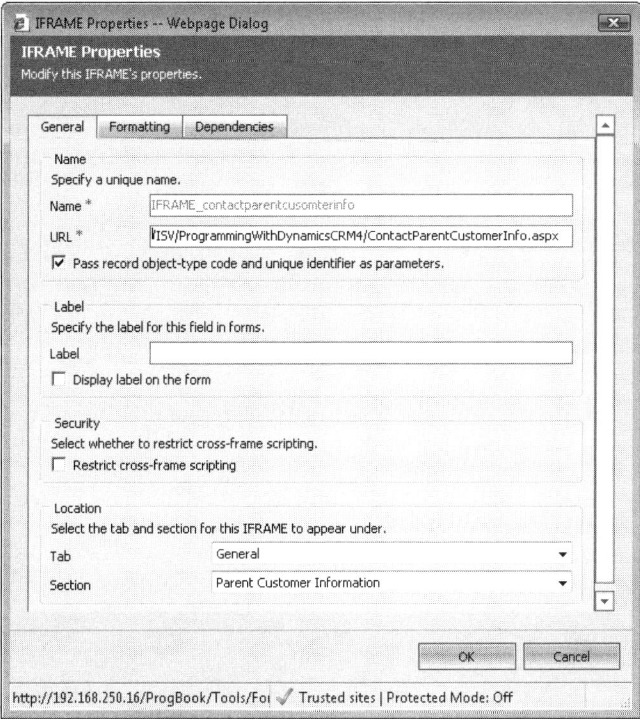

11. In the Formatting tab's Row Layout section, select the Automatically Expand To Use Available Space check box.

12. In the Formatting tab's Border section, clear the Display Border check box. This will make our IFrame integrate seamlessly into the form. Click OK.

13. Save the form and publish your customizations.

Now that our IFrame has been added to the Contact form, we will deploy our Web files to the server.

Deploying the Web files

Note If you have created a folder named ProgrammingWithDynamicsCrm4 under the ISV folder in a previous chapter, you can skip step 1 and move on to step 2.

1. Create a new folder named **ProgrammingWithDynamicsCrm4** under the ISV folder in the directory with your Microsoft Dynamics CRM Web files.

2. Copy the ContactParentCustomerInfo.aspx and ContactParentCustomerInfo.aspx.cs files into the ProgrammingWithDynamicsCrm4 folder on the server.

Warning Because this example uses the *MetadataUtility* class defined in Chapter 15, it requires the ProgrammingWithDynamicsCrm4.Utilities assembly to be copied into the Microsoft Dynamics CRM bin folder. You can obtain the ProgrammingWithDynamicsCrm4.Utilities assembly by opening the ProgrammingWithDynamicsCrm4 solution in Visual Studio and compiling the ProgrammingWithDynamicsCrm4.Utilities project.

Now we can test our IFrame. Navigate to the Contact grid in Microsoft Dynamics CRM and open an existing Contact record that has the parent customer field populated. Our IFrame at the bottom of the General tab shows the parent customer's information with the labels translated into the language currently set on your user record (Figure 11-4).

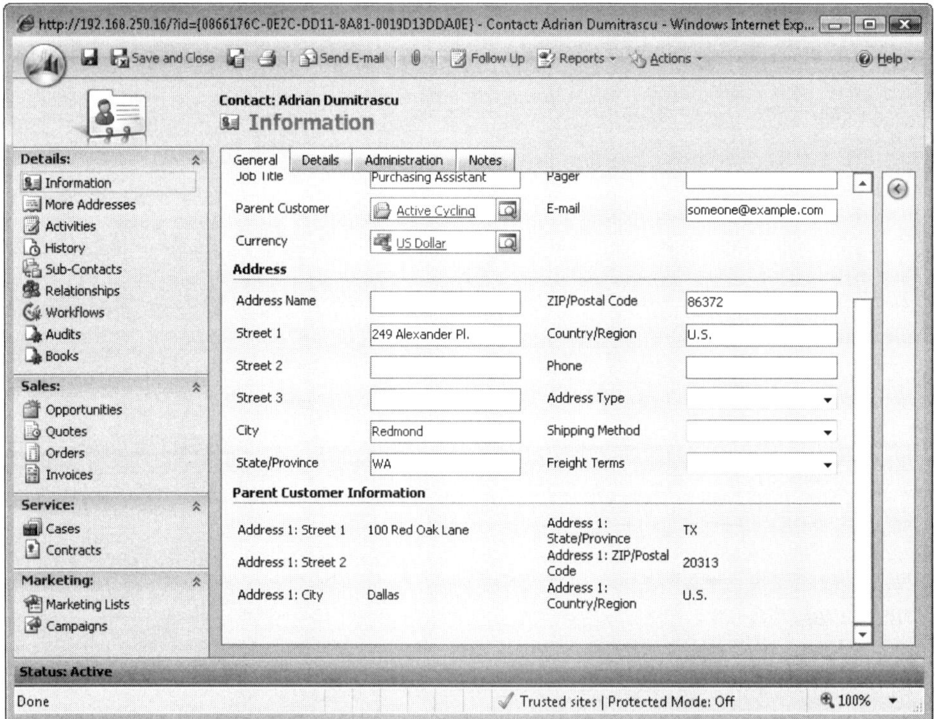

FIGURE 11-4 The Parent Customer IFrame in English

To test in a different language, go to the Tools menu on the main Microsoft Dynamics CRM toolbar and select Options. On the Languages tab of the Set Personal Options dialog box change your User Interface Language preference to Spanish and click OK. Now go back to the Contact record you just viewed and refresh the browser. The entity form and IFrame should now be displayed in your newly selected language (Figure 11-5).

Note If you are using a cache to store your metadata, you need to clear it before the updated labels will display.

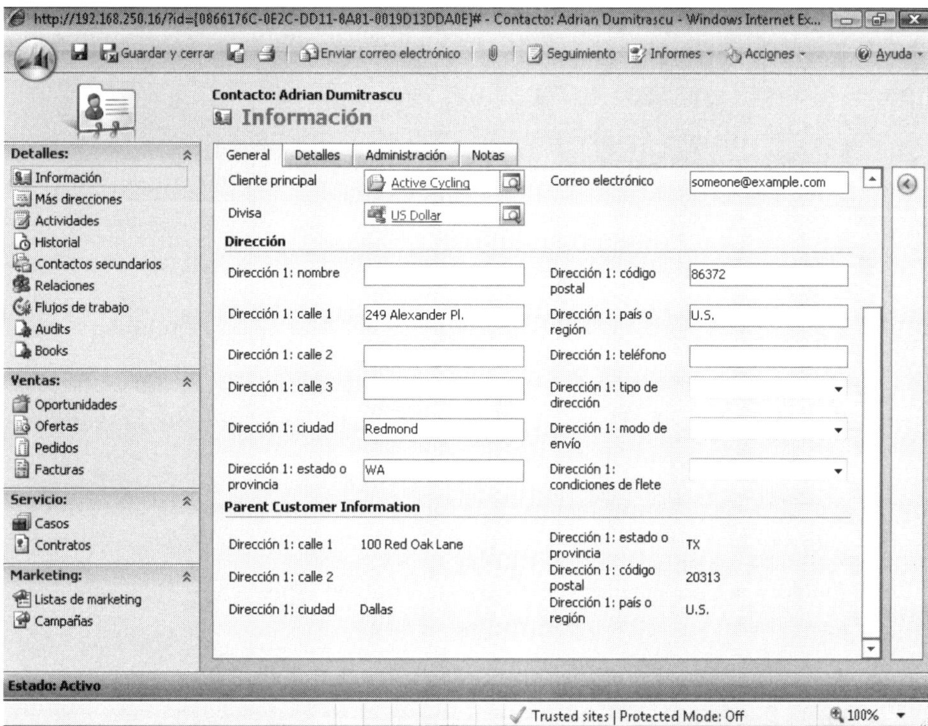

FIGURE 11-5 The translated Parent Customer IFrame in Spanish

Using Resource Assemblies for Multilingual Strings

In the example we just completed, we were able to use the Microsoft Dynamics CRM language packs to display the field labels because our IFrame displayed a field from the native account entity. Therefore, we did not need to provide a custom translation.

However, what about scenarios where we want to display multilingual text to the user but that text isn't stored in the Microsoft Dynamics CRM metadata? One way to handle this case is to use *resource files*. A resource file is just a file that contains nonexecutable text that we can use in our code. Resource files make localizing our text easy because they are external files and we can add as many new translated resource files as we need without having to update any code. To illustrate the use of resource files, we will update the previous example to display the warning message to the user in his or her preferred language.

Updating the Multilingual IFrame with Resource Files

In the IFrame we created in the previous section, we hard-coded an English warning message to the user if a new Contact record had not been saved yet. In this section we will learn how to use a resource file to localize this warning message so that users with Spanish as their language will see the warning in the localized language. To accomplish this we will add two resource files, one for English and one for Spanish translations.

Adding the resource files

1. Open the ProgrammingWithDynamicsCrm4 solution in Visual Studio 2008.
2. Right-click the ProgrammingMicrosoftDynamicsCrm4.Web project, select Add ASP.NET folder, and then click App_GlobalResources.
3. Right-click the App_GlobalResources folder and select Add New Item.
4. Select the Resource File template and type **Strings.resx** in the Name field. Click Add.
5. In our new resource file, type **IFrames_ContactParentCustomerInfo_Warning** as the name of the first string resource.
6. Type **The record must be saved before you can view the customer information.** in the Value field.
7. To add a resource file for the Spanish translation, repeat steps 3 through 5 replacing the resource file name with **Strings.es-ES.resx**.
8. In the Spanish resource file, type **El expediente debe ser ahorrado antes de que usted pueda ver la información del cliente.** in the Value field.
9. Save the two .resx files.

Now we will use a .NET utility named Resource File Generator (Resgen.exe). This tool converts a .resx file into a binary .resource file. The syntax for using the Resource File Generator looks like this:

```
Resgen <resource file name>
```

Important Always follow the correct naming convention when creating resource files. This allows your code to easily locate the resources at run time. The proper naming convention is: *<resource file name>*.*<culture>*.resources.

Tip You can find a list of valid culture strings at the following link: *http://msdn.microsoft.com/en-us/library/system.globalization.cultureinfo.aspx*.

Converting the .resx files to .resource files

1. Open the Visual Studio 2008 Command Prompt and navigate to the folder containing your .resx files.
2. Type in the following command: **Resgen Strings.resx**. This creates a file named Strings.resources in the App_GlobalResources folder.

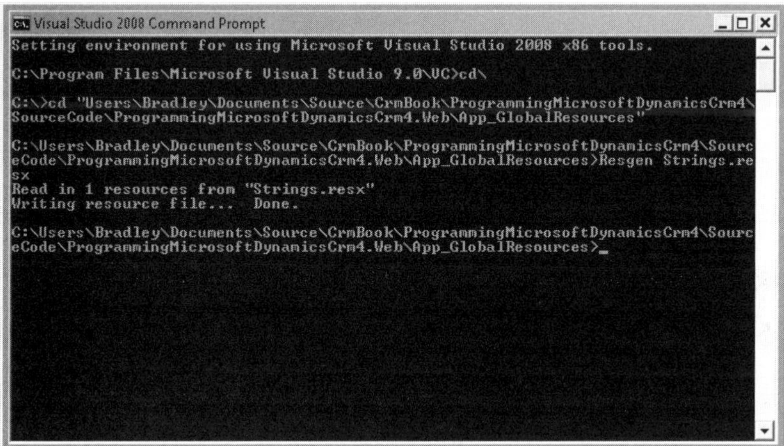

3. Now we need to run a command to create a .resource file for our Spanish translation. Run the following command: **Resgen Strings.es-ES.resx**.
4. Create a new folder in the Web site's folder hierarchy under the IFrames folder and name it **Resources**. Copy the two .resources files we just generated from the App_GlobalResources folder into our newly created Resources folder.

Now we need to update our IFrame's code-behind file to use the new resource files. Listing 11-4 contains the updated source code.

LISTING 11-4 ContactParentCustomerInfo.aspx.cs updated source code for resources

```
using System;
using System.Collections;
using System.Configuration;
using System.Data;
using System.Web;
using System.Web.Security;
using System.Web.UI;
using System.Web.UI.HtmlControls;
using System.Web.UI.WebControls;
using System.Web.UI.WebControls.WebParts;
using Microsoft.Crm.Sdk;
using Microsoft.Crm.SdkTypeProxy;
using Microsoft.Crm.Sdk.Query;
using Microsoft.Crm.SdkTypeProxy.Metadata;
```

```
using Microsoft.Crm.Sdk.Metadata;
using ProgrammingWithDynamicsCrm4.Utilities;
using System.Resources;
using System.Reflection;
using System.Globalization;
using System.Xml;
using System.Threading;

public partial class IFrames_ContactParentCustomerInfo : System.Web.UI.Page
{
    protected void Page_Load(object sender, EventArgs e)
    {
        string contactId = Request.QueryString["id"];
        string orgName = Request.QueryString["orgname"];

        CrmService crmService =
       CrmServiceUtility.GetCrmService(CrmServiceUtility.GetServerURLFromRegistry(),
                                       orgName);

        if (!string.IsNullOrEmpty(contactId))
        {

            MetadataService metadataService =
  CrmServiceUtility.GetMetadataService(CrmServiceUtility.GetServerURLFromRegistry(),
                                       orgName);

            ColumnSet contactColumns = new ColumnSet();
            contactColumns.AddColumn("parentcustomerid");

            contact crmContact =
                         (contact)crmService.Retrieve(EntityName.contact.ToString(),
                                                      new Guid(contactId),
                                                      contactColumns);

            if (crmContact.parentcustomerid != null)
            {
                string customerEntityName = crmContact.parentcustomerid.type;

                // set up labels using metadata
                AttributeMetadata addressLine1Metadata =
                          MetadataUtility.RetrieveAttributeMetadata(metadataService,
                                                                    customerEntityName,
                                                                    "address1_line1");
                this.street1Label.Text =
                               addressLine1Metadata.DisplayName.UserLocLabel.Label;

                AttributeMetadata addressLine2Metadata =
                          MetadataUtility.RetrieveAttributeMetadata(metadataService,
                                                                    customerEntityName,
                                                                     "address1_line2");
                this.street2Label.Text =
                                addressLine2Metadata.DisplayName.UserLocLabel.Label;
```

```
AttributeMetadata cityMetadata =
        MetadataUtility.RetrieveAttributeMetadata(metadataService,
                                                   customerEntityName,
                                                   "address1_city");

this.cityLabel.Text = cityMetadata.DisplayName.UserLocLabel.Label;

AttributeMetadata stateMetadata =
        MetadataUtility.RetrieveAttributeMetadata(metadataService,
                                                   customerEntityName,
                                          "address1_stateorprovince");

this.stateLabel.Text = stateMetadata.DisplayName.UserLocLabel.Label;

AttributeMetadata zipMetadata =
        MetadataUtility.RetrieveAttributeMetadata(metadataService,
                                                   customerEntityName,
                                               "address1_postalcode");

this.zipLabel.Text = zipMetadata.DisplayName.UserLocLabel.Label;

AttributeMetadata countryMetadata =
        MetadataUtility.RetrieveAttributeMetadata(metadataService,
                                                   customerEntityName,
                                                  "address1_country");

this.countryLabel.Text =
                    countryMetadata.DisplayName.UserLocLabel.Label;

// populate the form
TargetRetrieveDynamic targetRetrieve = new TargetRetrieveDynamic();
targetRetrieve.EntityName = crmContact.parentcustomerid.type;
targetRetrieve.EntityId = crmContact.parentcustomerid.Value;

ColumnSet customerColumns = new ColumnSet();
customerColumns.AddColumns("address1_line1",
                           "address1_line2",
                           "address1_city",
                           "address1_stateorprovince",
                           "address1_postalcode",
                           "address1_country");

RetrieveRequest retrieve = new RetrieveRequest();
retrieve.Target = targetRetrieve;
retrieve.ColumnSet = customerColumns;
retrieve.ReturnDynamicEntities = true;

RetrieveResponse retrieved =
                    (RetrieveResponse)crmService.Execute(retrieve);

DynamicEntity entity = (DynamicEntity)retrieved.BusinessEntity;

if (entity.Properties.Contains("address1_line1"))
    this.street1.Text =
                    entity.Properties["address1_line1"].ToString();
```

```
            if (entity.Properties.Contains("address1_line2"))
                this.street2.Text =
                                 entity.Properties["address1_line2"].ToString();
            if (entity.Properties.Contains("address1_city"))
                this.city.Text = entity.Properties["address1_city"].ToString();
            if (entity.Properties.Contains("address1_stateorprovince"))
                this.state.Text =
                       entity.Properties["address1_stateorprovince"].ToString();
            if (entity.Properties.Contains("address1_postalcode"))
                this.zip.Text =
                            entity.Properties["address1_postalcode"].ToString();
            if (entity.Properties.Contains("address1_country"))
                this.country.Text =
                               entity.Properties["address1_country"].ToString();
        }
    }
    else
    {
        ResourceManager resManager =
                     ResourceManager.CreateFileBasedResourceManager("Strings",
                                                  Server.MapPath("Resources"),
                                                                       null);

        WhoAmIRequest whoAmIRequest = new WhoAmIRequest();
        WhoAmIResponse whoAmIResponse =
                              (WhoAmIResponse)crmService.Execute(whoAmIRequest);

        Guid userId = whoAmIResponse.UserId;

        string fetchXml = String.Format(@"<fetch mapping='logical'>
                                   <entity name='usersettings'>
                                       <attribute name='uilanguageid' />
                                       <filter type='and'>
                <condition attribute='systemuserid' operator='eq' value='{0}' />
                                       </filter>
                                   </entity>
                                  </fetch>", userId.ToString());

        string fetchResults = crmService.Fetch(fetchXml);

        XmlDocument fetchDoc = new XmlDocument();
        fetchDoc.LoadXml(fetchResults);

        XmlNode resultNode =
                          fetchDoc.DocumentElement.SelectSingleNode("result");
        string languageCode =
                        resultNode.SelectSingleNode("uilanguageid").InnerText;

        CultureInfo cultureInfo = new CultureInfo(int.Parse(languageCode));

        string warningMessage =
resManager.GetString("IFrames_ContactParentCustomerInfo_Warning", cultureInfo);
```

```
                this.warning.InnerHtml = warningMessage;

                this.warning.Visible = true;
                this.main.Visible = false;
            }
        }
    }
```

Warning This example only works for on-premise because it doesn't use the *CrmImpersonator* class and uses a *WhoAmIRequest* to find the current user's ID.

The main changes to our code-behind file are in the *else* of our condition that checks whether the Contact record's ID was passed to the IFrame in the query string. The first thing we do is create a new *ResourceManager*. This object allows us to pull the string values from the .resources files we created earlier.

```
ResourceManager resManager =
                          ResourceManager.CreateFileBasedResourceManager("Strings",
                                                          Server.MapPath("Resources"),
                                                                               null);
```

We will copy our .resources files to the Microsoft Dynamics CRM server when we deploy our changes, so we will use a file-based resource manager. The first argument passed into the *CreateFileBasedResourceManager* method is the base name of our resource files. In our case this is "Strings", because we have two files: "Strings.resources" and "Strings.es-ES.resources". The second argument is the path to our .resources files. We will copy them into a folder named Resources in the next section.

Now that our *ResourceManager* is set up, we need to figure out the user's preferred language. To do this we use the *WhoAmI* message to find the current user's ID and some FetchXML to query the User Settings entity and find the language code. After we retrieve the language code we can create a new *CultureInfo* object and use it in the *ResourceManager* object's *GetString* method. The first argument is the name of the resource we want to return, and the second argument is our *CultureInfo* object.

```
resManager.GetString("IFrames_ContactParentCustomerInfo_Warning", cultureInfo);
```

This method either returns the English or Spanish translation, depending on which language code was set on the *CultureInfo* object. If a language code other than English or Spanish was used, the *GetString* method returns the default language because it could not find a resource for the specified language. In our case, this is English.

Deploying and Testing the Updated IFrame

Now we can test our updates on the Microsoft Dynamics CRM server.

Deploying the Web and Resource files

1. Copy the ContactParentCustomerInfo.aspx and ContactParentCustomerInfo.aspx.cs files from the IFrame folder to the ProgrammingMicrosoftDynamicsCrm4 folder on the Microsoft Dynamics CRM server.
2. Copy the Resources folder containing our two .resources files into the Programming-MicrosoftDynamicsCrm4 folder.

Because we are testing the warning message when a record has not been created, open Microsoft Dynamics CRM in a Web browser and navigate to the Contacts grid. Click the New button. The resulting window should display our IFrame with the warning message in your current language (Figure 11-6).

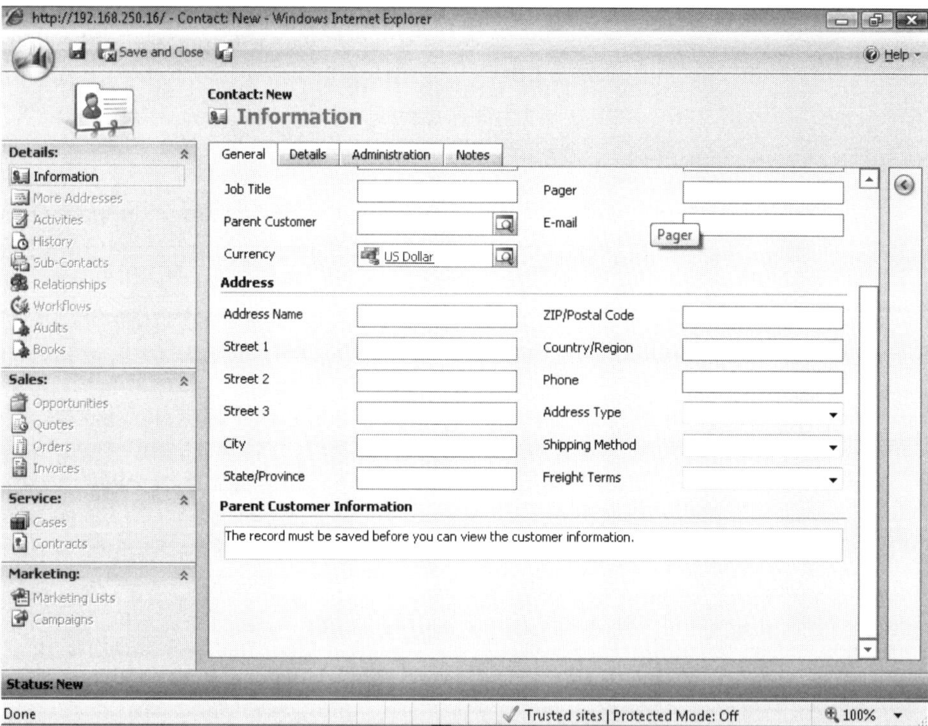

FIGURE 11-6 The Contact Parent Customer IFrame warning in English

Now change your language preference to Spanish in the Microsoft Dynamics CRM UI just like we did when testing the IFrame the first time. Once again, click the New button on the Contacts grid. The warning message should now be translated (Figure 11-7).

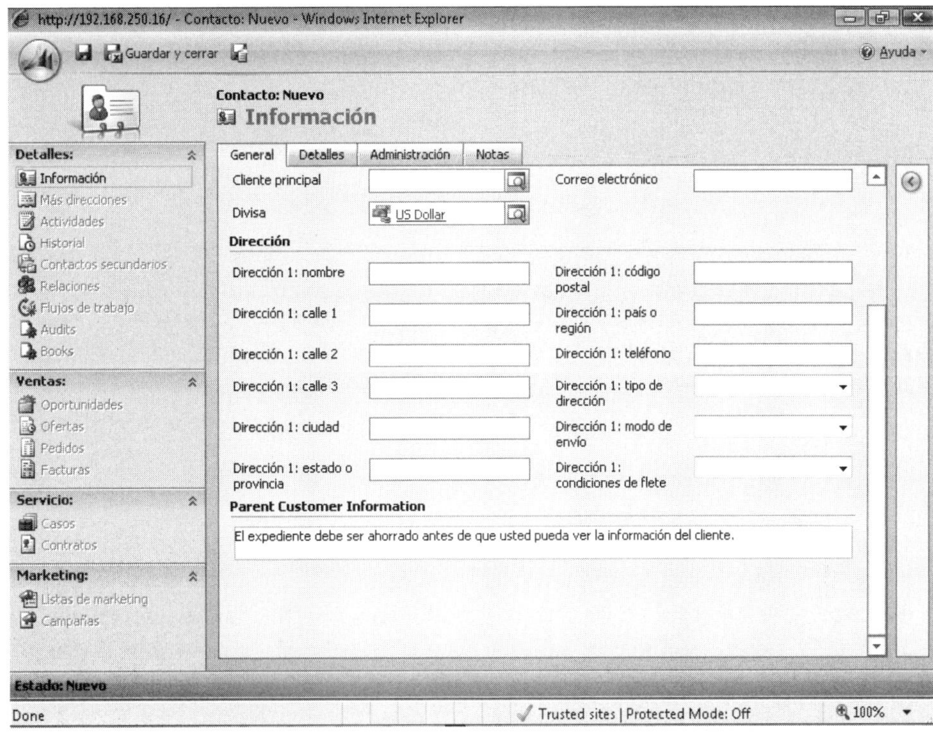

FIGURE 11-7 The Contact Parent Customer IFrame warning in Spanish

Note You might notice that the name of our Parent Customer Information section has not been translated. To add translations for IFrame section names, you must export the translations from Microsoft Dynamics CRM, open the XML file in Excel, and update the appropriate text on the Localized Labels sheet. After you do this, you can import your updated translations and publish your entity to see your changes.

Programming for Multi-Currency Applications

In addition to multilingual support, Microsoft Dynamics CRM supports multi-currency functionality for globally based deployments. Microsoft Dynamics CRM implements multiple currencies by allowing each record to be associated with its own currency. Microsoft Dynamics CRM calculates the value of the record in its specified currency in addition to calculating the record's values using the organization's base currency. This multi-currency functionality allows each user to work in his or her preferred currency, but it still allows users and management to report across the board in the base currency. Converting the currency values for each record into a base currency allows for greater efficiency when your organization runs reporting throughout the entire organization. Microsoft Dynamics CRM stores this base currency information in the *basecurrencyid* field of the OrganizationBase table in the database. Entity records that support a transaction currency will have a *transactioncurrencyid* attribute that specifies which Transaction Currency entity to use for the exchange rate between the transaction currency and the base currency.

Tip Add new currencies to your Microsoft Dynamics CRM organization through the Currencies link on the Business Management screen of the Settings section.

When programming with money attributes, you need to consider which value you need: the value converted to the base currency or the value in the currency selected on the record. Microsoft Dynamics CRM actually makes this very easy. Each money attribute created in the database also has a second field associated with it that contains the value converted into the base currency. These associated fields are named with the following format:

```
<fieldname>_base
```

These *_base* fields are also created for any custom attributes you create with the type of *money*. For example, let's say you want to write a piece of code that calculates the total estimated revenue from a user's open opportunities. Users can have opportunity records in multiple currencies, and you want the total returned in the base currency. The following code sample demonstrates how to accomplish this:

```
CrmService crmService = CrmServiceUtility.GetCrmService("ServerName", "OrgName");

QueryExpression query = new QueryExpression();
query.EntityName = EntityName.opportunity.ToString();

ColumnSet opportunityCols = new ColumnSet();
opportunityCols.AddColumns("estimatedvalue_base");

query.ColumnSet = opportunityCols;

ConditionExpression stateCondition = new ConditionExpression();
stateCondition.AttributeName = "statecode";
stateCondition.Operator = ConditionOperator.Equal;
stateCondition.Values = new object[] { 0 };

WhoAmIRequest whoAmIRequest = new WhoAmIRequest();
WhoAmIResponse whoAmIResponse = (WhoAmIResponse)crmService.Execute(whoAmIRequest);

Guid userId = whoAmIResponse.UserId;

ConditionExpression ownerCondition = new ConditionExpression();
ownerCondition.AttributeName = "ownerid";
ownerCondition.Operator = ConditionOperator.Equal;
ownerCondition.Values = new object[] { userId };

FilterExpression filter = new FilterExpression();
filter.FilterOperator = LogicalOperator.And;
filter.Conditions.Add(stateCondition);
```

```
filter.Conditions.Add(ownerCondition);

query.Criteria = filter;

BusinessEntityCollection bec = crmService.RetrieveMultiple(query);

decimal totalEstimatedValue = 0.0m;

foreach (BusinessEntity be in bec.BusinessEntities)
{
    opportunity crmOpportunity = (opportunity)be;

    totalEstimatedValue += crmOpportunity.estimatedvalue_base.Value;
}
```

The preceding example is pretty straightforward. You can see how we use the Opportunity entity's *estimatedvalue_base* field to calculate our estimated revenue in the base currency. Using this base field saves us from having to retrieve the exchange rate and do the conversion ourselves.

Summary

This chapter provided you with some ideas for writing custom code to deal with multiple languages and multiple currencies used by your Microsoft Dynamics CRM system. We discussed the *CrmService* messages that you can use to retrieve language information and update translations. The Metadata Service allows for easy access to attribute labels for all installed and enabled language packs. Any text added to custom pages in an application intended to be multilingual should be placed in a resource file and not hard-coded into your HTML or code-behind page. Microsoft Dynamics CRM is configured with a base currency, but allows for users to select a currency for their records. When programming for multiple currencies, remember that Microsoft Dynamics CRM gives you both the selected currency in the attribute and an additional attribute containing the currency value converted to the base currency.

Chapter 12

Advanced Workflow Programming

In Chapter 6, "Programming Workflow," we discussed how Microsoft Dynamics CRM 4.0 uses Windows Workflow Foundation (WF) to execute workflow instances defined by business users. We also looked at developing your own custom activities and how you can register them with the CRM server.

In this chapter, we'll dig deeper into the workflow implementation within Microsoft Dynamics CRM 4.0 to understand how the software stores workflow definitions within entities in CRM and how you can manipulate these definitions through the Microsoft Dynamics CRM Web services. Additionally, you will gain an understanding of workflow dependencies and how they affect workflow execution. Finally, we'll explore how CRM uses Extensible Application Markup Language (XAML) and declarative workflows, as well as how you can register your own workflows to execute within CRM.

We'll cover the following topics in this chapter:

- Custom workflow manager tool
- Workflows as entities
- Declarative workflows

Custom Workflow Manager Tool

To help assist the process of working with workflows, we created a custom desktop application that we refer to as the custom workflow management tool. You can use this application to explore and manipulate workflows on your Microsoft Dynamics CRM server. The tool is named ProgrammingWithDynamicsCrm4.WorkflowManager.exe, and you can find the source code on the book's companion Web site as detailed in the Introduction. Because this is a desktop application, we don't step through every line of code; instead, we just take a look at the methods that apply to managing workflows within Microsoft Dynamics CRM 4.0.

Let's take a quick look at the ProgrammingWithDynamicsCrm4.WorkflowManager user interface to better understand the code samples we'll be looking at throughout the chapter.

Using ProgrammingWithDynamicsCrm4.WorkflowManager

1. Download the source code for the book as described in the Introduction.
2. Open the ProgrammingWithDynamicsCrm.sln solution in Microsoft Visual Studio 2008.

3. Within the Solution Explorer, right-click the ProgrammingWithDynamicsCrm4.WorkflowManager project, and then select Set As StartUp Project.
4. Select Start Without Debugging from the Debug menu, or press Ctrl+F5 on the keyboard.
5. The Connection Details dialog box is displayed, prompting you to specify how to connect to your Microsoft Dynamics CRM server.

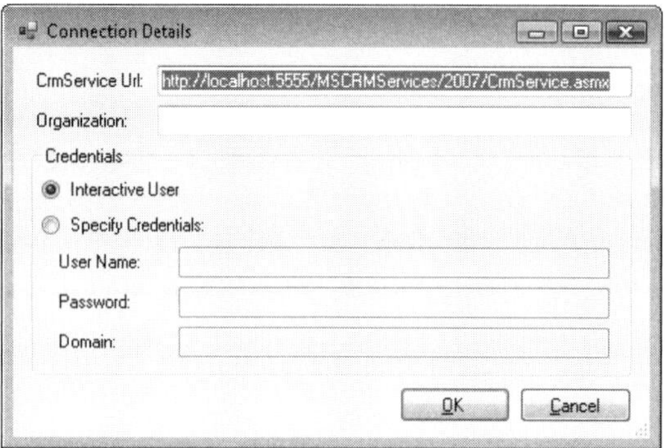

6. Update the CrmService Url field to the correct URL for your Microsoft Dynamics CRM server.
7. Type your organization name in the Organization field.
8. If you want to connect to the Microsoft Dynamics CRM server with the credentials that you are currently logged on to Windows with, just leave Interactive User selected. Otherwise you can select Specify Credentials and type in the user name, password, and domain you want to pass to the server. Click OK.

   All of the values in the Connection Details dialog box, with the exception of the Password field, are saved when you click OK. You don't need to enter them every time you use the ProgrammingWithDynamicsCrm4.WorkflowManager tool. If you select Specify Credentials, you must type in the password every time.

   After a few seconds, the main ProgrammingWithDynamicsCrm4.WorkflowManager window opens with a list of your current workflows. From here you can perform various operations, such as importing, exporting, and publishing workflow definitions. We examine this functionality as we progress through the chapter.

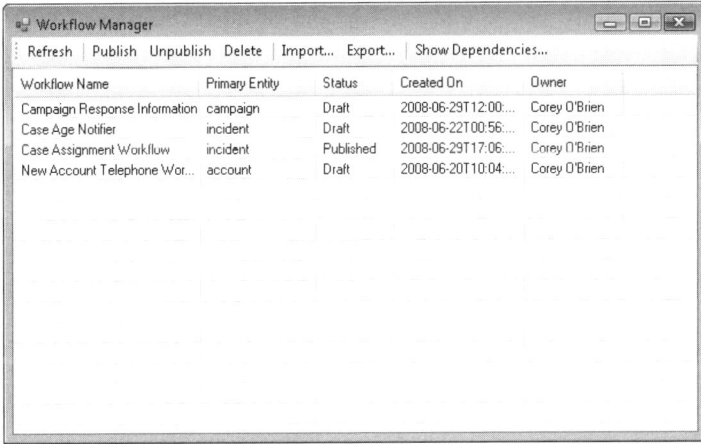

Workflows as Entities

It probably won't surprise you to learn that Microsoft Dynamics CRM stores workflow definitions in entities, just like most things in Microsoft Dynamics CRM. Conveniently, this allows developers to access and manipulate workflows through the familiar *CrmService* API.

The *workflow* Entity

The entity that contains most of the workflow definition is appropriately named *workflow*. Table 12-1 lists the attributes of the *workflow* entity.

TABLE 12-1 Attributes of the *workflow* Entity

name	Type	Description
activeworkflowid	*Lookup*	Only populated if the *workflow* has a *type* equal to *Definition* and a *statecode* of *Published*. Contains the *workflowid* for the compiled workflow that is executed when this workflow is triggered. See "Workflow Publication" later in this chapter for more information.
activities	*String*	Contains the declarative workflow definition in Extensible Application Markup Language (XAML). For workflows defined in the CRM workflow designer, this attribute is only populated after a workflow is published and only for the workflows with a *type* equal to *Activation*. See "Declarative Workflows" later in this chapter for more information.
createdby	*Lookup*	The *systemuser* that created the workflow.
createdon	*CrmDateTime*	The date and time the *workflow* was created.
description	*String*	The description of the *workflow* definition.

TABLE 12-1 Attributes of the *workflow* Entity

name	Type	Description
iscrmuiworkflow	*CrmBoolean*	True if the *workflow* was defined in the Microsoft Dynamics CRM 4.0 workflow designer; otherwise false.
modifiedby	*Lookup*	The *systemuser* that last modified the *workflow* definition.
modifiedon	*CrmDateTime*	The date and time the *workflow* was last modified.
name	*String*	The name of the *workflow.*
ondemand	*CrmBoolean*	True if this *workflow* is allowed to be executed on demand by users; otherwise false.
ownerid	*Owner*	The owner of the *workflow.*
owningbusiness-unit	*Lookup*	The *workflow* owner's business unit.
parentworkflowid	*Lookup*	If the *workflow* has a *type* of *Activation, parentworkflowid* references the *workflow* that represents the definition.
plugintypeid	*Lookup*	References the *plugintype* for a compiled *workflow.* Only populated for workflows with a *type* of *Activation.* See "Workflow Publication" later in this chapter for more information.
primaryentity	*EntityNameReference*	A reference to the type of the primary entity for the *workflow* definition.
rules	*String*	Contains the declarative *workflow*'s policy rules in XAML. For workflows defined in the CRM workflow designer, this is only populated after a *workflow* is published and only for the workflows with a *type* equal to *Activation.* See "Declarative Workflows" later in this chapter for more information.
scope	*Picklist*	The scope of the event that automatically triggers the *workflow.* Valid values are exposed as constant integer fields from the *WorkflowScope* class (User = 1, BusinessUnit = 2, Deep = 3, Global = 4). For example, if *scope* is set to *WorkflowScope.User,* the workflow only automatically executes if the primary entity is also owned by the workflow owner. See "Automatic Workflows" in Chapter 6 for more information.
statecode	*WorkflowStateInfo*	The state of the *workflow.* Valid values are exposed as constant integer fields from the *WorkflowState* class. (Draft = 0, Published = 1).
statuscode	*Status*	Additional information about the state of the *workflow.* Currently, each *statecode* only has a single valid value for *statuscode* (Draft = 1, Published = 2).
subprocess	*CrmBoolean*	Indicates whether the workflow can be included in other workflows as a child process.

TABLE 12-1 Attributes of the *workflow* Entity

name	Type	Description
type	*Picklist*	Used to determine the type of the *workflow*. Valid values are exposed as constant integer fields from the *WorkflowType* class (Definition = 1, Activation = 2, Template = 3). A workflow with *type* equal to Activation indicates that it has been compiled from a definition during publication. See "Workflow Publication" later in this chapter for more information.
uidata	*String*	When a *workflow* is defined in the Microsoft Dynamics CRM workflow designer (*iscrmuiworkflow* equals true), *uidata* contains proprietary information about the configuration of the steps and stages.
workflowid	*Key*	The primary key for the *workflow*.

If you have read Chapter 6, many of these attributes, such as *scope* and *ondemand*, are undoubtedly familiar to you because you worked directly with them in the Microsoft Dynamics CRM workflow designer. Others, such as *activities, activeworkflowid,* and *rules*, are not as obvious, and for that reason we examine them more closely later in this chapter.

Interacting with Workflows Through *CrmService*

Because Microsoft Dynamics CRM stores workflows within entities, you can access and manipulate them using the familiar *CrmService* methods. For example, ProgrammingWithDynamicsCrm4.WorkflowManager uses the code from Listing 12-1 whenever it needs to refresh the list of workflows.

LISTING 12-1 *WorkflowLogic's RetrieveWorkflows* method

```
public IEnumerable<workflow> RetrieveWorkflows(params string[] attributes)
{
    QueryExpression query = new QueryExpression();
    query.EntityName = "workflow";
    ColumnSet cols = new ColumnSet();
    cols.AddColumns(attributes);
    query.ColumnSet = cols;
    query.Criteria.AddCondition(
        "type", ConditionOperator.Equal, WorkflowType.Definition);

    BusinessEntityCollection results = this.CrmService.RetrieveMultiple(query);
    foreach (workflow w in results.BusinessEntities)
    {
        yield return w;
    }
}
```

This query returns all workflow definitions in the system, regardless of their state or owner. We use the results of this method to populate the *ListView* control in the main form of the ProgrammingWithDynamicsCrm4.WorkflowManager tool.

In addition to workflow retrieval and deletion, you can use the *CrmService* API for all of the other manipulations such as updating, deleting, and reassigning *workflow* entities to new owners. See Chapter 3, "Communicating with Microsoft CRM APIs," for more information on how to use the API to execute this functionality.

Workflow Publication

Once you begin managing workflows through the API, you will quickly find yourself needing to publish and unpublish workflows programmatically. Listing 12-2 demonstrates how easily you can accomplish this with the *SetStateWorkflowRequest*.

LISTING 12-2 *WorkflowLogic's PublishWorkflow* and *UnpublishWorkflow* methods

```
const int WorkflowStatusDraft = 1;
const int WorkflowStatusPublished = 2;

public void PublishWorkflow(Guid workflowId)
{
    SetStateWorkflowRequest publishRequest = new SetStateWorkflowRequest();
    publishRequest.EntityId = workflowId;
    publishRequest.WorkflowState = WorkflowState.Published;
    publishRequest.WorkflowStatus = WorkflowStatusPublished;

    this.CrmService.Execute(publishRequest);
}

public void UnpublishWorkflow(Guid workflowId)
{
    SetStateWorkflowRequest unpublishRequest = new SetStateWorkflowRequest();
    unpublishRequest.EntityId = workflowId;
    unpublishRequest.WorkflowState = WorkflowState.Draft;
    unpublishRequest.WorkflowStatus = WorkflowStatusDraft;

    this.CrmService.Execute(unpublishRequest);
}
```

Best Practices Notice that the *WorkflowStatusPublished* and *WorkflowStatusDraft* constants are defined locally in the *WorkflowLogic* class. Although the CRM SDK provides the *WorkflowState* class to access the *statecode* definitions, it does not provide a similar class for *statuscode*. To make your code more maintainable, it is a good idea to define some constants of your own to represent the values.

Although the two methods in Listing 12-2 are fairly straightforward, behind the scenes CRM is doing more than simply changing some attribute values in response to these calls.

Back in Listing 12-1, you saw that we added a condition to make sure we only retrieve workflows if the *type* equals *WorkflowType.Definition*. Without this condition, the *CrmService* appears to return duplicate workflow definitions to our *ListView*. In reality, a compiled copy of a workflow definition is created each time you publish a workflow. The compiled version is marked with *type* set to *WorkflowType.Activation* and the *activeworkflowid* attribute on the definition *workflow* is updated to reference this compiled copy.

Compilation takes the stages and steps you defined in the workflow designer out of the *uidata* attribute and converts them into XAML. We'll take a closer look at XAML in the section "Declarative Workflows" later in this chapter, but for now just understand that the XAML is XML that you use to describe the stages and steps.

XAML is combined with some generated code and compiled into a class in a new assembly. The new assembly and class are stored in a *pluginassembly* entity and a *plugintype* entity respectively. The resulting *plugintype* is associated with the compiled *workflow* through the *workflow*'s *plugintypeid* attribute.

In addition to compiling the *workflow*, a series of related entities of type *workflowdependency* are created during publication. These entities contain additional information about when to execute a workflow instance and what data it requires during execution. Because this is a vital and yet complex part of workflow execution, we discuss the *workflowdependency* entity in more depth in the next section.

The publication process enables Microsoft Dynamics CRM to streamline the execution of workflow instances by optimizing the *workflow* into a .NET assembly and preparing additional data to dictate how and when to execute it.

The *workflowdependency* Entity

As mentioned in the previous section, a series of *workflowdependency* entities are created during publication to instruct CRM both when a workflow should be executed and what data it needs during execution. A *workflowdependency* can be one of eight different types. You can use the *type* attribute to determine the type of the *workflowdependency*. The valid values for *type* can be found as constant integer values in the *WorkflowDependencyType* class, as shown in Table 12-2.

TABLE 12-2 *WorkflowDependencyType* Field Values

Field	Value	Description
AttributeDefinition	8	Creates a dependency on a custom attribute. A custom attribute cannot be deleted if a published workflow references it with this dependency.
CustomEntityDefinition	7	Creates a dependency on a custom entity. A custom entity cannot be deleted if a published workflow references it with this dependency.
LocalParameter	2	Used to define local parameters that exist as properties on the compiled workflow class. These properties are frequently modified and read by *PolicyActivity* instances as defined in the *workflow*'s *rules* attribute.
PrimaryEntityImage	3	Specifies which attributes of the primary entity should be passed in to the workflow instance.
PrimaryEntityPostImage	5	Specifies which attributes of the primary entity's post image should be passed in to the workflow instance.
PrimaryEntityPreImage	4	Specifies which attributes of the primary entity's pre image should be passed in to the workflow instance.
RelatedEntityImage	6	Specifies the attributes needed by this workflow from an entity directly related to the primary entity.
SdkAssociation	1	This dependency is used to define which SDK messages should cause the related *workflow* to execute.

With these dependency types in hand, we can take a look at the other attributes exposed from the *workflowdependency* entity. Table 12-3 lists all of the *workflowdependency* attributes and their uses.

TABLE 12-3 The *workflowdependency* Entity

property	Type	Description
createdby	*Lookup*	The user that created the *workflowdependency*.
createdon	*CrmDateTime*	The date and time the *workflowdependency* was created.
customentityname	*String*	If *type* is *CustomEntityDefinition*, this is the name of the custom entity the workflow is dependent upon.
dependentattribute-name	*String*	If *type* is *AttributeDefinition*, *dependentattributename* is the name of the attribute that is required.
dependententityname	*String*	If *type* is *AttributeDefinition*, *dependententityname* is the name of the entity that the required attribute must exist on.

TABLE 12-3 The *workflowdependency* Entity

property	Type	Description
entityattributes	*String*	The *entityattributes* property has multiple meanings depending on the *type* attribute. Regardless of the meaning, it always contains a comma-separated list of attribute names. If *type* is *SdkAssociation* and *sdkmessageid* references the *Update* message, *entityattributes* contains the names of the attributes that automatically trigger the workflow. For any of the entity image defining types, *entityattributes* contains the list of attributes that should be populated in the image.
modifiedby	*Lookup*	The user that last modified the *workflowdependency.*
modifiedon	*CrmDateTime*	The date and time the *workflowdependency* was last modified.
owningbusinessunit	*UniqueIdentifier*	The business unit that owns the *workflowdependency.*
owninguser	*UniqueIdentifier*	The user that owns the *workflowdependency.*
parametername	*String*	This identifies the name of a property that will be defined on the compiled workflow instance. These properties can be accessed from rules used by *PolicyActivity* instances.
parametertype	*String*	Only populated when *type* is set to *LocalParameter, parametertype* contains the name of the .NET type for the local property that is defined on the workflow.
relatedattributename	*String*	When *type* is set to *RelatedEntityImage*, the *relatedattributename* property is set to the name of the attribute on the primary entity that contains the related entity.
relatedentityname	*String*	When *type* is set to *RelatedEntityImage*, the *relatedentityname* property is set to the name of the related entity type.
sdkmessageid	*Lookup*	When *type* is set to *SdkAssociation*, *sdkmessageid* is the related message that automatically triggers the workflow execution.
type	*Picklist*	Determines the type of the *workflowdependency.* See Table 12-2 for a list of possible values.
workflowdependencyid	*Key*	The primary ID for the *workflowdependency.*
workflowid	*Lookup*	The *workflow* this dependency is associated with.

Workflow dependencies play an important but subtle role in the Microsoft Dynamics CRM workflow processing. To help understand the complexities of workflow dependencies, we will create a simple workflow through the native workflow designer and then examine the workflow dependencies generated as a result.

Examining workflow dependencies created by the native workflow designer

1. Using the native workflow designer, create a workflow named **Dependency Test** that automatically executes when an opportunity is created. (Refer to Chapter 6 if you need a refresher on using the native workflow designer.)
2. Set the workflow's scope to Organization.
3. Add a Check Condition step to check whether the opportunity's estimated revenue is greater than or equal to $10,000.
4. Add a Create Record step to create a follow-up phone call if the condition evaluates to true. Set the subject of the phone call to **Follow Up For New Opportunity** and set the due date to three days after the opportunity's creation date.

   At this point, your workflow should look like the following image:

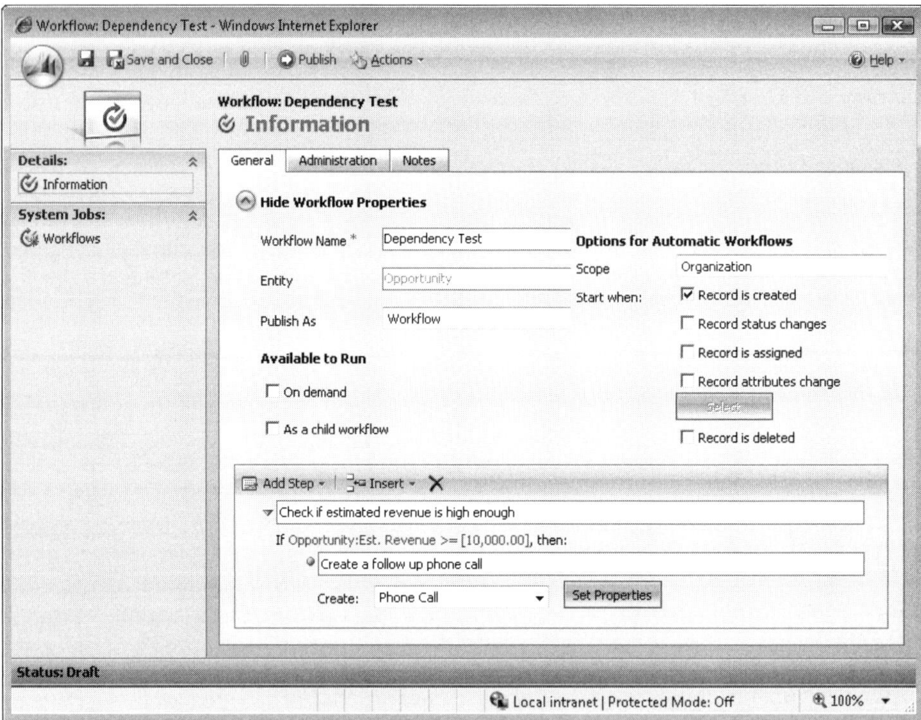

5. Publish the workflow.
6. Launch the ProgrammingWithDynamicsCrm4.WorkflowManager tool as described earlier in this chapter and connect to your Microsoft Dynamics CRM server.
7. Select the Dependency Test workflow from the list and click the Show Dependencies button.

8. You should see the workflow dependencies list in a grid as shown here. Resize the columns and scroll to examine all of the dependency properties.

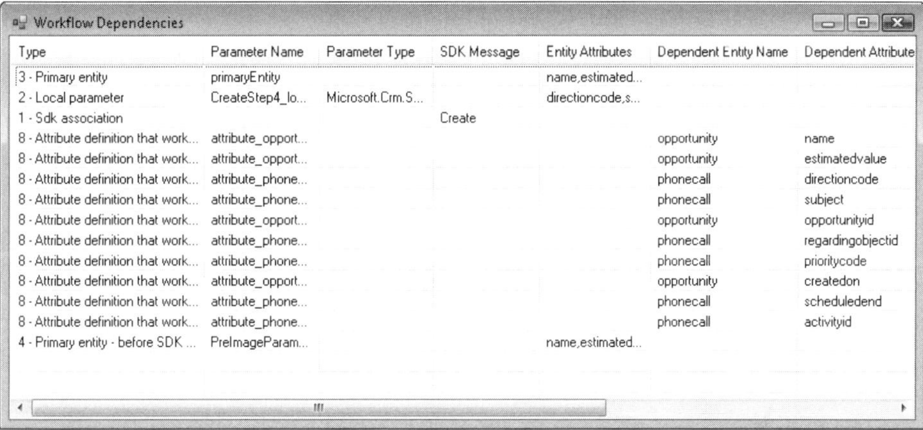

Type	Parameter Name	Parameter Type	SDK Message	Entity Attributes	Dependent Entity Name	Dependent Attribute
3 - Primary entity	primaryEntity			name,estimated...		
2 - Local parameter	CreateStep4_lo...	Microsoft.Crm.S...		directioncode,s...		
1 - Sdk association			Create			
8 - Attribute definition that work...	attribute_opport...				opportunity	name
8 - Attribute definition that work...	attribute_opport...				opportunity	estimatedvalue
8 - Attribute definition that work...	attribute_phone...				phonecall	directioncode
8 - Attribute definition that work...	attribute_phone...				phonecall	subject
8 - Attribute definition that work...	attribute_opport...				opportunity	opportunityid
8 - Attribute definition that work...	attribute_phone...				phonecall	regardingobjectid
8 - Attribute definition that work...	attribute_phone...				phonecall	prioritycode
8 - Attribute definition that work...	attribute_opport...				opportunity	createdon
8 - Attribute definition that work...	attribute_phone...				phonecall	scheduledend
8 - Attribute definition that work...	attribute_phone...				phonecall	activityid
4 - Primary entity - before SDK ...	PreImageParam...			name,estimated...		

By examining the workflow dependencies we can see that the majority of them have a *type* of *AttributeDefinition* (8) that defines attributes that need to exist for the workflow to run. Some of the attributes defined in the list are not directly referenced by anything we specified in our steps, but Microsoft Dynamics CRM uses them behind the scene regardless.

A dependency of *type SdkAssociation* (1) also dictates the workflow should be run in response to a Create message. If we had selected more messages to automatically trigger the workflow, they would show up as additional dependencies.

Two of the dependencies are used to request that images of the primary entity be passed in as local parameters during the workflow execution. These images allow our workflow to reference attributes off of the primary entity such as *estimatedrevenue* and *createdon* without needing to retrieve the data manually.

Note You may have noticed that the *name* and *opportunityid* attributes are also included in the primary entity image. This is because those attributes represent the primary attribute and primary key for the entity and they are always included in the primary entity image, regardless of whether you directly reference them.

The final dependency has a *type* of *LocalParameter* (2) and is used to define a local DynamicEntity property on the workflow itself. This property is referenced by *PolicyActivity* instances to populate and create the *phonecall* entity.

Retrieving Workflow Dependencies

Before we move on from workflow dependencies, let's look at how ProgrammingWithDynamics-Crm4.WorkflowManager retrieves the workflow dependencies from the *CrmService*. Listing 12-3 shows the *RetrieveWorkflowDependencies* method from the *WorkflowLogic* class.

LISTING 12-3 The *RetrieveWorkflowDependencies* method

```
public IEnumerable<workflowdependency> RetrieveWorkflowDependencies(
    Guid workflowId, params string[] attributes)
{
    QueryExpression query = new QueryExpression();
    query.EntityName = "workflowdependency";
    query.ColumnSet = new ColumnSet(attributes);
    query.Criteria.AddCondition("workflowid", ConditionOperator.Equal, workflowId);

    BusinessEntityCollection results = this.CrmService.RetrieveMultiple(query);
    foreach (workflowdependency dependency in results.BusinessEntities)
    {
        if (dependency.sdkmessageid != null)
        {
            RetrieveRequest request = new RetrieveRequest();
            request.ReturnDynamicEntities = true;
            request.ColumnSet = new ColumnSet(new string[] {"name"});
            request.Target = new TargetRetrieveDynamic()
            {
                EntityId = dependency.sdkmessageid.Value,
                EntityName = "sdkmessage"
            };

            RetrieveResponse response =
                (RetrieveResponse)this.CrmService.Execute(request);

            DynamicEntity message = (DynamicEntity)response.BusinessEntity;

            dependency.sdkmessageid.name = (string)message["name"];
        }

        yield return dependency;
    }
}
```

Note that the *workflowid* passed in to this method should be the *activeworkflowid* attribute of a *workflow* with a *type* equal to *Definition*. This is because workflow dependencies are created for the active workflows during publication, and are not tied to the definition itself.

Warning Notice that *RetrieveWorkflowDependencies* has special logic around populating the *name* property on the *sdkmessage* attribute. This is done to hide a rare inconsistency with the *CrmService RetrieveMultiple* message, where the name of a *Lookup* attribute is not populated. The problem is further compounded if you are referencing the CRM SDK assemblies instead of a Web Reference, because the *sdkmessage* entity is not deserialized correctly from *CrmService*. To get around this, you must request that a *DynamicEntity* be returned.

Now that you have an understanding of workflow dependencies and the tools to explore them more deeply when needed, you are ready to move on to the main topic of the chapter: declarative workflows.

Declarative Workflows

One of the main features of Windows Workflow Foundation is the ability to run declarative workflows, which are described in a specific XML format called Extensible Application Markup Language, or XAML.

By abstracting a workflow definition from a programming language, WF has opened the door to the creation of workflow designers that target business users and end users instead of software developers. In addition, a program that uses declarative workflows does not need to be aware of them until run time, which allows workflow definitions to be modified without recompiling the host application.

XAML Syntax

While you may typically depend on a workflow designer to generate the XAML for you, we recommend that you should take a look at a sample XAML file to gain a basic understanding of the syntax. Listing 12-4 demonstrates what a simple sequential workflow might look like in XAML.

LISTING 12-4 Sample XAML syntax

```
<SequentialWorkflowActivity
    x:Class="SampleWorkflowProject.SampleWorkflow"
    x:Name="SampleWorkflow"
    xmlns:x="http://schemas.microsoft.com/winfx/2006/xaml"
    xmlns="http://schemas.microsoft.com/winfx/2006/xaml/workflow">

     <DelayActivity TimeoutDuration="00:01:00" x:Name="DelayOneMinute" />

</SequentialWorkflowActivity>
```

This sample is not very useful other than serving as a demonstration of the XAML syntax. It simply waits for one minute and then exits.

In this case, both of the element names (*SequentialWorkflowActivity* and *DelayActivity*) map to classes in the .NET Framework. The .NET namespace is determined from the element's XML namespace. In this case the XML namespace *http://schemas.microsoft.com/winfx/2006/xaml/workflow* is mapped to the *System.Workflow.Activities* .NET namespace. This mapping comes from the application of the *XmlnsDefinitionAttribute* within the *System.Workflow.Activities* assembly.

The attributes with the *x:* prefix denote special XAML-specific properties that the XAML parser uses. The *x:Name* attribute assigns a name to the element that can be used to reference the elements later during execution. The *x:Class* attribute can only be assigned to the root element, and is used to define a class for that element that derives from the element's natural type. This is used to create code-behind files similar to ASP.NET pages.

The *TimeoutDuration* attribute maps to a .NET property with the same name of type *TimeSpan* on the *DelayActivity*. Various type converters are available to the XAML parser that can convert string values into complex types such as *TimeSpan*. Properties can also be contained in child elements prefixed with the parent element's name. For example, if you want to set a value to the *Description* property on the *DelayActivity*, you can add a *Description* attribute to the *DelayActivity* element, or you can assign a value by creating a child element inside the *DelayActivity* element shown by the following code:

```
<DelayActivity.Description>
    This is a one minute delay.
</DelayActivity.Description>
```

XAML is a powerful tool with an intuitive syntax that has many books and Web sites dedicated to it, but explaining the full details of XAML is outside the scope of this book. For more information on XAML, you can read about it at *http://msdn.microsoft.com/en-us/library/ms747122.aspx*. The topics in that section of MSDN specifically talk about XAML and its use in Windows Presentation Foundation (WPF), but the XAML syntax descriptions are excellent and still apply to WF.

XAML in Microsoft Dynamics CRM

Microsoft Dynamics CRM uses XAML behind the scenes during the publication of workflows defined within the native workflow designer. The XAML that describes the flow of activities is stored in the *activities* attribute in a *workflow* entity and the XAML that contains the policy rules are stored in the *policy* attribute (more on policy rules in a little bit).

The more interesting part is that Microsoft Dynamics CRM allows us to create workflow definitions and specify our own values for *activities* and *rules*.

The following benefits apply when you use XAML-based workflow definitions:

- Although Microsoft Dynamics CRM Online does not currently support custom workflow activities, you can deploy XAML-based workflows to Microsoft Dynamics CRM Online.
- You can access native WF activities that are not exposed by the native workflow designer in CRM (such as the *ConditionedActivityGroup* used for looping).
- If you are already familiar with a different stand-alone XAML-based WF designer, you can continue to use it.

Creating Your First Declarative Workflow

In this section, we'll create a declarative workflow in Visual Studio .NET that creates three follow-up tasks for a newly created lead. Each follow-up task is due a week apart. We use a simple loop to accomplish this. Looping is something that can only be accomplished in the native workflow designer by recursively calling the same workflow definition as a child process. By using a simple activity to achieve the same thing, we can create a more maintainable workflow that has less overhead.

Because we will only be uploading the XAML to the Microsoft Dynamics CRM server, we will not need to compile the workflow into an assembly. But in order to take advantage of the workflow designer in Visual Studio .NET, we'll still create a workflow project.

Creating a workflow project

1. In Visual Studio .NET, select File > New > Project... from the top menu.
2. In the New Project dialog box, click Workflow under the Visual C# group in the Project types tree.
3. Select Empty Workflow Project from the list of templates.
4. Type **SampleWorkflowProject** in the Name box and click OK.
5. Right-click SampleWorkflowProject in Solution Explorer and then click Add Reference.
6. On the Browse tab, navigate to the CRM SDK's bin folder and select microsoft.crm.sdk.dll and microsoft.crm.sdktypeproxy.dll. Click OK.

Now that we set up our project, we can add our workflow definition. Because there is not a CRM-specific workflow template in Visual Studio, we will tweak the files produced by the default WF template after we add them.

Adding a workflow definition

1. Right-click SampleWorkflowProject in Solution Explorer and select Add > Sequential Workflow.
2. Select Sequential Workflow (with code separation) from the list of Templates.
3. Change the name to **LeadFollowUpWorkflow.xoml** and click OK.

Note Even though the filename ends with .xoml instead of .xaml it is still a XAML file. The .xoml file extension is used to differentiate Windows Workflow Foundation XAML files from Windows Presentation Foundation XAML files. (WPF uses the .xaml file extension.)

You should now see something like this image:

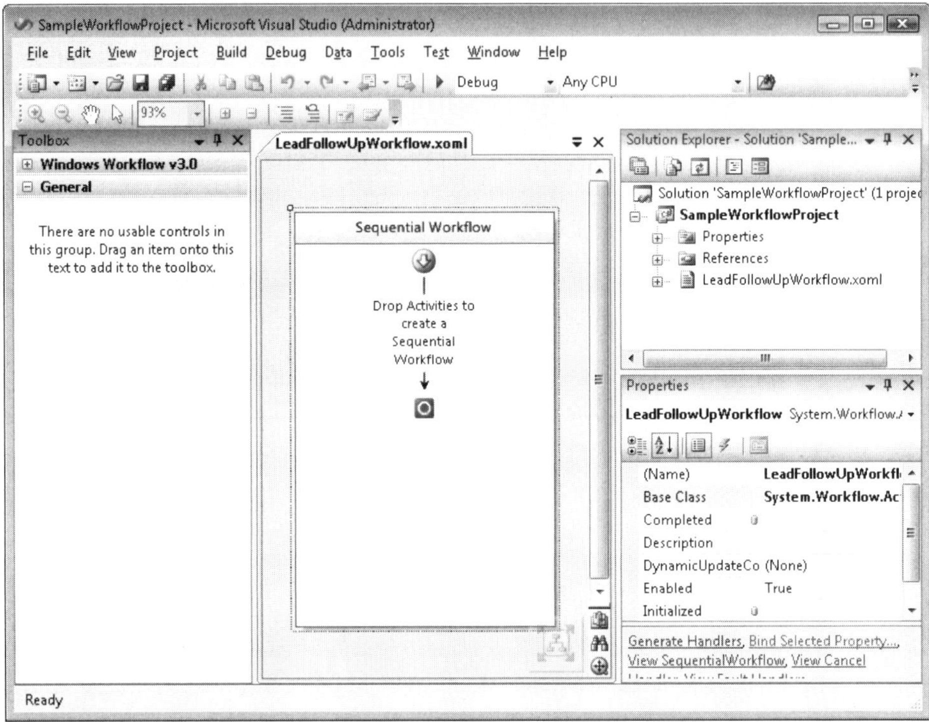

4. Right-click the background of the workflow and select Properties.
5. In the Properties window, click the Base Class property and click the ellipsis button that becomes visible.
6. Type **Microsoft.Crm.Workflow.CrmWorkflow** in the Type Name box and click OK.

You now have a workflow definition created that you can start to edit in the Visual Studio .NET workflow designer. Before we begin, though, let's add the CRM-specific activities to the Toolbox so that you can easily access them.

Adding the Microsoft Dynamics CRM assemblies to the Toolbox

1. Right-click inside the Toolbox and select Add Tab.
2. Type **Microsoft Dynamics CRM 4.0** for the tab name and press Enter.
3. Right-click within the new tab and select Choose Items.
4. Click the Browse button at the bottom of the .NET Framework Components tab.
5. Browse to the CRM SDK's bin folder, select the Microsoft.Crm.Sdk.dll, and then click OK.
6. Click OK to exit the Choose Toolbox Items dialog box.

You should now see the Toolbox populated with the familiar Microsoft Dynamics CRM workflow activities:

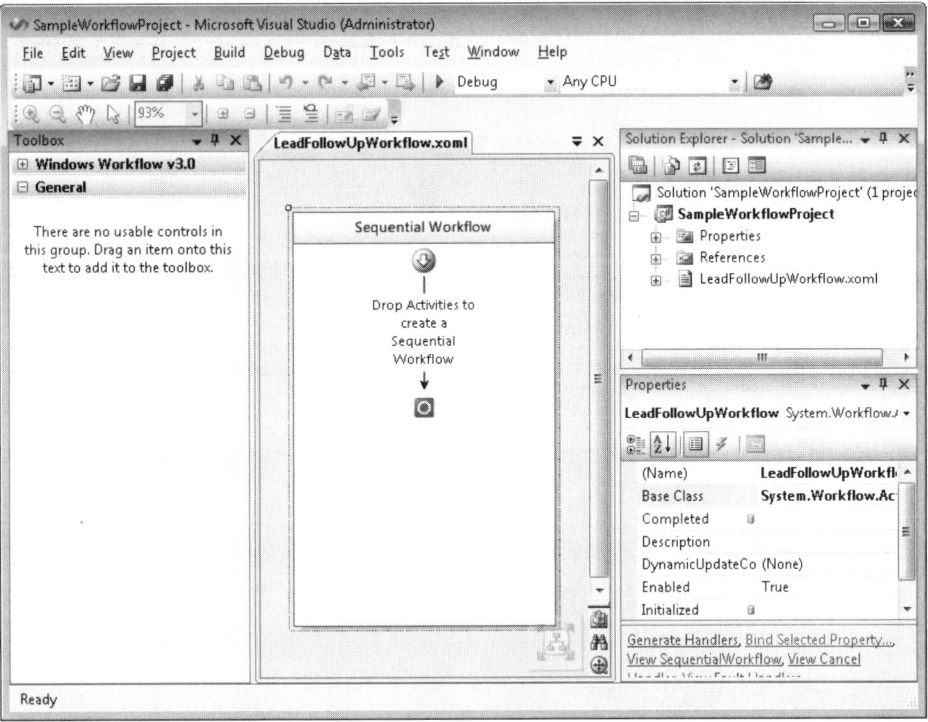

Now we are ready to start designing our workflow definition. One of the first things you should think about when starting on a new workflow definition is which local parameters you need. It is important to have these local parameters defined before you begin writing the workflow policies that reference them because the policy editor is not forgiving of invalid syntax. In our case we need two local parameters to serve as temporary storage for the task entities we will create and for the count of tasks we have created. We can use the existing *PrimaryEntity* property from the base *CrmWorkflow* class to hold the lead image we receive from CRM.

Ultimately these parameters will be defined using workflow dependencies, but to use the Visual Studio .NET workflow designer without errors, we need to define them in the code-behind file.

Important You should not put anything in the code-behind file that cannot be emulated with workflow dependencies. The C# file is not uploaded to the CRM server when you deploy the XAML, so properties in the code-behind file need to be re-created using workflow dependencies.

Defining local parameters on the workflow

1. Right-click the workflow in the designer and select View Code.
2. Add ***using Microsoft.Crm.Sdk;*** to the end of the existing *using* statements.
3. Within the class definition, add the following two properties:

```
public DynamicEntity TaskEntity { get; set; }
public int TaskCount { get; set; }
```

4. Save and close the code-behind file.

Now with our local parameters set up, we can begin designing our workflow. For now we will just lay out the activities and assign them names, and then come back and fill out the additional rules that control the local parameters.

Designing the LeadFollowUpWorkflow

1. Open the LeadFollowUpWorkflow.xoml file if it is not already open.
2. In the Toolbox, drag a *Policy* activity from the Windows Workflow 3.0 tab into the workflow definition.
3. In the Properties window for the newly created *Policy* activity, change the name to **InitializeLoop**. For now ignore the warning icon on the *Policy* activity and continue.
4. Drag a *ConditionedActivityGroup* activity from the Toolbox into the workflow directly beneath the Policy you just configured. *ConditionedActivityGroup* is one of the activities that allows looping in Windows Workflow Foundation. Other activities such as the *WhileActivity* are simpler, but are not included in the list of types supported by CRM for workflows and therefore aren't publishable. See the topic "Supported Types for Workflow" in the Microsoft Dynamics CRM 4.0 SDK for a list of supported workflow types.
5. In the Properties window for the *ConditionedActivityGroup*, change the Name property to **Loop**.
6. Drag a *Sequence* activity from the Toolbox into the *ConditionedActivityGroup*.
7. In the properties window, rename the *Sequence* activity **LoopSequence**.
8. Within the Loop activity, click the icon next to the text Previewing [1/1]. This switches *ConditionedActivityGroup* into edit mode and allows us to edit the contained activities.
9. Drag another *Policy* activity into the LoopSequence activity and name it **InitializeTask**. Again ignore the warning icon for now and continue.
10. From within the Microsoft Dynamics CRM 4.0 tab in the Toolbox, drag in a *CreateActivity* activity directly underneath the *InitializeTask* activity and then rename it **CreateTask**.

The following image shows what your workflow should look like now:

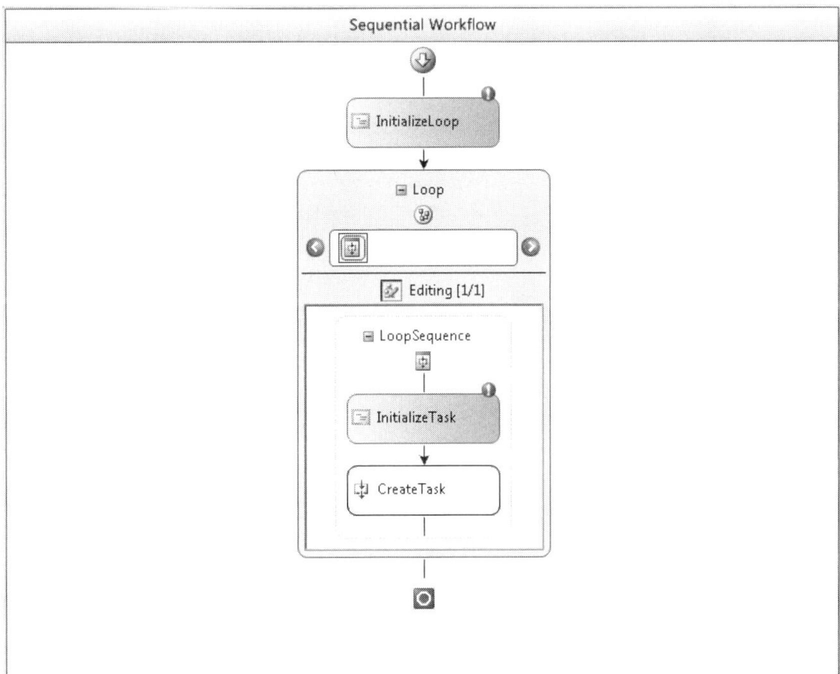

The next step is to go through and tie all the various activities together through the local parameters. We will make heavy use of the policy activities to update the local parameters. *PolicyActivity* references declarative rules located within a separate rules file to execute statements when a condition evaluates to *true*. The rules file is also written in XAML and can perform simple programmatic statements without the need for a compiled assembly. Fortunately for us, the Microsoft Visual Studio .NET workflow designer automatically creates and maintains the rules file as we type in simple code statements.

Adding rules to the workflow definition

1. Select the InitializeLoop activity in the workflow designer.
2. Click the RuleSetReference property in the Properties window and then click the ellipsis button that appears.
3. In the Select Rule Set dialog box, click the New toolbar button.
4. In the Rule Set Editor dialog box, click the Add Rule toolbar button.
5. Change the rule name from Rule1 to **InitializeLoopRule**.

6. Enter **true** in the Condition text area. By doing this we are saying that we want this rule to always be executed. This is fairly common practice when using rules to manipulate local parameters.
7. In the Then Actions text area, type **this.TaskCount = 0** and click OK.
8. In the Select Rule Set dialog box click the Rename toolbar button and type in the new name **InitalizeLoopRuleSet** when prompted. Click OK.
9. Click OK to exit the Select Rule Set dialog box.
10. Next you want to set up the LoopSequence so that it repeats three times. Click the LoopSequence activity, which is inside the Editing area of the Loop activity.
11. Set the WhenCondition property in the Properties window to Declarative Rule Condition.
12. Expand the WhenCondition property, click the ConditionName property beneath it, and then click the ellipsis button that appears.
13. In the Select Condition dialog box, click the New toolbar button.
14. Type **this.TaskCount < 3** in the Condition text area and then click OK.
15. Click Rename in the Select Condition dialog box and change the condition name to **ContinueCondition**. Click OK.
16. Click OK to exit the Select Condition dialog box.
17. Next you create a policy that increments the *TaskCount* local parameter and then initializes the TaskEntity local parameter so that it is ready for the CreateTask activity. Select the InitializeTask activity and click the ellipsis button for the RuleSetReference property.
18. Click the New toolbar button within the Select Rule Set dialog box.
19. Click the Add Rule toolbar button within the Rule Set Editor dialog box.
20. Rename the rule **InitializeTaskRule** and set the Condition to **True**.
21. Type the following code into the Then Actions text area and then click OK.

```
this.TaskCount = this.TaskCount + 1
this.TaskEntity = Microsoft.Crm.Workflow.CrmWorkflow.CreateEntity("task")
this.TaskEntity["subject"] = string.Format("Follow up with lead ({0} days old)",
    this.TaskCount * 7)
this.TaskEntity["scheduledend"] = Microsoft.Crm.Sdk.CrmDateTime.FromUser(
    System.DateTime.Now.AddDays(this.TaskCount * 7))
this.TaskEntity["regardingobjectid"] =
    Microsoft.Crm.Workflow.CrmWorkflow.ConvertToLookup(
    this.PrimaryEntity["leadid"], "lead")
```

Note Notice how the preceding code creates a new *DynamicEntity* and assigns it to the *TaskEntity* local parameter. It assigns values to the *subject, scheduledend,* and *regardingobjectid* attributes as well. For the *regardingobjectid* attribute, it gets the *leadid* from the primary entity image. This is a common pattern you will use whenever you need to create new entities in your custom workflows.

22. Rename the rule set **InitializeTaskRuleSet** and click OK to close the Select Rule Set dialog box.
23. The last thing we need to do is to associate the CreateTask with the TaskEntity local parameter. Start by clicking the CreateTask activity.
24. Click the Entity property in the Properties window and then click the ellipsis button that appears.
25. In the Bind dialog box, select TaskEntity from the Bind To An Existing Member tab and click OK.

At this point, we completely defined our workflow and the only thing that remains is deploying it to the CRM server. Fortunately the ProgrammingWithDynamicsCrm4.WorkflowManager tool can help with this process. The tool does, however, require us to set up an XML file to describe how the workflow should be deployed. Add a new XML file to your project named **LeadFollowUpWorkflow.config**. Type in the configuration text as it is shown in Listing 12-5 into the newly created file.,

LISTING 12-5 LeadFollowUpWorkflow.config contents

```
<?xml version="1.0" encoding="utf-8" ?>
<WorkflowConfiguration
  PrimaryEntity="lead"
  Name="Lead Follow Up">

  <Dependencies>
    <SdkAssociationDependency MessageName="Create" />
    <PrimaryEntityImageDependency
      ParameterName="PrimaryEntity" EntityAttributes="leadid" />
    <LocalParameterDependency
      ParameterName="TaskEntity" ParameterType="Microsoft.Crm.Sdk.DynamicEntity"/>
    <LocalParameterDependency
      ParameterName="TaskCount" ParameterType="System.Int32"/>
  </Dependencies>

</WorkflowConfiguration>
```

Here we define the *name* and *primaryentity* attributes for our *workflow* instance as well as four workflow dependencies. Notice that the two properties we created (*TaskEntity* and *TaskCount*) are represented here by the *LocalParameterDependency* elements. ProgrammingWithDynamicsCrm4.WorkflowManager looks for a .xoml and .rules file with the same name as the configuration file to assign the *activities* and *rules* attributes as well. If you have files that do not match that pattern for some reason, two attributes on the *WorkflowConfiguration* element, *ActivitiesFile* and *RulesFile*, allow you to specify the appropriate files.

Tip If you edit your configuration file in Visual Studio .NET you can include a reference to the schema file to get IntelliSense while working with the XML. To include the schema information, modify the opening *WorkflowConfiguration* element to match the following code:

```
<WorkflowConfiguration
  xmlns:xsi="http://www.w3.org/2001/XMLSchema-instance"
  xsi:noNamespaceSchemaLocation="workflow-config.xsd"
  PrimaryEntity="lead"
  Name="Lead Follow Up">
```

Copy the workflow-config.xsd file from the ProgrammingWithDynamicsCrm4.WorkflowManager folder into the folder that contains your workflow configuration file. Now when you start a new element or attribute you are prompted with possible values, as shown here:

Deploying the workflow

1. Make sure that all the files you have been working with are saved in Visual Studio .NET by selecting File and then Save All from the menu.
2. Launch ProgrammingWithDynamicsCrm4.WorkflowManager and connect to your CRM server as described earlier in the chapter.
3. Click the Import toolbar button.
4. Navigate to the LeadFollowUpWorkflow.config file and then click OK.

   Within a few seconds the list of workflows should refresh and include a new one with the name Lead Follow Up.

5. Select the Lead Follow Up workflow from the list and click the Publish toolbar button to publish it.

Now your declarative workflow is published and deployed. You can create a new lead in Microsoft Dynamics CRM, and after a few seconds the lead should have three tasks associated with it, each with due dates one week apart.

Declarative Workflow Deployment

Now that we have our first declarative workflow up and running, it is important to understand what is involved in deploying a declarative workflow. In this section we'll examine the code behind the import functionality within the ProgrammingWithDynamicsCrm4.WorkflowManager tool. Listing 12-6 shows the *ImportWorkflow* method of the *WorkflowLogic* class.

LISTING 12-6 The *ImportWorkflow* method

```
public void ImportWorkflow(string configurationFileName)
{
    WorkflowConfiguration config =
        WorkflowConfiguration.Load(configurationFileName);

    workflow workflow = config.ToEntity();

    Guid workflowId = this.CrmService.Create(workflow);
    foreach (WorkflowDependency dependencyConfig in config.Dependencies)
    {
        workflowdependency dependency = dependencyConfig.ToEntity(workflowId);

        if (dependency.sdkmessageid != null)
        {
            dependency.sdkmessageid.Value =
                GetSdkMessageId(dependency.sdkmessageid.name);
        }

        this.CrmService.Create(dependency);
    }
}
```

The method first loads the workflow configuration from the specified file and then asks the configuration class to generate a *workflow* instance, which it passes along to the *CrmService Create* method. Next, the method loops through the *Dependencies* property on the *WorkflowConfiguration* and gets a *workflowdependency* instance for each of them. If a value is provided for the *sdkmessageid* property, the actual ID is looked up by the *GetSdkMessageId* method based on the name of the SDK message. This is done so that the end user editing the configuration file does not need to know the message ID and can just specify the name. Finally, each *workflowdependency* is passed in to the *CrmService Create* method as well.

Let's continue by taking a look at the *WorkflowConfiguration* class *load* method, as shown in Listing 12-7.

LISTING 12-7 The *WorkflowConfiguration load* method

```
public class WorkflowConfiguration
{
    [XmlAttribute]
    public string Name { get; set; }

    [XmlAttribute]
    public string Description { get; set; }

    [XmlAttribute]
    public string PrimaryEntity { get; set; }

    [XmlAttribute]
    public string ActivitiesFile { get; set; }

    [XmlAttribute]
    public string RulesFile { get; set; }

    [XmlArrayItem(typeof(AttributeDefinitionDependency))]
    [XmlArrayItem(typeof(CustomEntityDefinitionDependency))]
    [XmlArrayItem(typeof(SdkAssociationDependency))]
    [XmlArrayItem(typeof(PrimaryEntityImageDependency))]
    [XmlArrayItem(typeof(PrimaryEntityPreImageDependency))]
    [XmlArrayItem(typeof(PrimaryEntityPostImageDependency))]
    [XmlArrayItem(typeof(RelatedEntityImageDependency))]
    [XmlArrayItem(typeof(LocalParameterDependency))]
    public WorkflowDependency[] Dependencies { get; set; }

    public static WorkflowConfiguration Load(string configurationFileName)
    {
        ...
    }

    public workflow ToEntity()
    {
        ...
    }


    public void Save(string configFileName)
    {
        ...
    }
}
```

The *WorkflowConfiguration* class mainly represents the state of a workflow configuration, but it does have a few methods that help in the loading, saving, and conversion to a *workflow* instance. We'll take a look at these methods shortly, but first notice the *XmlAttribute* and *XmlArrayItem* attributes assigned to the property definitions in *WorkflowConfiguration*. These attributes are used to aid serialization of the class to and from XML with the aid of the *System.Xml.Serialization.XmlSerializer* class. *XmlAttribute* tells *XmlSerializer* to use an xml attribute instead of a child element to contain the property value. *XmlArrayItem* is used to list the acceptable types that can be included in an array property. Listing 12-8 demonstrates how simple it is to load an XML file into an instance of *WorkflowConfiguration* when using *XmlSerializer*.

LISTING 12-8 *WorkflowConfiguration's Load* method

```
public static WorkflowConfiguration Load(string configurationFileName)
{
    XmlSerializer xmlSerializer = new XmlSerializer(typeof(WorkflowConfiguration));
    WorkflowConfiguration config;
    using(Stream file = File.OpenRead(configurationFileName))
    {
        config = (WorkflowConfiguration)xmlSerializer.Deserialize(file);
    }

    if (String.IsNullOrEmpty(config.PrimaryEntity))
    {
        throw new InvalidOperationException(
            "PrimaryEntity is a required attribute.");
    }

    if (String.IsNullOrEmpty(config.ActivitiesFile))
    {
        config.ActivitiesFile = Path.ChangeExtension(
            configurationFileName, ".xoml");
    }

    if (!Path.IsPathRooted(config.ActivitiesFile))
    {
        config.ActivitiesFile = Path.Combine(
            Path.GetDirectoryName(configurationFileName),
            config.ActivitiesFile);
    }

    if (String.IsNullOrEmpty(config.RulesFile))
    {
        string rulesFile = Path.ChangeExtension(config.ActivitiesFile, ".rules");
        if (File.Exists(rulesFile))
        {
            config.RulesFile = rulesFile;
        }
    }

    if (!String.IsNullOrEmpty(config.RulesFile) &&
          !Path.IsPathRooted(config.RulesFile))
    {
        config.RulesFile = Path.Combine(
            Path.GetDirectoryName(configurationFileName),
```

```
            config.RulesFile);
    }

    if (String.IsNullOrEmpty(config.Name))
    {
        config.Name = Path.GetFileNameWithoutExtension(config.ActivitiesFile);
    }

    return config;
}
```

The first six lines of the method de-serialize the XML file into a *WorkflowConfiguration* instance. Next the method confirms that a primary entity value was specified and then determines intelligent defaults for any other values that were omitted.

The *ToEntity* method is responsible for converting the *WorkflowConfiguration* into a *workflow* instance that can be passed along to *CrmService*'s *Create* method. After the *Load* method has set up all of the properties, performing this conversion is straightforward, as shown in Listing 12-9.

LISTING 12-9 *WorkflowConfiguration's ToEntity* method

```
public workflow ToEntity()
{
    workflow entity = new workflow();
    entity.name = this.Name;

    entity.type = new Picklist(WorkflowType.Definition);
    entity.primaryentity = new EntityNameReference(this.PrimaryEntity);
    entity.activities = File.ReadAllText(this.ActivitiesFile);

    if (!String.IsNullOrEmpty(this.RulesFile))
    {
        entity.rules = File.ReadAllText(this.RulesFile);
    }

    return entity;
}
```

The last method in *WorkflowConfiguration* is actually used during the workflow export process, and we examine it later in the chapter.

Next let's look at the dependencies and how they are imported. If you recall from Listing 12-6, the *ImportWorkflow* method loops through each of the *WorkflowDependency* instances in the *WorkflowConfiguration.Dependencies* property and calls *ToEntity* on each of them to generate a *workflowdependency* instance.

WorkflowDependency is an abstract base class that has no properties of its own. The *ToEntity* method it implements is only provided as a helper for the inherited classes. Listing 12-10 shows the simple *ToEntity* implementation on *WorkflowDependency.*

LISTING 12-10 *WorkflowDependency's ToEntity* method

```
public virtual workflowdependency ToEntity(Guid workflowId)
{
    workflowdependency entity = new workflowdependency();
    entity.workflowid = new Lookup("workflow", workflowId);
    return entity;
}
```

If you refer back to Listing 12-7 you can see eight applications of the *XmlArrayItem* attribute on the *WorkflowConfiguration.Dependencies* property. Each application of this attribute specifies a class that can be entered into the XML-based configuration file and ultimately passed in as an item to the *Dependencies* property.

You can specify the following eight valid types for the *Dependencies* property:

- *AttributeDefinitionDependency*
- *CustomEntityDefinitionDependency*
- *LocalParameterDependency*
- *SdkAssociationDependency*
- *PrimaryEntityImageDependency*
- *PrimaryEntityPreImageDependency*
- *PrimaryEntityPostImageDependency*
- *RelatedEntityImageDependency*

You have probably noticed that these dependencies correspond very closely to the values found on *WorkflowDependencyType* as shown in Table 12-2. This is because each of these classes is used to specify one of the different dependency types in the workflow configuration file. Let's take a brief look at each of the individual classes to get a better understanding of how the dependencies are mapped to their CRM counterparts.

The first of these classes, *AttributeDefinitionDependency*, is used when you want to keep a custom attribute from being deleted when you have a workflow that depends on it. The full source for *AttributeDefinitionDependency* is shown in Listing 12-11.

LISTING 12-11 The *AttributeDefinitionDependency* class

```
using System;
using System.Xml.Serialization;
using Microsoft.Crm.Sdk;
using Microsoft.Crm.SdkTypeProxy;

namespace ProgrammingWithDynamicsCrm4.WorkflowManager.Configuration
{
    public class AttributeDefinitionDependency: WorkflowDependency
    {
        public AttributeDefinitionDependency()
        {

        }

        public AttributeDefinitionDependency(workflowdependency dependency)
        {
            this.DependentEntityName = dependency.dependententityname;
            this.DependentAttributeName = dependency.dependentattributename;
        }

        [XmlAttribute]
        public string DependentEntityName { get; set; }

        [XmlAttribute]
        public string DependentAttributeName { get; set; }

        public override workflowdependency ToEntity(Guid workflowId)
        {
            workflowdependency entity = base.ToEntity(workflowId);
            entity.type = new Picklist(WorkflowDependencyType.AttributeDefinition);
            entity.dependententityname = this.DependentEntityName;
            entity.dependentattributename = this.DependentAttributeName;
            return entity;
        }

    }
}
```

This class is not very complex. During workflow import only the parameterless constructor is used. The other constructor, which accepts a *workflowdependency*, is used during workflow export. The two properties are both tagged with *XmlAttribute* again to ensure that they are both serialized as attributes instead of child elements.

The method of most interest, however, is *ToEntity*, which calls the base implementation to create an instance of *workflowdependency* and assign the proper *workflowid*. It then proceeds to set the *type* attribute to *WorkflowDependencyType.AttributeDefinition*. The remaining attribute assignments, *dependententityname* and *dependentattributename* both have one-to-one mappings with properties on *AttributeDefinitionDependency*.

The next workflow dependency configuration class is *CustomEntityDefinitionDependency*, which you use when you want to keep users from deleting custom entities that your workflow depends on. Listing 12-12 shows *CustomEntityDefinitionDependency* in its entirety.

LISTING 12-12 The *CustomEntityDefinitionDependency* class

```
using System;
using System.Xml.Serialization;
using Microsoft.Crm.Sdk;
using Microsoft.Crm.SdkTypeProxy;

namespace ProgrammingWithDynamicsCrm4.WorkflowManager.Configuration
{
    public class CustomEntityDefinitionDependency: WorkflowDependency
    {
        public CustomEntityDefinitionDependency()
        {

        }

        public CustomEntityDefinitionDependency(workflowdependency dependency)
        {
            this.CustomEntityName = dependency.customentityname;
        }

        [XmlAttribute]
        public string CustomEntityName { get; set; }

        public override workflowdependency ToEntity(Guid workflowId)
        {
            workflowdependency entity = base.ToEntity(workflowId);
            entity.type =
                new Picklist(WorkflowDependencyType.CustomEntityDefinition);
            entity.customentityname = this.CustomEntityName;
            return entity;
        }
    }
}
```

CustomEntityDefinitionDependency follows the same pattern as *AttributeDefinitionDependency*, but assigns a different value to the *type* attribute and then only populates the *customentityname* attribute.

Both *CustomEntityDefinitionDependency* and *AttributeDefinitionDependency* define workflow dependencies on the CRM metadata. You can use these to verify that the metadata is in an acceptable state for your workflow to execute, but they do not modify the workflow definition or change when it executes. Because of this, you only need to apply these dependencies to prevent a user from deleting custom entities and attributes that your workflow depends on. If you do not apply these dependencies, and a custom entity or attribute that your workflow requires is deleted, Microsoft Dynamics CRM 4.0 will raise an error and put the workflow instance in a suspended state when it tries to access the unavailable attribute or entity.

Next we take a look at *SdkAssociationDependency*. You can use this configuration entry to specify one or more system messages that should automatically trigger workflow execution. Listing 12-13 shows the full source code for *SdkAssociationDependency*.

LISTING 12-13 The *SdkAssociationDependency* class

```
using System;
using System.Xml.Serialization;
using Microsoft.Crm.Sdk;
using Microsoft.Crm.SdkTypeProxy;

namespace ProgrammingWithDynamicsCrm4.WorkflowManager.Configuration
{
    public class SdkAssociationDependency : WorkflowDependency
    {
        public SdkAssociationDependency()
        {
        }

        public SdkAssociationDependency(workflowdependency dependency)
        {
            if (dependency.sdkmessageid != null)
            {
                this.MessageName = dependency.sdkmessageid.name;
            }
            this.EntityAttributes = dependency.entityattributes;
        }

        [XmlAttribute]
        public string MessageName { get; set; }

        [XmlAttribute]
        public string EntityAttributes { get; set; }

        public override workflowdependency ToEntity(Guid workflowId)
        {
            workflowdependency entity = base.ToEntity(workflowId);

            entity.type = new Picklist(WorkflowDependencyType.SdkAssociation);
            entity.sdkmessageid = new Lookup("message", Guid.Empty);
            entity.sdkmessageid.name = this.MessageName;
            entity.entityattributes = this.EntityAttributes;

            return entity;
        }
    }
}
```

SdkAssociationDependency is provided with a message name, but ultimately needs to map the human-readable name to the internal CRM SDK message ID. It creates the *Lookup* and populates the *name* property, but assumes that the caller will look up the ID if needed. *SdkAssociationDependency* also can assign a value to the *entityattributes* attribute. This is used for the *Update* message so that the workflow is only executed if the specified attributes are modified.

Next up is the *LocalParameterDependency* class, which you can use to add local parameters to the workflow definition. We used these in our first declarative workflow sample to create the *TaskEntity* and *TaskCount* parameters. Listing 12-14 shows the source code for the *LocalParameterDependency* class.

LISTING 12-14 The *LocalParameterDependency* class

```
using System;
using System.Xml.Serialization;
using Microsoft.Crm.Sdk;
using Microsoft.Crm.SdkTypeProxy;

namespace ProgrammingWithDynamicsCrm4.WorkflowManager.Configuration
{
    public class LocalParameterDependency : WorkflowDependency
    {
        public LocalParameterDependency()
        {

        }

        public LocalParameterDependency(workflowdependency dependency)
        {
            this.ParameterName = dependency.parametername;
            this.ParameterType = dependency.parametertype;
        }

        [XmlAttribute]
        public string ParameterName { get; set; }

        [XmlAttribute]
        public string ParameterType { get; set; }

        public override workflowdependency ToEntity(Guid workflowId)
        {
            workflowdependency entity = base.ToEntity(workflowId);
            entity.type = new Picklist(WorkflowDependencyType.LocalParameter);
            entity.parametername = this.ParameterName;
            entity.parametertype = this.ParameterType;
            return entity;
        }
    }
}
```

The only unique aspect of *LocalParameterDependency* is the *ParameterType* property, which you use to specify the .NET type for the parameter. The name should include the namespace, but exclude the assembly information. You can find the full list of supported types in the CRM SDK under the topic "Supported Types for Workflow."

The remaining workflow dependency configuration classes are similar to each other because they are all related to entity images of one form or another. Therefore they have an additional abstract class they inherit from that implements the common functionality they share. *EntityImageDependency* is the base class that provides population of the *parametername* and *entityattributes* attributes on the *workflowdependency*. This class is shown in Listing 12-15.

LISTING 12-15 The *EntityImageDependency* class

```
using System;
using System.Xml.Serialization;
using Microsoft.Crm.SdkTypeProxy;
namespace ProgrammingWithDynamicsCrm4.WorkflowManager.Configuration
{
    public abstract class EntityImageDependency : WorkflowDependency
    {
        public EntityImageDependency()
        {
        }

        public EntityImageDependency(workflowdependency dependency)
        {
            this.ParameterName = dependency.parametername;
            this.EntityAttributes = dependency.entityattributes;
        }

        [XmlAttribute]
        public string ParameterName { get; set; }

        [XmlAttribute]
        public string EntityAttributes { get; set; }

        public override workflowdependency ToEntity(Guid workflowId)
        {
            workflowdependency entity = base.ToEntity(workflowId);
            entity.parametername = this.ParameterName;
            entity.entityattributes = this.EntityAttributes;
            return entity;
        }
    }
}
```

All of the entity image dependencies need to specify a local parameter name that will be populated with the entity image. This parameter is always of type *DynamicEntity*. The attributes that should be included in the image are also handled by the *EntityImageDependency* base class.

The first and most commonly used entity image dependency is *PrimaryEntityImageDependency*. By adding this dependency to your workflow you can request which attributes from the workflow's primary entity should be populated on the *CrmWorkflow*'s

PrimaryEntity property. You'll frequently want to access attributes off of the primary entity, and your workflow can run faster if you register a dependency for those attributes instead of retrieving them during execution yourself. Listing 12-16 shows the full source code for *PrimaryEntityImageDependency*.

LISTING 12-16 The *PrimaryEntityImageDependency* class

```
using System;
using Microsoft.Crm.Sdk;
using Microsoft.Crm.SdkTypeProxy;

namespace ProgrammingWithDynamicsCrm4.WorkflowManager.Configuration
{
    public class PrimaryEntityImageDependency : EntityImageDependency
    {
        public PrimaryEntityImageDependency()
        {

        }

        public PrimaryEntityImageDependency(workflowdependency dependency)
            : base(dependency)
        {

        }

        public override workflowdependency ToEntity(Guid workflowId)
        {
            workflowdependency entity = base.ToEntity(workflowId);
            entity.type = new Picklist(WorkflowDependencyType.PrimaryEntityImage);
            return entity;
        }
    }
}
```

PrimaryEntityImageDependency has almost everything done by its base class. It is only responsible for setting the appropriate *WorkflowDependencyType* value.

The next two dependency configuration classes are very similar to *PrimaryEntityImage-Dependency*. You can use *PrimaryEntityPreImageDependency* and *PrimaryEntityPostImage-Dependency* to request images of the primary entity as it existed before the core operation is performed and after it is completed. Because these two classes are so similar to each other and to the previous example, they are both included in Listing 12-17.

LISTING 12-17 The *PrimaryEntityPreImageDependency* and *PrimaryEntityPostImageDependency* classes

```
using System;
using Microsoft.Crm.Sdk;
using Microsoft.Crm.SdkTypeProxy;

namespace ProgrammingWithDynamicsCrm4.WorkflowManager.Configuration
{
    public class PrimaryEntityPreImageDependency : EntityImageDependency
    {
        public PrimaryEntityPreImageDependency()
        {

        }

        public PrimaryEntityPreImageDependency(workflowdependency dependency)
            : base(dependency)
        {

        }

        public override workflowdependency ToEntity(Guid workflowId)
        {
            workflowdependency entity = base.ToEntity(workflowId);
            entity.type = new
                Picklist(WorkflowDependencyType.PrimaryEntityPreImage);
            return entity;
        }
    }

    public class PrimaryEntityPostImageDependency : EntityImageDependency
    {
        public PrimaryEntityPostImageDependency()
        {

        }

        public PrimaryEntityPostImageDependency(workflowdependency dependency)
            : base(dependency)
        {

        }

        public override workflowdependency ToEntity(Guid workflowId)
        {
            workflowdependency entity = base.ToEntity(workflowId);
            entity.type = new
                Picklist(WorkflowDependencyType.PrimaryEntityPostImage);
            return entity;
        }
    }
}
```

The last of the entity image dependency classes is slightly different. You use *RelatedEntityImageDependency* to specify that your workflow would like an image of an entity directly related to the workflow's primary entity. This is useful when you need access to the attributes on the related entity. For example, if you want to generate an e-mail message when a case is open too long, you can use a *RelatedEntityImageDependency* in your configuration file to get the e-mail address of the case's owner. Listing 12-18 shows the full source code for the *RelatedEntityImageDependency* class.

LISTING 12-18 The *RelatedEntityImageDependency* class

```
using System;
using System.Xml.Serialization;
using Microsoft.Crm.Sdk;
using Microsoft.Crm.SdkTypeProxy;

namespace ProgrammingWithDynamicsCrm4.WorkflowManager.Configuration
{
    public class RelatedEntityImageDependency : EntityImageDependency
    {
        public RelatedEntityImageDependency()
        {

        }

        public RelatedEntityImageDependency(workflowdependency dependency)
            : base(dependency)
        {
            this.RelatedEntityName = dependency.relatedentityname;
            this.RelatedAttributeName = dependency.relatedattributename;
        }

        [XmlAttribute]
        public string RelatedEntityName { get; set; }

        [XmlAttribute]
        public string RelatedAttributeName { get; set; }

        public override workflowdependency ToEntity(Guid workflowId)
        {
            workflowdependency entity = base.ToEntity(workflowId);
            entity.type = new Picklist(WorkflowDependencyType.RelatedEntityImage);
            entity.relatedentityname = this.RelatedEntityName;
            entity.relatedattributename = this.RelatedAttributeName;
            return entity;
        }
    }
}
```

RelatedEntityImageDependency has two additional attributes beyond the other *EntityImageDependency*-derived classes. *RelatedAttributeName* is the name of the *Lookup* attribute on the primary entity that references the related entity. *RelatedEntityName* is the name of the related entity type. The name of the local parameter that is populated—as well as which attributes are included in the image—are handled by the base *EntityImageDependency* class.

Workflow dependencies are fairly advanced and not well-documented in the CRM SDK. Although the approach used in ProgrammingWithDynamicsCrm4.WorkflowManager uses many classes to accomplish workflow dependency management, none of them is very complicated and the end result is a very user-friendly configuration file. Now that you have an understanding of declarative workflow deployment, you can use the concepts described in this section to implement your own deployment tools that may be more streamlined for your environment.

Examining Native Workflow XAML

You may find yourself trying to emulate a workflow that you created in the native CRM workflow designer in a declarative workflow. The natively designed workflows still generate XAML behind the scenes during publication, and you can retrieve the XAML and inspect it when you need some inspiration for your own declarative workflows.

ProgrammingWithDynamicsCrm4.WorkflowManager has a feature that allows workflows to be exported as XAML even if they were originally created in the native designer. We'll demonstrate this by exporting the Dependency Test workflow created earlier in this chapter and adding it to the sample workflow project we created.

Adding a natively designed workflow to a declarative workflow project

1. Start ProgrammingWithDynamicsCrm4.WorkflowManager and connect to your CRM server as described earlier in the chapter.
2. Select the Dependency Test workflow from the list and click the Export toolbar button.

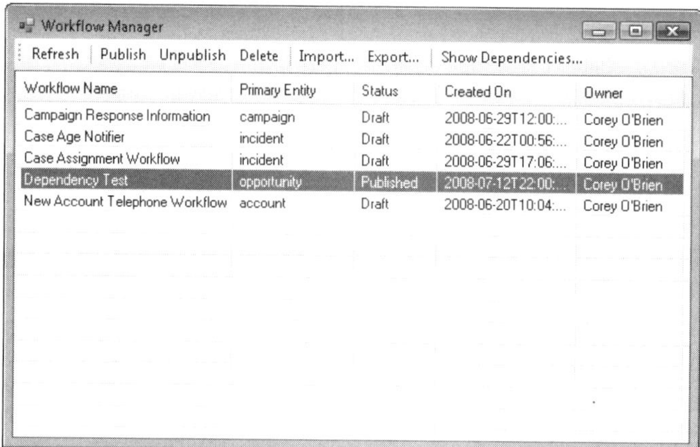

3. In the Browse For Folder dialog box, navigate to your SampleWorkflowProject folder that contains the NewLeadFollowUp.xoml file and click OK.
4. Close the ProgrammingWithDynamicsCrm4.WorkflowManager.
5. Launch Visual Studio .NET and open the SampleWorkflowProject you created earlier.
6. Right-click SampleWorkflowProject within Solution Explorer and select Add > Existing Item.
7. In your project folder you should see the recently exported files DependencyTest.xoml, DependencyTest.rules, and DependencyTest.config. Select them all and click Add.
8. At this point if you open the DependencyTest.xoml file in Visual Studio .NET you will see a workflow like the one shown here:

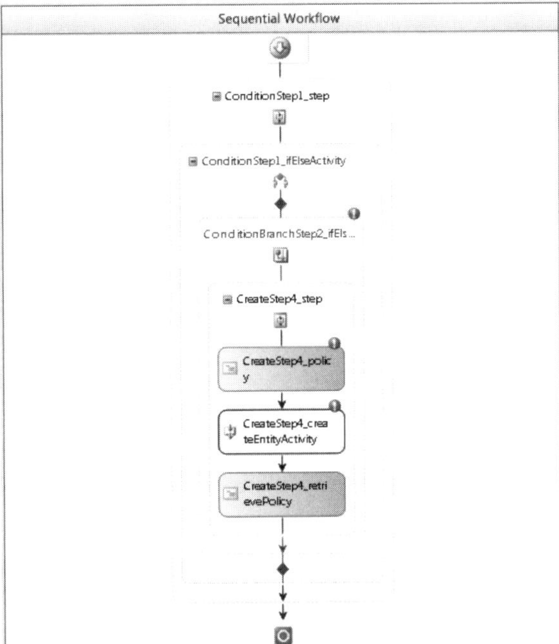

The workflow designer indicates errors within the rules. This is because the local parameters that are normally created on the fly during workflow compilation do not exist in our declarative workflow. To get rid of the errors in the workflow designer we need to add a code-behind file to define the local parameters.

9. Right-click SampleWorkflowProject in Solution Explorer and select Add > Class.
10. Type in the name **DependencyTest.xoml.cs** and click Add.

11. Update the contents of DependencyTest.xoml.cs to match the following code:

```
using System;
using System.Collections.Generic;
using System.Text;
using Microsoft.Crm.Workflow;
using Microsoft.Crm.Sdk;

namespace SampleWorkflowProject
{
  public partial class DependencyTest: CrmWorkflow
  {
        public DynamicEntity primaryEntity { get; set; }
        public DynamicEntity CreateStep4_localParameter { get; set; }
        public DynamicEntity PreImageParameter { get; set; }
  }
}
```

12. Determine the names of the properties you need by looking at the DependencyTest.config file and using the *ParameterName* attributes off of the *LocalParameterDependency*, *PrimaryEntityImageDependency*, *PrimaryEntityPreImageDependency*, *PrimaryEntity-PostImageDependency*, and *RelatedEntityImageDependency* elements.

13. Next, update the .xoml file to reference the code-behind file. Right-click DependencyTest.xoml in Solution Explorer and select Open With.

14. Select XML Editor from the list and click OK. If you already have DependencyTest.xoml open in the workflow designer, you may receive a warning asking if you want to close it. If that happens click Yes and continue.

15. In the root element in DependencyTest.xoml, find the *x:Name* attribute and add **x:Class="SampleWorkflowProject.DependencyTest"** directly after it. This ties the declarative workflow definition to the code-behind class.

16. Close the DependencyTest.xoml file in the XML Editor and then double-click it in Solution Explorer to open it in the workflow designer. The workflow definition now contains no errors and you can inspect the native workflow designer's version of a declarative workflow.

Exporting Workflows Programmatically

The code that allows ProgrammingWithDynamicsCrm4.WorkflowManager to export the XAML behind CRM's workflows uses all of the same classes that we reviewed during our examination of the import process. However, a few unique methods are worth taking a look at.

The main method, *ExportWorkflow*, is found in the *WorkflowLogic* class. Listing 12-19 displays the contents of this method.

LISTING 12-19 *WorkflowLogic's ExportWorkflow* method

```
public void ExportWorkflow(Guid workflowId, string exportFolder)
{
    ColumnSet cols = new ColumnSet();
    cols.AddColumns(
        "name",
        "description",
        "primaryentity",
        "activities",
        "rules",
        "plugintypeid");

    workflow workflow = (workflow)this.CrmService.Retrieve(
        "workflow", workflowId, cols);

    String configFileName = Path.Combine(exportFolder, String.Concat(
        Regex.Replace(workflow.name, "[^a-zA-Z0-9]", ""),
        ".config"));

    WorkflowConfiguration config = new WorkflowConfiguration();
    config.Name = workflow.name;
    config.Description = workflow.description;
    config.PrimaryEntity = workflow.primaryentity.Value;

    File.WriteAllText(
        Path.ChangeExtension(configFileName, ".xoml"), workflow.activities,
        Encoding.Unicode);

    if (!String.IsNullOrEmpty(workflow.rules))
    {
        File.WriteAllText(
            Path.ChangeExtension(configFileName, ".rules"), workflow.rules,
            Encoding.Unicode);
    }

    IEnumerable<workflowdependency> dependencies =
        this.RetrieveWorkflowDependencies(workflowId,
        "type",
        "parametername",
        "parametertype",
        "relatedentityname",
        "relatedattributename",
        "sdkmessageid",
        "entityattributes",
        "customentityname",
        "dependententityname",
        "dependentattributename");

    List<WorkflowDependency> configDependencies = new List<WorkflowDependency>();
    foreach (workflowdependency dependency in dependencies)
    {
        WorkflowDependency configDependency =
```

```
                WorkflowDependency.FromEntity(dependency);

            if (configDependency != null)
            {
                configDependencies.Add(configDependency);
            }
        }

        config.Dependencies = configDependencies.ToArray();
        config.Save(configFileName);
    }
```

ExportWorkflow starts by retrieving the workflow with all of the required attributes. It then strips out all non-alphanumeric characters from the workflow name to use as a base name for the three files that will be created. Next, the method creates an instance of *WorkflowConfiguration* and populates its properties using values from the retrieved *workflow*. After this, the activities (.xoml) and rules files are written from the appropriate attributes on the *workflow*.

The next section of *ExportWorkflow* retrieves the *workflowdependency* entities associated with the *workflow* and uses the static *WorkflowDependency FromEntity* method to convert them into their *WorkflowDependency*-derived counterparts. All of these dependencies are passed in to the original *WorkflowConfiguration* object and the *Save* method is called, which is responsible for generating the .config file.

The *Save* method is quite simple, thanks to the *XmlSerializer* class. Listing 12-20 shows the *Save* method using the *XmlSerializer* to generate an XML file based on a *WorkflowConfiguration* instance.

LISTING 12-20 *WorkflowConfiguration's Save* method

```
public void Save(string configFileName)
{
    XmlSerializer xmlSerializer = new XmlSerializer(typeof(WorkflowConfiguration));
    using (Stream file = File.Create(configFileName))
    {
        xmlSerializer.Serialize(file, this);
    }
}
```

The *WorkflowDependency FromEntity* method is a straightforward class factory that creates the appropriate instance of a *WorkflowDependency*-derived class. Listing 12-21 demonstrates how this is accomplished.

LISTING 12-21 *WorkflowDependency's FromEntity* method

```
public static WorkflowDependency FromEntity(workflowdependency dependency)
{
    switch (dependency.type.Value)
    {
        case WorkflowDependencyType.SdkAssociation:
            return new SdkAssociationDependency(dependency);

        case WorkflowDependencyType.PrimaryEntityImage:
            return new PrimaryEntityImageDependency(dependency);

        case WorkflowDependencyType.PrimaryEntityPreImage:
            return new PrimaryEntityPreImageDependency(dependency);

        case WorkflowDependencyType.PrimaryEntityPostImage:
            return new PrimaryEntityPostImageDependency(dependency);

        case WorkflowDependencyType.RelatedEntityImage:
            return new RelatedEntityImageDependency(dependency);

        case WorkflowDependencyType.LocalParameter:
            return new LocalParameterDependency(dependency);

        case WorkflowDependencyType.CustomEntityDefinition:
            return new CustomEntityDefinitionDependency(dependency);

        case WorkflowDependencyType.AttributeDefinition:
            return new AttributeDefinitionDependency(dependency);

        default:
            return null;
    }
}
```

FromEntity uses the *type* attribute off the passed-in *workflowdependency* to determine which derived class to create. It uses the overloaded version of the constructor that takes a *workflowdependency* as an argument so that the derived class can populate its properties appropriately.

If at any point you need inspiration regarding how to re-create something in a declarative workflow that you know how to do in CRM's native workflow designer, you can use the export functionality in ProgrammingWithDynamicsCrm4.WorkflowManager to export the workflow and then inspect the dependencies and declarative workflow definition generated by CRM.

Summary

We started this chapter by digging into the entities behind workflow support within Microsoft Dynamics CRM. We then looked at the various types of workflow dependencies and how they can affect when workflows are executed as well as what data they receive during execution. Next, we explored declarative workflows and XAML. After creating our first declarative workflow and deploying it, we wrapped up by looking at the deployment process for declarative workflows.

Chapter 13

Emulating User Interface with ASP.NET Development

Throughout this book, we explained various ways in which you can programmatically interact with Microsoft Dynamics CRM in areas such as creating plug-ins, leveraging custom workflow assemblies, and manipulating the metadata API. These tools provide great options for you to implement your own custom business logic and processes within Microsoft Dynamics CRM.

However, you will probably encounter business requirements and scenarios for which you want to extend Microsoft Dynamics CRM beyond the tools we've explained so far. Some examples might include:

- Creating a custom dashboard
- Adding buttons and dialog boxes that users can access
- Using a custom form layout for an entity
- Adding entirely new Web pages to the user interface

Fortunately, Microsoft Dynamics CRM allows you to create your own custom Web pages that you can embed in the user interface to accomplish these types of customizations. If you create these custom Web pages and style them to appear like the Microsoft Dynamics CRM Web pages, they will blend seamlessly with the user interface, and your users might not even realize they are working with a custom Web page!

This chapter offers examples of extending Microsoft Dynamics CRM using the following techniques:

- ASP.NET page for an IFrame
- ASP.NET page for a dialog box
- ASP.NET page for a stand-alone page added to the Microsoft Dynamics CRM navigational features

Further, we will explain how to style these pages properly so that they mimic the native Microsoft Dynamics CRM Web pages.

Note Chapter 9, "Deployment," discusses deploying custom ASP.NET pages to the server under the ISV folder in Microsoft CRM's root folder. All of the examples in this chapter follow this deployment model.

IFrame Development

You can use the Microsoft Dynamics CRM form editor to modify the layout of a form by adding fields, moving tabs, removing sections, and so on. However, the form editor does restrict your layout customization options because you can only use data fields from the entity, and you can only select from the predefined form layouts.

However, Microsoft Dynamics CRM also allows you to embed Inline Frames (IFrames) in your entity forms. This IFrame functionality opens up an almost unlimited world of customization options because you can display any Web page you want. For example, you can use IFrames to display pages such as the following:

- Commercial Web sites
- Web pages from a Microsoft SharePoint site
- Custom Web pages that you create
- Web pages from an alternative application

In this section we focus on displaying custom application pages within an IFrame on an entity form.

More Info You might remember from Chapter 10, "Developing Offline Solutions," that we created a simple IFrame to display Contact information on the Account Form.

When you add an IFrame to a form, you have the option to choose the check box Pass Record Object-Type Code And Unique Identifier As Parameters. When you select this check box, Microsoft Dynamics CRM automatically appends query string parameters to the specified IFrame URL. By appending this information to the query string, your custom Web pages can read the parameters and then use those parameters to display information relevant to the specific record that the user has open. Table 13-1 lists all of the parameters that are passed to your custom IFrame page.

TABLE 13-1 IFrame Query String Parameters

Name	Description
Typename	The schema name of the entity. For example, this value would be *account* for the Account entity.
Type	The entity type code, which is an integer that can be used to identify the entity.
Id	The *Guid* of the entity record.
OrgName	The organization name.
UserLCID	The language code of the currently logged-on user.
OrgLCID	The language code of the base language set for the organization.

Warning When your custom code reads the query string parameters, we recommend that you use the *typename* parameter to identify an entity. The *typename* value stays the same across Microsoft Dynamics CRM environments. The *type* parameter's value differs across environments for custom entities, so if you use the entity type codes anywhere in your code, be sure to not hard-code them for custom entities.

The IFrame example that we created in Chapter 10 was a simple read-only display. In this section we will create an IFrame that actually writes data back to Microsoft Dynamics CRM.

Programming the IFrame

As we mentioned earlier, one constraint of the entity form editor is that you can only display attributes from the entity. You cannot display attributes from related entities (such as displaying account fields on a contact form). However, sometimes your users might want the entity form to display these types of related values. Fortunately, you can take advantage of the IFrame feature to enable this type of functionality.

In this section we create an IFrame on the Opportunity entity that allows an end user to update address information on the Opportunity's selected Potential Customer without actually opening the Potential Customer record. Customizations like this can speed up data entry because they eliminate the need to open multiple windows to edit data on other entities.

Note This example assumes that once an Opportunity record is created, the end users cannot update the Potential Customer field. This can be done by adding script to the Opportunity form's *onload* event. See Chapter 7, "Form Scripting," for more information on adding this type of script.

Before we start the development, let's create a new Microsoft Visual Studio project.

Creating the Chapter 13 project in Visual Studio 2008

1. Open Visual Studio 2008.
2. On the File Menu, select New and then click Project.
3. In the New Project dialog box, select the Visual C# Web type and then select the ASP.NET Web Application template.
4. Type **Chapter13** in the Name box, and then click OK.
5. Right-click the Chapter13 project in Solution Explorer, and select Add Reference.
6. Browse to the location of the Microsoft.Crm.Sdk.dll and Microsoft.Crm.SdkTypeProxy.dll assemblies, select these two assemblies, and then click OK.

We will also need to add a utilities assembly to handle some common tasks. This ProgrammingWithDynamicsCrm4.Utilities.dll assembly can be obtained by compiling the ProgrammingWithDynamicsCrm4.Utilities project included in the source code for this book.

7. Right-click the Chapter 13 project in Solution Explorer, and select Add Reference.
8. Browse to the location of the ProgrammingWithDynamicsCrm4.Utilities.dll assembly, select it, and then click OK.

Now we will create a style sheet to use with our entity IFrames so that they blend in with the native Microsoft Dynamics CRM entity forms.

Adding the Styles folder and the IFrame.css file

1. Right-click the Chapter13 project in Solution Explorer, select Add, and then click New Folder.
2. Type **Styles** as the name of the new folder.
3. Right-click the Styles folder, select Add, and then click New Item.
4. Select the Style Sheet template and type **IFrame.css** in the Name box. Click Add.

Listing 13-1 contains the source code for the IFrame.css style sheet. This style sheet will be referenced from our IFrame page. Table 13-2 lists all of the styles along with a description of their use.

LISTING 13-1 IFrame.css

```
BODY
{
    background-color: #EAF3FF;
    font-family: Tahoma;
    margin: 0px;
    border: 0px;
}
INPUT
{
    background-color: White;
    border: 1px solid #6699CC;
    width: 100%;
    height: 19px;
    font-size: 11px;
}

TD
{
    font-size: 11px;
    height: 27px;
}
```

```
TABLE.IFrame
{
    width: 100%;
    table-layout: fixed;
}

DIV.warning
{
    background-color: #FFFFAE;
    height: 26px;
    border: 1px solid #C5C5C5;
    font-size: 11px;
}
```

TABLE 13-2 IFrame.css Styles

Name	Description
BODY	Sets the borders and margins of the body to zero. It also sets the background color and font family for the page.
INPUT	Styles HTML input controls to look like the input controls used on the Microsoft Dynamics CRM entity forms.
TD	Sets the table cell height and font size used in the cell.
TABLE.Iframe	Sets the width to expand the length of the window and gives the table a fixed layout.
DIV.warning	Styles a *DIV* tag to look like a Microsoft Dynamics CRM alert banner.

Tip You can find all of the styles (colors, sizes, dimensions, and so on) in the Microsoft Dynamics CRM UI Style Guide that comes included in the Microsoft Dynamics CRM SDK.

We will now create the ASP.NET Web Form to use as our IFrame page.

Adding the PotentialCustomerInfo.aspx page

1. Right-click the Chapter13 project in Solution Explorer, select Add, and then click New Item.
2. On the Add New Item dialog box, select the Web Form template.
3. Enter **PotentialCustomerInfo.aspx** into the Name field and click Add.

Your project should now contain two new files, PotentialCustomerInfo.aspx and PotentialCustomerInfo.aspx.cs. Listings 13-2 and 13-3 contain the source code for the Web Form and its code-behind file respectively.

LISTING 13-2 PotentialCustomerInfo.aspx

```
<%@ Page Language="C#"
        AutoEventWireup="true"
        CodeBehind="PotentialCustomerInfo.aspx.cs"
        Inherits="Chapter13.PotentialCustomerInfo" %>

<html>
<head runat="server">
    <title>Untitled Page</title>
    <link href="Styles/IFrame.css" rel="Stylesheet" type="text/css" />
</head>
<body>
    <form id="form1" runat="server">
    <div id="warning" visible="false" class="warning" runat="server">
       The record must be saved before you can update customer information.
    </div>
    <div id="main" runat="server">
        <table cellspacing="1" cellpadding="0" border="0" class="IFrame">
            <colgroup>
                <col style="width: 111px;" />
                <col />
                <col style="width: 115px; padding-left: 23px;" />
                <col />
            </colgroup>
            <tr>
                <td>
                    Street 1
                </td>
                <td>
                    <input type="text" id="street1" runat="server" />
                </td>
                <td>
                    State/Province
                </td>
                <td>
                    <input type="text" id="state" runat="server" />
                </td>
            </tr>
            <tr>
                <td>
                    Street 2
                </td>
                <td>
                    <input type="text" id="street2" runat="server" />
                </td>
                <td>
                    Zip/Postal Code
                </td>
                <td>
                    <input type="text" id="zip" runat="server" />
                </td>
            </tr>
            <tr>
```

```
                <td>
                    City
                </td>
                <td>
                    <input type="text" id="city" runat="server" />
                </td>
                <td>
                    Country
                </td>
                <td>
                    <input type="text" id="country" runat="server" />
                </td>
            </tr>
        </table>
    </div>
    </form>
</body>
</html>
```

Notice the reference to our IFrame.css file at the top of the PotentialCustomerInfo.aspx page. We divided the form into two sections. The first section is the *div* tag with an *id* of "warning". The "warning" *div* is used to send an alert message to the user. It defaults to invisible. (We will discuss when this *div* becomes visible later on in this section.) The second section of the page is the *div* tag with an *id* of "main". This second *div* contains a table with all of our address input fields.

LISTING 13-3 PotentialCustomerInfo.aspx.cs

```
using System;
using System.Collections;
using System.Configuration;
using System.Data;
using System.Web;
using System.Web.Security;
using System.Web.UI;
using System.Web.UI.HtmlControls;
using System.Web.UI.WebControls;
using System.Web.UI.WebControls.WebParts;
using Microsoft.Crm.SdkTypeProxy;
using Microsoft.Crm.Sdk.Query;
using Microsoft.Crm.Sdk;
using ProgrammingWithDynamicsCrm4.Utilities;

namespace Chapter13
{
    public partial class PotentialCustomerInfo : System.Web.UI.Page
    {

        private string _opportunityId;
        private string _orgName;
```

```
protected override void OnInit(EventArgs e)
{
    _opportunityId = Request.QueryString["id"];
    _orgName = Request.QueryString["orgname"];

    base.OnInit(e);
}


protected void Page_Load(object sender, EventArgs e)
{
    if (IsPostBack)
    {
        using (new CrmImpersonator())
        {
            CrmService crmService =
CrmServiceUtility.GetCrmService(CrmServiceUtility.GetServerURLFromRegistry(),
                                _orgName);

            ColumnSet opportunityColumns = new ColumnSet();
            opportunityColumns.AddColumn("customerid");

            opportunity crmOpportunity =
          (opportunity)crmService.Retrieve(EntityName.opportunity.ToString(),
                                    new Guid(_opportunityId),
                                    opportunityColumns);

            if (crmOpportunity.customerid != null)
            {
                DynamicEntity entity = new DynamicEntity();
                entity.Name = crmOpportunity.customerid.type;

                KeyProperty entityIdProp = new KeyProperty();
                entityIdProp.Name = string.Format("{0}id",
                                        crmOpportunity.customerid.type);
                entityIdProp.Value =
                                new Key(crmOpportunity.customerid.Value);

                entity.Properties.Add(entityIdProp);

                StringProperty addressLine1Prop = new StringProperty();
                addressLine1Prop.Name = "address1_line1";
                addressLine1Prop.Value = this.street1.Value;

                entity.Properties.Add(addressLine1Prop);

                StringProperty addressLine2Prop = new StringProperty();
                addressLine2Prop.Name = "address1_line2";
                addressLine2Prop.Value = this.street2.Value;

                entity.Properties.Add(addressLine2Prop);
```

```
                    StringProperty cityProp = new StringProperty();
                    cityProp.Name = "address1_city";
                    cityProp.Value = this.city.Value;

                    entity.Properties.Add(cityProp);

                    StringProperty stateProp = new StringProperty();
                    stateProp.Name = "address1_stateorprovince";
                    stateProp.Value = this.state.Value;

                    entity.Properties.Add(stateProp);

                    StringProperty zipProp = new StringProperty();
                    zipProp.Name = "address1_postalcode";
                    zipProp.Value = this.zip.Value;

                    entity.Properties.Add(zipProp);

                    StringProperty countryProp = new StringProperty();
                    countryProp.Name = "address1_country";
                    countryProp.Value = this.country.Value;

                    entity.Properties.Add(countryProp);

                    crmService.Update(entity);
                }
            }
        }
    }

    protected override void OnPreRender(EventArgs e)
    {
        if (!string.IsNullOrEmpty(_opportunityId))
        {
            using (new CrmImpersonator())
            {
                CrmService crmService =
CrmServiceUtility.GetCrmService(CrmServiceUtility.GetServerURLFromRegistry(),
                                  _orgName);

                ColumnSet opportunityColumns = new ColumnSet();
                opportunityColumns.AddColumn("customerid");

                opportunity crmOpportunity =
             (opportunity)crmService.Retrieve(EntityName.opportunity.ToString(),
                                              new Guid(_opportunityId),
                                              opportunityColumns);

                if (crmOpportunity.customerid != null)
                {
                    TargetRetrieveDynamic targetRetrieve =
                                              new TargetRetrieveDynamic();
                    targetRetrieve.EntityName = crmOpportunity.customerid.type;
                    targetRetrieve.EntityId = crmOpportunity.customerid.Value;
```

```
                        ColumnSet customerColumns = new ColumnSet();
                        customerColumns.AddColumns("address1_line1",
                                                   "address1_line2",
                                                   "address1_city",
                                                   "address1_stateorprovince",
                                                   "address1_postalcode",
                                                   "address1_country");

                        RetrieveRequest retrieve = new RetrieveRequest();
                        retrieve.Target = targetRetrieve;
                        retrieve.ColumnSet = customerColumns;
                        retrieve.ReturnDynamicEntities = true;

                        RetrieveResponse retrieved =
                                   (RetrieveResponse)crmService.Execute(retrieve);

                        DynamicEntity entity =
                                         (DynamicEntity)retrieved.BusinessEntity;

                        if (entity.Properties.Contains("address1_line1"))
                            this.street1.Value =
                                   entity.Properties["address1_line1"].ToString();
                        if (entity.Properties.Contains("address1_line2"))
                            this.street2.Value =
                                   entity.Properties["address1_line2"].ToString();
                        if (entity.Properties.Contains("address1_city"))
                            this.city.Value =
                                    entity.Properties["address1_city"].ToString();
                        if (entity.Properties.Contains("address1_stateorprovince"))
                            this.state.Value =
                           entity.Properties["address1_stateorprovince"].ToString();
                        if (entity.Properties.Contains("address1_postalcode"))
                            this.zip.Value =
                                entity.Properties["address1_postalcode"].ToString();
                        if (entity.Properties.Contains("address1_country"))
                            this.country.Value =
                                 entity.Properties["address1_country"].ToString();
                    }
                }
            }
            else
            {
                this.warning.Visible = true;
                this.main.Visible = false;
            }

            base.OnPreRender(e);
        }
    }
}
```

The first thing we do in the code-behind is grab two query string parameters, *id* and *orgname*, that we need for our IFrame functionality. If the *id* parameter is empty, it means the Opportunity record has not been saved yet. Because we need the Opportunity record's *Guid* to retrieve information on the record, we display a message to the user stating that she must first save the record before she can update the customer information and hide the main form elements:

```
this.warning.Visible = true;
this.main.Visible = false;
```

Populating the Form

If the *id* parameter contains the *Guid* of the Opportunity record, we can then retrieve the *customerid* attribute. An Opportunity's customer can be an Account or a Contact. If you take a look at the *OnPreRender* method in Listing 13-3, you can see how we handle the retrieval of the customer information used to pre-populate our form. Because we don't know up front whether the Opportunity's customer is a Contact or Account, we use the *TargetRetrieveDynamic* class. This allows us to retrieve the entity instance as a *DynamicEntity*. We set the *EntityId* and *EntityName* properties of the *TargetRetrieveDynamic* class using the Opportunity's *customerid* attribute:

```
TargetRetrieveDynamic targetRetrieve = new TargetRetrieveDynamic();
targetRetrieve.EntityName = crmOpportunity.customerid.type;
targetRetrieve.EntityId = crmOpportunity.customerid.Value;
```

The *customerid* attribute is of type *customer*, which is a *Lookup* attribute that can contain either an Account or a Contact. The attribute has a property *type* that contains the schema name of the customer entity type and a property named *Value* that contains the entity instance's *Guid*. You can see from the preceding code snippet how we use these properties to set up our instance of *TargetRetrieveDynamic*.

Next we create an instance of the *RetrieveRequest* class and set its *Target* property to our instance of *TargetRetrieveDynamic*. Note that we set the *ReturnDynamicEntities* property to "true" on the *RetrieveRequest*:

```
retrieve.ReturnDynamicEntities = true;
```

Using the *AddColumns* method for the *ColumnSet*, we add the columns we would like returned, and then we can execute the request. The returned response contains a *BusinessEntity* which we then cast to a *DynamicEntity*. Now all we need to do is loop through our entity's *Properties* collection and populate our form elements.

Handling a Form Submit

Now that we have our form elements on the page and code to populate them, we need to write some code to handle updating these fields in the database. We could add a submit button to our IFrame page that would require the user to submit only the IFrame when they make changes, but one of our goals is to make this IFrame seamlessly integrate into our Opportunity form. Therefore, we will create the code so that the user only has to save the opportunity record, but that action will update both the opportunity and the related customer record. In the next section we will attach our form submit to the entity form's *onsave* event. The remainder of this section focuses on writing code to handle the save.

Again, we do not know if the entity being updated is an Account or a Contact, so we use a *DynamicEntity* and the Opportunity's *customerid* attribute to configure our entity for the save. Next, we simply add a property for each input control to the *DynamicEntity* instance's *Properties* collection and call the *CrmService* instance's *Update* method.

Deploying and Testing the IFrame

Now that the coding of our page is finished, we can deploy it to the server and run a test. We start by adding the IFrame to the Opportunity form.

Adding the IFrame to the Opportunity form

1. Open Microsoft Dynamics CRM in a Web browser and navigate to the Opportunity entity's form customizations screen.
2. Click Add A Tab on the Common Tasks menu.
3. Type **Potential Customer** in the Name box and click OK.
4. An IFrame must be housed in a section, so click Add A Section on the Common Tasks menu.
5. Type **Customer Information** in the Name field.
6. Select both the Show The Name Of This Section On The Form and the Show Divider Line Below The Section Name check boxes and verify that the Tab is set to our new Potential Customer tab. Click OK.

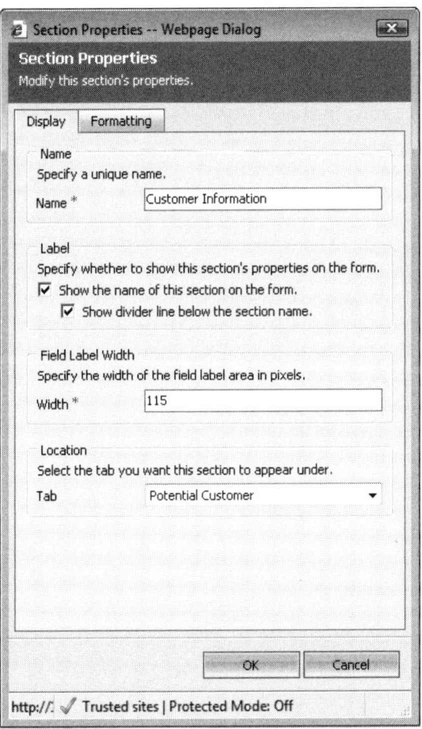

7. Select our new section and click Add An IFrame on the Common Tasks menu.
8. Type **potentialcustomerinfo** in the Name field.
9. Type **/ISV/Chapter13/PotentialCustomerInfo.aspx** in the URL field.
10. Select the Pass Record Object-Type Code And Unique Identifier As Parameters check box.
11. Clear the Restrict Cross-Frame Scripting check box.
12. Verify that Tab is set to Potential Customer and Section is set to Customer Information.

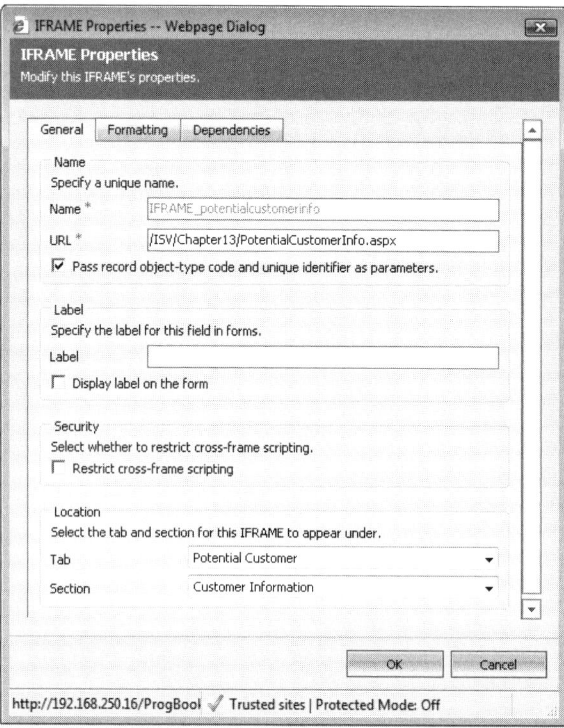

13. In the Formatting tab's Row Layout section, select the Automatically Expand To Use Available Space check box.
14. In the Formatting tab's Border section, clear the Display Border check box. This makes our IFrame integrate seamlessly into the form. Click OK.
15. Save the form and publish your customizations.

Next we need to copy our Style Sheet, Web Form, and assembly to the Microsoft Dynamics CRM server.

Deploying the Web files

1. Create a new folder named **Chapter13** under the ISV folder in the directory with your Microsoft Dynamics CRM Web files.
2. Compile the Chapter 13 project in Visual Studio.
3. Copy the PotentialCustomerInfo.aspx file into the newly created folder.
4. Copy the Styles folder from the Chapter13 project into the newly created folder.
5. Copy the Chapter13.dll and ProgrammingWithDynamicsCrm4.Utilities.dll assemblies into the Microsoft Dynamics CRM bin folder.

Finally, we need to add script to the Opportunity form's *onsave* event to trigger our IFrame page's form submit. Navigate to the Opportunity entity form customizations screen and click Form Properties. Make sure that the Event Is Enabled check box is selected and enter the following script into the *onsave* event. Save the form and publish the Opportunity customizations.

```
var crmFormTypeUpdate = 2;
var potentialCustomerIFrame = document.frames("IFRAME_potentialcustomerinfo");

if ( crmForm.FormType == crmFormTypeUpdate )
{
        if ( potentialCustomerIFrame != null && potentialCustomerIFrame.document != null
             && potentialCustomerIFrame.document.form1 != null )
        {
            potentialCustomerIFrame.document.form1.submit();
        }
}
```

Now we can test our IFrame. Navigate to the Opportunity grid in Microsoft Dynamics CRM and click the New button. If you click the Potential Customer tab you see a message alerting you that you must save the record before you can update the customer information (Figure 13-1).

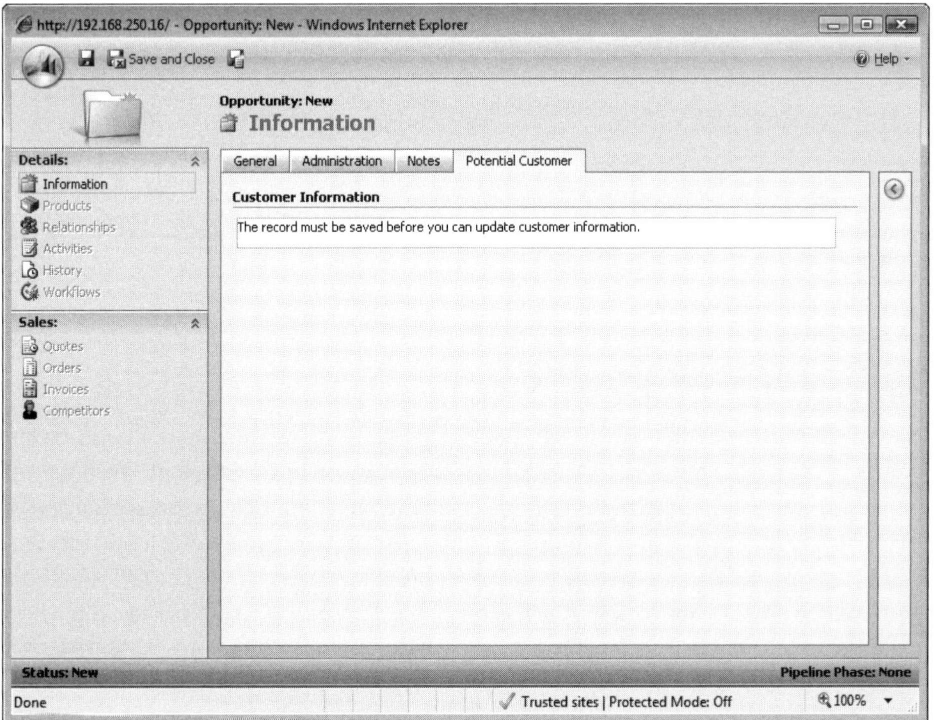

FIGURE 13-1 Potential Customer IFrame warning message

Populate the Opportunity's required fields and save the record. Now click the Potential Customer tab again. You can see the populated form with the selected customer's information (Figure 13-2). Now you can make changes to the main Opportunity form and the fields in the IFrame and click Save or Save And Close. Both the Opportunity and Customer fields are updated.

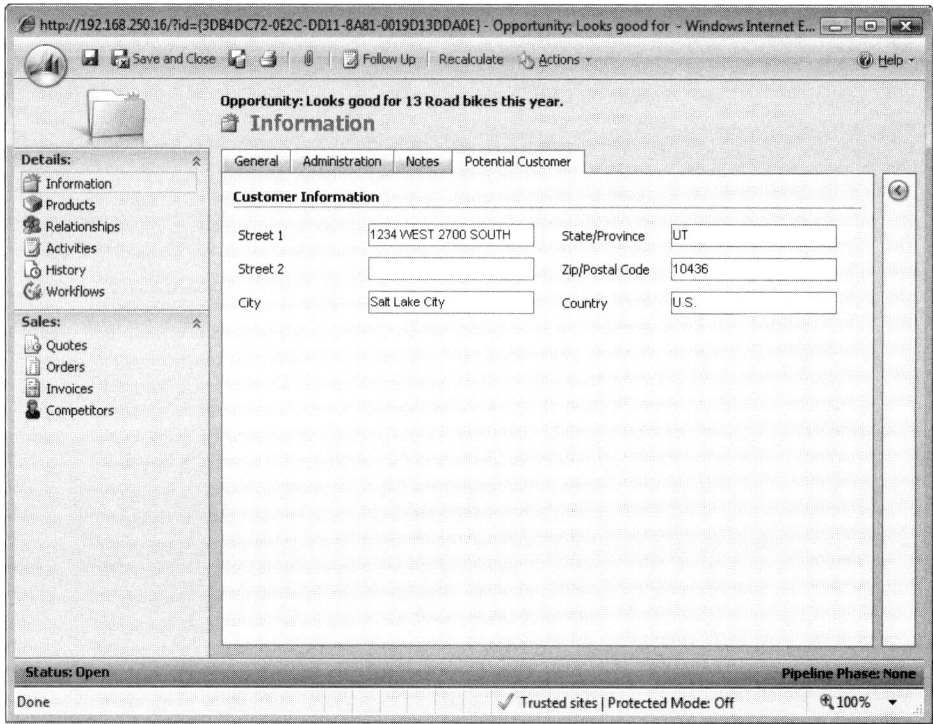

FIGURE 13-2 Potential Customer IFrame

Dialog Box Development

In addition to embedding a custom Web page within an IFrame, you can also create custom Web pages that users access by clicking a button in the grid or toolbar. From the user perspective, it will appear to them as if they launched a dialog box. In this section we will show you how to create a custom Web page that has the look and feel of a Microsoft Dynamics CRM dialog box. Like the IFrame page we created in the previous section, one of our goals is to make the dialog box look so much like a native Microsoft Dynamics CRM page (Figure 13-3) that the end user has no idea it is a custom page.

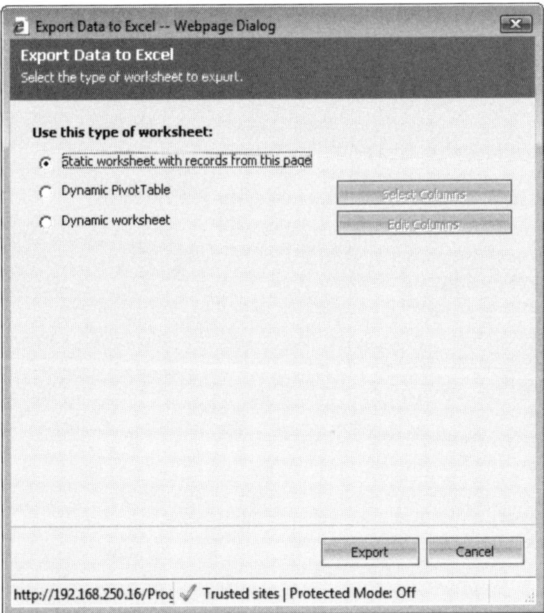

FIGURE 13-3 Native Microsoft Dynamics CRM dialog box

Programming the Dialog Box

We begin by creating a style sheet for our dialog boxes. This style sheet will allow our custom Web pages to match the style and formatting of the native Microsoft Dynamics CRM pages and dialogs. Listing 13-4 shows the source for this style sheet.

Important Even though you could technically reference the Microsoft Dynamics CRM style sheets directly, this would not be considered a supported or upgradeable customization. Create and reference your own style sheets.

Adding Styles folder and Dialog.css file

1. Our *BUTTON* style requires an image, so we need to add a new folder. Right-click the Chapter13 project in Solution Explorer, select Add, and click New Folder.
2. Type **Images** as the name of the new folder.
3. Right-click the Images folder, select Add, and click Existing Item.

Tip You can find images like the one we use as a background for our dialog buttons (btn_rest.gif) in the client\images folder that comes with the Microsoft Dynamics CRM SDK.

4. Navigate to the location of the Microsoft Dynamics CRM SDK files, open the client\images folder, and select the btn_rest.gif image file.
5. Click Add.
6. Right-click the Styles folder, select Add, and click New Item.
7. Select the Style Sheet template and type **Dialog.css** in the Name box.
8. Click Add.

LISTING 13-4 Dialog.css source code

```
HTML
{
    height: 100%;
    margin: 0;
    padding: 0;
    border: 0;
}

BODY
{
    background-color: #E3EFFF;
    margin: 0;
    padding: 0;
    border: 0;
    height: 100%;
    font-family: Tahoma;
    font-size: 11px;
}

DIV.DialogTitle
{
    font-family: Tahoma;
    font-size: 14px;
    font-weight: bold;
    color: #FFFFFF;
    padding-top: 4px;
    padding-right: 5px;
    padding-left: 5px;
}

DIV.DialogDescription
{
    font-family: Tahoma;
    font-size: 11px;
    color: #FFFFFF;
    padding-top: 4px;
    padding-right: 5px;
    padding-left: 5px;
}
```

```
DIV.DialogHeader
{
    position: absolute;
    top: 0;
    left: 0;
    background-color: #6693CF;
    width: 100%;
    height: 51px;
    border-bottom: 1px solid #6693CF;
}

DIV.DialogMain
{
    margin: 0px;
    padding-top: 30px;
    padding-left: 12px;
    position: absolute;
    top: 51px;
    bottom: 44px;
    width: 100%;
    border-bottom: 1px solid #A7CDF0;
}

DIV.DialogFooter
{
    position: absolute;
    bottom: 0;
    left: 0;
    height: 43px;
    width: 100%;
    border-top: 1px solid #ffffff;
}

DIV.Buttons
{
    text-align: right;
    vertical-align: middle;
    padding-top: 11px;
    padding-right: 12px;
}

BUTTON
{
    font-family: Tahoma;
    font-size: 11px;
    line-height: 18px;
    height: 22px;
    width: 84px;
    text-align: center;
    cursor: pointer;
    border: 1px #3366CC solid;
    background-color: #CEE7FF;
    background-image: url(Images/btn_rest.gif);
    background-repeat: repeat-x;
```

```
        border: 1px #3366CC solid;
        padding-left: 5px;
        padding-right: 5px;
    }

    .Spacer
    {
        padding-right: 3px;
    }
```

Table 13-3 contains the name of each style with a brief description of what it is used for.

TABLE 13-3 Dialog.css Styles

Name	Description
HTML	Sets the borders, margins, and padding of the page to zero.
BODY	Sets the borders, margins, and padding of the body to zero. Also, sets the height to 100 percent to ensure that the content fills the window. The background color and font size and type are also set here.
DIV.DialogTitle	Sets the font size, weight, and color for the dialog box's main title.
DIV.DialogDescription	Sets the font size, weight, and color for the description that appears right below the dialog title.
DIV.DialogHeader	Sets the background color and height of the dialog header and positions it at the top of the page. Also adds a thin border line to the bottom of the header *DIV*.
DIV.DialogMain	Positions the main content *DIV* of the dialog box to fit between the header and footer *DIV* tags. Also adds a thin border to the bottom of the main dialog *DIV*.
DIV.DialogFooter	Positions the footer *DIV* at the bottom of the window and sets its height. Also adds a thin border to the top of the *DIV*.
DIV.Buttons	Adds padding and alignment for the buttons added to the footer *DIV*.
BUTTON	Adds styles to make the buttons the same size and look as the standard Microsoft Dynamics CRM dialog buttons.
.Spacer	This style is used to add a three-pixel padding between HTML elements. It is most commonly used as a spacer between buttons.

Since you may want to create multiple dialog boxes in one project, the next thing to do is create an ASP.NET Master Page that defines our dialog box page structure. Listing 13-5 contains the source for our master page.

Adding the Dialog.Master master page

1. Right-click the Chapter 13 project in Solution Explorer, select Add, and click New Item.

2. Select the Master Page template and type **Dialog.Master** into the name box.

3. Click Add.

LISTING 13-5 Dialog.Master source code

```
    <%@ Master Language="C#"
           AutoEventWireup="true"
           CodeBehind="Dialog.master.cs"
           Inherits="Chapter13.Dialog" %>

<!DOCTYPE html PUBLIC "-//W3C//DTD XHTML 1.0 Transitional//EN"
                        "http://www.w3.org/TR/xhtml1/DTD/xhtml1-transitional.dtd">

<html>
<head id="Head1" runat="server">
<base target="_self" />
    <title>Untitled Page</title>

    <link rel="Stylesheet" href="Styles/Dialog.css" type="text/css" />

    <asp:ContentPlaceHolder ID="ScriptContent" runat="server" />

</head>
<body>
    <form id="DialogForm" runat="server">
    <div class="DialogHeader">
        <div class="DialogTitle">
            <asp:ContentPlaceHolder ID="DialogTitleContent" runat="server" />
        </div>
        <div class="DialogDescription">
            <asp:ContentPlaceHolder ID="DialogDescriptionContent" runat="server" />
        </div>
    </div>
    <div class="DialogMain">
        <asp:ContentPlaceHolder ID="MainContent" runat="server" />
    </div>
    <div class="DialogFooter">
        <div class="Buttons">
               <asp:ContentPlaceHolder ID="ButtonContent" runat="server" />
        </div>
    </div>
    </form>
</body>
</html>
```

Tip We will be opening this window as a dialog box, so the *base* tag was added to the *head* tag of the master page. Setting the *target* attribute of the *base* tag prevents the page from opening a second window on postback.

You can see that we divided our master page into three main sections: header, main content area, and footer. The header includes two subsections, one for the title and one for the description, and the footer has one subsection for buttons. Each section or subsection contains an ASP.NET *ContentPlaceHolder* control. We use these controls to add content to our dialog box at a later time in pages that implement our master page. Now that we have constructed a master page, setting up new dialog boxes that match the style and interface of Microsoft Dynamics CRM will be easy.

Now it's time to put our new master page to use. As a real-world example, we will add a button to the Activities grid that allows a user to mark a Task Activity as Completed or Canceled without actually opening the record. This saves the user from having to take the extra step and time to actually open each record in order to simply mark the record as Completed or Canceled. Our custom button will open a dialog box that gives the user a choice of completing or canceling the selected records. Now we will add a new Web form for our dialog. Listing 13-6 contains the source code for our new page.

Adding the CompleteActivity.aspx page

1. Right-click the Chapter13 project in Solution Explorer, select Add, and then click New Item.
2. On the Add New Item dialog, select the Web Form template.
3. Enter **CompleteActivity.aspx** into the Name field and click Add.

LISTING 13-6 CompleteActivity.aspx source code

```
<%@ Page Language="C#"
         MasterPageFile="Dialog.Master"
         AutoEventWireup="true"
         CodeBehind="CompleteActivity.aspx.cs"
         Inherits="Chapter13.CompleteActivity" %>

<asp:Content ID="Title"
             ContentPlaceHolderID="DialogTitleContent"
             runat="server">
    Complete Activity
</asp:Content>

<asp:Content ID="Description"
             ContentPlaceHolderID="DialogDescriptionContent"
             runat="server">
    Mark selected Activity as completed.
</asp:Content>

<asp:Content ID="Main"
             ContentPlaceHolderID="MainContent"
             runat="server">
        <input type="hidden" id="ActivityId" runat="server" />
```

```
        <asp:Label id="Message" runat="server" Visible="false" />

        <asp:label ID="StatusLabel" Text="Status" runat="server" />

        <asp:DropDownList ID="Status"
                          style="width: 85%; font-size: 11px;"
                          runat="server">
            <asp:ListItem Value="5" Text="Completed" />
            <asp:ListItem Value="6" Text="Canceled" />
        </asp:DropDownList>

</asp:Content>

<asp:Content ID="Buttons" ContentPlaceHolderID="ButtonContent" runat="server">
    <button type="submit" id="btnOK" runat="server">
        OK
    </button>
    <span class="Spacer" />
    <button id="btnClose" onclick="close_click()">
        Close
    </button>
</asp:Content>

<asp:Content ID="Scripts" ContentPlaceHolderID="ScriptContent" runat="server">
    <script type="text/javascript">

        function window.onload()
        {

            var arrActivityIds = window.dialogArguments;
            var hdnActivityId =
                           document.getElementById("ctl00_MainContent_ActivityId");

            if ( arrActivityIds.length > 1 )
            {
                alert( "You have selected more than one record." );
                window.close();
            }
            else
            {
                hdnActivityId.value = arrActivityIds[0];
            }

        }

        function close_click()
        {
            window.close();
        }

    </script>
</asp:Content>
```

The CompleteActivity.aspx page implements our Master Page by setting the *MasterPageFile* attribute in the Page directive.

```
<%@ Page Language="C#"
        MasterPageFile="Dialog.Master"
        AutoEventWireup="true"
        CodeBehind="CompleteActivity.aspx.cs"
        Inherits="Chapter13.CompleteActivity" %>
```

Because we are using the Master Page, we no longer need the *html* and *form* tags in our Web Form file. Notice that our Web Form simply contains ASP.NET *Content* controls. When the page is rendered, these content controls are combined with the *html* tags used in the Master Page.

We have added a *Content* control for each *ContentPlaceHolder* control contained in the Master Page.

Tip A full description of how master pages and *Content* controls work is beyond the scope of this book, but to set up a *Content* control, simply set its *ContentPlaceHolderID* property to the ID of the *ContentPlaceHolder* control on the Master Page that you are trying to populate.

Setting the dialog box's title and description is pretty straightforward. Their *Content* controls just contain the text that will be styled and displayed. The main content area of our dialog box is a little more complex and contains actual controls. This is the *Content* control with an ID of "Main" from Listing 13-6. It contains a hidden input to store the activity ID that will be passed to our dialog box from the Microsoft Dynamics CRM Activities grid, an ASP.NET *Label* control that we will use to send messages back to the end user, and an ASP.NET *DropDown* control that is populated with a few activity status values.

Tip For simplicity this example uses a hard-coded list in our drop-down list, however, your system might contain customized values. To make this example more dynamic and to account for customized values, you could update the code to make the appropriate calls to the *MetadataService* and populate your list items. Chapter 14, "Developing Custom Microsoft CRM Controls," goes into more detail on how to accomplish this.

The next *Content* control is for our dialog buttons. This example has two buttons: an OK button used to submit the form, and a Close button used to close the window. The OK button is of type *submit* and will cause a postback when clicked. The Close button has its *onclick* attribute set to call a script function that we discuss next. The *Content* control that contains our script code starts off with a standard *script* tag. Inside it has three functions. The first is for the page load. When the page loads, we grab the activity ID from the window's dialog arguments. Because the dialog arguments are an array, we check the length to make sure that only one record was selected. If we find more than one, we alert the user and close the dialog.

If everything looks good, we set the value of our hidden input in the main content section to the activity ID. Notice that the hidden input's ID is set to "ActivityId" in the main content section, but when you grab an instance of the control from script we use the ID "ctl00_MainContent_ActivityId".

```
var hdnActivityId = document.getElementById("ctl00_MainContent_ActivityId");
```

We can't use "ActivityId" because when the page is rendered, the IDs of our controls contained in the *Content* controls change. An easy way to figure out what your IDs will be is to open the page in Internet Explorer, right-click, and select View Source.

The other function in our script is the *click* event for the Close buttons we added. The function *close_click* closes the browser window.

Now that our UI is complete, we can examine the functionality contained in our code-behind file. Listing 13-7 contains the source code for the code-behind file.

LISTING 13-7 CompleteActivity.aspx.cs source code

```
using System;
using System.Collections;
using System.Configuration;
using System.Data;
using System.Web;
using System.Web.Security;
using System.Web.UI;
using System.Web.UI.HtmlControls;
using System.Web.UI.WebControls;
using System.Web.UI.WebControls.WebParts;
using Microsoft.Crm.SdkTypeProxy;
using Microsoft.Crm.Sdk.Query;
using Microsoft.Crm.Sdk;
using System.Text;
using System.Xml;
using ProgrammingWithDynamicsCrm4.Utilities;

namespace Chapter13
{
    public partial class CompleteActivity : System.Web.UI.Page
    {
        private const int _completedStatus = 5;
        private const int _canceledStatus = 6;

        protected void Page_Load(object sender, EventArgs e)
        {
            if (IsPostBack)
            {
                string orgName = Request.QueryString["orgname"];
```

```
            using (new CrmImpersonator())
            {
                CrmService crmService =
        CrmServiceUtility.GetCrmService(CrmServiceUtility.GetServerURLFromRegistry(),
                                        orgName);


                Guid activityId = new Guid(this.ActivityId.Value);

                string fetchXml = String.Format(@"<fetch mapping='logical'>
                                    <entity name='activitypointer'>
                                        <attribute name='statecode' />
                                        <attribute name='activitytypecode' />
                                        <filter type='and'>
                 <condition attribute='activityid' operator='eq' value='{0}' />
                                        </filter>
                                    </entity>
                                </fetch>", activityId);


                string fetchResults = crmService.Fetch(fetchXml);

                XmlDocument fetchResultDoc = new XmlDocument();
                fetchResultDoc.LoadXml(fetchResults);

                XmlNode resultNode = fetchResultDoc.DocumentElement.FirstChild;

                string stateCodeName =
              resultNode.SelectSingleNode("statecode").Attributes["name"].Value;
                string activityType =
        resultNode.SelectSingleNode("activitytypecode").Attributes["name"].Value;

                if (activityType != "Task")
                {
                    ShowMessage("The select activity is not a Task.");
                    return;
                }

                if (stateCodeName != ActivityPointerState.Open.ToString())
                {
                    ShowMessage("The selected activity is not Open.");
                    return;
                }

                TaskState newState;
                int selectedStatus = int.Parse(this.Status.SelectedValue);

                if (selectedStatus == _completedStatus)
                    newState = TaskState.Completed;
                else
                    newState = TaskState.Canceled;
```

```
                SetStateTaskRequest stateRequest = new SetStateTaskRequest();
                stateRequest.EntityId = activityId;
                stateRequest.TaskStatus = selectedStatus;
                stateRequest.TaskState = newState;

                SetStateTaskResponse stateResponse =
                        (SetStateTaskResponse)crmService.Execute(stateRequest);

                ShowMessage(
                      "The status of the selected activity has been updated.");
            }
        }
    }

    private void ShowMessage(string message)
    {
        StatusLabel.Visible = false;
        Status.Visible = false;

        Message.Text = message;
        Message.Visible = true;

        btnOK.Visible = false;
    }
  }
}
```

Tip The code from this example can be easily extended to handle more than the Task Activity type and can also be updated to complete more than one activity at once.

The *Page_Load* method of our code-behind file is set up to handle a postback. The first thing we do when the page is posted is grab the organization name from the query string and create an instance of the *CrmService*. Next, we use a Fetch Xml query to retrieve the activity type and its current state.

Note At the time of this writing, the *CrmService Retrieve* and *RetrieveMultiple* methods were throwing the following error when used with the *activitypointer* entity: "The specified type was not recognized: name='activitypointer', namespace='http://schemas.microsoft.com/crm/2007/WebServices', at <BusinessEntity xmlns='http://schemas.microsoft.com/crm/2006/WebServices'>.", so Fetch Xml was used instead.

Because our page is only coded to handle task activities, we need to check the selected Activity's type. If it is not Task, we can call the *ShowMessage* method and exit out of the *Page_Load* method. The *ShowMessage* method hides the OK button and Status drop-down list and displays a message in the *Label* control. If the Activity is a Task, we can then check its current state. If the Activity is not open, we cannot mark it complete. Once again, we can use the *ShowMessage* method to display a message to the user. If the Activity passed our validation, we can then change its state using the *SetStateTaskRequest* message.

Now that our functionality is coded, we can demonstrate how to deploy our files, and how to call our dialog box from Microsoft Dynamics CRM.

Deploying and Testing the Dialog Box

First, we deploy our Web files to the server. The files will be deployed to the same Chapter13 folder we created when we deployed our IFrame sample pages.

Deploying the Web files

1. Compile the Chapter 13 project in Visual Studio.
2. Copy the CompleteActivity.aspx and Dialog.Master files into the Chapter13 folder on the server.
3. Copy the Dialog.css file into the Styles folder located under the Chapter13 folder on the server.
4. Copy the Images folder from your Chapter13 project into the Chapter13 folder on the server.
4. Copy the Chapter13.dll assembly into the Microsoft Dynamics CRM bin folder.

Next we need to update the ISV Config to add a Complete Task button to the Activities grid. Export the ISV Config customization from Microsoft Dynamics CRM. Open the customizations.xml file in Visual Studio or your preferred XML editor. Add the following code under the *Entities* node located under the *IsvConfig* node:

```
<Entity name="activitypointer">
    <Grid>
        <MenuBar>
            <Buttons>
                <Button Icon=""
                        Url="/ISV/Chapter13/CompleteActivity.aspx"
                        WinMode="2"
                        WinParams="dialogWidth:300px;dialogHeight:200px"
                        PassParams="1">
                    <Titles>
                        <Title LCID="1033" Text="Complete Task" />
                    </Titles>
                </Button>
            </Buttons>
        </MenuBar>
    </Grid>
</Entity>
```

After you add the preceding code and save the file, import the updated ISV Config. Open Microsoft Dynamics CRM in a Web browser and navigate to the main Activities grid. You should see our new button now (Figure 13-4).

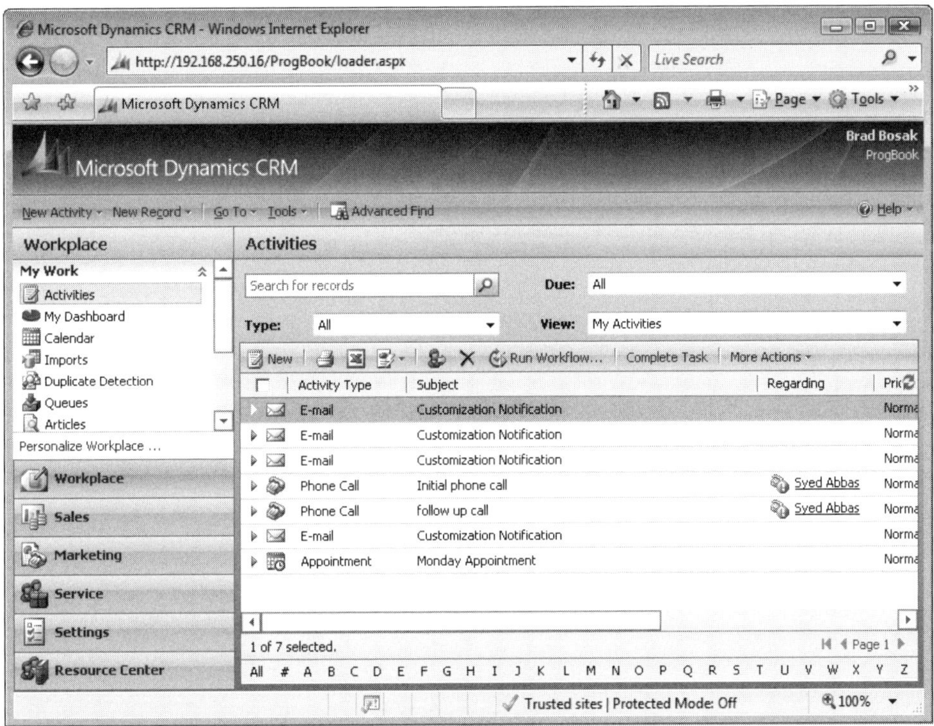

FIGURE 13-4 Microsoft Dynamics CRM Activities grid with ISV button

To test the functionality, select an Activity row in the grid and click our new button. If you select more than one record, you are alerted and then the window closes. If you select only one record, you should see our new dialog box. Notice that it appears almost identical to a native Microsoft Dynamics CRM dialog box (Figure 13-5). A user probably won't even realize that this dialog is a custom Web page, which is exactly what we want.

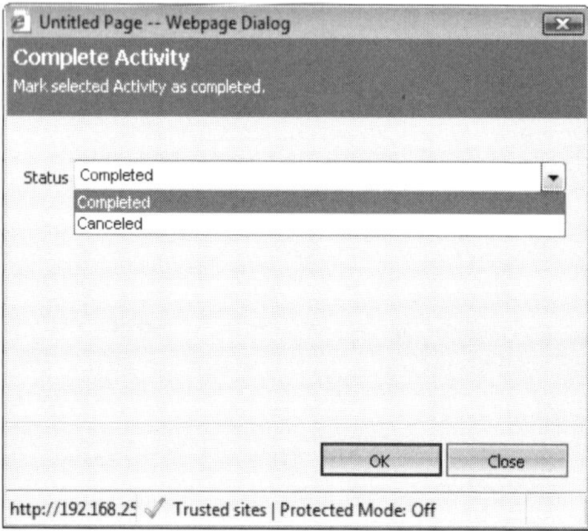

FIGURE 13-5 Complete Activities dialog box

Choose the status you would like to update the Task to and click OK. You should then see a message telling you that your activity's status has been updated. Notice also that the OK button is hidden. Now you can close the window.

ISV Page Development

In addition to embedding custom Web pages into IFrames and creating custom dialogs, you can also add entirely new Web pages into the Microsoft Dynamics CRM navigation. We refer to this type of customization as ISV page development. To demonstrate this type of customization, we will create a custom dashboard. A dashboard page gives users a quick overview of data from types of records. For this example, we'll create a simple dashboard to display the following information to the user:

- Top five most recent leads
- Top five Activities due this week
- Top five Opportunities with a status of In Progress

Figure 13-6 shows what the finished product will look like.

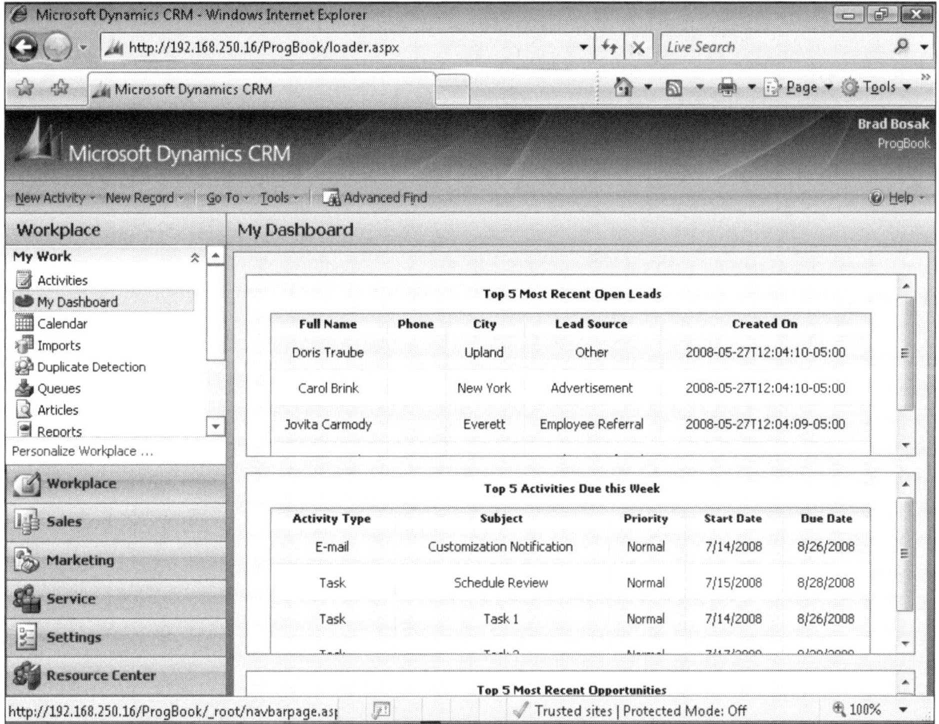

FIGURE 13-6 Dashboard

Programming the ISV Page

Now we will add a new Web Form to the Chapter13 project for our dashboard page. Listing 13-8 contains the source code for the new dashboard page.

Adding the Dashboard.aspx page

1. Right-click the Chapter13 project in Solution Explorer, select Add, and then click New Item.
2. On the Add New Item dialog, select the Web Form template.
3. Enter **Dashboard.aspx** into the Name field, and then click Add.

LISTING 13-8 Dashboard.aspx source code

```
<%@ Page Language="C#"
         AutoEventWireup="true"
         CodeBehind="Dashboard.aspx.cs"
         Inherits="Chapter13.Dashboard" %>
```

```
<!DOCTYPE html PUBLIC "-//W3C//DTD XHTML 1.0 Transitional//EN"
                              "http://www.w3.org/TR/xhtml1/DTD/xhtml1-transitional.dtd">
<html xmlns="http://www.w3.org/1999/xhtml">
<head runat="server">
    <title>Untitled Page</title>
    <style type="text/css">
        BODY
        {
            background-image: url(/_imgs/app_back.gif);
            background-repeat: repeat-x;
            border-top: 1px solid #6693cf;
            font-family: Tahoma;
            font-size: 11px;
            height: 100%;
            margin: 0;
            padding: 0;
        }
        #MainDiv
        {
            margin: 5px;
            padding: 5px;
            border: 1px solid #6893CF;
            background-color: #eaf3ff;
            display: table;
            text-align: center;
        }
        DIV.ContentDiv
        {
            height: 150px;
            width: 98%;
            text-align: center;
            border: 1px solid #6893CF;
            background-color: #F3F8FF;
            overflow: auto;
        }
        table
        {
            width: 90%;
            margin-top: 10px;
            margin-bottom: 10px;
            border: 1px solid #6893CF;
        }
        th
        {
            font-size: 7pt;
            filter: progid:DXImageTransform.Microsoft.Gradient(GradientType=0,
                    StartColorStr=#DBEBFF, EndColorStr=#FFFFFF; )
                    background-image:url(/_imgs/nav_header_back.gif);
                    background-repeat:repeat-x;padding:3px;
                    border-top:1pxsolid#ffffff;border-bottom:1pxsolid#DDECFF;
        }
        th, td
        {
            border-left: 1px solid #DDECFF;
        }
```

```
        td
        {
            padding-top: 8px;
            padding-bottom: 8px;
            border-bottom: 1px solid #DDECFF;
        }
        .MainRow
        {
            background-color: #edf4fc;
        }
        .AltRow
        {
            background-color: #ffffff;
        }
        .TableHeader
        {
            font-size: 7pt;
            font-weight: bold;
            padding-top: 10px;
        }
    </style>
</head>
<body>
    <form id="form1" runat="server">
    <div id="MainDiv">
        <div>
             
            <div id="LeadDiv" class="ContentDiv">
                <div class="TableHeader">
                    Top 5 Most Recent Open Leads</div>
                <asp:Table ID="LeadTable"
                           runat="server"
                           CellPadding="0"
                           CellSpacing="0">
                    <asp:TableHeaderRow>
                        <asp:TableHeaderCell>Full Name</asp:TableHeaderCell>
                        <asp:TableHeaderCell>Phone</asp:TableHeaderCell>
                        <asp:TableHeaderCell>City</asp:TableHeaderCell>
                        <asp:TableHeaderCell>Lead Source</asp:TableHeaderCell>
                        <asp:TableHeaderCell>Created On</asp:TableHeaderCell>
                    </asp:TableHeaderRow>
                </asp:Table>
            </div>
             
            <div id="ActivityDiv" class="ContentDiv">
                <div class="TableHeader">
                    Top 5 Activities Due this Week</div>
                <asp:Table ID="ActivityTable"
                        runat="server"
                        CellPadding="0"
                        CellSpacing="0">
                    <asp:TableHeaderRow>
                        <asp:TableHeaderCell>Activity Type</asp:TableHeaderCell>
                        <asp:TableHeaderCell>Subject</asp:TableHeaderCell>
                        <asp:TableHeaderCell>Priority</asp:TableHeaderCell>
```

```
                    <asp:TableHeaderCell>Start Date</asp:TableHeaderCell>
                    <asp:TableHeaderCell>Due Date</asp:TableHeaderCell>
                </asp:TableHeaderRow>
            </asp:Table>
        </div>
         
        <div id="OpportunityDiv" class="ContentDiv">
            <div class="TableHeader">
                Top 5 Most Recent Opportunities</div>
            <asp:Table ID="OpportunityTable"
                    runat="server"
                    CellPadding="0"
                    CellSpacing="0">
                <asp:TableHeaderRow>
                    <asp:TableHeaderCell>Topic</asp:TableHeaderCell>
                    <asp:TableHeaderCell>
                        Potential Customer
                    </asp:TableHeaderCell>
                    <asp:TableHeaderCell>Est. Close Date</asp:TableHeaderCell>
                    <asp:TableHeaderCell>Probability</asp:TableHeaderCell>
                </asp:TableHeaderRow>
            </asp:Table>
        </div>
    </div>
     
</div>
</form>
</body>
</html>
```

Note The styles in our dashboard page are contained in a *style* tag on the aspx page. We did this because once we add the page to the navigation using the site map, it has to go through Microsoft Dynamics CRM's Virtual Path Provider. If we were to put these styles in a separate style sheet referenced on the page, it would not be found when the page is rendered in the browser.

Just like the IFrame and the dialog box examples earlier in this chapter, we want our custom dashboard to match the style and formatting of the Microsoft Dynamics CRM user interface. Table 13-4 lists all the styles used on the dashboard along with a description.

TABLE 13-4 Dashboard.aspx Styles

Name	Description
BODY	Sets the background to the same repeated gradient image used by the native Microsoft Dynamics CRM pages. Also sets the margins and borders to zero and font family to Tahoma.
#MainDiv	Sets the background color, margins, and padding of a *div* tag with an ID of "Main". Used to create the outer shell of our dashboard.

TABLE 13-4 Dashboard.aspx Styles

Name	Description
DIV.ContentDiv	Styles the sections of the dashboard. Sets their background, borders, width, and scrolling.
table	Styles the tables we will use to display our dashboard data. Sets their border, width, and margins.
Th	Styles table header rows. Sets their font size and gives them a gradient background.
td	Adds a bottom border to table cells and sets their padding.
.MainRow	Our dashboard data tables use alternating row color. This style sets the background color of a table row.
.AltRow	Sets the background color for alternate table rows in our data tables.
.TableHeader	Sets font size and weight and adds padding to the *div* tags that contain the section titles in the dashboard.

The dashboard pages uses multiple *div* tags. The outer shell of the dashboard is the *div* tag with an id of "Main". Then each section is contained in its own *div.* Each section *div* has two parts: a header *div* containing the title of the section and an ASP.NET *Table* control. The *Table* control will be used in the code-behind page to dynamically add rows. We add an ASP.NET *TableHeaderCell* to define our columns. Now that we finished our page layout, we can discuss dynamically populating the data tables in the code-behind page. Listing 13-9 contains the source code for the code-behind page.

LISTING 13-9 Dashboard.aspx.cs source code

```
using System;
using System.Collections;
using System.Configuration;
using System.Data;
using System.Web;
using System.Web.Security;
using System.Web.UI;
using System.Web.UI.HtmlControls;
using System.Web.UI.WebControls;
using System.Web.UI.WebControls.WebParts;
using Microsoft.Crm.SdkTypeProxy;
using Microsoft.Crm.Sdk.Query;
using Microsoft.Crm.Sdk;
using System.Xml;
using ProgrammingWithDynamicsCrm4.Utilities;

namespace Chapter13
{
    public partial class Dashboard : System.Web.UI.Page
    {
        protected void Page_Load(object sender, EventArgs e)
        {
            string orgName = Request.QueryString["orgname"];
```

```
        CrmService crmService =
    CrmServiceUtility.GetCrmService(CrmServiceUtility.GetServerURLFromRegistry(),
                                    orgName);

        WhoAmIRequest whoAmI = new WhoAmIRequest();
        WhoAmIResponse whoAmIResponse =
                                    (WhoAmIResponse)crmService.Execute(whoAmI);

        Guid userId = whoAmIResponse.UserId;

        PopulateLeadTable(crmService, userId);
        PopulateActivityTable(crmService, userId);
        PopulateOpportunityTable(crmService, userId);
    }

    private void PopulateLeadTable(CrmService crmService, Guid userId)
    {
        QueryExpression leadQuery = new QueryExpression();
        leadQuery.EntityName = EntityName.lead.ToString();

        ColumnSet leadColumns = new ColumnSet();
        leadColumns.AddColumns("fullname",
                               "telephone1",
                               "address1_city",
                               "leadsourcecode",
                               "createdon");

        leadQuery.ColumnSet = leadColumns;

        ConditionExpression ownerCondition = new ConditionExpression();
        ownerCondition.AttributeName = "ownerid";
        ownerCondition.Operator = ConditionOperator.Equal;
        ownerCondition.Values = new object[] { userId };

        FilterExpression filter = new FilterExpression();
        filter.Conditions.Add(ownerCondition);
        filter.FilterOperator = LogicalOperator.And;

        leadQuery.Criteria = filter;

        OrderExpression order = new OrderExpression();
        order.AttributeName = "createdon";
        order.OrderType = OrderType.Descending;

        leadQuery.Orders.Add( order );

        BusinessEntityCollection bec = crmService.RetrieveMultiple(leadQuery);

        // add the top 5 leads
        for (int i = 0; i < bec.BusinessEntities.Count; i++)
        {
            lead crmLead = (lead)bec.BusinessEntities[i];

            string rowClass = "MainRow";
```

```
            if (i % 2 == 1)
                rowClass = "AltRow";

            TableRow tr = new TableRow();
            tr.CssClass = rowClass;

            TableCell fullNameCell = new TableCell();
            fullNameCell.Text = crmLead.fullname;

            tr.Cells.Add(fullNameCell);

            TableCell phoneCell = new TableCell();
            phoneCell.Text = crmLead.telephone1;

            tr.Cells.Add(phoneCell);

            TableCell cityCell = new TableCell();
            cityCell.Text = crmLead.address1_city;

            tr.Cells.Add(cityCell);

            TableCell leadSourceCell = new TableCell();
            if ( crmLead.leadsourcecode != null )
                leadSourceCell.Text = crmLead.leadsourcecode.name;

            tr.Cells.Add(leadSourceCell);

            TableCell createdOnCell = new TableCell();
            createdOnCell.Text = crmLead.createdon.Value;

            tr.Cells.Add(createdOnCell);

            this.LeadTable.Rows.Add(tr);

            if (i == 4)
                break;
        }
    }

    private void PopulateActivityTable(CrmService crmService, Guid userId)
    {
        string fetchXml = String.Format(@"<fetch mapping='logical'>
                                    <entity name='activitypointer'>
                                        <attribute name='activitytypecode' />
                                        <attribute name='subject' />
                                        <attribute name='scheduledstart' />
                                        <attribute name='scheduledend' />
                                        <attribute name='prioritycode' />
                                        <attribute name='createdon' />
                                        <filter type='and'>
                  <condition attribute='ownerid' operator='eq' value='{0}' />
                  <condition attribute='scheduledend' operator='this-week' />
                  <condition attribute='statecode' operator='eq' value='0' />
                                        </filter>
```

```
                                    <order attribute='createdon' />
                                </entity>
                            </fetch>", userId);

        string fetchResults = crmService.Fetch(fetchXml);

        XmlDocument fetchResultDoc = new XmlDocument();
        fetchResultDoc.LoadXml(fetchResults);

        XmlNodeList resultNodes =
                       fetchResultDoc.DocumentElement.SelectNodes("result");

        for (int i = 0; i < resultNodes.Count; i++)
        {
            string activityType = String.Empty;
            string subject = String.Empty;
            string scheduledStart = String.Empty;
            string scheduledEnd = String.Empty;
            string priorityCode = String.Empty;

            activityType =
    resultNodes[i].SelectSingleNode("activitytypecode").Attributes["name"].Value;

            subject = resultNodes[i].SelectSingleNode("subject").InnerText;

            XmlNode scheduledStartNode =
                           resultNodes[i].SelectSingleNode("scheduledstart");

            if (scheduledStartNode != null)
              scheduledStart = scheduledStartNode.Attributes["date"].Value;

            XmlNode scheduledEndNode =
                            resultNodes[i].SelectSingleNode("scheduledend");

            if (scheduledEndNode != null)
              scheduledEnd = scheduledEndNode.Attributes["date"].Value;

            priorityCode =
        resultNodes[i].SelectSingleNode("prioritycode").Attributes["name"].Value;

            string rowClass = "MainRow";

            if (i % 2 == 1)
              rowClass = "AltRow";

            TableRow tr = new TableRow();
            tr.CssClass = rowClass;

            TableCell activityTypeCell = new TableCell();
            activityTypeCell.Text = activityType;

            tr.Cells.Add(activityTypeCell);
```

```
            TableCell subjectCell = new TableCell();
            subjectCell.Text = subject;

            tr.Cells.Add(subjectCell);

            TableCell priorityCell = new TableCell();
            priorityCell.Text = priorityCode;

            tr.Cells.Add(priorityCell);

            TableCell scheduledStartCell = new TableCell();
            scheduledStartCell.Text = scheduledStart;

            tr.Cells.Add(scheduledStartCell);

            TableCell scheduledEndCell = new TableCell();
            scheduledEndCell.Text = scheduledEnd;

            tr.Cells.Add(scheduledEndCell);

            this.ActivityTable.Rows.Add(tr);

            if (i == 4)
                break;
        }
    }

    private void PopulateOpportunityTable(CrmService crmService, Guid userId)
    {
        QueryExpression opportunityQuery = new QueryExpression();
        opportunityQuery.EntityName = EntityName.opportunity.ToString();

        ColumnSet opportunityColumns = new ColumnSet();
        opportunityColumns.AddColumns("name",
                                      "customerid",
                                      "estimatedclosedate",
                                      "closeprobability");

        opportunityQuery.ColumnSet = opportunityColumns;

        ConditionExpression ownerCondition = new ConditionExpression();
        ownerCondition.AttributeName = "ownerid";
        ownerCondition.Operator = ConditionOperator.Equal;
        ownerCondition.Values = new object[] { userId };

        FilterExpression filter = new FilterExpression();
        filter.Conditions.Add(ownerCondition);
        filter.FilterOperator = LogicalOperator.And;

        opportunityQuery.Criteria = filter;

        OrderExpression order = new OrderExpression();
        order.AttributeName = "createdon";
        order.OrderType = OrderType.Descending;
```

```
            opportunityQuery.Orders.Add(order);

            BusinessEntityCollection bec =
                                      crmService.RetrieveMultiple(opportunityQuery);

            for (int i = 0; i < bec.BusinessEntities.Count; i++)
            {
                opportunity crmOpportunity = (opportunity)bec.BusinessEntities[i];

                string rowClass = "MainRow";

                if (i % 2 == 1)
                    rowClass = "AltRow";

                TableRow tr = new TableRow();
                tr.CssClass = rowClass;

                TableCell topicCell = new TableCell();
                topicCell.Text = crmOpportunity.name;

                tr.Cells.Add(topicCell);

                TableCell customerCell = new TableCell();
                if (crmOpportunity.customerid != null)
                    customerCell.Text = crmOpportunity.customerid.name;

                tr.Cells.Add(customerCell);

                TableCell closeDateCell = new TableCell();
                if ( crmOpportunity.estimatedclosedate != null )
                    closeDateCell.Text = crmOpportunity.estimatedclosedate.Value;

                tr.Cells.Add(closeDateCell);

                TableCell probabilityCell = new TableCell();
                if (crmOpportunity.closeprobability != null)
                    probabilityCell.Text =
                                crmOpportunity.closeprobability.Value.ToString();

                tr.Cells.Add(probabilityCell);

                this.OpportunityTable.Rows.Add(tr);

                if (i == 4)
                    break;
            }
        }
    }
}
```

The first thing we do in the *Page_Load* method is grab the organization name from the query string and then create an instance of the *CrmService*. Then we can use the *WhoAmIRequest* message to find the *Guid* of the currently logged-on user.

We need this *Guid* to help filter our dashboard data. Our code-behind also contains three private methods: *PopulateLeadTable*, *PopulateActivityTable*, and *PopulateOpportunityTable*. These are called from the *Page_Load* method and handle populating our dashboard data tables. All three methods take in the *CrmService* instance and the user ID *Guid* as arguments. We briefly discuss each of these methods in the next section.

Warning The *WhoAmIRequest* used in this code means this dashboard example will only work for on-premise deployments. You can update this code to use the *CrmImpersonator* class to make it work for both Internet-facing deployments (IFDs) and on-premise deployments. Then, instead of the *WhoAmIRequest*, you would use the *CalledId* property of the *CrmAuthenticationToken* to create your *CrmService* as the currently logged-on user ID.

PopulateLeadTable and *PopulateOpportunityTable*

The *PopulateLeadTable* and *PopulateOpportunityTable* methods are very similar in functionality. The methods begin with a *QueryExpression* to retrieve entity records that are owned by the currently logged-on user. The *ConditionExpression* added to the query makes sure that only records with the specified *ownerid* are returned. The query is also sorted on the date the record was created. This is important because our dashboard will only display the five most recent records.

Once the query executes, we can loop through the resulting records. To dynamically add the rows, we create a new ASP.NET *TableRow* object. Because we want to display alternating row colors, we need to check the index of the loop each time and use the modulus operator to determine which color to use.

```
string rowClass = "MainRow";

if (i % 2 == 1)
    rowClass = "AltRow";

TableRow tr = new TableRow();
tr.CssClass = rowClass;
```

Next we create *TableCell* objects for each cell and add them to the row's *Cells* collection. Notice that at the end of the loop a statement checks the index number. If the number is equal to four, we break the loop. This ensures that we only display the five most recent records.

```
if (i == 4)
    break;
```

Note You can improve the performance of your applications by using fetch queries and setting the *count* property on the *fetch* node to avoid retrieving more than the desired number of records.

PopulateActivityTable Method

Because the Activity table on our dashboard displays all types of Activities, we need to query against the Activity Pointer entity. Once we have the fetch results, we can load them into an *XmlDocument* object and use *XPath* to retrieve the data we need to populate our table. First we grab an *XmlNodeList* of the result nodes so that we can loop through and create our table rows. Inside of the loop, we use *XPath* to grab the attribute data.

```
subject = resultNodes[i].SelectSingleNode("subject").InnerText;
```

The remaining portion of this method uses the same *TableRow* and *TableCell* objects and functionality used in the previous two methods we discussed.

Deploying and Testing the ISV Page

Now that our code is complete, let's deploy the files and test our dashboard.

Deploying the dashboard Web files

1. Compile the Chapter 13 project in Visual Studio.
2. Copy the Dashboard.aspx file into the Chapter13 folder on the server.
3. Copy the Chapter13.dll assembly into the Microsoft Dynamics CRM bin folder.

Once we deploy the Web files, we need to update the Site Map entry to add a link to our dashboard in the Microsoft Dynamics CRM left navigation. To do this, export the Site Map customization and save it to your computer. Open this file in Visual Studio or another text editor and add the following code inside of the *Group* node on which you would like the dashboard to appear:

```
<SubArea Id="nav_mydashboard"
         Icon="/_imgs/area/18_reports.gif"
         Url="/ISV/Chapter13/Dashboard.aspx"
         Client="All"
         PassParams="1">
  <Titles>
    <Title LCID="1033" Title="My Dashboard" />
  </Titles>

</SubArea>
```

After you add the new *SubArea* node, save the file and import the updated Site Map customizations. Now you can view the completed dashboard in your system. Open Microsoft Dynamics CRM in the Web browser and browse to your newly added My Dashboard link. You should now see our dashboard as shown in Figure 13-7.

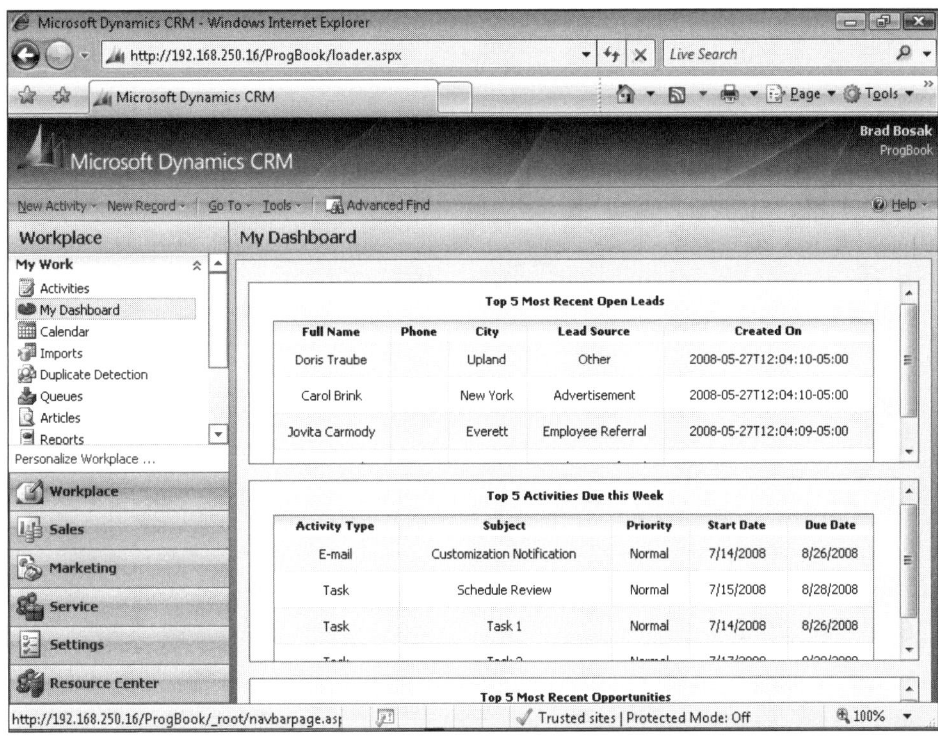

FIGURE 13-7 The final custom dashboard

Summary

This chapter introduced you to some of the ways you can extend your Microsoft Dynamics CRM system using ASP.NET development. In the first example, we created an IFrame page that blends with an existing entity form. The second example showed a custom dialog box using Master Pages that mimic the look and feel of native dialog boxes. The last example showed how to add an entirely new dashboard page that displays a custom ASP.NET page right within the Microsoft Dynamics CRM navigation. All of the examples showed how you can style your custom development to match the look and feel of the Microsoft Dynamics CRM user interface. In addition to our samples, please remember that the Microsoft Dynamics CRM SDK comes with an excellent style guide and a folder of images that provide great help when you emulate the Microsoft Dynamics CRM user interface with custom ASP.NET development.

Chapter 14

Developing Custom Microsoft CRM Controls

In Chapter 3, "Communicating with Microsoft CRM APIs," we showed you how to add references to the Microsoft Dynamics CRM APIs and use them to perform basic functions. In this chapter, we'll go further into customization by creating custom server controls that incorporate the Microsoft Dynamics CRM APIs. This chapter assumes that you have a basic working knowledge of server-control development.

Microsoft ASP.NET provides developers with many built-in server controls. When you're developing custom Web solutions with Microsoft Dynamics CRM, you may want to extend these server controls or build your own from scratch by inheriting from a control base class. We will do both of those things in this chapter. Because all of our custom controls will render a user interface component, they all inherit from the *System.Web.UI.WebControl* class or an existing control class that inherits from it.

Creating custom server controls can be time-consuming and might seem like a lot of work up front, but your upfront investment will pay offer later through benefits such as these:

- Speed of future development
- Encapsulation of common functionality
- Built-in validation

In this chapter, we'll cover the following topics:

- Overview of control development
- Developing a *CrmPicklistControl*
- Developing a *CrmBooleanControl*
- Developing a *CrmDateTimeControl*
- Developing a *CrmEntityPicklistControl*
- Developing a *CrmGridViewControl*

Overview

When you are developing custom IFrames or Web forms in a portal that interact with Microsoft Dynamics CRM, you may find yourself writing the same code in numerous places to handle the user interface for attributes. We will focus on creating custom server controls to handle some of the more complex attribute types:

- *Boolean*
- *Picklist*
- *DateTime*
- *Lookup*
- *Status*

After we create our attribute controls, we will finish by creating an editable grid view control that incorporates all of the other controls we develop in this chapter.

First we'll create a new Microsoft Visual Studio project for our custom server-controls development.

Creating the ProgrammingWithDynamicsCrm4.Controls project

1. Open the ProgrammingWithDynamicsCrm4 solution in Visual Studio 2008.
2. On the File Menu, select Add and then click New Project.
3. In the New Project dialog box, select the Visual C# project type targeting the .NET Framework 3.0 and then select the Class Library template.
4. Type in the name **ProgrammingWithDynamicsCrm4.Controls** and click OK.
5. Delete the default Class.cs file.
6. Right-click the ProgrammingWithDynamicsCrm4.Controls project in Solution Explorer, and then click Add Reference.
7. On the .NET tab of the Add Reference dialog box, select System.Configuration, System.Web, and System.Web.Services. Click OK.

We will also need to add a utilities assembly to handle some common tasks. This ProgrammingWithDynamicsCrm4.Utilities.dll assembly can be obtained by compiling the ProgrammingWithDynamicsCrm4.Utilities project included in the source code for this book.

1. Right-click the Chapter 13 project in Solution Explorer, and select Add Reference.
2. Browse to the location of the ProgrammingWithDynamicsCrm4.Utilities.dll assembly, select it, and click OK.

Now we have a Class Library project named ProgrammingWithDynamicsCrm4.Controls. During our custom server-control development, we need to test our code, so we'll add a Web site project to our solution for testing.

Adding a Web site project to the Visual Studio solution

1. On the File Menu, select Add and then click New Web Site.
2. In the New Web Site dialog box, select the ASP.NET Web Site template targeting the .NET Framework 3.0 and set the Location to File System and the Language to C#.
3. Click the Browse button, and select a file system location for the Web site. Change the Web site's name from WebSite1 to **ProgrammingWithDynamicsCrm4.Web** and click OK.
4. Delete the Default.aspx file.
5. Right-click the ProgrammingWithDynamicsCrm4.Web project in Solution Explorer, and click Add Reference.
6. On the Projects tab of the Add Reference dialog box, select the ProgrammingWithDynamicsCrm4.Controls project and click OK.

We'll use this Web site throughout the chapter to test the functionality of our custom controls. You can think of our test Web site as a portal application that interacts with Microsoft Dynamics CRM. As a CRM developer, one of the common tasks you will encounter is using Web portals to display and update data in Microsoft Dynamics CRM. The custom server controls we develop in this chapter will aid in this process.

Our controls will use the Microsoft Dynamics CRM SDK assemblies. Referencing these assemblies in our project allows our controls to tie into the entity and attribute metadata and provide the end user with a Microsoft Dynamics CRM–like user experience.

Adding references to the Microsoft Dynamics CRM SDK assemblies

1. Right-click the ProgrammingWithDynamicsCrm4.Controls Project in Solution Explorer, and click Add Reference.
2. On the Browse tab of the Add Reference dialog box, locate the *Microsoft.Crm.Sdk.dll* and *Microsoft.Crm.Sdk.TypeProxy.dll* assemblies. Click OK.

Because our custom server controls will use both the *CrmService* and *MetadataService* from the Microsoft Dynamics CRM SDK API, we need to add a few keys to the *AppSettings* section of the ProgrammingWithDynamicsCrm4.Web project's web.config file. These keys allow our controls to easily obtain the Microsoft Dynamics CRM server's name and your organization name.

Adding *CrmServer* and *OrgName* keys to the web.config

1. Open the web.config file in the ProgrammingWithDynamicsCrm4.Web project.
2. Find the *AppSettings* node.
3. Add **<add key="*CrmServer*" value="*YourCrmServerName*"/> and <add key="*OrgName*" value="*YourOrgName*"/>** under the *AppSettings* node, as shown here:

```
<appSettings>
    <add key="CrmServer" value="YourCrmServerName"/>
    <add key="OrgName" value="YourOrgName"/>
</appSettings>
```

Note Replace *YourCrmServerName* and *YourOrgName* in the preceding code with the names of your Microsoft Dynamics CRM server's name and your organization name, respectively.

CrmPicklistControl

The first control we will develop is the *CrmPicklistControl* control. This control renders a select box with all of the options defined in your Microsoft Dynamics CRM attribute. It supports the *Picklist* and *Status* attribute types.

Typically, when creating a drop-down list on a custom page that updates a picklist attribute, a developer needs to either hard-code the list options or make a call to the Microsoft Dynamics CRM metadata service to obtain them. If you have multiple drop-down lists like this in your Web application, writing code to retrieve the options and populate your lists can get tedious. The *CrmPicklistControl* handles all of this for you.

The *CrmPicklistControl* allows a developer to add the control, set the entity and attribute name, and then render a select box with all of the attributes defined in your Microsoft Dynamics CRM environment.

Programming the *CrmPicklistControl*

The first thing we will do is add a new Class file to our Controls project.

Adding the *CrmPicklistControl* class

1. Right-click the ProgrammingWithDynamicsCrm4.Controls Project in Solution Explorer. Under Add, click New Item.
2. In the Visual C# Items category, select the Class template.
3. Type **CrmPicklistControl.cs** in the Name box and click Add.

Listing 14-1 shows the full source code for the *CrmPicklistControl*. This control inherits from the *System.Web.UI.DropDownList* class. This class provides us with most of the functionality we need.

LISTING 14-1 *CrmPicklistControl* source code

```
using System;
using System.Collections.Generic;
using System.Text;
using System.Web.UI.HtmlControls;
using System.ComponentModel;
using System.Web.UI.WebControls;
using Microsoft.Crm.SdkTypeProxy.Metadata;
using Microsoft.Crm.Sdk.Metadata;
using System.Configuration;
using ProgrammingWithDynamicsCrm4.Utilities;

namespace ProgrammingWithDynamicsCrm4.Controls
{
    public class CrmPicklistControl : DropDownList
    {
        public string EntityName
        {
            get
            {
                object entityName = ViewState["EntityName"];

                if (entityName != null)
                    return (string)entityName;
                else
                    return String.Empty;
            }
            set
            {
                ViewState["EntityName"] = value;
            }
        }

        public string AttributeName
        {
            get
            {
                object attributeName = ViewState["AttributeName"];

                if (attributeName != null)
                    return (string)attributeName;
                else
                    return String.Empty;
            }
            set
            {
                ViewState["AttributeName"] = value;
            }
        }
```

```
public bool IncludeNullOption
{
    get
    {
        object includeNullOption = ViewState["IncludeNullOption"];

        if (includeNullOption != null)
            return (bool)includeNullOption;
        else
            return false;
    }
    set
    {
        ViewState["IncludeNullOption"] = value;
    }
}

[Browsable(false)]
[EditorBrowsable(EditorBrowsableState.Never)]
public override object DataSource
{
    get
    {
        return base.DataSource;
    }
    set
    {
        base.DataSource = value;
    }
}

[Browsable(false)]
[EditorBrowsable(EditorBrowsableState.Never)]
public override string DataSourceID
{
    get
    {
        return base.DataSourceID;
    }
    set
    {
        base.DataSourceID = value;
    }
}

[Browsable(false)]
[EditorBrowsable(EditorBrowsableState.Never)]
public override string DataTextField
{
    get
    {
        return base.DataTextField;
    }
```

```
        set
        {
            base.DataTextField = value;
        }
    }

    [Browsable(false)]
    [EditorBrowsable(EditorBrowsableState.Never)]
    public override string DataValueField
    {
        get
        {
            return base.DataValueField;
        }
        set
        {
            base.DataValueField = value;
        }
    }

    [Browsable(false)]
    [EditorBrowsable(EditorBrowsableState.Never)]
    public override ListItemCollection Items
    {
        get
        {
            if (base.Items.Count == 0)
                this.AddListItems();

            return base.Items;
        }
    }

    private void AddListItems()
    {
        MetadataService service = CrmServiceUtility.GetMetadataService(
                                  ConfigurationManager.AppSettings["CrmServer"],
                                  ConfigurationManager.AppSettings["OrgName"]);

        AttributeMetadata attributeMetadata =
MetadataUtility.RetrieveAttributeMetadata(service,
    EntityName, AttributeName);
        // Verify that the attribute is a valid picklist
        switch (attributeMetadata.AttributeType.Value)
        {
            case AttributeType.Picklist:
            case AttributeType.Status:
                break;
            default:
                throw new Exception(String.Format(
                       "{0} is not a valid attribute for the Picklist control.",
                        attributeMetadata.AttributeType));
        }
```

```
                if (this.IncludeNullOption)
                {
                    base.Items.Add(String.Empty);
                }

                PicklistAttributeMetadata picklistMetadata =
                                        (PicklistAttributeMetadata)attributeMetadata;

                foreach (Option option in picklistMetadata.Options)
                {
                    base.Items.Add(new ListItem(option.Label.UserLocLabel.Label,
                                option.Value.Value.ToString()));
                }

                if (String.IsNullOrEmpty(this.SelectedValue))
                    this.SelectedValue = picklistMetadata.DefaultValue.ToString();
            }
        }
    }
```

Note A detailed description of the *MetadataUtility* used in Listing 14-1 can be found in Chapter 15 "Additional Samples and Utilities."

CrmPicklistControl Properties

The *System.Web.UI.DropDownList* gives us a good start, but does not provide us with everything we need. Table 14-1 lists all of the properties we need to add for our *CrmPicklistControl*.

TABLE 14-1 ***CrmPicklistControl* Properties**

Property Name	Type	Description
EntityName	*string*	Name of the Microsoft Dynamics CRM entity that the picklist attribute belongs to
AttributeName	*string*	Name of the picklist attribute
IncludeNullOption	*bool*	Determines whether to render a null option in the select box

Because we are adding the options that have already been defined in Microsoft Dynamics CRM for the specified attribute, we want to hide some of the built-in properties inherited from the *DropDownList* class. To do this, we override the property and add the following attributes to prevent programmers from using them during development:

```
[Browsable(false)]
[EditorBrowsable(EditorBrowsableState.Never)]
public override string DataSourceID
{
    get
      {
        return base.DataSourceID;
```

```
        }
      set
        {
          base.DataSourceID = value;
        }
}
```

Setting the *Browsable* attribute to false hides the property in the Visual Studio Properties window and in the Visual Studio designer's IntelliSense. To prevent the property from being shown in the Visual Studio C# code editor's IntelliSense, we add the *EditorBrowsable* attribute and set it to *EditorBrowsableState.Never*. The following properties are hidden on the *CrmPicklistControl*:

- *DataSource*
- *DataSourceID*
- *DataTextField*
- *DataValueField*
- *Items*

Note If your class library project is in the same Visual Studio solution as your Web project and both are referenced using a project reference, setting the *EditorBrowable* attribute set to *EditorBrowsableState.Never* will *not* hide properties from the C# code editor's IntelliSense. The logic behind this is that you want to hide these attributes from outside developers using your assembly but not from the developers actually developing your controls library.

Adding Options to the *CrmPicklistControl*

In the "get" of our overridden Items property, we check the base *DropDownList* class *Items* collection and if it is empty, we call the *AddListItems* method. When the control renders, it checks the control's *Items* collection and triggers the call to *AddListItems*. In the *AddListItems* method, we make a call to the Microsoft Dynamics CRM *MetadataService* to retrieve the metadata for the attribute specified in the *AttributeName* property on the *CrmPicklistControl*. Next we check the attribute type to verify that the retrieved attribute is of the type *Picklist* or *Status*. If it is, the attribute metadata is then converted to the type of *PicklistAttributeMetadata*. The *PicklistAttributeMetadata* contains a collection of options that we then loop through and add to the base *DropDownList* class's *Items* collection.

We use each *Microsoft.Crm.Sdk.Metadata.Option* to add a new *ListItem* to the *DropDownList Items* collection. Because the installation of Microsoft Dynamics CRM can have multiple language packs installed, we use the user's local label on the *Option* for the list item's text. Using the *UserLocLabel* value will give us the text translated into the preferred language of the user making the *MetadataService* call.

```
option.Label.UserLocLabel.Label
```

For more information on this, see Chapter 11, "Multilingual and Multi-Currency Applications." Using the user's local label ensures that the user sees the correct label for each *Picklist* option. The list item's value will be set to the *Value* of the *Option*.

Testing the *CrmPicklistControl*

Adding the *CrmPicklistControl* test page

1. Open the ProgrammingWithDynamicsCrm4.Web project in Visual Studio.
2. Right-click the project name in Solution Explorer, and click Add New Item.
3. Select the Web Form template, and type the name **CrmPicklistControlPage.aspx** in the Name box. Click Add.

The next thing we need to do is register a tag prefix for our custom controls library. To register a tag prefix for this page only, under the page directive on the CrmPicklistControl-Page.aspx add **<%@ Register TagPrefix="crm" Assembly="ProgrammingWithDynamics-Crm4.Controls" Namespace="ProgrammingWithDynamicsCrm4.Controls" %>**. Now you can access our *CrmPicklistControl* just like you would any ASP.NET control. Because we will be adding multiple pages to our Web project, we can alternatively register the tag prefix for all of the pages at once in the web.config. Under the *system.web* node, add **<pages><controls><add namespace="ProgrammingWithDynamicsCrm4.Controls" assembly="ProgrammingWithDynamicsCrm4.Controls" tagPrefix="crm"/> </controls></pages>**. Now our "crm" tag prefix will be available on each of our .aspx pages.

```
<pages>
      <controls>
        <add namespace="ProgrammingWithDynamicsCrm4.Controls"
             assembly="ProgrammingWithDynamicsCrm4.Controls"
             tagPrefix="crm"/>
      </controls>
</pages>
```

To test the control, we add a *CrmPicklistControl* for the Lead entity's *leadsourcecode* attribute. Delete the *div* tag that was added by Visual Studio when the page was created. Inside the form tag, add **<crm:CrmPicklistControl ID="picklist" EntityName="lead" Attribute-Name="leadsourcecode" IncludeNullOption="true" runat="server" />**.

```
<form id="form1" runat="server">
    <crm:CrmPicklistControl ID="picklist"
                            EntityName="lead"
                            AttributeName="leadsourcecode"
                            IncludeNullOption="true" runat="server" />
</form>
```

Compile your solution, right-click the CrmPicklistControlPage.aspx, and select View in Browser to view the page in your Web browser. You'll see an HTML select box populated with all of the options defined on your Lead entity's *leadsourcecode* attribute (Figure 14-1).

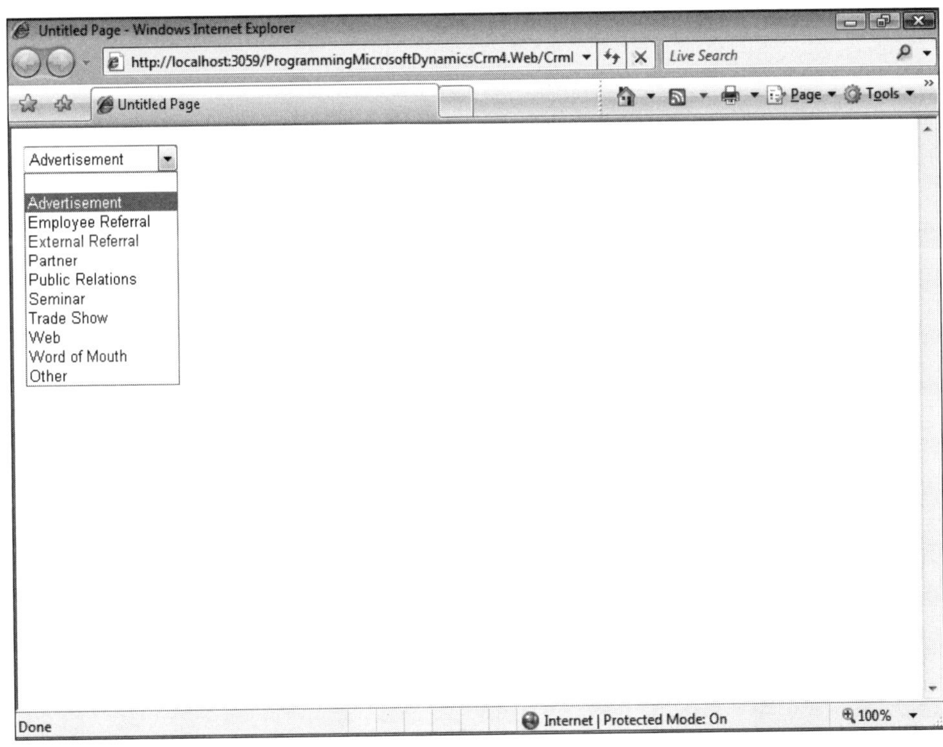

FIGURE 14-1 CrmPicklist control

CrmBooleanControl

We will now create a control to handle the *Boolean* attribute type. The *CrmBooleanControl* functions similarly to our *CrmPicklistControl*. Instead of a select box, this control will render radio buttons with labels and values based on the options defined in the Microsoft Dynamics CRM attribute.

Programming the *CrmBooleanControl*

Adding the *CrmBooleanControl* class

1. Right-click the ProgrammingWithDynamicsCrm4.Controls Project in Solution Explorer, and then, under Add, click New Item.
2. In the Visual C# Items category, select the Class template.
3. Type **CrmBooleanControl.cs** in the Name box and click OK.

The *CrmBooleanControl* extends another existing ASP.NET control, the *RadioButtonList*. We inherit the *CrmBooleanControl* class from the *System.Web.UI.RadioButtonList* class. Listing 14-2 provides the full source code for the *CrmBoolean* control.

LISTING 14-2 *CrmBoolean* control source code

```
using System;
using System.Collections.Generic;
using System.Text;
using System.Web.UI.WebControls;
using System.ComponentModel;
using System.Configuration;
using Microsoft.Crm.SdkTypeProxy.Metadata;
using Microsoft.Crm.Sdk.Metadata;
using ProgrammingWithDynamicsCrm4.Utilities;

namespace ProgrammingWithDynamicsCrm4.Controls
{
    public class CrmBooleanControl : RadioButtonList
    {
        public string EntityName
        {
            get
            {
                object entityName = ViewState["EntityName"];

                if (entityName != null)
                    return (string)entityName;
                else
                    return String.Empty;
            }
            set
            {
                ViewState["EntityName"] = value;
            }
        }

        public string AttributeName
        {
            get
            {
                object attributeName = ViewState["AttributeName"];

                if (attributeName != null)
                    return (string)attributeName;
                else
                    return String.Empty;
            }
            set
            {
                ViewState["AttributeName"] = value;
            }
        }
```

```
        [Browsable(false)]
        [EditorBrowsable(EditorBrowsableState.Never)]
        public override ListItemCollection Items
        {
            get
            {
                if (base.Items.Count == 0)
                    this.AddListItems();

                return base.Items;
            }
        }

        private void AddListItems()
        {
            MetadataService metadataService =
    CrmServiceUtility.GetMetadataService(
        ConfigurationManager.AppSettings["CrmServer"],
        ConfigurationManager.AppSettings["OrgName"]);

            AttributeMetadata attributeMetadata =
        MetadataUtility.RetrieveAttributeMetadata(metadataService, EntityName,
           AttributeName);

            // Verify that the attribute is a valid picklist
            if (attributeMetadata.AttributeType.Value != AttributeType.Boolean)
                throw new Exception(
    String.Format("{0} is not a valid attribute for the Picklist control.",
    attributeMetadata.AttributeType));

            BooleanAttributeMetadata booleanMetadata =
    (BooleanAttributeMetadata)attributeMetadata;

            base.Items.Add(
    new ListItem(booleanMetadata.TrueOption.Label.UserLocLabel.Label, "1"));
            base.Items.Add(
    new ListItem(booleanMetadata.FalseOption.Label.UserLocLabel.Label, "0"));
        }
    }
}
```

CrmBooleanControl Properties

We need to add two properties to the *CrmBooleanControl* to enable the integration with the Microsoft Dynamics CRM metadata. Table 14-2 lists the properties we need to add to our control.

TABLE 14-2 *CrmBooleanControl* Properties

Property Name	Type	Description
EntityName	*string*	Name of the Microsoft Dynamics CRM entity that the picklist attribute belongs to
AttributeName	*string*	Name of the picklist attribute

Just like we did in the *CrmPicklistControl*, we need to override and hide a property for the *CrmBooleanControl*. Because we only want this control to display the options defined on our attribute, we need to override and hide the *Items* collection.

Adding Options to the *CrmBooleanControl*

We add items to the *CrmBooleanControl* in the same way we added the select options to the *CrmPicklistControl*. This time we verify that the specified attribute has a type of *Boolean*. We then convert the attribute metadata to *BooleanAttributeMetadata*. The *BooleanAttributeMetadata* contains a *TrueOption* and a *FalseOption*. We add two new list items using the option's label and the value of "0" for the false option and "1" for the true option.

Testing the *CrmBooleanControl*

Adding the *CrmBooleanControl* test page

1. Open the ProgrammingWithDynamicsCrm4.Web project in Visual Studio.
2. Right-click the project name in Solution Explorer, and click Add New Item.
3. Select the Web Form template, and type the name **CrmBooleanControlPage.aspx** in the Name box. Click OK.
4. Delete the *div* tag that was added by Visual Studio when the page was created.

If you have not added the tag prefix to your web.config, you need to register a tag prefix for this page as previously described in the section "*CrmPicklistControl*." We can test the *CrmBooleanControl* using the Lead entity's *donotemail* attribute by adding **<crm:CrmBooleanControl ID="CrmBoolean" runat="server" EntityName="lead" AttributeName="donotemail" />** inside of the *form* tag of the CrmBooleanControlPage.aspx:

```
<crm:CrmBooleanControl ID="CrmBoolean"
                       runat="server"
                       EntityName="lead"
                       AttributeName="donotemail" />
```

Compile your solution, and view the page in your browser. You will see two radio buttons, one for each option defined on the attribute (Figure 14-2).

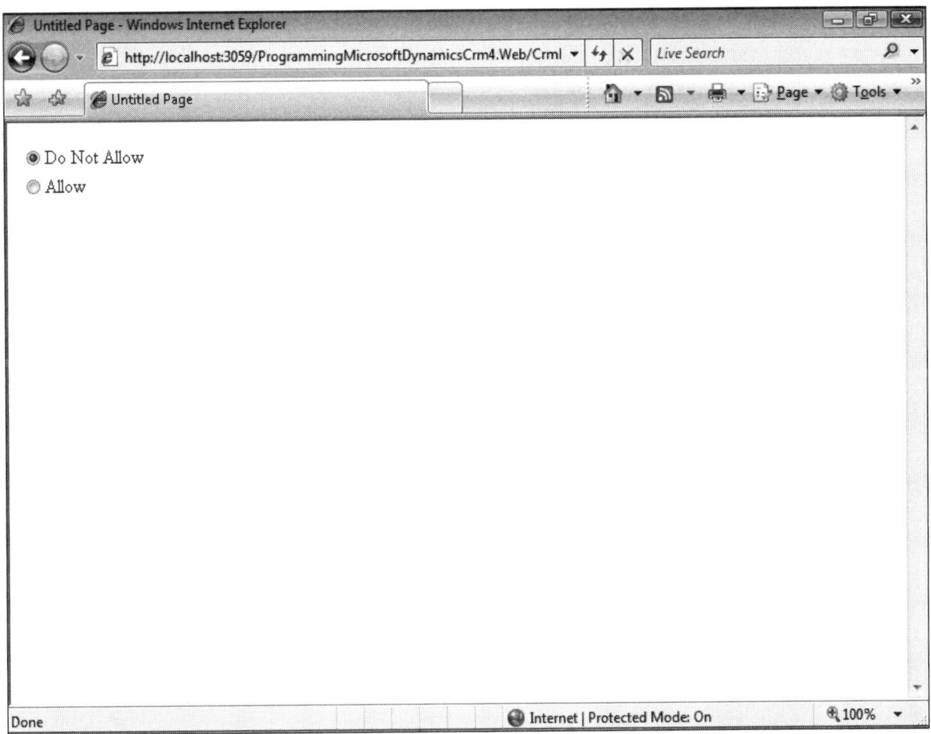

FIGURE 14-2 *CrmBooleanControl*

CrmDateTimeControl

Now we will develop a date and time control to work with Microsoft Dynamics CRM's *CrmDateTime* attribute type. The *CrmDateTime* control we will develop takes care of formatting the date and time in the user's preferred format as defined in Microsoft Dynamics CRM. Based on the attribute's metadata, we render an HTML input for entering the date or an HTML input for the date and a select box populated with time options. We also add a pop-up calendar to make it easy for the end user to select a date.

Programming the *CrmDateTimeControl*

Adding the *CrmDateTimeControl* class

1. Right-click the ProgrammingWithDynamicsCrm4.Controls Project in Solution Explorer. Under Add, click New Item.
2. In the Visual C# Items category, select the Class template.
3. Enter **CrmDateTimeControl.cs** in the Name box and click OK.

The *CrmDateTimeControl* inherits from the *System.Web.UI.CompositeControl* class. In this case we use *CompositeControl* because the *CrmDateTimeControl* is composed of multiple child controls. As you will see, we will use these controls to handle the rendering of our final output. Listing 14-3 provides the full source code for this control.

LISTING 14-3 *CrmDateTimeControl* source code

```
using System;
using System.Collections.Generic;
using System.Text;
using System.Web.UI.WebControls;
using Microsoft.Crm.SdkTypeProxy;
using System.Web.UI.HtmlControls;
using System.Xml;
using Microsoft.Crm.Sdk.Metadata;
using Microsoft.Crm.SdkTypeProxy.Metadata;
using System.Configuration;
using ProgrammingWithDynamicsCrm4.Utilities;

namespace ProgrammingWithDynamicsCrm4.Controls
{
    public class CrmDateTimeControl : CompositeControl
    {
        public string EntityName
        {
            get
            {
                object entityName = ViewState["EntityName"];

                if (entityName != null)
                    return (string)entityName;
                else
                    return String.Empty;
            }
            set
            {
                ViewState["EntityName"] = value;
            }
        }

        public string AttributeName
        {
            get
            {
                object attributeName = ViewState["AttributeName"];

                if (attributeName != null)
                    return (string)attributeName;
                else
                    return String.Empty;
            }
            set
            {
                ViewState["AttributeName"] = value;
```

```
        }
    }

    private DateTime _value = DateTime.MinValue;
    public DateTime Value
    {
        get
        {
            DateTime returnVal = DateTime.MinValue;
            string dateTime = String.Empty;

            Table table = (Table)this.Controls[0];

            // get an instance of the date input
            HtmlInputText dateInput =
                            (HtmlInputText)table.Rows[0].Cells[0].Controls[0];

            dateTime = dateInput.Value;

            if (table.Rows[0].Cells.Count > 2)
            {
                // get an instance of the time select
                HtmlSelect timeSelect =
                            (HtmlSelect)table.Rows[0].Cells[1].Controls[0];
                dateTime += " " + timeSelect.Value;
            }

            if (!string.IsNullOrEmpty(dateTime))
                returnVal = Convert.ToDateTime(dateTime);

            return returnVal;
        }
        set
        {
            _value = value;
        }
    }

    private void AddTimeOptions(HtmlSelect timeSelect, string timeFormat)
    {
        for (int hour = 0; hour < 24; hour++)
        {
            for (int minute = 0; minute < 60; minute += 30)
            {
                DateTime time = new DateTime(2008, 5, 1, hour, minute, 0);
                string formattedTime = time.ToString(timeFormat);

                timeSelect.Items.Add(new ListItem(formattedTime));
            }
        }
    }

    protected override void CreateChildControls()
    {
        Controls.Clear();
```

```
            CreateControlHierarchy();
            ClearChildViewState();
        }

        private void CreateControlHierarchy()
        {
            CrmService service =
      CrmServiceUtility.GetCrmService(ConfigurationManager.AppSettings["CrmServer"],
                                      ConfigurationManager.AppSettings["OrgName"]);

            // find the user's id
            WhoAmIRequest userRequest = new WhoAmIRequest();
            WhoAmIResponse userResponse =
                                       (WhoAmIResponse)service.Execute(userRequest);

            string fetch = String.Format(@"<fetch mapping='logical'>
                                           <entity name='usersettings'>
                                              <attribute name='timeformatstring' />
                                              <attribute name='dateformatstring' />
                                               <filter type='and'>
                                                   <condition
                                                        attribute='systemuserid'
                                                        operator='eq'
                                                        value='{0}' />
                                               </filter>
                                           </entity>
                                          </fetch>",
                                          userResponse.UserId.ToString());

            string fetchResults = service.Fetch(fetch);

            XmlDocument resultDoc = new XmlDocument();
            resultDoc.LoadXml(fetchResults);

            string timeFormat = resultDoc
                                  .DocumentElement
                                  .FirstChild
                                  .SelectSingleNode("timeformatstring").InnerText;
            string dateFormat = resultDoc
                                  .DocumentElement
                                  .FirstChild
                                  .SelectSingleNode("dateformatstring").InnerText;

            Table table = new Table();
            TableRow tr = new TableRow();

            table.Rows.Add(tr);

            TableCell dateTD = new TableCell();
            HtmlInputText dateInput = new HtmlInputText();
            dateInput.ID = "dateinput";

            if (this._value != DateTime.MinValue)
                dateInput.Value = this._value.ToString(dateFormat);
```

```
            dateTD.Controls.Add(dateInput);

            tr.Cells.Add(dateTD);

            TableCell calendarTD = new TableCell();
            HtmlInputButton calButton = new HtmlInputButton();
            calButton.Value = "Cal";
            calButton.Attributes.Add("onclick",
    String.Format(@"window.open('crmdatetimecalendar.aspx?datecontrol='
                + this.parentElement.previousSibling.firstChild.id
                + '&dateformat={0}','cal','width=250,height=225,left=270,top=180');"
              , dateFormat));

            calendarTD.Controls.Add(calButton);

            tr.Cells.Add(calendarTD);

            MetadataService metadataService = CrmServiceUtility
                   .GetMetadataService(ConfigurationManager.AppSettings["CrmServer"],
                                       ConfigurationManager.AppSettings["OrgName"]);

            RetrieveAttributeRequest attributeRequest =
                                                    new RetrieveAttributeRequest();
            attributeRequest.EntityLogicalName = EntityName;
            attributeRequest.LogicalName = AttributeName;

            RetrieveAttributeResponse attributeResponse =
               (RetrieveAttributeResponse)metadataService.Execute(attributeRequest);
            AttributeMetadata attributeMetadata =
                                               attributeResponse.AttributeMetadata;

            DateTimeAttributeMetadata dateTimeAttribute =
                                         (DateTimeAttributeMetadata)attributeMetadata;

            if (dateTimeAttribute.Format.Value == DateTimeFormat.DateAndTime)
            {
                TableCell timeTD = new TableCell();

                HtmlSelect timeSelect = new HtmlSelect();
                AddTimeOptions(timeSelect, timeFormat);

                if (this._value != DateTime.MinValue)
                    timeSelect.Value = this._value.ToString(timeFormat);

                timeTD.Controls.Add(timeSelect);
                tr.Cells.Add(timeTD);
            }

            this.Controls.Add(table);
        }
    }
}
```

CrmDateTimeControl Properties

The *CompositeControl* base class provides us with a good starting point, but we still need to add some properties to our control. Table 14-3 lists all of the properties we need to add.

TABLE 14-3 *CrmDateTimeControl* Properties

Property Name	Type	Description
EntityName	*string*	Name of the Microsoft Dynamics CRM entity that the CrmDateTime attribute belongs to
AttributeName	*string*	Name of the CrmDateTime attribute
Value	*DateTime*	Gets or sets the value of the *CrmDateTime* control

Adding the Child Controls

The *CrmDateTimeControl* is composed of an outer HTML table that holds an HTML text input, a button for our calendar pop-up, and an HTML select box for the time options. These are all created and added to the *Controls* collection in the *CreateControlHierarchy* method.

The first thing we do in the *CreateControlHierarchy* method is find the current user's *systemuserid* by making a *WhoAmI* call to the *CrmService*. Next we use a Fetch XML query to retrieve the user's preferred date and time formats. Fetch XML is used in this case because *QueryExpression* does not support queries made against the *usersettings* entity.

After we create a *Table* control, we create the cell to hold the HTML text input for the date. If a value has been set on the *CrmDateTimeControl*, the user's preferred date format is used to add the formatted date value to the input control.

The next table cell will hold the button for our calendar pop-up. Because we are creating a class library of controls and want to make deployment and use as easy as possible, it is essential that we keep everything contained in our assembly. To create our pop-up calendar window without having to deploy any extra files, in the "Creating the Calendar Pop-Up" section, we will create a new *CrmDateTimeCalendar* class that inherits from *Page* and add an *HttpHandler* to our web.config to serve the page.

The final table cell contains the HTML select box of time options. We only add this cell for *CrmDateTime* attributes the have the Format set to "Date and Time". The select options range from 12:00 A.M. to 11:30 P.M. and are formatted based on the user's preferred time format.

Creating the Calendar Pop-Up

We use the ASP.NET calendar control in the calendar pop-up. First we add a new Class file to the Controls project.

Adding the *CrmDateTimeCalendar* class

1. Right-click the ProgrammingWithDynamicsCrm4.Controls Project in Solution Explorer. Under Add, click New Item.
2. In the Visual C# Items category, select the Class template.
3. Type **CrmDateTimeCalendar.cs** in the Name box and click Add.

Because this is an actual page, we inherit the *CrmDateTimeCalendar* class from *System.Web.UI.Page*. We do not have an aspx file to work with, so we build our page's control hierarchy in our newly added class file. Listing 14-4 shows the source code for the *CrmDateTimeCalendar* class.

LISTING 14-4 *CrmDateTimeCalendar* source code

```
using System;
using System.Collections.Generic;
using System.Text;
using System.Web.UI.WebControls;
using System.Web.UI.HtmlControls;

namespace ProgrammingWithDynamicsCrm4.Controls
{
    public class CrmDateTimeCalendar : System.Web.UI.Page
    {
        protected override void OnInit(EventArgs e)
        {
            HtmlForm form = new HtmlForm();
            this.Controls.Add(form);

            // add the calendar control
            Calendar calendar = new Calendar();
            calendar.ID = "datepicker";
            calendar.Style.Add("width", "100%");
            calendar.Style.Add("height", "100%");
            calendar.SelectionChanged +=
                                  new EventHandler(Calendar_SelectionChanged);

            form.Controls.Add(calendar);

            // add a hidden input to store the date control's id
            HtmlInputHidden hdnDateControl = new HtmlInputHidden();
            hdnDateControl.ID = "datecontrol";
            hdnDateControl.Value = Request.QueryString["datecontrol"];

            form.Controls.Add(hdnDateControl);

            // add a hidden input to store the user's date format
            HtmlInputHidden hdnDateFormat = new HtmlInputHidden();
            hdnDateFormat.ID = "dateformat";
            hdnDateFormat.Value = Request.QueryString["dateformat"];
```

```
            form.Controls.Add(hdnDateFormat);

            base.OnInit(e);
        }

        protected void Calendar_SelectionChanged(object sender, EventArgs e)
        {
            HtmlForm form = this.Form;
            Calendar calendar = (Calendar)form.Controls[0];
            HtmlInputHidden hdnDateControl = (HtmlInputHidden)form.Controls[1];
            HtmlInputHidden hdnDateFormat = (HtmlInputHidden)form.Controls[2];

            StringBuilder updateScript = new StringBuilder();
            updateScript.Append("<script>");
            updateScript.AppendFormat("window.opener.document.all.{0}.value =
                               '{1}';",
                               hdnDateControl.Value,
                               calendar.SelectedDate.ToString(hdnDateFormat.Value));
            updateScript.Append("self.close();");
            updateScript.Append("</script>");

            ClientScript.RegisterClientScriptBlock(this.GetType(),
                                                   "updatescript",
                                                   updateScript.ToString());
        }
    }
}
```

We build the HTML form and controls for our pop-up page in the *OnInit* method of the *CrmDateTimeCalendar* class. First we create an ASP.NET *Calendar* control with the height and width set to *100%* so that it will fill our entire window. The *Calendar* control also needs an *EventHandler* to handle when the user selects a date. Next we create two hidden HTML inputs to store the id of the date input from the *CrmDateTimeControl* and the user's preferred date format string that are passed to the window in the query string. If you look back at Listing 14-3, you will notice that our calendar button has an *onclick* event set to open a page named "CrmDateTimeCalendar.aspx" and it passes a value for the date control id and date format string in the query string.

```
calButton.Attributes.Add("onclick",
    String.Format(@"window.open('crmdatetimecalendar.aspx?datecontrol='
            + this.parentElement.previousSibling.firstChild.id
            + '&dateformat={0}','cal','width=250,height=225,left=270,top=180');",
            dateFormat))
```

The *Calendar_SelectionChanged* method is called when the user makes a selection. This method gets an instance of all of the controls we created on this page and then adds a block of JavaScript that populates the date input on the pop-up window's opener and then closes the calendar window.

Testing the *CrmDateTimeControl*

Adding the *CrmDateTimeControl* test page

1. Open the ProgrammingWithDynamicsCrm4.Web project in Visual Studio.
2. Right-click the project name in Solution Explorer, and click Add New Item.
3. Select the Web Form template and type the name **CrmDateTimeControlPage.aspx** in the Name box. Click OK.

We need to make an addition to our web.config file to handle opening our calendar pop-up window. Under the *system.web* node add **<httpHandlers ><add verb="*" path="crmdatetimecalendar.aspx" type="ProgrammingWithDynamicsCrm4.Controls.CrmDateTimeCalendar" /></httpHandlers>**. When the request for the crmdatetimecalendar.aspx page comes in, this code will direct it to our *CrmDateTimeCalendar* class.

```
<httpHandlers >
    <add verb="*"
         path="crmdatetimecalendar.aspx"
         type="ProgrammingWithDynamicsCrm4.Controls.CrmDateTimeCalendar" />
</httpHandlers>
```

After we add the *HttpHandler*, we can add the *CrmDateTimeControl* to our page. Add **<crm:CrmDateTimeControl ID="crmDateTimeControl" EntityName="lead" AttributeName ="estimatedclosedate" runat="server" />** to our page to test with the Lead's *estimatedclosedate* attribute. If you view this page in the browser, you can see the HTML input for date along with our calendar button. Clicking the button pops up our ASP.NET *Calendar* control and allows you to select a date (Figure 14-3).

```
<crm:CrmDateTimeControl ID="crmDateTimeControl"
                        EntityName="lead"
                        AttributeName="estimatedclosedate"
                        runat="server" />
```

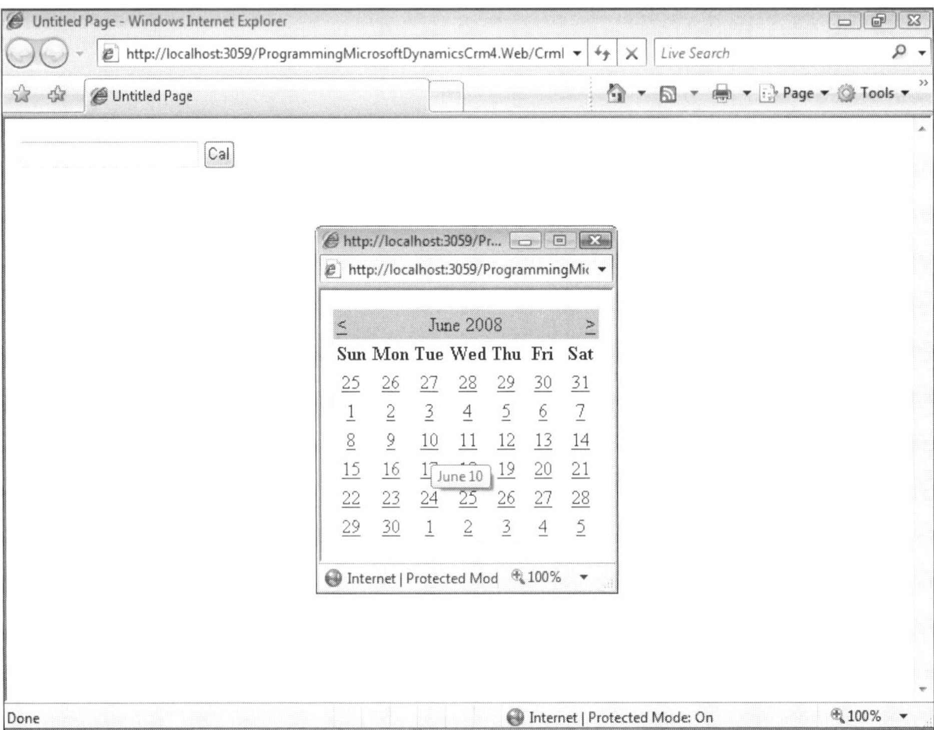

FIGURE 14-3 *CrmDateTimeControl*

CrmEntityPicklistControl

The next control we will create handles *Lookup* attributes. Instead of a CRM-style lookup control, the *CrmEntityPicklistControl* renders a drop-down list just like our *CrmPicklistControl*. However, this control doesn't use the Microsoft Dynamics CRM metadata to populate its option list. It instead uses a query to retrieve records from an entity. The end user can then select the appropriate record from the drop-down list. The *CrmEntityPicklistControl* also gives you the ability to filter the results returned to populate the drop-down options.

Programming the *CrmEntityPicklistControl*

Adding the *CrmEntityPicklist* class

1. Right-click the ProgrammingWithDynamicsCrm4.Controls Project in Solution Explorer. Under Add, click New Item.
2. In the Visual C# Items category, select the Class template.
3. Type **CrmEntityPicklist.cs** in the Name box and click Add.

The *CrmEntityPicklistControl* inherits from the *System.Web.UI.DropDownList* class. Listing 14-5 shows the full source code.

LISTING 14-5 *CrmEntityPicklistControl* source code

```
using System;
using System.Collections.Generic;
using System.Text;
using System.Web.UI.WebControls;
using Microsoft.Crm.Sdk.Query;
using Microsoft.Crm.SdkTypeProxy;
using System.ComponentModel;
using Microsoft.Crm.Sdk;
using System.Configuration;
using ProgrammingWithDynamicsCrm4.Utilities;

namespace ProgrammingWithDynamicsCrm4.Controls
{
    public class CrmEntityPicklistControl : DropDownList
    {
        public string EntityName
        {
            get
            {
                object entityName = ViewState["EntityName"];

                if (entityName != null)
                    return (string)entityName;
                else
                    return String.Empty;
            }
            set
            {
                ViewState["EntityName"] = value;
            }
        }

        public bool IncludeNullOption
        {
            get
            {
                object includeNullOption = ViewState["IncludeNullOption"];

                if (includeNullOption != null)
                    return (bool)includeNullOption;
                else
                    return false;
            }
            set
            {
                ViewState["IncludeNullOption"] = value;
            }
        }
```

```
public FilterExpression Filter { get; set; }

[Browsable(false)]
[EditorBrowsable(EditorBrowsableState.Never)]
public override object DataSource
{
    get
    {
        return base.DataSource;
    }
    set
    {
        base.DataSource = value;
    }
}

[Browsable(false)]
[EditorBrowsable(EditorBrowsableState.Never)]
public override string DataSourceID
{
    get
    {
        return base.DataSourceID;
    }
    set
    {
        base.DataSourceID = value;
    }
}

[Browsable(false)]
[EditorBrowsable(EditorBrowsableState.Never)]
public override ListItemCollection Items
{
    get
    {
        return base.Items;
    }



}

protected override void OnLoad(EventArgs e)
{
    this.DataBind();
}

public override void DataBind()
{
    if (String.IsNullOrEmpty(EntityName))
        throw new Exception(
```

```
                    String.Format("{0}: Please provide a value for EntityName.",
                                  this.ID));
            if (String.IsNullOrEmpty(DataTextField))
                throw new Exception(
                    String.Format("{0}: Please provide a value for DataTextField.",
                                  this.DataTextField));
            if (String.IsNullOrEmpty(DataValueField))
                throw new Exception(
                    String.Format("{0}: Please provide a value for DataValueField.",
                                  this.DataValueField));

            QueryExpression query = new QueryExpression();
            query.EntityName = this.EntityName;

            ColumnSet columns = new ColumnSet();
            columns.Attributes.Add(this.DataValueField);
            columns.Attributes.Add(this.DataTextField);

            query.ColumnSet = columns;

            if (this.Filter != null)
                query.Criteria = this.Filter;

            CrmService service =
      CrmServiceUtility.GetCrmService(ConfigurationManager.AppSettings["CrmServer"],
                                  ConfigurationSettings.AppSettings["OrgName"]);

            RetrieveMultipleRequest request = new RetrieveMultipleRequest();
            request.Query = query;
            request.ReturnDynamicEntities = true;

            RetrieveMultipleResponse response =
                           (RetrieveMultipleResponse)service.Execute(request);

            foreach (BusinessEntity be
                           in response.BusinessEntityCollection.BusinessEntities)
            {
                DynamicEntity de = (DynamicEntity)be;

                string text =
           DynamicEntityUtility.GetPropertyValue(de.Properties[this.DataTextField]);
                string value =
          DynamicEntityUtility.GetPropertyValue(de.Properties[this.DataValueField]);

                ListItem newItem = new ListItem(text, value);

                if (!this.Items.Contains(newItem))
                    this.Items.Add(newItem);
            }
        }
    }
}
```

Note A detailed description of the *DynamicEntityUtility* used in Listing 14-5 can be found in Chapter 15.

CrmEntityPicklistControl Properties

Table 14-4 lists the three properties we need to add to our *CrmEntityPicklistControl* class.

TABLE 14-4 ***CrmEntityPicklistControl* Properties**

Property Name	Type	Description
EntityName	*string*	Name of the Microsoft Dynamics CRM entity that will be queried
IncludeNullOption	*bool*	Determines whether to render a null option in the select box
Filter	*FilterExpression*	Used to add filtering to the *QueryExpression* that populates the drop-down list

We use the inherited *DataTextField* and *DataValueField* properties along with our added *EntityName* and *Filter* properties to build the *QueryExpression* that populates our list items:

```
QueryExpression query = new QueryExpression();
query.EntityName = this.EntityName;
ColumnSet columns = new ColumnSet();
columns.Attributes.Add(this.DataValueField);
columns.Attributes.Add(this.DataTextField);

query.ColumnSet = columns;

if (this.Filter != null)
    query.Criteria = this.Filter;
```

As with our other controls that inherit from existing ASP.NET controls, we need to hide some of the inherited properties. Because we will be handling the data binding, we hide the *DataSource*, *DataSourceID*, and *Items* properties.

Binding the Data

We override the *DataBind* method to handle adding the list items. As stated earlier we build a *QueryExpression* based on the property values provided. Because this control works with all entities, including custom entities, we use the *DynamicEntity* class. This is why our *RetrieveMultipleRequest* has the *ReturnDynamicEntities* property set to true:

```
RetrieveMultipleRequest request = new RetrieveMultipleRequest();
request.Query = query;
request.ReturnDynamicEntities = true;
```

The returned dynamic entities have the attributes specified in the *DataTextField* and *DataValueField* properties populated. We can grab these values and use them to add new list items to the *DropDownList Items* collection.

Note The source code for the *DynamicEntityUtility* used in the *CrmEntityPicklistControl* control's *DataBind* method can be found in Chapter 15.

Testing the *CrmEntityPicklistControl*

Adding the *CrmEntityPicklistControl* test page

1. Open the ProgrammingWithDynamicsCrm4.Web project in Visual Studio.
2. Right-click the project name in Solution Explorer, and click Add New Item.
3. Select the Web Form template and type the name **CrmEntityPicklistControlPage.aspx** in the Name box. Click OK.
4. Delete the *div* tag that was added by Visual Studio when the page was created.

We can test our *CrmEntityPicklist* control by adding **<crm:CrmEntityPicklistControl ID="entityPicklist" runat="server" EntityName="lead" DataTextField="fullname" DataValueField="leadid" />** inside of the form tag. Now if you view the CrmEntityPicklist-ControlPage.aspx in the browser, you can see a list of all Leads from your Microsoft Dynamics CRM system (Figure 14-4).

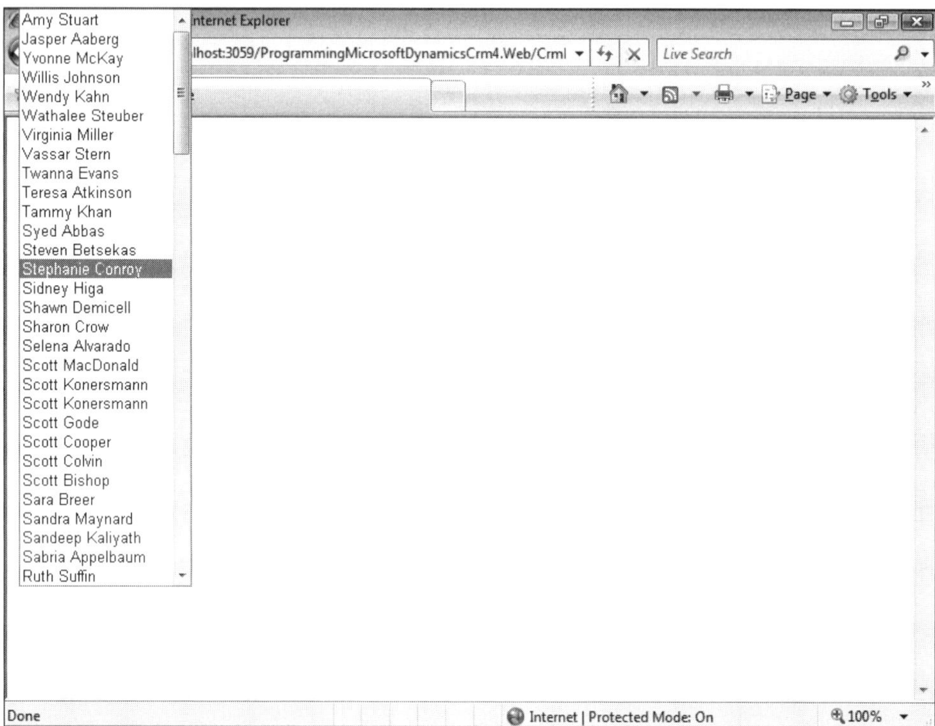

FIGURE 14-4 *EntityPicklistControl* unfiltered

In some cases you may not want to return all of the records for your entity. We can add some filtering by setting the *Filter* property. Let's set a filter so that our control only shows Leads with a company name of "Adventure Works." Add the following code block to the *Page_Load* method of your code-behind file. Compile your solution and view the page in the browser again. Now you can only see the Lead records that have the value "Adventure Works" in the *companyname* attribute (Figure 14-5).

```
ConditionExpression condition = new ConditionExpression();
condition.AttributeName = "companyname";
condition.Operator = ConditionOperator.Equal;
condition.Values = new object[] { "Adventure Works" };

FilterExpression filter = new FilterExpression();
filter.FilterOperator = LogicalOperator.And;
filter.Conditions.Add(condition);

this.entityPicklist.Filter = filter;
```

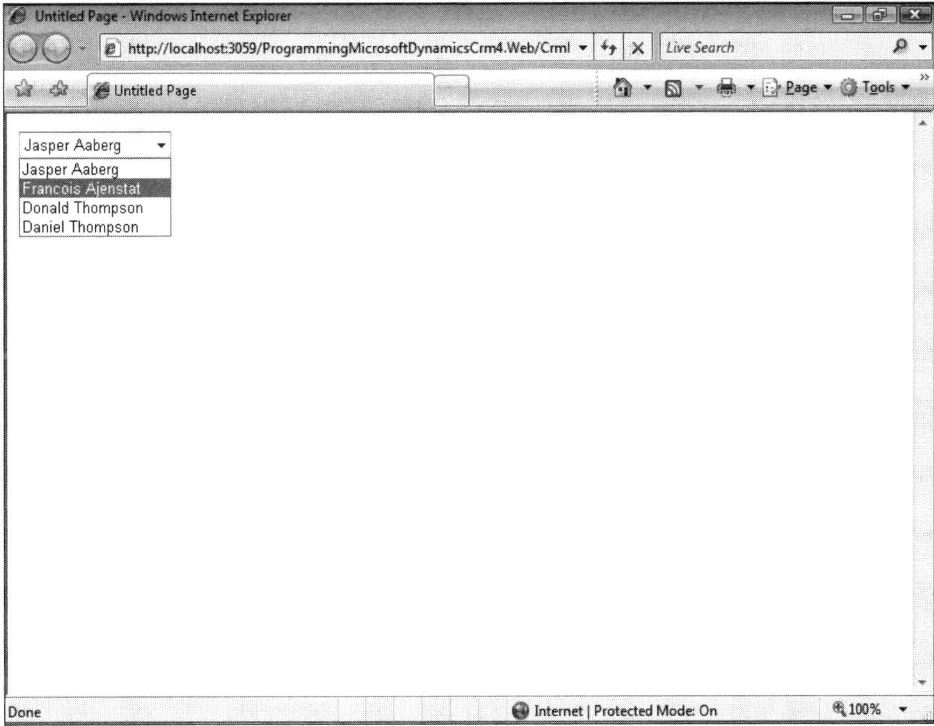

FIGURE 14-5 *EntityPicklistControl* with filtering

CrmGridViewControl

Now we will take all of the controls we have built in this chapter and use them to create an editable grid control. We'll use the *CrmGridViewControl* to quickly update records in Microsoft Dynamics CRM from an external Web page.

Programming the *CrmGridViewControl*

Adding the *CrmGridViewControl* class

1. Right-click the ProgrammingWithDynamicsCrm4.Controls Project in Solution Explorer. Under Add, click New Item.
2. In the Visual C# Items category, select the Class template.
3. Type **CrmGridViewControl.cs** in the Name box and click Add.

The *CrmGridViewControl* inherits from the ASP.NET *GridView* control. As you can see from Listing 14-6, we use a great deal of the inherited functionality.

Note The code in Listing 14-6 uses a few *static* variables for caching metadata. The performance of this control can be greatly increased by using a full metadata cache in your application. See Chapter 8 "Developing with the Metadata Service," for more details on how to build a metadata cache.

LISTING 14-6 *CrmGridViewControl* source code

```
using System;
using System.Collections.Generic;
using System.Text;
using System.Xml;
using Microsoft.Crm.SdkTypeProxy;
using Microsoft.Crm.Sdk.Query;
using System.ComponentModel;
using System.Web.UI.WebControls;
using Microsoft.Crm.SdkTypeProxy.Metadata;
using System.Web.UI;
using Microsoft.Crm.Sdk.Metadata;
using System.Data;
using Microsoft.Crm.Sdk;
using System.Configuration;
using ProgrammingWithDynamicsCrm4.Utilities;

namespace ProgrammingWithDynamicsCrm4.Controls
{
    public class CrmGridViewControl : GridView
    {
        private static IDictionary<String, AttributeMetadata> _attributeCache =
    new Dictionary<String, AttributeMetadata>();
        private static object _attributeCacheLock = new object();
        private static IDictionary<String, EntityMetadata> _entityCache =
    new Dictionary<String, EntityMetadata>();
        private static object _entityCacheLock = new object();
        private MetadataService _metadataService =
    CrmServiceUtility.GetMetadataService(
        ConfigurationManager.AppSettings["CrmServer"],
        ConfigurationManager.AppSettings["OrgName"]);
        private CrmService _crmService =
    CrmServiceUtility.GetCrmService(ConfigurationManager.AppSettings["CrmServer"],
        ConfigurationManager.AppSettings["OrgName"]);

        private string _entityName;
        private string _fetchXml;

        public Guid? ViewId
        {
            get
            {
                object viewId = ViewState["ViewId"];

                if (viewId != null)
                    return (Guid)ViewState["ViewId"];
                else
```

```
                return null;
            }
            set
            {
                ViewState["ViewId"] = value;
            }
        }

        public bool IsUserQuery
        {
            get
            {
                object isUserQuery = ViewState["IsUserQuery"];

                if (isUserQuery != null)
                    return (bool)ViewState["IsUserQuery"];
                else
                    return false;
            }
            set
            {
                ViewState["IsUserQuery"] = value;
            }
        }

        [Browsable(false)]
        [EditorBrowsable(EditorBrowsableState.Never)]
        public override object DataSource
        {
            get
            {
                return base.DataSource;
            }
            set
            {
                base.DataSource = value;
            }
        }

        [Browsable(false)]
        [EditorBrowsable(EditorBrowsableState.Never)]
        public override string DataSourceID
        {
            get
            {
                return base.DataSourceID;
            }
            set
            {
                base.DataSourceID = value;
            }
        }

        [Browsable(false)]
```

```
        [EditorBrowsable(EditorBrowsableState.Never)]
        public override bool AutoGenerateColumns
        {
            get
            {
                return base.AutoGenerateColumns;
            }
            set
            {
                base.AutoGenerateColumns = value;
            }
        }

        [Browsable(false)]
        [EditorBrowsable(EditorBrowsableState.Never)]
        public override DataControlFieldCollection Columns
        {
            get
            {
                if (base.Columns.Count == 0)
                    this.AddColumns();

                return base.Columns;
            }
        }

        private void AddColumns()
        {
            if (string.IsNullOrEmpty(_fetchXml))
                GetFetchXmlFromView();

            XmlDocument fetchDoc = new XmlDocument();
            fetchDoc.LoadXml(_fetchXml);

            XmlNode entityNode =
    fetchDoc.DocumentElement.SelectSingleNode("entity");

            _entityName = entityNode.Attributes["name"].Value;

            XmlNodeList attributes = entityNode.SelectNodes("attribute");

            string[] attributeNames = new string[attributes.Count];

            for (int i = 0; i < attributes.Count; i++)
            {
                attributeNames[i] = attributes[i].Attributes["name"].Value;
            }

            // add the edit/update column
            CommandField editColumn = new CommandField();
            editColumn.ButtonType = ButtonType.Link;
            editColumn.CausesValidation = false;
            editColumn.ShowEditButton = true;
            editColumn.ShowCancelButton = true;
            editColumn.EditText = "Edit";
```

```
        editColumn.UpdateText = "Update";
        editColumn.CancelText = "Cancel";

        base.Columns.Add(editColumn);

        foreach( string attributeName in attributeNames )
        {
            AttributeMetadata attributeMetadata =
GetAttributeMetadata(_entityName, attributeName);

            TemplateField templateField = new TemplateField();
            templateField.HeaderText =
attributeMetadata.DisplayName.UserLocLabel.Label;

            if (attributeMetadata.AttributeType.Value ==
AttributeType.PrimaryKey)
                templateField.Visible = false;

            templateField.ItemTemplate =
new CrmGridViewTemplate(ListItemType.Item, _entityName, attributeName,
attributeMetadata.AttributeType.Value, attributeMetadata.ValidForUpdate.Value);

            CrmGridViewTemplate editTemplate =
new CrmGridViewTemplate(ListItemType.EditItem, _entityName, attributeName,
attributeMetadata.AttributeType.Value, attributeMetadata.ValidForUpdate.Value);

            switch (attributeMetadata.AttributeType.Value)
            {
                case AttributeType.Lookup:
                {
                    LookupAttributeMetadata lookupAttribute =
(LookupAttributeMetadata)attributeMetadata;
                string lookupEntity = lookupAttribute.Targets[0].ToString();

                EntityMetadata lookupEntityMetadata =
GetEntityMetadata(lookupEntity, EntityItems.EntityOnly);

                editTemplate.EntityPicklistEntityName =
lookupEntityMetadata.LogicalName;
                editTemplate.EntityPicklistTextField =
lookupEntityMetadata.PrimaryField;
                editTemplate.EntityPicklistValueField =
lookupEntityMetadata.PrimaryKey;
                }
                break;
            }

            templateField.EditItemTemplate = editTemplate;

            base.Columns.Add(templateField);
        }
    }

    private void GetFetchXmlFromView()
    {
```

```
        if (!this.ViewId.HasValue)
            throw new Exception(
String.Format("{0}: Please provide a value for ViewId.", this.ID));

        ColumnSet cols = new ColumnSet();
        cols.AddColumn("fetchxml");

        if (this.IsUserQuery)
        {
            userquery userQuery =
(userquery)_crmService.Retrieve(EntityName.userquery.ToString(), ViewId.Value,
     cols);
            _fetchXml = userQuery.fetchxml;
        }
        else
        {
            savedquery savedQuery =
(savedquery)_crmService.Retrieve(EntityName.savedquery.ToString(), ViewId.Value,
     cols);
            _fetchXml = savedQuery.fetchxml;
        }
    }

    private void CreateDataSource()
    {
        if (string.IsNullOrEmpty(_fetchXml))
            this.GetFetchXmlFromView();

        XmlDocument fetchDoc = new XmlDocument();
        fetchDoc.LoadXml(_fetchXml);

        XmlNode entityNode =
fetchDoc.DocumentElement.SelectSingleNode("entity");

        _entityName = entityNode.Attributes["name"].Value;

        XmlNodeList attributes = entityNode.SelectNodes("attribute");

        string[] attributeNames = new string[attributes.Count];

        for (int i = 0; i < attributes.Count; i++)
        {
            attributeNames[i] = attributes[i].Attributes["name"].Value;
        }

        DataTable dt = new DataTable();

        // add columns to the new data table
        for (int i = 0; i < attributeNames.Length; i++)
        {
            dt.Columns.Add(attributeNames[i]);

            // check the metadata for each attribute
            // we will want to store the name attribute as well as the value for
```

```
            // certain attributes
            AttributeMetadata attributeMetadata =
this.GetAttributeMetadata(_entityName, attributeNames[i]);

            switch (attributeMetadata.AttributeType.Value)
            {
                case AttributeType.Boolean:
                case AttributeType.Lookup:
                case AttributeType.Picklist:
                case AttributeType.Status:
                    {
                        dt.Columns.Add(String.Format("{0}name",
 attributeNames[i]));
                    }
                    break;
            }
        }

        string fetchResults = _crmService.Fetch(_fetchXml);

        XmlDocument resultsDoc = new XmlDocument();
        resultsDoc.LoadXml(fetchResults);

        XmlNodeList results = resultsDoc.DocumentElement.SelectNodes("result");

        foreach (XmlNode result in results)
        {
            DataRow dr = dt.NewRow();

            foreach( DataColumn column in dt.Columns )
            {
                string columnName = column.ColumnName;

                XmlNode columnNode = result.SelectSingleNode(columnName);

                if (columnNode != null)
                {
                    AttributeMetadata resultAttributeMetadata =
this.GetAttributeMetadata(_entityName, columnName);

                    switch (resultAttributeMetadata.AttributeType.Value)
                    {
                        case AttributeType.Boolean:
                        case AttributeType.Lookup:
                        case AttributeType.Picklist:
                        case AttributeType.Status:
                            {
                                dr[columnName] = columnNode.InnerText;
                                dr[columnName + "name"] =
columnNode.Attributes["name"].Value;
                            }
                            break;
                        case AttributeType.DateTime:
                            {
```

```
                        dr[columnName] = columnNode.InnerText;
                    }
                    break;
                default:
                    {
                        dr[columnName] = columnNode.InnerText;
                    }
                    break;
            }
        }
    }

    dt.Rows.Add(dr);
}

this.DataSource = dt;
}


    private AttributeMetadata GetAttributeMetadata(string entityName,
string attributeName)
    {
        string key = GetAttributeKey(entityName, attributeName);
        AttributeMetadata attributeMetadata = null;

        if (!_attributeCache.TryGetValue(key, out attributeMetadata))
        {
            lock (_attributeCacheLock)
            {
                if (!_attributeCache.TryGetValue(key, out attributeMetadata))
                {
                    RetrieveAttributeRequest attributeRequest =
new RetrieveAttributeRequest();
                    attributeRequest.EntityLogicalName = entityName;
                    attributeRequest.LogicalName = attributeName;
                    RetrieveAttributeResponse attributeResponse =
(RetrieveAttributeResponse)_metadataService.Execute(attributeRequest);
                    attributeMetadata = attributeResponse.AttributeMetadata;

                    _attributeCache.Add(key, attributeMetadata);
                }
            }
        }
        return attributeMetadata;
    }

    private string GetAttributeKey(string entityName, string attributeName)
    {
        return String.Format("{0}|{1}", entityName, attributeName);
    }

    private EntityMetadata GetEntityMetadata(string entityName,
EntityItems entityItems)
    {
        string key = GetEntityKey(entityName, entityItems);
```

```
        EntityMetadata entityMetadata = null;

        if (!_entityCache.TryGetValue(key, out entityMetadata))
        {
            lock (_entityCacheLock)
            {
                if (!_entityCache.TryGetValue(key, out entityMetadata))
                {
                    RetrieveEntityRequest entityRequest =
new RetrieveEntityRequest();
                    entityRequest.LogicalName = entityName;
                    entityRequest.EntityItems = entityItems;
                    entityRequest.RetrieveAsIfPublished = false;

                    RetrieveEntityResponse entityResponse =
 (RetrieveEntityResponse)_metadataService.Execute(entityRequest);

                    entityMetadata = entityResponse.EntityMetadata;

                    _entityCache.Add(key, entityMetadata);
                }
            }
        }
        return entityMetadata;
    }

    private string GetEntityKey(string entityName, EntityItems entityItems)
    {
        return String.Format("{0}|{1}", entityName, entityItems.ToString());
    }

    protected override void OnLoad(EventArgs e)
    {
        if (!Page.IsPostBack)
        {
            this.AutoGenerateColumns = false;
            this.AddColumns();
            this.CreateDataSource();
            this.DataBind();
        }

        base.OnLoad(e);
    }

    protected override void OnRowEditing(GridViewEditEventArgs e)
    {
        this.EditIndex = e.NewEditIndex;
        this.CreateDataSource();
        this.DataBind();
    }

    protected override void OnRowUpdating(GridViewUpdateEventArgs e)
    {
        DynamicEntity updateEntity = new DynamicEntity();
        updateEntity.Name = _entityName;
```

```
        GridViewRow row = this.Rows[e.RowIndex];

        foreach( TableCell cell in row.Cells )
        {
            if (cell.Controls.Count > 0)
            {
                Control control = cell.Controls[0];

                if (control is Label)
                {
                    Label label = (Label)control;

                    if (label.ID == String.Format("{0}id", _entityName))
                    {
                        KeyProperty key = new KeyProperty();
                        key.Name = label.ID;
                        key.Value = new Key();
                        key.Value.Value = new Guid(label.Text);

                        updateEntity.Properties.Add(key);
                    }

                    continue;
                }

                if (control is TextBox)
                {
                    TextBox textBox = (TextBox)control;

                    StringProperty stringProp = new StringProperty();
                    stringProp.Name = textBox.ID;
                    stringProp.Value = textBox.Text;

                    updateEntity.Properties.Add(stringProp);

                    continue;
                }

                if (control is CrmBooleanControl)
                {
                    CrmBooleanControl crmBoolean = (CrmBooleanControl)control;

                    CrmBooleanProperty booleanProp = new CrmBooleanProperty();
                    booleanProp.Name = crmBoolean.ID;
                    booleanProp.Value = new CrmBoolean();

                    bool value = false;
                    if (crmBoolean.SelectedValue == "1")
                        value = true;

                    booleanProp.Value.Value = value;

                    updateEntity.Properties.Add(booleanProp);

                    continue;
```

```
            }

            if (control is CrmDateTimeControl)
            {
                CrmDateTimeControl crmDateTime =
(CrmDateTimeControl)control;

                if (crmDateTime.Value != DateTime.MinValue)
                {
                    CrmDateTimeProperty dateTimeProp =
new CrmDateTimeProperty();
                    dateTimeProp.Name = crmDateTime.ID;
                    dateTimeProp.Value = new CrmDateTime();
                    dateTimeProp.Value.Value = crmDateTime.Value.ToString();

                    updateEntity.Properties.Add(dateTimeProp);
                }

                continue;
            }

            if (control is CrmEntityPicklistControl)
            {
                CrmEntityPicklistControl crmEntityPicklist =
(CrmEntityPicklistControl)control;

                LookupProperty lookupProp = new LookupProperty();
                lookupProp.Name = crmEntityPicklist.ID;

                Lookup lookup = new Lookup();
                lookup.name = crmEntityPicklist.SelectedItem.Text;
                lookup.Value = new Guid(crmEntityPicklist.SelectedValue);

                lookupProp.Value = lookup;

                updateEntity.Properties.Add(lookupProp);

                continue;
            }

            if (control is CrmPicklistControl)
            {
                CrmPicklistControl crmPicklist =
(CrmPicklistControl)control;

                string attributeName = crmPicklist.ID;
                AttributeMetadata attributeMetadata =
this.GetAttributeMetadata(_entityName, attributeName);

                if (!string.IsNullOrEmpty(crmPicklist.SelectedValue))
                {
                    switch (attributeMetadata.AttributeType.Value)
                    {
                        case AttributeType.Picklist:
                            {
```

```
                                    PicklistProperty picklist =
new PicklistProperty();
                                    picklist.Name = attributeName;
                                    picklist.Value = new Picklist();
                                    picklist.Value.Value =
int.Parse(crmPicklist.SelectedValue);

                                    updateEntity.Properties.Add(picklist);
                                }
                                break;
                            case AttributeType.Status:
                                {
                                    StatusProperty status =
new StatusProperty();
                                    status.Name = attributeName;
                                    status.Value = new Status();
                                    status.Value.Value =
int.Parse(crmPicklist.SelectedValue);

                                    updateEntity.Properties.Add(status);
                                }
                                break;
                        }
                    }

                    continue;
                }
            }
        }

        TargetUpdateDynamic targetUpdateDynamic = new TargetUpdateDynamic();
        targetUpdateDynamic.Entity = updateEntity;

        UpdateRequest updateRequest = new UpdateRequest();
        updateRequest.Target = targetUpdateDynamic;

        UpdateResponse updateResponse =
 (UpdateResponse)_crmService.Execute(updateRequest);

        this.EditIndex = -1;
        this.CreateDataSource();
        this.DataBind();
    }

    protected override void OnRowCancelingEdit(GridViewCancelEditEventArgs e)
    {
        this.EditIndex = -1;
        this.CreateDataSource();
        this.DataBind();
    }
  }
}
```

CrmGridViewControl Properties

Table 14-5 lists the properties added to the *CrmGridViewControl*. We'll populate the grid using a saved query from Microsoft Dynamics CRM. This can either be a system view or a saved Advanced Find. The unique identifier (*Guid*) of this record is set in the *ViewId* property and then the grid uses the value set in the *IsUserQuery* property to determine which type of record it is.

TABLE 14-5 ***CrmGridViewControl* Properties**

Property Name	Type	Description
ViewId	*Guid*	Unique identifier of the system view or advanced find view used to populate the grid
IsUserQuery	*bool*	Determines whether the view being used is a system view or a saved advanced find

Because we are adding the columns and setting up the data source based on the *ViewId*, we need to override and hide the following properties from the Visual Studio designer and C# code editor's IntelliSense:

- *DataSource*
- *DataSourceID*
- *AutoGenerateColumns*
- *Columns*

Adding the Columns

The *CrmGridViewControl* overrides the *Columns* collection inherited from the *System.Web.UI.GridView* class. In the "get" of this property, if the base class's column collection is empty, we call our *AddColumns* method.

Before we can actually add the columns, we need to retrieve the Fetch XML query that drives the view specified in the *ViewId* property. From the retrieved Fetch XML, we can determine the entity and the list of attributes that will be returned for that entity.

The first column we add is for the command buttons. This column adds the Edit, Update, and Cancel buttons to the first column of our grid.

```
// add the edit/update column
CommandField editColumn = new CommandField();
editColumn.ButtonType = ButtonType.Link;
editColumn.CausesValidation = false;
editColumn.ShowEditButton = true;
editColumn.ShowCancelButton = true;
editColumn.EditText = "Edit";
editColumn.UpdateText = "Update";
editColumn.CancelText = "Cancel";
```

Next we loop through the attributes and add a column for each. Inside the loop we retrieve the *AttributeMetadata* for the current attribute. We will be making many calls to the retrieve the metadata, so we create a method that stores the *AttributeMetadata* in a *Dictionary*. The *GetAttributeMetadata* method checks the *Dictionary* to see whether we have already retrieved metadata for that attribute, and either returns the stored metadata or makes a call the *MetadataService*.

Warning Since the *_attributeCache Dictionary* is *static*, it will need to be refreshed if any changes to the metadata occur.

```
private AttributeMetadata GetAttributeMetadata(string entityName, string attributeName)
{
    string key = GetAttributeKey(entityName, attributeName);
    AttributeMetadata attributeMetadata = null;

    if (!_attributeCache.TryGetValue(key, out attributeMetadata))
    {
        lock (_attributeCacheLock)
        {
            if (!_attributeCache.TryGetValue(key, out attributeMetadata))
            {
                RetrieveAttributeRequest attributeRequest = new RetrieveAttributeRequest();
                attributeRequest.EntityLogicalName = entityName;
                attributeRequest.LogicalName = attributeName;
                RetrieveAttributeResponse attributeResponse =
     (RetrieveAttributeResponse)_metadataService.Execute(attributeRequest);
                attributeMetadata = attributeResponse.AttributeMetadata;

                _attributeCache.Add(key, attributeMetadata);
            }
        }
    }
    return attributeMetadata;
}
```

After we have the *AttributeMetadata*, we first check to see whether it is the entity's primary key. To do this we simply check to see whether the *AttributeType* equals *PrimaryKey*. If it does, we want to add it as a hidden column. We'll use this later when we are updating the record in Microsoft Dynamics CRM. The columns will all be added as ASP.NET *TemplateFields*. Because we are going to have some pretty complex logic in our columns, we need to create our own template.

Creating the *CrmGridViewTemplate*

Adding the *CrmGridViewTemplate* class

1. Right-click the ProgrammingWithDynamicsCrm4.Controls Project in Solution Explorer. Under Add, click New Item.
2. In the Visual C# Items category, select the Class template.
3. Type **CrmGridViewTemplate.cs** in the Name box and click Add.

The *CrmGridViewControl* has two modes, Read Only and Edit. The *CrmGridViewTemplate* controls what gets rendered for each grid mode. For the Read Only display, we want to render an ASP.NET Label control that displays the value, and in Edit mode we want to render a control that allows the end user to update the values in that row. We will render a different edit control based on the *AttributeType* of the current column's *AttributeMetadata*. Listing 14-7 has the source code for the *CrmGridViewTemplate*. This class implements the *ITemplate* interface, which forces us to add the *InstantiateIn* method.

LISTING 14-7 *CrmGridViewTemplate* source code

```
using System;
using System.Collections.Generic;
using System.Text;
using System.Web.UI;
using System.Web.UI.WebControls;
using Microsoft.Crm.Sdk.Metadata;

namespace ProgrammingWithDynamicsCrm4.Controls
{
    public class CrmGridViewTemplate : ITemplate
    {
        private ListItemType _itemType;
        string _entityName;
        private string _fieldName;
        private AttributeType _attributeType;
        private bool _validForUpdate;

        public string EntityPicklistEntityName { get; set; }
        public string EntityPicklistTextField { get; set; }
        public string EntityPicklistValueField { get; set; }

        public CrmGridViewTemplate(ListItemType itemType,
                                   string entityName,
                                   string fieldName,
                                   AttributeType attributeType,
                                   bool validForUpdate)
        {
            _itemType = itemType;
            _entityName = entityName;
            _fieldName = fieldName;
            _attributeType = attributeType;
```

```
        _validForUpdate = validForUpdate;
    }

    public void InstantiateIn(Control container)
    {
        switch (_itemType)
        {
            case ListItemType.Item:
                {
                    Label label = new Label();
                    label.ID = _fieldName;
                    label.DataBinding +=
                                     new EventHandler(Control_DataBinding);
                    container.Controls.Add(label);
                }
                break;
            case ListItemType.EditItem:
                {
                    if (_validForUpdate &&
                                _attributeType != AttributeType.PrimaryKey)
                    {

                        switch (_attributeType)
                        {
                            case AttributeType.Boolean:
                                {
                                    CrmBooleanControl crmBoolean =
                                                     new CrmBooleanControl();
                                    crmBoolean.ID = _fieldName;
                                    crmBoolean.EntityName = _entityName;
                                    crmBoolean.AttributeName = _fieldName;
                                    crmBoolean.DataBinding +=
                                          new EventHandler(Control_DataBinding);
                                    container.Controls.Add(crmBoolean);
                                }
                                break;
                            case AttributeType.DateTime:
                                {
                                    CrmDateTimeControl crmDateTime =
                                                   new CrmDateTimeControl();
                                    crmDateTime.ID = _fieldName;
                                    crmDateTime.EntityName = _entityName;
                                    crmDateTime.AttributeName = _fieldName;
                                    crmDateTime.DataBinding +=
                                          new EventHandler(Control_DataBinding);
                                    container.Controls.Add(crmDateTime);
                                }
                                break;
                            case AttributeType.Lookup:
                                {
                                    CrmEntityPicklistControl crmEntityPicklist =
                                                 new CrmEntityPicklistControl();
                                    crmEntityPicklist.ID = _fieldName;
                                    crmEntityPicklist.EntityName =
                                                 this.EntityPicklistEntityName;
                                    crmEntityPicklist.DataValueField =
```

```
                                    this.EntityPicklistValueField;
                            crmEntityPicklist.DataTextField =
                                    this.EntityPicklistTextField;
                            crmEntityPicklist.DataBinding +=
                                new EventHandler(Control_DataBinding);
                            container.Controls.Add(crmEntityPicklist);
                        }
                        break;
                    case AttributeType.Picklist:
                    case AttributeType.Status:
                        {
                            CrmPicklistControl crmPicklist =
                                        new CrmPicklistControl();
                            crmPicklist.ID = _fieldName;
                            crmPicklist.EntityName = _entityName;
                            crmPicklist.AttributeName = _fieldName;
                            crmPicklist.DataBinding +=
                                new EventHandler(Control_DataBinding);
                            container.Controls.Add(crmPicklist);
                        }
                        break;
                    default:
                        {
                            TextBox textBox = new TextBox();
                            textBox.ID = _fieldName;
                            textBox.DataBinding +=
                                new EventHandler(Control_DataBinding);
                            container.Controls.Add(textBox);
                        }
                        break;
                }
            }
            else
            {
                Label label = new Label();
                label.ID = _fieldName;
                label.DataBinding +=
                                new EventHandler(Control_DataBinding);
                container.Controls.Add(label);
            }

        }
        break;
    }
}

private void Control_DataBinding(object sender, EventArgs e)
{
    switch (_itemType)
    {
        case ListItemType.Item:
            {
                Label label = (Label)sender;
                GridViewRow container = (GridViewRow)label.NamingContainer;
                object value = null;
```

```
                    switch (_attributeType)
                    {
                        case AttributeType.Boolean:
                        case AttributeType.Lookup:
                        case AttributeType.Picklist:
                        case AttributeType.Status:
                            {
                                value = DataBinder.Eval(container.DataItem,
                                                String.Format("{0}name",
                                                _fieldName));
                            }
                            break;
                        default:
                            {
                                value = DataBinder.Eval(container.DataItem,
                                                _fieldName);
                            }
                            break;
                    }

                    if (value != null && value.GetType() != typeof(DBNull))
                    {
                        label.Text = (string)value;
                    }
                }
                break;
            case ListItemType.EditItem:
                {
                    WebControl editControl = (WebControl)sender;
                    GridViewRow container =
                                (GridViewRow)editControl.NamingContainer;

                    object value = DataBinder.Eval(container.DataItem,
                                            _fieldName);

                    if (value.GetType() != typeof(DBNull))
                    {
                        if (_validForUpdate)
                        {
                            switch (_attributeType)
                            {
                                case AttributeType.Boolean:
                                    {
                                        CrmBooleanControl crmBoolean =
                                            (CrmBooleanControl)editControl;
                                        crmBoolean.SelectedValue =
                                                            (string)value;
                                    }
                                    break;
                                case AttributeType.DateTime:
                                    {
                                        CrmDateTimeControl crmDateTime =
                                            (CrmDateTimeControl)editControl;
                                        crmDateTime.Value =
                                                Convert.ToDateTime(value);
                                    }
```

```
                                break;
                            case AttributeType.Lookup:
                                {
                                    CrmEntityPicklistControl
                                                    crmEntityPicklist =
                                      (CrmEntityPicklistControl)editControl;
                                    crmEntityPicklist.SelectedValue =
                                                             (string)value;
                                }
                                break;
                            case AttributeType.Picklist:
                            case AttributeType.Status:
                                {
                                    CrmPicklistControl crmPicklist =
                                            (CrmPicklistControl)editControl;
                                    crmPicklist.SelectedValue =
                                                             (string)value;
                                }
                                break;
                            default:
                                {
                                    TextBox textBox = (TextBox)editControl;
                                    textBox.Text = (string)value;
                                }
                                break;
                        }
                    }
                    else
                    {
                        Label label = (Label)editControl;

                        switch (_attributeType)
                        {
                            case AttributeType.Boolean:
                            case AttributeType.Lookup:
                            case AttributeType.Picklist:
                            case AttributeType.Status:
                                {
                                    value =
                                        DataBinder.Eval(container.DataItem,
                                                    String.Format("{0}name",
                                                    _fieldName));
                                }
                                break;
                        }

                        if (value.GetType() != typeof(DBNull))
                            label.Text = (string)value;
                    }
                }
                break;
            }
        }
    }
}
}
```

Each Template field takes two templates, one for the item template and one for the edit template. The values passed into the *CrmGridViewTemplate* constructor allow us to determine which type of template is being created. Table 14-6 lists the members that are set based on the arguments from the constructor.

TABLE 14-6 *CrmGridViewTemplate* Members

Member Name	Type	Description
_itemType	*ListItemType*	The type of item being set. Valid values are *Edit* and *EditItem*.
_entityName	*string*	The entity name to retrieve records from.
_fieldName	*string*	The schema name of the attribute used for the current column.
_attributeType	*AttributeType*	The *AttributeType* value from the current column's *AttributeMetadata*. Use this to determine which type of control to render.
_validForUpdate	*bool*	Determines whether the column should render an edit control. This property's value is based on the *AttributeMetadata's ValidForUpdate* property.

Adding the *Item* template for each *AttributeType* will be accomplished in the same manner.

```
templateField.ItemTemplate = new CrmGridViewTemplate(ListItemType.Item,
                                    _entityName,
                                    attributeNames[i],
                                    attributeMetadata.AttributeType.Value,
                                    attributeMetadata.ValidForUpdate.Value);
```

Each attribute renders a Label containing the data for that column. Notice that we add a new *EventHandler* to the *DataBinding* event on the *Label* control. This allows us to add the correct value to the *Label* control's *Text* property during data binding. For attributes with the types *Picklist*, *Status*, *Boolean*, and *Lookup* we want to display the text name for the value instead of the underlying *int* or *Guid*. We will talk more about how this is accomplished in the next section, "Creating the DataSource." If you look in the *Control_DataBinding* method of the *CrmGridViewTemplate*, you can see that we grab our value for these attribute types from a column named by concatenating the field name and the text "name".

The Edit Item logic is a little more complicated than the read-only items. Based on the *AttributeType* we render a different control. However, if the attribute is not valid for an update through the Microsoft Dynamics CRM SDK API, we render a read-only label. Table 14-7 lists the attribute types and which server control they render in the *CrmGridViewControl* control's edit mode.

TABLE 14-7 ***CrmGridVeiwTemplate*** **Control Mapping**

AttributeType	Control
Boolean	*CrmBooleanControl*
DateTime	*CrmDateTimeControl*
Picklist	*CrmPicklistControl*
Status	*CrmPicklistControl*
String	*TextBox*

These controls are all created in the *InstantiateIn* method. The properties of the newly created controls are set to the values of the members of the *CrmGridViewControl*, and the *Control_DataBinding* method is added to the *DataBinding* event. The *Lookup AttributeType* is a special case. Because our *CrmEntityPicklistControl* is used to grab records for an entity other than the one being used to populate the grid, we need to add a few extra properties to the *CrmGridViewTemplate* class. These properties are listed in Table 14-8.

TABLE 14-8 ***CrmGridViewTemplate*** **Properties**

Property Name	Type	Description
EntityPicklistEntityName	*string*	Entity name to be set on the *CrmEntityPicklistControl*
EntityPicklistTextField	*string*	Field name to be set for the *CrmEntityPicklistControl's DataTextField*
EntityPicklistValueField	*string*	Field name to be set for the *CrmEntityPicklistControl's DataValueField.*

If you look back to the source code of the *AddColumn* method, you can see where these properties are being set for attributes of type Lookup:

```
case AttributeType.Lookup:
    {
        LookupAttributeMetadata lookupAttribute =
    (LookupAttributeMetadata)attributeMetadata;
        string lookupEntity = lookupAttribute.Targets[0].ToString();

        EntityMetadata lookupEntityMetadata = GetEntityMetadata(lookupEntity,
     EntityItems.EntityOnly);

        editTemplate.EntityPicklistEntityName = lookupEntityMetadata.LogicalName;
        editTemplate.EntityPicklistTextField = lookupEntityMetadata.PrimaryField;
        editTemplate.EntityPicklistValueField = lookupEntityMetadata.PrimaryKey;
    }
    break;
```

We use the *LookupAttributeMetadata* target as the *EntityPicklistEntityName*, and then we retrieve the *EntityMetadata* for that target entity. We can then use the entity's primary field and primary key for the *EntityPicklistTextField* and *EntityPicklistValueField*, respectively.

Inside of the *Control_DataBinding* method, we grab the value from the *DataSource* and populate our control if need be. Now that the template is set, we can create a data source.

Creating the *DataSource*

In the *CreateDataSource* method (Listing 14-6), we create a *DataTable* that we can bind our grid to. We add the columns for our *DataTable* by grabbing the attributes from the Fetch XML in the same way we did for the grid columns. Each attribute has a corresponding column in the *DataTable*. Attributes for the types *Boolean*, *Picklist*, *Status*, and *Lookup* have an extra column. Because these attribute types return an integer or *Guid* value, we need to add an extra column to store the text value to display to the user:

```
switch (attributeMetadata.AttributeType.Value)
                {
                    case AttributeType.Boolean:
                    case AttributeType.Lookup:
                    case AttributeType.Picklist:
                    case AttributeType.Status:
                        {
                            dt.Columns.Add(String.Format("{0}name", attributeNames[i]));
                        }
                        break;
                }
```

Next we call the *CrmService Fetch* method to retrieve our results. We can then use *XPath* to loop through our result set and populate the *DataTable*.

Updating the Record in Microsoft Dynamics CRM

To enable the row editing on the grid, we added an override for the *OnRowEditing* method. In this method, we set the edit index for the grid and then bind the data. The page then renders the grid populated with our edit controls along with an Update and Cancel button in place of the Edit button. Handling the Cancel button is easy: We add an override to the *OnRowCancelingEdit* method and set the edit index to -1. This renders our grid in read-only mode without making any changes to the underlying data. The *OnRowUpdating* method is added to handle when the end user clicks the Update button.

In the *OnRowUpdating* method we create a *DynamicEntity* and loop through each of our grid cells adding properties to the *Properties* collection on the *DynamicEntity*. While looping through the cells we will use reflection to figure out the type of control contained in the cell. After we have this, we can retrieve the updated values and add the property. After we've added all of the properties, we use the *CrmService* to update our entity record and then set the grid's edit index back to -1.

Testing the *CrmGridViewControl*

Adding the *CrmGridViewControl* test page

1. Open the ProgrammingWithDynamicsCrm4.Web project in Visual Studio.
2. Right-click the project name in Solution Explorer, and click Add New Item.
3. Select the Web Form template and type the name **CrmGridViewControlPage.aspx** in the Name box. Click OK.

To ensure that we test with each of the custom server controls we created in this chapter, we first create an Advanced Find in Microsoft Dynamics CRM. Create a new Advanced Find query that returns the following columns on the Lead entity:

- Name
- Source Campaign
- Do Not Allow E-mail
- Est. Close Date
- Lead Source Code

Save the Advanced Find query. Now you can obtain the *Guid* of your saved query, which can be found in the *UserQueryBase* table of your Microsoft Dynamics CRM database.

Add **<crm:CrmGridViewControl id="crmGrid" ViewId="2A1E0690-1B1D-DD11-8839-0019B9F8F548" IsUserQuery="true" runat="server" />** inside of the form tag of the CrmGridViewControlPage.aspx file:

```
<crm:CrmGridViewControl id="crmGrid"
                        ViewId="2A1E0690-1B1D-DD11-8839-0019B9F8F548"
                        IsUserQuery="true"
                        runat="server" />
```

Note Replace the *ViewId* value in the preceding code snippet with the *Guid* from your saved query.

You can now see a read-only grid of Lead records returned from the Advanced Find query (Figure 14-6).

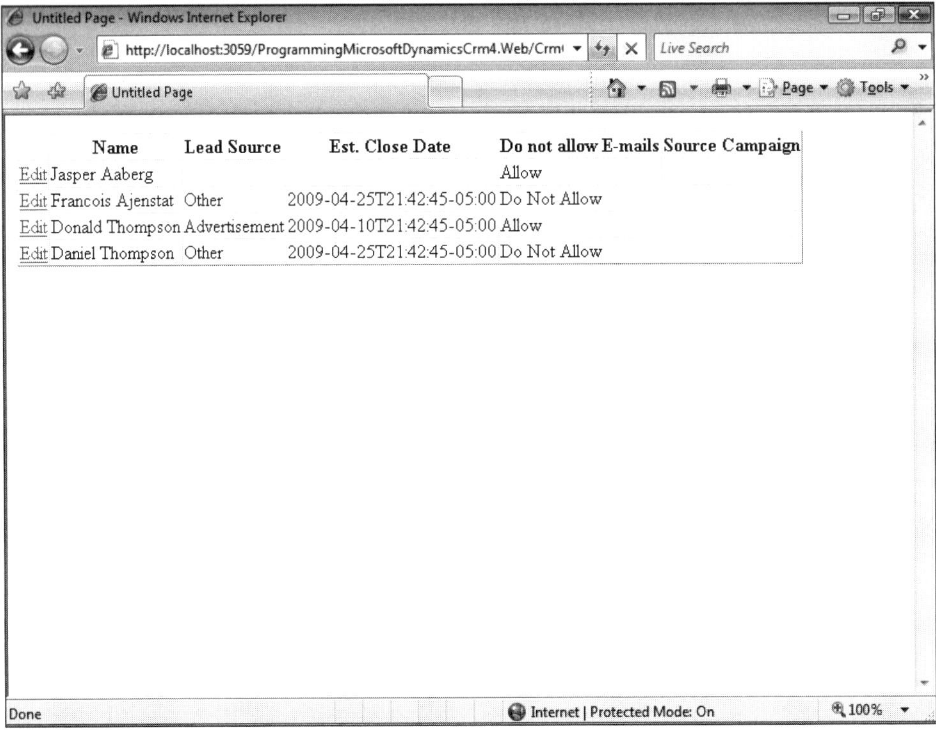

FIGURE 14-6 *CrmGridViewControl*

Click the Edit button on one of the grid rows to turn on that row's edit mode (Figure 14-7).

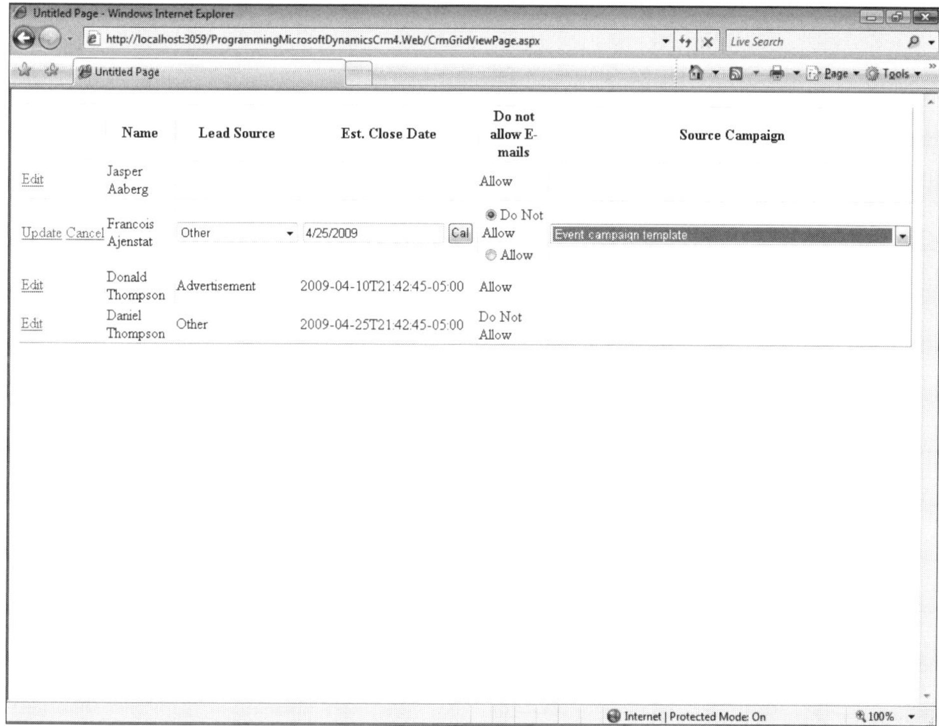

FIGURE 14-7 *CrmGridViewControl* in edit mode

Now you can see all of our edit controls rendered for each of the different attribute types we returned in our query. Notice that the Name column is still read-only. The *fullname* attribute on the Lead is not valid for updates through the Microsoft Dynamics CRM SDK API. Update the values in the edit mode row and click Update (Figure 14-8).

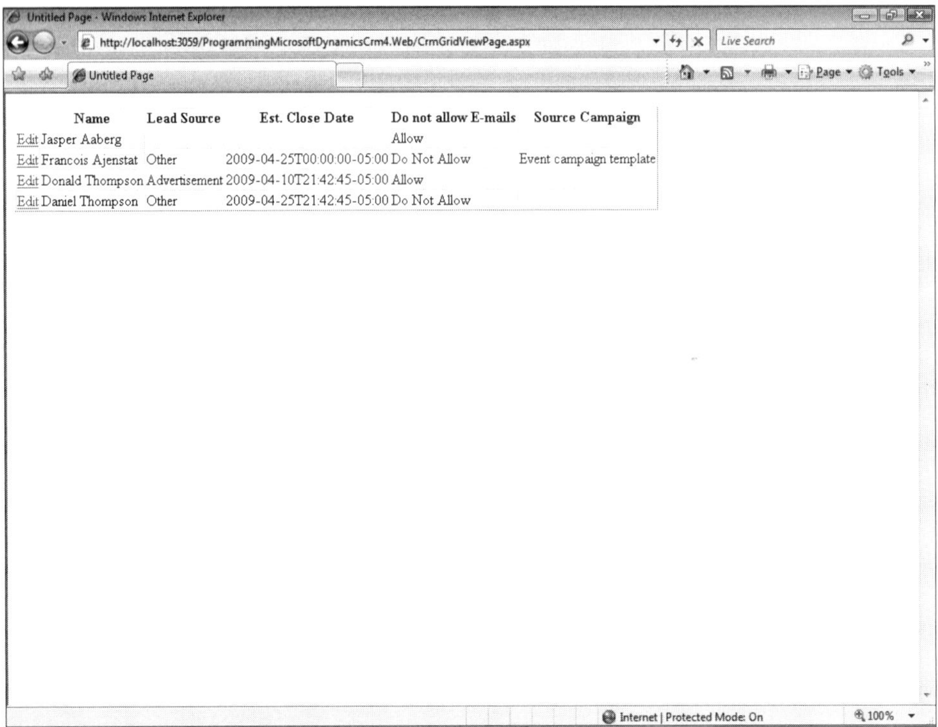

FIGURE 14-8 *CrmGridViewControl* after editing

Now the values in that record have been updated in Microsoft Dynamics CRM.

Summary

This chapter provided you with some techniques for creating custom server controls using the Microsoft Dynamics CRM SDK API. You can use the controls presented in this chapter as is, or you can easily enhance them for your own custom development needs. Because all of these example controls inherit from ASP.NET Web controls, you can use any of the styling techniques that you use for your other ASP.NET controls. If you plan to do a lot of custom Microsoft Dynamics CRM development, developing a custom server-control library like the one we just created will prove to be a valuable tool down the road.

Chapter 15

Additional Samples and Utilities

By now you are well versed in how to extend and develop custom business logic with Microsoft Dynamics CRM 4.0. To conclude, we want to share some additional code examples and useful utilities. This chapter will describe some helpful classes and an export customizations utility that you can immediately use with your Microsoft Dynamics CRM development. Lastly, we will delve into some additional sample script ideas, including a full demonstration of using script and two custom entities to implement basic form-based, field-level security.

Remember that you can download all of the source code for your own use. Please see the Introduction for the download URL.

This chapter covers the following topics:

- Various utility classes
- Customizations utility
- Additional script examples
- Field-level security

Utility Classes

This section provides a few helpful utility classes that you can include in your projects. These classes, included in the following list, provide common actions you will take during the course of your development with Microsoft Dynamics CRM:

- *CrmServiceUtility*
- *DynamicEntityUtility*
- *MetadataUtility*

Listing 15-1 demonstrates a class that exposes three static methods:

- *GetCrmService*
- *GetMetadataService*
- *GetServerUrlFromRegistry*

GetCrmService allows you to easily return an instance of the *CrmService* object using the current user's default credentials. This service works for both IFD and on-premise deployments. Similarly, the *GetMetadataService* method returns an instance of the *MetadataService* object. The *GetServerURLFromRegistry* method provides a quick way to access the Microsoft Dynamics CRM Web server *ServerUrl* value from the registry.

LISTING 15-1 The *CrmServiceUtility* class

```
public static class CrmServiceUtility
{
  /// <summary>
  /// Creates an instance of a CrmService.
  /// </summary>
  /// <param name="crmServerUrl">The URL of the CRM server.
  /// Path does not need to be included.</param>
  /// <param name="organizationName">The name of the CRM organization.</param>
  /// <returns>A new CrmService instance.</returns>
  public static CrmService GetCrmService(string crmServerUrl,
   string organizationName)
  {
    CrmAuthenticationToken token = new CrmAuthenticationToken();
    token.OrganizationName = organizationName;

    CrmService service = new CrmService();

    if (!String.IsNullOrEmpty(crmServerUrl))
    {
      UriBuilder builder = new UriBuilder(crmServerUrl);
      builder.Path = "/MSCRMServices/2007/CrmService.asmx";
      service.Url = builder.Uri.ToString();
    }

    service.UseDefaultCredentials = true;
    service.CrmAuthenticationTokenValue = token;

    return service;
  }

  /// <summary>
  /// Creates an instance of a MetadataService.
  /// </summary>
  /// <param name="crmServerUrl">The URL of the CRM server.
  /// Path does not need to be included.</param>
  /// <param name="organizationName">The name of the CRM organization.</param>
  /// <returns>A new MetadataService instance.</returns>
  public static MetadataService GetMetadataService(string crmServerUrl,
    string organizationName)
  {
    CrmAuthenticationToken token = new CrmAuthenticationToken();
    token.OrganizationName = organizationName;

    MetadataService service = new MetadataService();

    if (!String.IsNullOrEmpty(crmServerUrl))
    {
      UriBuilder builder = new UriBuilder(crmServerUrl);
      builder.Path = "/MSCRMServices/2007/MetadataService.asmx";
```

```
      service.Url = builder.Uri.ToString();
    }

    service.UseDefaultCredentials = true;
    service.CrmAuthenticationTokenValue = token;

    return service;
  }

  public static string GetServerURLFromRegistry()
  {
    using (RegistryKey mscrmKey =
     Registry.LocalMachine.OpenSubKey(@"SOFTWARE\Microsoft\MSCRM"))
    {
      if (mscrmKey != null)
      {
        string serverUrl = (string)mscrmKey.GetValue("ServerUrl");
        if (!String.IsNullOrEmpty(serverUrl))
        {
          return serverUrl;
        }
      }
    }

    return String.Empty;
  }
}
```

Listing 15-2 shows that the *DynamicEntityUtility* class provides one static method, *GetPropertyValue*, which uses reflection to return the value from a dynamic entity property.

LISTING 15-2 The *DynamicEntityUtility* class

```
public static class DynamicEntityUtility
{
  public static string GetPropertyValue(object value)
  {
    string returnValue = String.Empty;

    // checking for a name property
    // this way we can show the text value instead of a guid
    // for types of lookup, customer, and owner
    PropertyInfo prop = value.GetType().GetProperty("name");

    if (prop != null)
    {
      value = prop.GetValue(value, null);
    }
    else
    {
      prop = value.GetType().GetProperty("Value");
```

```
        if (prop != null)
        {
            value = prop.GetValue(value, null);
        }
    }

    returnValue = value.ToString();

    return returnValue;
  }
}
```

MetadataUtility Class

The *MetadataUtility* class provides a couple of helpful utilities for working with Microsoft Dynamics CRM's metadata. The class provides a way to easily retrieve and, more importantly, cache the metadata. Listing 15-3 shows the source code for this class.

LISTING 15-3 The *MetadataUtility* class

```
public static class MetadataUtility
{
  private static Dictionary<string, AttributeMetadata> _attributeCache;
  private static object _attributeCacheLock = null;

  static MetadataUtility()
  {
    _attributeCache = new Dictionary<string, AttributeMetadata>();
    _attributeCacheLock = new object();
  }


  public static AttributeMetadata RetrieveAttributeMetadata(
   MetadataService metadataService, string entityName, string attributeName)
  {
    string key = GetAttributeKey(entityName, attributeName);
    AttributeMetadata attributeMetadata = null;

    if (!_attributeCache.TryGetValue(key, out attributeMetadata))
    {
      lock (_attributeCacheLock)
      {
        if (!_attributeCache.TryGetValue(key, out attributeMetadata))
        {
          RetrieveAttributeRequest attributeRequest =
           new RetrieveAttributeRequest();
          attributeRequest.EntityLogicalName = entityName;
          attributeRequest.LogicalName = attributeName;
          RetrieveAttributeResponse attributeResponse =
           (RetrieveAttributeResponse)metadataService.Execute(attributeRequest);
          attributeMetadata = attributeResponse.AttributeMetadata;
```

```
                _attributeCache.Add(key, attributeMetadata);
              }
            }
          }
          return attributeMetadata;
        }

        private static string GetAttributeKey(string entityName, string attributeName)
        {
          return String.Format("{0}.{1}", entityName, attributeName);
        }
      }
```

Customizations Utility

The Microsoft Dynamics CRM customizations file can encapsulate the application's configuration and schema, workflow rules, and security roles. As mentioned in Chapter 2, "Development Overview and Environment," during the development process you should plan to have regular software builds as well as copies of the customizations file available for rollback purposes. This utility will automatically export all of the customizations for an organization and save the information to a file. You can then save this file in your source control system for backups, restores, and auditing. By setting up this utility to run automatically, you can create scheduled backups of the organization's customizations in case you ever need to go back and retrieve an older version. Technically, you could also back up the _mscrm database to provide a complete snapshot of the customizations, but we think you'll find it more useful to have backups of the full customizations XML available.

The code in Listing 15-4 provides a simple application to extract the entire customizations file from a system and store it on the file system.

More Information See Chapter 5, "Plug-ins," for an example of how to use a similar technique with a plug-in to save the customizations each time someone publishes changes.

LISTING 15-4 The customizations utility

```
using System;
using System.Collections.Generic;
using System.Text;
using Microsoft.Crm.Sdk;
using Microsoft.Crm.SdkTypeProxy;

namespace ExportCustomizations
{
  class Program
  {
```

```
static void Main(string[] args)
{
  if (args.Length != 2)
  {
    Console.Error.WriteLine(
      "usage: ExportCustomizationsXml <crmServerUrl> <organizationName>");
    Environment.Exit(1);
  }

  try
  {
    string crmServerUrl = args[0];
    string orgName = args[1];
    string filename = string.Format("customizations_{0}_{1}.zip",
        orgName, DateTime.Today.ToString("yyyyMMddhhmmss"));

    CrmService service = GetCrmService(crmServerUrl, orgName);

    ExportCompressedAllXmlRequest request = new ExportCompressedAllXmlRequest();
    request.EmbeddedFileName = "customizations.xml";
    ExportCompressedAllXmlResponse response =
      (ExportCompressedAllXmlResponse)service.Execute(request);

    System.IO.File.WriteAllBytes(filename, response.ExportCompressedXml);
  }
  catch (System.Web.Services.Protocols.SoapException ex)
  {
    Console.Error.WriteLine(ex.Detail.InnerText);
    Environment.Exit(-1);
  }
  catch (Exception e)
  {
    Console.Error.WriteLine(e.Message);
    Environment.Exit(-1);
  }
}

/// <summary>
/// Creates an instance of a CrmService.
/// </summary>
/// <param name="crmServerUrl">The URL of the CRM server.
/// Path does not need to be included.</param>
/// <param name="organizationName">The name of the CRM organization.</param>
/// <returns>A new CrmService instance.</returns>
public static CrmService GetCrmService(string crmServerUrl,
  string organizationName)
{
  CrmAuthenticationToken token = new CrmAuthenticationToken();
  token.OrganizationName = organizationName;

  CrmService service = new CrmService();

  if (!String.IsNullOrEmpty(crmServerUrl))
  {
    UriBuilder builder = new UriBuilder(crmServerUrl);
```

```
            builder.Path = "/MSCRMServices/2007/CrmService.asmx";
            service.Url = builder.Uri.ToString();
        }

        service.UseDefaultCredentials = true;
        service.CrmAuthenticationTokenValue = token;

        return service;
    }
  }
}
```

The following example demonstrates how to create a simple utility application to export customizations from a Microsoft Dynamics CRM system.

Creating a new console project

1. Open Visual Studio 2008.
2. On the File menu, click New, and then click Project.
3. Under Project Types, select Visual C# Projects, and then click Console Application under Templates.
4. In the Name box, type **ExportCustomizations** and click OK.
5. Using the techniques discussed in Chapter 3, "Communicating with Microsoft CRM APIs," add references to the Microsoft.Crm.Sdk and Microsoft.Crm.SdkTypeProxy assemblies.
6. Add a reference to Microsoft.Web.Services.
7. Replace the contents of the Program.cs file with the code in Listing 15-4.
8. Save and then build the application.
9. Open a command window and navigate to the proper output folder to find the application.
10. Enter the following statement:

```
exportcustomizations "http://<crmserver>" "<organizationname>"
```

Important You must run the application as a valid Microsoft Dynamics CRM user who has the ability to export customizations and has permission to write to the file system.

11. The following output zip file will then appear with an xml file with all of your customizations.

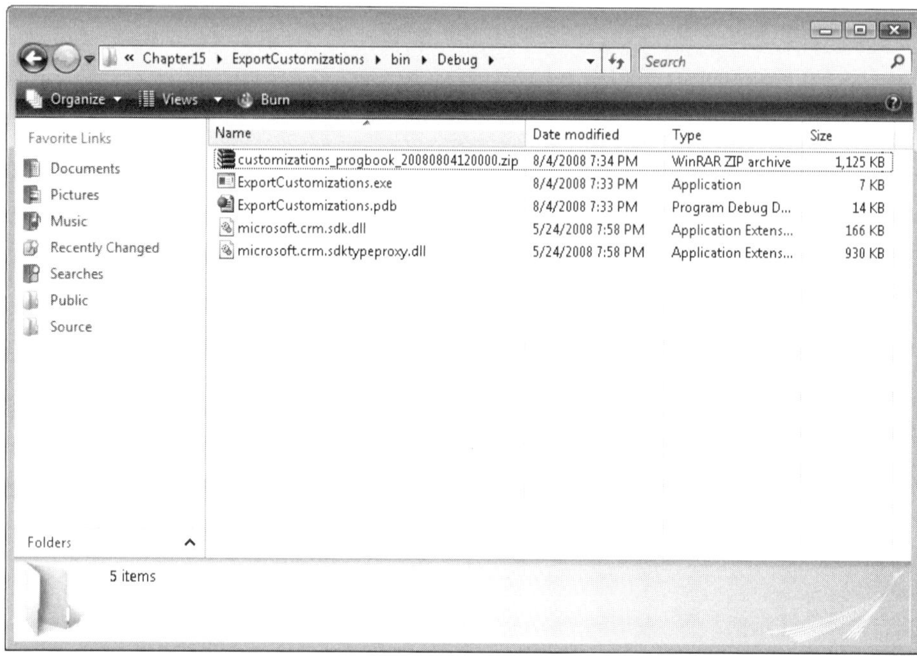

Additional Script Samples

Chapter 7, "Form Scripting," described how you can use scripting techniques to further extend Microsoft Dynamics CRM. The next two examples demonstrate how to perform the following common application requests using scripts:

- Conditionally enabling attributes
- Hiding navigation links on a form

Conditionally Enabling Attributes

When you configure attributes in Microsoft Dynamics CRM, you can specify a requirement level for each attribute: no constraint, business recommended, or business required. However, you will probably encounter scenarios where you want to dynamically change the requirement level of an attribute based on the value of a different attribute. For example, you might require an account number for your customers (account entity), but you may not require an account number for your prospects, vendors, suppliers, etc. Since all of these types of records use the account entity, you can't use the entity editor to set the requirement level of the account number attribute without impacting *all* types of accounts. Fortunately, you can take advantage of form scripting techniques and the *SetRequiredLevel()* method to implement this type of customization in Microsoft Dynamics CRM. Listing 15-5 shows a simple example of enabling the Account's account number attribute when the Account's relationship type attribute is set to the value of *Customer*.

LISTING 15-5 Conditionally enabling the Account's account number attribute

```
if (crmForm.all.customertypecode.DataValue == 3) {
  crmForm.SetFieldReqLevel("accountnumber", 1);
}
else {
  crmForm.SetFieldReqLevel("accountnumber", 0);
}
```

You will need to add the script in Listing 15-5 to both the Account form's *onLoad* event and the *Relationship Type* attribute's *onChange* event. Figure 15-1 shows that when a user selects Customer for the Relationship Type, the account number field becomes required.

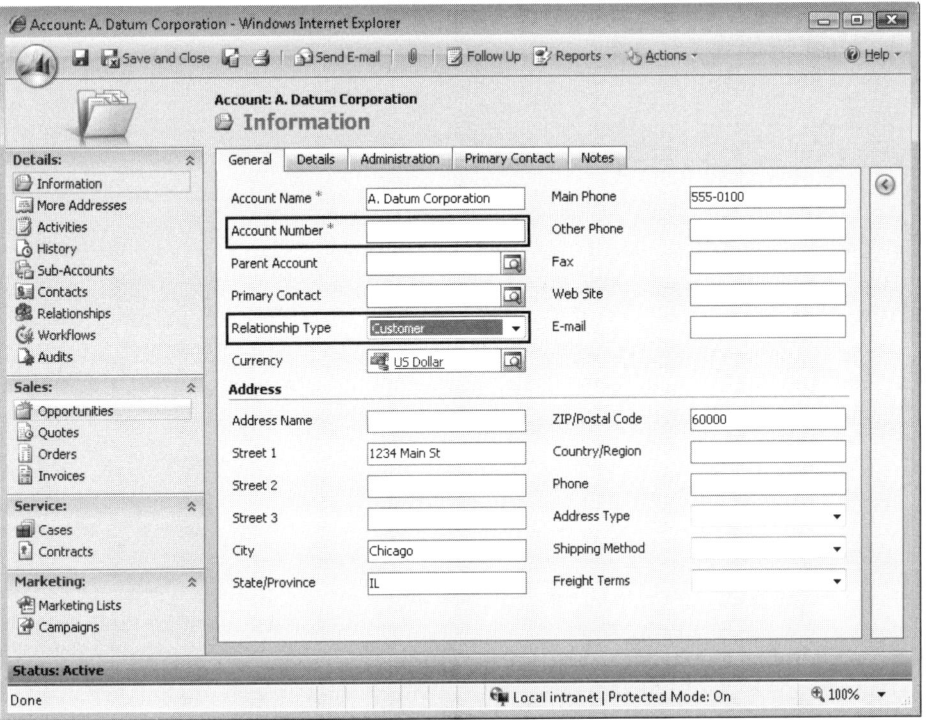

FIGURE 15-1 Conditionally requiring the account number attribute

Warning This type of form manipulation might not upgrade to future versions of Microsoft Dynamics CRM without additional work.

Hiding Navigation Links on a Form

Each entity's form contains one or more related links located on the form's left navigation links. Figure 15-2 shows the default left navigation links of the Account form.

FIGURE 15-2 The Account form's left navigation links

When you create a new custom relationship between entities, Microsoft Dynamics CRM allows you to configure whether you want to display a link on the referenced entity to the referencing entity or a link on each entity in a many-to-many relationship, as shown in Figure 15-3.

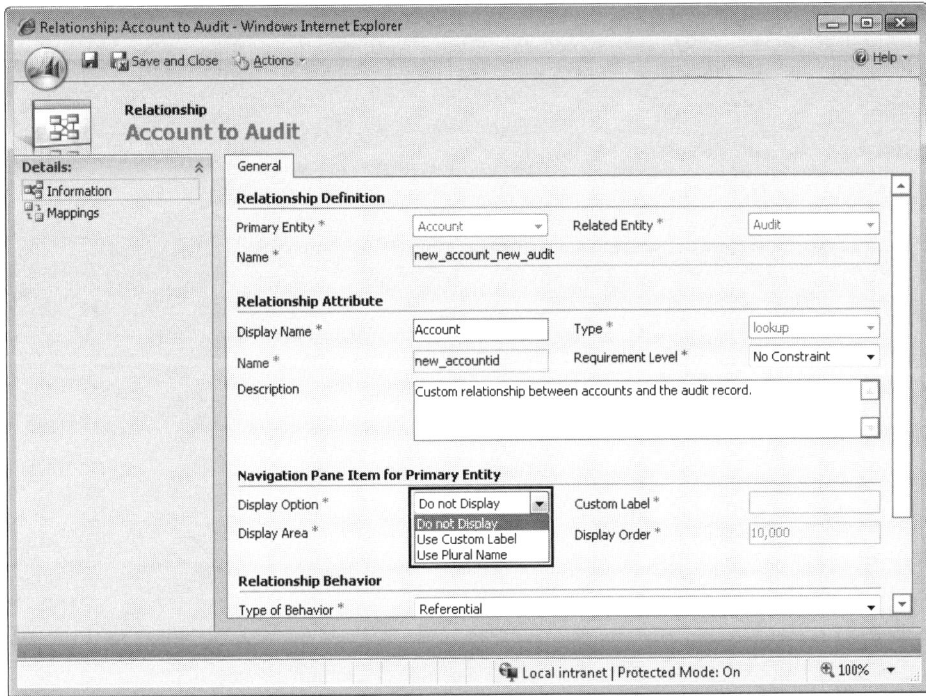

FIGURE 15-3 Configuring the left navigation links of a custom relationship

By default, the native Microsoft Dynamics CRM security settings determine most of the related links that a user will see when they open a record. If the user viewing the record does not have minimum Read access to a related entity, Microsoft Dynamics CRM automatically removes the link from the record. However, some of the links, such as an Account's Relationships, More Addresses, or Sub-Accounts, always display on the form's left navigation. In the following situations, the ability to hide or disable the form's system links may be useful:

- You may wish to hide the system links that are not used in your implementation.
- You want to replace the purpose of those links with your own implementation and don't need two links displayed.
- You want to enable the links for only certain users or roles.
- You need to enable the links only when certain business criteria are met.

Unfortunately, toggling the security roles will not hide some of these links from the navigation pane. Fortunately, you can use form scripting to programmatically hide or disable the related links. If you want to, you could further extend this script example to dynamically modify the navigation pane links based on the security role of the user viewing the record. Listing 15-6 shows a series of script functions you can use to hide/show and enable/disable a form's system left navigation links. You can easily reuse these functions with any entity.

Warning This type of customization might not upgrade to future versions of Microsoft Dynamics CRM without additional work.

LISTING 15-6 Left navigation link display functions

```
// Removes a specified left navigation link on a form
function hideLeftNavItem(leftNavItemText)
{
  displayLeftNavItem(leftNavItemText, false)
}

// Displays a hidden left navigation link on a form
function showLeftNavItem(leftNavItemText)
{
  displayLeftNavItem(leftNavItemText, true)
}

// Show/hide helper function
function displayLeftNavItem(leftNavItemText, showItem)
{
  // left nav items have two extra trailing spaces
  leftNavItemText += "  ";

  var leftNav = document.getElementById("crmNavBar");
  if (leftNav)
  {
    var items = leftNav.all;
    var itemsLength = items.length;

    for (var i = 0; i < itemsLength; i++)
    {
      var leftNavItem = items[i];

      if (leftNavItem.tagName == "LI" && leftNavItem.innerText == leftNavItemText)
      {
        // set display value based on the value of showItem
        leftNavItem.style.display = (showItem) ? "" : "none";
        return;
      }
    }
  }
}

// Disables a left navigation link
//  (will gray out the text of the left nav item as well as the image)
function disableLeftNavItem(leftNavItemText)
{
  setLeftNavItemState(leftNavItemText, true);

}
```

```
// Enables left navigation link
function enableLeftNavItem(leftNavItemText)
{
  setLeftNavItemState(leftNavItemText, false);
}

// Enable/disable helper function
function setLeftNavItemState(leftNavItemText, disableLink)
{
  // left nav items have two extra trailing spaces
  leftNavItemText += "  ";

  var leftNav = document.getElementById("crmNavBar");
  if (leftNav)
  {
    var items = leftNav.all;
    var itemsLength = items.length;

    for (var i = 0; i < itemsLength; i++)
    {
      var leftNavItem = items[i];

      if (leftNavItem.tagName == "LI" && leftNavItem.innerText == leftNavItemText &&
        leftNavItem.firstChild != null)
      {
        // Disable the item based on the value of disableLink
        leftNavItem.firstChild.disabled = disableLink;

        var leftNavItemChildren = leftNavItem.all;
        var leftNavItemChildrenLength = leftNavItemChildren.length;

        for (var j = 0; j < leftNavItemChildrenLength; j++)
        {
          var leftNavItemChild = leftNavItemChildren[j];
          if (leftNavItemChild.tagName == "IMG")
          {
            // Set filter style based on value of disableLink
            leftNavItemChild.style.filter = (disableLink) ? "gray" : "";
            break;
          }
        }
        return;
      }
    }
  }
}
```

To use the display-related links logic, you need to include the appropriate script functions to the *onLoad* event of the form. You also need to pass the display name of the link into the function.

The following sample demonstrates how to use the script in Listing 15-6 to disable the Relationships link from the Account form's left navigation links. Insert the following line of code preceding the script shown in Listing 15-6 into the *onLoad* event of the Account form:

```
disableLeftNavItem("Relationships");
```

Publish your changes and then open an account record. Figure 15-4 shows the Relationships link disabled after you apply the script.

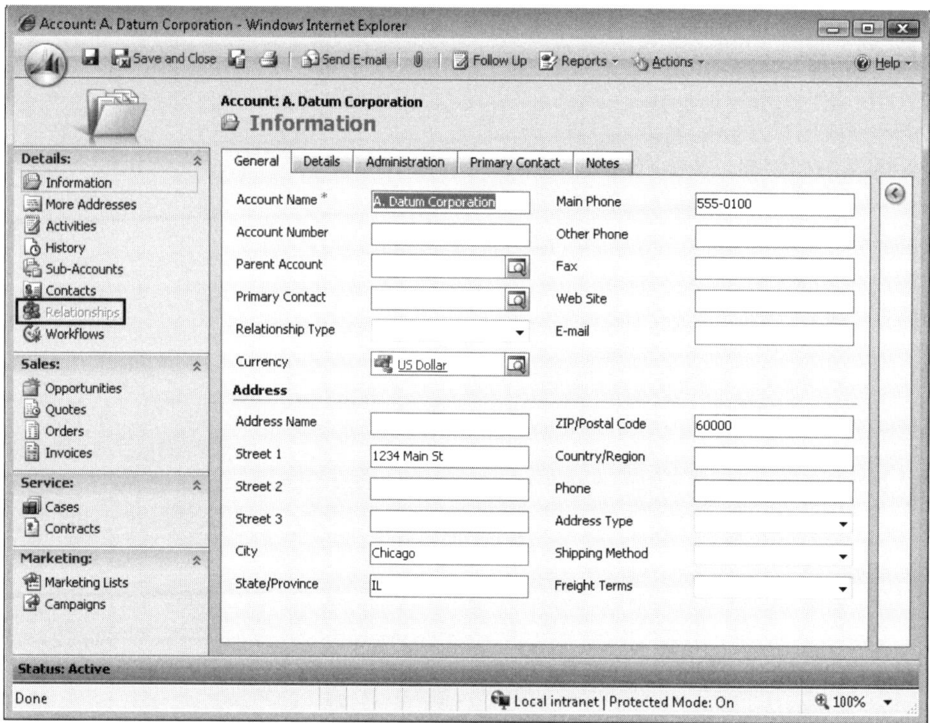

FIGURE 15-4 Account with the Relationships link disabled

Real World One particular scenario where you might want to use the script in Listing 15-6 is to hide the Quotes link from the Opportunity form. Even if your organization does not use the Quote entity, Microsoft Dynamics CRM requires that a user have Read access to the Quotes entity in order to close an opportunity (because it needs to ensure that no active quotes exist prior to closing an opportunity). If you grant users read access to the Quote entity, they will see the Quotes link in the navigation pane, which might not be desirable if your organization doesn't use quotes. You can use the script above to hide the Quote link from the opportunity record for your users.

Field-Level Security

When you configure security roles in Microsoft Dynamics CRM, you grant the user privileges to the entire entity. If someone can read an account record, they can read *all* of the values in the account record. If they can edit a contact record, they can edit *all* of the values in the contact record. As you might guess, many organizations want to lock down specific attributes of a record depending on the permissions of a specific user. This request is typically referred to as *field-level security.*

Although you can't accommodate this field-level security request by configuring security roles, you could implement this type of field-level security through a variety of methods, such as:

- **Custom entities** Create custom entities that contain the attributes that you want to restrict, relate the custom entities to the parent entity, and then use the native security roles to restrict access to the custom entities.
- **Form scripting** Use form scripting to hide or show fields and tabs on the Microsoft Dynamics CRM
- **Custom IFrame** Create a custom Web page that you display in an IFrame within the entity's form.

Each option has advantages and disadvantages. In this sample, we will focus on the form script–based approach. Unlike the other options described, the form script approach allows for the following:

- You can define security at the field level or tab level.
- It provides a more seamless user experience because the user does not need to access data from a related entity
- It keeps the data model simpler, allowing for easier access to the data in views, reporting, and advanced find queries.

However, using JavaScript to enable field-level security brings with it the following drawbacks:

- Restricting rights on the form only limits the rights to edit and view data on the entity's main form. The user is not restricted from seeing a record's data through print preview, views, an export to Excel, reports, etc. Therefore, you should not attempt to use this technique to hide attributes from users, but it should work well for restricting their ability to edit a field.
- Form scripting might not prevent a user from updating a record value via a workflow rule.

- To prevent the protected data from being exported, a user's right to export to Excel needs to be removed. This action eliminates that user's ability to export all data throughout the application. You cannot configure the export to Excel security privilege for specific entities; it is an across-the-board privilege.
- This approach may not be seamlessly upgradeable in future Microsoft Dynamics CRM releases.

Even though this technique includes considerable constraints, we still think it's worthwhile to share as an example of what's possible with form scripting. This example will also show you how to store and retrieve configuration data in custom entities (instead of a custom database or configuration file). By storing the field-level security settings in custom entities, you can allow business users to modify the security settings in the Microsoft Dynamics CRM Web interface without needing to write new scripts and deploy them. Before we continue with our implementation of form-based field-level security, we want to remind you about hiding fields and tabs with Microsoft Dynamics CRM.

Hiding Tabs and Fields on a Form

Microsoft Dynamics CRM 4.0 does not allow you to create forms based on a user's security role or some other custom logic natively; everyone sees the same form. Some customers want to display different information on the entity form depending on the security role of the user viewing the form. One technique to accomplish this is to implement your own business logic and use DHTML to hide form tabs and fields based on the user's security role.

Tip Remember that when an item is hidden it does not receive any events.

Hiding a Tab

To hide a tab, we recommend you use the *display* property of the element's *style* attribute. The following JavaScript example can be used to hide a tab:

```
tabnTab.style.display = 'none';
```

tabnTab refers to the ID of the tab. The *n* is the number of the tab starting with 0 from the left. In Figure 15-5, the Administration tab is *tab2Tab*.

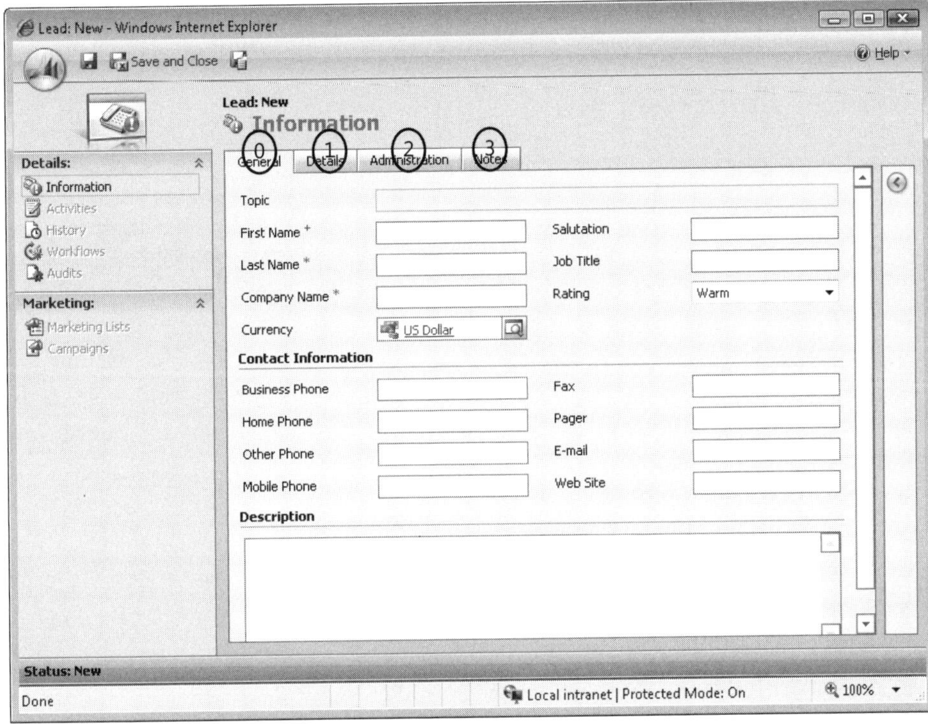

FIGURE 15-5 Determining a tab's ID on the Lead form

To show a hidden tab, you can use the following script:

```
tabnTab.style.display = 'inline';
```

Caution This approach assumes that the tab order won't change in the future. For instance, if someone were to add another tab in between the first one and the tab you are using, you would end up hiding the wrong tab.

Hiding and Showing a Field and Label

You can use the same approach to hide and show a field and its label that you use to hide a tab. However, unlike the tab example, you may not want to collapse the area because the fields on the form might shift around unexpectedly. Therefore, you might want to set the style's *visibility* property instead. Just as with the tab, you need to find the ID of the element you wish to toggle and set its *visibility* property to *hidden* or *visible* as appropriate.

Use the following script to hide a field and label, replacing *attributename* with the name of the attribute you wish to hide:

```
crmForm.all.attributename_c.style.visibility = 'hidden'; //label
crmForm.all.attributename_d.style.visibility = 'hidden'; //data
```

You can use the following script to show a field and label by replacing *attributename* with the name of the attribute you wish to show:

```
crmForm.all.attributename_c.style.visibility = 'visible'; //label
crmForm.all.attributename_d.style.visibility = 'visible'; //data
```

Important As a reminder, when the *display* property is set to *none*, the browser removes the entire element from the page upon rendering and shifts all remaining elements as appropriate. The *visibility* property can also hide an element, but the element still occupies its proper space on the page.

We next discuss how to use this approach with script to apply basic field-level security. Then, we walk through a simple example of how to apply this functionality to your Microsoft Dynamics CRM application.

Field-Level Security Script

Before we step through our example, let's review the script that provides the logic behind the field-level security implementation. We will break up the script into multiple listings to describe each method. Please refer to the source code download for the full script. We start with Listing 15-7, which simply sets up the security level variables and the two types of objects that can be secured. Then we call the *SetPageSecurity()* function to execute the field-level security logic for the form.

LISTING 15-7 Field-level security script setup

```
// security levels
var HIDDEN = 1;
var READ_ONLY = 2;
var EDIT = 3;

// object types
var FIELD = 1;
var TAB = 2;

SetPageSecurity();
```

Listing 15-8 defines the main *SetPageSecurity()* function. The *SetPageSecurity()* function retrieves the current roles for the logged-on user. Then the script retrieves the custom security settings for the entity form and loops through the returned objects, setting the field or tab security based on the object type.

LISTING 15-8 The *SetPageSecurity()* function

```
// Main page security routine
function SetPageSecurity()
{
  var formObj = document.all.crmForm;
  var formType = formObj.FormType;

  // Retrieve user roles and security configuration for the form type.
  var userRoles = GetUserRoles(currentUser);
  var securityObjects = GetSecurityObjects(formObj.ObjectTypeName, userRoles);

  // loop through returned security objects and set up form security
  for ( var i = 0; i < securityObjects.length; i++ ) {
    switch( securityObjects[i].objectType ) {
      case FIELD:
        if ( formType == 4 )
          return;
        SetFieldSecurity( securityObjects[i] );
        break;
      case TAB:
        SetTabSecurity( securityObjects[i] );
        break;
      default:
        alert( "Unhandled object type in SetPageSecurity()" );
        break;
    }
  }
}
```

Listing 15-9 shows the *SetFieldSecurity()*, *SetTabSecurity()*, and *SecurityShowField()* functions. These functions set the custom security level based on the user.

LISTING 15-9 The *SetFieldSecurity()*, *SetTabSecurity()*, and *SecurityShowField()* functions

```
// Configures the form security for fields
function SetFieldSecurity( securityObject )
{
  var fieldObj = document.getElementById( securityObject.objectName );

  if ( fieldObj != null ) {
    switch( securityObject.securityLevel ) {
      case EDIT:
        SecurityShowField( fieldObj.id, false );
        fieldObj.Disabled = false;
        break;
      case READ_ONLY:
        SecurityShowField( fieldObj.id, false );
        fieldObj.Disabled = true;
        break;
      case HIDDEN:
        SecurityShowField( fieldObj.id, true );
        fieldObj.Disabled = true;
```

```
            break;
          default:
            alert( "Unhandled Security Level in SetFieldSecurity." );
            break;
        }
      }
      else {
        alert( "An error occurred while attempting to set security on " + securityObject.
objectName );
      }
    }

    // Configures the form security for tabs
    function SetTabSecurity( securityObject )
    {
      //don't hide tab on quick create
      if(crmForm.FormType > 0 && crmForm.FormType == 5)
        return;

      var tab = document.getElementById( securityObject.objectName );

      if ( tab != null ) {
        switch( securityObject.securityLevel ) {
          case HIDDEN:
            tab.style.display = "none";
            break;
          case EDIT:
          case READ_ONLY:
          default:
            break;
        }
      }
      else
        alert( "An error occurred while setting security on " + securityObject.objectName
);
    }

    // Method that displays or hides fields.
    function SecurityShowField( fieldName, isHidden )
    {
      var fieldObjTcLabel = document.getElementById( fieldName + "_d" );
      var fieldObjTcControl = document.getElementById( fieldName + "_c" );

      if ( isHidden ) {
        fieldObjTcLabel.style.display = "none";
        fieldObjTcControl.style.display = "none";
      }
      else {
        fieldObjTcLabel.style.display = "inline";
        fieldObjTcControl.style.display = "inline";
      }
    }
```

The *GetUserRoles()* function returns an array of all of the Microsoft Dynamics CRM security roles for the currently logged-on user. The script accomplishes this by using the *EqualUserId* operator telling Microsoft Dynamics CRM to use the current user. Listing 15-10 shows the script for both of these functions.

LISTING 15-10 The *GetUserRoles()* function

```
// Helper method to return the CRM security roles of a user
function GetUserRoles(userId)
{
  // Define SOAP message
  var xml =
  [
  "<?xml version='1.0' encoding='utf-8'?>",
  "<soap:Envelope xmlns:soap=\"http://schemas.xmlsoap.org/soap/envelope/\" ",
  "xmlns:xsi=\"http://www.w3.org/2001/XMLSchema-instance\"
  "xmlns:xsd=\"http://www.w3.org/2001/XMLSchema\">",
  GenerateAuthenticationHeader(),
  "<soap:Body>",
  "<RetrieveMultiple xmlns='http://schemas.microsoft.com/crm/2007/WebServices'>",
  "<query xmlns:q1='http://schemas.microsoft.com/crm/2006/Query' ",
  "xsi:type='q1:QueryExpression'>",
  "<q1:EntityName>role</q1:EntityName>",
  "<q1:ColumnSet xsi:type='q1:ColumnSet'>",
  "<q1:Attributes><q1:Attribute>name</q1:Attribute></q1:Attributes>",
  "</q1:ColumnSet>",
  "<q1:Distinct>false</q1:Distinct>",
  "<q1:LinkEntities>",
  "<q1:LinkEntity>",
  "<q1:LinkFromAttributeName>roleid</q1:LinkFromAttributeName>",
  "<q1:LinkFromEntityName>role</q1:LinkFromEntityName>",
  "<q1:LinkToEntityName>systemuserroles</q1:LinkToEntityName>",
  "<q1:LinkToAttributeName>roleid</q1:LinkToAttributeName>",
  "<q1:JoinOperator>Inner</q1:JoinOperator>",
  "<q1:LinkCriteria>",
  "<q1:FilterOperator>And</q1:FilterOperator>",
  "<q1:Conditions>",
  "<q1:Condition>",
  "<q1:AttributeName>systemuserid</q1:AttributeName>",
  "<q1:Operator>EqualUserId</q1:Operator>",
  "</q1:Condition>",
  "</q1:Conditions>",
  "</q1:LinkCriteria>",
  "</q1:LinkEntity>",
  "</q1:LinkEntities>",
  "</query>",
  "</RetrieveMultiple>",
  "</soap:Body>",
  "</soap:Envelope>"
  ].join("");

  var resultXml = executeSoapRequest("RetrieveMultiple",xml);
  return getMultipleNodeValues(resultXml, "q1:name");
}
```

The *GetSecurityObjects()* function shown in Listing 15-11 retrieves the custom security behavior records for an entity and array of Microsoft Dynamics CRM security roles. It then loops through the records and sets an array of *SecurityObjects*.

LISTING 15-11 The *GetSecurityObjects()* function

```
// Helper method to custom security objects
function GetSecurityObjects(entity, userRoles)
{
  // Define SOAP message
  var xml =
  [
    "<?xml version='1.0' encoding='utf-8'?>",
    "<soap:Envelope xmlns:soap=\"http://schemas.xmlsoap.org/soap/envelope/\" ",
    "xmlns:xsi=\"http://www.w3.org/2001/XMLSchema-instance\" ",
    "xmlns:xsd=\"http://www.w3.org/2001/XMLSchema\">",
    GenerateAuthenticationHeader(),
    "<soap:Body>",
    "<RetrieveMultiple xmlns=\"http://schemas.microsoft.com/crm/2007/WebServices\">",
    "<query xmlns:q1=\"http://schemas.microsoft.com/crm/2006/Query\" xsi:type=\"q1:
QueryExpression\">",
    "<q1:EntityName>sonoma_securitybehavior</q1:EntityName>",
    "<q1:ColumnSet xsi:type=\"q1:AllColumns\" />",
    "<q1:Distinct>false</q1:Distinct>",
    "<q1:LinkEntities><q1:LinkEntity>",
    "<q1:LinkFromAttributeName>sonoma_securitybehaviorid</q1:LinkFromAttributeName>",
    "<q1:LinkFromEntityName>sonoma_securitybehavior</q1:LinkFromEntityName>",
    "<q1:LinkToEntityName>sonoma_securitybehaviorrole</q1:LinkToEntityName>",
    "q1:LinkToAttributeName>sonoma_securitybehaviorid</q1:LinkToAttributeName>",
    "<q1:JoinOperator>Inner</q1:JoinOperator>",
    "<q1:LinkCriteria><q1:FilterOperator>And</q1:FilterOperator>",
    "<q1:Conditions><q1:Condition>",
    "<q1:AttributeName>sonoma_rolename</q1:AttributeName>",
    "<q1:Operator>In</q1:Operator>",
    "<q1:Values>"
  ].join("");

  for (var i = 0; i < userRoles.length; i++)
  {
    xml += "<q1:Value xsi:type=\"xsd:string\">" + userRoles[i] + "</q1:Value>"
  }

  xml +=
  [
    "</q1:Values></q1:Condition></q1:Conditions>",
    "</q1:LinkCriteria></q1:LinkEntity></q1:LinkEntities>",
    "<q1:Criteria><q1:FilterOperator>And</q1:FilterOperator>",
    "<q1:Conditions><q1:Condition>",
    "<q1:AttributeName>sonoma_entityname</q1:AttributeName>",
    "<q1:Operator>Equal</q1:Operator><q1:Values>",
    "<q1:Value xsi:type=\"xsd:string\">",
    entity,
    "</q1:Value></q1:Values></q1:Condition></q1:Conditions></q1:Criteria>",
    "</query>",
```

```
    "</RetrieveMultiple>",
    "</soap:Body>",
    "</soap:Envelope>"
  ].join("");

  var resultXml = executeSoapRequest("RetrieveMultiple",xml);

  var securityObjects = new Array();
  if( (resultXml.xml) != null && (resultXml.xml.toString().length) > 0)
  {
    var objectNodes = resultXml.getElementsByTagName( "BusinessEntity" );

    // create an array of SecurityObject objects to deserialize the
    // XML returned from the webservice
    for ( var i = 0; i < objectNodes.length; i++ )
    {
      securityObjects[i] = new SecurityObject();
      securityObjects[i].objectName = objectNodes[i].selectSingleNode( "q1:sonoma_
        targetname"
        ).text;
      securityObjects[i].objectType = Number(objectNodes[i].selectSingleNode(
        "q1:sonoma_targettype" ).text);
      securityObjects[i].securityLevel = Number(objectNodes[i].selectSingleNode(
       "q1:sonoma_behaviortype" ).text);
    }
  }
  return securityObjects;
}
```

Finally, the last part of the script contains the helper methods used earlier. These methods range from defining the *SecurityObject* properties to extracting the node values from XML. You also have a helper method that builds and executes the SOAP requests. Listing 15-12 describes these four helper methods.

LISTING 15-12 Helper functions

```
// SecurityObject properties
function SecurityObject()
{
  this.objectName;
  this.objectType;
  this.securityLevel;
}

// Helper method to execute a SOAP request
function executeSoapRequest(action, xml)
{
  var actionUrl = "http://schemas.microsoft.com/crm/2007/WebServices/";
  actionUrl += action;

  var xmlHttpRequest = new ActiveXObject("Msxml2.XMLHTTP");
  xmlHttpRequest.Open("POST", "/mscrmservices/2007/CrmService.asmx", false);
  xmlHttpRequest.setRequestHeader("SOAPAction",actionUrl);
```

```
    xmlHttpRequest.setRequestHeader("Content-Type", "text/xml; charset=utf-8");
    xmlHttpRequest.setRequestHeader("Content-Length", xml.length);
    xmlHttpRequest.send(xml);

    var resultXml = xmlHttpRequest.responseXML;
    return resultXml;
}

// Helper method to return a single node value from XML
function getNodeValue(tree, el)
{
    var retVal = null;
    var e = null;
    e = tree.getElementsByTagName(el);

    if (e != null && e[0] != null) {
      retVal = e[0].firstChild.nodeValue;
    }
    return retVal;
}

// Helper method to return a multiple node value from XML
function getMultipleNodeValues(tree, el)
{
    var retVal = new Array();
    var e = null;
    e = tree.getElementsByTagName(el);

    for(i = 0; i < e.length; i++) {
      retVal[i] = e[i].firstChild.nodeValue;
    }

    return retVal;
}
```

Field-Level Security Script Example

In this example, we demonstrate how to use the field-level security script described previously. You apply the script to the *onLoad* event of the Account form and then configure the security settings using two custom entities. You can accomplish this example by performing the following steps:

- Import two custom security entities.
- Add the field-level security script to the *onLoad* event the Account entity.
- Create security records to define authorization.

First, you need to import and publish the custom security entities located with the source code download. These two entities allow you to configure the security of the form without changing any code.

Import custom security entities

1. Download the source code mentioned in the book's Introduction.
2. Open Microsoft Dynamics CRM in a Web browser and click Settings in the Application Area.
3. Click Customizations, and then click Import Customizations.
4. Click Browse and select the fieldlevelsecurity_customizations.xml file located in the Chapter15 folder of your source code download.
5. Click Upload, and you should see two new entities.

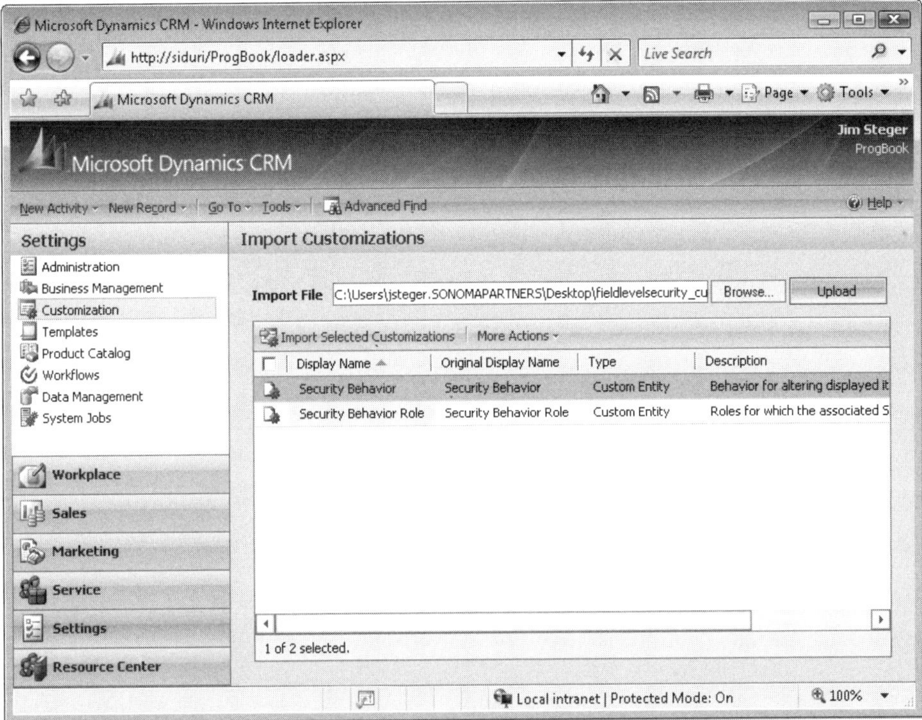

6. On the Customizations toolbar, click More Actions and then select Import All Customizations.
7. Click OK in the Import Customizations dialog box after Microsoft Dynamics CRM successfully imports the entities.
8. Return to the Customization area, and click Customize Entities.
9. Open the Security Behavior entity. On the General tab, under Areas That Display This Entity, ensure that Settings is selected. If not, select Settings and click Save And Close.

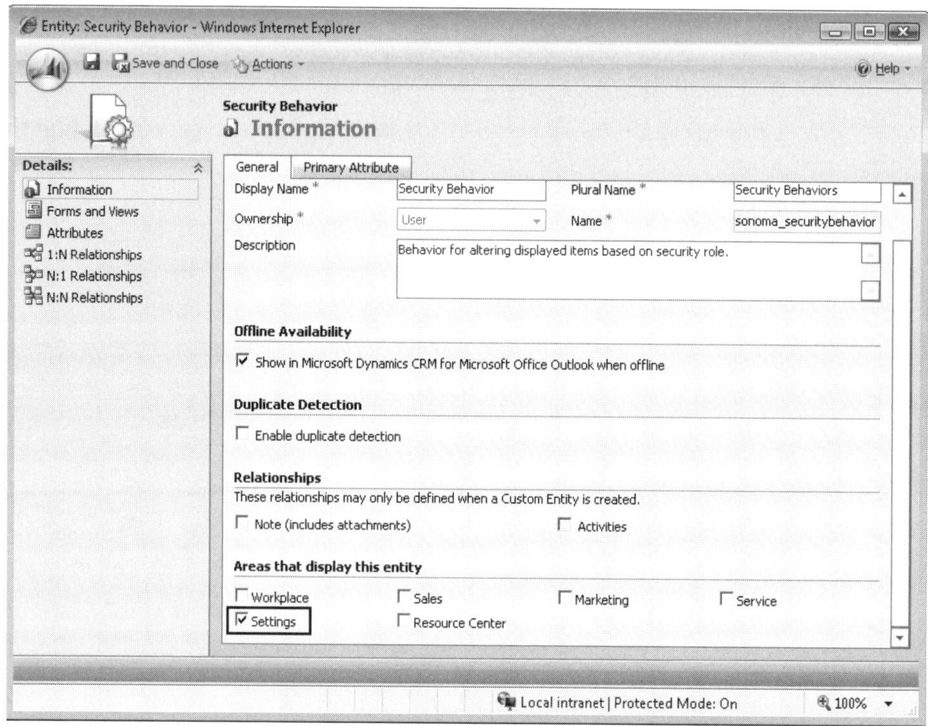

10. On the Customize Entities grid, select the two new security entities and click Publish on the grid toolbar.

This field-level security example can apply to different types of entities in the system, so you will need to decide which entities you want to set up. To add field-level security to an entity, you will need to add the field-level security script to the *onLoad* event of the entity form. For this example, we chose the Account entity, but you could apply this to multiple entities if you desired.

Add script to the *onLoad* event of Account entity's form

1. Open Microsoft Dynamics CRM in a Web browser and click Settings in the Application Area.
2. Click Customizations, and then click Customize Entities.
3. Double-click the Account entity.
4. Click Forms and Views, and then double-click the Form record.
5. Click Form Properties, select the *onLoad* event, and click Edit.
6. Select the Event Is Enabled option, and then copy and paste the script in the fieldlevelsecurity.js file located in the Chapter15 folder of your source code download.

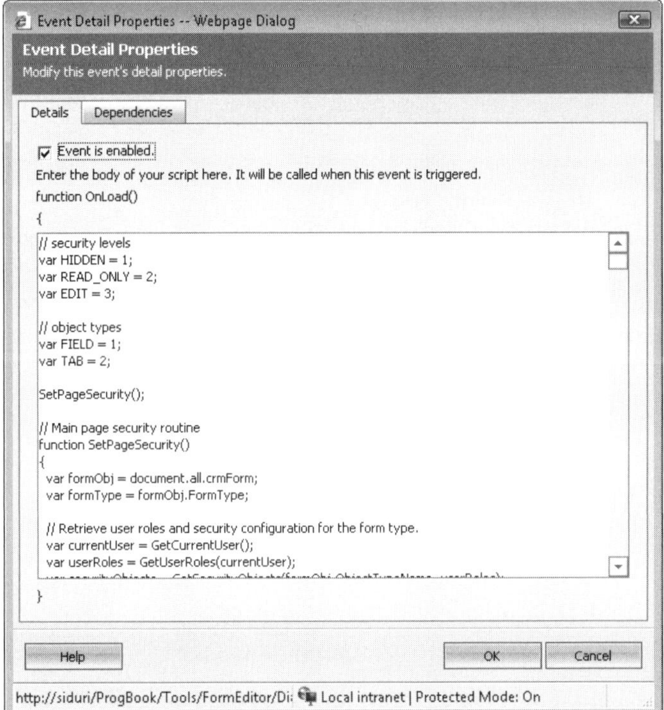

More Info For more information regarding the field-level security script, please refer to listings 15-7 through 15-12.

7. When you are finished, click OK to close the Event Detail Properties window, and then click OK on the Form Properties window.
8. Save the form and publish the Account entity.

The custom security entities that you previously imported allow you to configure how you wish the form to display for each role without having to change any source code. You need to create records for each attribute that you want to include in the field-level security solution and then configure the roles that have access.

Important Only Microsoft Dynamics CRM users with the System Administrator role can see the Security Behavior and Security Behavior Roles entities. If you want other users to configure security, you need to update the security role to allow access to these two new entities.

Table 15-1 describes the values the security behavior record expects.

TABLE 15-1 Security Behavior Form Attributes

Attribute	Description
Name	Name of the security behavior record; provides a descriptive way to find security behavior records in Microsoft Dynamics CRM. Not used by the field-level security script.
Entity	The name of the entity.
Behavior Type	*Behavior Type* describes what should be done to the attribute or tab. Possible values include *Hide*, *Make Read Only*, and *Make Editable*. ■ *Hide indicates* that the target attribute or tab is hidden from any users with the related Security Behavior Roles. ■ *Make Read Only* indicates that the target attribute or tab is not editable by any users with the related Security Behavior Roles. ■ *Make Editable* indicates that the target attribute or tab that is marked as read-only on the entity form is available to edit by any users with the related Security Behavior Roles.
Target Name	Schema name of the attribute or tab name. For tabs, use the format tab*n*Tab, where *n* represents the order in which the tab appears on the page from the left starting with 0. For example, if you want to apply field level access to the first tab, type **tab0Tab** in the Target Name field.
Target Type	Available options include *Attribute* and *Tab*.

In the following procedure, you prevent users who only have the salesperson security role from editing the account number field and seeing the Administration tab.

Configure security records

1. Open Microsoft Dynamics CRM in a Web browser and click Settings in the Application Area.
2. Click the Security Behavior link.
3. Click New to launch the Security Behavior form.
4. Complete the form as follows:
    - In the Name field, type **account-accountnumber**.
    - In the Entity Name field, type **account**.
    - In the Target Name field, type **accountnumber**.
    - For Behavior Type, select Make Read Only.
    - For Target Type, select Attribute.

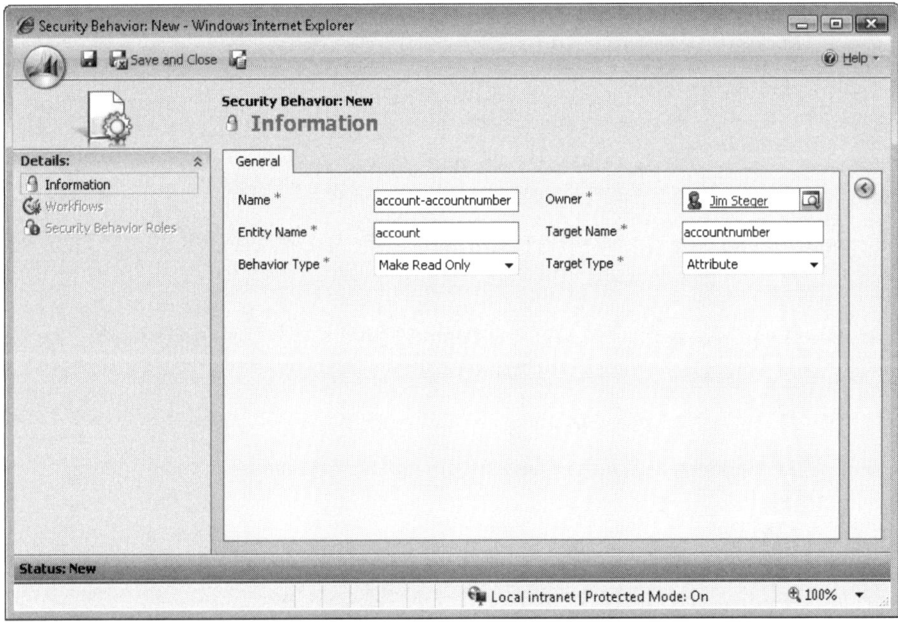

5. Click Save.
6. From the form's left navigation links, click Security Behavior Roles.
7. Click New to launch the Security Behavior Role form.
8. In the Name field, type **Salesperson-Read Only**. In the Role Name field, type **Salesperson**. The Security Behavior field should already default to your newly created security behavior record.

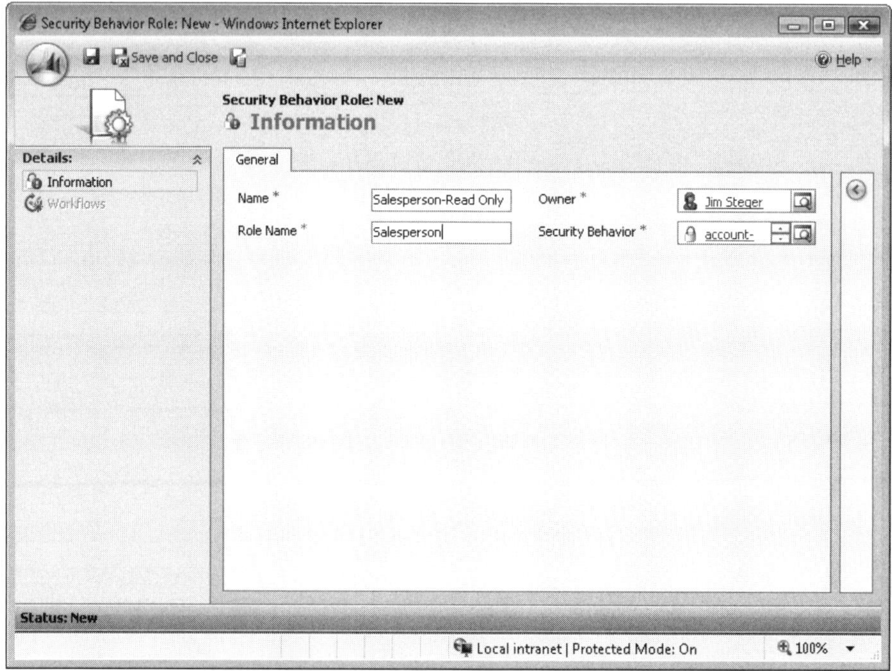

9. Click Save And Close on the Security Behavior Role form and then click Save And Close on the parent Security Behavior form.

10. Repeat the same steps to hide the Administration tab. Click New to launch the Security Behavior form.

11. In the new Security Behavior form, enter the following:

    - In the Name field, type **account-admin tab**.
    - In the Entity Name field, type **account**.
    - In the Target Name field, type **tab2Tab**.
    - For Behavior Type, select Hide.
    - For Target Type, select Tab.

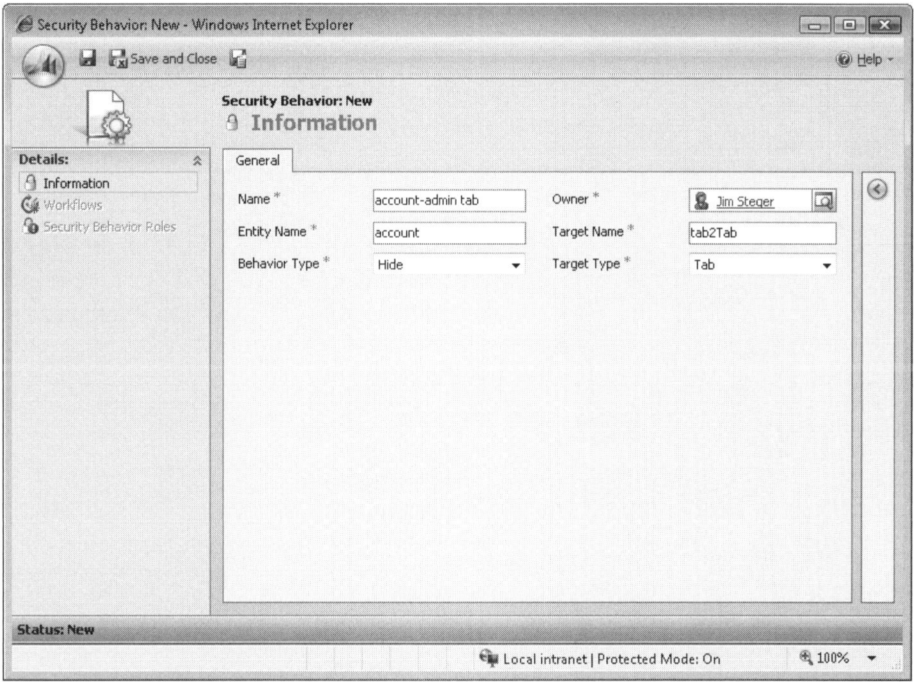

12. Click Save and then repeat the process in step 8 to set up the Security Behavior Role record for a salesperson.

> **Tip** You can create the records in Microsoft Office Excel and use Microsoft Dynamics CRM import functionality to quickly configure your field-level security records. Alternatively, you could create your own custom interface to make this process easier.

Figure 15-6 shows an example of an Account record when accessed from a user with a Salesperson role after the field-level security changes are applied. The salesperson cannot alter the Account Number field and does not see the Administration tab.

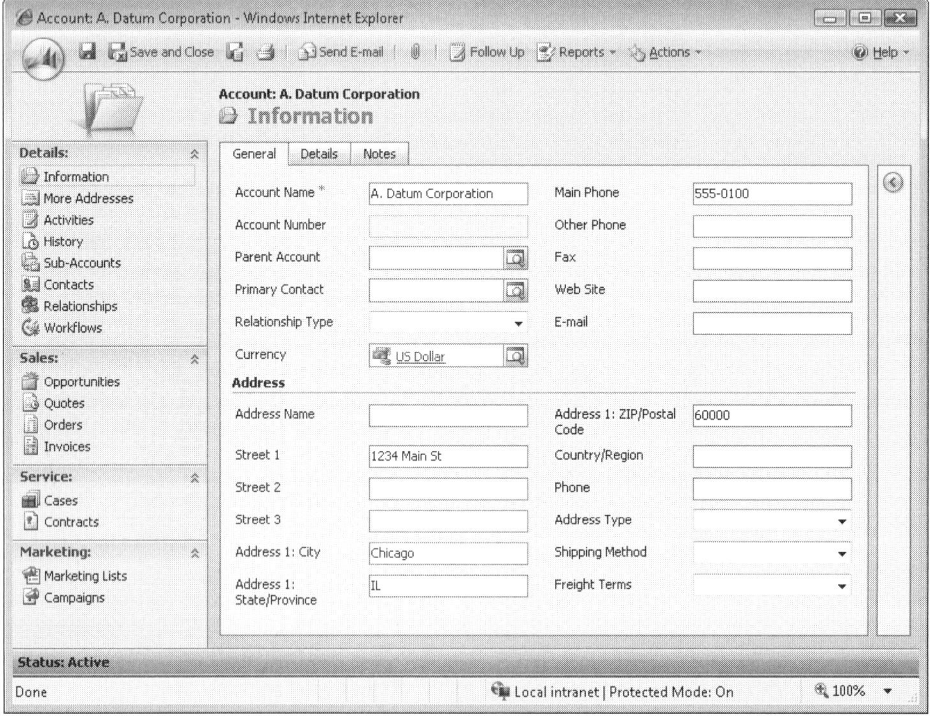

FIGURE 15-6 Account form with field-level security applied

Summary

This chapter showed you additional examples of how you can apply standard .NET and scripting techniques to create a more creative and advanced Microsoft Dynamics CRM system. We showed you some useful coding utilities and explained how to programmatically export all of a system's customizations for backup and restore purposes. Lastly, we gave an example of how you can leverage form scripting to implement a more dynamic record security that restricts user's access on an attribute-by-attribute basis. Even better, you can easily configure this field-level security code example by creating and editing custom entities in the Web interface (so you don't have to write more code to configure more security rules).

Index

A

B

C

D

G

H

I

J

K

L

M

N

Q

R

S

W

X

About the Authors

Jim Steger

Jim Steger is cofounder and principal of Sonoma Partners, a Chicago-based consulting firm that specializes in Microsoft Dynamics CRM implementations. Sonoma Partners won the Global Microsoft CRM Partner of the Year award in both 2003 and 2005 and was a finalist in 2008. He is a Microsoft Certified Professional and has architected multiple award-winning Microsoft Dynamics CRM deployments, including complex enterprise integration projects. He has been developing solutions for Microsoft Dynamics CRM since the version 1.0 beta.

Before starting Sonoma Partners, Jim designed and led various global software development projects at Motorola and ACCO Office Products. Jim earned his bachelor's degree in engineering from Northwestern University. He currently lives in Naperville, Illinois, with his wife and two children.

Mike Snyder

Mike Snyder is cofounder and principal of Sonoma Partners. Recognized as one of the industry's leading Microsoft Dynamics CRM experts, Mike is a member of the Microsoft Dynamics Partner Advisory Council, and he writes a popular blog about Microsoft Dynamics CRM.

Before starting Sonoma Partners, Mike led multiple product development teams at Motorola and Fortune Brands. Mike graduated with honors from Northwestern's Kellogg Graduate School of Management with a Master of Business Administration degree, majoring in marketing and entrepreneurship. He has a bachelor's degree in engineering from the University of Notre Dame. Mike lives in Naperville, Illinois, with his wife and three children. He enjoys ice hockey and playing with his kids in his free time.

Brad Bosak

Brad Bosak is a lead architect at Sonoma Partners, and he has been developing client solutions on Microsoft Dynamics CRM since version 1.2. Brad works on the most complex CRM projects at Sonoma Partners, using his deep product experience to meet various types of customer requirements.

Before starting at Sonoma Partners, Brad worked for several years as a .NET application developer and consultant. Brad earned his bachelor's degree in computer technology from Purdue University. He currently lives in Chicago, Illinois. In his free time, he enjoys taekwondo and playing guitar.

Corey O'Brien

Corey O'Brien is a lead architect at Sonoma Partners and certified in Microsoft Dynamics CRM. Corey has designed numerous Microsoft Dynamics CRM solutions for clients in a wide range of industries.

Corey has more than 10 years of experience designing and developing software solutions using Microsoft technologies. Corey holds patents for software concepts in both the Industrial Automation and Education industries. Corey earned his bachelor's degree in computer science from Hope College in Holland, Michigan. He currently lives in Hanover Park, Illinois with his wife and child. He enjoys volleyball and basking in the warm glow of his various electronic devices.

Philip Richardson

Philip Richardson has worked at Microsoft since 2000 and currently works as a Senior Program Manager in the Cloud Services team. Prior to his current role he was a lead on the Dynamics CRM team for the 4.0 release and for the first milestone of the next release (codename: CRM5). He is passionate about sales and marketing business systems and the positive impact they can have on a organization and its end customers

Philip is a native of Sydney, Australia, and currently resides (with his wife, son, and dog) near Microsoft's global headquarters in Redmond, Washington. In 2007 his blog (*http://www.philiprichardson.org/blog*) took the #4 position on *InsideCRM*'s Top 20 CRM bloggers.

About Sonoma Partners

This book's authors, Jim Steger, Mike Snyder, Brad Bosak, and Corey O'Brien, are executives at the Chicago-based consulting firm Sonoma Partners. Sonoma Partners is a Microsoft Gold Certified Partner that sells, customizes, and implements Microsoft Dynamics CRM for enterprise and midsize companies throughout the United States. Sonoma Partners has worked exclusively with Microsoft Dynamics CRM since the version 1.0 pre-release beta software. Founded in 2001, Sonoma Partners possesses extensive experience in several industries, including financial services, professional services, health care, and real estate.

Sonoma Partners is unique for the following reasons:

- We are focused 100 percent on the Microsoft Dynamics CRM software product. We do not spread our resources over any other products or services.
- We have successfully implemented more than 150 Microsoft Dynamics CRM deployments.
- Microsoft awarded Sonoma Partners as the Global Microsoft Dynamics CRM Partner of the Year in 2005 and 2003. Microsoft recognized Sonoma Partners as one of three finalists for the 2008 Microsoft Dynamics CRM Partner of the Year award.
- More than half of our staff includes application and database developers so that we can perform very complex Microsoft Dynamics CRM customizations and integrations.
- We were named one of 101 Best and Brightest Companies to Work for in Chicago in 2007 and 2008.
- We are a member of Microsoft Dynamics Partner Advisory Council.

In addition to the books we've written for Microsoft Press, we share our Microsoft Dynamics CRM product knowledge through our e-mail newsletter and online blog. If you're interested in receiving this information, you can find out more on our Web site at *http://www.sonomapartners.com.*

Even though our headquarters is in Chicago, Illinois, we work with customers throughout the United States. If you're interested in discussing your Microsoft Dynamics CRM system with us, please don't hesitate to contact us! In addition to working with customers who want to deploy Microsoft Dynamics CRM for themselves, we also act as a technology provider for independent software vendors (ISVs) looking to develop solutions for the Microsoft Dynamics CRM platform.

Sometimes people ask us where we got our name. The name *Sonoma Partners* was inspired by Sonoma County in the wine-producing region of northern California. The wineries in Sonoma County are smaller than their more well-known competitors in Napa Valley, but they have a reputation for producing some of the highest quality wines in the world. We think that their smaller size allows the Sonoma winemakers to be more intimately involved with creating the wine. By using this hands-on approach, the Sonoma County wineries can deliver a superior product to their customers—and that's what we strive to do as well.

What do you think of this book?

We want to hear from you!

Your feedback will help us continually improve our books and learning resources for you. To participate in a brief online survey, please visit:

microsoft.com/learning/booksurvey

...and enter this book's ISBN-10 or ISBN-13 number (appears above barcode on back cover). As a thank-you to survey participants in the U.S. and Canada, each month we'll randomly select five respondents to win one of five $100 gift certificates from a leading online merchant. At the conclusion of the survey, you can enter the drawing by providing your e-mail address, which will be used for prize notification only.*

Thank you in advance for your input!

Where to find the ISBN on back cover

Example only. Each book has unique ISBN.

Microsoft Press

* No purchase necessary. Void where prohibited. Open only to residents of the 50 United States (includes District of Columbia) and Canada (void in Quebec). For official rules and entry dates see: **microsoft.com/learning/booksurvey**

Stay in touch!

To subscribe to the *Microsoft Press® Book Connection Newsletter*—for news on upcoming books, events, and special offers—please visit:

microsoft.com/learning/books/newsletter